Social Change

Richard T. LaPiere

Professor of Sociology
Stanford University

McGraw-Hill Book Company

New York
St. Louis
San Francisco
Toronto
London

II

SOCIAL CHANGE

Library of Congress Catalog Card Number: 64–22194

36366

Preface

Forty years ago the term "sociologist" was still being used in the public print to invoke the image of a sanctimonious reformer who thought he knew the cause of every social ill and had a cure for it, and many who should have known much better were still confusing sociology with socialism. Sociology as a discipline was tolerated to some degree in the major American universities; but elsewhere it was ignored or else tucked away as an appendage to some other, more sanctioned, social science, and neither private foundations nor governmental agencies had much enthusiasm for the support of sociological investigations. As a consequence, sociologists were few in number; and they either belligerently insisted on the worthiness of their discipline or meekly apologized for its existence, depending presumably upon their personal response to its academically inferior status.

Today, by marked and gratifying contrast, sociology has achieved something of the status that its founder, Auguste Comte, anticipated for it. The term has lost its derogatory connotations, and a large and thriving department of sociology is now a status symbol for college and university alike. Today sociologists are accepted as scientists, differing from economists, psychologists, biologists, chemists, and the like only in the area of their specialty. Today the counsel of sociologists is sought by leaders in many walks of life, the demand for competent sociologists seems insatiable, and money for the support of sociological research is available from many sources, private and public.

The status of sociology today as a respected field of scientific endeavor is a reflection of its growth in stature. Much knowledge has been slowly and laboriously accumulated; and in many respects present-day sociology differs as much from what it was thirty or forty years ago—in method, in content, and in concept—as its present status differs from its status then. The great advances in knowledge that have brought sociology to its present state have, however, been advances in knowledge and understanding of social structure, of the forms of social life. No comparable advances have occurred in knowledge and understanding of the processes by which and the conditions under which these forms change through time.

It is easy to understand why most of the advances have been in the field of social structure, where the dimension of time is relatively unimportant. Very early, historical sociology bogged down in a series of sterile dichotomous concepts, in vast and vague theories of history, and in the no doubt inspiring but scientifically unfruitful doctrine of social evolution. Subsequent and less pretentious attempts to introduce the dimension of time into sociological analysis have produced only particularistic fallacies, such as geographic, biological, technological, and ideological determinism. These conceptual cul-de-sacs have no doubt discouraged interest in social change and diverted attention from it; but the fact that nothing much has yet been done about the subject does not mean that sociologists can long afford to ignore it. If sociology is to maintain the status that it has so recently and laboriously won and to secure the full social support that is essential to its continued growth, sociologists must attack the study of social change with the same zest and conceptual ingenuity that have characterized the study of social structure; for in the long run the status of sociology will depend upon the ability of sociologists to provide decision makers, political and otherwise, with probability predictions of the consequences to society of various alternative courses of action.

Man has fumbled along for thousands of years solving, or failing to solve, the problems of his collective survival by empirical procedures. It is only two centuries or so ago that man began to utilize that systematic method of ascertaining the probable consequences of a given act that is known as science, and so far man has applied science mainly to his adjustment to and use of physical and biological nature. The need to have scientific knowledge about social life and the need to apply it to social life are not, therefore, historically self-evident; but there are good reasons to believe, reasons that will be explored in the following pages, that modern man cannot long survive if political and other policy decisions continue to be made on an empirical basis. The kings of old could do little wrong, if only because their whims and fancies had such slight effect on the course of social history; but under the vast and encompassing organizations of the modern world any error can be disastrous, and foresight is a social necessity. Ability to predict the consequences of a law, an administrative ruling, or a decision to produce or not produce some new device or product is fast becoming the *sine qua non* of social survival; and ability to predict with some assurance rests on a full understanding of the ways through which and the conditions under which social change comes about.

The theory upon which the following analysis is based, and which for reasons of personal preference is kept more implicit than explicit, constitutes a sharp break with the traditional theories that have in the past served as barriers rather than pathways to an exploration of social change. It rejects the vague idea, derived from the nineteenth century, of change as a socially normal process that arises, inevitably and effortlessly, out of the conditions that are thereby modified. It builds rather on the view, advanced a decade and more ago by H. G. Barnett, that social change is worked by the efforts of individuals—functioning in various capacities as innovators, advocates, or adopters—who have in some small measure and in some specific respect been freed from the conventionalizing effects of social ideology and of organizational membership; and it endeavors to specify the kinds of social circumstances that are favorable to the emergence of such individuals and the kinds of forces that bring those circumstances about.

Richard T. LaPiere

Contents

chapter 1 *Theories of Change*

Every innovation, whether it be a new mechanical device, a new form of human relationship, an addition to the stock of knowledge, or a theory, such as that which will be presented here, is at once a utilization of established cultural elements and a violation of some aspect of the social *status quo*. It may be well, therefore, to preface this analysis of the processes and conditions of social change with an examination of ideas, old and new, concerning the desirability of social change, the ways it comes about, and its consequences to the welfare of mankind.

Through most of recorded social history men have apparently considered that change per se is undesirable and that the ideal social condition is stability. Whether society as they have known it has been stable or whether it has been undergoing rapid change, they have sought to maintain or to achieve continuity of social life—to preserve for their descendants what they have inherited from their ancestors. Folklore, myth, legend, theology, social philosophy, ethical and aesthetic standards, and other symbolic constructs have, for the most part, reflected the traditional modes of social conduct and have operated as social controls, subtly or overtly coercing the individual members of society to conform to the traditional ways of life. Even the philosophers of change, such as Plato and Marx, have usually granted the desirability of change only as a means to the achievement of the good—and stable—social order; men have, in fact, through most of social history maintained a considerable degree of social stability. Wars, invasions, and other disasters, natural or social, have been a commonplace in most times and places; but periods of pronounced social change have been few and of short duration, and during these periods only limited areas of the social system have been affected, while the vast bulk of the social heritage has persisted, generation after generation, more or less intact.

1

The conclusion is inescapable, therefore, that stability has been not only the social ideal but also the normal social condition. Quantitatively and qualitatively, social change has been the atypical, if not the abnormal. Only within the past three hundred years, and until very recently only among Western peoples, has change secured any general social sanction. Over the past three hundred years Western society has changed at an unsteady but ever-increasing rate; and the idea of a new normal—one in which change is the typical and stability is the abnormal—has become tenable if not generally acceptable. Even now, in the midst of the most rapid social change that man has ever experienced, the social *ideal* would seem to lean toward the glorification of stability and the depreciation of change, as witness the fact that most contemporary sociological writing is concerned with structure rather than process, with the state of things as they are rather than with how they came to be that way and in what directions they are going.

THE CONCEPT OF SOCIAL PROGRESS

During the Middle Ages the social thought, secular as well as sacred, of Western society (and also, incidentally, of Byzantine and Islamic society) was hardly more than a rationalization of the social *status quo;* it endeavored to explain and justify things as they were, whatever they might happen to be at the moment—the authority of dukes and kings, the existence of slavery, the position of serfs, the universality of poverty, the frequency of war, etc. In the sixteenth century the historian Jean Bodin did, it is true, break from this practice of mere rationalization and offer a cyclical interpretation of history, his eye on the decline of ancient Rome; but it was centuries later before this approach was adopted by others. Even such an enterprising product of the Italian Renaissance as Machiavelli, who is often characterized as the first social scientist after Aristotle, thought only of preserving the power of princes, which he assumed would be accomplished by sly and crafty political preservation of the *status quo.* The Reformation of the sixteenth century was a marked change in religious ideas and organization that reflected many antecedent changes—the general breakup of the medieval system; but Luther's intention was to return religion to the purity of the good old days, and Calvin's theocratic state was designed specifically to produce and maintain social stability. Not until Locke (1632–1704) did there appear a social philosopher who directly and consistently sanctioned change, in this case through political revolt, as a desirable and justifiable process; and Locke considered revolution, as did Marx two centuries later, to be a means by which the people could recapture the equable social conditions they had lost through changes that had been wrought by political tyranny.

It was not, in fact, until well toward the close of the eighteenth century that the idea emerged in Western Europe that change per se is desirable; and it was well into the nineteenth century before the further idea emerged that desirable social change is also inevitable. The former was a product of French intellectualism; the latter, of British science.[1]

Late in the eighteenth century the French essayist Condorcet advanced the view that men could apply their minds to a deliberate improvement of their social relationships, even as they had already applied themselves to improvement of their material technology. Princes, kings, and emperors had, of course, always proceeded upon the assumption that they could by legal fiat prevent changes that were in process, that is, changes that seemed to jeopardize their rule, and an occasional ruler had endeavored by the same means to improve the lot of his subjects. But Condorcet advanced the very novel thesis that men could by scientific study of social life discover the laws by which it operated and devise social improvements in accordance with these laws. Condorcet was perhaps the first positivist, the first of those who have believed that men can plan and bring into being efficient social organizations and procedures in the same basic fashion in which they design and then build bridges, ships, and other material edifices and devices. It was, at any event, upon this assumption that Saint-Simon and others in early nineteenth-century France initiated the socialist movement that, after many modifications, was to be translated into action in postrevolutionary Russia; and it was upon this same assumption, derived from common roots but differently developed, that the founders of the American commonwealth formulated the Constitution of the United States as a rational design for *the* good and effective system of government.

The idea of social progress, that men could by their own efforts and through the application of reason to human affairs work improvements in their social life, constituted a sharp break with the social thought that had prevailed throughout the Middle Ages. It was, in the terms that will be used later in this analysis, a major ideological innovation. It involved a rejection of the traditional idea—an idea that had been sanctioned and propagated by the medieval Church and that had for the most part been validated by the actions of secular authority—that life in this world is inherently and inevitably wretched, a sort of trial by ordeal that has been ordained by God as punishment for man's fall from grace. To what extent this morbid view of life actually affected the conduct of medieval peoples is impossible to say; but

[1] A general account of this development is provided by J. B. Bury in *The Idea of Progress: An Inquiry into Its Origin and Growth*, Dover Publications, Inc., New York, 1955. For the French intellectuals who contributed to the idea of progress, see Frank E. Manuel, *The Prophets of Paris*, Harvard University Press, Cambridge, Mass., 1962. The impact of the idea on American thought is examined in Stow Persons (ed.), *Evolutionary Thought in America*, Yale University Press, New Haven, Conn., 1950.

it reflected, if it did not induce, their characteristic passivity toward social and other forms of adversity. The idea of social progress also involved a rejection of the belief, so long maintained by the medieval Church, that forms of social life have been designated by divine will and are therefore inviolable and that, such being the case, any attempt by mere man to change the conditions of his life, even to escape slavery or violate the bonds of feudal serfdom, is a sinful evasion of the design that God has wrought for man.

The men who contributed to the emergence of the idea of social progress —Locke, Condorcet, Saint-Simon, and the many others—were both ingenious and courageous; for it required great courage and profound contempt for the traditional to assert that not God but man himself had created society and that what man had wrought man could change to suit his needs and his conveniences. It is difficult now to appreciate how radical, how subversive in the eyes of authority, how strikingly adventurous, this idea must have seemed to most men of eighteenth-century Europe. It rejected and ran counter to a vast collection of myths, legends, superstitions, laws, and theological proscriptions.

The idea of social progress did not of itself produce the many and profound changes that distinguish contemporary social life from that of the later Middle Ages; but it did give ideological sanction to the changes that occurred and at the same time provided a favorable ideological climate for the making of further changes, for it elevated to a central position in social thought the view that God helps most those who help themselves. The correlates of this view are many and equally at variance with medieval thought: that man is a rational animal; that through systematic application of reason—i.e., through science—man can extend his powers to control his destiny; that the purpose of life is to live and to live as long and as comfortably and as enjoyably as possible. The idea of social progress was, moreover, variously applied. The socialists, early and late, believed that progress was to be achieved through political planning and enforcement of the good life; the laissez-faire economists, on the other hand, believed that it was to be achieved through the removal of all political restraints on individual enterprise. Furthermore, there was, inevitably perhaps, considerable difference of opinion regarding what kinds of change constitute progress.

Evolutionism

The idea that it is possible to improve society through deliberate human effort has persisted in one form or another and among various segments of society down to the present day. It has been the ideological basis for all sorts of efforts at social reform, legal and otherwise; but it does not define the course of social development. According to it, men can work improvements in their society; but whether they will do so and, if they do, of what these improvements will consist are unpredictable, the uncertain consequence of individual endeavor. Such indeterminacy was evidently uncongenial to the systematic minds of many nineteenth-century philosophers; moreover, it ran counter to the growing faith in the existence of a great, cosmic design in nature. In order to fit man and his society into that design, many social philosophers began to conceive of social progress as the manifestation of a natural law. Of these, Auguste Comte (1798–1857) is perhaps the most notable, not only because he coined the term "sociology" and thereby became the titular founder of a field of science, but also because his theory has in part survived the test of time. To the idea of social progress by deliberate endeavor Comte added the concept of fixed stages—from the theological to the scientific— through which each society must progress; it is only when the final stage, the scientific, is reached that rational control of human affairs becomes possible. Already, he believed, Western peoples had reached the scientific stage in respect to nature, and they were on the threshold of that stage in regard to social relations. Soon sociology, the scientific study of the laws of social life, would make it possible for social technicians to devise improved systems of social life through which men would ultimately achieve the good, because highly efficient, society.

Less optimistic was the cosmic philosophy of Herbert Spencer (1820– 1903). Every society, he thought, goes through a series of fixed and immutable stages, not because of deliberate effort on the part of man himself, but as a consequence of a cosmic design over which man has no control. With Spencer, therefore, the idea of social progress by human endeavor gives way to that of inevitable evolutionary development in directions dictated by natural law. With the publication of Darwin's *On the Origin of Species,* the concept of evolutionary development, social as well as biological, captured the minds of many nineteenth-century intellectuals, and much attention was devoted to speculative consideration of the course and mechanism of social evolution. In all such speculation the idea of inevitability was strong; and although men differed greatly as to where evolution was taking them and how the process worked, they were inclined to accept constant social change as good—if only because it was thought to be inevitable. That idea was staunchly resisted by Protestant theologians, by philosophers of doom, and by uninformed laymen, all of whom, as is usual, preferred to hold to things as they were rather than assume the risk of things as they might become. For most intellectuals, however, the concept of inevitable evolutionary development of society provided a reassuring mental scheme by which to order and interpret the many and extensive changes that were actually occurring in their society. It made all such changes meaningful and desirable; moreover, it offered a "scientific" justification for events, such as war, and for conditions, such as the impoverishment of the masses, that would appear to run counter to the belief that society was progressing.

Many quite contradictory theories of social evolution were developed, each, presumably, providing its originator with a satisfactory rationalization of those particular changes that were of interest to him. Many of these theories, such as those of the Austrian Gumplowicz and the Englishman Kidd, played variations on the Darwinian concept of the survival of the fittest, the fittest being defined as the most effective social system or element thereof. Many others, especially those developed by antiquarians and anthropologists, such as Morgan, Maine, and Westermarck, incorporated the idea of stages that Comte and Spencer had propounded. Thus Westermarck, whose attention was focused on the institution of marriage, saw that institution as having evolved over the ages and through the fixed stages of primitive promiscuity, group marriage, polygamy, and polyandry to monogamy in which the uncertainty of fatherhood led to inheritance through the maternal line (the matrilinear system) and finally to the patriarchal family, the last, the perfected stage. In its evolution each society, he thought, must progress through these same fixed stages of family development.

Neo-evolutionism

The idea of social change as the normal and as proceeding inevitably from bad to good and from good toward better on the way to social perfection was an intellectual heritage from which the early modern sociologists could not entirely escape. The American Lester F. Ward blended Comtian positivism with Darwinism and the traditional American faith in the social benefits of public school education to produce his concept of "telic progress." Comte had expected the achievement of the scientific stage of social thought to lead to the emergence of a new social elite, the social engineers, who would apply to human welfare the findings of science, including those of the new science of society. Comte's perfected society would be autocratic and authoritarian in nature; for the social engineers would take over the directive functions that had previously been fulfilled by ignorant and self-seeking politicians and authoritatively apply law and government with scientific efficiency. Ward, on the other hand, believed that the application of scientific knowledge, about social as well as natural phenomena, was to come about through increasingly rational, i.e., expedient, conduct on the part of the individual members of society, conduct made possible by the fact that they had been taught in public schools the scientific facts of life—physical, biological, and social. Thus each individual would be a "social engineer"; and the good society, the society that would in this way be brought into being, would be both democratic and equalitarian.

Since Ward's concept of telic progress made public school education second in importance only to science itself, the educators of America found in it justification for the indefinite expansion of educational facilities; and even today Ward is considered by educators as the father of educational theory. There may be good reason to doubt the validity of the concept of telic progress; but there can be no doubt that public school education is one of the dominant values of contemporary American society, and to an almost equal extent of European. Whatever the realities, Americans quite generally believe that formal education is *a* means, and possibly *the* means, to social progress; the current attempt to solve the racial problem in our Southern states by forcible integration of Negro and white schools, for example, is only one of the many manifestations of American faith in the efficacy of education.

Ward was the only notable American sociologist to make the evolutionary concept his primary concern; indeed, as will shortly become evident, American sociologists have been inclined to ignore the phenomenon of social change. Most of the early German sociologists, such as Weber, Tönnies, and Simmel, on the other hand, were much interested in the processes of change and were in one way or another evolutionary in their outlook. All believed that society, specifically Western society, was moving inexorably from one stage or phase toward another, better one. Weber's theory of the role of the Protestant ethic in the emergence of capitalistic society, which will be given considerable attention later, had no evolutionary implications; it was, in fact, a truly scientific hypothesis of specific historical sequences; and while it has its limitations, it is one of the few usable concepts of social change that have been advanced by sociologists. Weber's theory of bureaucracy, however, incorporates the central concept of evolutionism—that change proceeds in some specified and irreversible direction.[2] For Weber this direction is one of ever-increasing rationality in social arrangements and practices. Capitalistic forms of social organization, produced by the rational conduct of individuals qua individuals, would, he thought, in due course give way to bureaucratic society in which collective rationality would replace that of an individual character. The result would be the ultimate, if not perfect, society, a society in which all the various social functions would be efficiently fulfilled through bureaucratic organizations.

The *Gemeinschaft-Gesellschaft* theory that was advanced by Tönnies is even more clearly an expression of nineteenth-century faith in evolution.[3] Although couched in the language of a hypothesis designed to put into order

[2] A summary of Weber's thesis is provided by H. G. Gerth and C. Wright Mills in *From Max Weber*, Oxford University Press, Fair Lawn, N.J., 1946, chap. VIII, "Bureaucracy." According to Weber, even the arts were evolving in the direction of greater rationality through increasing application of scientific thought and the scientific method. See Max Weber, *The Rational and Social Foundations of Music*, Don Martindale et al. (trans.), Southern Illinois University Press, Carbondale, Ill., 1960.

[3] Ferdinand Tönnies, *Community and Society*, Charles P. Loomis (trans.), The Michigan State University Press, East Lansing, Mich., 1957.

the observed facts of social change, it is actually an assumption that in the past men have always and everywhere lived together in tradition-bound modes of life (*Gemeinschaft*) but have now finally begun to evolve a new, more fruitful system of organization (*Gesellschaft*). In this new system the individual members will be relatively free to exercise reason in the conduct of their affairs; and they will be held together in loose collectivities, not through the dead hand of the past, but from a conscious awareness of the advantage to them of organization of this sort. As a crude description, in ideal-type terms, of some aspects of the changes that have recently been occurring in Western societies, Tönnies's *Gemeinschaft-Gesellshaft* dichotomy has some value; but when it is used as an explanation for the emergence of modern society, as it has been used by Tönnies and his followers, it is hardly more than a warmed-over version of Comtian positivism. Nevertheless, this theory has been used by many contemporary sociologists and anthropologists explicitly as an explanatory device; it occupies a rather strong place in the folklore of American sociology, and it appears in a variety of guises, such as the sacred-secular typology that was so long and so staunchly advocated by Howard Becker.

The imprint of evolutionism is also to be found in the theories of a number of early modern French sociologists, most clearly in the writings of Durkheim. Like Tönnies, Durkheim advanced a concept of social change that involved two stages. In the first stage, which has been characteristic of all premodern peoples, there is little division of labor, the members of a society are very much one like another, and they are all held together in social groups through what he termed "mechanical solidarity." The second, recently achieved stage has been forced into being by population pressures; it involves a progressive division of labor, which in turn produces marked and sharp differentiation of the members. The now highly divergent individuals are bound together in groups not, as Tönnies saw it, through rational self-interest but rather through a subrational acceptance of group ideology, through "collective representations." Durkheim did not consider that the historical trend from small, homogeneous, custom-bound forms of group life toward large, differentiated, and ideologically unified forms was necessarily progress— from inferior to superior; but he believed that the trend was a historical imperative and that the latter phase or state of social development was the ultimate one.

In Britain the rather pessimistic evolutionism of Spencer was given an optimistic turn by such early twentieth-century social scientists as Graham Wallas, Leonard Hobhouse, and Morris Ginsberg.[4] They all believed that social change is inevitable; they all held that the direction of social change

[4] Morris Ginsberg, *The Idea of Progress: A Revaluation*, Beacon Press, Boston, 1953.

is from simple, relatively ineffectual forms of organization (tribal, feudal, familistic, etc.) toward the highly differentiated, but at the same time highly integrated, forms of organization that they believed to be the emergent characteristic of modern society; and they all regarded this change as desirable as well as inevitable, since it was bringing about greater human welfare.

SOCIALISTIC CONCEPTS OF CHANGE

Evolutionism tended to dominate Western social thought through the nineteenth and well into the present century; but it was often combined, particularly by men of impetuous temperament, with the earlier concept of progress through rational and deliberate social action to justify some sort of reformistic program. Such reformers usually accepted to some degree or other the idea that society does change inexorably and in the direction of perfection. They deviated from the true evolutionists, who were content to let natural law work itself out, in the belief that the evolutionary process was being thwarted by those who had a strong vested interest in the *status quo*—by persons and classes of persons who profited by the inadequacies of the existing, and imperfect, social system. They were far from agreed, however, upon who or what it was that hampered the course of progress and, thus, upon what should be done to speed the evolutionary process.

Particularly here in America, the evolutionary reformers were prone to focus their attention upon specific social conditions that they defined as bad, rather than upon a class of persons presumed to be responsible for those conditions, and to direct their attacks toward amelioration of those conditions. The reforms that they advocated—the elimination of ignorance, of slavery, of poverty, and of drinking; the liberation of women; the unionization of workers; improvements in the penal system; etc.—often became the cores of strong social movements and somewhat less often may actually have speeded changes in social organization. In Europe, on the other hand, the tendency was for social thinkers to take a broader and longer view and to advocate sweeping and systematic, rather than piecemeal, reform programs.

Anarchism

Building somewhat on the theories of Saint-Simon, but taking their cue mainly from Rousseau, a school of French social thinkers and reformers developed around the idea that the barrier to social progress is government (a view that was also held, in more moderate degree, by the English economist Adam Smith). In this view, government is always and everywhere inimical to change, since it invariably represents the social elite, a parasitic class that has a vested interest in preserving those traditional forms of social life which enable them to live well on the miseries of common people. Political revolution is not the solution; for parliamentary government is no better than monarchial, as is attested by the venality and the upper-class bias of the First Republic. Progress can come only when government per se is eliminated; the resulting condition will be that of anarchy, in which the true nature of man is permitted to become manifest. Since the advocates of anarchy accepted Rousseau's dictum that "natural man" is altruistic and that the evil deeds of men are all a manifestation of political constraint and repression, they believed that a state of social anarchy would be one of willing and blissful cooperation among individuals—that is, that once government was destroyed, the truly natural and perfected society would quickly come into being.

Although the term "anarchy" currently implies total social chaos, a reversion to presocial barbarism, to the anarchists of the nineteenth century, mainly French and some Russian, it meant quite the opposite. They often advocated violent and destructive attacks upon property, private and public, but only as a means toward the liquidation of government; for they considered property to be the material manifestation of the political order—i.e., that it is mainly through forcible preservation of the legal, hence entirely fictitious, rights of property ownership that government maintains its power and its ability to prevent social progress. To destroy property—sabotage of industrial plants was a favored device among active anarchists—was simply a means of undermining governmental authority. Their goal, as is the professed goal of all revolutionists and the actual goal of most social reformers, was the achievement of a utopian society.

The assumption that government is inherently evil was not peculiar to the anarchists; it ran through much of the social thought of the late eighteenth and the nineteenth centuries, and it probably stemmed from the fact that for the most part the political constraints on individual action that had grown up through the later Middle Ages were inimical to the technological and other changes that were bringing industrial society into being. Thus even the stolid, and in many respects solidly conservative, framers of the Constitution of the United States subscribed to the view that government is an evil, although a necessary one; and they endeavored to devise a political system that would provide the necessary minimum of government but that could not be extended beyond this point to become an unnecessary evil. Marx, whose theories are now used to justify harsh and rigorous political control by communistic governments, also considered government a necessary evil; but for him government was necessary only during the short transitional period that would occur between the revolutionary destruction of the capitalistic system and the emergence of the utopian, the communal, one. As the latter, the final, evolutionary stage was reached, government would wither away, never to appear again.

What the anarchists did was to deny that the evil of government is in fact a necessary one, even temporarily, and to put their faith in man himself. For them, man the individual is inherently good. If left to his own devices, he will live and work with his fellow men in peace, plenty, and contentment. The end of government will not bring social chaos; on the contrary, it will bring the end of strife, including war, and the end of meanness and evil conduct of every sort, both individual and collective; and it will enable men to evolve, as nature has intended that they should, efficient and equable forms of non-political social life. Specifically, the end of government will enable all men to live and work together in the same idealistic, self-sacrificing, and coopera-tive ways in which man now lives and works, despite the repressive force of government, within his family membership. All men will then be truly brothers. Although the anarchists considered organized religion as a servant of evil government, in the good society that they envisioned the individual members would conduct themselves very much in accordance with the Ten Commandments; and it is not without reason that a latter-day offshoot of the anarchistic movement in France took the name of Christian socialism.

Marxism

Karl Marx was directly in the evolutionary tradition. He saw society moving inevitably through predetermined phases or stages as a consequence of a mystic force that he called "historical imperatives." The nineteenth-century phase, capitalism, was one which had brought a solution to the age-old prob-lem of production—the provision of material wealth sufficient to free men from bondage to nature. But this phase, which, by freeing the forces of indi-vidual initiative, had wrought such great advances in the techniques of produc-tion, had also made possible the systematic exploitation of the majority of the members of society by the holders of the tools of production (the capitalists), with the result that, while these few profited hugely from the improvement of productive techniques, the masses (the workers) whose labor created wealth profited not at all.

The power of the capitalists to exploit the masses, to retain for their own use the surplus value (those goods and services that were not essential to the sheer physical survival of the workers), stemmed, Marx thought, from the fact that the capitalists controlled government, directing it, even as they did religion, to their own ends. In accordance with "historical imperatives," the industrial workers, then unaware of the extent to which they were being exploited, would eventually develop a class consciousness, realize that their interests as a class were antithetical to those of their capitalistic exploiters, and finally revolt. The revolution would be directed toward the destruction of the existing political system and the liquidation of the exploitative class. Out of the chaos of revolution there would arise a government of, for, and by the workers; and this government would legislate into existence a communal economic system that would operate on the principle of "from each according to his abilities, to each according to his need." During this transitional phase in the evolution of the good society, what Marx called the tutorial period, political control would dominate; but once the inherently good people, the workers, had learned to live together in the proper communal manner and had discovered the advantages of doing so, the need for political enforcement of the good life would disappear. In the end, therefore, communal forms of life would be self-maintaining and thus stable. For Marx, as for so many others, social change was only a means of achieving social stability at a utopian level.[5]

So far, Marx differed from other true evolutionists only in the particular sequence of stages through which he thought society was moving and would move. The fact that he believed political revolution to be one of the events in the evolutionary process does not make him any less an evolutionist. With the publication of the *Communist Manifesto*, however, he became the advocate of action intended to speed up the evolutionary process and thereby entered the ranks of the social reformers.

Fabian Socialism

It is frequently asserted that of all the theories of change advanced during the nineteenth century, Marxism is the only one that proved to have predictive value—i.e., that was actually realized; and it is probably assumed by many laymen, here as well as in Russia, that Marxism caused the Russian Revolution and the emergence of communistic society. Neither the first assertion nor the second assumption, however, has any validity. There is no doubt that the early Bolsheviks got their inspiration, perhaps even their courage, from Marx's assurance that revolution was an evolutionary imperative; nor is there any doubt that Lenin and his successors have paid lip service to Marxian doctrine; but for the rest, everything has gone contrary to Marx's expectations. The early Bolsheviks did not bring about the revolution in Russia; they simply grasped power during the chaos and political vacuum that the revolution induced. The revolution itself occurred, not as Marx had predicted it would, in the most industrialized country of the West (in England), but instead in the least industrialized. Rather than being a spontaneous uprising of a class-conscious industrial proletariat against their capitalistic exploiters, it began as a rebellion of soldiers and sailors against their bumbling aristocratic officers and was never more than an attack upon a postfeudal elite (the czarist regime). Not until the later Bolsheviks took over did the relatively small bourgeois class (the villains in

[5] For one of many recent reevaluations of Marxian theory see Robert C. Tucker, *Philosophy and Myth in Karl Marx*, Cambridge University Press, New York, 1961.

Marxian drama) become the object of attack. Moreover, the Russian Revolution did not lead, and has not led in nearly a half century since, to the establishment of a classless society. On the contrary, the class distinctions of contemporary Russia are at least as clear as those in any modern Western society and the range in powers, privileges, etc., from highest to lowest class fully as great. The revolution did not, furthermore, bring into being a socioeconomic system that operated on the principle of to each according to his need. On the contrary, the governments of both Communist Russia and China have been endeavoring to maintain the principle of to each according to his political worth. Finally, the revolution did not lead into a tutorial period, with government as the tutor, a temporary evil that would disappear when a new and uncontaminated generation of members had grown to maturity. On the contrary, after two generations the role of government is vastly greater than it was in czarist days. The Russians are currently ruled by the strongest, most durable, most inclusive, and least representative political dictatorship that the world has ever known.

Actually, it is the theory of the Fabian socialists which came closest to predicting what has come to pass in Western societies during the present century. The Fabians, taking their name from the Roman general Quintus Fabius Maximus, whose nibbling tactics eventually brought the downfall of the conquering Hannibal, were mainly British intellectuals (Bernard Shaw was among their numbers) who were discouraged by some aspects of capitalistic society and yet violently opposed to Marx's solution.[6] They rejected the idea that revolution was necessary in order to bring about the evolution of the good society; they held, rather, that the transition from capitalism to socialism would and should be gradual and piecemeal. They were indifferent to the presumed class struggle; indeed, they did not perceive any sharp and irreconcilable conflict in interests among the various classes. The real struggle, the vital conflict, as they viewed the problem, was between old ideas of what is right and proper and rational perception of the advantages of a socialistic system of life. Bit by bit, they thought, the logical desirability of socialism would be discovered and socialistic forms would evolve. They were not clear concerning the role of government in this process; but on the whole they seem to have believed that it would be through specific political actions, as distinct from all-inclusive political action, that socialistic principles would be put into practice. Moreover, they considered that the core principle of socialism—the greatest good to the greatest number—was already implicit in many of the social reforms, such as the establishment of minimum standards of safety in mines and the construction of public housing for the poor, that had already been undertaken in England.

[6] Margaret Cole, *The Story of Fabian Socialism*, Stanford University Press, Stanford, Calif., 1962.

Fabian socialism was, thus, a projection into the future of certain of the changes that were already occurring in highly industrialized societies; and it has so happened that the kinds of changes that the Fabians considered to be socialistic in nature, mainly the assumption by governmental agencies of responsibility for the welfare of special classes of the population, in fact continued to occur and still continue to occur at a rate that the Fabians did not anticipate. Every modern Western country is today even less individualistic and capitalistic and even more socialistic than was the Fabian ideal; and the process by which socialistic principles have come into practice is very much that which the Fabians advocated—a piecemeal reduction of the personal rights of the individual and a concomitant piecemeal extension of his social right to economic maintenance.

Moralistic Reformism

Neither Marxism nor Fabian socialism acquired much of a following in the United States. For one thing, the comparatively high rates of change in this country during the latter half of the nineteenth century made any concerted and deliberate effort to produce changes seem redundant; organized resistance to changes in process was, perhaps, more appropriate to the times. For another, the opportunities for personal advancement, even for members of the working classes, were so great that social malcontents and the exceptionally ambitious may have found it easier and more rewarding to better their positions within the existing social system than to undertake reformation of the system. Moreover, faith in the powers of public school education to rectify social inadequacies remained strong. Thus, for many, the mechanism of social progress was already at work and needed no supplementary aids.

As was mentioned earlier, nineteenth-century America did, however, generate a great number and variety of short-lived mass movements, usually reformistic in nature, and an even greater number of crusades against some specific social condition or in favor of some specific social change. Of the movements, that against the use of alcoholic beverages (the temperance movement) was the most durable, the most vociferant, the most widespread, and, in the long run, the least effective. Of the crusades, that in favor of the political enfranchisement of women, which probably reflected fundamental underlying social changes, was one of the most effective. The goals of the various crusades were infinitely varied: liberation of the Negro slaves, unionization of labor, free coinage of silver, protection of farmers against the inroads of industrialization, liberalization of the divorce laws, elimination of prostitution, etc.

What the various movements and crusades had in common was faith in the power of organized minority groups to bring about calculated social change and to prevent changes that were already in progress. That faith was, and in some degree still is, one of the distinguishing characteristics of American society. The second quality that they had in common was the moral basis upon which the movements and crusades generally justified their endeavors. In America, by contrast with Europe, most reform movements and many crusades had as their avowed goal, not the economic improvement of the condition of the masses, but moral elevation. Thus the primary charge against slavery was its immoral character; that against liquor, that its use was sinful; that against prostitution, not that it made for human misery, but that it was in violation of divine law. In America the Protestant pulpit was commonly used to propagandize in favor of some social change or in protest against some other change. American churches were, therefore, often centers of social reform and of resistance to change, whereas in Europe the churches, both Catholic and Protestant, tended to remain outside the arena of organized social strife.

At the same time churchmen, both American and European, were exceedingly busy reforming the natives of various non-Western lands by inducting them into the religious and social practices of the West. The missionaries proceeded on the assumption, not generally held at home, that Western society had been brought to perfection and that the remaining task was to spread the benefits of Western society to all the people of the world. As agents of social change, they played an important role during the latter half of the nineteenth century and well into the twentieth, although the changes that they actually helped to bring about were seldom those that they had contemplated and often in the long run succeeded only in creating more problems than they solved. Nevertheless, in spite of the experiences of the past, the missionary spirit and the belief in reform still persist; since World War II, the United States, with some reluctant aid from Western Europe, has been embarked upon a vast, new, but this time distinctly political, endeavor to bring the material benefits of Western society to the heathens—now euphemistically described as the underdeveloped peoples of the world.

THEORIES OF CYCLICAL CHANGE

To support the theory of social evolution—or, as it is now usually described, the hypothesis that social change is constant and in the direction of perfection—appeal was made to historical data. What the evolutionists, including Marx, did was to present selected facts (and, inevitably, fictions) from recent historical developments or to point out contrasts between primitive societies and contemporary Western societies. They could do no more; for any searching study of historical and comparative materials would emphatically have disproved the thesis that societies move constantly in the direction of perfection and would have revealed that the rates of social change have varied widely from society to society and from time to time within a given society and that the directions of such changes as have occurred, by whatever standard of measurement, also have varied. A monogamous people may, as did the Mormons, adopt polygamy; a lawful society may evolve a high crime rate; a democratic political system may become autocratic; an expanding system may, in the course of time, become a contracting one; and so on.

Theory of History

The antithesis to the theory that social change is toward perfection is the old and intriguing idea that societies change, not toward perfection, but toward extinction. When attention is focused on human culture in general, particularly when it is focused on the material technology, which often leaves records in the form of artifacts, it is possible to trace over long periods of time a progressive refinement—a movement from the crude, simple, and inefficient toward ever-increasing complexity and efficiency. Thus ten thousand or so years ago, the best housing used by man was the natural cave; today, after many developments, he may live in a vast, complex, efficient man-made structure—a modern apartment house. Where once a fire of fagots, burning in the center of his cave, was the most effective use of fire man could achieve, today, after thousands of years of development, he can ride his contrived heat waves through the stratosphere. Where once the best tool that man could muster was a stone, selected from those available in the riverbed, today he has at his command all the vast and complex instruments of modern industry. In many instances, developments of this order can be traced, step by step, through countless centuries. Such evidences lead quite logically to the idea of evolutionary progress.[7]

[7] It is through the mustering of just such evidence that anthropologist Leslie A. White (*Evolution of Culture*, McGraw-Hill Book Company, New York, 1959) has endeavored to revive and revitalize evolutionary theory. He and his disciples treat culture very abstractly and do not hesitate to jump from society to society and century to century in tracing the "evolution" of a given device or social practice. The result is a sort of museum view of cultural elements, with the element under study entirely removed from its operational context. It was to correct for this very artificial procedure and to bring anthropological study and analysis down to earth that Bronislaw Malinowski developed his functional concept of cultural elements, a concept that has had profound effects upon American sociology. Ironically, Talcott Parsons and his disciples have elevated Malinowski's functionalism to such a rarefied level of abstraction that it, too, has now lost all touch with social realities.

The following are in the cultural-evolution tradition: V. Gordon Child, *Social Evolution*, C. A. Watts & Co., Ltd., London, 1950; Julian H. Steward, *Theory of*

When, however, attention is directed to the life of specific peoples—of a single tribe, family line, town, or even the whole of a civilization—quite a different story emerges. The evolution of tools and other aspects of the material culture of the world was not accomplished by a single people, but rather by a great many peoples, each having made its own limited contribution and most having vanished from the earth. Culture in general may have evolved; but various peoples and their particular ways of social life have come and gone. Where now are the ancient Greeks with their city-states and many very human gods? Where now are the Romans with their flowing togas and their love of gladiatorial contests to the death? There remain Greek philosophy and Roman law, the ruins of temples and colosseums, and fragmentary records of their long and turbulent histories; but modern Greeks and modern Romans have little more in common with the Greeks and Romans of antiquity than do the cities that they occupy. Not even the "blood" of the ancients has survived.

Students of social history, particularly of that of the Mediterranean area, could hardly fail to be impressed by the transitory character of societies —of groups of people living together in accordance with a fairly common, although ever-changing, way of life. Within the brief (as geologists measure time) span of five thousand years, a great many civilizations seem to have arisen, to have flourished for a time, and then to have disappeared more or less from the historical record—Egyptian, Babylonian, Cretan, Greek, Carthaginian, Roman, Byzantine, and Islamic. In each of these and in many others, such as the Aztec and Mayan civilizations of central Mexico, an inconspicuous people has at some point begun through wars and expansion and other activities to make their imprint on the historical record. Often they have built upon the ruins of an antecedent society, as the Romans did upon that of Greece. In time, also, they have come to dominate recorded history, in many instances, in fact, to write it. In due course the record begins to show them losing wars, losing political control of territory, and perhaps being invaded by more virulent and less civilized peoples. In a

---

Cultural Change: The Methodology of Multilinear Evolution, The University of Illinois Press, Urbana, Ill., 1955; Marshal D. Sahlins and Elman R. Service (eds.), *Evolution and Culture*, The University of Michigan Press, Ann Arbor, Mich., 1960.

On the rare occasions when Talcott Parsons has acknowledged that social systems are subject to structural change, he has offered a vaguely evolutionary point of view in which social systems move through time from an original condition of "ascriptive solidarity" to one characterized by "functional differentiation," an idea that he no doubt borrowed directly from Durkheim but one that has very deep roots in Western social thought. See, for example, Parsons's discussion of "systems change" in Talcott Parsons et al. (eds.), *Theories of Society*, The Free Press of Glencoe, New York, 1961, vol. 1, pp. 242–263.

century or so, then, the book of history has been closed for them; they have more or less completely disappeared from the record; they are of the past.

The apparent rise and subsequent decline of the civilizations of the past is all too easily equated with the life cycle of the individual human being, who is born, grows to maturity, ages, and then dies. The idea of a rise and decline fits neatly, perhaps too neatly, into the mental framework through which, for evident reasons, all men view the phenomena of life. At any event a great many philosopher-historians have been inclined to impute a life cycle to societies, to their own as well as to those of peoples known to have preceded them. The result is a theory of social history that differs only in minor detail from man to man and from century to century. The Greek Heraclitus, the Moslem Khaldun, the German Leibnitz, and the contemporary Englishman Toynbee had greatly differing historical materials with which to work; but their theories of history, and those of many other scholars, are hardly more than an extension to societies of the characteristic progression of the individual through the organic life cycle.

Like the evolutionists, these theorists of history have considered social change to be normal and inevitable; but whereas the evolutionists believed that a society changes in the constant direction of perfection (upon reaching which, presumably, it then lives happily ever after), the theorists of history have been convinced that the contrary is the case; for the records of history demonstrate that, whatever may have happened to the world at large, every specific society has had—and by projection current societies will have—a comparatively brief period of glory and has then slid into obscurity. Professional historians with theoretical leanings were not, therefore, impressed by the eighteenth-century idea of progress or by the succeeding vogue for the evolutionary concept. They tended, as a consequence, to remain aloof from the stream of thought that gave rise to the social sciences; and in part perhaps in retaliation, social scientists, notably sociologists, have been inclined to depreciate historical materials.

Recent Theories of History

In any study of social change the cyclical theory cannot, however, be ignored. It has persisted in some forms, and it continually reappears in others; and it has, moreover, an inherent appeal in that it gives order and meaning to the otherwise chaotic and conflicting records of the past. Perhaps the earliest of the modern versions was that which was presented in 1725 by Giovanni Battista Vico, who was apparently untouched by the growing hope that was soon to be codified as the idea of progress. Later in the same century Edward Gibbon documented the cyclical theory of history in his monumental and very influential *Decline and Fall of the Roman Empire.* For nearly two centuries thereafter, Gibbon's cyclical concept was the major, although not the only, theoretical framework that was used by historians. Thus in 1920, when H. G. Wells compressed the known history of the world into his *Outline of History*, each of the many civilizations that he discussed followed the standard rise-and-fall pattern.

About the same time, Oswald Spengler advanced a special application of the cyclical concept: The West, which had given birth to industrial society, was now, he contended, losing vigor and beginning to stagnate.[8] The outcome of World War I had clearly demonstrated the venality of Western society—that Western society had come to depreciate strength, military and otherwise, and to sanction weakness and timidity, both individual and collective. Meanwhile, the peoples of Asia had emerged from their centuries of lethargy and were on the march, challenging the power and effectiveness of the West. Political, military, technological, and organizational dominance was, therefore, about to shift from West to East. The next historic epoch would belong to Asia and the Asians, just as long centuries before it had shifted from the venal Greeks to the vigorous Romans.

Spengler's gloomy view of the future of Western society was shared during the early post-World War I years by many writers. Stoddard, for example, forecast that the West would shortly be overwhelmed by a "rising tide of color" (i.e., by Asiatic peoples). Two generations and another great war later, a variety of circumstances—the communization of China, the emergence of nationalistic movements in India and throughout Africa, and the spectacular increase in the populations of these and other underdeveloped regions of the world—lent a certain prophetic quality to such fearful forecasts. The cyclical frame of reference has not, however, always led to pessimism regarding the future of society. As with any heuristic device, a skillful intellectual craftsman can make with it what he will. Thus both the sociological theoretician Sorokin and the historian Toynbee have found in it cause to hope that Western civilization may survive.[9]

Sorokin came to his reassuring conclusion by an ingenious route. He rejected the standard rise-and-fall approach to the history of civilizations, with its stress upon such aspects of social life as the growth and contraction of political and military power, the expansion and loss of territory, the rise and decline of population, and evaluated the social histories of various peoples in terms of degrees of goodness and badness. Moreover, he focused not upon political and related events, but upon such cultural phenomena as art forms, music, literature, and modes of life, and upon the nature and frequency of wars and other evidences of social disorder. All societies, he

[8] Oswald Spengler, *The Decline of the West*, 2 vols., Alfred A. Knopf, Inc., New York, 1939.

[9] Pitirim Sorokin, *Social and Cultural Dynamics*, 4 vols., American Book Company, New York, 1937–1941. A one-volume edition of this work is available under the same title published by Porter Sargent Publisher, Boston, 1957. For Toynbee's position, see Arnold J. Toynbee, *A Study of History*, one-volume abridgement by D. C. Somervell, Oxford University Press, Fair Lawn, N.J., 1947.

decided, fluctuate through time and between two polar extremes—the ideational (the good) and the sensate (the bad). In its ideational phase, the members of a society are guided by idealistic considerations and tend therefore to subordinate crass, personal concerns to the social good; in its sensate phase, on the other hand, they are guided mainly by self-interest and thus put their own individual welfare above that of the common good. The whole of a social system does not move in one coordinated swing toward one pole or the other; one aspect of the system, such as sexual conduct, may be moving in the direction of the sensate while another, such as art forms, may be changing toward the ideational.

Sorokin thought, however, that he saw through the history of Western peoples a long-run general trend: During the Middle Ages life had been in many, if not all, respects ideational; through the last few centuries Western society had been moving generally toward the sensate pole; now, however, Western society was giving evidence of beginning to veer again toward the ideational. Science and scientism are dominant today, and religious idealism has all but vanished from Western life; our art is pornographic, our music is sensual and erotic; our prized buildings are temples of commerce and government; we honor generals and successful politicians and ignore the few saints who appear among us; wealth is power, and most men strive only to achieve it. But whereas these qualities of social life are regarded in the standard theory of history as the prelude to, if not the direct causes of, the disappearance of a society from the historical record, Sorokin held that they are evidence that Western society has more or less completed the swing toward the sensate and is about to reverse its historical course. He was hopeful, therefore, that Western people would survive by moving, slowly and in piecemeal fashion, back toward the ideational pole. It is hardly necessary to add that Sorokin's theory of social change actually differed only in one major respect from that of his predecessors: where they saw a succession of peoples entering and eventually departing from the cycle of history, Sorokin held to a version of collective reincarnation—that is, a given people, in this case the people of the West, runs its life course and is then reborn.

It is also through the concept of rebirth—in what he calls the "response to the challenge of imminent destruction"—that the historian Toynbee has found cause to hope for the future of Western civilization. His version of the history of civilization is considerably more sociological than is that of the sociologist Sorokin, for Toynbee is much interested in the mode and manner by which peoples are organized. Societies, he holds, change for a time by growing larger, stronger, and more productive in a manner somewhat analogous to the physical maturation of an organism; but as they in this sense approach maturity, they tend to develop organizational rigidity, until at length they become stiff and unyielding, even as does an organism in its later years. In this condition a society may persist until it encounters some major crisis—war, plague, loss of material resources, or the like. Such a crisis constitutes a "challenge" to which an aging society may, but not always will, "respond." If the society responds, it recaptures something of the dynamic, adaptive quality that it has lost—it is revitalized, reborn; if it does not respond, it continues down the historic path to oblivion. Western society, according to Toynbee, has passed its youth and is well along into maturity; it shows marked evidences of rigidity; and it is being challenged by a variety of circumstances, such as the rise of Communist Russia and China. Toynbee believes that it can and hopes that it will meet the crisis for survival rather than attempt to evade it; and for Toynbee this means not something simple and obvious, such as military victory over Communist peoples, but a revitalization of the spirit of Western society. Apparently Toynbee, like Sorokin before him, really means that Western society can be saved by a return to religious idealism.

Although sociological disregard of the cyclical theory may stem more from unfamiliarity with social history than from anything else, the theory is in fact of very dubious scientific value. It provides a way of looking upon, of ordering, the multitudinous and chaotic events of social history; but there is reason to suspect that the theory is itself in considerable measure responsible for the fact that the records give so much support to it. Men not only make history, they write it; and the history that is written is inevitably but a slight fraction of that which, over the centuries, men have made. In every phase of the writing process, from the original chronicle or base document to the final integrative history of civilizations, what men think and how they view their world no doubt determine far more what is written than do the events about which they write.[10] Millions of documents, each reflecting the recorder's selective perception of a minute part of what transpired about him, make up the record of the past. Many of these have survived only in fragmentary form; many others are known only through translation, twice or thrice removed; all must be interpreted for meaning and significance; and from them all only a small, residual fraction will actually be used in the writing of the historical record.

Even the process by which written records survive through time may conspire to save only that part of what is at any place and time recorded which fits in with preconceived notions of significance. A scribe may write diligently throughout his lifetime, but at his death his cupboards are cleared of all save a few documents that confirm the current view of man's affairs; these few, perhaps, find their way into a royal collection along with many others, similarly selected. In time, and as an aftermath of war, the library is burned; but all is not lost; in the rubble some unharmed manuscripts and fragments of others are found; and of these, some few, selectively, may

[10] Some idea of the many ways in which events become distorted by the theoretical and other preconceptions of their recorders and subsequent interpreters can be secured from Patrick Gardiner (ed.), *Theories of History*, The Free Press of Glencoe, New York, 1959.

be salvaged. Thus it goes down the centuries. A manuscript is translated into a newer or more virulent tongue, and in the translation selective perception determines what the meanings are and what is worth the saving. In the end, then, what is known of Greece, of Rome, and of Europe during the Middle Ages is at best only a very little and that little selected and distorted by the many men who have contributed to its survival.

It is therefore at least a possibility that what appears in the historical record as a rising and declining of peoples in a complex parallel to the life cycle of an organism is mainly a reflection of the fact that it is in this way that men always view the process of social as well as organic life. This is not to deny that a society is subject to change or that social change may, and over the long run often does, lead to the relative decline of a society vis-à-vis other societies in military strength and other criteria of power and position; but that there is a built-in cycle of change, a process inherent in the very nature of society, is to be doubted. If there were, and if the sequence and time intervals of that cycle could be ascertained in detail, prediction of the future course of a given society—the ultimate goal of the social sciences and the constant claim of social prognosticators, ancient and modern— would be a simple matter. In two thousand years and more, however, the theorists of history have brought us no closer to that goal than men were at the dawn of recorded history.

The cyclical theory can, moreover, be discredited by the very kinds of evidences upon which it is erected; for the historical record indicates that, even as whole civilizations seem to have risen and fallen, so, too, but in an inconsistent fashion, have many of the places and parts within each civilization. Thus the social history of Granada in southern Spain runs as a sort of contrapuntal theme against that of the history of Islam, of which it was once a part. Thus, too, such centers of commerce and the arts as Venice, Genoa, Florence, Bruges, and Montpellier "rose and fell" while Western civilization as a whole was only beginning its rise from obscurity. A close reading of the historical record gives an impression not just of great cycles of history, but of innumerable cycles within cycles, within each of which there are still smaller cycles, such as those of the rise and fall of specific arts or ruling families; and the closer the record is read, the more confused the reader becomes, until the order that is imposed upon it by the cyclical interpretation resolves again into the chaos of a multitude of unique events.

PARTICULARISTIC THEORIES OF SOCIAL CHANGE

During the past fifty years a number of theories of social change, less sweeping and less inclusive than those of evolution and the cyclical course of social history, have been advanced by men qualified as scientists in one field or another. Perhaps only because they have been couched in scientific terms and have been offered by men of science have these theories been granted the serious attention that should be reserved for the truly scientific hypothesis. Nevertheless, they illustrate a common hazard in the analysis of social change—that of applying the scientifically untenable concept of simple cause and effect. In each instance, the theory involves an assumption that social change is the product of some particular variable, some single "cause," and that not only is every change attributable to that cause, but every change in that cause will produce a concomitant change in society.

Incorporate: Culture/Innovations diffuse into urban areas, & then gradually to rural sectors.

Diffusionism

It has often been observed that in some historical periods some one people has maintained a sort of cultural dominance over many others, usually by providing them with new ideas, devices, and forms of organization. At one time, for example, the Sumerians seem to have set the cultural tone for most of the peoples of the Near East, just as centuries later France was to set the fashion in clothes, manners, and morals for the aristocratic elite of all Western Europe. Athens, too, was for a century or more culturally dominant; it provided Rome, its successor, with such varied cultural attributes as philosophy, art, and construction techniques.

During the early years of this century the idea of culturally dominant centers was elaborated and made into a theory of social change by G. Elliot Smith, an Egyptologist. About 3000 B.C., according to Smith, an unusual constellation of circumstances produced a great spurt in cultural development among the people of the Nile Valley; agricultural technology was rapidly improved, geometry was invented, metalworking and toolmaking processes were evolved, a new and effective political order was devised, etc. From this center of cultural innovation new and improved cultural devices spread throughout the Mediterranean and thence to all the peoples of the world. Smith concluded that it was the inventiveness of the Egyptians of that period that was the "cause" of social change in the various societies of the world, that what the Egyptians invented was *diffused* to and adopted by these other societies.

To validate his theory, Smith tried to find cultural similarities between the early Egyptians and peoples as far removed in space and time as the Incas of Peru and the Melanesians of the South Pacific. The cultural characteristics of these and other later peoples were presumed to be cultural survivals from the waves of cultural diffusion that had, ages ago, swept about the world. Since few if any of the social practices of these later peoples were directly comparable to those of the ancient Egyptians, Smith resorted to the cabalistic principle that things—in this case cultural traits—are never what they seem, that beneath the evident lies the true reality (to be ascertained, of course, by Smith himself). Through the application of this formula Smith was able to demonstrate to his and his disciples' satisfaction that a bone fishhook in Melanesia had been derived from a bronze spear developed by the Egyptians, that the Mayan practice of building pyramidal stone structures upon which to hold blood sacrifices to the sun-god was but a transmutation of the Egyptian practice of mummifying their dead and burying them in the great pyramids, etc.

For a generation cultural anthropologists were split into two camps: the diffusionists, who tried to trace everything cultural to some particular center, most often Egypt, and the parallelists, who were inclined to think that each people had independently developed its own cultural devices. The former insisted that man is rarely original; the latter, that originality is a very common characteristic of man. The former held that there is but one history of culture—that of Egypt, or of wherever the center was located, and the world at large; the latter, that each people has its own special and independent history. Time, new evidences, and sober reflection have led to the conclusion that both positions are in error and that, on the other hand, there is a grain of truth in each of them.

Geographic Determinism

In many lands it is a durable folk belief that those who live in the northern part of the area (in the Southern Hemisphere, those in the southern part) are typically of stern and sturdy character, reticent, somewhat dour of disposition, industrious, provident to the point of stinginess, and in these and related ways the antithesis of those who live in the southern section. In accordance with this belief, the latter are characteristically easygoing, tend to be somewhat indolent as befits people who live in a warm climate, and are of open mien, talkative, and of cheerful disposition. This folk belief exists among such varied peoples as the Japanese, the Chinese, the Indians, the Italians, the Germans, the Spanish, and the English. Even in little Holland there is no doubt in the minds of the populace that the people of Groningen (to the north) are sturdy and energetic, dour and uncommunicative, etc., while those of Limburg, scarcely a hundred miles to the south, have the casual characteristics that we in the United States associate with the people of the Deep South.

The apparent universality of this folk dichotomization of people north and south does not mean that it is necessarily valid, and so far no one has attempted to test it systematically; but its implication—that climate determines a people's character—has often been used by social theorists to explain observed differences between societies. The result is a more or less inclusive theory of geographic determinism.

It was an American geographer, Ellsworth Huntington, who used the geographic factor to explain, not just why peoples differ, but why societies change.[11] If, he argued, some geographic condition or some combination of geographic conditions determines the characteristics of a people, then it follows that only as geographic conditions change will their society be changed—unless, of course, they should migrate to some new location having different geographic characteristics. Huntington accepted uncritically the cyclical interpretation of the rise and fall of civilizations about the Mediterranean and set about to explain all such social change in terms of changing climatic conditions. Like Smith, he believed that the cradle of civilization was the valley of the Nile, where there had existed for a time a unique combination of conditions favorable to the development of highly complex and efficient modes of life. For Huntington, these favorable circumstances were a temperate climate, adequate but not excessive rainfall spread equably throughout the year, freedom from violent storms, and sufficient cloud cover to protect the land and its people from the sun. Thus for Huntington the cradle of civilization is a geographic setting such as most human beings dream about but never actually experience.

In this perfect climatic setting men are freed from the normal necessity of diverting time and effort into protecting themselves from climatic adversity; their crops and herds thrive without undue attention; and men therefore have the opportunity to devote themselves to the finer things in life—to devising new tools, developing the arts, working out elaborate and effective systems of organization, etc. It was in just such a physical setting and for just these reasons, according to Huntington, that the Egyptians evolved their complex, civilized mode of life. In time Egyptian civilization faded; the Sumerians rose to civilized estate, and then, they, too, returned to barbarism; and over the centuries the center of civilization shifted from people to people and region to region. Why?

Because, Huntington concluded, climatic changes had reduced the valley of the Nile to a brutally hot, brilliantly lit, exceedingly dry land which in these and other ways had become climatically unfavorable to the maintenance of civilized life. Meanwhile related climatic changes had made the valley of the Euphrates into a climatic cradle of civilization, with the consequence that a civilization arose there to replace that of Egypt; and so on. As the ideal climatic conditions shifted, the center of civilization moved—to Crete, Greece, Rome, Constantinople; and then in due course the physical springs of civilization dried up, and the peoples of the Western world receded into universal barbarism. Presumably, although Huntington did not pursue his theory to this point, it was the reappearance of newly favorable climatic

[11] Ellsworth Huntington, *Climate and Civilization*, 3d ed., Yale University Press, New Haven, Conn., 1924, and *Mainsprings of Civilization*, John Wiley & Sons, Inc., New York, 1945.

conditions that enabled the feudal peoples of Europe to shake off their lethargy, pick up the pieces of Roman civilization, and begin the development of modern Western society.

To validate his theory, Huntington advanced a variety of evidences intended to prove that there had actually occurred profound climatic changes about the Mediterranean basin over the three thousand years or so preceding the fall of Rome. Some of these evidences are indisputable, but the interpretation that Huntington made of them is not. The valley of the Euphrates was once fertile and productive and is now mostly desert wasteland; the hills of Palestine were once heavily forested (from them Caesar obtained the spars for his ships of war) and are now wind-swept and barren; the plains of Carthage were lush with grain in Roman times and are now dry, eroded, and unproductive. Huntington cited these and similar facts as proof that it was natural changes in local climate that had *caused* civilizations to rise and fall. (In due course it will be shown that these geographic changes and many others like them have actually been the work of man himself.) Moreover, to make the history of civilizations fit his theory, Huntington had to ignore a good deal of it; thus he neglected to incorporate in his theory such historical facts as that long after the valley of the Nile had lost its salubrious climate it became once again the center of a great civilization, that of Islam from the seventh to the eleventh century.

Theories of the geographic determination of social change less sweeping and less inclusive than that of Huntington have been advanced from time to time, usually by geographers or other physical scientists who have had slight acquaintance with social history. One that is worth considering and that will be discussed in detail later is that all societies eventually come to a bad end through soil erosion, that, in effect, societies eat themselves out of topsoil. In this view it is not, of course, physical nature that causes the decline of the society; rather, the society destroys itself through bad management of the physical resources necessary for its maintenance.

Biological Determinism

During the nineteenth century the French savant J. A. de Gobineau advanced the thesis that the French were a decadent race who should, and in due course would, give way to the vigorous people of Germany. He thereby anticipated by nearly a century the chauvinistic argument for a war of conquest made by Adolph Hitler and the more devious, if no less chauvinistic, theories of the German geopoliticians. More significantly, De Gobineau gave a semblance of scientific respectability to the old folk idea that blood will tell. This idea has been almost universal, and the members of every tribe and nation have been inclined to subscribe to the view that they themselves are endowed with special and superior natural qualities.

The core of biological determinism is the assumption that the peoples of the world are divided into races, biologically distinct groups, that races have markedly different inherent abilities to develop and maintain social life, and that the forms and quality of the social life that a people lead are indications of the racial qualities of that people. In this way it is possible to explain not only the differences between social systems, but also changes that may occur within a given social system, especially deteriorative changes. Deteriorative changes may logically be traced either to mongrelization, the adulteration of the racial bloodline by the infusion of inferior racial stock (the danger of which was the justification used by the Nazis for their program of exterminating the Jews); to the downbreeding of the race; or to something called the "running out" of racial qualities. Conversely, the rise of a society can be traced to the flowering of latent racial greatness or to the appearance, presumably through the evolutionary process, of superior biological qualities in a population that has formerly been undistinguished.

The idea that a racial stock may deteriorate through downbreeding is based upon the very old and persistent assumption that class differences within a society reflect different biological qualities—that is, that the rich are rich because they are biologically superior to the poor.[12] Even the ancient Greeks, who evidently did not draw the color line, believed that some men are born to rule and most are born to obey. In comparatively modern times the idea that social stratification is simply the social manifestation of biological differences has been used to justify inequalities in educational and other kinds of opportunity, inequality in income, and resistance to social changes that have seemed to jeopardize the position of social elites. It has also been the basis for a major proposal of social reform by deliberate upbreeding of the racial stock.

If, the argument runs, the well to do, the educated, and the most socially productive members of society are what they are because they are biologically superior to their social inferiors, then social progress will come about through a numerical reduction of the latter and an increase in the numbers of the former. Unfortunately, Western societies have of late tended to downbreed; the best biological stocks (the rich, the educated, etc.) have had a considerably lower birth rate than have the poor and ineffectual members of society. The result is a progressive deterioration of the biological quality of the social population—a progressive rise in the proportion of those of inferior quality. This is bringing about or ultimately will bring about a deterioration of social life. To prevent such social decline (comparable, perhaps, to that which in the end brought Rome and other great civilizations to bankruptcy) and reverse the trend—i.e., to assure social progress rather than retrogression—it is necessary only to reduce the lower-class birth rate and increase that of the

[12] The very dubious thesis that modern society encourages the survival of unfit members and is therefore jeopardizing the survival of society itself has been unequivocally stated by E. A. Hooton in *Twilight of Man*, The Macmillan Company, New York, 1939.

upper classes. Such was, in substance, the goal of the eugenics movement, a movement for social reform that a few decades ago had many staunch supporters in England and America.

Neither the biological determinists nor the eugenists have at present any standing among American social scientists, although biological determinism did provide the excuse for the American restrictive immigration legislation that was enacted shortly after World War I and is currently used as the basis for their position by the more extreme opponents to the desegregation of the schools in our Southern states. There are, however, some scientists, mainly biologists, who accept, if only in a tentative way, a latter-day version of biological determinism. In this more devious theory, the character and tempo of social life are thought to be determined not by the innate biological qualities of the people, but by the level of their health. Many diseases, it is pointed out, have a severely debilitating effect upon the individual; and some of these diseases have become at times epidemic or endemic. Conversely, some other diseases seem to have a stimulating effect; were not, for example, many of the great artists, poets, and men of letters of the nineteenth century tubercular?

What has ironically been termed the "syphilitic interpretation of history" takes off from this view. Roman society, it is said, and perhaps other civilizations before it, may have declined as a result of the weakening effects of endemic malaria (which is known to have bothered the Romans). Because the Romans in this way became weak, they lost wars, declined in numbers, and lost the ability to maintain their cities and modes of life. Conversely, the plagues that swept through Europe in the fifteenth century may have been the indirect cause of the Renaissance; for they sharply reduced the population and thereby opened lands and new occupational opportunities to the survivors. Moreover, the sixteenth century saw the introduction to Western Europe of a new and more virulent form of syphilis, which seems to have operated, as tuberculosis was supposed to have done centuries later, to stimulate men to exceptional endeavors.

The complex role of the biological habitat—plants and animals, plant and animal diseases, and diseases that affect man himself—in both the maintenance and the modification of society will be analyzed later. At this point it need only be said that changes in the biological habitat—and the same is true of changes in the physical habitat—are not the *cause* of social change, although they may be important intervening variables in the chain of interdependent factors which together produce changes in a social system.

SOCIOLOGICAL THEORIES OF SOCIAL CHANGE

Such nineteenth-century predecessors of modern sociology as Comte, Spencer, and Ward were preoccupied with the problem of social change. Their self-assigned task was to chart the past course of social development, using as their guide the idea of social evolution, in order to predict the future of Western civilization. To this task they applied themselves with vigor, ingenuity, and immense self-confidence in their ability to ascertain the laws that regulate man's affairs. The systems of interpretation that they produced, however, were grandiose social philosophies rather than scientific hypotheses— testaments of faith neither derived from nor testable against the evidences of social history or the observable facts of social life. Each system of interpretation was in its turn given considerable attention by both scientists and laymen; but none, save only some elements of Comte's positive philosophy, contributed to knowledge and understanding of social change.

By the opening of this century the vogue that had been so much pronounced during the eighteenth and nineteenth centuries for the building of quasi-scientific systems of interpretation had largely passed; and the failure of the social philosophers to have produced workable scientific concepts was in part responsible for a general abandonment of the historical approach to social change and, perhaps incidentally, of the sociological study of change itself. In Germany sociologists continued for a time to take the long view and to study, or at least speculate about, the changes that were occurring in Western society. In America, however, where sociology as a special discipline within the social sciences developed with considerable rapidity, the attention of sociologists was directed almost exclusively to the study of and theorizing about things as they are and the processes, such as socialization and social control, by which the social system is maintained; and so it has, for the most part, remained to the present day. As a consequence, very little sociological attention has been devoted to the study of how Western society came into being; and current theories about and knowledge of social change are but little advanced beyond what they were a quarter century and more ago.

Assimilation

Use concept of Assimi. — rural & urban culture — dichotomy

A number of early sociologists, of whom W. I. Thomas was the outstanding representative, were interested in the scientific analysis of the process by which immigrants to America take over the customs, manners, values, etc., of American society. This process, assimilation, came to sociological attention mainly because it was not operating with the speed and effectiveness that had been expected. America had long held to the belief that the United States could make stalwart citizens out of any kind of human material, that the American melting pot could render into good Americans people of any color, creed, or condition of servitude. Almost until the close of the nineteenth century all the immigrants except the Irish had in fact been absorbed with comparative ease; but the hordes of central and southern Europeans who toward the close of the century and during the two decades following came to make their fortunes in American industry formed into somewhat isolated foreign ghettos and proved resistant to assimilation.

The study of assimilation, of which a great deal was undertaken by sociologists, was tangential to that of social change per se. It was a sociological parallel to the study, which currently so much concerns anthropologists, of the acculturation of primitive and peasant peoples into the techniques, values, etc., of industrial life. The findings of such studies, old and new, have had some value to the study of change itself; for individual and group resistance to assimilation or acculturation is not unlike the resistance that a new social element may encounter; but in such studies attention has been on the spread to new people of social elements that are already well established in another social system, rather than on the essential problem of social change, on how various new elements come into being and gain acceptance in the society of their origin.

Social Ecology

During the 1920s American sociology was to a considerable extent dominated by what was known as the Chicago School. This school, under the stimulus of Robert E. Park, was concerned mainly with ascertaining the processes of social life, as distinct from the present American concentration on structure.[13] Many of the processes were looked upon as processes of maintenance rather than change; and others, such as Park's own "race relation cycle," were looked upon as variants on the process of assimilation; but Park and his associates did undertake one venture into the study of change per se under the rubric "social ecology."

From plant and animal ecology the social ecologists drew the concepts of competition and conflict between species and of invasion of an ecological area by a new species with a consequent change in which species dominated. They applied these concepts to the study of the spatial relationships and changes in spatial relationships of the various classes in an urban population, each class being conceived of as comparable to a plant or animal species. Their study and theorizing need not be detailed here, for the unfruitfulness of the approach has long since become evident. There is, however, profit to be derived from this unfruitfulness, that profit being an indication of the reasons why the few American sociologists who have studied social change have made so very little headway.

The social ecologists were endeavoring to ascertain the ways in which cities grow and, in the growing, change. They brought to this study the idea that the population of a city is governed by the same laws that regulate bac-

[13] The base document of what came to be known as the Chicago School of American sociology was *Introduction to the Science of Sociology* by Robert E. Park and Ernest W. Burgess, The University of Chicago Press, Chicago, 1921.

teria, plants, and animals in their use of a piece of land. Thus they assumed that the social life of man and the subsocial actions of lower organisms are subject to the same basic laws. They tended to disregard the significant differences between man and other organisms—that men have a culture and live in social ways, that men can upon occasion act to some extent as self-determining individuals rather than as members of a species, and that when men do act as individuals, they sometimes devise new forms of conduct.

Because they expected social change to conform to a few simple, unvarying laws, the social ecologists discovered little about the processes of social change. They failed to recognize that social change is an exceedingly complex and uncertain phenomenon which at least so far cannot be explained in terms comparable to those by which the physicist describes the attraction of matter for matter or even to those used by the biologist to describe the transmission of genetic characteristics.

Social Lag

A consequence of tech. innovation : soc. change thru stress/strain ...

It was, however, to provide a law of social change comparable to the laws of physics and biology that William F. Ogburn in 1922 advanced his theory of social lag.[14] The concept of social lag struck the fancy of American sociologists and was for long, and possibly indeed still is, the major idea regarding social change in the folklore of sociology. Ogburn pointed out, quite soundly, that social changes always originate in the invention by some individual of a new way of doing something or of something new to do. So far he was following in the tradition established by Gabriel Tarde; but Ogburn then began to wander in the tracks of Marx. Historically, he argued, inventions occur most often in the field of material technology, if only because the advantages of an improvement in technology are self-evident. With each development in technology there comes, however, some disturbance to the effective working of the existing social order. A strain or stress is set up between the new technique and various organizational aspects of the social system, changes in which come slowly if at all; the result, disequilibrium between new technology and old social organization, is social lag. (Ogburn was not clear regarding the process by which changes in social organization come about; he did not, at any event, consider them to be inventions comparable to those of new techniques.)

The core of Ogburn's theory is the idea that change first occurs in the material technology, an idea borrowed directly from Marx and indirectly from Saint-Simon, Condorcet, and other French founders of the idea of progress. Ogburn eventually qualified his original statement, in reply to con-

[14] William F. Ogburn, *Social Change with Respect to Culture and Original Nature*, B. W. Huebsch, Inc., New York, 1922. A new edition has been issued under the same title by The Viking Press, Inc., New York, 1950.

trary evidences, to make it apply specifically to Western society since the industrial revolution; but even as a theory of change for this special time and place, the concept of social lag so oversimplifies historical realities that it contributes very little.[15]

Cultural Acceleration

Tarde had observed that, other things being equal, the more complex the society and therefore the more numerous the elements of a society, the greater the likelihood that two or more elements will meet and be synthesized into a unique combination—i.e., an invention.[16] In 1931 Hornell Hart used this idea as the basis for a new statement of the old idea of social progress. Culture, he held, accumulates through the addition of new inventions; and with each such addition, the chances are increased that still more inventions will occur. As a consequence, culture accumulates at an accelerative rate, much as money in the bank grows through compound interest. To substantiate his hypothesis, Hart offered in evidence historical data on such matters as the increasing range and destructive power of guns, the increasing efficiency of the cutting tools used by man, the increasing speed at which could cover distance, the increasing power of steam-generating plants, and the increasing use of coal, oil, and such other industrial materials as steel. The rate of increase in these and other instances, he pointed out, has been constantly increasing; and when the changing distance, speed, size, or use is plotted over time, the result is in each case a close approximation to geometric progression. Hart concluded, therefore, that social change is linear and accelerative and that the direction of change is invariably toward increasing efficiency or effectiveness.[17]

The inadequacy of Hart's theory of change is easily demonstrated. If it were a universal principle that societies moved constantly and acceleratively

[15] This contrary evidence, the first serious criticism of the social-lag concept, was advanced by Richard T. LaPiere and Cheng Wang in "The Incidence and Sequence of Social Change," *American Journal of Sociology*, vol. 37, pp. 399–409, November, 1931. They demonstrated that the major change in Chinese society that had occurred within recent years had been ideological rather than technological and that the probable sequence would be ideological-organizational-technological, rather than the reverse. The social history of China since then has tended to confirm this view.

[16] G. Tarde, *The Laws of Imitation*, Holt, New York, 1903.

[17] Hornell Hart, *The Technique of Social Progress*, Holt, Rinehart and Winston, Inc., New York, 1931; "Acceleration in Social Change," in Francis R. Allen et al. (eds.), *Technology and Social Change*, Appleton-Century-Crofts, Inc., New York, 1957; and "Social Theory and Social Change," in Llewellyn Gross (ed.), *Symposium on Sociological Theory*, Harper & Row, Publishers, Incorporated, New York, 1959.

toward greater effectiveness, how could the regression of specific societies, such as Roman, be explained? How, further, could the fact be explained that China, which at the opening of the Christian era was by far the most complex society on earth in that it had the largest number of cultural elements, has remained comparatively stable for nearly two thousand years?

Hart's basic error was his use of selected quantitative criteria as indications of rates of change in the structure of society. The fact that guns can shoot farther, trains go faster, and airplanes fly higher and faster undoubtedly reflects technological accomplishments; but data on such matters tell nothing at all about the nature of the techniques themselves or how changes in them were brought about and they do not provide even inferential evidence regarding the nature of, or changes in, such other vital aspects of social life as ideology and organization. Quite possibly the monetary costs of government have risen in Western societies over the past century at something like an accelerative rate; but does this mean that the functional effectiveness of governmental organization is rapidly approaching perfection? The divorce rate has also risen considerably, if not so rapidly as the range of guns and the speed of airplanes; but does this mean that the efficiency of family life has increased (or, perhaps, decreased) proportionately?

Generalizing from a relatively few cases to the entire class of such cases is an established and acceptable scientific procedure. It is not necessary to analyze every grain of sand on the beach to ascertain the composition of beach sand; a small sample will suffice. The sample must, however, be representative of the material or phenomenon under study; and Hart violated this basic rule of the scientific method. His data, his sample material, consisted of quantitative changes in the *consequences* of some few technological elements of society (e.g., military weapons, modes of transportation); but the conclusions he drew from his data concern the nature of all elements, not only of those of a technological character, but of those of an ideological and organizational character as well. Even as the character of a boy cannot be deduced from how far he can throw a stone, the social life of a people cannot be determined from how far they can shoot an arrow or a rocket into space.

Sociology and Social Change

The foregoing is not a representative sample of American sociological theory regarding social change but comes close to being the sum total of that theory. For in spite of the fact that contemporary American society is probably the most rapidly changing society the world has ever known, its sociologists have been and continue to be almost totally preoccupied with social stability. They study and theorize about many of the processes of social life—the induction of the young into social membership, the movement of individuals from one status position to another, the formation and operation of family units, peer groups, and such larger forms of organization as industrial and political bureaucracies, etc. They are much concerned with the ways through which the society is maintained; and they speculate a great deal about the presumed universal tendency of societies to maintain a functional equilibrium both within the social system and between the social system and other social systems with which the society is articulated. In all the empirical research and theorizing, attention is almost always centered upon the here and now of society—upon what is its structure, what part is related to what other part, and how each of the various parts operates to make up the whole. Rarely do modern American sociologists include in their studies and theory making what happens over time; society, as they are prone to see it, is a quick-frozen slice of the life of a people at one given moment and one given place.

The preoccupation of American sociologists with structure and with the maintenance processes that occur within the social system is evident in all aspects of the sociological literature.[18] Writers of introductory textbooks seldom devote more than a short final chapter to the subject of social change, and many texts fail to mention change at all. Perhaps not more than one out of twenty articles in the technical journals bears in the slightest degree on the subject; the scant reference to the technical literature of sociology in the

[18] Of the hundreds of books that were published over the past decade by American sociologists about sociological matters, only nine are specifically on social change. Of these, two [John E. Nordskog (ed.), *Social Change*, McGraw-Hill Book Company, New York, 1960; and George K. Zollschan and Walter Hirsch (eds.), *Explorations in Social Change*, Houghton Mifflin Company, Boston, 1964] are collections of discrete essays and articles. Three [Everett M. Rogers, *Social Change in Rural Society*, Appleton-Century-Crofts, Inc., New York, 1960; David E. Lindstrom, *Rural Social Change*, Stipes Publishing Co., Champaign, Ill., 1961; and Everett M. Rogers, *Diffusion of Innovations*, The Free Press of Glencoe, New York, 1962] are by rural sociologists and apply only to change in the rural sector of contemporary American life. Of the other four, one [Francis R. Allen et al., *Technology and Social Change*, Appleton-Century-Crofts, Inc., New York, 1957] is a very simple and dogmatic restatement of Ogburn's idea that change comes through inventions in technology and that it is such change that is the cause of subsequent change in social organization; while another [Neil J. Smelser, *Social Change in the Industrial Revolution*, The University of Chicago Press, Chicago, 1959] is a meticulous historical analysis of social change in a particular time and place rather than a contribution to general theory. Only Don Martindale's *Social Life and Cultural Change*, D. Van Nostrand Company, Inc., Princeton, N.J., 1962, and Wilbert E. Moore's *Social Change*, Prentice-Hall, Inc., Englewood Cliffs, N.J., 1963, in any way qualify as sociological contributions to a general theory of social change. The former book, however, is only an elaboration of certain aspects of Max Weber's theory of the role of religion in the determination of social stability and change; and the latter is a new version of the old thesis that change is a manifestation of inherent qualities of that which is changed—i.e., the old idea of immanent as distinct from emergent development.

pages that follow stems from this fact. Sociological theorists and an occasional research worker sometimes refer to the *Gemeinschaft-Gesellschaft* concept of Tönnies, even if they do not utilize it; in addition, there is a general assumption in sociology that modern industrial society is different in kind from all the societies that have preceded it, an assumption that reflects the inability of sociologists as well as others to avoid the bias of ethnocentrism; but the body of sociological theory deals with the here and now, not with how the here and now came to be what it is.

The preoccupation of American sociologists with structure and maintenance processes has not gone unremarked.[19] Occasionally a sociologist has

[19] That preoccupation has been justified by Parsons, who is as responsible as any other single person for it, on the grounds that "A general theory of the processes of change of social systems is not possible in the present state of knowledge" (Talcott Parsons, *The Social System*, The Free Press of Glencoe, New York, 1951, p. 486). Parsons here ignores the fact that scientific knowledge and theory grow hand in hand and that knowledge of change will not be increased until testable theories about it are formulated.

The extent of current sociological preoccupation with the social here and now ("social structure," "social systems," "equilibrium models" are some of the terms applied to it) is indicated by the total absence of concern with social change in *Sociology Today: Problems and Prospects* (Robert K. Merton, Leonard Broom, and Leonard S. Cottrell (eds.), Basic Books, Inc., Publishers, New York, 1959) and the very little material on this subject that could be mustered by Charles P. Loomis and Zona K. Loomis for *Modern Social Theories*, D. Van Nostrand Company, Inc., Princeton, N.J., 1961.

Criticism of American sociological preoccupation with social structure and equilibrium models has been voiced by Harry Elmer Barnes in *Historical Sociology: Its Origins and Development*, Philosophical Library, Inc., New York, 1948; by Barrington Moore, Jr., in *Political Power and Social Theory: Six Studies*, Harvard University Press, Cambridge, Mass., 1958; by Peter A. Munch in *A Study of Cultural Change: Rural-Urban Conflicts in Norway*, H. Ascheboug & Company, Oslo, 1956; by C. Wright Mills in *The Sociological Imagination*, Oxford University Press, Fair Lawn, N.J., 1959; and by J. A. Ponsioen in *The Analysis of Social Change Reconsidered: A Sociological Study*, Mouton & Co., The Hague, 1962. In a searching analysis of the problem Wilbert E. Moore ("A Reconsideration of Theories of Social Change," *American Sociological Review*, vol. 25, pp. 810-818, December, 1960) has pointed out that there is nothing irreconcilable about the currently popular structural-functional approach to the study of society and a much-needed development of theories of social change; the two should, in his view, be complementary. (But see the comment on Moore's concept of the nature of change in the preceding footnote.)

The idea that the structural-functional approach does not preclude a concern with social change has also been expressed by Reinhard Bendix and Bennett Berger. They say, in part, "And to do this [to include in sociological concern the changes that may occur within the social system] attention must be focused on the boundary-extending as well as upon the boundary-maintaining activities of

noted the futility of conceptually freezing what is in reality a highly fluid state, a procedure that assures that much that is learned about society today will be antiquated tomorrow. But this preoccupation with static models, with equilibrium theory, and with research into what exists now and may be gone tomorrow has dominated and continues to dominate American sociology and has had its staunch defenders. Some have maintained that the forces that make for social change are all embedded in the present, and thus through the study of the present everything will become known—present, past, and future. Still others have defended the current sociological fashion on negative grounds; they hold that we must restrict ourselves to the scientific, by which they mean quantitative, investigation of the present because knowledge of the social past is both fragmentary and uncertain. What they mean is that since questionnaires and other objective techniques of measurement (such as panel reports on what is observed through a one-way window) cannot be applied to people now dead, a truly scientific science of society can deal only with the present. What they assume—that current methods for the investigation of current social life yield data that are neither fragmentary nor uncertain—does not, however, stand up under careful scrutiny.

Just why modern American sociology so studiously ignores the phenomenon of social change is itself a rather interesting problem in social change. It may be that the spectacular failure of the nineteenth-century evolutionists to produce testable concepts of social change has cast a constraining influence on sociologists of the twentieth century; perhaps the fact that America is a relatively new society with a short history, as history measures time, may predispose Americans, sociologists and otherwise, to a present-time view of things; or possibly the heroic, if largely unsuccessful, effort of American sociologists to avoid an ideological commitment, to remain, in Mannheim's terms, "free-floating intellectuals," may be the deterrent to their study of social change. At any event, with some few exceptions those American sociologists who have in recent years taken a long view and probed the past for an understanding of the present have been Marxist in their personal preferences and inclined to find in the social past and present what they are apparently looking for—confirmation of the Marxian evolutionary thesis.[20]

---

individuals, on the permissive aspects of culture and society which enable individuals *to experiment with what is possible* as well as upon the social controls which limit the range of tolerated behavior without defining that range clearly" ["Images of Sociology and Problems of Concept Formulation in Sociology," in Llewellyn Gross (ed.), *Symposium on Sociological Theory,* Harper & Row, Publishers, Incorporated, New York, 1959, p. 112].

[20] See, for example, Seymour Martin Lipset, *Political Man: The Social Bases of Politics,* Doubleday & Company, Inc., Garden City, N. Y., 1960; C. Wright Mills, *The Power Elite,* Oxford University Press, Fair Lawn, N.J., 1956; and Ralf Dahrendorf, *Class and Class Conflict in Industrial Society,* Stanford University Press, Stanford, Calif., 1959.

There is, however, still another and more likely possibility, one that is congenial to the scientific mind: it may be that a fundamental misconception regarding social change has closed the door to sociological exploration of the field. Over and over and in all the various disciplines false conceptions have for a time checked advance in both theory and empirical investigation. Thus it was a blinding misconception of the elements that kept the alchemists busy in a cul-de-sac and delayed the emergence of chemistry for centuries on end. Thus, too, it was the surge theory of the motion of the blood in the human body that closed the minds of medical men for a century or more to the evidences of their senses, and so delayed by a century or more the discovery of the circulation of blood.

The nineteenth-century evolutionists, unlike their predecessors who put their faith in progress through rational means, assumed that social change comes about through the working of some process that is built into society, some inherent social process. They often endeavored to specify this process and reduce it to a unitary law of change. Some, such as Marx and Gumplowicz, found in the conflict of classes or of interests the force that moves society along its predetermined path from the past to the present and from the present to the perfected future. Others, such as Comte and Ward, saw in the continuing accumulation of knowledge the mechanism by which society improves itself. Still others, such as Spencer, believed that cosmic law as embodied in the social system controls the destiny of man even as it does the movement of the stars. All of them, however, no matter how varied were the laws of change that they thought they discerned, found in society itself the immediate, if not final, explanation for the changes that occur, or were supposed to occur, in it.

Those few twentieth-century sociologists who have offered theories of social change have for the most part also assigned to society (more or less abstractly conceived) the cause of its own modification.[21] Even Ogburn, who initially stressed the role of the individual inventor in the making of technological changes, fell under the spell of this nineteenth-century concept and

[21] A recent example of this fallacy is provided by Charles P. Loomis in *Social Systems: Essays on Their Persistence and Change*, D. Van Nostrand Company, Inc., Princeton, N.J., 1960. In "Evolution, Function, and Change" (*American Sociological Review*, vol. 28, pp. 229–237, April, 1963) Kenneth E. Bock analyzes in some detail the stultifying effects of evolutionary theory, shows how modern functionalists are subject to the same conceptual error, and urges that sociologists recognize that social changes come about through events rather than, as is so commonly assumed, being the manifestation of forces that are inherent in the existing structure of society. He does not, however, venture to designate what particular kinds of events are contributory to social changes, a problem that is as vital to the development of a workable theory of social change as is his recognition that changes come to, rather than out of, a social system.

was fond of citing incidents of simultaneous invention as proof that society produces innovations and that the inventor acts only as an agent of social forces. Anyone, it is implied, could serve in this capacity; for given the appropriate circumstances, the innovation will emerge as a social, not an individual, product.[22]

The Asocial Nature of Social Change

It is the thesis of this book that the changes that occur within a society are asocial; that they are not in any sense a product of the society per se or a consequence of some universal and unvarying law of social life. Social change is not comparable to the changes that invariably occur through time in a living organism, to the normal changes that are involved in growth, maturity, and decline. The changes that may occur in a society are, on the contrary, far more comparable to those violations of the normal organic processes that follow when, for reasons yet unknown, a cell goes wild—when it breaks from the "laws" that control its growth and reproduction and, multiplying, disturbs the functioning of the entire organism. The forces that make for social change are, if the organic analogy be pursued, abnormal—a violation of the

[22] Perhaps it is because they have not been hampered by this blocking preconception that economists have made the major contributions to the development of a general theory of social change in recent years. Their interest in the subject has been stimulated by the post-World War II efforts of the United States government to retard the spread of communistic ideology by giving economic and technical aid to many of the so-called underdeveloped peoples of the world. Economists have often served as advisers or field workers in this endeavor, and they have apparently been amazed to discover that underdeveloped peoples often resist American efforts to bring them the boons of industrial technology and the free-enterprise system of economic life. The search for an explanation of this resistance has not yet produced a general theory of social change that is sociologically acceptable, but it has led to a consensus among economists who are interested in economic stability and growth that it is the character and activities of individual members of society, not the social system itself, that distinguishes the stable from the dynamic society, a view that is in general accord with that which will be developed in the present work.

Among the many recent contributors to economic thought about social change are: W. Arthur Lewis, *The Theory of Economic Growth*, George Allen & Unwin, Ltd., London, 1955; C. P. Kindleberger, *Economic Development*, McGraw-Hill Book Company, New York, 1958; Harvey Leibenstein, *Economic Backwardness and Economic Growth*, John Wiley & Sons, Inc., New York, 1957; Nicholas Kaldor, *Essays on Economic Stability and Growth*, Gerald Duckworth & Co., Ltd., London, 1960; David C. McClelland, *The Achieving Society*, D. Van Nostrand Company, Inc., Princeton, N.J., 1961; and Everett E. Hagen, *On the Theory of Social Change*, The Dorsey Press, Inc., Homewood, Ill., 1962.

normal process by which the social system is transmitted from generation to generation of members. A change in society comes, even as does a tumor in an organism, as a foreign and unwanted agent, not necessarily of destruction, but always of disturbance to the established and organizationally preferred structures and processes of life.

The idea that social change emerges directly out of the society that is thereby changed has long delayed recognition of the fact that society in all its various aspects operates constantly and consistently toward self-maintenance; that all social organization, formal and informal, is as organization inherently resistant to change; and that social change is the work of socially deviant individuals acting in asocial ways. That social change is not directly produced by the society so changed was implicit in a theory of collective behavior that was advanced in 1921 by Robert E. Park.[23] Change comes about, in this theory, as an incidental consequence of the fortuitous interaction of numbers of people who have become desocialized—that is, stripped of their normal social characteristics—through participation in mass milling. In the milling process new modes of social conduct are sometimes created and, he thought, sometimes established in the social system as the end product of a mass movement. Had Park turned his attention to deviant individuals rather than to deviant masses of individuals, he might have broken the conceptual barrier that has retarded sociological study of social change and thereby inaugurated a fruitful change in American sociology.

[23] Robert E. Park and Ernest W. Burgess, *Introduction to the Science of Sociology*, The University of Chicago Press, Chicago, 1921, pp. 865–952.

chapter **2** *The Dimension of Social Change*

A society may change at varying rates, in various respects, and in a variety of ways. Although a society is often described as a social system in order to stress the interdependence of its several elements, it is never in fact a single system that is all this or all that—communistic or capitalistic, totalitarian or democratic, Christian or Moslem, prosperous or impoverished. Categorizing societies, especially categorizing one's own as this and all others as that, is a normal social process; in addition, typifying societies or elements of societies in terms of their more or less normative characteristics can be a scientifically useful heuristic device. But just as people are never, whatever the criteria used, all good or all bad, so societies are never actually one thing to the exclusion of all else; nor do they ever change at one rate, in one way, and in all respects.

It was in some measure the failure of the social evolutionists to distinguish between the various kinds of changes that enabled them to accept the idea of inevitable change toward social improvement. For they regarded such different changes as growth in population, increasing literacy, mechanization of the processes of production, increasing class mobility, growth of nationalism, and decreasing frequency of wars and revolutions as equal in kind, extent, and significance. On the other hand, it is in part because they have centered their attention upon political power and other evidences of governmental activity, such as the scope and role of law, that so many social historians have been convinced that societies go through a predetermined cycle of growth and decline. Perhaps if their attention were directed toward the importance and integrity of family life, and if adequate data were available to them, they would find a similar but contravening cycle—for example, that as a society grows politically, it declines familistically, and vice versa. At any event, whatever cycle were perceived would certainly depend upon the particular phenomena that were viewed and the particular criteria that were used.

40

The tendency to treat change as change, and the resulting failure to distinguish between various kinds of changes, has been characteristic of many theorists. Marx could not see society as a system of interdependent relationships because of his preoccupation with class differences in economic income; Ogburn hinged his entire theory of social lag upon an unrealistic distinction between the technological and the organizational, a dichotomization that in turn led him to lump together such varied phenomena as spatial movements of people and movements for social reform; and Hart, it will be recalled, identified certain quantitative indexes of technological changes (the increasing speed of bullets, planes, etc.) with those changes themselves and, indeed, with change per se.

THE NORMAL DYNAMICS OF SOCIAL LIFE

The term "static" or "stable" is ordinarily used to refer to a society or an aspect of a society that is for a given period comparatively free from significant changes. Thus the entire social system of China was fairly stable from about the sixth century of the Christian era until well into the eighteenth; and the educational system of England was fairly stable during the nineteenth century and the first half of the twentieth, although during this period English society was changing markedly in most other respects. In the midst of many radical changes, the English academicians, especially at Oxford and Cambridge, continued to adhere to the salient elements of an intellectual tradition and academic organization that had evolved in the later Middle Ages. In 1950, as in 1800 and long before, the curriculum at both institutions was primarily classical; and the preservation of long-dead languages and of equally moribund ideas and philosophical concerns was still the primary concern of both teachers and students. The don of 1950 might have been driving a modern automobile, wearing a modern watch, and spreading hydrogenated whale oil on his breakfast toast; but his quarters had changed little since the eighteenth century, his relations with his fellow scholars even less, and his intellectual values and interests were, the few modern scientists aside, hardly distinguishable from those of his predecessors seven or eight generations removed.

Although a social system or particular aspects of a social system may be fairly stable through many generations, social life is nonetheless life. It exists only through the actions of the members of the society, and those actions are not in any real sense static or stable. Actions are motion; motion is fleeting; and the instant the members of a society cease acting, that society ceases to exist. A shoemaker may make the same kinds of shoes, using the same kind of leather and cutting and stitching with the same tools in the same way all the days of his life; he may greet his customers year after year with the same opening phrases, gossip with them over the same kinds of events, and eat the same bread day after day. What he does may be abstracted from the doing, reduced to forms, structures, or procedures, and thus seen to be stable through time; but the shoemaker's life, like that of all members of a society and so of the society itself, is in reality highly dynamic.

The kinds of changes that are normal to all societies are not social change; but since they loom large in the minds of the members of society and are the object of constant interest, they may be mistaken for, or at the very least distract attention from, the kinds of changes that are socially significant. It may be well, therefore, to analyze the normative changes in social life as a prelude to the specification of the particular phenomena that are incorporated within the dimension of social change.

Normal Cycles of Activity

Perhaps initially only because the sun rises and sets and because in most habitable parts of the earth the seasons change, men have everywhere developed and embodied in their culture daily and other cycles of activity. For primitive hunters and simple farmers the daily cycle has necessarily been geared to the rising and setting of the sun; for other people, especially urban people, it has varied from class to class and from occupation to occupation and has differed widely from place to place and from time to time. In all instances the daily cycle has ranged between the extremes of minimal activity, rest or sleep, and peaks of maximum activity, work, play, or some such activity as the daily homeward rush of urban commuters. It has generally involved regular changes in activity—from work to play, usually intermixed in premodern societies, but often separated into discrete time periods in modern society; from eating and caring for one's person to going through such rituals as the reciting of a bedtime prayer or the drinking of a predinner cocktail; and so on.

The changes in activity that make up the daily cycle—i.e., the regular daily events, such as going off to work and returning home—are not sociologically significant; but changes in the pattern of the daily cycle may be, for they are sometimes indicative of antecedent and related changes in the technology, organization, or perhaps even the ideology of the society. Thus the shift, mainly in the past two centuries, of many social activities, especially those of a recreational nature, from daylight to the hours of darkness was evidently an adaptation of the daily cycle to such fundamental changes as industrialization and urbanization and the concomitant separation of work and play. The recent shift, particularly marked in Britain and America, in the time of the major meal from midday to evening (in most societies, primitive and civilized, the main meal has come at midday) seems to be an adjustment to the fairly recent separation of place of work and place of residence, with the consequent commuting of workers to and from work.

Although the weekly cycle of activities that is deeply embedded in the culture of all Western peoples is not universal, most peoples have had some sort of cycle of activities larger than the daily cycle. In many agricultural societies every third day has been market day, with a resulting three-day cycle. The seven-day cycle of Western people would seem to be a heritage from Judaism that came into the West along with Christianity and that has been preserved in spite of many subsequent changes in social life. Perhaps it once had a functional basis, religious and otherwise; but it has long since lost most of its religious significance and is responsible for such social malfunctioning as having the productive plant lie idle every seventh day, and, more and more of late, every sixth as well as seventh day, while recreational facilities, including many of the road and highway systems, are overloaded two days a week and underused five.

A cycle of seasonal activities, imposed on agricultural peoples by natural changes in the weather, is also a heritage from the past that has slight relevance to the conditions of modern urban life. In premodern societies many aspects of life necessarily changed with the seasons. For both hunting and agricultural peoples the annual work load reached a peak in the spring and early fall weeks; and winter weather drove people into their habitations where, in many times and places, they could do little but await the coming of spring. Their food supplies, too, waxed and waned with the passing seasons; for most, winter was a time of near, if not actual, starvation; and even in fairly recent times, the winter diet in many places was restricted in variety if not in quantity, so much so that the first greens to sprout in spring, such as dandelions, were often welcomed as a break in the monotony of bread, potatoes, and preserved meat and regarded as a tonic that would revive the sluggish bodies of the entire family. For most peoples in times past and for many nonindustrialized peoples of the present there have also been longer than seasonal cycles, years when the crops or the hunting or fishing were unusually poor, years when they ran above the long-range average, cycles of feast and famine, of well-being and adversity. Cycles of this sort have not been regular, since they have stemmed from such variables in natural phenomena as drought and flood, cold and warm summers, early and late frosts, and the invasion or recession of plant and animal diseases and pests, over which premodern peoples have had little if any control; but the changes in activity that they have involved have been repeated with every shift from well-being to adversity.

Modern men cannot entirely ignore seasonal variations in the weather; modern as well as premodern farmers must gear their activities to them. Seasonal variations in the weather, however, have little direct effect upon the activities of modern urban and suburban people, many of whom now live and work well-insulated from both excessive heat and cold; and a host of social changes, technological and organizational, have considerably reduced seasonal

The dimension of social change   **43**

variations in the food supply and periodic cycles of famine. Nevertheless, modern urban people follow many seasonal variations in activity that no longer have a basis in climatic variations and in such dependent activities as planting and harvesting.[1] Thanksgiving was the American version of the harvest festival that is found in all agricultural societies—a relaxing and rejoicing that the harvest is in. Its current celebration has no such function; it is maintained simply from force of cultural habit. The practice of closing down the educational plant from June to September or October, until recently almost universal in Western societies, is another survival from the past that no longer has any function. This school cycle, which apparently originated with the medieval universities, had some point when the students were mainly country boys needed back on the farm for the planting and harvesting seasons; but it has led to the now-traditional practice of everyone's crowding the now-traditional two-week annual vacation into the period from mid-June to mid-August, even though millions of people are without school children to consider.

Changes of a Personal Character

The various cycles of social activity, whatever their particular character, provide a more or less effective adaptation to nature, they give variety to the lives of all the members of the society, and they often contribute directly to the maintenance of the social system. Even more important to the individual members of a society are those changes that are involved in the maintenance of the social population, as distinct from the social system. However stable a society, the social population is constantly changing and highly dynamic; for the membership of each individual in it is transient and the life of each individual is affected by the changes implicit in growth, maturity, decline, and death.

In addition to the unescapable biological events of birth and death, the maintenance of a social population involves a considerable variety of other events that mark changes in the lives of its individual members. These events have varied from society to society. Marriage and its preludes, such as falling in love or being engaged through parental arrangement, have been universal, as have parenthood and ceremonial disposal of the bodies of the dead, an event for the kith and kin of the deceased, if not for the deceased. In many primitive societies ritual induction at puberty into adult society has been one of the great and painful events in the life of an individual. In our own society some of the major events that mark changes in the lives of the majority of individuals are graduation from high school, entrance into and graduation

[1] E. O. James, *Seasonal Feasts and Festivals*, Barnes & Noble, Inc., New York, 1961.

from a college or university, and, particularly for men, getting a position in business, industry, or one of the professions, and securing from time to time promotions and other rewards for excellence.

The changes that stem from events of the foregoing kind are of primary personal importance to the individual members of a society. They are a major subject of discussion, they constitute much of the news of the day, they pose the problems that must be solved, and they are the source of most personal pleasures and sorrows. An individual may be only vaguely aware of the socially significant changes that occur in his society; but he is vitally concerned with, and intensely aware of, the fact that he did or did not win an academic scholarship, get the position that he wanted, secure the hoped-for promotion, etc. Moreover, changes that directly affect other individuals may often have considerable indirect effect upon him. The death of a friend or relative may disturb him in many ways, the marriage of his son may add to or lessen his financial burdens, the illness of his wife may force him to take on responsibility for keeping the household running and will certainly call for many readjustments in his personal life.

Changes of this individual character are inherent in life and living; they are socially normal, they occur in one form or another in all societies, and they are endlessly repeated. They do not, however, constitute changes in the social system itself or necessarily lead to changes; like the rising and setting of the sun, they may go on and on without, as it were, getting anywhere. For while the members of a society are constantly coming and going and during their brief stay experiencing a multitude of changes in their personal lives, the social system itself may run on and on generation after generation more or less unchanged.

SOCIAL EVENTS AND SOCIAL CHANGE

In every society, stable or changing, the individual members live out their lives following the established seasonal and other cycles of activity and engrossed in the normative personal events in which they are directly or indirectly involved. In any society, however, the members will from time to time be distracted from their personal concerns by an event that transcends the personal and that has or is supposed to have significance for all or a considerable proportion of the social population. Such events, of which the election of a new president, the advent of war, the enactment of new legislation, and the calling of a nationwide transportation strike are modern examples, have a significance that is social rather than just personal; and it is events of this sort that usually become embodied in written records and thus in time become the data of history. Historians describe them as unique events on the assumption that they are not repetitious, as are personal events, and that no two of them ever follow the same course or have comparable effects on the society.

Any occurrence of such exceptional character or such great magnitude that it is defined, either by the members of the society at large or by those who chronicle the events of the time, as a crisis, the outcome of which will affect the life and welfare of the society as a whole, constitutes a social event. What particular events will be so defined depends in part upon the character of the society; for what is exceptional from the point of view of one society may be quite normal from that of another. In contemporary America an outbreak of smallpox, for example, would be defined as a crisis: it would be announced in the newspapers; prompt emergency measures would be undertaken to prevent spread of the disease; and until it was brought under control, there would be considerable concern over the danger of a runaway epidemic. In many times and places, however, smallpox has been endemic and so commonplace that infection was a personal rather than social event.

Recorded history is for the most part accounts of what were at the time of their occurrence considered to be crises, and it is for this reason that the history of a people is far less the record of changes within the society than of social events that may or may not have had long-range social consequences.[2] The new king—or president or premier or dictator—who was proclaimed at the time as savior may turn out to have been just another king; the treaty that was to bring an end to war may have ended in war; the military victory that was to inaugurate a new and more fruitful era may have resulted in the same old problems and predicaments. Nevertheless, the role of some kinds of social events—wars and revolutions, invasions and migrations, and major plagues and other natural catastrophes—in the making of social changes cannot be ignored; and that role will be explored in later chapters.

The historical record is cluttered, however, with what from the point of view of social change are trivia, and the effect on a society of those events that do contribute to the making of social changes is varied and uncertain. For any social event represents but a fraction of the total forces that are operating in the given time and place, and it is the remainder, those not of record, that determine the significance of what is defined as a crisis. Thus the effect of a war on the social system may, depending upon the nature and magnitude of the war and upon the condition of the society engaged in that war, be either to discourage social change, to accelerate social change, or to have no enduring consequences whatsoever to the social system. Most of the wars of the early Middle Ages no doubt reflected the disequilibrium between small,

[2] The nature of the historical record is examined in great detail by Harry E. Barnes in *A History of Historical Writing*, reprint ed., Dover Publications, Inc., New York, 1962. For a semipopular analysis of the values and limitations of historical data see Edward Carr, *What is History?* Alfred A. Knopf, Inc., New York, 1962.

postfeudal political units and the growing web of economic interdependence; nevertheless, most of those wars did nothing either to facilitate or to impede the growth of economic interdependence or the enlargement of the units of political organization. The American Civil War was ostensibly fought over the slavery issue, and the victory of the North was presumed to result in the liberation of the Southern slaves from political bondage. The actual consequences to American society, however, are even now far from clear. The Negroes were legally liberated, but not in any real sense freed. The war probably served as the final straw to break the economic back of the Southern plantation economy; perhaps more important, it gave various and vital incentives to the industrialization of the Northern states; but to what extent and in what specific ways the Civil War was responsible for the social changes that have made American society of today so markedly different from American society of a century ago, no one can say.

Great Men and Social Events

Even as the record of social events does not constitute an adequate account of the changes that have occurred in a society over time, interpretations of those events by chroniclers and later historians do not contribute much to an understanding of the way in which changes come about. Perhaps all societies have some few members who are as socially sophisticated as contemporary social scientists would like to be; but in all societies, including our own, it is the cultural practice to hold some person or class of persons, real or symbolic, responsible for deviations from the normal course of events. In this process the actual forces that are responsible for a change from the normal, which are unknown and perhaps unknowable, are given personal representation. Thus a natural disaster may be interpreted as a sign or consequence of God's wrath: He sent the drought that destroyed the crops and led to widespread famine; He sent the plague to decimate the people; He sent the violent storms that flooded their fields and washed out their towns and villages. Conversely, God or some other supernaturalistic symbol may be credited with a social event that is welcomed and enjoyed; thus God granted His children the bountiful harvest that assures them a prosperous year.

With social events that clearly involve actions of actual, as distinct from symbolic, persons, cause is often attributed to a particular person or a particular class of persons. It was in this way, for example, that President Lincoln became for a time at least the Great Liberator, the agency that liberated the Southern slaves, a hero to those who believed that the slaves should be free men and a villain to those who did not. The idea that President Lincoln through his own personal actions liberated the slaves of the South is childlike in its naïveté. Nevertheless, it is only a gross example of the characteristic way in which the members of society, the chroniclers of their times, and the writers of history attribute social events to the actions of outstanding figures of the period in which the events occur.

The embodiment in persons or personifications of the conditions and forces that determine phenomena, both natural and social, occurs at all levels of social thought and on varying levels of complexity. Belief in theological and metaphysical explanations for the universe or a part thereof differs only in degree of complexity from belief that a campaigning candidate is the paragon who can, as he claims, drive the scoundrels from the White House, restore good, cheap government, and with it bring about enduring peace and prosperity for everyone. That God, the saints, and the devil are symbols that personify the unknown forces that produce phenomena may be evident to a metaphysician; but that his own explanations of conditions and forces— Destiny, Racial Character, Emergent Evolution, the Imperatives of History, etc.—are merely less humanized symbols of the same order is quite likely to escape his notice.

As has been indicated, many historians have come to the view that political dynasties, indeed entire societies, run a long-term course that is somewhat comparable to the life cycle of an individual and that this cyclical course of events is built into society, a part of its inherent nature. The idea that, whatever the long-run course of a society, all social events of a given time or period are wrought by the endeavors, benevolent or evil, of the political, military, ideological, or economic leader of the period in which the events occurred is somewhat more primitive and perhaps for that reason even more commonly encountered in historical writings.[3] According to this idea, which is usually described as the great-man theory of history, the king, prince, caliph, emir, vizier, tyrant, general, or other recognized leader reorganized the army and led it to success in battle, built aqueducts and paved the streets of the city, liberated the slaves and serfs and brought warring feudal lords under his jurisdiction, and in these or other ways brought peace and prosperity to his people; or, perhaps, he waged war against the independent city-states, slaughtered the inhabitants, leveled palaces and humble dwellings alike, burned the libraries, pillaged fields and storehouses, and so brought to pass a time of darkness and despair.

The temptation to impute to one or another of the recognized leaders of a period the social events that occurred during that period is evidently height-

[3] Even the philosopher Will Durant, who is explicitly aware of the fallacy of imputing great and complex social events to the endeavor of single individuals, frequently does so in his capacity as a writer of history. Thus, to cite but one instance, he explains the tenth-century revival of Arab political power in Africa and the Near East by constant reference to the personal characteristics and activities of Saladin, Sultan of Egypt and Syria. See Will Durant, *The Story of Civilization:* vol. IV, *The Age of Faith,* Simon and Schuster, Inc., New York, 1950.

ened by the fact that most of the documents of history are couched in great-man terms. For one thing, the scribes, both past and present, have thought in these terms; and what they have recorded for the use of future historians has been or has tended to be causally imputed to one or another of the leaders of the time. Thus what was done in Caesar's time becomes, in the record, what Caesar did, even as what is happening in the political arena today becomes, in the newspaper account, what the President or some other notable is doing. For another thing, what is preserved for the historians of the future from the records of the past is more likely to be a dramatic personalized account of events rather than a diffused, complex, and perhaps more realistic documentation.

There can be slight doubt that political and other leaders exercise an influence on their times that is disproportionate to their numbers or that social elites, such as nobles and capitalists, play a larger role in the making of social events than their numbers would imply. It does not follow, however, that great men or influential elites are *the* determinant of social events or, what is more pertinent to the present inquiry, that they are the *cause* of social change.[4]

[4] Vilfredo Pareto, Italian economist and sociologist, advanced a significant variation on the idea that the social elite of a society determines the course of social events. In *The Mind and Society*, A. Livingston and A. Bongiorno (trans.), Harcourt, Brace & World, Inc., New York, 1935, Pareto advanced a rather devious thesis in which it is held that changes within a society make for the rise to elite position of men whose personal characteristics are appropriate to leadership under the circumstances of the times and who in turn strongly affect those times. Interwoven with this idea of the interdependence of the social elite and society is a cyclical concept of social change involving three stages, political, economic, and ideological. During the depression years of the 1930s, when American business-men were commonly being blamed for the economic troubles of the times, Pareto's "circulation of the elite" theory enjoyed a considerable vogue; and it was widely held that the age of the great industrialist had passed. It was not clear, however, whether the new elite would consist of politicians or priests; and at the time no one seems to have anticipated that a second world war would in fact elevate military men to an elite position.

Recent writing on the role of elites in the maintenance and change of society has been more in the straightforward cause-and-effect tradition of G. Mosca, *The Ruling Class*, Hannah D. Kahn (trans.), McGraw-Hill Book Company, New York, 1939, than in that developed by Pareto. See, for example, Floyd Hunter, *Community Power Structure: A Study of Decision Makers*, The University of North Carolina Press, Chapel Hill, N.C., 1953; C. Wright Mills, *The Power Elite*, Alfred A. Knopf, Inc., New York, 1956; Daniel Bell, "The Power Elite—Reconsidered," *American Journal of Sociology*, vol. 64, pp. 238–250, November, 1958; Floyd Hunter, *Top Leadership, U.S.A.*, The University of North Carolina Press, Chapel Hill, N.C., 1959; and Harry Eckstein, *Pressure Group Politics: The Case of the British Medical Association*, Stanford University Press, Stanford, Calif.,

What a king or president or other recognized leader is and does depends mainly upon the social circumstances into which he was born and by which he was socialized; for to a very marked degree, times do produce the kinds of men appropriate to those times. Moreover, the social conditions of the times largely determine what particular kinds of men will rise to positions of leadership; in times of peace and general security, for example, ruthless and forceful men are neither wanted nor, for the most part, forthcoming. Even with hereditary rulers some selection occurs; for if a ruler is weak and the times call for a strong one, his reign will be short or his power usurped. Furthermore, the social consequences of the actions of a leader, whatever they may be, are determined by circumstances beyond his control. No doubt Caesar could, at the height of his power, decree that the streets of Rome be paved; but unless there were artisans to do the actual work, an economic surplus to apply to this specific endeavor, reasonable freedom from such distractions as war, and a general acceptance of the desirability of paved streets, nothing whatever would come of that decree.

This is not to deny that social change is brought about by individual endeavor, but to point out that those who are acclaimed as great men by their society or who are singled out by subsequent historians as the determinants of the events of their day are not for the most part those who work changes in their society. The unknown Englishman who first put together in tandem a number of spindles and powered them with a horse may have contributed far more to the making of modern English society than have any of the kings of England; and the unknown man who first thought to modernize the Roman legal fiction of the corporation, producing the joint-stock company, may well have done more to the Western world than have any of the generals since the time of Alexander.

Social change comes for the most part inconspicuously, and for the most part it is worked by unimpressive little men whose names and achievements are rarely entered in the records of social history. While these men are laboriously modifying some aspect of the social system, public attention, and ultimately that of the historians, is distracted by the pomp and ceremony of status leaders and by the drama of events associated with their names. Kings and presidents, generals and admirals, financial giants and industrial rulers are not without their sociological significance. But just as the social events that are imputed to such men neither constitute nor cause social change, so the great men of history are neither the determinants of social change nor an important source of data on such change as may in fact have occurred during their times.

1960. For a highly sophisticated and hence tempered analysis of the ways in which and the extent to which elites, political and otherwise, influence their times, see Robert M. MacIver, *The Web of Government*, The Macmillan Company, New York, 1947.

Need for a Sociological Time Perspective

Because social events and the lives of great men of the past have limited importance in the study of social change, it does not follow that the student of social change can dispense with social history. Socially significant changes occur through time; they and the conditions that produce them can be known, if at all, only by comparing the social phenomena under investigation as they are at one time with how they are at another, which generally means as they are in the present with how they were at some time—a year, a decade, or a century or more ago—in the past. Some highly limited and very short-lived changes have been studied as they have occurred; but for reasons that will shortly be evident, such changes are seldom sociologically significant. The inadequacy of historical data regarding the social past makes the study of social change precarious and difficult; this inadequacy, while it may not have been responsible for the general neglect by American sociologists of the field, has at least been used as a rationalization for it.[5] The structuralists and experimentalists, who examine society as of here and now, hold that since only the most intensive study of current social phenomena yields scientifically acceptable data, knowledge of times past is prescientific; and that, hence, no comparisons with times past are scientifically valid. They presume that the sociologist has no more need to probe into the social past than the physicist has need to ascertain the history of the atoms, electrons, protons, etc., that he studies.

Many American sociological studies do, in fact, lack a time perspective; and as a consequence the data that they yield often have the character of a social inventory, a simple and relatively meaningless description of how many of what existed at the moment and in the place under investigation. Most sociological studies, however, are either undertaken with some implicit if unstated historical frame of reference or else acquire one as the investigation proceeds. In the former case the study is *de facto* a test of a hypothesis derived from social history, whether recognized as such or not; in the latter the findings are compared, not necessarily with clear recognition of what is being done, with a hypothetical base line derived from or imputed to the past.[6] In

[5] The neglect of the historical approach to the study of society by American sociologists is analyzed by Harry E. Barnes in *Historical Sociology: Its Origins and Development*, Philosophical Library, Inc., New York, 1948. Aside from Barnes, the chief exponent of the historical approach in America was for long Howard Becker, who proved, for a variety of reasons, a very poor advocate. See his chapter on historical sociology in Harry E. Barnes, Howard Becker, and Frances B. Becker, *Contemporary Social Theory*, Appleton-Century-Crofts, Inc., New York, 1940, pp. 491–542.

[6] Thus the extensive and meticulous studies of American soldier morale during World War II that were conducted under the direction of S. A. Stouffer for

either case failure or unwillingness on the part of the investigator to examine his historical frame of reference is likely to result in the grossest sort of error.

Those who endeavor to dispense with a historical perspective in the study of society frequently point out in their defense that anything and everything and hence nothing can be proved or disproved by properly selected historical evidence; and so, indeed, it can, as Marx so ably demonstrated. At the same time, anything and everything and hence nothing can also be proved by objective, quantitative data statistically manipulated; the fact that statistical procedures are at present highly fashionable in sociology does not assure that what is derived from them has scientific validity. No tool, intellectual or manual, is better than the craftsman who applies it; the finest tool may be used ineptly, or a crude tool with consummate skill. The quantitative and experimental methods that sociologists have borrowed from physics may have the inherent potentiality of yielding testable data about contemporary society that is far superior scientifically to what can possibly be ascertained about the social past; but this possibility does not eliminate the need for a time perspective.

Of late there has been a growing body of historical analysis that transcends the conventional. It is being developed by institutional and social historians and by others who have perceived the inadequacy for social scientists of the artistic or literary approach to the social past. They direct their attention neither to wars, elections, the passing of pieces of legislation, and other social events nor to the lives and times of great men, but, rather, to the economic, political, religious, and other institutions of a given time and place—to the history of science or medicine or of such special forms of social organization as labor unionism. Always in studies of this sort the incompleteness of the

---

the Army were predicated on the assumption that the desertion, malingering, conspiring to evade orders, etc., that were found to occur among soldiers on active duty were indicators of abnormally low morale. This low military morale was in turn related to the high level of industrialization of American society and the presumed depersonalized "mass" character of social life in industrialized society. The base line used in the evaluation of the data on military morale was an implicit assumption that in previous wars American soldiers had had high morale— that is, that they had accepted and acted upon the idea that there is no greater honor than to lay down one's life on behalf of one's country. In point of historical fact, however, such high military morale is no more than a myth. Quantitative data on morale of the sort obtained in the World War II studies are lacking for previous wars that involved Americans; but there is ample historical evidence that, long before the United States became a highly industrialized nation and, by presumption, a mass society, its soldiers often fought with great reluctance, deserted in considerable numbers, and behaved generally as human beings rather than as the heroic soldiers of romantic fiction. See S. A. Stouffer et al., *Studies in Social Psychology in World War II*, 3 vols., Princeton University Press, Princeton, N.J., 1949.

historical records is evident; always the interpretation of such records as are available is subject to doubt and debate. Nevertheless, studies of this sort do provide raw materials from which tentative comparisons of how men have lived from time to time can be made and thus from which some equally tentative hypotheses regarding the ways in which societies are changed may be derived.

QUANTITATIVE VERSUS QUALITATIVE SOCIAL CHANGES

Western society of today, American society in particular, or any specific element of either differs from what it was fifty or a hundred years ago both quantitatively and qualitatively. There are at present, for example, more than twice as many members of American society as there were in 1900, nearly seven times as many as there were at the outbreak of the Civil War. There has perhaps been a corresponding increase in the number of family units and a considerable if not equivalent increase in the number of business, educational, and recreational organizations. Perhaps three times as much land is in cultivation now as at the time of the Civil War; the consumption of coal has increased more than fiftyfold; and while petroleum products were almost unknown in 1860, modern America is powered mainly by the hydrocarbons pumped from the ground. The quantitative changes that have occurred have not all been in the direction of increase and growth. Both the birth and the death rates of the American people, as of all Western peoples, have fallen spectacularly since 1860; the number of farm establishments has declined during this century; and during the same period the average number of persons per household has also diminished, as has the per capita consumption of grain, animal fat, and certain other commodities.

Quantitative changes that have occurred over the past are much easier to ascertain with some degree of exactitude than are those of a qualitative nature, in part because counting is simpler than evaluating and in part because record keepers usually have practical and immediate reasons for notating the numbers and magnitudes of things rather than their character. Thus while the Roman scribes boasted much about the numbers of Caesar's legions, the distances they could march, and the enemies they destroyed, the records tell very little, and that largely through inference, about the way in which the legions were organized; and while there is a fair idea of the number and distribution of American colonists on the eve of the Revolution and even of their birth and death rates, far too little is known about their family life, their community organization, and the ways through which they made their livelihood.

Data on quantitative changes, changes in population numbers and composition, in population distribution, in per capita consumption of fuel and food, in passenger miles flown per year by commercial airlines, etc., are often valuable for purposes of predicting the future quantitative needs of a society. Thus in attempting to decide today how many public school classrooms, how many family dwellings, or how much iron ore will be needed a year or a decade hence, or, more accurately, what the social demand for these things will be, projections of past quantitative changes can be used with some degree of confidence. In order to know not just how many Americans will be living in the American manner a year or a decade from now, but what kind of manner that manner will be, it would be necessary, however, to predict what qualitative changes in American society were going to occur during the next year or decade.

Qualitative Changes

Qualitative changes may occur in any aspect of the social system—in the tools and other artifacts used by the members; in their technological processes; in their informal or formal modes of association; in their language and its supplements, writing, pictorial representation, etc.; in their modes of socialization and social control, including law; in the body of myths, legends, and ideologies; in their moral concepts; or in their sentiments, opinions, values, tastes, prejudices, or the like.

One of the more obvious of the qualitative changes that have recently occurred in our own social system is the development and use of the elaborate technique of power production from fossil fuels—from coal, oil, and natural gas. This technique, compounded of many new skills and knowledges, varied and complex mechanisms and devices, and equally complex usages, is one of the vital elements of all modern industrial societies. Quantitative indexes to the increased application of this technique to work and other tasks are the previously mentioned consumption rates of the fossil fuels. The qualitative changes that these growing consumption rates reflect can perhaps be suggested by the contrast between the sailing ship and the jet airplane and between the horse-drawn carriage and the automobile; between the household spinning wheel and the modern textile factory; between the whale-oil lamp and the fluorescent light; between the charcoal brazier and the gas-fired heating plant; between the three-man iron smelter and the vast contemporary steel mill.

Two hundred years ago, Western peoples made almost no use of the hydrocarbons that were stored in the earth some hundreds of thousands of years ago. Peat, an immature form of coal, was used for household heating and cooking in some parts of Western Europe, and here and there outcroppings of coal were used in a small way for similar purposes. Nowhere had either peat or coal been put to the production of power. At that time the greatest single source of power at man's command was the sail of the sailing ship; on land, the draft animal—horse, ox, or donkey—aided in plowing, transport, water lifting for irrigation, and some few mechanical tasks, such as the grinding of grain; the water wheel was the source of some power for like mechanical tasks; and for the rest, power was the strength of man's own body. Even in the middle of the eighteenth century, when the industrial revolution was well under way, coal was not used for power; and the smelting of iron ore was accomplished by the traditional use of charcoal.

As the use of iron increased—a consequence of a host of antecedent and related social changes—charcoal making became a major industry; and toward the close of the eighteenth century, England in particular and Western Europe in general were becoming deforested. It seemed to many that the new age of iron would soon be brought to an end by the scarcity of fuel for the smelters; but there then occurred a major technological development, a qualitative change in one aspect of the social system. It was discovered that coal can be converted to charcoal-like form, to coke. A new form of fuel thus replaced charcoal in the smelting of iron; coal mining began on a large scale, and there was inaugurated a sequence of subsequent changes that are still going on in fuel, fuel converters, and power usages.

Meanwhile, equally radical qualitative changes were being worked in various forms of social organization, one of the more important of which was the development of life insurance and other kinds of commercial insurance. At the time of the American Revolution, insurance was practically unknown, whereas today it is the major means by which economically responsible men protect themselves, their properties, and their dependents from financial adversity. The highly complex organizations and procedures through which the modern American can purchase assurance that he will be financially protected in the event that disaster strikes him or his possessions are a commonplace and accepted part of our social system; by such insurance a man can modulate the economic consequences of sudden death, disability, old age, fire, accident, and many other of the hazards of life. Two hundred years ago little of the sort was available. Financial security rested, none too solidly, upon accumulated real property (a home, a farmstead, or other tangible property), upon the familial sentiments that would induce a brother to support a widowed sister-in-law and her children, upon the good services of neighbors in case the house or barn caught fire, etc.

Although the development of modern forms of insurance is less well documented than is that of power sources and usages, the records show that the process was fully as complex and that the consequences have been equally significant; and the two developments were no doubt interdependent.[7] The

[7] A brief account of the conditions that gave rise to various forms of insurance and of how each developed is provided by Alfred Manes, "Insurance: Principles and History," *The Encyclopedia of the Social Sciences*, vol. 8, 1932, pp. 95–99. A detailed analysis of early efforts to provide economic security to early

underlying incentive for the development of commercial insurance was, apparently, a decline in the effectiveness of the traditional familistic and community assistance in time of adversity. This decline, in turn, seems to have arisen from changes in the structure of family and community life, from increased individual mobility, both spatial and social, from progressive urbanization, and from the growth of a money economy. Insurance against sea risks had developed on a rather haphazard basis in England as early as the seventeenth century, a beginning from which in time evolved the world-famous Lloyd's of London. Toward the close of the eighteenth century commercial fire insurance was available to householders in the major cities of the West, including New York; but since the insuring companies were often financially irresponsible, a consequence, in part, of their inability to calculate risks and rates realistically, the major value of an establishment's being insured was the plaque on the building that marked it as insured and hence worth saving from fire, since the insurance company would reward the volunteer fire companies for their labors. (Such plaques are still to be found on many of the older buildings in European cities, where they are cherished as mementos of times past.)

During the early nineteenth century the practice of forming mutual life insurance associations developed and became popular, although in the end this form of insurance did little more than demonstrate that good intentions do not provide security. In the early, highly experimental mutual life insurance associations, a number of responsible heads of families would enter into a contract, each with all the others, to assure that should any one of them die before his sons were grown and his properties sufficient to support his widow, the others would jointly maintain his family in the manner to which it had been accustomed. Possibly some of these associations functioned effectively; but for the most part they broke down under increasing adversity. Nine survivors might be able and willing to support the family of one deceased member; perhaps eight would bear up under the requirement that they provide for the families of two former members; but there usually came a point at which the self-interests of the survivors were stronger than their contractual obligations, and at that point widows and children had to turn elsewhere for aid. Yet out of these mutual associations and a variety of other organizational experiments, there gradually developed the modern forms of life insurance and the many and varied kinds of supplementary insurance that are now available commercially and, indeed, those forms of assurance against individual adversity that are now provided by many modern governments.

It is qualitative changes such as the foregoing that make the social system at one period in time different from what it is at a subsequent period;

industrial workers through voluntary friendly societies is given by Neil J. Smelser in *Social Change in the Industrial Revolution,* The University of Chicago Press, Chicago, 1959, pp. 342–383.

hence it is qualitative rather than quantitative changes that are of primary significance in social change. Quantitative changes, however, cannot be ignored; for there is a complex, uncertain, and variable relationship between the qualitative and the quantitative changes that occur in society. In some instances, no doubt, a quantitative change is no more than that. Thus upon a number of occasions during the settlement of the North American continent, an increase in the number of family units indicated only that more land was being brought into cultivation, that the food supply was growing, and that the death rate was declining and the total numbers of the population consequently increasing. Through this period few if any significant qualitative changes occurred in agricultural technology, in religious and other beliefs, or in the family system. In other instances, however, a quantitative change may indicate that some antecedent qualitative change has taken place, the exact nature of which is never self-evident and can be ascertained only by intensive investigation, if at all. The sharp rise in the American birth rate during and following World War II, for example, undoubtedly reflected changes in American society of a qualitative nature, although just what these changes were remains, years and much study later, mainly a matter of conjecture.[8] Some investigators have concluded that economic affluence, itself stemming from improved productive techniques, more efficient methods of work organization, etc., was the antecedent; others, equally competent and well-informed, have held that it was a change in the middle-class value system —that large families came back into fashion, that the bourgeois value on prudence and foresight, economic and otherwise, disappeared, and that the threat of impending atomic warfare encouraged the younger generation to take a more hedonistic view of life than had their fathers.

Moreover, there is some evidence, albeit uncertain, that some kinds of quantitative changes do more than just reflect qualitative changes, that they actually implement qualitative changes. Where this is the case, the quantitative change would appear to operate as an *intervening variable*, a link between two orders of qualitative changes, although not in any sense the cause of the changes that are second in time. The concept of intervening variables will be examined in detail later; their role in change can be suggested, however, by what has in recent years been happening in many of the so-called underdeveloped, i.e., preindustrial, societies of the world. In Egypt, in India, and in many parts of tribal Africa, native peoples have been revolting against the established political order (often European-dominated) and endeavoring to establish new (to them) forms of political organization. In some, but far from all, of these politically restive societies there has occurred or is occurring considerable industrialization of the productive processes, with such corollary

[8] Ronald Freedman, Pascal K. Whelpton, and Arthur A. Campbell attempt to evaluate these changes in *Family Planning, Sterility, and Population Growth,* McGraw-Hill Book Company, New York, 1959.

changes as growing urbanization and decline in individual attachment to tribal, family, and other traditional forms of organization. The easy explanation for all these qualitative changes is that these peoples have rather suddenly perceived the advantages to them of political self-determination and of industrialization. If so, why did they not make this discovery fifty or a hundred years ago? What antecedent change has made political independence and industrialization appear desirable only now at this late date?

One possible answer to the latter question might be found in the recent, very rapid growth in the population of each of these societies, the postwar population explosion. That growth seems to have been lowering a standard of living that was already at a near-subsistence level; and it may well be that the drive toward political self-determination is an attempt to offset the economic consequences of the increase in population. Still unexplained, however, would be the rise in population. From the evidence that the postwar growth in native populations is a consequence of declining death rates rather than rising birth rates, which in most instances have always been close to maximum, comes the inference that certain qualitative changes are antecedent; specifically, that the adoption by native peoples of some Western public health measures during and just after the war brought about a sharp reduction in such natural and, for these peoples, normal checks on population growth as plague and epidemic diseases. In this view, thus, the population explosion becomes a variable that has intervened between qualitative changes that had the effect of lowering death rates and later qualitative changes in political and economic organization.[9]

There is still another way in which the uncertain relationship between quantitative and qualitative social changes makes for difficulty in analysis. Every qualitative change, be it a new tool or technique, a new idea or belief, a new form of human relationship or method of organization, begins in the mind and action of one man. At that point it is most certainly not a significant change; indeed, as will be seen, it is often socially defined as the product of mental aberration. If, however, others adopt the new, if it gains more and more adherents, a kind of quantitative change is then occurring; in simple terms, the new tool, idea, or method of organization is being diffused through the membership of the society. But the question then arises: at what point in this quantitative change is the qualitative change accomplished? when 10 per cent of the population have adopted the new? when over 50 per cent have adopted it?

To this question there is no easy answer, for there would seem to be no constant relationship between what proportion of the population adopt some-

[9] See *The Determinants and Consequences of Population Trends*, United Nations, Department of Public Information, New York, 1953, chap. IV, "Economic and Social Factors Affecting Mortality."

thing new and the life span of the new. No doubt there are some sorts of minimal limits. Unless a new technique in the field of medicine is accepted and used by a considerable proportion of medical men, it will not become a durable part of the medical heritage. Unless many young middle-class families adopt the practice of buying houses, furniture, motorcars, vacations, etc., on time, this practice can hardly be considered a normal social practice and will certainly not endure. Some middle-class families have no doubt always lived, insofar as they could, on credit; but until more and more middle-class people adopted the practice, it was not established as a norm of middle-class life. Indeed, it may even now be debated whether or not a sufficient proportion of middle-class people rely upon consumers' credit to justify its being so considered.

TRANSITORY SOCIAL CHANGES

The uncertain relationship between the extent to which something new is adopted and its life span is most evident in those transitory changes of a qualitative nature that appear as fads, fashions, vogues, cults, and movements. The new is in many instances adopted with great rapidity until the majority of the members of at least a class of the population have become involved; its appearance and spread are invariably recognized; and, like births and deaths and other events, it is usually the subject of much reporting and comment.[10] At the time of its occurrence the new may have a considerable impact on social life; but it may be abandoned even more rapidly than it came into use, with the result that it never becomes an established part of the social system and rarely leaves any durable imprint.

Faddish Changes

The more trivial, unpredictable, rapidly spreading, and rapidly disappearing changes are those of a faddish character. Changes of this sort occur when the value of the new to the individual who adopts it arises, not from what the new is or does, but from the fact that, being new, it attracts favorable attention from others. As more and more adopt it, its value rapidly diminishes, so

[10] Transitory social changes, on the other hand, have been little studied by psychologists and sociologists. During the 1930s there was something of a vogue among social psychologists for the analysis of fads, fashions, crowds, crazes, and mass movements of one sort and another; but in the years since then understanding of such phenomena has not greatly increased. Compare, for example, the interpretations of Richard T. LaPiere (*Collective Behavior*, McGraw-Hill Book Company, New York, 1938) with those advanced much later by Kurt Lang and Gladys Lang (*Collective Dynamics*, Thomas Y. Crowell Company, New York, 1961).

that within weeks or months of its initial appearance, the new has become old and uninteresting; and the change has come to an end.

In the societies of the past and the predominantly peasant and primitive societies of today, changes of a faddish character seem to have occurred only in conversational topics, in the subjects and nature of rumors and stories, and to have spread by word of mouth. Today, especially when the normal avenues of communication break down, faddish changes in topics of conversation may occasionally spread from person to person by word of mouth; but for the most part they stem from the news, both local and international, that is provided by newspapers, the radio, and television programs. Within these agencies an erratic process of selection operates on the basis of what is thought to be attention-getting value by those who disseminate the news. Of all the events of the day, week, or month, only a very small fraction come to be reported on the news-service wires; and of these, again only a fraction get into print or on the air. The selection is, in both instances, largely determined by the news values of the moment. At some times, as at the approach of Easter, for example, the reason why a given kind of news is news may be fairly evident; but in most instances a given kind of news has no better basis for being news than have the word vogues of the local adolescents. Thus one international conference of statesmen will be given heavy coverage and the next five or ten largely ignored; and for a time it may seem from the news sources that rape is becoming a commonplace or that most of the children in the land are being suffocated in abandoned refrigerators.

Faddish changes occur in many aspects of modern society, particularly those aspects that are unessential to the survival or welfare of individuals or to the maintenance of the social population. All peoples have dialects, patois, argots, or occupational or other jargons that tend to be stable. Slang, on the other hand, which usually consists of a distortion of the traditional language, often the imputation of a new meaning to an old word, usually has very brief currency. Slang words, expressions, sentence structures, etc., appear, spread within the membership of some more or less defined age, sex, class, or other category of the population, and drop out of use. As a consequence yesteryear's slang dates the person who uses it; indeed outdated slang may be deliberately used in fiction and the drama to invoke a sense of some particular time of the past.

The popularity of some games, such as bridge, baseball, and football, persists over the decades, although it may wax and wane over the years; but many games—Monopoly, mah-jongg, backgammon, battledore and shuttlecock, to name but a few—have been devised or resurrected and become extremely popular for a very limited time. Of recent years, faddish changes have occurred both in the games and in the play roles of small children. Thus for one horrifying season almost every small boy had to have his beaver-tailed hat in order to play Davy Crockett; another season it was Superman;

and still another somebody or other who was supposed to have been the quickest man on the draw of all time.

What are called "health foods" evidently have a continuing appeal to many people in modern American society; but what constitutes a health food is a matter of social whimsy and changes from time to time. Fermented milk had a great vogue in the 1920s, when it was called "Bulgarian milk," and again in the 1950s, when it acquired the name "yoghurt." Stimulated, perhaps, by the apparent increase in deaths from heart failure and sanctioned by some medical findings, the fad for polyunsaturated fats swept through the ranks of middle-aged Americans during the late 1950s; and about the same time it became something of a fad for overweight Americans to shift from solid to semiliquid foods, such as Metrecal.

Faddish changes are particularly noticeable in dance music, dance forms, mechanical gadgets, ornamental devices, minor items of clothing and jewelry, and hair and make-up styles. In all these areas the new can be adopted at slight cost in either time, effort, or money; and because it can, the fact that the new will soon be antiquated is of little consequence to the individual.

Fashion Changes and Vogues

Less rapid and somewhat more orderly than transitory changes of a faddish sort are those that occur in the realm of women's clothing, interior decoration, architectural design, automobile styling, and many other fields. Wherever adopting something new is costly in time, effort, or money, most individuals will refrain from doing so unless given some assurance that the new will endure (in the case of women's clothing, for a season or two at least). That assurance is provided, in each of the several fields in which fashion changes occur, by recognized authorities—by clothing stylists, interior decorators, architects, etc.; and in each such field there is a more or less stable structure of personal, institutional, and promotional mediums (fashion magazines, house and garden journals, etc.).

Fashion changes occur most often in aspects of social life that are relatively independent and that can therefore change without seriously affecting other aspects of society. Changes of a similar sort do sometimes occur, however, in more integrated areas of contemporary life—scientific, educational, medical, and organizational. Scientists, physicians, educators, and business executives ordinarily proceed about their official tasks in an orderly manner; but as persons they are as subject to whims and fancies as is everybody else and from time to time become victims of a seemingly contagious enthusiasm for this or that new field of study, method of study, curative agent, pedagogical gadget, organizational procedure, or what not. The result is a vogue or fashion-like change in science, medicine, education, or business procedure.

Fashion-like changes in interest, in techniques, and in speculative theory occur in every field of science.[11] The enthusiasm for the new never affects the entire scientific community, nor does it ever preempt the field; but for a time the new will be considered by many as the key to the scientific future, it will be the most talked-about development, it will tend to secure the most ready financial support, articles on it will flood the journals, and so on. Fields of applied scientific knowledge, such as medical practice, are even more susceptible to fashion-like changes than are the sciences themselves, perhaps because practitioners are under constant pressure to accomplish socially designated ends. There will be occasion later to refer to the history of medicine for illustrations of the ways in which significant social changes arise; but a great deal of the history of medicine illustrates only that most of the quickly recognized and applied "discoveries" in medicine have turned out to be excitements without substance. There may not be an inverse relationship between the welcome accorded a new medical discovery and its duration, but it does often happen that the more excitement that attends the appearance of a new surgical technique, a new drug, or a new theory of cause and cure, the sooner it is abandoned. Moreover, in medical practice, mechanical engineering, criminology, psychotherapy, and other fields of applied science, the really significant changes have usually come about slowly and with little clamor. One is therefore tempted to posit the thesis that, at least in such areas of modern society, the greater the fanfare with which something new is greeted, the less significant it will in time prove to be.

Possibly because they deal with intangibles, are constantly subject to public pressures, and have no real way of testing the validity of their theories and practices, educators—or, at least, most of the philosophers of education and the teachers of teachers—seem particularly prone to accept whatever new idea comes along. They may steadfastly and rather uniformly subscribe to the belief that education is a major factor in the improvement of society or, at any event, that it is good for the individual, if not for the

[11] The vogue in American sociology for equilibrium theory and structural-functional analysis was discussed in the preceding chapter. The concurrent and dependent vogue for the application to the study of society of the research methods and conceptual tools—e.g., mathematical model building—that have proved so fruitful in physics may also turn out to be a transitory phenomenon rather than a major and vital step in the development of sociology. It is not yet, at any event, a firmly established aspect of the sociologist's culture and is still subject to criticism by doubting sociologists. See, for example, Pitirim A. Sorokin, *Fads and Foibles in Modern Sociology and Related Sciences*, Henry Regnery Company, Chicago, 1956; C. Wright Mills, *The Sociological Imagination*, Oxford University Press, Fair Lawn, N.J., 1959; and Helmut Schoeck and James W. Wiggins (eds.), *Scientism and Values*, D. Van Nostrand Company, Inc., Princeton, N.J., 1960.

society as a whole; but when it comes to such matters as the desirable goal of education, the best pedagogical procedures, the most useful curricula, etc., they evidence no constancy. As a result, today's vogue is hotly disputed and soon discarded for some other, and equally transitory, theory or practice. At the moment there is some tendency toward a consensus among professional educators that the educational goal should be the adjustment of the student to the station in life assigned to him by society, that the educational process should proceed in accordance with "democratic principles," and that care should be exercised to avoid imposing stresses and strains upon the student. There are, however, a variety of other current theories, many of them conflicting; and what the dominant vogues and the secondary ones will be in a year or two is quite unpredictable.

Even the colleges and universities are subject to whims and fancies. For the most part they move along in stately adherence to time-worn traditions; but academic administrators and managerially inclined academicians are often busy advocating the adoption of some new organizational gadget or educational procedure that has caught their fancy. The idea that there is too much specialization, especially in the sciences, for the good of the student or for the good of science is one such vogue; it was current in the universities during the early 1930s, was soon supplanted by new and equally transitory concerns, and was revived and refurbished as a new idea during the 1950s. In both instances, acceptance of the idea led to the establishment for a time of interdepartmental courses (for example, "a survey of social science" and "an introduction to the physical sciences"), of cross-departmental programs for the A.B. or for higher degrees, and of degrees at large and in nothing in particular. During the 1920s there was a great and equally transitory vogue for the division of the college program into two phases, the first two years ("Lower Division," it was often called) to be devoted to general education as locally defined, the last two years to specialized, semiprofessional studies. During the 1950s a comparable vogue arose for integrating the general and specialized programs through the mechanism of a "core curriculum."

Cults and Movements

Our own social history, like that of many other peoples, has seen the rise and fall of numerous religious, political, aesthetic, economic, and generally unclassifiable cults and movements. They may concern almost anything—how to raise children or how to get oneself into heaven, how to live the good life or how to live a long life, how to find political short cuts to utopia or how to find quick and sure roads to riches.

The proportion of the social population that becomes involved in a given cult or movement is usually small; but what the membership lacks in size, it typically makes up for in intensity of faith and vigor of action. A cult or movement (the former term is usually applied to those who are engaged in personal salvation of one sort or another, the latter to an endeavor to change some aspect of the social system or the whole of it) centers about a new or refurbished idea of how to do something, an idea that is in direct violation of the traditional way to accomplish this end. Thus a get-rich-quick cult invariably involves a rejection of established ways to wealth—they are too difficult and too uncertain—and the provision of an easy and certain alternative. A religious cult involves a rejection of the traditional theologies in favor of a new one or one that has been borrowed from some other society.

Since the ideological basis of a cult or movement always violates reason, or empirical experience, or good taste as locally and currently defined, those who accept it are socially suspect; they are considered as belonging to the lunatic fringe, a suspicion that is confirmed when such people are found drifting from cult to cult and movement to movement. Those who join cults and movements are, certainly, unstable in comparison to the general run of the population, who are inclined to plod along established routes to health, wealth, and happiness and to put their faith in the powers of established government to bring about the good society.

For the most part, the ideas that men hold as valid reflect the activities that they accept as normal, rather than the other way around. The cult or movement reverses this order; it evolves around a new idea, and those who join the cult or movement are encouraged by the new idea to act in new ways.[12] Often, of course, the action is little more than talk; this is notably the case with short-lived religious or supernaturalistic cults. The action may, however, take such deviant and vigorous forms as retiring to the wilderness to live without clothing (as those involved in "back to nature" movements have done); purchasing some land and settling down on it with a hen and a rooster (as those who joined the One Acre and Independence did); and growing a beard, going unwashed, and sitting about in smoke-filled rooms spouting gibberish in the name of poetry (as the self-styled beatniks of the postwar years continue to do).

The Limited Effects of Transitory Changes

In spite of the fact that much attention is being devoted to it, a fashion or vogue may have little effect on any aspect of social life. The fact that a physician is following a current vogue in diagnosis or therapy does, of course, have considerable significance for his patients. From the point of view of medicine

[12] See Neil J. Smelser, *Theory of Collective Behavior*, The Free Press of Glencoe, New York, 1963.

as a whole, however, its significance may be very slight indeed; for medical vogues occur mainly in the uncertain realms of medical practice. A responsible physician may become enamored of the latest, highly touted antibiotic and for a few months use it widely; but he will do so only with patients whose difficulties cannot be clearly diagnosed or as a therapy for clearly diagnosed troubles for which no certain therapy is available. The vogues in science, in education, and in organizational procedures likewise occur mainly in frontier areas about which there is little real knowledge. Cults and movements often involve conduct of considerable significance to those directly involved and sometimes of limited significance to the society at large. Nevertheless, a cult or movement is always concerned with matters regarding which there is, in the particular time and place, a weakened tradition and considerable lack of social consensus. Religious cults rise and fall only when and where the established religion is failing to satisfy social needs; economic and other social movements generate and gain a following only among people who have become detached from and disillusioned with that which the movement promises to replace.

Most fads, fashions, cults, and movements simply give way to some newer fad, fashion, cult, or movement. Occasionally, however, a word, game, or mechanical gadget that begins as a fad may survive to become established in the social system. A fashionable garment, idea, scientific concern, etc., may lose its fashionable quality but persist as an established part of the social heritage. A cult or movement may leave behind something besides disappointment, broken faith, and a record of futility. In all such instances what survives is a modulated, refined, or fragmentary part; and what survives lacks the excitement or attention-getting value that it formerly possessed.

Although any given transitory change usually contributes little, if anything, to changes in the social system, the occurrence of transitory changes in a society is symptomatic of conditions that are conducive to the appearance of significant changes in that society. In the modern world trying out something new is one way in which individuals attempt to resolve their frustrations or to secure satisfactions that are not otherwise forthcoming; and the occurrence of a great number of transitory changes is thus an indication that the felt needs of many of the members of the society are not being satisfied by the established practices of social life, that for many of the members of the society life is in some respects frustrating or inadequate.

It does not follow, however, that in a society in which many transitory changes are occurring changes of a socially significant sort will also occur. Transitory changes may operate as a substitute for socially significant changes by dispelling the tensions of individual discontent and by diverting into socially fruitless channels energies and abilities that might otherwise have been applied to the solving of problems. Just as a woman who is not happy in her marital life may find interest and gratification in the role of a woman of fashion or in involvement in the latest religious cult and so abandon the attempt to make her marriage work, a social population may become so much engrossed in the excitements of transitory changes that it tends to ignore and neglect the inadequacies of the social system itself.

SOCIALLY SIGNIFICANT CHANGES

What constitute the really significant changes that occur in a society are, clearly, a matter of perspective. To every member of a society it is the changes in his personal life and the social events of his times that are of paramount significance; for within the framework of his particular society these are what determine whether he will live out his life in peace and comfort, live long but miserably, or die young of famine, disease, or the misfortunes of war. For the individual, what his society was a generation or a century ago or what it will be a generation or a century hence is significant only to the extent that the social past and the social future affect the social present. For the student of social change, on the other hand, what is significant is of a quite different and considerably less self-evident order.

To constitute a socially significant change, the new must be not only adopted by a sufficient number of the members of a social population to give it currency, but so integrated into the social system that it will endure. Thus the student of social change must eschew the worm's-eye view of social life that is usually taken by the members of a society, by their spokesmen, such as journalists, and by their leaders, political and otherwise, and adopt a fairly long-range time perspective. If he does not, he is likely to mistake transitory changes for significant ones and to project a current but short-run trend in social affairs into the indefinite future. A fairly satisfactory rule-of-thumb position is that no change may justly be deemed socially significant until the new has been so effectively transmitted from the generation in which it occurs to the next generation that it is thereafter considered as the normal and is taken for granted as an integral part of things as they are.[13]

On the whole, socially significant changes would seem to be accomplished before they become apparent and to be unheralded rather than welcomed with public acclaim. It is, thus, seldom possible to detect and recognize those current developments that will in the course of time become significant social changes. Only in the main, by looking backward after such a change has been accomplished, can something of its origins and the factors that have

[13] For a more highly formalized conceptualization of what constitutes significant social change, see Alvin Boskoff, "Social Change: Major Problems in the Emergence of Theoretical and Research Foci," in Howard Becker and Alvin Boskoff (eds.), *Modern Sociological Theory*, Holt, Rinehart and Winston, Inc., New York, 1957, pp. 260–302.

brought it about be ascertained. The student of social change does not, for the present at least, have the powers of foresight; among the many endeavors that are no doubt at the moment under way to discover new things about the universe, to invent new mechanical devices, to create new ideas, to design new forms of social organization and patterns of human relation, to formulate new laws, etc., he cannot possibly distinguish which will bear fruit; nor can he possibly anticipate which of the products of these endeavors will be adopted and put into use and, in use, prove sufficiently gratifying to assure their survival in competition with other, and perhaps even newer, devices, ideas, etc., to the end that they become more or less enduring elements of the social system.

Accumulation and Synthesis

Significant social changes come about slowly, even in the most rapidly changing society. Since, however, numbers of such changes may accumulate over time and be synthesized into an operational whole, the end product may appear to be a general and radical advance over what preceded it. Modern medicine, for example, is obviously more effective than was that of a century ago in preventing and delaying death. Today few infants are stillborn and few need die during their first year, whereas a century ago about one out of five were stillborn and about one out of three died during the first year of life. Today very few Americans die of smallpox, scarlet fever, diphtheria, malaria, yellow fever, typhoid, or other contagious diseases, whereas a century ago comparatively few escaped relatively early death from one or another of these diseases. Modern medicine did not, however, suddenly appear in the modern world as a spectacular new discovery. On the contrary, it grew up as a gradual synthesis of bits and pieces of knowledge and skill that had accumulated over the centuries. The contagious diseases of man were conquered one by one, each after long effort by many men; and each conquest was built upon a variety of antecedent discoveries about organic life. The change that has occurred in medicine is enormous, but it is a change that has been wrought over the centuries by small advances first here and then there, segmental advances in knowledge and its application.

Although major social change, such as that from medicine of a century ago to that of today, is accomplished through the accumulation and synthesis of a multitude of segmental changes, casual observation and conventional modes of thinking tend to obscure this fact. A modern hobbyist may look over his woodworking shop with its neat and efficient power tools and think to himself that they represent the recent mechanization of woodworking; they do, but only in a gross manner of speaking. They did not develop simultaneously from the hand tools that were their predecessors, nor did they come into being within a time span that can be delimited. On the contrary, each of the machines, the circular saw, the planer, the drill, and the sander, has a long and complex history of its own; and the development of each has not been concurrent with that of all the others. Each of the several parts and of the various materials from which they are made also has its own long and complex history. The electric motors by which the machines are powered are a modern development that was begun in the seventeenth century and that grew out of devices that were in limited use more than a century ago; and just one of the very many developments that made possible the small electric motor of today was the discovery of a method for producing electric brushes to ride on copper commutators that would neither disintegrate with heat nor wear down the copper over which they traveled. Thus the workshop equipment represents the summation of a multitude of specific and, from the larger point of view, minuscule and discrete discoveries, inventions, and developments, no one of which was actually directed specifically toward providing the hobbyist with efficient tools. The history of the ball bearings used in the motors does not run parallel to that of their brushes, to that of the steel from which the cutting tools are made, to that of the controlled electrical energy that drives the motors, or to that of the reinforced concrete upon which the equipment stands.

Similarly, a modern supermarket operator and his customers may see the supermarket as a single entity (and, indeed, it operates in this way) and, contrasting it with some actual or remembered old-fashioned food store, assume that the former grew up or was devised as a whole. Like the woodworking shop of a modern hobbyist, a modern supermarket is, however, the summation of a great many small, highly specific changes, each one of which has a social history of its own. The concept and practice of fixed and clearly marked prices developed very slowly during the early decades of the present century and quite independently of such now closely related practices in the merchandising of foods as standardized prepackaged products, self-service, cash and carry, etc. Until well into the present century, merchants of foods as well as of other consumers' goods followed the ancient and almost universal practice of haggling with their customers over the price of each item that was sold, a practice that is only now, mainly through the introduction of American-type supermarkets and department stores, disappearing in Europe. Just where and when the practice of fixed prices for goods emerged is unknown. It became necessary, at any event, with the development in America of the mail-order house, for it was impossible for a merchant and customer to bargain over prices by mail. Its spread to various kinds of retail merchandising was very gradual, and it was long before it was combined with the many other and separate merchandising developments which together constitute the supermarket form of selling foods and related products.

Even as conventional modes of thinking reflect the view that major social change comes about abruptly and in a unitary manner, so, too, do conventional explanations for changes. It is commonly said, for example, that James

Watt invented the steam engine and that the Federal welfare program was the creation of President Roosevelt. Actually, however, the steam engine, political welfare programs, and all the other devices, ideas, and forms of social organization that have emerged in recent or fairly recent times are a synthesis of a very large number of highly specific changes, no one of which was in itself a major change from that of the past.

Programmed Change and the Planned Society

There is throughout much of the world today a prevailing hope that men can take deliberate and effective charge of their social destiny and by one means or another, usually by programmed changes to be governmentally enforced, shape the social future to accord with current desires. Social planning has become an honored and sanctioned endeavor, a sort of modern substitute for the prayers and incantations by which medieval peoples endeavored to control the world about them. In almost all the countries of the modern world, including those that have only recently gained their political independence, there is a quite general acceptance of the view that government can and should assume major responsibility for the economic and social welfare of its citizens. This view involves the assumption, usually implicit, that through political action desirable social changes can be calculated and put into effect; and in accordance with it and upon this assumption modern governments are all busily at work.

It is, of course, conceivable that man has at long last discovered a technique whereby planned, generalized changes can be brought to successful fruition and that, as a result of this discovery, new laws of social change are presently at work; but there is no evidence to this effect, and so far those deliberate changes that have been attempted have had unascertainable or unanticipated consequences. It is therefore to be expected that the significant social changes of the future will come about, as they have in the past, in a random and segmental fashion and that most of the legislated and other grandiose attempts to shape the social future will in the perspective of time turn out to be no more than social events. This is not to imply that such endeavors are without significance, for obviously they often have considerable effect on social life. In due course the role of government and other control organizations, both as agents of society and as agencies affecting society, will be analyzed. At this point, however, it may suffice to say that one of the underlying assumptions of the present analysis is that man has not yet discovered a unique and effective means by which to determine his social future and that thus the same processes that have shaped the social present from the social past are working and will continue to work to make the social future from the social present.

chapter 3 Models of Change and Stability

Although the study of social change centers upon the rise, adoption, and establishment in a social system of new social elements, the new is significant only in terms of its consequences. A new tool, a new idea, a new procedure, technological or otherwise, or a new pattern of human relationships becomes socially significant only through the way in which and the extent to which it functions differently from the old; and this difference depends, not only on the new element itself, but also upon the context in which it operates. The introduction of a new kind of tool or a new kind of social relationship might have fruitful consequences in one society, whereas the same tool or social relationship might bring only disutility when incorporated into another.

The discovery that the functional effectiveness of a social element is not inherent in the element itself antedates the emergence of the science of sociology—it is to be found, for example, in the writings of Montesquieu; but although it is one of the major intellectual discoveries of all times, it has not been effectively incorporated into the intellectual heritage in the same way that such innovations as the wheel and the arch have been incorporated in the technological heritage. As a consequence, men are inclined today, as in times past, to regard their various social practices, techniques, ideas, etc., as entities unto themselves and to evaluate them in absolutistic and universalistic terms of good or bad—for example, to regard racial segregation as bad in all places and at all times, and public school education as good for all people under all conditions.

No certain means has yet been discovered by which to measure objectively the functional effectiveness of a social system or of any of its elements; and insofar as changes are concerned, sociologists can for the present do no more than make an informed guess regarding the functional consequences of a change that is occurring—such as the socialization of medicine

—and can do but little better in evaluating the consequences of a change that has occurred in the past. Even so, such guesses and evaluations are far more reliable than are the views, opinions, and explanations of the members of a society, including such authoritative leaders as churchmen, politicians, lawmakers, and the philosophers of the period; for the members of a society are seldom aware of the functional relativity of their social practices.

Functional Relativity

The functional effectiveness of some social elements is determined largely if not entirely by the value that the members of the society impute to them, by how they are socially defined. The aesthetic functions of pictures, musical compositions, household decor, etc., are thus determined; for the gratification of owning or observing such objects arises from the fact that they are socially and personally defined as beautiful. Religious icons, magic potions (including the placebos that even modern physicians may prescribe), rites (such as that of baptism), and many other kinds of ceremonials also derive most of, if not all, their functional effectiveness from how they are socially defined. In these and similar instances, a change in social definition may be all that is necessary to bring about a change in the functional effectiveness.

Most of the devices, procedures, concepts, relationships, etc., of a social system, however, are so interdependent that the function of each depends fully as much upon other elements as upon itself, and a change of any one of them may markedly modify the functioning of the others. A spinning wheel has the capacity of aiding in the conversion of fibers into thread; but it will function to this end only in combination with fibers, human skill, and the human desire to make thread by this particular means. In many of the societies of the past the spinning wheel was one of the important elements of the many related technological and other elements by which textiles were produced. In modern society the spinning wheel is an antiquated device; it is still capable of being used to make thread, but it does not actually function in this way. Thread is now made by far faster and far more efficient powered machinery; no one wants to make thread with a spinning wheel, and few indeed would have the skill to do so.

The original functions of social practices, of ideas, and even of values and sentiments may in like manner be modified or destroyed by changes in the social elements with which they are interdependently related. A century ago the formal debut was an integral part of a system of practices by which upper-middle-class and upper-class American girls were brought to social maturity and into marriage and motherhood. The formal presentation of a girl who had just reached marriageable age then functioned to impress upon her that she had come of age socially (even as do the puberty rites of many primitive societies), to announce to the community that she was now available for proper courting attentions, and to introduce her under the most favorable circumstances to the eligible young men of the community and their parents, who may not have seen her since she was a child and who would not, at any event, know her intimately. In modern America the daughters of wealthy and socially prominent parents often make formal debuts; but the function is no longer what it once was. The sexual segregation that once made the debut a socially useful device has entirely disappeared. Boys and girls now grow up together in frequent and casual association, and girls are out long before their formal coming out. Moreover, parental jurisdiction over courtship and parental selection of marital companions is also a thing of the past. When, therefore, a modern girl makes a formal debut, the function of the affair is not to introduce her to society, but to demonstrate her social position and the wealth and position of her parents. It may also, if incidentally, constitute an enjoyable occasion for all concerned, much as a pseudo barn dance may be good fun for modern urban people, even though none of them works on the land and the barn is only a country clubhouse draped with sheaves of corn.

Many of the inconveniences and some of the major problems of modern society may be traced to the preservation of social elements that have lost their original functions as the result of changes in interdependently related elements. Thus it is the retention by modern peoples of traditional but now quite inappropriate values, sentiments, attitudes, and practices regarding procreation that is at the basis of the current problem of overpopulation. In premodern societies infant mortality was very high, and the average life span was very short. Under these conditions, which in times past were nearly universal, attitudes and practices that encouraged conceptions—such as early marriage, discouragement of coitus interruptus (the major form of premodern birth control), idealization of parenthood, and a high valuation on children—functioned toward the survival of the group. Many changes, especially in public sanitation and medical technology, have eliminated the need for these old attitudes, sentiments, and practices as aids to group survival. Today a population can be maintained by a very low birth rate. Nonetheless, the old values and sentiments everywhere persist to some extent, and in many places their current effect is to jeopardize rather than preserve the society. In southern Italy and Puerto Rico, for example, where the traditional values and sentiments are fully operative and the birth rate is close to maximal, population pressure precludes a rise in the standard of living; for gains in social productivity are promptly canceled by an increase in population numbers. In both these areas, the real stumbling block to conscious control of the population is not the anachronistic insistence by the Church that birth control is contrary to the will of God, but the deeply embedded traditional sentiments, such as that which makes it a point of pride and a demonstration of his virility for a man to become a father just as often as his poor wife can bear children. Even a sophisticated modern American would probably be shocked by the bald assertion that, far from being an unmitigated blessing, a newborn infant can be an unmitigated social disutility; and yet such, from the functional point of view, is often the case in modern society.

MODELS OF FUNCTIONAL CONSEQUENCE

The social evolutionists, it will be recalled, believed that every change that occurs in a society is a refinement and improvement upon what preceded it and that a society therefore moves constantly and inevitably toward social perfection. Although evolutionary theory may now be dismissed on a variety of grounds, including the fact that the evolutionists did not recognize the relativity of the functions of social elements, the idea of progress has persisted. Its latest and perhaps most sociologically sophisticated version is that of equilibrium theory. In this theory, which recognizes and indeed devolves upon the variations in the functional effectiveness of social elements, changes in social practices, ideas, techniques, etc., are viewed as efforts—by what or by whom is not indicated—to resolve antecedent disequilibriums and are presumed to lead inevitably and directly to greater functional equilibrium.[1] The idea that change usually occurs when disequilibriums have arisen may be valid; but that change is invariably or even normally conducive to better functioning runs counter to much historical and a good deal of contemporary evidence.

Functional Equivalents

Because the members of society, including those in positions of leadership, are inclined to be preoccupied with social elements themselves rather than

[1] See Talcott Parsons, *The Social System*, The Free Press of Glencoe, New York, 1951, and his many prior and subsequent books. A carefully qualified version of equilibrium theory is offered by Robert K. Merton in *Social Theory and Social Structure*, rev. ed., The Free Press of Glencoe, New York, 1957. Equilibrium theory is dependent upon functionalism; but the recognition that most of the elements of a society operate within and in terms of a context of other elements—which is the orignal functional concept—does not lead directly and necessarily to acceptance of equilibrium theory. It is this use of the functional concept as a steppingstone to that theory, rather than the concept itself, that has been subjected recently to a good deal of criticism. See, for example, Kingsley Davis, "The Myth of Functional Analysis as a Special Method in Sociology and Anthropology," *American Sociological Review*, vol. 24, pp. 752–772, December, 1957; and Harold Fallding, "Functional Analysis in Sociology," *American Sociological Review*, vol. 28, pp. 5–13, February, 1963.

with their functional effectiveness, changes are in many instances merely substitutions of one element for another, with the result that the new is the functional equivalent of the element that it replaces. A simple example of a change of this sort is the development and use of the cigarette lighter. For many smokers, who presumably find it a more convenient or somehow more gratifying means of striking fire, the lighter has replaced the match; but since many other smokers continue to use the match, the advantages of the lighter—whatever they may be—are evidently very slight. At any event, the adoption of the lighter has not in any way affected the practice of smoking; a smoker can shift from lighter to match and back again in accordance with the momentary availability of the one or the other and without in any way disturbing the procedure by which he burns tobacco.

More complex, but otherwise comparable, are the many changes that have occurred in the forms of prostitution in Western society, mainly as a consequence of repressive laws. Since the early Middle Ages, moralists have recurrently deplored the existence of prostitution, and many medieval towns enacted stringent laws prohibiting the particular form of prostitution that was current in that time and place. During the nineteenth century moralistic concerns in the endeavor to abolish prostitution gave way to a more practical concern for physical health, and the idea developed that licensed and regularly inspected brothels are the best means of preventing the spread of the venereal diseases, if not of stamping out prostitution. Experience eventually discredited this idea, and first in Britain and then in the United States, the licensing of brothels was discontinued and their existence made illegal. Recently both France and Italy have followed our example of legislating against brothels. In the meantime the English have found it necessary—or at least aesthetically desirable—to prohibit open solicitation by streetwalkers and have been forcing them to adopt those covert forms of prostitution (such as the call-girl system) that have replaced the legalized brothel in America. All the many efforts that have been made over the centuries to abolish or at least reduce the practice of prostitution have resulted only in changing the particular form by which sexual services are sold. Each such change has undoubtedly occasioned considerable trouble for prostitutes, their clients, and the officials who have been charged with the enforcement of the laws; but no one of these changes, nor all of them together, has abolished prostitution or demonstrably improved the health of prostitutes or their clients.

Deliberate attempts to make sweeping changes in society through reformistic appeals, legislative action, or administrative fiat, have often resulted in no more than the substitution of one social element for another without any change in its functional effectiveness. Although many changes with profound functional consequences have occurred over the centuries in the governments of Western societies, political reform movements, most especially those of a local, municipal type, have seldom contributed to them. Reform movements have usually arisen when the party or clique that has held political power has grown old and slothful and indifferent to the obligations through which, in the particular system, political power was obtained or retained. A reform party has then made its appearance, promising to rectify all the presumed evils of the system; and upon election to office, the reform candidates have proceeded to make a variety of changes in the structure of the municipal government. Whatever their intentions, and no matter how sincere they may have been, the new political leaders have usually succeeded, however, only in substituting equivalent organizations and procedures for the old discredited ones. A police force may be reorganized; but before long it is functioning in the same old way—e.g., covertly sanctioning illegal gambling, prostitution, and pay-offs for special privileges. The established method of awarding contracts for municipal works may be replaced by one claimed to be graftproof; but in a matter of months municipal business will be back to normal. Bureaus and departmental organizations deemed unessential may be legislated out of existence, and various political sinecures abolished; but the end result is more likely to be a changing of titles than a reduction in the city payroll, for it is far easier to change the name of a bureau or a public office than to liquidate it. American cities have repeatedly undergone vigorous political reforms of this sort; but the important changes in the actual functioning of American municipal government have for the most part come by other, less spectacular and more gradual means.

Dysfunctional Changes

Every change is experimental in the sense that, whatever its proponents may claim for it, its functional consequences are not predictable. The social sciences have developed upon the premise that eventually it will be possible to predict with some assurance what will follow should men individually or collectively do this or that—for example, eliminate the death penalty for first-degree murder, sterilize women who live on public bounty, or clamp down harshly on juvenile delinquents. So far in human history, however, every new technological device and procedure, new idea, and new form of social organization and social relationship has been adopted without any real foreknowledge of how it will affect the working of the society. The adoption of the new is always expedited, as will later be noted in detail, by claims that the new will bring this or that desired result; but the claims are invariably spurious, if only because no one knows in advance how the new will actually function in its particular context.

It is, therefore, only through empirical experience with the new that its functional effectiveness can be determined—i.e., only through empirical testing can the errors in social experimentation be distinguished from the successes. The empirical process, particularly when applied to the testing out of new ideas and social practices, is exceedingly crude and uncertain; and the criteria by which the members of society or their political or other leaders judge the success or failure of the new may be vague and are often conflicting. Moreover, a recognized functional disutility may be ascribed to some social element, old or new, which is not in fact a contributor to that disutility; and the empirical testing may be so much protracted that the new becomes firmly established in the social system and thus ceases to be on trial.

The preservation of social elements that have lost their original functions has already been remarked. Such elements often acquire new if minor functional significance; an antiquated building, for example, may become a historical monument and an old device, such as a spinning wheel, may become a museum piece. Old buildings, old devices, and most especially old social practices and forms of organization may also be preserved after they have lost their original functions because they are cherished by, and serve the special interests of, some small but socially powerful segment of the society. Such survivals from the past are usually dysfunctional from the point of view of the society as a whole, whether the members of the society are clearly aware of the fact or not. Likewise new social elements that become established because they serve the interests of some particular group may, once established, be preserved even though they are dysfunctional from the point of view of the society as a whole.

One of the by-products of the development of large-scale commerce between Western Europe and the Orient during the eighteenth century was the introduction of opium to Western people. This drug gained wide adoption as a new cure-all for physical ills and as a magic potion that stimulated the mind and gave the user exceptional abilities, both physical and intellectual. The fact that opium and all its derivatives, such as morphine and heroin, are habit-forming and have severely deleterious effects upon both the body and mind—and hence, ultimately, the conduct—of the habitual user was not generally recognized for nearly a century. Once the disutility was recognized, efforts were made by Western governments to prevent nonmedical use of opium and its derivatives. By then, however, these drugs and their nonmedical uses had become established social elements; and today, as fifty and a hundred years ago, the problem of drug addiction is still with us, with no certain and final solution in sight.

Changes that have proved to be dysfunctional have often been forced on or foisted on a people, sometimes with the best of intentions. Christian missionaries to the South Seas, for example, were evidently distressed by the near nudity of the natives; to them it was an indication of sexual immorality, for in Western society clothing not only is a protection of the body against the elements, but is also, although perhaps only incidentally, a requisite for virtue. On the assumption that lack of clothing stimulated sexual desire, they attempted to improve the sexual morality of the natives by inducing them to clothe their bodies. It may be doubted that putting clothes on the natives had any significant effects upon their sex conduct; but there is no doubt that it contributed, along with newly introduced diseases, alcohol, and Western food practices, to the decimation and sometimes total extermination of native populations. For as is now clear, under the high temperature and humidity conditions of tropical regions, clothing has markedly adverse effects upon physical welfare.

Politically sponsored and governmentally enforced changes are quite common in modern societies; the proportion of them that turn out to be dysfunctional is exceedingly high, perhaps because they are usually put into effect by political fiat and do not undergo prolonged preliminary and gradual test. The Eighteenth Amendment to the Constitution of the United States was one of the more spectacular changes of this sort. For forty years and more, sentiment against the use of alcoholic beverages had been growing in the United States, and by 1919, when Federal prohibition went into effect, a considerable proportion of the American people, especially those of middle-class status, were morally opposed to the use of alcohol. Those responsible for the enactment of this legislation promised and expected that it would bring about an end not only to drinking, but also to various presumed social consequences of drinking—such as financial improvidence, marital discord, and crime. What actually came about was a new, extralegal system for the production and distribution of alcoholic beverages, almost universal corruption of officials charged with the enforcement of prohibition, the rise of underworld leaders to positions of wealth and great power, a widespread disdain for law, and a pronounced change in the attitude toward drinking. By the time the Eighteenth Amendment was repealed, the long-standing disapproval of the use of alcoholic beverages had largely disappeared, and the use of alcohol was socially sanctioned even among the middle classes. The dysfunctional character of this particular legislated change was soon recognized, but not sufficiently soon to prevent its having an effect exactly the reverse of what its advocates had anticipated.

Federal subsidy and the control of agricultural products has been equally dysfunctional, at least from the point of view of the Department of Agriculture. For more than half a century, the Federal government through the Department had encouraged the improvement of American agricultural techniques, but during the general economic crisis of the 1930s a reversal of policy and practices occurred. The new goal became that of arresting one order of change that was then under way—the decline in the number of small family farms and the concurrent rise of large-scale commercial farming—by inaugurating another order of change. To this end, attempts were made to bring agricultural production under control by law, to maintain agricultural prices by withdrawing produce from the open market and by subsidizing the small agricultural unit in various ways. For three decades the Department of Agriculture experimented with methods by which to achieve this goal; and through all this time the small family farm continued steadily to give way to large commercial production. In terms of the avowed goal, therefore, Federal agricultural policy and practices were totally unsuccessful. What was accomplished, if anything, was an acceleration of changes that were judged to be undesirable. From this point of view—which is not shared, however, by the nonfarm population or the more successful farming entrepreneurs—the many laws and administrative enactments affecting American agriculture were changes of a dysfunctional order.

Eufunctional Changes

In the short run every socially significant change is probably dysfunctional in some respects; and over the very long run even the most successful change may produce some dysfunctional by-products. Thus the adoption of a new labor-saving device may promptly result in the displacement of those whose labor it saves; and in time its use may contribute to the pollution of the atmosphere, which is one of the disutilities of industrial society. Whether or not a change is adjudged as dysfunctional will, of course, depend on what criteria are used and on whether evaluation is in terms of the welfare of the society as a whole or of some special segment of it. A conceptual distinction, however, may be drawn between a change that is mainly dysfunctional and one that is mainly eufunctional—i.e., one that proves over time to increase the production of social satisfactions more than it decreases them. Eufunctional changes are the successes in the trial-and-error procedure by which social change is effected, although, as has been noted, the determination of which trials are failures and which are successes is a very inexact process.

The way in which something new may be functionally more effective than its predecessor is easily demonstrated in terms of technological changes, less easily in the case of organizational and ideological changes. When cutting edges of bronze replaced those of flint and obsidian, the work of cutting wood, leather, meat, stone, etc., was reduced by one-half or more; when, centuries later, cutting edges of iron replaced the bronze, a further and greater reduction in work was achieved. Today, with a great variety of cutting edges of steel available, even an amateur craftsman can cut almost anything with ease and accuracy, even glass and metal. In the past thirty years the tractor has largely replaced the horse and the mule in American and, to a lesser extent, in European agriculture. As a traction device it can do ten times and more work than could its predecessors; it can plow ten acres of land for every one that could be plowed in a given time by a horse or a mule. In terms of work accomplishment, at least, its adoption has been a eufunctional change. In other terms, however, especially power consumption per unit of work, the tractor is far less efficient than is the horse or the mule, which can, as it were, produce more power from a pound of hay than a tractor can from a pound of gasoline; but as long as the petroleum supplies hold out, the tractor is far less costly in human time and effort than is the horse or mule.

The eufunctional nature of many changes in medical practice is also clear and undisputable. Mosquito control has practically eliminated malaria in the United States and over many parts of the world. Typhoid, once a major cause of death in the United States, has been reduced to a rare disease by improved techniques of water supply and, where water may be contaminated, by the processing of the water with chlorine. The development of sterile surgical techniques has made possible operations on the abdominal cavity (once certain death) with such eufunctional consequences as that death from appendicitis is now rare and that a surgeon can now even correct some congenital or acquired heart disorders. The progressive lengthening of the average life span of the members of Western societies is in considerable part the consequence of these and other changes in medical and public health techniques; and to the extent that people value a long and relatively comfortable life, those changes are eufunctional changes. The dysfunctional consequences of the lengthening life span—such as the growing proportion of old people in the population and the acceleration in the rate of population growth—will from this point of view appear incidental and minor.

The way in which new forms of organization and new organizational procedures may prove to be eufunctional substitutes for those that they replace is illustrated by the efficiency with which modern public fire-fighting agencies respond to an alarm and the frequency with which they put out fires that were not prevented. The historical predecessor of the modern system was the volunteer fire company. In rural hamlets and small towns it was at least better than nothing; but in cities such as Boston and New York volunteer fire companies often proved to be worse than nothing. The companies were usually staffed by the more rowdy young men of the city; and the companies often came into conflict with one another during the course of a fire for the honor—and reward—of saving insured buildings, with the result that in many instances all the hoses were cut and equipment was smashed while the fire ran on unchecked. Modern forms of commercial fire, life, and old-age insurance also have proved functionally superior to their fraternal or mutual predecessors; and modern hospitals have certainly proved more efficient and efficacious in caring for the seriously ill than the early hospitals, in which care was often more dangerous than no care at all, or the home, which until recently was the usual agency for tending the sick.

In terms of work efficiency at least, and perhaps of nutrition, the rise of industrial food processing and distribution has been a change of a eufunctional order. The epicure may well despair of modern processed foods;

they are highly standardized, they lack subtleties of flavor, and so to the old-fashioned palate they are bland, dull, and insipid; but they are produced far more efficiently than they could be by any housewife, and they are relatively stable. Because of the development of industrial production and mass distribution of foods, even the workingman can today secure a varied diet throughout the year. Consider, for example, just one of the many interrelated changes that have come about over the past half century—the change from the small, independent grocery store to the supermarket. In almost every respect the supermarket is more efficient and for most buyers more convenient than was the old grocery store. The range of available foods and food products is far greater; the foods, mostly packaged, are more sanitary and dependable (the crackers in the box are almost always fresh; those in the grocer's barrel were often stale); and the cost of getting the food from wholesaler to customer is proportionately but a fraction of what it was fifty years ago.

In the area of social organization, the development of the joint-stock company is a clear indication of how the new may function more effectively than what it replaces. A common form of business association in nineteenth-century America was the partnership, which made possible the joint undertaking by two or three men, each with limited capital, of a business venture that no one of them could undertake alone. But the partnership had its limitations. For one thing, since each of the partners was wholly liable for the actions of the other or others, it had to operate upon mutual trust; and not all partners proved trustworthy. For another, since partners had to trust one another, there was a limit to the number of partners who might be banded into one enterprise; no one would enter a partnership unless he knew intimately those with whom he would be associated. In time, therefore, the partnership form of organization gave way to the limited joint-stock company—an association of a number of contributors of capital, each of whom was responsible only to the extent of his contribution. The joint-stock company made possible the large capital outlays that were necessary for full exploitation of industrial technology. Railways, steamship lines, steel mills, etc., were all initially financed in this way; it is difficult to see how they could have been financed by the partnership form of capital pooling.

The eufunctional nature of new tools, techniques, organizations, etc., that supplement rather than replace the old is illustrated by such various things as the bicycle and the public school system. Whereas the automobile became in time a substitute for the horse and buggy, the bicycle was from the first and still is a supplement to walking; it is, in fact, a sort of walking on wheels. As a supplement or adjunct to the rider's own legs, the bicycle on favorable terrain gives about a fivefold increase in efficiency. A fairly accomplished walker can cover about 30 miles in a walking day; an equally accomplished cyclist can do upwards of 150 miles. Even for the ordinary user, a bicycle is much faster and much less tiring than walking.

The public school system in America was initially a supplement to the family in the socialization of children. It was intended to do what the family could seldom accomplish—i.e., induct the child into the knowledges, skills, values, attitudes, sentiments, and actions of the larger society, to make him an American, even as his family made him a Jones. The effectiveness of public school education in serving this function has often been doubted, probably because what is expected of the school system has continually increased. Yet there is no doubt whatever that the development of the professional schools—medical, legal, engineering, etc.—was a change of a eufunctional nature. The early physician who learned his trade from his father, or a father surrogate, learned very little that was of use to his patients, whereas the product of a modern medical school is highly trained in medical technology. Moreover, as a sort of social bonus, the medical schools that were gradually established came to be centers of discovery as well as of training.

MODELS OF FUNCTIONAL INTERDEPENDENCE

Until much more is known about how the multitudinous elements that go to make up a modern society are functionally related one to the others and to factors—physical and biological—external to the society itself, all social changes must continue to be, as they have always been in the past, experimental, with many of them proving to be dysfunctional or at least to have unanticipated or unwanted dysfunctional side effects. At present it is known that most of the elements of any society are functionally interdependent, but it is not known in what specific ways and to what specific degrees. Certain general inferences may be made from historical materials, and some tentative models of functional interdependence may be constructed as analytical tools. The models are purely heuristic and should not be thought of as scientific hypotheses to be tested against empirical data. The models that will be described here are derived in part from mechanics; they could just as well be based on biological concepts of functional interdependence.

Functional Interdependence

The functional interdependence of social elements and the unanticipatable consequences of changes in various related elements can be seen in the history of the whaling industry as it developed and changed in Western society over the past two centuries. In antiquity the major fat used both in cooking and in producing artificial light had been olive oil. During the Middle Ages, mutton tallow, a by-product of wool and meat production, came into use in the making of candles; and until well into the eighteenth century, the mutton-tallow candle was the standard means of artificial illumination. With the growth of urban life and the increasing demand for artificial light, candles became increasingly expensive. An improvement in the efficiency of the candle, the braided and mineralized wick, which consumes itself and does not require frequent trimming to avoid wastage of tallow, was eventually achieved; but the real solution to the demand for more artificial light came with the discovery that whale oil, extracted from the blubber of the sperm whale and a liquid at ordinary temperatures, could be burned in lamps, the lamps themselves being a modified version of those of Greece and Rome. There then developed an elaborate industry in whaling; whalers roamed the seas searching for sperm whales, killed the whales with hand-flung harpoons from small boats, and floated them to the side of the ship, where the blubber was removed, hoisted aboard ship, and cooked down into oil.

The whaling industry reached its peak about 1850, when it was producing most of the oil for the lamps of the Western world. In the years immediately following 1850, overhunting so reduced the supply of sperm whales in the seas that the cost of whale oil rose rapidly, oil became scarce, and some pessimists predicted that the lights of Europe and America were destined to go out from lack of fuel. The unsatisfied demand for lamp fuel led to the development, not long after the discovery of petroleum oil in Pennsylvania, of a method of distilling a liquid but not too volatile fuel (kerosene) from natural petroleum. Within a decade, kerosene had replaced whale oil in lamps. Meanwhile, carbon monoxide, a by-product of the coking of coal, came into use first for street lighting and, later and slowly, for the illumination of buildings. In the end, artificial gas and subsequently electricity replaced the kerosene lamp as the major means of illumination; but that is another, if closely related, development.

From about 1865 until well into the present century, whaling was a dead industry. The supply of sperm whales gradually returned toward normal; but there was little demand for their oil for illumination, and it could not be used as an edible fat. There were plenty of other kinds of whales in the seas, the fat of which was known to be edible; but they were too large, too fast, and sank too promptly upon killing to be hunted as sperm whales had been. Toward the close of the century, a Norwegian devised a harpoon gun with an explosive head; subsequently a mechanical, powered grab, the *hval kla*, was devised whereby the carcass of a large whale could be winched, tail first, through a slot in the end of the ship onto the deck, where it could be dismembered conveniently and without need to fight off the killer whales that liked to feed on a whale tied to the side of a ship. These two devices, together with large steam-powered factory ships, motorized hunting boats, and compressed air pumps, made it possible to kill, keep afloat, strip, and render the blubber of the large, fast, and numerous blue whales and other whales whose oil is edible.[2] Meanwhile, growing populations, rising

[2] The description of modern whaling techniques is taken from R. B. Robertson, *Of Whales and Men*, C. A. Watts & Co., Ltd., London, 1953.

standards of living, and related changes combined to provide a good market for this edible whale oil. In some countries whale oil has in recent years become the major edible fat; one reason for this was the development fairly early in the century of the technique of hydrogenating oils to make them solid. In America margarine, as well as cooking fats, is made mainly of soybean, peanut, and cottonseed oils; in Britain and some other countries, however, whale oil is the main oil used.

Today large-scale factory ships roam the antarctic seas each year hunting and reducing to oil thousands of great whales, not for the lamps of the Western world, but for the stomachs of Western people. An interesting sidelight on modern whaling is that it is an elaborate, ingenious, and in terms of human effort costly method of exchanging one kind of oil for another. A modern factory ship leaves for the whaling waters with its tanks full of fuel oil and returns, if the season has been good, with these same tanks filled with whale oil, all because at the present time a gallon of edible oil is valued far more highly than is a gallon of petroleum oil. Whether or not modern whaling techniques will continue to be functionally effective—or from the point of view of the whaling industry, whether or not a profit will continue to be made—depends upon a large number of circumstances, many of which are external to whaling itself and no one of which is likely to remain constant. Overhunting may in time deplete the supply of blue whales and other large whales, as it did that of the sperm whale a century ago; increased efficiency in the production of vegetable oils may reduce their relative costs in comparison to whale oil; or the constantly increasing use of petroleum may so deplete the supply and increase its cost that the exchange, in effect, of fuel oil for whale oil may become uneconomic. Any such change would disturb the entire whaling industry and, perhaps, call for a new series of changes in whaling techniques and organization.

Social Accessories

Some few social elements are not functionally interrelated with the rest and may therefore change without disturbance to the context in which they operate. It probably makes no difference what style of clothing whalers wear if it protects them from the rigors of the weather or whether they believe in Christianity or communism, as the Russian whalers presumably do. Whether they do or do not wear beards, drink coffee or tea with their meals, sleep in swinging hammocks or wooden bunks, say a prayer or curse before setting off in pursuit of a whale, or sing sea chanteys or play cards in their leisure hours cannot affect the efficiency of whaling operations. Insofar as the killing and processing of whales is concerned, these and some other aspects of the daily life of whalers, past and present, are extraneous variables. All social elements that are in this sense functionally independent of their social context may be thought of as social accessories—

bits and pieces that are attached, simply because they are for the moment valued for themselves, to elements of the social system that are functionally interrelated.

Since changes in social accessories do not disturb the context in which they operate, it is these social elements that are most subject to the rapid and transitory changes that were discussed earlier. Some elements that are independent of their immediate context and are to this extent social accessories may, however, at the same time be functionally integrated into other aspects of the social system. Thus while the political or religious beliefs of the whalers matter little insofar as whaling is concerned, those beliefs—whether, for example, in Christianity or in communism—will have considerable bearing on the welfare of the whalers, if not directly upon their conduct, when they return to their home ports.

Parts and Complexes

Unlike social accessories, most social elements do not function except in relationship to other elements; they are integral parts—anthropologists usually describe them as cultural traits—of a complex of parts that together makes a functioning social unit. The clipper ship, used by Americans in the early period of whaling, was the fastest and most efficient sailing ship then in existence. Each of the various parts—the hull, the rudder, the spars, the sails, etc.—was functionally integrated with all the others to the end that a change in any one of them would have modified the functioning of the whole and the loss of any one would have incapacitated the ship. The same thing is true, in varying degrees, of all mechanical devices—the automobile, the watch, the radio, the television set, etc. In each instance the device is a complex of parts, no one of which will function independently of the others.

The complex of interdependent parts that constitutes a functioning organizational unit or political or religious practice is less apparent and is perhaps most easily perceived as a system of specific social roles, each different from all the others but functionally dependent upon them. Viewed in this way, a modern American family operates as a system of interrelated roles—the various roles of a father, those of a mother, and those of a child or children. No one of these roles is as clearly and rigidly defined as is a part of a mechanical device, but the functional dependence of each role upon the others is at least conceptually clear. Apart from the make-believe of the drama a man cannot occupy the role of husband without someone in the role of wife, nor can he occupy the role of father without someone in the role of child, or that of head of a household without wife and children (and, possibly, servant or elderly relative) to make the role of householder functionally meaningful. In the same way a religious organization, such as a local church, cannot operate without someone in the role of priest or minister and a variety of other people in the role of parishioner.

Social roles are not, however, equivalent to individuals; one man may fill many roles, and many individuals may occupy the same role. Father of a family, for example, is not a single role but a number of roles, each somewhat dependent on all the others and each dependent upon the roles of other members of the family—mother, children, indigent relatives, etc. At the dinner table the father may be something of a disciplinarian, endeavoring to teach his children proper conduct at the table; at bedtime he may be a playful parent or a prayerful one; alone at last with his wife he may become briefly a lover, while at breakfast the next morning he may be the irritable master of a household. The life of the family as a unit of organization consists of the personal interrelations that are required by many such roles; and a change in any one of these roles will to some extent affect the operation of the entire complex, even as a change in one part of a mechanical device will modify, for good or ill, the functioning of all the others.

Assemblies

A complex of social parts, such as a clipper ship or a modern family, always operates in conjunction with other complexes with which it is functionally articulated to form a larger social unit—an assembly. The interdependence of the complexes that constitute an assembly is considerably less, however, than is that of the parts of the complex. The loss of its sails would incapacitate a clipper ship, and the loss of the father would profoundly disturb the functioning of a family unit. On the other hand, a clipper ship could be and was effectively operated in conjunction with a variety of other complexes. Always, of course, it sailed the sea and was dependent upon wind for motive power; but it sailed on many a sea as an integral part of many an economic assembly—whaling, the tea trade, the grain trade, and even in passenger transport.

Similarly, the modern family as a unit of organization always functions within some assembly of other related complexes; but a change in one of the related complexes does not necessarily—although, of course, it may—have as profound consequences to the functioning of the family as does a change within the family itself. Although the family in its present form could not operate in a nonindustrial society, it can operate with comparative effectiveness in an urban, suburban, or even rural context and, without much variation, in conjunction with such different religious complexes as Protestantism, Catholicism, and Judaism.

The difference in the degree of interdependence between the parts of a complex and between the complexes of an assembly is well illustrated in recent social history. The gradual liberation of women in Western society, especially in America, from their traditional position as homebound wives and mothers, brought about a radical change in the character of the family. As daughters and wives were released from the traditional obligations of these roles and took on others of a nonfamilistic character, the entire complex of family organization was disturbed; and all the various parts of the complex were profoundly affected. By contrast, many marked changes have in recent years occurred in some of the complexes that make up the assembly within which many modern families function without comparable effects upon the family itself. The neighborhood community, one of those complexes, has in many instances become weak and transitory—in part because of changing residential practices and an increased use of the automobile—without, apparently, profound disturbance to the family itself; and in the past two decades there have been marked changes in the merchandising complex by which many families are supplied with foods and other commodities without necessitating equally marked changes in the organization of family life. It is possible, for example, for a family to move out of an urban center or a small town and settle down in one of the new suburban residential communities with its modern shopping center and supermarkets and discount stores without major changes in the family structure. The members of the family will of necessity learn new ways of getting along with neighbors and develop new shopping and related practices; but their relations to one another can remain very much what they were when they lived in a city apartment or a small-town home.

Social Components

Complexes of parts and assemblies of complexes are models that are based upon differences in the degree of interdependence that exists among social elements or social units. In both models the relationship—of the parts of a complex or of the complexes of an assembly—is an interactional one. Since a change in one part or in one complex will to greater or lesser extent disturb the functional effectiveness of the others, those others must change to a corresponding extent if the effectiveness of the whole is to be maintained, while at the same time changes in the others will necessitate further change in that part or complex that first changed. As the role of wife in its various aspects has changed over time, it has been necessary for those of husband, father, son, and daughter also to change if the family complex was to continue functioning. The changes in these roles have constituted a modification of the context in which the role of wife operates, a modification that has in turn required further change in the role of wife. Once started, therefore, change within a complex and to a lesser extent within an assembly may continue indefinitely.

A different kind of relationship exists between the elements of a social component, a model that is commonly encountered in anthropological and sociological analysis and that will be utilized in later chapters of this book. The social elements of a social component are functionally interdependent in varying degree, but their relationship is reactional rather than interactional. Thus a change in one element may make possible a comparable change in another or others, but does not then necessitate compensating changes in the first. Such is the relationship of the various elements that together comprise the technology of a society, which may be simple or intricate; of those that comprise its organization, which is always intricate and consists of a considerable number of assemblies; and of those that comprise its ideology, which includes language and its supplements, and beliefs, knowledge, and other symbolic constructs.

The reactional, as distinct from interactional, nature of the relationship of the elements of a social component is perhaps most clearly illustrated in the technological, for any technological complex or assembly depends more or less on the entire technology of the times. A clipper ship, the killer boats, and the various devices and techniques that were used in whaling in 1850 could be re-created today, even as the *Mayflower* was recently reproduced for historical purposes. It would, however, obviously have been impossible in 1850 either to build and operate a modern factory ship or to conduct modern whaling operations. A modern factory ship is in a sense a summary of modern industrial technology; the ship and its boats are metal, they are powered by steam and internal-combustion motors, the harpoon is fired from a small cannon and is equipped with an explosive head, the killed whale is filled with air from a modern compressor (the whole history of artificial refrigeration lies behind this single device used in whaling), and radio communication coordinates the work of the killer boats.

While modern whaling depends upon the factory ship and many other technological complexes of modern society, those complexes are not, however, in a like way dependent upon whaling. A change in the arts of motive power, such as from the steam engine to the Diesel, might lead to a modification of whaling techniques; but the fact that whaling ships came to be powered by Diesel rather than steam engines would not disturb the functional effectiveness of Diesel engines and thereby call for a modification of Diesel techniques; nor, to carry the example one step further, would the incorporation of improved steels in the fabrication of Diesel engines disturb the function of the metallurgical complex.

Subsystems

In actual operation, however, a social component does not function as an entity. Modern technology, or organization, or ideology may as such be contrasted with the technology, or organization, or ideology that existed at some previous time; but what actually operates in any one place or time is a social unit that is composed of certain elements of each of these three components, related interactionally into complexes and assemblies. Thus the life of a household, of a commercial establishment, of an industrial plant, of an amusement center, or of any other tangible manifestation of the social system will incorporate some technological, some organizational, and some ideological elements. Such a working whole may, for purposes of analysis, be thought of as a social subsystem.

The practice of medicine, for example, constitutes one of the important subsystems of the American social system. It utilizes various elements of the technological component, from which it derives such modern devices as clinics and hospital buildings, ambulances and private automobiles, surgical and other tools, x-ray and other complex apparatus for diagnosis and treatment, and the many synthetic drugs that are now used in place of the herbs and other natural substances of times past. It also draws upon and is dependent upon an increasingly large fraction of the ideological component, specifically the sciences of anatomy, physiology, pathology, etc.; and it operates in terms of such other aspects of the ideology as the high value that is currently placed upon human life, the concept and values of the professional man, the belief that scientific medicine is efficacious while other kinds are not, and the correlate idea, very new in Western society, that man is an animal subject to the same biological laws as are other organisms. Moreover, it incorporates many organizational elements, ranging in form from the informal association of a private practitioner with fellow physicians and the local hospital to the elaborately bureaucratic organization of a large clinic, private or public, a large hospital, a medical school, etc.; it also operates through a variety of professional organizations, such as the staff of a medical school, the clique that dominates a local hospital, the medical society of a county, the American Medical Association, and other comparable national associations of medical specialists. The medical subsystem is, furthermore, functionally interrelated with such nonmedical organizations as the pharmaceutical houses, surgical-supply companies, and the commercial or governmental agencies that help patients pay for medical care. Almost any change in the social system will have some implications for the medical subsystem, for that system is functionally interrelated with most of the other subsystems of the society, even as the complexes and assemblies of which the subsystem is composed are functionally dependent each one upon the others.

MODELS OF FUNCTIONAL INTEGRATION

Not only are the parts, complexes, assemblies, components, and subsystems of a society in varying degrees and in varying ways functionally interdependent, but any one of these social units may be more or less integrated into a functional whole. The unit will be integrated to the extent that its elements are congruent with one another; and to that extent it will operate effectively, producing high social rewards at minimal social cost and providing those who are involved with a high level of social welfare. The unit will be poorly integrated and will operate ineffectively to the extent that its elements are incongruent; those whom it concerns will experience stresses and strains of various sorts—frustrations, conflicts, discontent, or, as has been the case in many times and places, even hunger and death.

Various terms are currently used by sociologists and others to distinguish between a condition in which functionally interdependent elements are congruent and hence reasonably well integrated and that in which they are not—terms such as "organizaton" versus "disorganization." Other terms are commonly used to designate one or another of the consequences of each of these conditions; thus on the assumption that the forces—psychological or otherwise—that are operative within an integrated social unit are in balance, these forces are often characterized as constituting a social equilibrium, the antithesis to which is a social disequilibrium. The latter circumstance is, in turn, often thought of as pathological and occasionally as analogous to a morbid organism—as a "sick" society.

In the study of social change what is of primary importance is the likelihood that functionally interdependent social elements will become the object of significant change; and for this purpose it is not sufficient just to distinguish between that condition in which functionally interdependent elements are congruent and that in which they are not; for it often happens that when incongruence exists, circumstances are of such a character that they preclude efforts on the part of the members of society to rectify it. In the analysis of social change, therefore, such dichotomous concepts as social organization and disorganization and social equilibrium and disequilibrium have limited value. Much more useful in such analysis is a triad of abstract models, or ideal-type conditions, that are based not only upon the congruence or incongruence of interdependent social elements but also upon the susceptibility of those that are incongruent to significant change of a eufunctional nature. For convenience, and to avoid confusion with the many traditional dichotomous models of society, these three conceptually distinct kinds of social circumstances will be termed "stable congruence," "static incongruence," and "dynamic incongruence."

Stable Congruence

A watch that is in good condition, that runs well and keeps time with reasonable accuracy, is usually in little danger of being tinkered with by its owner, unless its owner is a curious child, in which case destructive changes will probably occur. In a somewhat similar fashion, a social complex or other unit within which the various parts or other elements are functionally congruent is not likely to be modified by forces from within that unit—i.e., by those who are involved in its operation—although there is always the possibility that its operation may be disturbed by external factors of a social, physical, or biological character. All the internal forces, which are ultimately reducible to the motivations, interests, attitudes, sentiments, beliefs, etc., of those involved, would be in balance; and the system would run along unmodified generation after generation.[3] A social system or social unit in this condition might, therefore, be described as being in a state of stable congruence.

It has been just such an idyllic condition of affairs that has been envisioned by all the utopianists from Confucius to Marx. A society, whatever its particular form, would in this ideal-type condition run along smoothly, providing a steady and adequate flow of social values, just as a perfectly adjusted watch constantly provides the correct time, and would need only a steady replacement of the individual members of the population as the aged died out. In such circumstances, every individual would be perfectly socialized in his childhood and youth, and he would be so well adjusted to his various and changing roles that he would never experience stress or come

[3] It is this condition, sometimes described as "moving equilibrium," that the equilibrium theorists seem to have in mind. They tend to assume, however, that all societies are in this particular condition most if not all of the time, whereas historically this condition has in actual fact obtained only in certain places and then for only limited times.

For a highly theoretical analysis of equilibrium models and their inherent limitations, see Everett E. Hagen, *On the Theory of Social Change*, The Dorsey Press, Inc., Homewood, Ill., 1962, pp. 505–513.

The inadequacy of the equilibrium model as a useful theoretical construct in the analysis of modern societies should be obvious, for modern societies are all undergoing constant and marked change. According to John C. Harsanyi, the concept is too artificial even to be useful in the analysis of any society. He says, in part, "Social scientists who make use of a static explanation often do not sufficiently realize how restrictive their assumptions are to which they are committed by adopting this type of explanation. A static explanation implies a static model of the social system. That is, it implies the assumption that all social variables relevant to the problem on hand always adjust to one another (and to the variables defining the natural environment) without any considerable time lag. . . . If nothing else, at least the evident inertia of cultural traditions and of social institutions must prevent any immediate over-all adjustment to changing conditions as would be required of a static model. Therefore, in general we have to use dynamic models, which allow for slow, delayed or staggering adjustment, and which include those social conditions of earlier periods . . . among their explanatory variables" (John C. Harsanyi, "Explanations and Comparative Dynamics in Social Science," *Behavioral Science*, vol. 5, p. 137, May, 1961.

into conflict with anyone. All the members of the society would, therefore, live out their lives in happiness and contentment; and since all would be happy and content, no one would be inclined to work changes either in the system itself or in his own status and position within the system.

While no actual society or unit within a society ever completely achieves a condition of stable congruence, some societies have for a time approached it; and in any society some of the complexes, assemblies, components, and subsystems will be about as functionally effective as man can ever hope to make them. The romantic idea of primitives as healthy and sturdy creatures leading the perfect life is no longer tenable, for the anthropologists have taken the romance out of primitive society and shown the variable and none-too-charming realities of life among primitive peoples. Nevertheless, some primitive societies do seem to have been comparatively stable and functionally effective before external factors—mainly the advent of Westerners and their devices and diseases—disturbed them. As was mentioned earlier, the Chinese social system was in all salient aspects in a condition of fairly stable congruence for some twelve hundred years—from about 500 to 1700. During this long period the Chinese spread from the Middle Kingdom to the whole of Eastern Asia and increased in numbers from perhaps ten million to about two hundred million. Nevertheless, in the eighteenth century as in the sixth, Chinese peasants used a hoe type of cultivation; the fabrication of goods was everywhere conducted on the basis of handicraft techniques; and transportation, both via land and via water, was much the same. For the whole of the period Confucianism was the official ideology; the written language and the character of what was written by the scholars remained unchanged; and the scholar class was recruited and trained and subsequently worked in very much the same ways at the end as at the beginning. Throughout these twelve centuries the family, with its supporting clan organization, was the basic unit of social life; filiality was the highest value; and although the political system grew larger and more intricate, it maintained the original Confucian principles of organization and political rule. The Chinese were conquered many times by barbarian hordes from Central Asia, but in due course they Chinafied each barbaric horde and thus preserved more or less intact their cherished forms of social life.

It should not be imagined that the Chinese social system kept everyone in a constant state of bliss, but there is scant evidence to indicate that there was any considerable amount of discontent or discontent for any considerable length of time. Occasionally over the centuries the citizens of a locality would revolt against the current magistrate, but revolt of this sort seems to have been resistance against the threat of change, such as rising taxes and governmental proposals for social reform; and the ability of the system to digest such foreign peoples as Jews, Mohammedans, and barbarian conquerors and such foreign religions as Buddhism and return in time to its prior normal, suggests its effectiveness in satisfying the individual members and classes of members of the society. It did not work perfectly, of course; floods, famines, epidemics, and high death rates were a part of life; and no doubt some fathers ruled their sons with ruthlessness, some wives nagged, and some sons were wayward; but whatever the lot of the individual, the system seems to have been able to reconcile him to it or at least to prevent him from doing anything to change it.

The stable congruence of the various units of the old Chinese social system is well illustrated in the operation of the family. The Chinese family was patriarchal in type, marriages were arranged between families for their children, and daughters-in-law normally went to live and serve in the households of their husbands. For ideological reasons, related to ancestor worship, it was imperative that a family should not die out; but inevitably marriages sometimes failed to produce children and sometimes produced only daughters. Should either of these circumstances occur too frequently, especially in successive generations, a family might find itself without a son to carry on the family line. One defense against this danger was the supplementary practice of concubinage; if a daughter-in-law produced no sons, even she would urge her husband to take (actually to purchase) a peasant girl as concubine. A secondary line of defense was to arrange with some family that for the moment had a surplus of sons a reversal of the normal procedure in marriage, so that the husband would join his wife's family, where he became son, and she, poor girl, was reduced in her own home to the formal status of daughter-in-law. In such ways each of the various units of the old Chinese social system tended to maintain itself in a state of fairly stable congruence and to be so compatible with the others that Chinese society as a whole remained both functionally effective and stable for a longer period than any other known society.

Even in a society in which rapid changes are occurring in many of the various social units, some of the complexes or assemblies or subsystems may remain in a condition of fairly stable congruence for considerable periods. In view at least of the rapidity with which changes were occurring in most aspects of our technology, textile technology remained remarkably stable from about 1850 until the development of synthetic fibers in the period immediately following World War I. In medicine tremendous advances were made in surgery during the same period, with very little change occurring in chemotherapy, an area that has, however, changed far more rapidly than has surgery since World War II. Although Western societies have undergone political and technological revolution over the past few centuries, the Roman Catholic Church has remained in this context of change organizationally and ideologically quite stable; since the Church achieved perfection in the later Middle Ages, as churchmen might say, there has been no cause for change.

A condition of stable congruence does not, however, imply complete structural rigidity; for even as a bridge must be pliant enough to adjust to changing stresses induced by wind, varying temperatures, and the traffic that moves across it, so a social system and each of its several constituent units must have sufficient flexibility to adapt to fortuitous variations in the context within which it operates or its functional effectiveness will be impaired and its survival as a structure jeopardized. Occasionally the means of adaptation are built into the system itself, as concubinage and son adoption were in the old Chinese family. More often, perhaps, adaptation is accomplished through a violation, temporary and limited, by the members of the society of some aspect of the established social system—through what might be described as a concession to expediency. In both cases the adaptation operates to preserve the structure that is involved rather than to effect changes in it, and the adaptive process is a social analog to the biological phenomenon of homeostasis, through which the integrity of the organism is preserved.

Static Incongruence

In contrast to a condition of stable congruence is that of static incongruence, a condition in which incongruencies exist within a social system or social unit and are perpetuated over a considerable period of time. Incongruencies are normally the result of dysfunctional change in one or more elements of the society or unit—often, but not necessarily, in response to changes in the context of the society or unit. Further and corrective change is then precluded either because the social system fails to produce individuals who are motivated to work such change or because the organizational and ideological components of the society as a whole operate to discourage change, or, as is usually the case, because of both.

A rough analogy to a condition of static incongruence is chronic organic ill-health that for a considerable time leads neither to death nor to recovery. A person who is sick is in a condition of organic incongruence; some, at least, of the various parts of his body function poorly in terms of the whole, and he feels pain and operates at a low level of efficiency. Although in the modern world an attempt to alleviate this condition is usually made, it is not always possible to restore the body's normal functional effectiveness; and frequently a patient must resign himself to being a chronic invalid, to living with his disabilities. The members of a society may likewise, if for quite different reasons, learn to live with social arrangements that are functionally ineffective.

Static incongruence in the technological component may arise from failure to modify a technique that has lost its functional value as a consequence of changes in related techniques. The English people today have a road system that was probably adequate for its usage thirty years ago but which, in view of the large number of automobiles that are now used in England, makes for chronic congestion to a degree that would be intolerable to American motorists. The English motorist does not enjoy this congestion, but nothing much is being done to change the road system; consequently a state of relatively static incongruence exists.

Incongruence in the organizational component may arise and persist in much the same way. The monogamous family system has lost much of its old functional value with the industrialization of food processing, the separation of work and play, the removal of work from the home, declining birth rates, etc. As a consequence, economic imperatives for the maintenance of marital relations have weakened, and a marriage in which the partners are incompatible need not be perpetuated. Here in the United States these changes in the context have been recognized by a gradual liberalization of the divorce laws and corresponding changes in the sentiments regarding marriage and divorce. In England such is not the case; divorce is almost as difficult to secure now as a hundred years ago. The result is that many English marriages exist in an enduring condition of marked disharmony.

Many aspects of contemporary French society are also in a state of comparatively static incongruence.[4] Although the peasants are heavily subsidized by the French government, their economic condition has steadily deteriorated, at least relatively, for the last half century; and they have frequently rioted and otherwise evidenced their discontent. One of a number of the circumstances that keeps them poor is the law, embodied in the Napoleonic Code and strictly enforced since the time of Napoleon, that the property of a man must on his death be divided equally among all his children. That law was intended to preserve the French family farm system; but the major consequence has been *morcellement*, the recurrent subdivision of farm lands. The result is that the land-usage complex remains in a condition of static incongruence, which in turn discourages the adoption by impoverished peasant proprietors of the more modern means of land cultivation. An almost equivalent condition of static incongruence has existed for decades past in the housing complex of French society. Since World War II, during which a good deal of housing was damaged or destroyed, there has been a considerable increase in urban populations and a marked revival of the tourist trade; but for many reasons, such as restrictive labor rules, devious property laws, and antiquated building techniques, comparatively little new housing has been built. No one is happy with the result—urban families crowded together in hotel rooms or sharing with others a shabby

---

[4] For recent books on the state of French society see Edward M. Earle (ed.), *Modern France*, Princeton University Press, Princeton, N.J., 1951; Paul Combe, *Niveau de vie et progrès technique en France depuis 1860*, Presses Universitaires de France, Paris, 1956; and Nathan Leites, *Du Malaise politique en France*, Librairie Peon, Paris, 1958.

apartment, tourists forced to make do with prewar and mostly pretwentieth-century hotel accommodations, etc.—but nothing is done to correct for it.

Functional incongruence is very common, perhaps especially so in modern societies, between the ideological and the organizational aspects of various complexes and assemblies, and it has often persisted for decades unresolved. The so-called American dilemma is one striking instance of an enduring contradiction between what men believe, or at least profess to believe, and what they actually do. The Declaration of Independence of the United States puts forth the dictum that all men are created equal, and most Americans seem to cling to the illusion that in America all men are in fact equal. Nevertheless, social inequality is universal; and here in contemporary America some kinds of enforced inequality, most notably perhaps that between Negroes and whites, has constituted a recognized incongruence between ideal and real that a century of sporadic effort has done relatively little to correct.

Although a static incongruence is usually limited to this or that complex of social parts, this or that assembly, or this or that subsystem, occasionally an entire social system has entered into and long remained in a condition of general incongruence. Spain is perhaps the best current example. During the later Middle Ages Spain rose to international power through military conquest and systematic pillage; but unlike her successors, France and Britain, Spain did not acquire the military, political, and economic techniques of empire building and instead settled into chronic impoverishment. Today Spain is the least industrialized country of Western Europe; her people are by any measure the poorest and least productive; her family, class, economic, and other forms of organization are in some respects more akin to those of medieval Europe than to those of modern Europe; and although her people may be disgruntled with things as they are, relatively little has been done to change them.[5] The usual explanation for this condition—that

---

[5] This statement, like any generalization about social matters, needs extensive qualification. The more urbanized and industrialized parts of contemporary Spain—Madrid, Barcelona, the north central coast—although few in number, are in many respects almost as modern as are those of France and Italy; and over the past decade and a half Spain as a whole has shown signs of awakening from its centuries-old apathy. See, for example, Sheila M. O'Callaghan, *Cinderella of Europe: Spain Explained*, Philosophical Library, Inc., New York, 1951; Americo Castro, *The Structure of Spanish History*, Edmund L. King (trans.), Princeton University Press, Princeton, N.J., 1954; and John A. Crow, *Spain: The Root and the Flower*, Harper & Row, Publishers, Incorporated, New York, 1963. An excellent analysis of the way Spanish social factors have contributed to the stability of Latin America is provided by Woodrow Borah in *New Spain's Century of Depression*, University of California Press, Berkeley, Calif., 1951.

Possibly the best example of static incongruence in the contemporary West

since the civil war of 1936–1939 the Spanish social system has been held in bondage to the past by ruthless political dictatorship—actually explains nothing. Here as elsewhere, the explanation for static incongruence lies not in the existence of some one factor but in the coexistence of many organizational and ideological conditions that are deterrents to change in any aspect of the society.

Incongruence and the Vitiation of Social Elements

All societies have devices for dispelling the more or less normal tensions of social life—devices such as the orgiastic dances of primitives, the peasant festivals, and the games and mock battles (such as football) of urban societies. These devices are inadequate, however, when a society is in a condition of marked incongruence, for the tensions produced by severe malfunctioning are in excess of the ability of the system to absorb or dissipate them. Those tensions—which may be described as individual discontent with personal circumstances and status, frustrated ambition, or disillusionment with the ideals and values of the society—may then be dispelled, depending upon the relevant characteristics of the society, either in efforts to rectify the incongruence or in efforts to maximize personal returns through exploitation of the existing social circumstances.[6] Exploitation of this sort

---

is provided by Sicily, where, aside from such semi-industrial towns as Messina and Catania and such tourist centers as Taormina and Siracusa, social life limps along on the basis of agricultural and fabricative techniques that were abandoned elsewhere in Europe a century or two ago, in terms of religious, political, familial, etc., ideologies that have hardly changed since the Middle Ages, and with the doubtful aid of forms of social organization that may have functioned fairly well during the time of the Crusades but ill serve human needs today. As a consequence, population pressure is acute and the standard of living barely that of subsistence; there is almost no social or spatial mobility, although individuals do escape the system by migrating elsewhere; illiteracy is common; and the status of women is still that of chattels, and outside the larger cities the women are kept secluded within domestic establishments. In *The Awakening of Southern Italy* (Oxford University Press, Fair Lawn, N.J., 1950) Margaret Carlyle makes the most of the modest changes that have occurred since World War II but succeeds mainly in showing how very malfunctional and highly stable the social life of Sicily has been.

[6] The effectiveness of war and other forms of intergroup conflict as tension-dispelling alternatives to social change will be discussed in a later chapter. The occurrence of short-lived cults, religious and otherwise, and the more transitory kinds of movements is an indication of the existence of excessive social tensions; and although these cults and movements are not normal tension-dispelling devices, they no doubt aid in the dissipation of excessive tensions.

results in a vitiation of social parts or elements; and while it further reduces their functional effectiveness—as measured by the social values produced—it does not modify them. Indeed, from one point of view, it is the expending of energies in exploitation of existing social circumstances that permits a condition of static incongruence to persist.

Presumably in any society, and most certainly in our own, some vitiation of social elements is the result of simple apathy or ineptitude. A father who is lazy, ignorant, or indifferent in respect to his obligations as a father may vitiate the family subsystem by transferring responsibility for the education and discipline of his children to his neighbors or to society at large. More commonly, perhaps, vitiation of established social elements is the result of calculated exploitation, as is the case when an exceptionally ambitious, greedy, self-centered, or cynical politician vitiates the powers of his office by using them for his own personal profit.

Although exploitation of existing social circumstances undoubtedly occurs in all societies and at all levels within the society, incentives to, as well as opportunities for, exploitation are far greater under a condition of incongruence than under one of congruence; for the resultant malfunctioning produces what is individually, and often socially, defined as inequity. A slave may not actively enjoy his subordinate status and the work demanded of him; but in a functionally effective system of slavery he has rights of a sort and is more or less reconciled to the inevitablity of his position. In the malfunctioning system of slavery that came about in our Southern states with the decline of the old plantation form of organization, the treatment of slaves became increasingly harsh, and many of them struggled against the felt inequity of their position. Some took flight, thus contributing slightly to the eventual abandonment of the slave system. Many more of them discovered the art—and such it was—of exploiting the role of slave; they cultivated the reputation of being inherently irresponsible, indolent, and incompetent. So successful were they in doing this that, long before slavery was abolished, the work value of slaves had fallen far below the cost of maintaining them.

When, as has occurred in many times and places, malfunctioning has led to a general sense of inequity—or, as it is usually now described, of social demoralization—calculated exploitation may become progressive. The consequences to the social system are somewhat analogous to the deterioration that occurs in a dwelling which the inhabitants find inconvenient and distasteful and therefore misuse and abuse—it changes constantly for the worse, until it finally becomes uninhabitable. A progressive vitiation of social techniques, ideas, and practices as the result of increasing frequency and scope of the exploitation is no doubt self-limiting. A decline in the effectiveness of the social system cannot proceed indefinitely, since the point would ultimately be reached where social life would falter through sheer lack of the means to sustain life. Historically, the process seems usually to have been interrupted long before this point either by external factors, such as the barbarian invasion that disrupted venal Roman society, or by revolt from within. Internal revolt may, as did the Reformation, inaugurate a period of eufunctional changes; or it may, as did the French revolutions, only aggravate the conditions that gave rise to it and so lead to counter-revolution.

For a century and more prior to the Reformation the organization and operations of the Roman Catholic Church were in many respects incompatible with other aspects of society. The medieval social values, practices, and ideas, of which the Church was the major organizational representative, had been gradually changing under the impact of commerce, world exploration, and the rediscovery and elaboration of the knowledge of the ancients. The Church, which had failed to adapt to these changes, had lost much of its functional effectiveness; both internally and in its relations to the rest of society its condition had become one of static incongruence. In part, no doubt, because of this condition, secular authority was beginning to strip the Church of many of its traditional functions; in addition, the early scientists were beginning to question the basic premises upon which the entire system of Church organization rested. For these and related reasons, the position of churchman was losing much of its prestige and gratification, the morale of churchmen was steadily deteriorating, and increasingly churchmen were exploiting their waning powers for personal gain. They squabbled among themselves for promotion and especially lucrative posts; and like the secular politicians, they often were not hesitant to use crass methods to dispose of their opponents. They played upon the religious fears and sentiments of princes and commoners to extort wealth and to get edifices erected to their own glory; they sold indulgences—freedom from Church law—and other special privileges; and, it has been claimed, they so far forgot their priestly vows that they took mistresses and fathered children.

French society during the period preceding the First Revolution was, if Voltaire and other social critics of the day are to be believed, permeated with corrupt practices. The French court, ruled over by a series of incompetent wastrels, lived in debauchery; and the hereditary aristocracy as a whole, which had long since lost its functional effectiveness, exploited peasant and townsman alike. Manners and fine clothing, Voltaire reports, had replaced morals; and the most honored ladies of the land were little better than high-priced whores. French political bureaucracy was but organized brigandry; it was cheaper to pay bribes than taxes, and it was safer to be a knowledgeable thief than an honest man. Business could only be conducted through black-market means, for antiquated laws and hampering administrative regulations made almost any profitable business transaction illegal. Aping their social superiors, workingmen were as demanding and unproductive as possible.

No doubt historical evidences tend to overdramatize, as do contemporary newspapers, the venality of the members of a society, ignoring in their reports the unspectacular conduct of those members—the skilled and industrious craftsmen, the kind and generous husbands, the reasonably honest politicians and bureaucrats—who do what their social roles demand in the socially specified manner. Nevertheless, there is good reason to believe that in some times and places exploitation has become so commonplace that the society as a whole would have collapsed had the process not been checked by the shock of revolution, war, or some other social upheaval.

Dynamic Incongruence

When the characteristics of the social system are such that the psychological tensions generated by incongruence between functionally interdependent social elements tend to be directed toward a modification of those elements, rather than an exploitation of them, a condition of what may be termed dynamic incongruence exists.[7] It is only under a state of dynamic incongruence that eufunctional changes occur; and it is mainly to the analysis of this condition and how eufunctional changes arise that the remainder of this book will be devoted.

[7] What is here described as a condition of dynamic incongruence is sometimes designated as an open society. Economists usually refer to a stage or period of economic growth, although Hagen (*On the Theory of Social Change*, The Dorsey Press, Inc., Homewood, Ill., 1962) usually refers to the condition as one of creativity. Some economists have thought that they discerned stages through which a society may progress from stability to dynamism. W. W. Rostow (*The Stages of Economic Growth*, Cambridge University Press, New York, 1960) has offered a five-stage model of the transition of society from a condition of what is here termed stable congruence to that of dynamic incongruence. In his terms, the stages are: the traditional one, the period during which the preconditions for takeoff develop, the takeoff, the drive to maturity, and the "high mass consumption" society. His concern is, of course, with levels of economic productivity and changes in the nature of that activity; and his attention is on the transition from the preindustrial to the industrial society of contemporary peoples.

Hagen thinks that there are three historical sequences through which many, if not all, societies progress. The starting condition, and by implication the historical normal, is authoritarianism, which corresponds roughly with what is here described as a condition of stable congruence. Change begins when disturbances to the system bring a withdrawal of "status respect" for various classes of individuals; those who suffer status loss first withdraw from social participation—the stage of retreatism; and then, failing to gratify their needs in this way, they or their children begin to take action against the social system, working changes in it (*op. cit.*, pp. 185–236).

Functional incongruence, whether confined to a single complex within the society or existing in the social system as a whole, will be perpetuated to the extent to which the ideology of the society and the various forms of organization constrain the individual members from exercising their initiative in efforts to rectify it. Under absolute ideological and organizational constraint, the only freedom that the individual has is that of becoming psychopathic. He can discharge his psychological tensions only in socially established channels; and if the society is in a state of incongruence, he must for the rest endure the inconveniences, the indignities, and the dissatisfactions of living under such conditions. Such, for example, is the plight of a motorist in contemporary Britain. He may blow his horn at the long line of stationary cars ahead of him, and he may write bitter complaints about traffic congestion to the *Times;* but short of selling his car and resigning from the ranks of motorists, he must put up with inadequate, overloaded roads; for those ideological and organizational aspects that are relevant to roads, their uses and construction, prevent eufunctional changes.

Specifically, the reasons why the British have not undertaken, and probably will not undertake, an effective road-building program commensurate with the postwar increase in automobile ownership is that no one concerned, least of all those government engineers who have been assigned to the task, has had the freedom or the incentive to get such a program under way. In the first place, the political and bureaucratic organizations of England are all deeply entrenched; each is a tight little organizational island that can neither move nor be moved in new directions. In the second place, should the government actually undertake a large-scale program of highway building, it would find almost the whole of English society against it. All motorists in England presumably want wider and better roads; but each motorist has in fact some vested interest as homeowner, businessman, or just busybody in preventing local changes in the road system. Each would, for example, be appalled by the idea that the little road before his house might be enlarged to make a major highway. Moreover, most motorists in England would be temperamentally opposed to the destruction of the countryside, of ancient buildings, and of the quaint winding lanes through villages and towns that would be necessary to relieve the current traffic congestion. Each motorist would, as an individual and as a member of one of the two powerful automobile associations, fight to preserve historic England against the inroads of "progress." So, too, would every village, town, and county through its various informal as well as its political organizations fight against any threat to the physical *status quo.* Knowing this, and probably secretly sympathizing with it, no government engineer would dare to suggest that the correction for local traffic congestion would be to rip out the tiny sixteenth-century stone bridge that spans the local stream and install a broad, new concrete one. Furthermore, the contractors and workers who build roads in England—or, more accurately, fail to build roads—are tnemseives in part responsible for the present state of affairs. They are so highly organized, in both formal and informal ways, that they have prevented the adoption of modern, mechanical road-building techniques.

The ideological and organizational factors that keep Spain in a state of relatively static incongruence are, of course, both more general and more complex; but they are of much the same order. In Spain almost every aspect of organized life, formal and informal, seems to be unalterably resistant to change; and every aspect of life is organized in one way or another. The family unit has a tenacious hold on its members, however discontented and dissentious they may be among themselves. Peer groups of all ages and classes exercise a powerful normalizing control over their members; communities, rural and urban, are comparatively closed and are tightly organized; each occupational and professional group, local or national, is highly monopolistic and enforces its traditional practices upon every member; businesses are relatively uncompetitive; much of the economy, rural and urban, is geared to the maintenance of the *status quo*, however unprofitable; and over all is the dead hand of the past, as represented by Church and State, forcing the individual to conform, the one by supernaturalistic controls, the other by coercive.

In the relatively frozen organizational morass that is contemporary, but far from modern, Spain, it is almost impossible for the individual to break loose, should he wish to do so, and attempt to exceed some one of the various organizational norms to which he is subject. He can rarely escape even physically from the organizations into which he was born and subsequently inducted; and should he do so and move into a new social context, he would meet with acute suspicion until such time as he had proved himself a good—i.e., complacent and conforming—Spaniard.

By way of contrast, the organizational units of contemporary America are comparatively loose. The family is, on the whole, so weak that it is unable to tie down its sons and daughters or even in many cases its husbands and wives, either psychologically or physically. Peer groups, both those of the young and those of the mature, tend to be temporary rather than permanent; and the individual is usually able, in any event, to escape a group whose constraints are irksome and join one more to his liking. The class system is vague, confused, and unstable. The ideological units of the society, like the organizational, are variable, conflicting, and always uncertain. No single religion holds a monopoly over supernaturalistic beliefs, social values and sentiments are mixed and unstable, public school education is fraught with contrast and constant dissension, etc. In sum, American society is markedly and remarkably disorganized; and because it is, American society is at the present time in a condition of general dynamic incongruence. It is thus possible for the individual to a significant degree and in at least some one respect to escape organizational and ideological constraints and strike out in new ways. Those ways are often futile, often socially and individually dysfunctional; but occasionally they bring into being a new and eufunctional change—a new and better tool, a new and more appropriate technical procedure, a new and more effective mode of organizing men, a new scientific discovery, or a new and socially relevant idea.

chapter 4 *Innovation and the Innovator*

Each of the multitude of social elements which together constitute a social system is the product of human ingenuity; it has originated at some time or other, in some place or other, in the mind of some one individual. Until very recently, manmade explanations, naturalistic and supernaturalistic, for social elements have disguised this fact and, from the point of view of the social system, with good reason; for belief that God or Nature has decreed that men should adhere to the particular set of social elements that constitutes their social system has everywhere operated as a major means of social control, aiding in the perpetuation of those elements through the generations, preventing atrophic change in the society, and discouraging the acceptance—if not always the appearance—of new and competitive elements.

It is commonly accepted today that man's ability to devise for himself methods of relating himself to nature and to his fellows is what most clearly distinguishes him from the lower animals. The contrast between the instinctive, and hence unchanging, social life of ants and some other insects and the learned, and hence changeable, forms of human association is frequently observed; and its corollary—that of all the organisms on earth man is the only one that can and to some extent actually does shape his own destiny—is generally recognized. Nevertheless, whether the gap between man and the nearest of the lower animals—the primates—looms large or small depends entirely upon one's point of view. The culture of the primates is, in comparison with that of man, slight and rigid. On the other hand, man has rarely, and then only in limited ways, exercised his capacity to devise new and functionally more effective forms of social life; and his failure in this respect provides an impressive basis for the view that man's biological superiority over the apes and chimpanzees is slight and tenuous and that the time may well come when

103

his dominant position on earth will be successfully challenged by apes or elephants, ants or aphids.

Consider, for example, that the wheel, which from the modern point of view is so simple and so necessary a device, was unknown to most of the peoples of the world throughout most of known social history; that the principle of the abutted arch, upon which all modern construction depends, was discovered—and then, evidently, only in one place by one man—less than three thousand years ago; that it was nearly fifteen hundred years after the discovery that the earth is round before anyone thought to go west to get east; that the Chinese, who may have invented it, did not learn to use gunpowder for anything more important than making noise to frighten evil spirits away; that men made tools of bone and stone for thousands of years before anyone discovered the superiority of metal as a material; that Europeans were dependent upon the primitive smelters of Africa for iron until well into the Middle Ages; that generation after generation of surgeons watched their patients die of infection from wounds without losing their conviction that the suppuration of flesh is a part of the healing process; and that not even yet has anyone discovered a means of preventing men from going to war against their fellows as they did when they lived in caves.

Seen in this perspective, man is only slightly less stupid than the primates, only slightly more capable of ordering his affairs to the fulfillment of his own interests. From this point of view, an entirely tenable one, the social history of man is the history of his ineptitude. There is, however, another and more fruitful way to view what man has and has not done. The painful slowness with which he has developed his social systems, the infrequency with which he has discovered new facts about the world in which he lives, and the stubbornness with which he has everywhere and always clung to the established, however poorly the established may have served his interests, can be all taken as measures of the inherent difficulty of innovating anything—of devising a new tool, of discovering a new fact about nature, or of inventing a new form of human relationship.

Once it is recognized that the innovative process is inherently difficult, the rarity of innovation becomes comprehensible; the human history may then be viewed as a demonstration of man's unique capacity to create a culture, rather than as a record of his stupidity. Thus the wheel, which is such an obvious device today, is obvious and commonplace only because somewhere, sometime, someone perceived that it takes less effort to roll an object over the ground than to drag it along; because someone, building upon this discovery, invented the disk and the axle, which have no example in nature; and because someone discovered that burdens may be mounted above such a disk. Where and when these various innovations were made is not known; but the development of the wheel, upon which modern civilization moves and operates, was certainly a major human achievement. Such is the case with all the countless social devices, procedures, concepts, and practices which are today taken more or less for granted and which seem so natural and often so simple. There is nothing natural about them; and if they seem simple, it is only because they come ready-made. In the making of each of them there was nothing simple, nothing obvious, and nothing easy. Each was a man-made innovation; and the sum of them all, our present society, is to be viewed with awe and admiration.

One may well marvel at the intricate design of a human body, at the complexity and efficiency of the processes of organic life, at the near-absolute accuracy of the chemical controls that enable cells to reproduce themselves and that make possible the reproduction of members of a species generation after generation. Even now, after centuries of increasingly intensive and scientific study, precious little is known about the mechanics of organic life; and the little that is known inspires wonder that anything so complex as life can have evolved. By comparison with any organism, even man, any society, even the most simple, is, however, vastly more complex in both structure and processes; and for that reason, if no other, far less is presently known about social than organic life. It is known that society, the most complex phenomenon within the ken of man, is made by man; but just how man makes and changes the elements of his society is still imperfectly understood.

Cultural Borrowing

If left to themselves v. little cult. borrowing would take place amongst villagers: ineffective comms + little inherent desire to ↑.

Even as it is sometimes easier to steal wealth from others than to produce it through labor, it has often been simpler for a given people to derive new social elements from the stock of another people than to invent their own. The process, which has been and is being much studied by anthropologists, is usually described as cultural borrowing. Most of the elements of many societies, and certainly many of the elements of all modern societies, have been derived in this fashion from the cultures of other times or places. Thus very few of the words used by modern Americans were invented by modern Americans; none of the plants—cotton, corn, wheat, soybean, potato, etc.— that are used for food or fiber was discovered and developed by modern Americans (indigenous Americans discovered the value of the potato and of corn); the major forms of American social organization—the family, the corporation, the church, parliamentary government, etc.—were all derived from European sources; and many of the ideologies, both sacred and secular, were current in Europe before Columbus set out on his voyage of discovery. What proportion of the totality of the contemporary American social system originated outside America is anyone's guess; but it may be said with confidence that one of the reasons why American society has changed with such great rapidity during the past hundred and fifty years is that the

American people have been in a favorable position, geographically and socially, for borrowing tools, techniques, ideas, and modes of organization that were devised and developed in another place or at another time.

Cultural borrowing is innovative in the limited sense that it involves the perception that a foreign element can with advantage be incorporated into one's own way of life. Such perception is by no means automatic; markedly different societies have for centuries lived side by side—indeed, have engaged in trade and even in an interchange of members—without blending their various forms of life. The people of Switzerland speak four distinct languages and lead four rather different modes of life, although the process of political integration began seven hundred years ago. The peoples of Britain have been herded together for centuries; they have fought among themselves, been conquered by outsiders, and otherwise intermixed; and yet today the English, the Welsh, and the Scottish are sufficiently distinct in language, in manner, and even in political, economic, and social outlook that each considers the others foreigners of a sort. All the peoples of the Western world and increasingly of the entire globe have adopted to some degree the techniques of industrial production; they all know and use, again in varying degrees, such products of modern technology as the railroad, the automobile, the telephone, the electric light, radio, television, etc. As they have adopted these devices, their historical isolation as distinct peoples has sharply diminished: they travel in foreign places, and foreigners visit among them; and they read—and now via television, see—how other peoples live. Nevertheless, the people of the Western world are still divided into a great variety of linguistic, nationalistic, ethnic, religious, and other cultural and subcultural groupings.

To perceive that a tool used by the members of a neighboring tribe is more effective than one's own because it accomplishes the same end with less effort, to recognize that the domesticated cattle of an adjacent society provide a better supply of meat because a more certain one than do the wild game of the forest, or to discover that another people's magic brings more rain than does one's own is a major intellectual accomplishment. It is the equivalent to the first phase of the innovative process; and it presupposes circumstances, both social and psychological, akin to those that are necessary for innovative endeavor. Perception of the advantages of a foreign element over a native one does not, however, lead directly and certainly to its being borrowed. The foreign element, even as a native innovation, must be advocated if converts to it are to be secured and it is to become incorporated into the social system. The nature of advocacy, the characteristics of advocates, and the conditions that hamper and those that facilitate adoption will be analyzed in subsequent chapters. It may noted here, however, that the borrowing of a foreign element very often has innovative consequences; for a borrowed element may disturb the complex, assembly, or component that is involved, producing within it a condition of dynamic incongruence that is conducive to native innovation. Moreover, a borrowed element may be combined with native ones in a new way to produce something entirely new.

Since borrowing may in turn stimulate innovation and since the conditions that foster borrowing are very much like those that facilitate innovation, there is a tendency for the two to go together. Most societies that have been during a given period eager borrowers of elements from other societies have also been exceptionally innovative. (One of the striking exceptions to this generalization was Japanese society during the late nineteenth and early twentieth centuries. Japan borrowed very heavily from Western society, especially in technology, but tended to superimpose the new upon the old system rather than adapt the old system to what had been borrowed. Even now, the Japanese are better at imitation than innovation.) Such societies are, in anthropological terms, "cultural centers." Florence and Venice were such centers of social change during the fourteenth and fifteenth centuries, when they were crossroads of trade and travel; they borrowed from all the peoples with whom they came in contact and also, and for much the same reasons, produced many indigenous innovations. Southern Germany and the Low Countries were the major cultural centers during the century or two preceding the industrial revolution; and England became the major cultural center—most of the new techniques of production occurred there— during the revolution itself. In the modern world every city is to some extent a cultural center; for modern means of communication and transportation have so reduced isolation that it is no longer necessary to live in this or that place in order to draw on the varied cultures of the world. Today the circumstances are such that contributions to the culture of the world can occur in many places. Thus it may be said that in the modern world innovations will occur wherever there are innovators.

INNOVATION

An innovation is an idea for accomplishing some recognized social end in a new way or for a means of accomplishing some new social end. The idea or pattern of ideas may become manifest as a new kind of tool or mechanical device, as a new process or technical procedure, as a new material or substance, as a place or terrain previously unknown to man, as a new mode of human action, or as a new concept or belief. Whatever the manifestation, the innovating consists of the creation of a unique and to a significant degree unprecedented mental construct, the idea that makes possible the "thing." An idea of how to construct a new tool, how to live a tribal or other form of life, how to pacify the gods, or how to make music on a violin is not, of course, socially significant apart from its actual manifestation. Nevertheless, it is invariably antecedent to the latter—antecedent both in the sense that the manifestation originates in the idea and that in operation it is the idea that makes the manifestation possible. Thus his possessing a set of modern carpenter's tools would not make a carpenter out of a primitive African, nor would the fact that he played the part of a man of finance make an actor a financier. The tools of a carpenter are only the material manifestations of the skills and knowledges that in use make the tools effective. Should a qualified carpenter be deprived of his tools, he could, presumably, make do with makeshift devices. Should a society be stripped of its capital plant and even of a majority of its members, the social system could be reconstructed in all physical and operational manifestations as long as there were some survivors with knowledge of the mental heritage of the society.

It is mainly from the history of technology that what knowledge there is of the innovative process is derived. Artifacts of one sort and another, plus in some instances pictorial representations, provide some evidence, however crude and fragmentary, of the technology of prehistoric peoples, while there is nothing at all to indicate anything of their social life, their religious beliefs, and their knowledge and understanding of the universe. The material ruins of ancient civilizations, such as Greece and Rome, tell a good deal about the technologies of these civilizations, whereas their written records provide relatively little information regarding their family and political organizations, their philosophies, and their knowledge and beliefs. As the modern period is approached, the record of technological development is always clearer and more detailed than is that of developments in other aspects of life, even the ideological, which by its nature tends to be embodied in writing. Thus there are fairly detailed accounts of the invention and development of the steam engine, whereas knowledge concerning the invention and development of the joint-stock company as a form of economic organization must in the main be inferred; and although who discovered the technique of anesthesia is known, who first thought of the clinic as a new form of organized medical practice is not.

Whereas the analysis of the innovative process and the conditions that make for innovation that follows is derived mainly from the history of mechanics, the fine arts, medicine, world exploration, and the physical and biological sciences, there is no reason to believe that innovation in social organization or ideology follows a different course.[1] Wherever there

[1] The following are especially useful on the history of innovations in technology: R. J. Forbes, *Man the Maker: a History of Technology and Engineering*, Abelard-Schuman, Limited, New York, 1950; T. K. Derry and T. I. Williams, *A Short History of Technology*, Oxford University Press, Fairlawn, N.J., 1961; Charles Singer et al. (eds.), *A History of Technology*, 5 vols., Oxford University Press, Fairlawn, N.J., 1953–58, most particularly vols. IV and V, which deal with technological

is detailed evidence on innovation in these realms, the conditions and procedures seem very much the same. Some exceptions are to be noted in the case of innovations in organization. For one thing, innovations in organization are often very crude to begin with and must go through a longer period of developmental refinement than is necessary with most innovations in technology and ideology.[2] Thus parliamentary government was for long hardly more than a principle toward which to work, and modern forms of parliamentary government bear far less resemblance to the early efforts to achieve government of this sort than the modern jet transport plane does to the first biplane of the Wright brothers. For another, the number of individuals who are involved in the invention and development of a technique is usually far smaller than the number who in some way or other contribute to the emergence of a new form of social organization. Although some new organizational elements are innovated and developed in a manner not significantly distinct from that of a new tool or technological process, others, such as a new form of family life or a new system of merchandising, evolve so slowly and gradually that no one person can be identified as *the* innovator. In such instances, and they are many, the new element is produced piecemeal by contributions, each a very minuscule innovation, made by a comparatively large number of individuals, each contribution consisting of a personal decision to do something in a slightly unconventional manner. The process can be illustrated by simple analogy: It has often happened, or did happen in the days before streets and walks were paved, that a new path or route was gradually beaten through rough earth to become in time the accepted route from one place to another. That new route was created by many individuals, each of whom decided on some occasion or other to take a short cut rather than the customary path. In a comparable but vastly more complex manner the extended family system was historically changed into the modern nuclear family system. The latter was not invented as were the steam engine and sterile surgery; rather, it evolved through a multitude of decisions by a multitude of young married couples, parents, and elderly persons—such as

---

innovations and developments since 1750; Edward D. Churchill (ed.), *To Work in the Vineyard of Surgery: The Reminiscences of J. Collins Warren, 1842–1927*, Harvard University Press, Cambridge, Mass., 1958; Felix Marti-Ibañez, *Henry E. Sigerist on the History of Medicine*, MD Publications, Inc., New York, 1960; and Lester S. King, *The Medical World of the 18th Century*, The University of Chicago Press, Chicago, 1958.

[2] Two markedly contrasting accounts of the lengthy developmental period that seems characteristic of new social practices and forms of organization are provided by Negley K. Teeters and John D. Shearer, *The Prison at Philadelphia— Cherry Hill: 1829–1913*, Columbia University Press, New York, 1957; and Robert W. Habenstein and William M. Lambers, *The History of American Funeral Directing*, Bulfin Printers, Milwaukee, Wis., 1955.

the decision to set up housekeeping in a separate and independent establishment, the decision to resolve an unhappy marriage through divorce, the decision to restrict family size through birth control, and the decision to take refuge in a home for the aged rather than impose oneself upon a son and his family.

Innovation versus Development

The evolvement of new forms of social organization is a slow and laborious parallel to the development that normally follows upon innovation in any realm. Few innovations are perfected at their inception; most, sometimes even the simplest of new mechanical devices, must go through a more or less prolonged period of development before they become established elements in the social system. During this development the innovation is refined, and ordinarily its functional effectiveness is greatly increased; and often the developed innovation bears little structural resemblance to the original. A modern fire insurance company is very much larger and far more complex both in its organization and its operations than its early prototypes; the modern Woolworth's, than the first ten-cent store devised and established by F. W. Woolworth; the current intercontinental rockets, than the best devised by inventor Goddard; the present-day electronic computer, than the original multiple variable calculator; and the steam engine that drives a modern steamship or electrogenerating plant, than that invented by James Watt.

The development of an innovation involves considerable creativity; but it is of such a specific and piecemeal character that, unlike innovation per se, it can be accomplished through organized endeavor that involves a more or less elaborate division of labor and monetary incentives for workers. Development of innovations, particularly of technological devices and processes and of scientific discoveries, can therefore be purchased; the United States, for example, purchased, at a cost of many billions of dollars, the development of the atomic bomb during World War II. Innovation, on the other hand, does not occur in a piecemeal fashion; it cannot be facilitated by organization and a division of labor; and it cannot be forced by financial or other extraneous incentives. The distinction between the process of innovation and that of development is not always clear; for the development of an innovation is sometimes accelerated by a secondary innovation, as was that of the steam engine by John M'Naught's addition in 1845 of a high-pressure cylinder to Watt's original beam-type device. Secondary innovations, however, valuable though they may be, never overshadow the original; for a man who makes an improvement, however marked, upon something that already exists encounters far less difficulty, mental and social, than does one who tries to create something that has no precedent.

It is in considerable measure the failure to distinguish conceptually between the process of innovation and that of development that has led many writers, including some sociologists, to advance the view that innovation is a normative social process. In this view innovation is thought of either very abstractly as the emergence of new cultural items out of antecedent ones or as the result of organized social endeavor to produce something new—in the modern world, for example, the endeavor of commercial or nonprofit research institutes. There is no doubt that the development of innovations is currently facilitated by organized support; but there is good reason to believe that innovations themselves are for the most part today as in times past the product of individual endeavor that is more likely to be hampered than facilitated by membership in a business, industrial, or scientific organization.[3]

The *development* of the modern space rocket has been accomplished through organized means; but the *invention* of the rocket was the work of two individuals, neither of whom worked in an organizational context. A Russian schoolteacher, Konstantine Tsiolkovsky, proposed the rocket device in 1898; he applied Newtonic laws to its design, suggested the use of a liquid fuel, and made rough calculations of the speeds that might be achieved by rocket propulsion. The rocket engine was actually invented, and to a considerable extent developed, by American university professor Robert H. Goddard. He built a solid-propellant rocket in 1915 and thereby won a small grant from the Smithsonian Institution. This institution made a report on Goddard's endeavor in 1919; the report was vigorously attacked by various physical scientists on the grounds that the rocket propulsion would not work in empty space. By 1922 Goddard had constructed the world's first liquid-fuel rocket (the fireworks rocket is, of course, very old). With little financial support and much discouragement by his scientific peers, he persisted. In 1925 one of his rockets rose to ninety feet; by 1935 he was able to get one up to 7,500 feet. His rockets were small, but hardly crude. They had all the basic features of the liquid rockets of today, including gyroscopic guidance

[3] Such are the findings of John Jewkes, David Sawers, and Richard Stillerman (*The Sources of Invention*, St Martin's Press, Inc., New York, 1958). They made an elaborate case study of the origins of some of the most significant technological innovations that have appeared over the past half century and found that with few exceptions—and those mainly in the field of industrial chemistry—an innovation, as distinct from the subsequent development of it, was the product of one man working as an individual with little if any organizational encouragement or support. They found that the recent rise of large industrial and governmental research organizations and of governmentally subsidized academic research organizations has not as yet brought forth the expected flood of new discoveries, either in basic science or in technology. The theme running through their report is that men, not "social forces," produce inventions, a view in marked contrast to that advanced by S. C. Gilfillan in *The Sociology of Invention*, Follett Publishing Company, Chicago, 1935, and widely accepted by sociologists.

and combustion chambers cooled by flowing fuel. The German V-2s were simply larger versions of those invented by Goddard, and the great rockets of today have been developed from what he invented.

Scientists and technicians attached to and supported by research and other organizations have often achieved innovations; but there is much reason to suspect that they have done so because of what they were as individuals rather than because they were members of a research team. William Thaler, for example, was a physicist on the staff of the Office of Naval Research when, in 1956, he conceived the idea of using the backscatter of radio beams circling the globe as a means of detecting atom-bomb tests and rocket blasts. The Office of Naval Research was officially disinterested; but Thaler made preliminary experiments with borrowed equipment and in time demonstrated (by very accurate tracking of a Polaris missile) the superiority of his procedure over any then in use. Then, and not until then, was the Office of Naval Research willing to provide funds for the development of the technique.

Invention and Discovery

The unique mental construct that constitutes an innovation may be either an invention or a discovery. A discovery is a mental construct that gives recognition to the existence of something previously unknown, something that exists in nature or in society but that has not previously been identified. Thus Newton's law of gravity was a discovery; although men had always been subject to the force of gravity and early scientists had experimented with its various manifestations, Newton was the first to encompass all gravitational phenomena within one conceptual framework. An invention, on the other hand, is the creation of something that has not previously existed by the synthesizing of preexisting cultural elements (technological, ideological, or organizational) into a new pattern. Thus rayon, initially called "artificial silk," was an invention; nothing of its chemical character and physical structure had existed prior to Chardonnet's synthesis in 1884.

Although the distinction between invention and discovery is sometimes useful, especially perhaps in the analysis of contemporary scientific endeavor, the actual processes involved in invention and discovery are much the same, the social conditions that give rise to them are much alike, and the characteristics of inventors and discoverers are identical. It has sometimes been said that inventors are more practical than discoverers, probably because basic or pure science is devoted to discovery, while applied science is directed toward invention using scientific discoveries. Practicality does not, however, distinguish inventors from discoverers. No one could have been more practical than was Columbus, who discovered the New World, and few innovators can have been less practical than was the inventor of the jet engine.

From the social point of view, there is no distinction between an invention and a discovery, for insofar as the members of society are concerned, nothing exists until it has been discovered. Discovering a hitherto unknown piece of land, an unknown fact about nature, etc., is thus just as innovative as is devising a new tool or a new mode of human association. Moreover, what is discovered may be as much a contribution to the social heritage as is what is invented; and it may, like the latter, affect human conduct in some way or other. It has now been discovered that man has always been aided, harried, and often destroyed by bacteria of various sorts; but until somewhat over a century ago the existence of bacteria was unknown, and the visible effects of bacteria, such as death from infection, were explained in other terms. Until then, the social reality was not bacteria but evil spirits, the wrath of God, a miasma, or whatever it was that was by social definition the cause of death. It was what was defined as the cause of death, rather than the existence of bacteria, that affected human conduct (that, for example, led to the exorcising of evil spirits) and that was, therefore, an element of the social system. Conversely, there is even now no empirical proof of the existence of God, of a life after death, or of free and willful spirits who can haunt graves, knock on walls, incite men to murder, or otherwise affect the affairs of the living. Yet all the peoples of the world have created (i.e., invented) some such supernaturalistic entities and have been influenced in their behavior, often to a major degree, by belief in the existence of these entities.

Necessity as the Mother of Innovation

Innovations have come so rapidly in Western societies during the past century and a half that Western peoples are inclined to assume that change through innovation is a certain, indeed an almost automatic, process. "Necessity," it is often said, "is the mother of invention." This cliché may reflect current Western confidence in the ability of men to improve their society; but it ignores the fact that what constitutes necessity is a matter of social definition, and hence a variable, that the dominant necessity for any society is the preservation of the *status quo,* and that even under the most favorable conditions an individual who can transcend the definitions of his society and perceive as a necessity something that is not socially designated as such is a rarity. In our own society hunger is defined as a condition that necessitates effort to relieve it. Currently it is considered not only bad but inexcusable; and on this premise the American people have attempted to assure that no one amongst them lacks adequate food (by the school lunch program, the distribution of agricultural surpluses to the unemployed, etc.) and have from time to time sent vast supplies of grain to the hungry millions of other societies. Indeed, the postwar American attempt to bring productive benefits of modern agricultural technology to the so-called underdeveloped peoples of the world has been justified—whatever the ulterior political motivations—on the grounds that no one, even the prodigiously fecund peoples of India, needs to go hungry. Most of the peoples of times past and many of those of the contemporary world, however, have over long periods endured chronic and recurrently severe hunger without making any effort to find new sources of food, to increase the production of established foodstuffs, or to rearrange the distribution of whatever food has been available. For them, hunger has been by social definition a normal and unescapable condition of life, just as normal and to be taken for granted as the lice that fed upon their bodies, the epidemics that struck them down, the floods that destroyed their fields, and the babies that came each year, mostly to die before the year was out. Fatalistic resignation to things as they are, however painful and from our present point of view unnecessary, has been far more characteristic of societies than is the current American belief that man can and should take offensive action against those conditions that are distressing.

The tremendous power of the established definitions over the minds of men can perhaps be most effectively illustrated by an incident or two in the fairly recent history of surgery. Since at least the time of Hippocrates, physicians in the Western world have been ostensibly, and to a considerable degree actually, dedicated to the preservation of human life and the amelioration of physical misery. To the latter end, there had very early developed some use of narcotic substances in the relief of pain; with the introduction of opium from the Orient a great advance occurred in this particular respect. The widespread use of opium as a painkiller would seem to indicate that Western peoples, or at least their physicians, did not consider pain either desirable or inevitable. Nevertheless, when in 1844 dentist Horace Wells attempted to convince American surgeons that anesthesia could be safely induced by means of nitrous oxide gas, he was ignored by the medical profession and subsequently pilloried by the public. He was vilified by editorial writers, charged by preachers with tampering with God's will, and scoffed at by everyone. Implicit in much of the objection to his proposal was the assumption that relief from the pain of surgery is contrary to God or to nature or to both. Much later, long after the use of anesthesia had gained social and medical sanctions, the use of aspirin as a pain reliever encountered similar, if not so violent and enduring, resistance on the grounds that common headache, the pain of neuralgia, etc., are natural and that anything that dulls such pain is artificial and hence dangerous.

The Perception of a Problem

It is not some inherent necessity that mothers innovation but, rather, an asocial perception of the existence of a problem that is susceptible of solution. This perception may be either a specific redefinition of a socially recognized inadequacy or, as is much more common, the definition as a problem of what has not previously been defined as such. Puerperal fever, for example, had apparently always been considered one of the inevitable hazards of childbearing until the Hungarian obstetrician Semmelweis in the 1840s perceived it as a medical problem that could and should be solved and thereupon inaugurated investigations that led ultimately to the recognition of the bacterial cause of infectious diseases. From time to time in any society, vague discontent with things as they are on the part of some individuals or class of individuals may lead to political or some other form of rebellion; but a general and vague discontent does not result in the kind of asocial perception that fosters innovative efforts to change the system. It is, rather, discontent of a specific and individual nature that leads to perception of this sort, the discontent of some individual with some specific condition of life—with chronic hunger, too many babies, too intense pain, early death, dust in the road, flies on the bread, or some other circumstance that is accepted as normal by the other members of the society.[4]

No doubt an asocial perception of a problem always has complex social antecedents; it does not arise out of nothing. Changes or disturbances in the social value system, reflecting other changes in the society, are no doubt often involved. An attempt to analyze the social circumstances that culminated in Dr. Semmelweis's perception that puerperal fever was a problem about which something could be done would, for example, take us back at least to the plagues of medieval Europe. These plagues disturbed medieval society by sharply reducing populations; that reduction in turn led to a scarcity of labor and a rise in the value of labor; and this, in concordance with a great many other factors of which there is only limited knowledge, gradually led to the emergence of a new and higher value on human life and dignity. In all the subsistence societies of the past, the value that has been placed upon life has been, except perhaps to the possessor himself, relatively low. In ancient Rome, China, and India and during the

[4] Sometimes it is a very odd combination of circumstances that leads a man to reject the normal—i.e., the established—and seek to devise or discover something new. Almon B. Strowger, for example, in 1889 invented the step-by-step electronic procedure by which dial telephone connections were first made. He was by occupation an undertaker, and he evidently became obsessed with the idea that his competitor was bribing the local telephone operators to direct calls for his services to that competitor. It was to eliminate the bribable operators that he turned his efforts to the invention of a dial system. Incidentally, the local Bell company refused to consider his invention. He set up a telephone company of his own; and although some of the smaller independent companies adopted his dial system, it was years before the great American Telephone and Telegraph Company recognized its merits.

Middle Ages slavery kept a considerable proportion of the population in a condition hardly better than that of the cows and horses. So low was the value placed on life and dignity that death or dismemberment was the penalty for crimes which are today considered minor. In such societies ceremonialized murder, as in the Roman gladiatorial contests, was often sanctioned; and death from starvation, brutality, and easily avoided accidents was everywhere accepted with complacence. With the Reformation there began to emerge a new and viable idea of the dignity of the individual and the sanctity of life; with the industrial revolution the standard of living of Western peoples began to rise above that of sheer subsistence; and in time these two developments led to the placing of an ever-rising value on life and individual freedom, including freedom from human misery. Early in the nineteenth century a large number of innovations appeared that were predicated upon the perception that a life condition long taken for granted was in fact a problem to be solved. In England, for example, criminal court procedure was renovated in the interests of justice for the accused and protection for the society at large, prison reforms were undertaken, and differential treatment by the courts of the juvenile and the adult offender was established.

Dr. Semmelweis's perception of puerperal fever as a problem susceptible of solution was no doubt fathered by the humanitarian trend of his times; but it was the man, not the trend of the times themselves, that made this unique perception. Such, it would seem, is the case with all new perceptions that lead to innovative endeavor. Although they reflect the trend of the times in which they are made, they are made by some individual who because of peculiarities of personal experience and character is hypersensitive to some specific circumstance of his time and place. From the present vantage point, it is easy enough to perceive that in the late eighteenth century there existed a critical need for some new, larger, and more efficient source of motive power than any then existing. A series of changes—the increasing use of iron, the near exhaustion of the forests of Europe by the smelting industry, and the discovery of the technique of coking coal—had led to the opening up of coal fields in the northeastern part of England. The mines were fairly shallow, but they were plagued by surface waters. Pumps of a design that had long been used in the tin mines of Cornwall were brought into use; but while in hilly Cornwall surface streams could be used to provide power for such pumps, in the lowlands of Northumberland power of this sort was not available; the only existing alternatives were windmills and horses. Both were applied, and although there was clear recognition that more power was needed, it remained for James Watt to perceive that windmills and horses were insufficient to supply the power needed to keep the mines dry. That perception was the first step toward what proved to be a major innovation—a modification of Newcomen's atmospheric engine that increased its efficiency threefold.

The Innovative Process

An asocial perception of a problem does not, of course, ensure that an innovation will in due course be forthcoming. Some of the problems that men pose themselves may conceivably be unsolvable. Centuries of effort have not yet produced one authenticated instance of communication with the spirit world, the persistent search for perpetual motion has been unavailing, and the massive and very costly effort to find a cure for cancer has yielded an increasing body of knowledge about malignancies but nothing as yet in the way of a cure. Although the fact that a problem has not yet been solved does not mean, as the history of innovation has demonstrated, that no solution is possible, it may at least be hypothesized that one reason for failure is that the problem does not admit of solution—or, more realistically, that the problem cannot be solved with the existent knowledge and abilities. Thus the problem that the alchemists of the Middle Ages posed themselves— that of the transmutation of base metals into gold or silver—was at that time unsolvable, although with present-day knowledge and equipment the problem can be and has been solved.

For the most part, however, failure of innovative endeavor to solve a problem seems to have stemmed from one or both of two circumstances: the fact that innovation is inherently difficult and the fact that social preconceptions of one sort or another inhibit the innovative process. Little is actually known about innovative endeavor, aside from the fact that it is not standardized, that it is difficult, and that it is a random trial-and-error procedure that involves for the most part the use of symbols rather than things.[5] Although a graphic artist may use graphic images, a composer or arranger of music may use auditory symbols (mental sounds), and no doubt a mechanical innovator may experiment in his mind's eye with mental pictures of his tools and materials, it would appear that most of the new ideas that men have come upon have been achieved through the manipulation of verbal symbols —i.e., words, written or spoken or both—supplemented, especially in the modern world, by mathematical representations.

Trial-and-error experimentation in the arrangement of symbols is in contrast to the process of routine thinking in which all men engage and through which they solve, more or less satisfactorily, the ordinary problems of daily life. Routine thinking or calculating, which is the sort of problem solving that a modern electronic computer can do so rapidly and accurately, proceeds in accordance with fairly rigid formulas and with symbols of

[5] The major attempt to develop a theory of the innovative process is Homer Barnett's *Innovation: The Basis of Cultural Change*, McGraw-Hill Book Company, New York, 1953. His work has been exceedingly useful in the formulation of the concepts presented in this and the following chapters, and it was to a considerable extent the inspiration for the present effort to devise a general theory of social change.

known, or accepted, value; little if any trial and error is involved. It is through such thinking that a motorist decides whether he can or cannot beat another motorist to a crossing, that a housewife decides whether to buy beans or tomatoes, and that an accountant determines whether a business enterprise has made a profit or incurred a loss. Creative thinking, the kind that is necessary if a unique solution to a problem or any solution to a unique problem is to be achieved, involves a more or less random synthesizing of symbols that are themselves often of vague and uncertain meaning. Each such putting together constitutes a trial that, upon evaluation by the creative thinker, usually proves to be an error. Essential to this process is the ability to ascertain all the possible permutations in the arrangement of the symbols that are being manipulated and the capacity to evaluate each permutation in turn in terms of its relevance to the problem. Equally essential is the ability to continue the endeavor trial after trial and error after error until a workable solution has been found, even though the solution may not be reached for weeks, months, or years. These, then, are the difficulties inherent in innovative endeavor.[6]

To engage in creative thinking presupposes, moreover, an inherently contradictory state of mind—it presupposes knowledge relevant to the problem in hand but freedom from the preconceptions that knowledge of anything normally brings, a skill in the manipulation of symbols but at the same time ability to apply that skill in random ways, and a conviction that the problem can be solved but no fixed ideas regarding the nature of the solution. Such is the ideal. The actuality, of course, always falls far short of this perfect combination of mental contradictions and usually too far short to result in truly creative thinking. Consider, by way of example, just one of the contradictions involved: To think at all presupposes considerable knowledge of and skill in the use of that part of the vocabulary which represents the field in which the problem lies. Even as it is inconceivable that anyone who knows nothing at all about music should be able to compose music, so it is impossible for an illiterate to write or for someone untrained in mathematics to make mathematical computations. As he acquires the vocabulary of a subject, however, the individual tends also to acquire preconceptions about that subject that inhibit his manipulating the vocabulary in a random, trial-and-error way. Words are, after all, but the building blocks of speech and thought and of writing and computing; and a language consists, in addition to the words, of more or less standardized formulas for combining them into phrases and sentences and concepts. The grammatical form of the language tends to determine, or at least to limit, the formulas

[6] In *Horseless Carriage Days* (reprint ed., Dover Publications, Inc., 1962) Hiram P. Maxim recounts the difficulties and dangers that he and others encountered in the endeavor to devise a workable automobile.

that are used in discourse, especially argumentative or conclusion-reaching; and these in turn provide more or less standardized patterns of thinking that are difficult to escape. Thus the more skilled and informed an individual is in the symbols of a given subject, whether it be theology or penology, electronics or embryology, the more habituated he is to the established ways of thinking of that field and the more inhibited he is from manipulating those symbols in a random, trial-and-error way. This is the reason why highly trained and recognized experts in any field of endeavor rarely innovate in that field, why an academic artist or man of letters is notoriously traditionalistic, and why innovations so often come from the unexpected rather than the expected source—that is, from talented amateurs rather than members of a heavily staffed and subsidized research institute.[7]

It is also in part the reason why the innovative process cannot be organized and why innovators cannot be deliberately produced by educational or other institutions, why a school of innovation or an institute for the production of innovators cannot exist. To the extent that an individual is educated or trained, he is inducted not only into the acceptance and use of the existing knowledge and skills, but also into the beliefs, devices, etc., of the field and in both ways constrained from innovating and adding to that body. The confusion, contradiction, and inefficiency of the American system of higher education no doubt detract from its ability to turn out highly qualified technicians, engineers, physicians, developmental scientists,

[7] This is not to invoke the folk image of the unschooled tinkerer who invents a perpetual-motion machine in defiance of all the experts and of the laws of physics. A talented amateur must have at his command the knowledge and skills that are necessary to innovation, and today that usually means that he must be a scientist or at least well versed in the relevant science. What the term "talented amateur" is intended to indicate is one who is not by training and membership attached to the particular profession or industry for which the particular innovation is most relevant. Robert Goddard was a physicist; but he was not associated with the military, for whom his rocket proved a major advance in technology. The Englishman who invented the jet motor was associated with neither the military nor the aircraft-engine industry, for both of which it has had revolutionary consequences. Russel Varian, who in 1938 devised the klystron tube that became the basis for radar, was at the time associated neither with the military nor the electronics industry; nor was he, or these others, a member of a research team or foundation. In 1953 Michael Ventris, a young architect and amateur cryptographer, cracked the Cretan Linear B code that had mystified professional archeologists for years.

How often it has been a talented amateur rather than a professional who has achieved a significant advance in science or technology is not known; however, the many cases of innovation by talented amateurs that are on record indicate the constricting and constraining effects of organizational membership and of the subculture of professional life.

economists, and political bureaucrats; and in this respect it may, as has been so often charged, lag behind that of contemporary Russia. On the other hand, it is just because American universities are in this respect somewhat ineffective that they occasionally produce a scholar, scientist, or technician who is qualified to do innovative work in his field and yet not so fully indoctrinated in the established beliefs, preconceptions, and ways of thinking of that field to preclude his engaging in fairly random trial-and-error experimentation.

The power of established beliefs, preconceptions, and ways of thinking over the mind of man is much easier to illustrate than it is to analyze. During the fifteenth century there were many men who recognized the desirability of finding a new water route from Europe to the Orient, but it was not until well toward the close of that century that any one of them was able to escape the socially imposed logic of going east to get east. So for a century and more Spanish and Portuguese explorers worked their way down the west coast of Africa seeking a channel eastward; eventually they rounded the tip of that continent and reached Madagascar, which for a time was mistaken for the Orient. Only Columbus was able to ignore the traditional idea of how to solve the problem of getting east and to seek a solution to that problem in an entirely new way and direction. The failure of early endeavors to design a heavier-than-air flying machine was also due in considerable part to the inability of men to break with precedent and strike out in a new and radical direction. The precedent had been set in ancient Greece by the mythological Daedalus, who with his son Icarus made themselves wings of feathers so that they might fly like birds. All the earlier attempts to devise a means of flying through the air followed the bird model, whereas the actual solution to the problem of flight, perhaps first suggested by Henson in 1842, turned out to be stable wings and forward motion provided by an airscrew.

The power of social preconceptions, etc., to constrain the minds of men and so deter them from venturing in new directions is seldom realized until some ingenious individual breaks the barriers and succeeds in some unprecedented way. Then men may say, "How obvious!" What is obvious today, however, may have been unthought of yesterday; and what may be considered impossible today or, indeed, may not even be considered at all may seem simple and obvious tomorrow. Society in general and in all its organizational aspects circumscribes the minds of its members, even as it inducts them into its particular forms of action. It prescribes the proper and permissible channels of behavior, overt and mental, and establishes sentiments, superstitious and otherwise, to restrain the individual who is tempted to stray into the unexplored and so to protect the social system from the disorganizing effects of change. As long as a particular social system is in a condition of relatively stable congruence, the inhibiting effects of mental circumscription may be functionally desirable; but when a social system is already in a state of incongruence, social constraints upon independent thought operate only to perpetuate dysfunctioning.

Many of the inhibiting beliefs and patterns of thinking of any society are innovative errors that at some time became established in the culture; such is the case with much of what is currently described as superstition. Other inhibiting beliefs and patterns of thinking may have originated as the embodiment in a mental construct of empirical experience; adverse experience with a dangerous cave, for example, may have led to the belief that the cave is inhabited with evil spirits. Before the development during the fifteenth century of the large, keeled sailing ship and the adoption by Westerners of the compass, it was probably the fate of most sailors who ventured far into the Atlantic to die becalmed, to become hopelessly lost in fog or storm, or, if they dropped below the thirty-fifth parallel, to be driven westward to disaster by the prevailing winds, since their ships could not sail crosswind or upwind. At any event, few ventured far into the Atlantic, for the belief prevailed that just beyond the horizon the sea ended in space and was, at any event, filled with monsters. By Columbus's time, however, ships could weather heavy seas and work their way back to land against the prevailing winds; and the persistence of this belief operated, not as a protection against ill-advised ventures, but as an inhibition to the exploration of the western Atlantic. No doubt it was experience also that led to the idea, prevalent until well into the nineteenth century, that surgical incision of the abdomen would inevitably result in death; for, as is now known, bacterial infection spreads rapidly in this region of the body. For quite some time after the development of the technique of sterile surgery, however, that idea continued to prevent surgeons from attempting corrective work in the abdominal cavity; and still later, the idea, no doubt also empirical in origin, that exposure of brain tissue meant instant death for long precluded surgical attempts to correct brain damage.

Inadvertent Innovation

It has sometimes happened that success in innovation, particularly in technological innovation, has seemingly come by inadvertence.[8] Goodyear is sup-

---

[8] R. Taton, *Reason and Chance in Scientific Discovery*, A. J. Pomerans (trans.), Philosophical Library, Inc., New York, 1957, gives many illustrations of the fruitful error in scientific discovery. In technology, the error that led to the discovery of the antiknock qualities of tetraethyl lead has become something of a classic. One of the limitations of the early internal-combustion motor was its tendency to knock—actually, for the fuel to explode rather than burn—under heavy loads. While trying to find a fuel additive that would retard the burning rate, Thomas Midgley conceived the idea that if gasoline were colored red, the

posed to have discovered the process of vulcanizing rubber by the accident of having a mess of materials he was heating run over and fry on his hot stove; Dr. Fleming came upon the substance penicillin while in pursuit of quite another objective; and Columbus discovered the Americas while en route, so he thought, to the Orient. In all these and many other known instances, it is obvious that the innovation was inadvertent in the sense that the innovator was not at that moment deliberately experimenting toward the end to which he came. The innovator was, however, experimenting; had he not been doing so, he could not possibly have achieved that or any other innovation. Moreover, had he not recognized what had happened, that is, had he not perceived that something new had been discovered or something unprecedented had occurred, nothing would have come of it. No innovation, that is to say, would have been made. In the case of penicillin, Dr. Fleming did note the antibacterial powers of the substance that his mold had produced, although it was long afterwards that the discovery was followed up. Goodyear's accident produced the solution to the problem of stabilizing rubber that he had long been seeking. Columbus could not, of course, have failed to observe the land that he encountered; and his own definition of that land—the sought-for Orient—was entirely false. Nevertheless, it was only because he was attempting to find land by sailing west that he in fact did find it.

In some instances innovations can be traced directly to false hypotheses or errors in calculation. The modern technique of fingerprint identification, for example, grew out of the false doctrine, promulgated by Lombroso, that there is a direct correlation between an individual's physiognomy and his character and that, this being so, criminals both actual and potential can be identified by their possession of criminal-type facial characteristics. Bertillon, proceeding on this false concept, worked out an elaborate system for the measurement of such characteristics, a system that came to be used for record-keeping purposes. It was but a step from there to the discovery that the swirls of the fingertips are the most distinctive physical attributes of

---

heat of flash firing would be partially absorbed and the explosive effect in the motor cylinder thereby reduced. The only red material immediately available was iodine, and this additive did somewhat reduce the knock. Red aniline dye, on the other hand, was ineffective, disproving his original hypothesis; but the fact that iodine had helped to reduce knock proved to him that a fuel additive was the answer to knock and set him on the search that led ultimately to tetraethyl lead.

In the early 1890s the chemist Ferdinand Tiemann isolated a ketone from orris root (an irone) which had a violet odor similar to that of oil of violets, then highly valued in the perfume industry. He miscalculated the chemical composition and structure of this substance and, in trying to reproduce it artificially, created a substance unknown in nature—an ionone, the first of the synthetic perfume chemicals. See Edward Sagarin, *The Science and Art of Perfumery*, McGraw-Hill Book Company, New York, 1945, pp. 84–89.

an individual. Perhaps the most fruitful miscalculation of social history was Columbus's rejection of the calculation of the circumference of the earth that had been made by the Roman Pliny in the first century of the Christian era. Pliny's calculation, which was fairly accurate, was accepted in Columbus's time by those few who did not concur with folklore and Church dogma in the belief that the earth was flat. Although Columbus was among these few, he decided, possibly only because he wanted things to be that way, that the circumference of the earth was only one-third that which Pliny's measurements made it appear to be and that, this being so, it was possible for a ship to cross the Western Ocean and reach Cathay before running out of food and water. Had he not made this error, it is unlikely that he would have ventured on his voyage of discovery.

In a sense, all innovation is inadvertent. It cannot be predicted; if it could, it would be known, hence not subject to invention or discovery. Even in modern scientific exploration the hypothesis that is subjected to tests is not a prediction but a projection of the known into the unknown. As will be seen, an innovator must operate upon the assumption that there is a solution to his problem and, furthermore, that the solution lies outside the conventional realms and in some particular unconventional direction; but just where success will lie, only trial after trial will tell. For this reason the preliminaries to many critical inventions and discoveries would seem, upon looking back, to have been utterly fantastic performances. In his efforts to find a means of converting electricity to light, for example, Edison tried out every material that came to hand, including filaments of silk and bamboo, before arriving at his final solution—a soft iron wire in a vacuum.

Current Myths Regarding Innovation

Innovation has often been described as a synthesis of existing social elements into a unique pattern, the innovative aspect being the pattern, not the elements. Some writers prefer to speak of innovation as "creative synthesis," a reference to the well-known fact that by definition a synthesis is more than a sum of its separate parts. Thus a modern watch, it might be said, is a creative synthesis of cogwheels, shafts, and springs which together have the valuable faculty of running at a constant speed and thus of measuring time. This way of putting the matter conveys, or may convey, the entirely false impression that a modern watch was an invention achieved in a single "creative synthesis," whereas it was in fact a synthesis of a long series of specific innovations, each prerequisite to those that followed. Thus there came a time in the development of clocks when it was possible to manufacture small portable ones. Since a clock at that time had to be powered by falling weights and depended upon the swing of a pendulum to measure out time periods, moving it temporarily brought its action to a stop. Before the watch was possible, two more inventions were necessary: one was the use of a coiled flat spring as the motive power of the device and the other, equally essential, was the idea of the spring-wheel escapement which measured off time intervals without reference to gravity. The second was without the slightest precedent in mechanics and was the later to come; but when it did, the watch became a reality. After its invention, very little except refinement occurred to the watch until the invention of the device for winding the main spring by centrifugal force, by the motion of the watch on the wrist of the wearer; and before this last invention was possible, the watch had had to move, by social decree, from the pocket of the wearer to his wrist.

There is currently a good deal of talk about breakthrough in science and technology, the assumption being that a major barrier to technological advance will be suddenly shattered and that the way will thereafter be clear for tremendous developments. This idea is but a current version of the rather traditional myth of the great inventor and his revolutionary discovery; it reaches its highest expression in the imputing of charisma to radical political, religious, and other leaders, as is exemplified in the belief, so prevalent in Germany during the 1930s, that Hitler had found the magic way to German supremacy over the entire world. As was indicated in another connection, actual innovations do not occur, however, in this spectacular way and are not general in nature or world-shaking in character; they are, rather, both specific and slight, each a moderate advance upon the known. In the realm of fiction or purely abstract ideas, an innovation may be of a grandiose sort, and an innovator may run free and unrestrained by anything except the limitations of the language; for innovations in this area are syntheses of words without concrete reference, spoken or written fantasies that do not translate into action.

Even the remarkably predictive ideas of Jules Verne were innovative only as fiction. Verne projected into fantasy some of the then-current trends in mechanics and engineering, much as modern science-fiction writers do with current knowledge and hypotheses regarding the universe. He did not invent the submarine; the base invention had long since been made. What he did was to imagine, unrestrained by realities, what the submarine might be when it was fully developed. The actual development of the submarine came through a series of specific innovations, no one of which was even suggested by Verne's fictional projection.

The myth of the breakthrough, of the great and general innovation, is sometimes linked with another myth about the innovative process—that it can be a group or collective activity. This latter myth is especially agreeable to idealists who confuse the democratic political process with what is currently derided as togetherness and to sentimentalists who idealize the common man and resent the fact that, however they may have been born, all men are not equal. The myth of collective creativity has been given pseudoscientific validation by certain social psychologists, who think that they have found proof positive that four or five heads can solve any kind of problem quicker and better than can one. It has also become institution-alized in the practice, now so common in American business, industry, poli-tics, and other realms of life, of holding conferences on problems of joint concern and of setting up a committee to deal with any organizational matter that is too controversial for forthright administrative decision. In recent years, the myth of collective creativity has invaded the sciences, es-pecially the social sciences; and it is presently the vogue for research to be conducted by a team, preferably one composed of members of various dis-ciplines, such as economics, anthropology, psychiatry, sociology, psychology, and political science.

As a device of advocacy, the committee, the conference, or the team may be useful in securing group sanction for the adoption of some innova-tion; and it is to this end that committees and conferences are mainly, if covertly, used by business and other administrators. No such indirect value would seem to obtain for scientific teamwork, if by teamwork is meant any-thing more than a simple division of research labors. Two heads are certainly better than one when knowledge is to be pooled, as it is in the compilation of a dictionary or an encyclopedia, or when data are to be gathered as a prelude to the making of a judgment or decision. The actual making of a judgment or decision is presumably something more than a simple addition of facts, understandings, or opinions; it is a synthesis that is accomplished only within one mind.

Under the stimulation of group interaction, an individual may be aroused from his normal mental torpidity to the end that he recalls facts and ideas that he otherwise might not, at that moment, recall; and when numbers of individuals are so aroused, the total of what they mobilize to pool may be more than they could otherwise muster. Evidently it was this possibility that gave rise to the much-touted brainstorming sessions among advertising copywriters a few years ago. Creative thinking, as distinct from simple re-calling, is not, however, facilitated by stimulation of this sort; on the con-trary it is more likely to be inhibited. Under stress, social or circumstantial, an individual may solve a routine problem in a routine manner more quickly than he otherwise would; this is what happens when a motorist suc-cessfully extricates himself from a traffic crisis. Routine problem solving does not, however, require the repetitive and exhaustive trial and error that is involved in creative thinking and that is only interrupted and disrupted by external stimulation.

The idea that numbers of people assembled can be more innovative than can any one of them alone, that a decision produced by a group is somehow superior to one arrived at by a single individual, and that the great virtue of what is known as the democratic process is that it furthers creativity is no more than a convenient fiction. In actuality it has been an individual mind, not some synthetic mind produced through the interaction of the various members of a group, that has upon occasion come to an asocial perception of a problem, proceeded through laborious and inherently discouraging trial and error to solve it in an unconventional way, and ultimately hit upon a trial that was judged worthy of test.

The myth of group creativity blends imperceptibly into the even more metaphysical belief that innovations are social imperatives. This belief is reflected in extreme form in the theory of emergent evolution, which would have the changes that occur within a social system roughly comparable to the flowering of a plant—that is, the theory that changes are but the manifestation of forces inherent in the social system, as the growth and flowering of a plant are but the expression of the genetic characteristics of the seed from which the plant grew. A slightly more earthy version of the same idea is that innovations come about spontaneously when the slow and gradual accumulation of knowledge makes them possible. Scientists especially have favored this concept of the innovative process, perhaps because it seems to justify the more routine forms of scientific investigation. Moreover, it gratifyingly depreciates the potential importance of a deviant individual who does not share and hold to the values, sentiments, beliefs, and scientific preconceptions of the run-of-the-mill scientists.

The evidence—and evidence is vital to scientists—that is advanced in support of spontaneous occurrence of innovations is that upon many occasions two or more individuals, often widely separated in space, have come upon a discovery or invention simultaneously, the classical instance being that of Darwin and Wallace, who independently conceived the idea of biological evolution through environmental selection. It is rather unscientific, however, to conclude from the fact that two or more minds, struggling to solve the same problem and possessed of or having access to the same body of knowledge, have on some occasions come independently to much the same solution to that problem, that the solution sprang directly from the knowledge and would have made its appearance without the effort of the two or three men who claim credit for it. In point of fact, actual simultaneous innovation is exceedingly rare; for innovations are seldom identical, and "simultaneous" usually means any time within a year or two. What the occurrence of more or less simultaneous innovations does indicate is that the knowledge, skills, and other elements that go to make up a creative synthesis must be available before a synthesis is possible; but the fact that an innovation does not come in advance of them does not mean that the existence of these necessary knowledges, skills, etc., automatically leads to the innovation.

THE INNOVATOR

The vast majority of the members of any society live out their lives in conventional fashion, using and profiting from the innovations of others, mostly unknown and long dead, but adding nothing to the social heritage. They act as social functionaries, complex human puppets who behave and think and feel and believe mainly in the ways established for them in their society. A given individual may feel more keenly than is socially normal about this or that aspect of his society, he may work a little harder than is socially demanded of him, he may even in an uncommon and quite illegal fit of rage murder an annoying neighbor; for although most of the members of any society have no enduring impact upon the character of the society, and from the abstract point of view serve only to maintain and transmit the established social ways to a successive generation, each member fulfills his social roles with more or less effectiveness, with more or less zest, and with at least some slight idiosyncratic deviations from the social standards in tempo, timing, and tone. Just as no two English-speaking persons will speak English in such an identical manner that their friends cannot distinguish them by voice alone, so no two members of a society, a class, an age or sex grouping, or an occupation ever really behave exactly alike. Each is an individual; each has some individuality.

Most of the individual deviations from the social standards, which contribute so much to the spice of daily life, do not, however, change the basic forms of social life any more than do highly individualistic renditions of a Beethoven sonata change that musical composition. Nor does such deviation from the social standards as that of eccentric religious or other cults, of such subcultural groupings as thieves and prostitutes, and of those men of distinction who have distinguished themselves by exceptional endeavor and achievement of a conventional sort. Deviation per se does not, contrary to the pretensions of the many self-proclaimed geniuses who plague the modern world, make for creativity and social change.[9]

Stereotypes of the Innovator

In modern folklore, an innovator is either a born genius or a self-made eccentric. The idea of the born genius, or more properly, the inevitable, if

[9] Robert K. Merton, *Social Theory and Social Structure*, rev. ed., The Free Press of Glencoe, New York, 1957, has presented a fourfold typology of deviant behavior (only one type of which is conducive to social change): ritualism, retreatism, rebellion, and innovation. Robert Dubin, "Deviant Behavior and Social Structure," *American Sociological Review*, vol. 24, pp. 147–164, April, 1959, has elaborated and refined the Mertonian typology and finds that there are fourteen possible modes of deviant active adaptation, of which twelve have potentialities for social change.

For a detailed analysis of one real-life type of noninnovative adaptation, see Francis J. Regney and L. Douglas Smith, *The Real Bohemia: A Sociological and Psychological Study of the "Beats,"* Basic Books, Inc., Publishers, New York, 1961.

not innate, genius, is apparently very old. The Chinese had a stereotype of such an individual—Lao-tse, who resembled in many respects the Western image of the creative artist, man of letters, poet, or musical composer as a special personality type. The creative individual, in this image of him, is a social irresponsible who, if he is to express his creative abilities, must be permitted to, and at any event will, fail to fulfill the filial, marital, and financial obligations of an ordinary man; he must be allowed to enjoy to the full, as a sort of compensation for his creative labors, such sensuous satisfactions as are available to him; and he should, to fit the image that society has of him, die young through his excesses of drinking, wenching, and other enjoyable bad habits.

The social concessions that this stereotype grants would appear to reflect a kind of social awe and respect for those who work in such socially undisturbing areas of society as the arts. The stereotype has been effectively exploited, perhaps inevitably, both in old China and the modern West by generations of social incompetents. China had its pretentious and mendacious scholar-poets who sat about the teashops nursing their hemorrhoids and long fingernails—both symbols of the Chinese intellectual—and discoursing grandly about nothing at all; modern Western people have their Left Bank Bohemians, their Village intellectuals, and the self-styled beatniks of the postwar decades. Such pretenders to genius are for the most part uncreatively enjoying the socially sanctioned privileges of artistic and literary creativity rather than creating anything new. At any event, they work or fail to work in those arts in which success is not measured by any objective criteria. Such pretenders to genius do not, for evident reasons, play at being creative scientists or technicians.

The second stereotype of the innovator, that of a person who is eccentric, impractical, and irresponsible, or at least so unsociable that he is unable to participate in the ordinary relations of social life, has been invoked whenever the innovative endeavors or products have seemed to violate the sensitivities or to endanger the established self-interests of members of society. Hence this stereotype has been applied mainly to those who innovate, or attempt to innovate, in science, in technology, in ideology, or in social organization rather than in the arts. Even the members of his immediate family may be able to accept and justify the atypical conduct of an artist, musician, or novelist; for in our society, as in most societies, efforts to be creative in these realms are socially sanctioned, although, of course, even here sanction extends only to creativity that consists of the playing of minor variations on traditional themes and styles. Atypical conduct has seldom, however, been tolerated in an individual who is attempting to devise a better mousetrap, to discover why seeds sprout in moist, warm soil, or to find a new way to stimulate the production of economic values. If in the interests of such endeavor he arrives late to dinner, ignores his children, demands quiet in his home, and refuses to participate in community affairs, he is regarded as inconsiderate and selfish. Should he persist in his unconventional conduct, he may be judged somewhat unbalanced; and should he, perchance, succeed in his innovative endeavor and urge others to adopt what he has devised, he may very well be defined as mad. Such has been the reward of many of the most important contributors to the technology, ideology, and organization of modern society. The differential treatment that is commonly accorded the creative artist and the innovator in other fields and that is reflected in the two contrasting stereotypes of the genius is but a reflection of the many ways in which organized society manifests its inherent resistance to socially significant change.

It is no doubt true that occasionally a would-be innovator has become psychopathic in his failure to achieve his objective and that a successful innovator has been made psychopathic by the refusal of his society to grant him recognition. It is also no doubt true that many psychopaths have imagined themselves to be innovators. Innovation is certainly a socially atypical kind of achievement, and except in the arts the innovative process is definitely one that is not sanctioned by society. Moreover, it is also true that until and unless he succeeds, the endeavors of an innovator are hardly distinguishable from those of a psychopath who is under the delusion that he is an innovator. The stereotyped idea of the innovator as an eccentric does not, however, bear much resemblance to the personality of any real innovator, living or dead. Even a man who makes a career of innovation, as did the early scientist Copernicus and the modern inventor Thomas A. Edison, is likely to be recognizably human and normal in all respects excepting those which impinge on his innovative endeavors. His personality will not conform, even crudely, either to the stereotype of the born genius or to that of the self-made eccentric. Indeed, to the extent that it does approach one or the other of these stereotypes, he may be suspected of trying to play a role rather than trying to create something new.[10]

[10] This analysis of the sociopsychological characteristics of innovators is necessarily speculative and is based mainly upon biographical and autobiographical materials. In late years there have been many attempts to study creativity, mainly by small-group researchers; and there are currently a number of organized projects at work on the problem—e.g., at the Center for the Study of Creativity and Mental Health at the University of Chicago and at the Institute of Personality Assessment and Research of the University of California. Ultimately these efforts may contribute to an understanding of the processes involved in creativity and of the personal characteristics that are essential to creative achievement. So far, however, the findings, such as they are, have been limited by the very artificial criteria of creativity that have been used in experiments and the painfully contrived nature of experimental circumstances. A survey of some hundreds of books and articles on this subject by Morris I. Stein and Shirley J. Heinze (*Creativity*

The Innovator as a Nonconformist

One of the qualities that does seem to distinguish most successful innovators is an unconventionality of mind, as distinct from oddity of overt conduct. The body of beliefs, ideas, opinions, and ways of thinking of each society and each subcultural group in the society are highly standardized and fairly stable. They are officially represented by those in positions of authority who serve to correct errors in the thinking of group members, to provide proper interpretations of events, and to resolve whatever mental doubts and conflicts may arise. Thus the local priest may arbitrate sacred matters, while the local wiseman, scholar, or magistrate shapes local opinion, maintains traditional beliefs, or guides the inept into the proper ways of thinking. In the modern world there is a great assortment of more or less accepted authorities on correct thinking—newspaper and magazine editors, authors of all sorts, schoolteachers, scientists, political pontificators, news commentators, and, omnipresent if not omnipotent, commercial propagandists. The power for good or ill of all such contemporary thinkers for the masses has been grossly exaggerated by those who believe that modern means of communication have brought about the emergence of a new and authoritarian form of social life. Nonetheless, it is undoubtedly true that most men, now as in times past, learn to think in traditional fashion and to respect and therefore follow the opinions and thought processes of established leaders.

If a person is to be innovative in any specific regard, he must not only reject the conventional thinking in that regard, but, it would seem, be somewhat skeptical of the validity of conventional thinking in general. Should his skepticism be apparent, it will most likely be decried by his

---

and the Individual, The Free Press of Glencoe, New York, 1961) indicates how limited has been the contribution of the experimental method to an understanding of innovation and innovators.

The September, 1958, issue of *The Scientific American* was devoted to innovation in science. Some of the articles included in this issue are highly suggestive. In "The Psychology of the Imagination," for example, Frank Barron discusses the necessity of rejection of or detachment from conventional modes of thinking before an individual can hope to be creative; and in "The Encouragement of Science," Warren Weaver advances evidence to indicate that creativity cannot be purchased or induced by organizational means.

Harvey C. Lehman, *Age and Achievement,* Princeton University Press, Princeton, N.J., 1953, has advanced evidence that there is an inverse relation between age and creative ability, a finding that accords with common-sense observations but that cannot be accepted without much qualification. The tendency for innovators to be atypically egocentric and socially detached is at least partially borne out by the findings of Bernice T. Eiduson, *Scientists: Their Psychological World,* Basic Books, Inc., Publishers, New York, 1962.

contemporaries as the result of ignorance, as a sign that he is opinionated if not bigoted, or as evidence that he thinks in an illogical fashion. Mental nonconformity of this sort certainly tends to isolate the individual intellectually from his fellows; in ordinary discourse he may seem to them unpleasantly cynical or at least unpredictable, even as they may seem to him dull and uncomprehending.

Just what atypicalities of personal experience may make for mental nonconformity is not clear. It is unlikely that any single factor—such as failure to pass the College Board examinations—is ever solely responsible; and the impact of a given factor will depend upon the context in which it operates.[11] Although the English upper-middle-class family and the English public school system have together produced generations of highly conventional minds, they have also occasionally produced an intellectual deviant—a mind that has rejected in whole or in part the ways of thinking of the old school and the classic tradition and has struck out for itself. In some instances, perhaps, the rejection of traditional opinions, beliefs, and ways of thinking may be a rebellion against a too firm subjugation to authority; here the theory of frustration-aggression may possibly apply. On the other hand, it is quite as likely that the mental deviant is simply one who did not learn his lessons properly—or, alternatively, learned too well two conflicting sets of lessons and resolved the conflict by partially rejecting both.

Innate ability to learn no doubt varies widely from person to person, although so far no means has been devised for distinguishing accurately what has been learned from ability to learn. Since innovation is a mental accomplishment, and since it involves the synthesis of learned elements, there must be some relation between innate mental ability and innovativeness; but there is no evidence to support the idea that innovators, compared to those who do not innovate, are necessarily persons with innate mental superiority. What evidence there is suggests that a person who learns with unusual rapidity, either because he has superior innate capacity or because

[11] This is a fact that Everett E. Hagen (*On the Theory of Social Change*, The Dorsey Press, Inc., Homewood, Ill., 1962) tends to overlook. He stresses, and up to a point validly, the role of the family in producing conventional—in his terms "authoritarian"—individuals; but he fails to recognize that the effects of family socialization, whatever they may happen to be, are modulated by an individual's membership in many other kinds of organizations, each of which makes some contribution to his personality and exercises some control over his conduct. The effects of being brought up in a highly authoritarian family may be more or less offset by participation in an open, "permissive" community; and the absence of authoritarianism in the family does not assure that an individual will be adaptable; for a community, class, occupational, or other organization may induce the authoritarian attributes that the family did not.

he has had exceptional opportunities for learning and has been encouraged to learn, tends to acquire an unusually conventional mentality. A child prodigy, the walking-encyclopedia sort of person who performed so spectacularly on the television quiz shows of a few years ago, and a college student who earns straight A's in courses that depend on rote memory are not those most likely to attempt innovation.[12] Evidently they learn too easily how to think in the socially established fashion or at least to recall what they have learned ever to learn to think in a nonconventional way. At any event, the innovators of the past have not, so far as evidence shows, been judged in childhood and youth as exceptionally bright; more often, they have been considered by their contemporaries as being a bit dull, if only because they have failed to grasp the fact that the world is flat, that two and two always make four, that an iron plow will poison the soil, or that the king can do no wrong.

The Desire to Innovate

Mental nonconformity does not of itself lead to innovative endeavor. A person may doubt and question the going opinions, the traditional answers, and the stock values all his life without bringing into being one new opinion, belief, value, or tangible object. Voltaire wrote bitingly, and in his modes of expression with some originality, of the morals and manners of eighteenth-century France. He doubted everything and judged almost everything to be debased, but he was not the innovator of any new idea in morals or manners; nor have many of the modern French, who so value their right to be individualistic in their thinking as well as their conduct, been notably innovative.

Ability to think in an other than conventional fashion must, apparently, be backed with an abnormally strong motivation to be innovative in whatever the particular field. Motivation of this sort differs both in kind and in degree from the usual motives of men. In every society and every class and other grouping of society there is some sort of normative motivation for each of the several activities in which the members may engage. A person may through malsocialization or other peculiarities of experience or circumstance be less strongly motivated in some respect and consequently be lazy or indifferent in that respect; or a person may be more strongly motivated than is normative and be ambitious or intensely energetic or interested. Hypermotivation of this sort, in conjunction with hyperactivity and

[12] The attempts that have been made to foster creativity in individuals either by formal or informal means do not seem to have increased the probability that an individual will actually be innovative, although it may improve his ability to solve routine-type problems. See William J. J. Gordon, *Synectics: The Development of Creative Capacity*, Harper & Row, Publishers, Incorporated, New York, 1961; and Jacob W. Getzels and Philip W. Jackson, *Creativity and Intelligence: Explorations with Gifted Students*, John Wiley & Sons, Inc., New York, 1962.

skill and luck, is what distinguishes a successful businessman from the ordinary run of businessmen, a man who advances rapidly in his occupation or profession from those who go up in sedate fashion, and a self-made man from those who live out their lives in the class to which they are born. The motivations and activities of such men differ, however, only quantitatively from the norm; they are more of, but more of the same, or much the same, thing.

No doubt would-be innovators are sometimes ambitious to improve their station in life—to win wealth and power or to demonstrate their superiority over their fellows; but a man who is simply ambitious to get ahead in the world would be most unlikely to select innovation as the means; and if he were to do so, he would soon discover that the most certain and easy way to wealth, position, renown, and other rewards for social achievement is through conventional channels. Some innovators have, it is true, gained wealth and recognition through mechanical innovations. Edison won renown, if not great wealth and recognition, through his invention of the incandescent lamp, the phonograph, and other merchandisable devices; Henry Ford made millions through the application of his highly unconventional idea that what was needed was a simple and cheap automobile and his invention—or at least application—of the assembly-line method of producing automobiles. Most of the great and a great many of the lesser innovations in mechanics, in science, and in ideas and organization, however, have brought little by way of reward to their innovators during their lifetimes and have, on the contrary, often brought them only condemnation and persecution. The idea of the innovator as an eccentric starving in his miserable garret is a stereotype; but the idea that the way to success as socially defined is through innovative endeavor is equally false. Copernicus, who demonstrated that the earth is not the center of the universe, was excommunicated by the Church and damned in the eyes of men and God. Robert Goddard, whose invention of the liquid-fueled rocket has had profound consequences for military technology and is the basis for space exploration, gained neither fame nor fortune from his efforts; in terms of income and personal prestige he might better have lived out his life as an unproductive member of the faculty of Clark University.

Although a would-be innovator may in some instances realistically expect that success in his particular endeavors will bring him material and status returns, innovation is still the hard and doubtful way; for there never is and never can be any certainty that innovative endeavors will be successful. A moderately competent literary craftsman can write fiction in one or another of the standard formulas—mystery story, western, light romance, historical romance, etc.—in the reasonable expectation that it will secure a publisher and pay for the labor he puts into it; if he writes industriously, he can probably earn a livelihood and will have a considerable chance of acquiring over the years a following and success in his field. Should the same craftsman

Innovation and the innovator   **133**

be bent upon producing a great novel, he could, however, have no such expectations. No one can possibly tell in advance what will be a great novel, although it presumably must be original in both content and form; and a writer can have no assurance that what he writes will be the great novel that no one can delineate in advance. He must proceed on hope and live in faith; he must, that is to say, so much want to write a really great novel that he can ignore the probability that he will fail. The same is true of a man who would invent a better mousetrap, devise a new concept of the structure of the heavens or the atom, or formulate a new theory of the political process.

The kind of hypermotivation that will drive an individual not only to undertake but also to persist in an endeavor that is inherently discouraging and that is by everyone's definition but his own certain to be unrewarding is distinctly asocial. The socially established motivations are all conducive to conventional conduct; they presuppose values that make the rewards for conventional conduct desirable and reasonably certain, and that make the punishments for failure to engage in such conduct—deprivation, status loss, legal penalties—both undesirable and reasonably certain. The acquisition of the kind of hypermotivation that leads to innovative endeavor may in a general way be related to the stresses and strains of a society in a condition of dynamic incongruence; and it may perhaps be inferred that an individual who, under such circumstances, becomes asocially hypermotivated has been inadequately socialized into the normal social motives. Just what specifics of personal experience produce hypermotivation of this sort cannot, however, be designated. It is certainly not genetically established or the product of a genetic accident (i.e., a biological sport); for if it were either, then the number of innovators who occur in every society would be fairly constant.[13] Nor is there any reason to suppose, as some venturesome minds have speculated, that it is expressive of physiological abnormality, such as might be produced by the toxins of diseases like syphilis, consumption, or, as one theory had it, gout.

[13] The frequency of the occurrence of innovations, hence of men with innovative inclinations and abilities, has varied widely from country to country and within a given country from time to time. The ferment of the Renaissance was limited mainly to Italy, which had for centuries produced nothing new of note and was soon to lapse back into cultural stagnation. France and southern Germany were the major contributors to the cultural turmoil that culminated in the Reformation. England was the major contributor to those changes, organizational and technological, that launched the age of the machine; and to what England started, the United States, Germany, and now again Italy have been large contributors. In the United States most of the innovations, technological and otherwise, have been produced north of the Mason-Dixon Line; and almost all the critical innovations in agricultural technology have come, and still do come, from the Middle Western states. Clearly, such national and regional variations in the flow of innovations cannot be explained in genetic terms.

Egocentricity and Social Insensitivity

From the very nature of the innovative process it may be inferred that an innovator must have exceptional confidence in his own judgment and, conversely, subnormal regard for the judgment of others, for the power of authority, and for the evidence of the past. He perceives as a problem what everyone else takes for granted, or he strives to solve a problem in directions that no one else considers reasonable. His very doing so is a demonstration of his confidence in himself and his disbelief in all else. No innovator has ever been able to describe precisely how he has gone about his creative thinking, how he has determined which of his trials to formulate a new construct are errors, and how he has finally judged one of them to be sufficiently promising to be tested.[14] Some successful innovators have claimed that the successful idea, i.e., the usable synthesis, came to them at some odd moment —upon awakening from a night's sleep, while walking in the woods, or while thinking about something else; and the term "inspiration" has often been used to suggest the suddenness of the creative moment. Edison, however, described innovative endeavor as 99 per cent perspiration and 1 per cent inspiration. What he meant, no doubt, was that an innovator must try countless times to achieve a synthesis in the hope that ultimately success will come. Wherever, as in mechanics and modern physics, the better of the mental trials are overtly tested—where, for example, a mechanical device is actually constructed or, in physics, a hypothesis is made the basis for an experiment—the trial-and-error nature of innovative endeavor and the amount of testing and rejecting that enters into innovation are clearly evident.

It is because innovation proceeds, even in modern scientific works, by undescribable and hence unregulatable trial and error that a would-be innovator has nothing to go on but his own self-confidence. Since for all he can really know, every one of his efforts will be misdirected and since he may experience many, perhaps thousands, of failures, his self-confidence must be unshakable; it must be, in a sense, so strong that it prevents him from learning from failure that he may not succeed. In some instances there may be through time a perceivable decline in the extent of successive failures. Such could be the case with a surgeon who was trying to devise a new method of operating on the heart; each trial, though a failure, might be encouraging if each successive patient lived a bit longer than did the previous one. Most innovators, however, cannot in this way mark their progress toward success; and the only way that they can reassure themselves that continuing is worthwhile is to believe that the next trial, unlike all those that have

[14] Two rather contrasting versions of the innovative process are offered by Walter B. Cannon, *The Way of an Investigator*, W. W. Norton & Company, Inc., New York, 1945; and Bernard Barber, *Science and the Social Order*, The Free Press of Glencoe, New York, 1952, chap. IX, "The Social Process of Invention and Discovery."

preceded it, will be the successful one. After a month, a year, or a decade of this without any evidence of progress, only the most determined and self-confident person is likely to persist. To others, persistence under these circumstances will no doubt seem incomprehensible and irrational; this may, perhaps, account for the tendency to stigmatize would-be innovators as fanatics.

No doubt most innovative endeavor ends in discouragement and its being abandoned before success has been achieved. The record, such as it is, gives evidence only of those innovators who persisted until they were successful—in their own terms, if not in those of society. To the discouragement that is inherent in the very process of innovative endeavor is always added in some measure or other the discouragement imposed by society. From the point of view of a person who is engaged in innovative endeavor, the unvarying goal of society—in the person of relatives, friends, neighbors, tax collectors, employers, and all the other people and social agencies by which he is surrounded—is to use up his time and exhaust his energies. The self-confidence of a would-be innovator may assure him that he is expending his time and effort in a potentially valuable direction; but unless he is insensitive to the social demands on his time and energies and the social disapproval of his activities that often obtains, he is not at all likely to become successful. Time and freedom from distractions do not of themselves make for innovation, as the history of monastery life demonstrates. Both, however, are undoubtedly prerequisite, and free time and energy are almost always in short supply.

In our mythology the great problem of the creative person is usually pictured as financial. No one wants him to do what he is trying to do, and he has as yet nothing of value to sell; and so he starves in a garret. It is certainly true that a would-be innovator must be financially subsidized in some way or other, for if he labors all day to earn a living, he will have no time or energy to apply himself to innovative endeavor. From the point of view of society, innovative endeavor is at best a leisure-time activity; and as will be observed later, it is only when and where considerable numbers of men are free from the need to earn their livelihood on a day-to-day basis that innovators make their appearance.

Today at least, economic deterrents to innovative endeavor are far less imposing than are noneconomic demands on time and energy. There are many positions in modern society that provide financial support without encumbering the individual with overly burdensome responsibilities. Of these the most favorable to innovative endeavor is, perhaps, that of faculty member of a university. The occupant of such a position, especially if he has a research professorship, is even expected to devote himself to creative endeavors and to some extent may actually be permitted to do so. Unless, however, he is atypically insensitive to social controls, even he will find a good part of his time absorbed in institutional and peer-group activities; and unless he is capable of somewhat ruthless evasion of social obligations, his world outside the university will do everything possible to normalize his conduct—which means preventing him from applying himself to the innovative task.

It has been reported of Edison that he used his deafness as a defense against those who would claim his time and of Henry Ford that he early won the valuable reputation of being rude and irascible.[15] Perhaps so; these men did at any event somehow find time to engage in innovative endeavor. Most men, including presumably most would-be innovators, are too sensitive to social pressures, too much concerned with their status, and too conventional regarding duties and social obligations to be able to concentrate their time and energies on tasks that are not sanctioned by society. This is in part why successful innovators never constitute more than an infinitesimal fraction of a social population and why the innovations that make for social change occur so infrequently, even in a society such as our own, which seems to change with such rapidity.

Even in modern society, few if any fathers would wish their sons to grow up to become obsessed with an idea that they can create what no one wants. A modern father might sanction his son's ambition to become a scientist of the organizationally secure sort, he might even approve of his son's ambition to become a great violinist; but unless he himself were a successful innovator, no father would willingly contemplate for his son a career which is asocial, in which achievement is self-defined rather than socially defined, and which to all others must seem fraught with disappointment and discouragement and without much chance of reward. The same point of view is held by the family as a whole, by childhood peers, and by the public school, the college, and even the university. In the latter realm there may be much airy talk of creative endeavor and much pretense that originality is encouraged and admired; but even here, only to a lesser degree than elsewhere, the easier and more profitable way for anyone is to learn his lessons well and to think in the currently approved style.

Dynamic Incongruence and the Innovator

Since the atypical personality attributes of innovators are not, clearly, a normal consequence of socialization, there has been a temptation to seek in other than social factors the cause of innovative endeavor. The idea that an innovator is a biological sport, a born genius or a born fool, depending upon

[15] A revealing and genial account of the many ingenious ways in which one inventor, Sir Hiram S. Maxim, evaded his marital and parental responsibilities is provided by his son, Hiram P. Maxim in *A Genius in the Family,* reprint ed., Dover Publications, Inc., New York, 1960.

the point of view, has already been mentioned and discarded as untenable; and the idea that the seemingly irrational endeavors of an innovative mind are the result of stimulating toxins from some pathological condition of the body has long since proved absurd. The obvious conclusion is that the atypical attributes of innovators are in fact socially developed, albeit by social inadvertence rather than intent. The life of any individual in any society is spotted with misadventures—with what are from the social point of view accidents. Thus a spanking, socially indicated as punishment for misconduct, may, contrary to parental intent, teach a boy to do rather than not to do; the behavior of the village drunkard, which should be a bad example, may be taken by one village lad as conduct to emulate; the social thesis that honesty pays may be learned in reverse from observation that the local horse trader thrives on the gullibility of those who do business with him.

Any society, that is, fails to some degree and in various ways to induct its individual members into scrupulous adherence to the dictates of the social heritage; and the less integrated and stable the social system, the greater the range and frequency of failure. In a society that is in a more or less general condition of static incongruence, the result of failure is that many persons learn to exploit various social elements to their personal advantage. Under conditions of dynamic incongruence, some learn to be social parasites—predatory criminals, social incompetents, and sexual and other antisocial deviants; others, possibly but by no means certainly in greater than normal proportion, learn to be neurotics and psychopaths; and some few learn to apply themselves more or less diligently and in spite of social discouragements to creative endeavors. Innovators are, thus, but one of the human by-products of failure in socialization in a society that is undergoing change. They are, however, the one by-product that can in turn contribute significantly to further change; and they appear only under particular conditions of change.

chapter 5 *Advocacy and the Advocate*

Although every significant social change begins as an innovation, the appearance of innovators and innovations does not directly and automatically result in changes in the social system. No innovation is ever more than the cornerstone upon which, given proper social acceptance, a new element of social life may be erected. The ideological cornerstone around and upon which has grown the modern American system of representative government was conceived during the seventeenth century by the English philosopher John Locke; the first powered, heavier-than-air craft from which our modern system of air transport derives was first flown at Kittyhawk in 1903 by the Wright brothers; the religious and ethical idea from which developed the vast, complex system of beliefs, practices, and organizations now known as Christianity goes back to the life and sayings of Jesus Christ. Seen thus, it is obvious that a social element does not immediately and automatically result from an innovation and that the distinction between the one and the other is multidimensional. The innovation is new, the social element established; the innovation is accepted only by its innovator, the social element by the society at large; the innovation is an idea in the mind of the innovator manifest, perhaps, in some material tool or device, while the social element is a functioning part of the social system, incorporated in the culture and embodied in the personalities, practices, or equipment of the members of the society.

The making of a new social element from an invention or discovery is at least as complex and uncertain a process as is that of innovation itself, and perhaps considerably more so. It is a process that is at present little understood; and as is often the case when knowledge is limited or lacking, it has frequently been encompassed by such vague and metaphysical terms as "immanent evolution," which is used to suggest that everything that happens between the achievement of an inno-

139

vation and the establishment of a new social element is inherent in the innovation itself. Just as much must happen between the laying of the cornerstone and the completion of the building, much that is not determined by the nature of the cornerstone itself, so much must happen to an innovation before it can become a new social element. There is, however, nothing mystical, magical, or mysterious about the process, any more than there is anything automatic about it. Like innovation itself, it is a product of human endeavor and human ingenuity.

This is not to imply that fortuitous factors, variable and largely unknown, do not enter into determining which of the innovations produced in a given time and place will secure the attention necessary to assure its social acceptance and what the course of that acceptance will be. They do; and it is because they do that the case histories of innovations which have been developed and incorporated into the social system often seem to be unpatterned and mainly a matter of accident. Many a book or technical manuscript which has subsequently been recognized as both original and valuable has wandered for months or even years from publisher to publisher before being accepted. How many manuscripts with equal potentialities never have got into print only because the author became discouraged in his search for a publisher, because he proceeded in that search in an ineffective way, or because some accident or incident, personal or social, intervened (for example, the author's death or the advent of war) is incalculable. Moreover, the mere publishing of a book or technical manuscript with potentialities does not assure that it will secure attention. Fleming's report of his discovery of a mold with bacteriostatic properties lay dormant for years before it was read by someone interested enough to explore its possibilities. If it had not been for the occurrence of World War II, DDT might never have become the famous and widely used insecticide that it presently is. It was first synthesized late in the nineteenth century, and it was again and independently synthesized, and its deadly properties noted, by a Swiss chemist in 1934; but it was not until the United States Army, in anticipation of a war-fostered outbreak of insect-borne diseases, undertook to find a more effective insecticide than any then in use that American chemists rediscovered the Swiss discovery and put it into use.

In a sense every innovation is ahead of the times and therefore at odds with the times; but whether the course of human events will catch up with a given innovation and foster its being utilized or veer off in some other direction is not determined by the innovation itself. Many known mechanical devices, production procedures, proposals for social reform, and theories and concepts have simply died of inattention; and for each of these there must surely have been many others that did not even get into the historical record. The history of sociological thought, for example, is littered with ideas and observations—hypotheses, theories, and interpretations—that were never developed beyond their original statement. Perhaps most of them were simply errors in the trial-and-error process by which science grows and could not have been incorporated into our emerging body of knowledge about society. On the other hand, the variable history of concepts that have been accepted suggests how great may be the role of fortuitous factors in determining which innovations will survive and be utilized. During his lifetime, the philosopher-psychologist George Mead was considered little more than a curiosity at the University of Chicago and was practically unknown elsewhere; he wrote little, and that very badly. After his death, however, a number of his former students collaborated in the publication of the notes that they had taken while attending his lectures, and the result, *Mind, Self and Society*, set off a significant vogue in sociological thinking.[1] By contrast, Charles H. Cooley, a near contemporary of Mead's, wrote clearly and extensively and gained wide recognition among sociologists during the early part of the century. Later, the times—in this case the wide popularity of the instinct concept and, subsequently, sociological preoccupation with mass society—turned away from the concepts that Cooley had advanced; and for nearly three decades those concepts languished in obscurity. That might well have been the end of them; but again a change in the times—specifically, war and sociopsychological concern with the morale of American soldiers—led to their rediscovery; and Cooley's concept of the primary group, retitled the "small group," became the center of much study and discussion.

THE ADVOCATE

The social potentialities of an innovation cannot be realized without the efforts of many men, who in terms of their function in the process may be conceptually divided into advocates and adopters—into those who foster the introduction of the innovation into the social system and those who utilize the innovation and so make it an operative part of the society.[2] For reasons that will shortly be evident, an innovation does not win its own way. Some member of the society must perceive its ultimate value and devote himself to its exploitation. His role—and if he is successful, all those who directly and indirectly join in the endeavor—is that of advocate.

Every advocate faces a dilemma: an innovation cannot be incorporated

[1] The University of Chicago Press, Chicago, 1934.

[2] The term "change agent" was applied to advocates by Ronald Lippitt (*The Dynamics of Planned Change*, Harcourt, Brace & World, Inc., New York, 1958) and has for some reason been adopted by other writers, including Everett M. Rogers. For a brief analysis of the advocatory role and an account of the research data available on the subject, see Rogers's *Diffusion of Innovations*, The Free Press of Glencoe, New York, 1962, pp. 254–284, "The Role of the Change Agent."

into the social system until it has been developed through empirical experience into a functionally effective part; but an innovation cannot be developed except as it comes to be adopted by the members of society. The first automobile was a crude, unreliable, and ineffectual device. Countless man-hours of effort, and hence vast sums of money, were necessary to develop it into a reasonably satisfactory means of transportation (i.e., into one that could successfully compete with horse-drawn vehicles) and still more to provide it with a context, such as roads, in which it could function efficiently. Money and endeavor could be devoted to this development, however, only to the extent that the automobile was accepted. Over and over, therefore, in the early history of the automobile someone had to do such things as convert a livery stable into a garage to service automobiles not yet built, to convince a banker that a profit could be made by financing a factory for the production of automobiles for which no visible market existed, to induce an engineer to devote his skills to the improving of a device that was then almost universally condemned as impractical, etc.

Characteristics of the Advocate

Occasionally an innovator has become the advocate—or the initial advocate—for his own innovation. Apparently F. W. Woolworth not only conceived the then-novel idea of self-service, fixed-price merchandising, but also put it into operation and thereby began a development in merchandising that became one of America's major contributions to Western society. Karl Marx, with the collaboration and perhaps at the instigation of Engels, began the advocacy of his utopian dream with the publication of *The Communist Manifesto*. Thomas A. Edison was as much advocate for his technological innovations as he was originator of them.[3]

Usually, however, an innovator does not serve as advocate for his own invention or discovery, for advocacy requires somewhat different personal characteristics than those that are essential to innovative endeavor. The advocate of an innovation, like an innovator, must be hypermotivated and unusually egocentric, for his endeavor is directed toward a distant, uncertain, and unconventional end. But in two notable respects advocates differ in character from innovators.[4] Whereas the latter work mainly with

[3] See Matthew Josephson, *Edison: A Biography*, McGraw-Hill Book Company, New York, 1959.

[4] The growth economists have not distinguished between innovators, advocates, and adopters. Thus the "achievement motivation" of McClelland (David E. McClelland, *The Achieving Society*, D. Van Nostrand Company, Inc., Princeton, N.J., 1961) and the "creativity" of Everett E. Hagen (*On the Theory of Social Change*, The Dorsey Press, Inc., Homewood, Ill., 1962) are blanket terms. The rural sociologists, such as Everett M. Rogers (*Diffusion of Innovations*, The Free

symbols, advocates work mainly with persons; and whereas innovators are in the main motivated in their activities by the sheer desire to create something new—to solve a self-set problem—advocates are more often motivated by such ulterior considerations as the acquisition of wealth and prestige.

The latter point has been hotly debated; and it cannot be denied that advocates have sometimes been idealistic and unselfish and have often become personally dedicated to the success of what they have advocated. St. Paul must have believed that the Christian Church that he advocated would bring eternal salvation to mankind; Henry Ford no doubt believed that his cheap Model T would bring freedom and convenience to millions of Americans; and William Booth undoubtedly believed that his Salvation Army organization would save countless human derelicts from premature death. It is even possible that some among the many politicians who have been self-proclaimed saviors of mankind have thought themselves dedicated to human welfare, although the history of politics gives little support to this view.

Nevertheless, successful advocates, unlike most successful innovators, do normally receive wealth or renown or both for their endeavors. Invariably, as acceptance is gained for what is being advocated, the advocate himself rises in power and position (usually organizational) and normally, but not invariably, in economic status. It would be strange, therefore, if an advocate were to labor at his task unaware of the comforting realization that success, if he achieves it, will bring him, in addition to the gratification of a worthwhile task well done, personal recognition and some financial reward. Moreover, an advocate can to some extent mark out his progress toward his goal—this convert gained, this practical problem solved, this financial backing secured—whereas an innovator, it will be recalled, ordinarily has no indication of his progress toward the solution of his problem until his final, successful trial.

Individual Initiative and Enterprise

What, therefore, mainly differentiates the advocate of an innovation from the common run of men—or, more specifically, from the common run of ambitious men within the society—is that he chooses to distinguish himself from his fellows by promoting or developing something new. In this respect he differs qualitatively as well as quantitatively from the norm. As has been indicated, there are many men in modern society, and some have appeared from time to time in the societies of the past, who differ quantitatively from

---

Press of Glencoe, New York, 1962), do on the other hand differentiate between advocates and adopters and recognize that both the personal characteristics and the roles of each are different in degree if not in kind.

the norms—men who are more ambitious, more resourceful, and more determined than is normative, who therefore work harder, longer, and more effectively than do their peers, and who may, as a consequence of their enterprise, gain wealth, stature, and power. What they do, however, is conventional in character, whether they excel in business, agriculture, manufacture, religion, scholarship, or any other area of social life. The role of such men in our society is not to be depreciated; it is enterprising men who set the competitive pace and thereby to some extent counteract the tendency of all organized activities to become monopolistic and lethargic. Through their endeavors they may, if they are free from political constraints, squeeze out the more incompetent individuals and so retard if not prevent the atrophy of established social elements, particularly established forms of organization. Thus an enterprising merchant may through unusual endeavor and skill in the traditional forms of merchandising bring his equally traditional but also relatively lazy and incompetent competitors to bankruptcy; and an exceptionally industrious and conscientious schoolteacher may set a standard of local performance that his colleagues must strive to equal if they are to hold their teaching positions.

The advocate of an innovation, on the other hand, in addition to being more enterprising and persevering than is the normal for his time and place, takes on the task of gaining social acceptance for a device, idea, procedure, or form of organization that is neither fully developed nor socially indicated or socially accepted. If he succeeds in his self-designated endeavor, he will then be said to have had great foresight; if he fails, he will be proclaimed a foolish visionary. In either event, what he does have is the personal initiative to attempt what no others (or, more realistically, perhaps, few others) consider worth trying to do.

Men with initiative of this sort, like innovators, are social deviants, by-products of malsocialization who appear in numbers only in societies that are in a state of dynamic incongruence and who are as necessary as are innovators to that state of affairs. Presumably enterprise can be and often is established in individuals by social training, most especially, it would appear, by their being subjected to conditions of comparative adversity in early life. Initiative, on the other hand, would seem to be established inadvertently. Our modern schools of business, engineering, law, etc., apparently endeavor to instill in their students, in addition to knowledge and skill, the ideal of enterprise; but they, like all established social agencies, whether formal or informal, do not deliberately attempt to develop the complex of ideas, sentiments, attitudes, values, and motivations that are encompassed by the term "individual initiative."

In due course the reasons why no established agency of society encourages individual initiative will be explored, the organizational and ideological conditions that have led to the emergence in modern times of an unusually high proportion of individuals with initiative will be analyzed, and the recent social developments that seem to jeopardize their continued appearance and, hence, the dynamism of our society will be described. For the moment, it is sufficient to say that there is a distinct concordance between the circumstances that foster the emergence of innovators and those that foster the appearance of men with sufficient initiative to become advocates of innovations.

Advocatory Roles

In most times and places, the role of advocate has been quite as asocial as has that of innovator, and the task of an advocate has been considerably greater than it is today. In modern society, the relatively large number of men with the requisite initiative has resulted in social recognition and acceptance of advocates; and in recent times men have been able to assume an advocatory role without fear of social disapproval. Moreover, under the circumstances that have obtained in Western societies during the past hundred years, any individual who has had sufficient initiative, the good fortune to come upon a promising innovation, and the ability to perceive its potentialities has been able to become an advocate. Henry Ford was the proprietor of a rather unprofitable bicycle shop when he became advocate of the idea (no doubt his own) that automobiles could be produced cheaply and in numbers and sold to the common man; Lenin was the son of a lower-middle-class Russian family, headed for a conventional career in law, when he became enamored of Marxian doctrine and set out on his self-set task of bringing Marx's program to fruition; and Andrew Carnegie, who began his work life as a bobbin boy in a cotton mill, became advocate for a mode of steel production that was not then used in the United States.

Humble origins are hardly essential to becoming a successful advocate; and at any event, whatever his origins, any individual who achieves success in his advocacy comes to be recognized, grudgingly at first, as an exceptional person in whatever his particular role. Very often in our society the role is that of businessman or industrialist who has won wealth and fame through the successful advocacy of some new mercantile procedure, financial operation, productive process, or commercial product. It has been mainly through the initiative of what have been called "progressive businessmen" that Western industrial technology and its handmaiden, large-scale commerce, have been developed; and it will be on the initiative of such men that will depend whether or not new inventions and discoveries in technology will in the future be put to effective use; for so far no organizational substitute for individual initiative has made its appearance.

Many of the changes in organization that have been brought about over the past few centuries have involved the advocacy of men in business and industry—the decline of the guild system of production and distribution and the emergence of the corporate form of organization; the growth of national and worldwide markets and the forms of organized transportation that have made such economic integration possible; the development of banks and other financial institutions and of such agencies of financial assurance as fire, life, and now medical insurance. Not all the changes in organization—or even in technology—that have come about with the advocacy of men in business and industry have in the long run proved functionally advantageous; for there is no certainty that what can be made profitable to one individual or to one organization will also be conducive to the general welfare. But to blame men in business and industry, as has become something of the current fashion, for perceived inadequacies in our social system is to overlook the role that has been played by other kinds of advocates, most especially political, and to ignore the fact that so much of what is acceptable in our society has been wrought by men in these fields.

Anyone who obtains a financial profit from advocacy, either for himself as an individual or for the organization that he represents, is by social definition a businessman.[5] Where the possibility of financial profit is either lacking or less evident, as it is in the case of an advocate for some new way of treating criminals, advocates are usually defined as reformers. The distinction between advocatory businessman and reformer is seldom clear; but the role of reformer is now quite standardized in modern society, and the advocate of any technological or organizational change who does not himself seem likely to profit financially from its adoption is usually characterized as such. The advocate of a new idea, on the other hand, is usually cast into the role of disciple or agitator, or at least described as one.

Social reformers, disciples, and agitators are presumed to be motivated by more selfless considerations than those of businessmen. But, as was noted earlier, success usually brings them recognition and power and often financial profit; thus it is probably no more than a social convention to assume that businessmen are always and exclusively crass and self-seeking and that reformers and disciples are wholly concerned with the welfare of mankind. Insofar as the consequences to society are concerned, it actually matters little what the motives and goals of advocates may be. Idealists have brought as much calamity to mankind as have self-seeking realists; and the latter have contributed as much as, if not far more than, the former to the

[5] The socially atypical characteristics of successful advocates in business and industry are suggested by the case histories provided by the following: William Miller (ed.), *Men in Business: Essays in the History of Entrepreneurship*, Harvard University Press, Cambridge, Mass., 1952; Thomas C. Cochran, *Railroad Leaders, 1845–1890*, Harvard University Press, Cambridge, Mass., 1953; and W. Lloyd Warner and James C. Abegglen, *Big Business Leaders in America*, Harper & Row, Publishers, Incorporated, New York, 1955.

emergence of modern society. What is significant in the study of social change is not the motives of men, but their actions; and it is clear that advocates, whether they are socially defined as businessmen, reformers, disciples, or agitators, have played a significant part in the changes that have been worked in our society and, by presumption, wherever changes have come about.

A reformer may advocate the adoption of a new technique in production (such as the use of commercial rather than organic fertilizer in agriculture), in public or private sanitation, in medical practice, in child care, in nutrition, or in any other aspect of man's relation to physical and biological nature.[6] He may advocate, and many reformers have done so, the adoption of some new form of human relationship, such as a new way of dealing with marital discord or juvenile delinquency; or he may advocate some new form of social organization, such as public school education and, more recently, the desegregation of our public schools. Not all those who are socially defined as reformers are, of course, advocates of changes. Many are, rather, resistant to changes that are being advocated by others. Their role in social change will be analyzed in the following chapter.

In that they advocate the adoption of an idea or set of beliefs, often regarding some technique or form of organization, disciples and agitators are agents of change in the ideological component of society—in religion, science, and philosophy. Their effect, potential and actual, on the technological and organizational aspects of social life is both variable and uncertain; but that they do often secure the social acceptance of some new idea about the universe in which man lives, about the ultimate purpose of life, about proper morals and manners, etc., cannot be doubted.

Whether businessman, reformer, or agitator, every advocate, it will be recalled, faces a dilemma in that the innovation that he advocates must be developed and made functionally effective before it will have inherent value to those who adopt it, while the innovation cannot be developed except as it gains acceptance. As a result of this dilemma, the efforts of an advocate are of a piecemeal, trial-and-error order and usually have no more pattern to them than have the activities of an innovator. Analytically, however, advocatory efforts may be divided into two conceptually distinct, although

[6] There is available a great deal of biographical material about social reformers of one sort or another and many general accounts of reformism. The following are more or less representative: Maxwell C. Raddock, *Portrait of an American Labor Leader: William L. Hutcheson*, American Institute of Social Sciences, Inc., New York, 1955; Harold Schwartz, *Samuel Gridley Howe: Social Reformer, 1801–1876*, Harvard University Press, Cambridge, Mass., 1956; Herman Ausubel, *In Hard Times: Reformers among the Late Victorians*, Columbia University Press, New York, 1960; and Otis Pease (ed.), *The Progressive Years: The Spirit and Achievement of American Reform*, George Braziller, Inc., New York, 1962.

operationally interwoven, aspects: the promotion of the innovation and its development into a functionally valuable social device.

PROMOTION

Whoever invented the saying "Build a better mousetrap and the world will beat a pathway to your door" evidently favored innovations and thought that all the world felt the same. Everywhere and always, however, true innovations are greeted with skepticism and either ignored or almost automatically rejected. The rejection may be unreasoned, but it may not be without empirical foundation. Consider, for example, that over the past fifty years and more the claim of having discovered a cancer cure has been made repeatedly, in some instances by men of sound professional standing. Experience has drummed into the mores of the medical profession, if not into the consciousness of the public at large, that no such sudden discovery is possible and that if any means of conquering the many kinds of cancerous growths is ever discovered, it will come slowly through the accumulating of scientific knowledge of the chemistry of cell life. An announcement of a suddenly discovered cure for cancerous growths will, therefore, be disclaimed by the vast majority of medical men without their even bothering to investigate the basis for the claim. Such is the case, in one way or another, with all true innovations, the qualification "true" here being used to distinguish what is new from what is only purportedly new—from such things as the so-called new and secret ingredient that a detergent manufacturer claims to be in his product, the basic "newness" of the latest popular tune, and the "originality" of the restatement of an old idea.

At the outset an innovation is valued only by its innovator. It invariably violates the established canons of what is reasonable, what constitutes good taste, what is morally permissible, or all three, in that it constitutes a breach of some established element of the social system. Initially, only its innovator, who has achieved this breach after much effort, is convinced that it is desirable as well as possible. Other people see no reason for a break with the established and do not consider it desirable, to say nothing of being possible; and they most certainly are not going to struggle to comprehend what the innovator offers as a substitute for what they value and what is familiar to them. Thus only to its composer who has found the conventional forms of music unsatisfactory and has worked out new forms acceptable to himself, is unconventional music, as was Bartok's during his lifetime, initially acceptable. Other people, including musicians, who have no objection to the conventional forms, are neither willing nor prepared to listen hopefully to his innovative compositions.

Even when there is a rather general recognition of the need for some new device, procedure, or whatever, what is offered to satisfy this need is not granted immediate acceptance but is, rather, looked upon with doubt and tried out, if at all, hesitantly and with an overly critical attitude. Thus the need for cheap, efficient, and convenient street and house lighting must have been self-evident to most people in Western cities during the early decades of the last century if they thought about it at all. City life was becoming more complicated, and work and other activities were being pushed further and further into the evening hours; but far from being welcomed as a practical solution to the lighting problem, coal-gas lighting was at first strongly resisted on such practical grounds as that it would be unhealthful and dangerous and on such moral grounds as that gas lighting would encourage late hours in children, increase the activities of criminals, and cause a general rise of sexual immorality. Half a century later, there was similar resistance to the next great change in lighting—the shift from gaslight to electricity.

Since an innovation violates preexisting attitudes, sentiments, and values, it arrives upon the social scene unsanctioned. At the outset it has nothing in support of it except the confidence of the innovator himself, who, for reasons previously indicated, is usually without authority. The weight of authority, abstract and personal, normally lies entirely with the established and so against the new. In many instances the recognized authorities in the field, even in the field of technology, have promptly mobilized against an innovation in defense of the *status quo*. The most noted surgeons both here and in Europe pooh-poohed dentist Wells's idea that nitrous oxide could safely be used as an anesthetic in surgery; and when, having been given reluctant permission to hold a demonstration, Wells failed in his first public trial (for reasons now clear but then not understood), the medical profession was overjoyed by this "proof" that the idea was that of a crackpot. Goddard's rocket was considered an impractical toy by American military men—and everyone else, for that matter, who had knowledge of it and might have been interested in it—until the Germans employed it in the shelling of London in 1944. Similar rejection by authority, if not always so dramatic or emphatic, has been the initial reception of almost all recent innovations in technology and probably of all those that have been offered in the ideological and organizational aspects of social life, where there is little possibility of immediate and empirical testing of usefulness.

Because the usual, if not invariable, response to an innovation is outright rejection, or at the very least indifference, the potentialities of an innovation—as seen first by the innovator himself and then by an advocate—need to be promoted. If the advocate is a free lance, rather than an operative member of some relevant organization, such as a business, his endeavor is to persuade those persons whose support will in his judgment be useful to his cause that the innovation has a chance for commercial profit, of bringing personal advancement, of general social advantage, or of whatever those persons may be thought to value. If the innovation is a mechanical device or other technological invention in need of development before it can be presented on the open market, he will ordinarily first seek to persuade some individual or financial agency to advance money for the development of the innovation and then, having secured financial backing, proceed to convince engineers and other technicians that the innovation is worth working on. In the process, he normally—in modern society, at any event—establishes and develops a business enterprise; and if all goes well, he and his organization then turn their attention to creating a market for the developed technological device or procedure. If the advocate is at the outset a member of a business or industrial organization, he may promote the innovation within the membership of that organization, trying to convince his superiors and subordinates that the organization should take on the development and marketing of the innovation.

The promotion of new ideas, beliefs, professional techniques and procedures, modes of human relationship, forms of organization, etc., also usually proceeds in one or the other of these same two ways. Either the advocate begins as a free lance and, if successful, builds an organization to implement his work—as Marxian advocate Lenin developed the Communist International, eugenics advocate Sanger the American Birth Control League, and inventor-founder Booth the Salvation Army—or else he works within an existing organizational framework and endeavors to persuade its leaders that the organization should adopt the innovation and assume responsibility for its further promotion and development. The latter has very commonly been the way in which forms of organization and organizational procedures have been changed. Thus it was as chief of one of the sections of the London police force that Robert Peel became the effective advocate for the professionalization of police forces and thereby inaugurated what in time amounted to a major change in the policing organizations and operations of all Western societies. And to go further back in history, it was as a priest of the Roman Catholic Church that Luther attempted to reform and revitalize the venal Church. When, like many advocates of change before and since, Luther failed in his endeavor, he struck out as a free lance to develop a new organization that would give expression to his views, thereby inaugurating an organizational and ideological change of far-reaching and long-lasting significance.

In some instances advocates have begun and continued to operate without the aid, or the hindrance, of any formal organization. This has most commonly occurred in the promotion of ideas, although it has also occasionally happened in the advocacy of techniques that are not subject to commercial exploitation, such as new surgical techniques, and in the advocacy of proposed changes in some aspect of human relationships, such as a liberalization of the divorce laws. The advocate of a new philosophical concept, of a new scientific discovery, or of a new theory of practice or procedure has often done no more than write and proclaim (as in the classroom or in public lectures) the validity or value of what he represents. It was in these ways that Sir Francis Galton promoted the idea of using fingerprints for criminal indentification and that Talcott Parsons endeavored to secure sociological converts to the theory of social equilibrium. The advocate of a new technique has sometimes, in addition to writing and speaking on its behalf, adopted it himself and thereby attempted to demonstrate its values. New medical techniques have frequently been promoted in this way, as, for example, were sterile techniques in surgery by Lister's adoption and application of them.

Propaganda through the Mass Media

The defenders of modern commercial advertising have long claimed that the very high social costs of the various forms of advertising and commercial publicity are justified by the fact that they bring new products to the attention of consumers. They hold, in effect, that it is advertising that is *the* means of promoting innovations in technology. A like claim is made for many kinds of political, religious, medical, and educational propaganda—that, for example, the publicizing of the dangers of cancer through newspapers, magazines, television, etc., is the way to get the public to make full use of modern means of early diagnosis. Some students of the mass media—i.e., newspapers, radio, television, etc.—are inclined not only to accept these views but to extend them into the thesis that in the mass society, as they presume ours to be, it is the mass media that are the major agency of social change.

There is just sufficient truth in the claim that advertising and other kinds of propaganda have developed markets for new products and have led to the adoption of new practices to obscure the subtle realities. Advertising and its supplements (articles, news stories, etc.) have no doubt aided in the diffusion of knowledge about many new commercial products—electric refrigeration, frozen foods, the vacuum cleaner, and so on. No doubt, too, the propaganda that was disseminated on behalf of personal hygiene two generations ago aided in establishing the idea that cleanliness has something to do with godliness; nor is there any doubt that the massive propaganda against alcohol was a factor in the passage of the Eighteenth Amendment to the Constitution, that the propaganda of the late polio foundation encouraged public contribution of funds for research, or that the publicity that has been given to the growing need for new methods of dealing socially with the aged members of our population has helped to define the later years of life as a problem.

It is a far cry, however, from the recognition that some propaganda via the mass media has had some advocatory consequences to the claim that it is per se the method by which changes are worked in our society. In the first place, the evidence is now clear that the impact of propaganda via the mass media on the thinking and actions of people is at most supplementary to other forces. When those other forces, which often include empirical experience, have made people marginal regarding some opinion, product, or mode of conduct, such propaganda may turn the balance in favor of the new; but it cannot of itself detach people from an established opinion, product, or mode of conduct and so make them marginal in respect to it.[7] In the second place, only an exceedingly small part of commercial and other propaganda is concerned with promoting innovations. By far the greater part is simply an effort to secure a larger part of the established market for goods, to secure more votes for this traditional party or that, or to secure more believers in this old idea rather than that old one. It is a device of competition rather than of social change. Competitors who resort to propaganda are competing among themselves for what is; they are not attempting to gain acceptance for something new. Thus in the early days of the automobile, advertising and other forms of publicizing the automobile as a means of transportation may have helped somewhat in getting people to accept this device. But long since the automobile has become established in our culture; and for the last quarter century or more the effect of advertising, etc., if any, has been to influence buyer decision toward a given make and model. It is not clear whether, as Galbraith and others have held, competitive advertising goes somewhat further and makes people discontented with what they have (or, as it is often put, inflates their wants) and so inclined to buy more and more often (of whatever make of automobile, washing machine, clothes, etc.) than they otherwise would. Even if it does, the consequence is not a qualitative change but a quantitative one. Much the same may be said for the still doubtful effects of propaganda via the mass media on political voting. Even if voting behavior can be changed to some extent, the result is at most a shift from one party to another, not a change in the established voting procedures or political ideas.

The Strategy of Promotion

The process by which an innovation is promoted is far more personal, far more complex and subtle, and far less certain to succeed than those who believe in the powers of the mass media realize. By and large, an advocate works directly with people, often but not exclusively, in intimate relation-

---

[7] As has been demonstrated by Joseph T. Klapper in *The Effects of Mass Communication*, The Free Press of Glencoe, New York, 1960.

ship.[8] He is the agricultural county agent who is trying to induce Farmer Brown to try out a new seed, new fertilizer, or new method of cultivation. He is the teacher of medicine who is trying to convince his students, contrary to all that they have already learned, that a new drug, surgical technique, or diagnostic procedure is worthy of trial. He is the disciple who insists at every opportunity that his master's voice is the sound of the future. She is the county nurse who, through years of rebuff and discouragement, patiently and persistently struggles to convince her ignorant patients that the trained physician is more competent than the local midwife. He is the businessman who wrangles with bankers, his own associates, and manufacturers' agents to get a new device into production and on the market. He is the political reformer who pleads and argues for years with his conventional fellows in the effort to get a new law enacted. He is the prison reformer who over a lifetime of struggle with wardens, politicians, criminologists, etc., may finally get a new and more rational program established. Occasionally he is the dramatic leader of a true mass movement, as Brigham Young was the leader of the deviant society that had been inspired by Joseph Smith.

Persuading people to abandon something familiar and adopt something new in its place is an art that cannot be reduced to rules of procedure, any more than can the art of raising a child or playing a violin. Probably no two successful advocates have proceeded in quite the same way, and the techniques that they have used have been infinitely varied. These techniques can, however, be reduced to goals and principles.

Before anything new will be accepted, the hold of the old over an individual must be weakened. That hold will, inevitably, vary considerably from member to member of the society. Some members may be largely detached from a given social element because they were ineffectively socialized into its use or acceptance, because they have had repeated adverse experience

[8] For some of the research that has been done, mainly by rural sociologists, on the importance of direct, person-to-person persuasion in the promotion of innovations, see Everett M. Rogers, *Diffusion of Innovations*, The Free Press of Glencoe, New York, 1962, pp. 217–253, "Importance of Personal Influence." The promotion of a change within an established organization is described by Robert H. Guest in *Organizational Change: The Effect of Successful Leadership*, The Dorsey Press, Inc., Homewood, Ill., 1962. And the following accounts indicate both how strong is the resistance to the acceptance of innovations and how personal, devious, and always uncertain are the efforts of advocates: Charles W. Clarke, *Taboo: The Story of the Pioneers in Social Hygiene*, Public Affairs Press, Washington, D.C., 1961; A. Gilbert, *Eskimo Doctor*, W. W. Norton & Company, Inc., New York, 1948; Josephine Goldmarks, *Impatient Crusader: Florence Kelley's Life Story*, The University of Illinois Press, Urbana, Ill., 1953; M. T. Sloop and L. Blythe, *Miracle in the Hills*, McGraw-Hill Book Company, New York, 1953; and Mary Einslow (ed.), *Women at Work: The Autobiography of Mary Anderson*, The University of Minnesota Press, Minneapolis, 1951.

with it, or because it represents to them a reason why they lack desired social status, or something else. Insofar as the particular social element is concerned, such persons are marginal—they are presumably susceptible to being converted to a substitute element. A disgruntled and incompetent student may be talked into momentarily accepting any idea, however fantastic; an underpaid and unhappy night watchman may be easily convinced that the company could make money by producing some new product; and an incompetent farmer may be induced to try out anything new, provided only that it costs him nothing.

Those who are most marginal in respect to some established device, procedure, idea, or form of social organization are, however, usually though not invariably the least likely to be useful as converts to it. What the advocate of an innovation needs as converts are people of sound position in their occupation, profession, community, etc. Such people will, if they can be induced to accept the new, provide financing for its development, give the new a favorable test, or at least lend it the prestige of their own positions. It is people of this sort, however, who are most firmly attached to the established, which from their point of view serves them well, and least likely to be detachable.

Some appreciation of how firmly attached people of sound position are to the established ways and ideas can be gained from consideration of just a few of the factors that were involved in the introduction of aseptic surgery. Demonstration that a bacterially clean wound heals rapidly was not enough to gain acceptance for the idea. Lister demonstrated this fact over and over; but the adoption of aseptic surgery was slow and long delayed, for a variety of values stood in the way. Among other things, the surgeons of the time took pride in the blood-spattered formal coats in which traditionally they performed their operations. Their coats, their flowing beards, their operating theater dramatics (which often included such theatrical business as testing the sharpness of the knife with finger, a last puff before laying aside a cigar, and jokes and comments to the audience of students) were an integral part of their way of life. Moreover, like everyone else at the time, surgeons took completely for granted their dirty hands and clothes and the work-soiled tools of their trade. To scrub their hands and work in boiled white gowns was from their point of view not only inconvenient but also unnecessary. Furthermore, the idea that pus was a normal and even beneficial part of the healing process was firmly fixed in their minds.[9] To some degree or other every member of a society is attached to various elements of his social system in the same way that the surgeon of old was to his frock coat, his theories, and to his faith in what he was doing. As a consequence, it has

[9] J. Thorwald, *The Century of the Surgeon*, Pantheon Books, New York, 1957.

often been necessary for an advocate to induce discontent with the old in order to open the way for acceptance of the value of the new.

One of the methods by which advocates have attempted to induce discontent with the old has been to depreciate the old by providing a new standard for evaluating it. Probably what convinced surgeons that their traditional techniques were somewhat less than perfect was the fact that Lister gained a reputation for saving a disproportionate number of patients. Lister may therefore have become a Jones for fellow surgeons to keep up with; and as they, no doubt one by one, became envious of his success and desirous of emulating it, they had no alternative but to abandon the familiar surgical procedures and adopt his.

The provision of a new standard for evaluating an existing social element has often been accomplished through the mechanism of what is sometimes described as a new "reference group." Most people have fairly fixed standards in evaluation, and shifts in these standards usually come only through time and as a result of actual experience. Since it is seldom possible to demonstrate the relative inadequacy of an old social element and contrived circumstances and verbal arguments have no effect at all, advocates have often used new reference groups with new standards to induce discontent with the old and thereby open the way to acceptance of the new. The new reference group has been one of the devices by which agricultural county agents have attempted, in the long run with success, to persuade farmers who in their own eyes and in terms of the local standards are successful and prospering that they might do even better and get an even higher return from the land if they were to use this or that new fertilizer, seed, cultivation technique, or the like. Just telling a farmer that other farmers elsewhere were, in this way, doing even better than he might not impress him; but if he can be induced to attend a meeting at which these other farmers are present, hear their stories, and be outboasted, he may begin to feel that there is some truth in the county agent's claim for the new technique.[10] On a larger scale, this is the persuasive procedure that has been attempted when, as has occurred frequently in recent years, groups of foreign farmers have been toured through the lush fields of the American Middle West.

There are many possible variants on the above procedure. A very simple and crude one that is often encountered is that of setting up a historic reference group by pointing to the history of successful promotions—for

[10] On the United States Department of Agriculture county agent, see Neal Gross and Eugene A. Wilkening, *Sociological Research on the Diffusion and Adoption of New Farm Practices*, Kentucky Agricultural Experiment Station, Lexington, Ky., 1952; Eugene Wilkening, "Informal Leaders and Innovators in Farm Practices," *Rural Sociology*, vol. 17, pp. 272–275, September, 1952; and Paul C. Marsh and Lee A. Coleman, "Group Influence and Agricultural Innovations," *American Journal of Sociology*, vol. 61, pp. 588–594, May, 1956.

example, those who invested in General Motors at its inception have had their dollars multiplied a thousandfold; therefore a thousand dollars invested in this new electronic gadget will in the course of time become a million. The argument may be reversed and the reference group a negative one—for example, the experts considered it a wild and disastrous scheme to give the people the vote back in the eighteenth century; therefore the experts can now be just as wrong about the proposal to give every worker a five-hundred-dollar pension at the age of fifty. A historic reference group, positive or negative, is not, however, likely to be half so effective in inducing discontent as is a current and live one. Thus an advocatory business-man may contrive to get those of his associates whom he would like to convert to his view of some innovation into the company of some of their peers who have profited by the development and promotion of another innovation and let their conversation do his work for him. Thus, too, an academic administrator might, as a prelude to some proposal for reorganization of the institution or a change in teaching procedures, worry audibly for months over the growing stature of some other university; the advocate of some new safety measure in industry might get his fellow administrators to shift their standards by inducing them to visit maimed company workers; and a prison reformer might conceivably make some impression on the state legislature by getting members to inspect the prisons.

Another method that is often used by advocates in trying to induce discontent with the established as a prelude to the acceptance of something new is appealing to the desire, no doubt very common under conditions of dynamic incongruence, for distinctive status. It is to this desire, of course, that women's clothing designers and other fashion-goods producers appeal in order to sell their products at inflated prices. When this appeal is used by the advocate of an innovation, the goal is to make the individual discontented, not with what the innovation is to displace, but with his own social status; and the argument or claim is that rejection of the old and acceptance of the new will distinguish him from the common run of men as one who is progressive, a leader in the community, or something equally rare and presumably desirable.

Appealing to the desire for distinction—for getting ahead of, rather than just keeping up with, the Joneses—is a common advertising device that reflects the current belief, fostered by so-called motivational research, that a consumer often buys for unconscious reasons and that these reasons range from an unaware desire for exceptional status to vicarious sexual gratification. In accordance with this belief, it is not what a product does, how it tastes, what it looks like, or any other direct value that determines a buyer's choosing it, but, rather, the derived values that may be secured from his using or possessing it. This belief is reflected in the frequent characterization of a product, such as an expensive automobile, as a status symbol. No one really knows to what extent, if any, purchasing decisions are affected by unaware considerations; but the advocates of innovations have often invoked the prospect of exceptional status as a reward for support of the innovations; and there are many evidences that support has in fact frequently been given an innovation for no better reason than that the innovation gives, or seems to give, status to the supporter. The Medici of medieval Florence can hardly be credited with having had a sincere and knowledgeable interest in the development of science; yet they often gave rather lavish support to scientific endeavors, evidently for much the same reason that they collected objects of art and built religious edifices.

In principle, if not in practice, the status appeal is a fairly simple one. It involves the implication, tacit or explicit, that while almost anyone can keep up with the Joneses—have a horse and buggy, go to the local church, believe in traditional medicine, invest in established enterprises, etc.—only an exceptional man will have the foresight and character to invest in an untried gadget, lend his name and prestige to a social reform, sponsor a proposed law, recognize the validity of a new theory of this or that, or otherwise come to the support of what the advocate is promoting; ergo, if you would be exceptional, leave the ranks of the conventional and do whatever it is the advocate wishes you to do. The status appeal is perhaps most fruitful when the prospective supporter is asked to make a heavy investment in time, money, or other values and the innovation offers very little in the way of direct gratifications. Such was the case with the early automobile. It was at once costly and had little value as a means of transportation; it was unreliable, difficult to operate, and troublesome to maintain, and neither so comfortable nor so fast as a horse and buggy. What, then, could be claimed for it? Its advocates (manufacturers, writers of articles in *Motor Age*, etc.) held out for the owner a variety of derived values, including that of the distinction of being the first, or at least one of the first, motorists in the community.

Specious Claims for the New

The appeal to distinctive status may not be effective, and at best it has only transitory value; for if and as the innovation becomes an established social element, it ceases to lend distinctiveness to those who have adopted it. The appeal to status does, however, initially have a quality of validity that is lacking in still another method that is widely used in promoting innovations— that of claiming values for an innovation that are largely, and often entirely, fictitious. Specious claims for established products or special brands of standard products are a commonplace in modern advertising. The specious claims for new devices, new ideas, proposals for social reform, etc., that are made by their advocates are usually somewhat more devious and less flamboyant and may perhaps be justified by the Machiavellian principle that people must be tricked into doing what is good for them. At any event, some innovations that have in due time become accepted and valued parts of the social system have been promoted by specious claims for them.

New religious cults and organizations, for example, are nearly always promoted through the claim of their providing the one and only way to eternal salvation; and although it is impossible to disprove that claim in any given instance, the multiplicity of such claims certainly casts doubt upon the validity of any one of them. Most proposed changes in organization—either reform of an existing organization or the establishment of a new form of organization—have been and currently are promoted on the basis of specious claims. Over and over through the centuries, the advocates of some new way to abolish prostitution have claimed that their particular way would solve forever the problems of sexual immorality, marital infidelity, venereal disease, and almost anything else considered to be a detriment to society. Although early agitation for the establishment of free public school education was based upon the theoretical assumption that a democratic society must have an enlightened citizenry, the values that its advocates claimed it would provide were personal, practical, and irrelevant.[11] Since, perhaps, it was expected that the middle classes would in actuality pay the major part of the cost of public school education while the children of the lower classes, being both more numerous and needy, would reap most of its actual benefits, appeal to the middle classes was on the basis of the claim that public school education would more than pay for its costs. As the school system grew, so ran the argument, the need for such other publicly supported agencies as jails, prisons, police, homes for indigents, etc., would diminish; for as men became educated, they would learn that honesty is the best policy and crime does not pay and would become so foresightful and industrious that neither they, their wives, nor their children would ever become public charges. Different, but equally specious, claims have since been made for every new proposal in educational organization or procedure—for compulsory as well as free education, for progressive education, and for the

[11] The utopian nature of the claims that were made by advocates for public school education, abolition of slavery, universal suffrage, and other changes in social life and organization are described by Arthur M. Schlesinger, Jr., in *The American as Reformer*, Harvard University Press, Cambridge, Mass., 1950. Currently advocates of urban renewal and slum clearance claim, as have their reforming predecessors, that it will work general wonders—*e.g.*, result in a marked lowering of juvenile and adult crime rates, increase domestic harmony, and lead to a more healthful and happier life for the residents of the new housing. Evidence indicates, however, that the actual welfare of people is not significantly improved by better housing. See John P. Dean, "The Myths of Housing Reform," *American Sociological Review*, vol. 14, pp. 281–288, April, 1949.

consolidated school. When Margaret Sanger undertook to advocate the use of birth control by the lower classes, she was motivated by the then popular eugenic thesis that the high birth rate of the lower classes was a threat to the biological quality of the population. The middle and upper classes, presumed to be biologically as well as socially superior, had already adopted birth control; and the resulting differential birth rate was favoring the inferior over the superior strains in the population. She did not, for very evident reasons, appeal to the lower classes on the grounds that their high birth rate was diluting the blood of the nation; rather, she argued the advantages of planned parenthood and talked, not about reducing the size of workers' families, but of the convenience and desirability of spacing the arrival of children. Currently, the advocates of space travel stress such specious and impressive reasons for pouring billions of dollars annually into our space program as the military advantages of gaining squatter's rights to the moon and the imperative need of finding new worlds to provide space for our excess population.

Since, as has been observed, the members of a society seldom evaluate their social elements in terms of their functional effectiveness, there is apparently little appeal in the claim that a new element will function more effectively than the old. Specious claims have tended, therefore, to be more impressive than valid ones and have been widely used by advocates in their efforts to secure abandonment of the old and acceptance of the new. Often the claim has been the grandiose one that the innovation will cure all— that the new, whatever it may be, will solve all problems and bring the acceptor health, wealth, and happiness, and whatever else it is he may think that he wants and does not have in sufficient degree. Cure-all claims have perhaps been most characteristic in the health field; and at one time or another almost everything has been offered as the certain way to general good health—mineral baths, raw foods, fresh air, nudity, this and that surgical procedure, and, of course, countless medications.

In some instances a cure-all claim has been the basis for a popular vogue that with the passage of years has turned out to have enduring social consequences, as the fashion for mineral baths, which was based on a cure-all claim, led into the present practice of bathing for reasons of cleanliness and the fresh-air vogue, similarly based, led to the modern realization that an airless room has deleterious effects on its occupants. In leading tentative adopters of innovations to expect far too much or the wrong things of them, some cure-all claims have, however, backfired. That has certainly been the case in America with the early claim that public school education would cure all the troubles of society. Public school education has gained complete social acceptance in America, and the public school has become an integral part of modern life; but so, too, has the claim that it would cure all the troubles of society. As a consequence, whenever doubt arises concerning the well-being of the American people, the cry almost invariably goes up that our school system has failed us. There may be a kind of social justice in the blaming of the schools, or more particularly schoolmen, for the persistence of crime, juvenile and adult, for individual incompetence, for the low level of public taste, and even for failure to eliminate the Russian threat to our peace of mind; for in spite of the experience of the past, schoolmen have not ceased to make cure-all claims for publicly supported and compulsory education.

Legitimatization of the Innovation

Every established social element is supported, as has been pointed out, by a relevant body of beliefs, attitudes, and values and by authority—the authority of the past, of God, or of persons in positions of leadership. Such support legitimatizes the social element and must be worn away before that element will be abandoned in favor of something new. Until the new has itself acquired support of this sort, its survival is always in doubt; and legitimatization of the new usually comes very slowly, often along with its gradual acceptance. In the case of the automobile, for example, acceptance and legitimatization were parallel processes. In 1900 there were exceedingly few automobiles in operation; and everything was, in a sense, against them: the horse was the accepted means of private transportation; roads and other facilities were designed for the convenience of the horse and buggy (or horse and wagon); the customs and laws governing the use of roads were those that had evolved to meet the needs of horse traffic; and everyone had come to take for granted, if not actively to appreciate, the smell of the stable, the clop of hooves, and the flies and sparrows that were integral parts of the horse complex. Into this the early automobile came as an unwelcome and distressing invader: it frightened horses and pedestrians; it produced noxious odors and shocking bangs; and it soon aroused the wrath of moralists, who charged that it was destructive of family life, religion, and everything else that men valued; and the resentment of politicians, who frequently attempted to legislate the automobile out of existence. In the course of thirty years the horse was relegated to back country roads; the automobile had gained general acceptance and become legitimatized as *the* proper mode of personal transportation. Legitimatization came bit by bit and involved such varied changes as political acceptance of the need for motor-worthy roads and highways, commercial acceptance of responsibility for the convenient provision of supplies and services, legal facilitation—as distinct from restriction—of ownership and use of the automobile, etc. Today, in fact, it is the horse that lacks legitimacy as anything but a recreational device.

The role of the advocate in establishing the legitimacy of an innovation seems to be quite varied.[12] When an advocate is an established authority in the field of the innovation, as has frequently been the case in the history of medicine, he may himself provide the innovation with an initial aura of respectability. Certainly an innovation that secures as advocate a recognized member of an accepted profession, occupational group, or other class of persons will have a greater advantage within that group than an innovation that is advocated only by an outsider. Thus it was in considerable measure because Sigmund Freud was himself a man of medicine and gathered around him disciples who also were physicians that Freudianism was able to become so rapidly legitimatized *as a science.* The fact that its advocates were, as they still mainly are, men of presumed scientific integrity gave rise to the social fiction that the Freudian theory of man's psychic nature has been proved and that the psychoanalytic method of treating mental disturbances is demonstrably superior to any other.

When, however, the advocate or advocates of an innovation have no prior claim to being authorities in the realm of that innovation, its legitimatization normally comes about with its acceptance. To this general rule there is one exception—that of an innovation that is advocated by charismatic authority. A political, religious, or other leader who is believed by his followers to possess extraordinary personal powers, usually attributed to divine endowment, can upon occasion use these imputed powers to sanction an innovation. The value of the innovation to those who adopt it then stems, not from the innovation itself, but from the person of the leader.

Charismatic authority achieves its highest form in the mass movement, political or otherwise, which is a sort of collective dream that is directed by a leader to whom charisma is imputed and that is acted upon, insofar as circumstances permit, by his followers. Usually little of enduring significance comes of mass movements; but incidental to the movement, some innovation may be adopted by participants in the movement simply because the leader has given it his benediction. Thus it was probably only because Hitler was believed by many Germans to be infallible that it was possible for the Nazis to undertake the program of systematic extermination of the Jews. The Jews had for centuries been a more or less despised and feared minority in Germany and had occasionally been subjected to violent repressive

[12] A classic example of the legitimatization of an innovation is the way in which British resistance, both professional and lay, to the acceptance of anesthesia, especially as an aid to childbirth, was broken when in 1853 Queen Victoria took chloroform to bear Prince Leopold. The news of this event created a violent controversy; but the prestige of the Queen overrode all doubts about the propriety and the safety of using an anesthetic, and within months painless childbirth and, more importantly, painless surgery became something of a fashion in Britain. See J. Thorwald, *The Century of the Surgeon,* Pantheon Books, New York, 1957, pp. 136–137.

measures; but deliberate extermination of them was so new and so very radical and violated traditional sentiments and values to such an extent that it would no doubt have been rejected by the German people had it not been given superhuman sanction by Hitler himself.

Mass movements centering about a leader with charismatic powers are comparatively rare; but it is not uncommon for an established leader or an upstart leader who has gained acceptance in an established position of leadership to be accorded some sort of charisma and thus empowered to exceed the normal functions of his position. It was, for example, enthusiasm for and faith in Napoleon that enabled him to put into effect in France the then novel practice of military conscription and such other innovations as the cutting of broad, straight streets through the historic clutter of Paris. Many of the programs of reform that were attempted during the early years of the Roosevelt administration, such as those of the National Recovery Act, were so radical that only the prevalence of the idea that F.D.R. could do no wrong made them at all acceptable to the American people. Minor instances of advocacy by those with charismatic authority are scattered through the history of medicine; and not a few business entrepreneurs have won such a reputation for infallibility that almost anything that they have sanctioned has been given a trial.

The Intrinsic Value of the Innovation

So far little has been said about the intrinsic values of innovations. Except in the case of simple mechanical devices, materials, productive procedures, and the like, the appeal of the advocate tends to be in terms of extrinsic rather than intrinsic values—in terms of values that are supposed to stem from accepting the innovation rather than values intrinsic in the innovation itself. No doubt the fact that the members of a society seldom think of the elements of their society in terms of intrinsic values is one reason why this is so. Another reason, and at times the major one, is that most innovations, even those of a mechanical character, must be greatly refined—i.e., developed —before they have any intrinsic value. Moreover, any innovation must be incorporated into a social complex, a process that may involve many related changes, before its intrinsic value can be realized.

The automobile provides a simple example of the development that is often necessary before the intrinsic value of an innovation is forthcoming. The critical invention consisted of the synthesis of a number of preexisting mechanical devices, each of which was in turn itself a synthesis of a number of preexisting elements—the traditional buggy, deprived of its shafts for the horse and equipped with a steering mechanism; the gasoline engine; gear and chain transmission of power to the rear wheels; the differential, permitting variable application of power to each rear wheel; and the gear shift, making possible variable ratios between engine and wheels. Just who made this synthesis of mechanical devices is still uncertain; a series of patent suits finally awarded the honor to a man named Seldon. The basic invention did not, however, lead immediately to a useful horseless carriage; it had to be developed through years of experimentation before a reasonably reliable and efficient transportation device came into being. Meanwhile, as has been mentioned, a favorable context of roads, services, social sentiments, etc., had to evolve before the device could be used with ease and convenience. During all this time the values of the automobile were mainly extrinsic.

Theoretically an advocate might begin his endeavor as a promoter, relying entirely upon appeals to extrinsic values for his innovation, and then, as he gained supporters, turn his efforts gradually toward development of the innovation. As the development proceeded, reliance on extrinsic values would decline until, as the process of advocacy approached its end and the innovation became a social element, intrinsic, functional values would be self-evident. In actuality, however, the processes of promotion and development are erratic and often interwoven, with sometimes the one and then the other taking precedence. In a given instance, the acceptance of an innovation may far outrun its development, as was recently the case with polio vaccine. The development of an innovation may, on the other hand, far outstrip its acceptance; such was the case, for example, with Fabian Socialism in England. Moreover, the rates of acceptance and development may vary through time. The automobile was developed more rapidly than it was accepted during the first two decades of this century; the next decade was that of rapid and wide acceptance; and in the years since, development and acceptance (now of such devices as independent wheel suspension, power brakes, and automatic gear shift) have run hand in hand.

DEVELOPMENT

The development of an innovation may involve no more than its refinement and perfection. More often, perhaps, it involves a succession of subsequent innovations. A modern cotton gin is little more than an enlarged, powered version of the device invented by Eli Whitney a century and a half ago. A modern steam engine, on the other hand, does not even embody the principle of the original steam engine; its development involved a number of innovations of a magnitude equal to that of the original steam engine itself.

The circumstances that in the eighteenth century fostered the effort to secure a new source of power have already been discussed. The first significant contribution to the solution of this problem was Savery's steam pump, in which the vacuum produced by the cooling of steam in a vessel was used to suck water from a well. Shortly thereafter, Newcomen applied this vacuum principle to the obtaining of traction power, by using in place of a vessel a cylinder in which a piston moved; as the steam cooled and created a vacuum in the cylinder, the piston was sucked into the cylinder. The device was, at its best, crude and inefficient. Among its other limitations were the time that it took for the steam to cool in the cylinder and the great heat loss that was occasioned by the need to chill the cylinder in preparation for the next stroke. Nearly fifty years later, during which considerable use was made of the Newcomen engine, James Watt solved both problems by adding to the cylinder a separate steam-cooling chamber; and it was his engine that became the powerhouse of the industrial revolution. The development of the steam engine had, however, only just begun. Watt himself made many refinements and some rather major improvements on his engine. Subsequently others devised higher and still higher pressure engines. With the introduction of the compound engine, in which the steam from a high-pressure cylinder is scavenged by a lower-pressure cylinder, vastly greater fuel efficiency was obtained. In the course of time so many innovations occurred that the modern turbine engine, such as is used in the generation of electricity for domestic and industrial use, has only steam in common with the original innovation. Moreover, as the steam engine developed, it provided the basis for a multitude of other inventions and developments— such as the steamship and the railroad. To bring all this about required the efforts not only of many ingenious mechanics and technicians, but also of many equally ingenious and persistent advocates.

Innovations in social organization frequently build one upon another with the result that the latest form may bear as little resemblance to the original as the steam turbine does to Newcomen's vacuum engine. The modern corporate form of economic organization, for example, began in modern Western society as an idea borrowed, or rediscovered, from ancient Rome. The Romans had devised, or perhaps themselves borrowed, the legal concept of a body corporate with a common treasury and with a legal personality separate and distinct from those of the actual individuals who formed and operated it and who as individuals were not responsible for its actions. Such in Roman law were the various municipal, religious, industrial, and trading associations known as *universitates*. The Roman concept of the *universitas personarum* reappeared in England during the sixteenth century as the legal basis for the organizational form within which traders could band together for their common good without any one's losing his rights as a private individual. It was another century, however, before financial participation in such associations through transferable certificates—stock—appeared, and still later before the corporation was granted such further rights and responsibilities of real individuals as that of bringing suit and being sued. In the modern corporation of today the Roman concept of the corporate body still exists, but the form of organization of the modern corporation and its place in the social system are very different even from the form and position of the trading association of sixteenth-century England.

Simplification and Refinement

In many instances, the development of an innovation involves no further innovations of a major order but a great many minor ones. The development of the automobile involved only four major innovations in basic structure— the self-starter, the low-pressure tire, the independent front-wheel suspension, and the automatic transmission. In addition, however, it involved a large number of slight changes that have made the unreliable and inefficient device of 1910 into the highly reliable and comfortable, but still inefficient device preferred by Americans today. Some of these small changes came about through innovation in other technological complexes, such as the invention of new metals and the invention of mechanically controlled cutting tools. Others came from within the automobile industry itself; such was the case, for example, with the connecting rod and bearing assembly that made possible compact eight-cylinder motors.

Development frequently consists, at least in technology, of progressive simplification of design, sometimes by a reduction in the number of parts, but more often perhaps by the making of each part less complicated, functionally more effective, or both. In recent years, simplification of design has often stemmed from improved materials. The frame of the early airplane, for example, was constructed out of wood, wire, and bolts and was covered with canvas. The frame of the modern airplane is simpler in the sense that it is all metal and is integrated into one continuous unit; as a result it is no longer necessary to check a large number of wires, their fastenings, spar joints, and canvas junctions before venturing off the ground. It has, of course, been developments in metallurgy and design engineering that have made possible the unitary structure of the frame of the modern airplane.

The operation or use of an innovation may be greatly simplified through improvements in design, and its attractiveness to potential adopters may be thus increased. Simplification may be accomplished, however, by the addition to the innovation of control or other supplementary devices. The self-starter, for example, was an accessory addition to the automobile that greatly simplified its use and that, incidentally, reduced the hazard of motoring. Before the introduction of the self-starter, only a fairly strong and agile man could get the motor running, and that always with some chance of a broken arm. The subsequent additions of the automatic choke and the automatic transmission have greatly reduced the amount of skill and knowledge necessary to drive an automobile, if not to drive it well. Anyone who can remember to turn on a switch and press down the accelerator can get a modern motorcar into motion.

The simplification of nonmechanical innovations occurs in a variety of ways. A new art form ordinarily is stripped of its subtleties and reduced to its fundamental, if stark, elements as it becomes widely adopted. It is in this way that the vulgar versions of music, pictorial arts, furniture design, and even architectural forms come into being. New ideas, too, may be stripped of their qualifications, complexities, and nuances and thereby be so much simplified that they can be adopted easily, if not acted upon. As it became popular, the original doctrine of Freudianism was so much simplified that probably about all that is now generally understood is that it is the theory that human conduct is motivated by unconscious and mainly sexual forces. Even scholars and scientists tend to simplify the ideas with which they deal, especially earlier ideas that have more or less gone out of fashion. As a consequence, a history of their discipline may be little more than a compilation of clichés couched in erudite language.

The whole of a philosophical system may in similar manner be rendered over the years into a collection of rules and precepts. This is undoubtedly what happened to the original pronouncements of Confucius, to early Christian doctrine, and to the social philosophy which gave rise to parliamentary forms of government. The framers of the Constitution of the United States probably had a fairly comprehensive understanding of that philosophy and of the adverse experiences with monarchial government that it was proposed to correct. Perhaps some modern political theorists and a few of the Supreme Court justices are equally aware of the philosophical and experiential background that led to our form of government; but it is perfectly clear that no President since Woodrow Wilson has had a comprehensive understanding of the history and philosophy of representative government and that no practical politician or political bureaucrat would bother to study it. They are all far too busy trying to make the system operate.

Organizational innovations and some mechanical and other technological innovations are not so much simplified during their development as refined. In theory, refinement consists of the progressive elimination of faults. In actuality, it frequently means the opposite to structural simplification, particularly in the case of forms of organization. In technology the process of refinement is sometimes spoken of as "taking the bugs out" of the device or process. In the development of a new form of organization, the "bugs" are unanticipated difficulties that must be resolved by modification of the new form of organization. Refinement is always accomplished piecemeal, and it involves a minimum of innovative endeavor. Moreover, the procedure is empirical; as the innovation is put into use, first this and then that limitation, failure, or other deficiency makes its appearance and is more or less promptly corrected by an ingenious mechanic, competent technician, or in the case of a new form of organization, an imaginative administrator.

With innovations in organization, formal or informal, refinement involves the piecemeal abandonment of rules or procedures that prove faulty, the making of new rules or procedures to correct for deficiencies in the new form, etc. In the modern world, all forms of organization are continually undergoing refinement, if not because of the appearance of internal inadequacies or inefficiencies, then because of changes in the context that necessitate adaptive modifications of the organization. Tangible evidence of changes of this order is provided by the unending stream of legislation and the constant flow of administrative orders by which political jurisdictions—municipal, county, state, and Federal—endeavor to keep up with the times, if not advance beyond the times. Business and other formal organizations, too, currently keep refining their organizational structures and procedures; and a comparable but more subtle process of refinement seems to go on in less formally organized groups, such as the family.

Something of the nature of the refinment process as it occurs in innovations in organization can be gathered from the history of Mormonism, the development of which is well documented. Joseph Smith was the innovator, and his innovation consisted of a divine revelation that became manifest as the Book of Mormon, a mixture of elements of the Old and New Testaments, with some additions and interpretations that were distinctly new. This innovation provided the ideological basis for the establishment of a theocratic community in which the forms of organization, in accordance with Smith's interpretation of the mandate of the Book of Mormon, were initially patterned on Old Testament life, communal and other tribal practices of American Indians (with which, presumably, Smith had some acquaintance), and the polygamous family. For a time Smith served as the sole advocate for his proposed theocratic society and both promoted and developed it, the first colony being established in New York State. As the number of converts grew, advocatory functions were assigned in part to a group of elders, and missionaries were sent out to make converts and establish colonies. The movement met with great opposition and generated a good deal of internal dissension; and it is clear that Smith was a better prophet than organizer—a better innovator than advocate. After many vicissitudes, including expulsion of the home colony from a succession of locations, Smith was murdered and leadership fell upon Brigham Young, perhaps the most energetic and resourceful of the Twelve Apostles of the Church. It was during the thirty years of Young's leadership that the Mormons moved to Utah, brought the arid lands under cultivation, developed the salient elements of the quasi-communal form of social life that they follow today, made their peace with the United States government, and were welcomed into the larger society. Young's role in all this development was considerable, for upon him as an individual rested for years the final determination of administrative policy; it was his responsibility to resolve conflicts within the community, to decide which of various alternative solutions to arising problems should be followed, and to provide inspiration as well as guidance to Mormon society. The measure of his success is the fact that he did bring the Mormon Church and the Mormon system of social life through its formative period so well that it has survived as a distinctive religion and social system.[13]

Contextual Adaptation

Since most social elements function in a larger context, the value of an innovation ultimately depends, not only upon the innovation itself, but also upon the context in which it operates; and very often an innovation cannot be widely adopted until adaptive changes have occurred in the context in which it will function. The initial impact of the new is, thus, an increase rather than a resolution of incongruence and a reduction of the functional effectiveness of the social unit. Clearly such was the case with the automobile. Even had the automobile been from the outset a reliable and efficient mechanism, its value as a transportation device would have been very small. As has been observed, not until road systems designed specifically for it were evolved, fuel and other services developed, and a variety of social practices and attitudes changed could the automobile actually become functionally superior to the horse and buggy. Meanwhile, the automobile had dysfunctional consequences—it progressively rendered roads, barns, stables, horses, etc., obsolete; even today it continues to make highways inadequate within a year or two after they have been built. The dysfunctional repercussions of the adoption of the automobile were many and varied, and in addition to the effects on highways, many are still uncorrected. One, now forgotten, may serve to illustrate how extensive the incongruencies that are brought about by the adoption of an innovation may be. The automobile and the truck eventually replaced the horse as the major means of local and cross-country transport of people and goods. (They have also to a considerable extent displaced the railroad and electric car for the same uses, but that is still another story.) At the same time, the tractor came to replace the horse for plowing and cultivating on the farm and for earth moving and other operations in heavy construction. With the sharp decline in horses there came, inevitably, an equal decline in the demand for feed hay and grains and for pasturage for brood mares and colts. In effect, the oil field was replacing the farm as a source of power; and it was this transition from farm to oil field which, as much as anything else, resulted in the sharp decline in national agricultural income that began shortly after World War I, a decline that was arrested by complex political controls and subsidies, which have in turn led to a variety of new problems—such as the problem of agricultural

[13] See Thomas F. O'Dea, *The Mormons*, The University of Chicago Press, Chicago, 1957.

surpluses—and to further changes—such as the development of industrial agriculture.

The rate and effectiveness of the changes in context that are inaugurated by an innovation are a fair index to the state of the social component that is involved and in some instances to the state of the entire social system. Thus the tendency for contemporary England to be technologically static by comparison with some countries of Europe and with America is evidenced by the fact that the English have made few, and these limited, adaptations to their many automobiles; their road system is still primitive, their supply and service agencies are still antiquated, and modern motorists are still dependent upon the same old inns, hotels, teashops, etc., that may have served their grandparents well but are inappropriate to travel by car.

Development versus Innovation

The development of an innovation normally waits upon the innovation's having gained at least tentative acceptance, if not by the society at large, then at least by those directly concerned—converts, scholars, scientists, technicians, or business entrepreneurs. In many instances, as has been seen, the primary task of the advocate is to secure backing for the innovation, financial or otherwise, in order to begin developing it. This is most frequently the case with technological innovations that have commercial application, for either in order to be made manifest or in order to be empirically tested, the new idea may require financing beyond the means of the innovator himself. Fulton, for example, conceived a way of using steam power in ships, but until he was provided with considerable financial support, he could not convert the idea into an actual steamship. The idea for the modern aircraft jet engine was initially made manifest by its inventor with the use of facilities lent to him by the Royal Air Force and materials largely salvaged from military dumps and at the cost of a few thousand pounds advanced to him by faithful, if doubtful, supporters; but the development of his invention into the effective and economic power source it now is required the investment of millions of dollars, pounds, and marks (the development was begun by the German military), the labor of countless engineers and other technicians, and the equipment and organization of the aircraft-engine industry in the United States as well as abroad. Many advocates were involved in mobilizing all the social resources that proved necessary for the development of the jet engine, the first being German scientists who saw in the jet a device that might assure victory to Germany in World War II and who finally, and belatedly as it turned out, converted members of the German General Staff to its support. After the effective demonstration during the war of the superiority of the jet over the reciprocating engine, and not until then, did American and British companies, subsidized by their governments, shift their attention from the production of the traditional engine to the development of this new one. The invention and development of the rocket followed an almost identical course: initially made manifest at slight monetary cost by its inventor, it was first but indifferently developed by the Germans as a weapon to use in World War II; and only when the war had ended and the cold war with Russia begun, did first Russia and then the United States make further development of the rocket a matter of national policy.

Once an innovation has gained initial social acceptance, its development is more or less assured, assuming, of course, that it proves to have intrinsic value; and those who contribute to its development operate in a social climate quite different from that of the innovator. They are socially—and usually also financially—encouraged to apply themselves to the task and do not need to struggle against social skepticism and disapproval. Moreover, as has been seen, the task of simplifying and refining a base design is a piece-meal one; and each problem encountered may be solved in relatively short order. Consequently those who develop an innovation, unlike innovators, need not work on faith alone; they can measure their achievements.

For a combination of reasons, therefore, the development of an innovation can be accomplished by men of a character quite different from those who innovate and in an organizational context that would only inhibit innovative endeavor. The development of an innovation is a creative process only in the sense that the end product differs in degree from the original; and unlike innovation, development is purchasable and can be organized and more or less systematized, with a division of labor. In modern technology it may even be programmed with some success; i.e., the development may be planned, and the various specific problems farmed out to individuals or sub-organizations.

The distinction between the innovative and the developmental processes is well illustrated in the history of aseptic surgery. Three major innovations were involved, each achieved by a different man. The first was Semmelweis's idea of what he designated "contact infection." He, unlike all the rest of the medical fraternity of his time, had perceived that puerperal fever was somehow related to maternity hospitals, a deduction from the fact that maternity patients attended only by midwives had little or none of it. For several years he floundered about trying to ascertain the cause of the very high rates of fever—and death from it—in those wards that were serviced by surgeons. His first conclusion was that the responsible agent was a miasma —simply a euphemism for something unknown—that generated over time in and around surgical wards, and that the solution was to use temporary hospitals and abandon them at the first sign of fever. Later, in 1848, he decided, quite correctly as it turned out, that the surgeons themselves were somehow responsible for introducing the fever by contact with their patients. Actually, what was happening was that surgeons, often coming directly from their investigation of cadavers, were bringing with them into the maternity wards bacteria that they transferred to their patients while examining them. Since bacteria were then unknown, Semmelweis had nothing to go on but empirical experience. He did, however, institute a regime of hand washing with chlorinated water that considerably reduced the rate of infection.

The second innovation in the history of aseptic surgery was accomplished by Pasteur as a rather incidental outcome of his efforts to save the French wine industry. Vintners had been losing much of their wine as a consequence of spoilage in casks; investigating, Pasteur traced the cause to a microorganism and thereupon discovered the existence of bacteria (a fact that had long been obscured by the prevailing belief in "spontaneous generation" of organic life) as an infectious agent in wine. It was the English surgeon Lister who then put together the contact-infection idea of Semmelweis and the discovery of the existence of bacteria by Pasteur, plus his own experiences with surgical patients, to reach the conclusion that infections following surgery were caused by bacteria introduced into the surgical wound. This, then, was the third basic innovation.

The development of aseptic surgery followed piecemeal upon this innovation. Lister himself thought that bacteria were introduced into surgical incisions from the air, and he endeavored to protect the patient from infection by spraying the air of the surgical arena with carbolic acid. Then in rather rapid succession came a series of small advances—identification of specific strains of bacteria; discovery that bacteria are not air-borne but are to be found on the surgeon's hands, his instruments, etc.; the invention of the rubber surgical glove; the discovery that heat is the best means of sterilizing instruments, bandages, sutures, etc.; and the eventual reduction of these various developments to systematic procedure.

Semmelweis, Pasteur, and Lister made their innovations with little encouragement and in opposition to the traditional values, beliefs, and knowledge of the medical profession of their times. Those who made their contributions to the development of aseptic surgery, on the other hand, including Lister, worked under relatively favorable circumstances, with the encouragement of medical colleagues and with considerable prior assurance that their efforts would be rewarded. Moreover, their individual contributions to that development were usually accomplished in comparatively quick order; the man who contributed the surgeons' rubber gloves, for example, hit upon the idea simply because he wished to protect his fiancée, a surgical nurse, from the hand-disfiguring effects of the harsh soaps and carbolic acid that were then being used to cleanse the hands before surgery.

The Organization of Development

The distinction between the innovative and developmental processes is of more than analytical interest. Upon it hinges much of the current concern of scientists over the progressive organization by industry, government, and academic institutions of the work of scientific research. Many factors, including the rising costs of research in the very complex problems of today, have tended to draw an increasing proportion of those trained in the sciences into developmental work of one sort or another (what is usually described as applied science) and away from individual quest for new knowledge—i.e., away from innovative endeavor.

The highly practical concerns of business and industry and the equally practical interests of military and other governmental organizations have led to the establishment of a great variety of commercial research agencies. Some are dependent parts of business or industrial organizations; some are themselves businesses offering the services of scientists to industry and government. In either case, they provide financially rewarding and secure positions to scientists and demand in return relatively routine performance. No one doubts that much of the work done in such agencies contributes in one way or another to the improvement of industrial products, to increased efficiency in merchandising, to refinements in the internal organization of business and industrial organizations, etc. The concern stems from fear that all such research is a consumer of scientific knowledge but not a contributor to it—which is one way of describing the fact that in such organizations scientists are engaged in development rather than innovation.

Probably not even the pure or basic scientists would be distressed by the use of scientists as developers by industrial and commercial agencies were it not that the universities, the source of scientific personnel, have meanwhile tended to change from centers of individual and independent scientific inquiry into financially subsidized centers of scientific development. The transition is only partial, but the trend in this direction is very strong and does not seem to be subject to correction.

In a later chapter there will be occasion to investigate some of the developments in organization that currently seem to jeopardize the dynamic character of our society. One of these is the decline in our universities of a social climate conducive to individual initiative in matters of scholarly investigation and scientific research. Many factors have of recent years contributed to this decline and to the emergence of organizational characteristics and of faculty values and sentiments that encourage at least the younger men to become research entrepreneurs or members of research teams. Whether they become one or the other, they are inevitably embroiled in organized activities that are at best simply developmental in character and at worst, and most commonly perhaps in the social sciences, no more than intellectual rituals. External factors that have contributed to this change have been the provision through governmental agencies, mainly military, of large sums of money for research under contract and the rise of large private foundations, such as the Ford Foundation, that subsidize research of one sort or another. Inevitably and for fairly evident reasons, both the governmental agencies and the foundations prefer the organized project that is directed by a scientist of recognized stature to that of an individual who can say for himself only that he has a hunch that if he were to have free time, he might be able to discover something as yet unknown.

As the weight of research funds has turned the balance away from innovative endeavors in favor of those of a developmental nature, more and more scientists have abandoned any slight hope that they might have had of doing something creative and have taken rewarding refuge under the organizational protection of well-financed team research. In a position of this sort, a scientist is free from the strains of innovative endeavor—the opposition of society, the uncertainty of success, the need to drive himself through countless failures to another and still another try; and in such a position he is rewarded both financially and in terms of recognition.

The diversion of trained scientists into developmental work even in the universities may not, as many scientists currently fear, lead to an actual decline in the number of men who devote themselves to pure science, to innovative endeavor. As has been noted, innovators have always labored under comparatively adverse circumstances, even in the universities; and it may well be that the innovative person actually thrives under adversity. What may be happening is that many men who a few decades ago would have entered some conventional occupation and lived out a conventional life are now being trained as scientists and simply find in organized developmental work a substitute for dentistry, routine medical practice, the law, or business. Today, as a few decades ago, it may only be those socially deviant individuals who have happened to acquire the personal characteristics making for innovative endeavor and who have happened also to become scientists who are both willing and able to use their scientific knowledge to extend that knowledge. As was observed in the preceding chapter, there is no occupation of innovator, no subculture of innovators, and hence no training school for men of innovative leanings. Thus it may well be that the employment in organized developmental work of a large proportion of the many young men who are currently being trained as scientists does not of itself deprive society of potential innovators.

chapter *Adoption and*
the Adopter

To the advocate of an innovation, the people to whom he
appeals for support may seem unbelievably stupid or else
completely indifferent to their own welfare. Whereas he is
convinced that the innovation has valuable potentialities—
that its promotion and development will yield a good commercial profit; that its adoption will bring the adopter improved health, wealth, or happiness; or that its acceptance
will be of inestimable benefit to society at large—almost
everyone he approaches turns a deaf ear. Experts, if experts
be involved, may say that it cannot be done and would not
be worth doing if it could; bankers may refuse to lend financial
support to an untried and unproved device; political or other
authorities may smile tolerantly at his folly; the public at large
may evidence a massive unconcern; and even his intimates
may in time lose faith in his judgment and the prospects of
eventual success. If what he is advocating is a radical departure
from the established, the chances of eventual success are, in
fact, exceedingly small; and if success does come, it may be
too late to profit him personally. Many an advocate has
exhausted himself in the effort to overcome the lethargy or
active resistance of his fellow men to an innovation that they
have ultimately accepted and found useful. Even when he is
advocating a proved device or procedure, years of patient
and persevering endeavor may be required to wear away the
barriers to acceptance. Of her three decades of effort to get the
hill people of North Carolina to accept the simplest of modern
medical techniques and her own services as a physician, Dr.
Sloop said, "It was like rowing upstream with a straw for a
paddle."[1]

Resistance to anything new, however frustrating to the ad-

[1] M. T. Sloop and L. Blythe, *Miracle in the Hills*, McGraw-
Hill Book Company, New York, 1953, p. 118.

vocate, is a normal expression of the fact that the members of society are for the most part creatures of society, not that they are innately stupid or indifferent to their welfare. The universal tendency for men to resist changes of any sort has often and for long prevented the adoption of functionally valuable innovations; but it has also, and perhaps quite as often, prevented men from destroying themselves by adopting malfunctional devices or procedures. Many battles and some wars have been lost because military leaders have refused to try out a new weapon or strategy; on the other hand, many lives have no doubt been saved for the very same reason. Innovators and advocates have offered the world some potentially disastrous proposals, and in spite of men's inherent resistance to things new, some have been put into practice that have proved to be disastrous. The normal resistance of men to change is, moreover, more than a protection against misadventure; it is one manifestation of the forces which bind the individual to society and make social life possible, without which there would be only chaos. If men were willing and able to change their social elements whenever an alternative were provided, they would in fact have no social system, since the essence of a social system is consensus and stability.

The attachment of the members of a society to the elements of their particular social system and their consequent tendency to resist any proposal of change can be described in a number of ways—in terms of individual socialization into the values, sentiments, and usages of the society; in terms of status or role involvement or some other order of "ego involvement"; in terms of custom, tradition, or sheer habituation; etc. In terms of the individual who resists adopting something new, the forces that impel his resistance may be roughly classified as emotional, moral, aesthetic, rational, and self-protective.

COVERT BASES FOR RESISTANCE

Active resistance to change will usually be justified in some more or less practical terms. Even a stolid and, to the sophisticate, unthinking peasant will find reasons for his refusal to try out a new tool, seed, fertilizer, or mode of cultivation. The new, he may insist, will only poison the soil, produce inferior grain, bring down the wrath of God, or cause his wife to bear only girls. A modern businessman may point to prior ventures with new things that failed to produce a profit; a military man, to the fact that the entire weight of military authority runs counter to what is proposed. A political bureaucrat will have a body of rules and precedents to justify his conservatism; a scholar, the whole of history to protect him from new ideas. And for everyone, primitive, peasant, and modern layman and expert alike, there is always as the final and ultimate defense against anything new some version or other of the thesis that what was good enough for father is good enough for son.

The actual basis for much of man's resistance to change, however, is the covert, nonverbalizable responses (emotions, mood tones, feeling states, tastes, etc.) that have been acquired through socialization and that are in concordance with the various elements of the *status quo*. In analyzing social structure and the operations of a fairly stable social system, the covert aspects of the personalities of the members of the society can be taken for granted; they can be treated simply as intervening variables, aspects of the psychological mechanism of socially determined conduct. In analyzing social change, however, these "intervening variables" cannot be ignored; for when there is pressure on people to change their conduct, covert aspects of personality become factors in determining conduct. Food tastes, for example, are simply the internalized aspects of the culturally determined food preferences and practices of the members of the society. Thus in the normal operations of a society the fact that food tastes are highly specific and fixed can be taken for granted. When a new food makes its appearance, however, these covert factors of taste cannot be ignored, for they then play an active role in determining the acceptance or rejection of the new food. If the new food accords with established food tastes, it will, other factors being favorable, be accepted; if it violates or offends established taste values, it will be rejected. The same is true with anything new; covert aspects of individual personality enter into its acceptance or rejection.

Since the covert aspects of the human personality can be known only by indirection—by inference from observed overt conduct, verbal or otherwise—they have been the object of a good deal of metaphysical speculation, in which the speculative system, such as Freudianism, predetermines what will be found. Moreover, the linguistic symbols that are used in attempts to designate one's own covert experiences and to explain the presumed covert conduct of others have no objective referents and are therefore poor tools for scientific analysis. Since, however, covert factors do enter into the acceptance of and resistance to innovations, they cannot be excluded from analysis of social change.

Fear of the Unfamiliar

Apparently the emotional and other covert attributes of the individual personality normally harmonize with the established conditions of social life to the end that the individual is covertly as well as overtly more or less well-adjusted. It may not be that a slave cherishes his lowly position and would not prefer to change status with his master, that a peasant positively enjoys his labors on the land, that a primitive does not at times grow weary of his circumscribed little world, or that a mechanic standing at his bench may not sometimes envy a clerk sitting at his desk. The adjustment of the individual is always less than perfect; and in some times and places, such as our own, it is far from perfect. Most men are, however, no doubt for the most part in covert concordance with their society and their particular place in it. Were this not so, resistance to social change would be the exception rather than the rule.

The member of a modern society who is more or less adjusted to modern social practices may be horrified by accounts of the elaborate scarification and distortion of the body that has been customary in many primitive societies, the butchering of maidens on the altar of the sun-god that occurred annually in ancient Mayan society, the combat to death of the Roman gladiators, the torture with which the priests of the Inquisition destroyed their victims, the punishment through mutilation that is still administered to criminals in some parts of the world, etc. To the modern mind the life of an individual in a society with any such practices must have been fraught with constant fear; but the evidence, such as it is, suggests that in its time and place each of these and many other practices that are from the modern point of view repugnant and horrifying have simply been taken for granted, even as men today, after some qualms, take for granted the possibility of an atomic holocaust and proceed about their personal affairs in disregard of it. One does not imagine that the virgin sacrificed to the sun-god, the heretic broken on the rack, the gladiator ripped open by his opponent, or the criminal deprived of his nose or hand felt less pain than a modern person would; but it is evident that these, like countless other conditions of life, such as decimating famine and recurrent plague, were accepted as normal hazards of life; otherwise, something would have been done to modify them.

Men always and everywhere accept with considerable complacence what is familiar to them, whatever it may be and however disagreeable it may seem to members of another, different society, apparently because almost anything familiar is less disturbing emotionally than is something unknown. It is an oversimplification to say that men fear the unknown; it would be better, perhaps, to say that what is designated as fear (or apprehension, dread, or the like) are those emotional disturbances that are induced by contemplation of or exposure to what is unknown or unfamiliar and hence unpredictable. That contemplation of the unknown normally induces distress is evidenced by the universality of man-made explanations for what man does not or cannot know—i.e., of beliefs, superstitions, and related symbolic constructs regarding final causation, life after death, the nature of the universe, etc. Sociologically, the function of such beliefs, etc., is social control of the conduct of the individual members of the society. Psychologically, on the other hand, their function is to reassure the individual members by making the unknown understandable.

Apparently a good deal of the initial resistance to any innovation stems directly from the fact that even in prospect what has not been tried and hence is unknown arouses apprehension. Fear of a given innovation may be no more than a vague and generalized response to the unfamiliar, as might perhaps be the case with a proposal for a new form of human relationship; or it may be a fairly specific response or expressible as a specific response, as might be the case with a new form of transportation. The railroad, the steamship, the automobile, and the airplane has each in its turn occasioned considerable fear, or at least expressions of fear, that it would sicken or destroy those who traveled by it; and perhaps if one were able to go far enough back into human history, one might find the men of antiquity expressing similar sentiments regarding the sailing barge, the chariot, the sedan chair, and the saddled donkey.

Fear of the unknown can even override the certainty of acute physical pain. In the early days of anesthesia, surgical patients were almost as hard to convince that they should be anesthetized during an operation as were the surgeons that they should use anesthetics, although the patient's only alternative was to be bound to the operating table so that his agonized struggles would not interfere with the surgeon's work. Evidently the known prospect of pain was for many less frightening than the unknown experience of chemically induced unconsciousness. Today, on the other hand, the exact reverse is the case: anesthesia is the known, if only by indirection, and acute pain, rarely experienced today except by accident, the unknown that is feared. The history of medicine provides many examples of resistance to new techniques that has stemmed in considerable part from simple fear of consequences unknown. Smallpox vaccination aroused a variety of apprehensions—that the prevention would be worse than the disease; that the introduction of cowpox into the human body would somehow make the individual cowlike; and that to thwart nature in this artificial way would be to court retributive action from nature.[2] (Incidentally, the idea that what is natural—or, alternatively, decreed by God—must not be interfered with by man is perhaps the most common rationalization for apprehension regarding things that are unfamiliar.) Blood transfusion, which has saved countless lives, met initially with similar fear, although the antithetical procedure of bloodletting, which unquestionably brought premature death to tens of thousands of patients, had been accepted for centuries.

Fear of the unknown has historically tied many peoples to the little area of the globe known to them and has until modern times retarded exploration and settlement of the underpopulated parts of the world. It was fear of the unknown parts of the world, a fear that the great arctic explorer Vilhjalmur Stefansson devoted his life to breaking down, that hampered

[2] For these and many other justifications that were advanced for resisting vaccination against smallpox, see Bernard J. Stern, *Should We Be Vaccinated?* Harper & Brothers, New York, 1927.

Columbus's advocacy of the idea of finding a westward water route to the Orient, and that for so long kept the continent of Africa dark. Fear has often prevented the use of particular plants as food; thus in parts of the United States the tomato was feared as poisonous as little as a century ago. Even such a minor change from the familiar as the use of aluminum in place of iron in cooking pots and pans has aroused considerable apprehension; housewives were afraid that the new metal would contaminate the food cooked in it, and for some time after the introduction of aluminum even medical men and other experts were doubtful about its use in kitchenware.

Moral Sentiments, Principles, and Precepts

With innovations in interpersonal relations, in social organization, and in philosophical ideas, fear of the unknown tends to be merged with apprehension concerning the moral consequences of adopting the new. Here resistance usually has as its rationale the claim that the new violates and so jeopardizes a valued moral principle or precept, one that is considered essential to the survival of the social system or of mankind in general.[3] Even today, the Catholic Church resists birth control on the grounds that contraception violates the sanctity of life. Other moral grounds that have at one time or another been used as the justification for rejection of social changes include the divine right of kings, the inalienable (and in the United States, constitutional) right of the individual freely to pursue his own interests, the integrity of the family, the welfare of the state, and the purity of the race. The latter is still the grounds used to justify protest against the efforts to desegregate the public schools of our Southern states, against legalization of miscegenation, and against other pressures to equalize the status and opportunities of whites and Negroes. The moral principle that a man's home is his castle was for long invoked in protest against the progressive encroachments by political authority upon the right of a householder to determine what could be done in his home. Such constraints upon the traditional rights of the householder as legal prohibition of private outhouses and of the raising of chickens and pigs in the family establishment, legal enforcement of building codes, and countless other restrictions that were necessitated by urbanization and rising standards of health and safety have been strongly resisted on the same moral grounds.

It was to a considerable extent the moral principle or sentiment that woman's rightful social role is that of housewife and mother, a sentiment derived from the patriarchal family system, that led to so much opposition to the extension of the franchise to women during the early part of this

[3] See Milton Rokeach, *The Open and Closed Mind: Investigations into the Nature of Belief Systems and Personality Systems*, Basic Books, Inc., Publishers, New York, 1960.

century. Against much resistance women had been entering into business and some professional activities and had gradually been gaining some of the economic rights—to property, in contractual arrangements, etc.—that had long been the prerogative of the male. The proposal and agitation for the right to vote, which reached serious proportions in the United States about 1910, seems to have triggered and given a target to the resentment that had been generated by all the preceding changes in the social status of women.[4] At any event, there was a great outcry against the idea of extending the franchise to women; and much of it was couched in moralistic language: the sanctity of the home would be destroyed, the innate purity of women would be sullied, and children would be neglected and let run wild should women leave hearth and home for voting booth. (Advocates of the extension of the franchise to women, on the other hand, claimed that women's vote would be pure and incorruptible and political activities therefore improved.) Familistic moral sentiments were also offended by the advocacy, first in one state and then another, of liberalization of the divorce laws. Divorce and sin were often equated by preachers and other moral leaders; and it was widely charged that easy divorce would encourage sexual promiscuity, bastardy, and the general disruption of family life.

The moral principle that life is sacred and that the individual has an inalienable right to live is a fairly recent concept. In most times and places in the past little value was placed on life as such; slaves, wives, and children were chattels that might, in theory at least, be mistreated at will, if not outright destroyed, by their masters, husbands, or fathers. The development of this particular moral principle was one of the major accomplishments of early modern society; and it is now often invoked in protest against a variety of proposed social reforms, such as the sterilization of imbeciles, the castration of rapists, and legalization of abortion. A rather distorted appeal to the same principle was made by those who for long resisted the development and enforcement of pure food and drug laws that were intended to protect the members of society from inadvertently ruining their health or causing their death.

Resistance to innovations on moral grounds stems from the fact that in every society the members are more or less effectively socialized into the feeling, as well as the mental set, that the established forms of conduct, especially those of an organizational nature, are the only ones that are right and proper. In a sense, the right and proper has become emotionally incorporated into the personality—an integral part of the self. Sex morality, filial loyalty, parental responsibility, self-reliance, and comparable terms refer fully as much to emotional attachments to established forms of conduct

[4] Eleanor Flexner, *Century of Struggle: The Women's Rights Movement in the United States,* Harvard University Press, Cambridge, Mass., 1959.

as to the conduct itself.[5] Change in conduct may therefore result in emotional disturbances, for it would seem that in general it is easier to acquire a new form of conduct than to acquire a new emotional set. Thus a modern middle-class American may establish his aged parent in one of the comparatively new facilities for the aged—such as a commercial nursing home—for the very practical reason that his parent cannot be comfortably accommodated in his home. In doing so, he may violate his deeply embedded sense of filial responsibility; emotionally he may feel that the right and proper thing to do is to take his parent, as was the old-fashioned way, into his home, although intellectually he knows that to do so would jeopardize the welfare of his wife, his children, and himself and might not even be conducive to the welfare of his aging parent.

Conduct can be shaped to some extent by cognition; moral feelings, on the other hand, are not at all subject to deliberate control. In this respect, they are comparable to food and other tastes—once acquired, they have a life somewhat of their own. An individual who is being persuaded to adopt something new may calculatingly decide that it is to his advantage to do so; but his moral attachment to the old will tend to deter him. He cannot, in a manner of speaking, argue with his conscience. The sense of guilt, a subject that occupies so much of Freudian thinking about the forces that determine conduct, is probably no more than a term for the emotional stress that inevitably arises within the personalities of the members of a changing society as a result of the difference between what they do and what they feel they should do. Relatively few people go to church these days, for very evident reasons, such as the counterattraction of such modern forms of recreation as golf and motoring; but it may be suspected that many who do not go to church feel, in a manner appropriate to an earlier day, that they ought to go to church rather than to the golf course or beach or mountains. Many of the various relatively new social practices, such as premarital sexual experience, divorce as the resolution of an unsatisfactory marriage, birth control, and the payment of income taxes, are not yet fully internalized in the personalities of many people and produce emotional stress because they run counter to old and persistent moral sentiments.

Innovations can, no doubt, be adopted in spite of the latent protest of established moral sentiments; but such sentiments, feelings, or emotional sensitivities tend to retard adoption and may for long even preclude it.

[5] In Puerto Rico, for example, as in many other places, the unwillingness to adopt birth-control practices has stemmed far more from the high emotional value placed upon children and the pride that men take in their procreative abilities (as is evidenced by the numbers of their offspring) than from the fear invoked by religious prohibition of birth control. See Reuben Hill et al., *The Family and Population Control: A Puerto Rican Experiment in Social Change*, The University of North Carolina Press, Chapel Hill, N.C., 1959.

Currently Western advisers are trying to persuade the peoples of India to convert their sacred cows into food, or, at the very least, to reduce them to token numbers. These cows have for centuries wandered at will over field and town, eating the grains and grasses and returning nothing to man except a poor fuel for his kitchen fires. They are a major break in the agricultural nitrogen cycle and account in considerable part for the progressive deterioration of Indian soils; but they are held sacred, and to kill one for food could be more disturbing than to kill off one's grandmother. Indeed, the Indian will let the cows destroy fields that are necessary for the survival of his parents, his wife, and his children. In doing so he does not deliberately equate cows with people, but it is evidently less distressing to him to see famine strike his people than it would be to kill and eat a sacred cow.

Modern people are, of course, far too rational to pamper cows in the midst of famine; but they are no less free than are the Indians from emotional and moral sentiments that can, upon occasion, stand in the way of the adoption of new forms of social conduct. One of the recognized problems of modern urban life is the continuing presence of a large number of often vicious and always costly juvenile delinquents. At least in recent times, no one has dared to suggest that a practical solution to this particular problem would be to apprehend and exterminate those juveniles who have forcibly demonstrated that they are dangerous to the welfare of more conventional people. In modern America, and to an almost equal degree in all of Western Europe, children are in a sense sacred cows; and the very idea of exterminating the lads with duck-tail haircuts and switch-blade knives arouses a feeling of horror. Thus because of the prevalence in our society of the feeling that every individual, however unproductive he may be, has the right to life, liberty, and the pursuit of pleasure, the delinquent youth is accorded considerations that are actually no more rational than are those that the Indian grants his sacred cows.

A good many socially recognized problems of modern society remain unsolved only because moral sentiments preclude the adoption of available solutions. The habitual criminal could be destroyed and he, at least, would commit no further crimes; the demonstrably accident-prone motorists could be barred from the highways, and the highway death rate would promptly fall; the delinquent mother could be sterilized before she bears half a dozen potential delinquents; the ailing elder could be eased painlessly out of this life; etc. It is obvious, however, why none of these things is done. For somewhat less obvious, but often quite as enduring, moral sentiments, many sorts of social innovations have been resisted. It was, for example, mainly because of countervailing moral sentiments that early in this century American fathers put up stiff, if in the end unavailing, resistance to compulsory public school education. The traditional feeling was that a man's children are his to guide and direct as he himself sees fit; thus to take them from him by force and place them in school for six hours or so a day was in violation of his moral rights.

Aesthetic Values

For an American woman to bare her breasts in public would be a violation of established ideas of propriety, and it would occasion considerable embarrassment to those who saw her. An advocate for a change of this sort would certainly meet resistance for this reason, if for no other. Different in degree if not in kind from resistance on the basis of moral sentiments is resistance that stems from the violation an innovation does to some established aesthetic value or system of values. Of these, food tastes, which were mentioned earlier, are perhaps the most firmly established and least subject to change. Next, perhaps, are some aesthetic values regarding personal sanitation. Both are acquired early in childhood; both are very much circumscribed—a rice eater, for example, will have little liking for wheat, and a well-washed individual a very low tolerance for the animal odor of the unwashed; and both are quite stable. An expatriate may take over many of the customs and even some of the moral sentiments and values of his adopted land, but he usually clings tenaciously insofar as he can to his native cuisine. Thus the Chinese immigrants to America brought with them rice and bean sprouts, noodles and dried shrimp, soy sauce and rank little sausages; and the missionaries to China baked their bread and longed for some butter to spread on it.

The past half century has brought radical changes in the diet of Western peoples, most especially the people of the United States. The providing of food has become highly industrialized; almost every food product is now elaborately processed, packaged, and made all but ready for the table. The food factory, with its complex machinery and its food chemists in place of cooks, has come between farm and consumer; and what the latter gets to eat has only slight resemblance to what the former produces. Looking backward, it might seem that these radical changes in diet have come about rapidly and have been avidly welcomed; but the fact is quite the opposite. Each new item of processed food that has entered into our present diet has had to win its way against considerable resistance, against prejudice against the new because of its taste, its appearance, or its composition. The transition, for example, from primary reliance upon lard as the standard cooking fat to the hydrogenated vegetable oils in use today began early in this century with the introduction of liquid cottonseed oil—a by-product of cotton-fiber production. Although this oil had the advantage over lard of being comparatively stable—it does not grow rancid as does lard—to most people it seemed tasteless, pastry and cakes prepared with it seemed inferior in texture, and housewives disliked its liquid form. It was not until World War I brought about a scarcity of lard that the consumption of cottonseed oil became of national significance; and lard was not effectively displaced as the preferred cooking fat until cottonseed and other vegetable oils were made, through hydrogenation, to look, if not taste, like lard. Such is the case with most other modern food products; acceptance of them has been quite recent and has been granted reluctantly. The packaged, prepared breakfast cereals now standard throughout the United States took two generations to gain ascendancy over home-cooked oatmeal and other unprocessed grains. The frozen meats, fruits, and vegetables which are the modern housewife's mainstay waited not only on the wide acceptance of the mechanical refrigerator and freezer but also on the very gradual adaptation of food tastes to these preserved commodities. Even today, a half century after the baking of bread began to be a large-scale industrial enterprise, enough Americans still prefer baker's bread to warrant the support in most communities of at least one small, only semi-industrialized bakery.

Food preferences are not, of course, the only aesthetic values that may be offended by changes proposed or in process. Most if not all of the objects, persons, and conditions—such as clear mountain air or congested city streets—that are the normal acquire some aesthetic value; and as a consequence each society and each occupational and other subcultural group within the society has something of its own particular set of aesthetic values. A slum dweller may dream about a Park Avenue penthouse; but he values the sounds, the smells, and the sights of the slum; to him they represent home. If he were transplanted to a Park Avenue penthouse, he and his family would rapidly begin to re-create in the penthouse the untidy congestion, the noise, and the cooking and other odors that were familiar and enjoyable to them. It is in part because of their slum-determined aesthetic values that the urban poor so rapidly reduce a modern housing project to a shambles. A craftsman usually values the sounds and smells of his particular trade—the cabinetmaker his glue, sawdust, and shrieking saw; the automobile mechanic his grease and gasoline; the machinist his hot oil and protesting metal.

Many innovations, particularly of a technological nature, have been resisted in some part because the change would deprive people of familiar smells, sounds, and sights and create others not to their liking. Modern urban people today accept and perhaps to a degree value the majestic flow of motor traffic on the highways and the swish of tires on pavement. Conversely, most of them would find the clop of horses' hooves and the clatter of iron-wheeled wagons more irritating than anything else; and the smell of horse sweat, urine, droppings, old harness leather, and street dust would be positively revolting. Two generations ago, however, the exact reverse was true; people then were accustomed to the sounds and smells of horse-borne traffic; and they found those of the automobile most disagreeable. They constantly complained that the automobile was a noisy, stinking device that offended the ear and violated the nose. Similar charges have been leveled against the factory, the railroad train, the steamship, and the streetcar, and, more recently, against first the piston and then the jet airplane. Each has violated some established aesthetic values.

Innovations in music, art, household decor, and architecture have usually encountered strong resistance and have gained adoption, if at all, quite slowly. Not all that resistance has stemmed from the violation that the new has done to the established aesthetic values; but such values have delayed adoption of the new and have often forced a compromise between the old and the new. Many aspects of what is now considered modern architecture were being advocated thirty years before they became socially accepted; and typical tract homes—popularized versions of current tastes in domestic building—have almost invariably been a blend of new ideas and traditional elements. Very often, too, what are proclaimed as major innovations turn out upon analysis to be no more than old things with new names. The modern family room is actually nothing but a new version of the traditional sitting room, and the term "living room" is now applied to what used to be called the parlor.

There have, of course, been many significant changes over the years in music, art, decor, and architecture, especially in the United States. The ideal type of home of the gaslight era, rambling, multistoried, ornate, and cluttered with elaborate, massive furniture, does contrast sharply with modern modes of house design and furnishing. It may seem tasteless to the modern mind, and the new would no doubt have struck the householder of the 1880s as barren and devoid of aesthetic merit. The transition from the old to the new did not, however, come all at once; rather, it came piecemeal over several generations. Each generation in turn was inclined to feel that the tastes of its successor were debased; and each generation resisted, or at the very least resented, the changes that were occurring in music, art, decor, and architecture.

Rationalizations

Moral philosophers and professional aesthetes, including musicologists, epicures, art critics, etc., frequently offer elaborate rationales for resisting changes that violate established emotional, moral, aesthetic, or other covert attributes of personality. However tightly reasoned, there is nothing reasonable about their justifications for preferring the old to the new; they can all be summed up by the phrase "the new offends me."[6] Thus the very consider-

6 Paul R. Farnsworth, *The Social Psychology of Music*, Holt, Rinehart and Winston, Inc., New York, 1958, has shown that there is no scientific evidence in support of the idea that any particular sound, timbre, pitch, or other element of

able literature of protest against divorce reflects moral disapproval of the abrogation of the marriage contract rather than the belief that divorce produces more problems than it solves. Those sociologists who have endeavored to study the rise of the divorce rate as a function of various structural changes in our society have, in fact, often been accused of sanctioning immorality.

Sometimes, of course, resistance to the adoption of an innovation has a very practical basis. Such has often been the case with innovations in technology; for until a technological innovation has been developed and its context functionally adapted to it, the device or process may actually be impractical, as measured against the established device or process. The early rayon fabrics were sleazy, sagged out of shape, and did not hold their dye; the first transatlantic steamships, although somewhat faster and more reliable than sail, were noisy, sooty, and pitched badly in a storm; the first telephones did carry the voice through space as could no other means, but the telegraph was a more certain means of getting a message through; the margarine of an early day was considerably cheaper than butter, but its taste and texture were unpredictable and often very poor.

New forms of social organization may also be resisted for a time on the sound grounds that they do not work or do not work well enough to justify their cost in time, effort, or money. The adversity experienced with early forms of fire, life, and other insurance has already been discussed; many decades and much trial and error were needed before insurance became economically advantageous, and during this period those who refused to participate had on the whole justification for refusing to do so. The resistance to cooperative agricultural colonies, so strongly advocated in the period following World War I, had sound basis, however often it may have sprung from prejudice. The colonies that were set up invariably collapsed, mainly because the participants expected benefits to accrue from the organizational system itself and were therefore loath to work the land. Socialism —Marxian, Fabian, or otherwise—can quite rationally be rejected on the grounds that it will not work until such time as some socialistic social system does prove to be more fruitful than other social systems. So far in the long history of attempts to establish them, socialistic societies have either promptly fallen apart or else survived as nonsocialistic societies claiming to be socialistic, as, for example, has Russia, which is politically autocratic but far from economically socialistic.

---

music has inherent value over any others. Nevertheless, musicologists invariably hold that the kind of music they happen to prefer is per se good and all else less than good. Usually, the professional musicologist, like the member of any other profession, is a traditionalist; hence he will usually approve of some long-established form of music—e.g., Bach's compositions for the clavichord—and disapprove of newer musical forms.

Many of the rationales for opposing an innovation during the period of its advocacy have been so fantastic, however, in terms of the understandings of the times, that they can be interpreted only as rationalizations for emotional or other covert objections. Such was clearly the case with the frequently heard claim that the speed of the early railroad, which was probably not in excess of 30 miles per hour, was more than the human body could bear and, a century later, with the claim that man could not endure supersonic speeds. A good deal of the rationale for resistance to commercially canned food was in actuality no more than an expression of fear of the unknown; and although the evidence is overwhelming that modern food processing and distribution have brought about a marked improvement in nutrition, the continuing resistance to the new, stemming presumably from taste preferences, is usually rationalized on the grounds that the new is adverse to physical welfare. Thus the food cultists depreciate all modern foods and advocate a return to a "natural" diet—which, in their minds, may be anything from fruit to nuts, provided that it is uncooked and unprocessed. One of the more fantastic and yet persistent of the rationales that were presented in opposition to the early automobile, one often sanctioned by medical men, was that use of it would lead to atrophy of the human legs. The man of the future, it was frequently said, would be incapable of motion without the aid of a horseless carriage. Some of the resistance to blood transfusion was rationalized in terms of a literal interpretation of the idea that blood will tell—i.e., that the character of a man depends upon his blood, and that if some other man's blood is injected into him, he may become like that other man.

Quite logically, no doubt, resistance to new political, religious, and philosophical ideas is usually expressed in rationalistic terms. Since in the end the test of an idea is its acceptance or rejection, the polemics of advocacy and of resistance can have nothing whatever to do with validity; they are simply rationalizations for or against the adoption of the new idea. Theological disputation is perhaps most clearly of this character, for there is no way to test objectively the value of one theological idea over another, except in those rare instances where it might be the basis for action. Political ideas may sometimes be tested as actual political forms or processes; but the testing of an idea comes only after the idea has been accepted, it takes an exceedingly long time, and it is never very conclusive, since the criteria of success are always vague and subjective. Thus neither the early proponents nor the early opponents of representative government were able to muster any real historical evidence in support of their contrasting positions; they argued from emotional bias or personal self-interest and in terms of assumptions—such as that all men are born equal or, conversely, that some men are born to rule and others to be ruled—that are not subject to test. The same may be said of all the arguments, pro and con, over Marxian communism; the arguments advanced may have had some bearing on the adoption or rejection of the Marxian idea of the good society, but they have had almost nothing to do with the known facts about society, past or present. Thus American opposition to the idea of communism, so strong that it has at times made adopting the idea a traitorous act, is no more rational and hence fully as emotional as is Russian insistence that the idea be accepted.

RATIONAL BASES FOR RESISTANCE

Although a good deal of the resistance to innovations, however rationalized, has an emotional, moral, or aesthetic basis, much of it stems from the vested interest of the individual in the various elements of his society and may reflect a more or less rational calculation on his part of what is to his personal advantage. The extent to which the individual has a vested interest in any particular element varies greatly according to his position— class, occupational, and otherwise—and according to his personal characteristics. A discontented son has, presumably, less interest in family life than has his contented brother; an impecunious man less interest in the maintenance of monetary stability than has one with money in the bank; a poor craftsman less interest in the existing craft techniques than has his skillful fellow worker. Likewise, a physician has both an economic and intellectual interest in illness (of others) that is not shared by the majority of people; shipbuilders and all those who have to do with ships have a special interest in ship technology and little, if any, in the devices and organizations of railroad transportation; and while most modern women presumably have at least a slight interest in the art of food preparation, only those persons, men or women, who are engaged in commercial food processing have very much interest in food chemistry.

As a rule it is those with the strongest interest in a given element that are in a position to adopt an alternative element. A new surgical technique is not and cannot be adopted by the general public and these days not even by surgeons in general. If it is to be adopted, it must be taken over by those surgical specialists who are the most likely to have a strong professional attachment to the specific technique that it is designed to replace or supplement. Such is the case with most new technological devices and processes, with many forms of organization, and with some kinds of ideas. Ideas concerning the operation of our economic system, for example, will be adopted, if at all, by professional economists or businessmen.

As a consequence, self-interest in the established almost always runs counter to the adoption of an innovation. Within some limits, the sick are willing to try anything that medical authority sanctions (and, all too often, anything that is advocated as a sure cure for every human ill). Medical authorities, on the other hand, including local practitioners, are more or less firmly attached to the existing body of medical theories and practices; hence a theoretical or therapeutic innovation usually comes head on against the self-interests of those in the profession who must adopt it if patients are to receive the benefits of the new (assuming that the new is an advance over the prior). Frequently the general public is the final arbiter of the success or failure of an innovation, particularly one in technology; but unless that innovation comes to be adopted by those whose self-interest, frequently commercial, is the most likely to make for resistance, the public may never have a chance to evaluate the innovation. Thus such currently commonplace synthetic fibers as rayon and nylon would not have been offered to consumers had not the advocates in the chemical industry finally worn down the strong self-interest-based resistance to the new fibers by spinners and weavers of cotton, silk, and wool.

Some innovations, technological or otherwise, go directly to the general membership of the society for adoption. Such was the case, for example, with early contraceptive devices, which came in, as it were, by the back door and without medical sponsorship. Such was the case, too, with labor unionism during its early phases, with the public school movement before it had given rise to a cadre of professional educators, and with the early automobile. The automobile was so radical a departure from the traditional that those who were concerned with the provision of personal transportation took little part in its development and exploitation; a new class of craftsmen, entrepreneurs, etc., evolved to displace hack drivers, horse breeders, carriage makers, etc., who were rarely able to make the transition to the motor age. Since, however, the membership of every modern society is stratified into occupational and other specialized activities, most innovations can directly affect only a limited proportion of the total population; and since modern societies are very much complicated and the functions of the members— technological, economic, financial, parental, religious, educational, etc.— highly segmented, the adoption of an innovation is almost always a matter for some specialized and fairly well organized minority of the population to determine.

It has often been assumed that the more differentiated and specialized the activities of the members of a society, the more likely that changes will occur in each of the various realms of action. Thus, it has been argued, only when there is minute division of labor in the productive processes is it at all likely that anyone will be able to institute a labor-saving device. It is pointed out that as long as wool was grown, carded, spun, dyed, and woven by the shepherd and his family, there was no possibility of technological improvements in the processes of making fabrics, but that with the development of occupational specialization (the cottage-industry system in eighteenth-century England), the chances improved, since the worker who did nothing but spin all day long might perceive the possibility of making a more efficient spinning wheel. There is probably a grain of truth in the idea that a highly specialized activity can more easily be mechanized or otherwise improved than a general one; but the theory that it was the division of labor that led to the industrial revolution and that all innovation stems from specialization is not tenable. It would be just as sound—hence, unsound— to hold that the division of labor and all specialization of social roles stems from technological innovations. What does seem generally valid is that, although the high degree of occupational and other specialization that obtains in modern societies facilitates the development of innovations, it does not facilitate either the adoption of innovations or the process of innovating. On the contrary, it does quite the reverse, for it is simply an expression of the high level of organization; and, as will be seen later, organization is inimical both to the appearance of innovations and to their adoption.

Vested Interests in Skills and Knowledge

Perhaps the simplest kind of self-interest that leads to resistance to innovations is that which is vested in the skills, manual and mental, that are involved in use of or conformity to the existing device, process, procedure, or idea. Craftsmen, ancient and modern, are almost invariably reluctant to adopt a new tool, material, or craft procedure, if only because doing so would render their existing skills obsolete and demand that they learn to utilize the new. The current unwillingness of the craft unions to sanction the adoption of labor-saving devices may stem from economic self-interest; but it is firmly grounded in the individual craftsman's normal distrust of anything new. He is aware, however dimly, that any change in craft techniques is to his personal disadvantage. It devaluates his skill as a craftsman and, at least in this particular respect, makes him an apprentice again. Moreover, it deprives him, if only temporarily, of such pride as he may take in his proficiency as a craftsman. Thus it was not without reason that house painters resisted, and at times actively rebelled against, the adoption a few years ago of the newly developed synthetic paints and of the roller technique of applying them. These developments did actually render many of the skills of the painter obsolete, and they made it possible for a slightly talented amateur to do as good a job of household decorating as could the professional. Before the advent of the roller and the new nondrip paints, a good deal of skill was required to paint a ceiling well and quickly. Today an amateur with a roller can do the job as quickly and perhaps as well as an experienced painter.[7] One of the reasons why so many

[7] It was for long a stock joke among house painters that any amateur could paint a ceiling provided he was equipped with an "elbow bucket"—i.e., with a bucket to catch the paint that ran down his upraised arm. This joke and the pride in craftsmanship it expressed are now quite obsolete.

surgeons of a century ago refused for long to adopt anesthesia was the devaluation it brought to their carefully cultivated and greatly prized speed in the completion of an operation. Before anesthesia, the success of an operation depended in part on the rapidity with which it was performed. The noted surgeons of the preanesthesia period were incredibly quick with the knife, proud of their ability to remove a bladder stone or amputate a leg in a brief time, and with good reason inclined to consider speed the most important factor in a successful operation. With the advent of anesthesia, meticulousness in cutting, suturing, etc., became more important. Thus the surgeon who had made his reputation because of his ability to work with exceptional speed was understandably reluctant to adopt, or even to grant value to, the new technique.

Since the beginnings of the industrial revolution those in almost every occupation—law and politics have been the major exceptions—have experienced a more or less constant devaluation of their skills and knowledge as a consequence of technological change, of organizational changes within the occupation, or of both. Neither individually nor collectively through union or professional organization have the members of an occupational group been able to prevent these changes from occurring; but they have both individually and collectively resisted them, delaying their general adoption as long as possible. Rarely if ever have any considerable proportion of the members of an occupational group willingly renounced their established skills and knowledge in favor of some innovation that required the development of new skills and understandings. Frequently, the change in occupational techniques or organization has been so rapid and radical that the old members were unable to make the transition and were displaced by a new generation of workers. The case of the automobile has already been mentioned. There are many other instances of this sort of displacement. The workers and managers of the wagon trains and river boats, for example, were replaced by railroad workers; the majority of the performers and even technicians of the silent motion picture were displaced when the sound picture came into being; and the rise of modern merchandising methods— as exemplified in the supermarket—has displaced and replaced many of those trained in the now old-fashioned arts of personal selling.

Although the devaluation of skills and knowledges by changes is most evident in occupational areas, it often occurs in other realms. Some of the resistance to the early typewriter was occupational—the typewriter displaced the old-time clerk, who had written letters and other documents by hand, and gave rise to a new occupation, that of the stenographer; but there was also considerable resentment of this new device because it devaluated skill at handwriting, which had been a prized ability of the educated man. No doubt some of the parental resistance to the advent of compulsory public schooling stemmed from an awareness that, as the school took over the child, the traditional skills of a parent were losing some of their importance. No man—whether as worker, husband, father, or citizen—will passively accept a change that destroys the value of hard-won skills and knowledge and that demands that he acquire a complex of new and different skills and knowledge if he is to hold his own. As a consequence, those who must adopt an innovation if it is to become an established element in the social heritage for the most part find it to their personal disadvantage to do so.

In some instances the self-interest value of preserving established skills and knowledge is augmented by a desire to preserve other values that seem to be jeopardized by the new. Any major change in technology or organization will have many, varied, and potentially disturbing side effects; for, as has been observed, there is considerable functional interdependence between most of the social elements of a society. Adopting an innovation will necessitate not only the acquisition of new skills in using it but also some adaptation in other aspects of social life. Thus as farmers replaced their horses and mules with tractors, they had not only to learn to operate and maintain tractors, but also to adjust their daily work cycle and even certain agricultural practices to the absence of horses. Tractors do not need thrice-daily feeding and watering, their stables cleaned out, etc.; they do not require pasturage and hayfields; and they do not provide manure with which to fertilize the land. For many a farmer who was contemplating the purchase of a tractor, one or another or all of these side effects might, to the extent that it was perceived, weigh as heavily in his decision as the more direct ones. The disturbance that it brings to a housewife's daily cycle and her community relations has been one of the factors that in European countries have retarded the acceptance of the supermarket as a merchandising form. For most European housewives, as for American housewives of two generations ago, food purchasing is a daily task that takes a woman out of the home and enables her to meet neighbors and friendly merchants. For her it is an integral and valued part of her social life. Shopping for food supplies at a modern supermarket not only demands new buying skills—e.g., making one's own selection from the the many, visible alternatives—but largely depersonalizes the entire operation. The clerks are efficient automatons, and the supermarket is not as a place particularly conducive to gossip between neighbors. To the European housewife, therefore, the lower costs, the greater variety of goods available, and the convenience of the supermarket have tended to be outweighed by the loss it brings in secondary values—the enjoyable process of wandering from shop to shop, haggling with the clerks, gossiping with friends and acquaintances, etc.

Status Interests

Interwoven with, but conceptually distinct from, the devaluation that change may bring to established skills and knowledge is the attendant loss of status, occupational or otherwise. Where craft techniques are stable, the elder craftsman is without question the master craftsman; but where, as in recent times, technological changes render the skills of the elder craftsman obsolete, his work may be no better and may even be less effective than that of a young apprentice. As a consequence, occupational status and age are no longer correlated. The preference of modern business and industry for young employees is simply an organizational acknowledgment of the fact that social change has in many instances devaluated experience, and the long-standing endeavor of labor unions to make simple seniority the criterion of the relative value of workers is merely an attempt to offset the consequences to status of that change.

In all the more stable societies of the past, the passing years brought the individual some improvement in his social status; he became the master craftsman, the wise old father, the village or tribal elder. As his physical stamina and prowess declined, he was increasingly respected for his other skills, knowledge, and judgment. This rise in social status was more than a social reward for past performance; it was a social recognition of his growing value to society. In the changing societies of the modern world, however, past experience often has no relevance for the present; hence those who have earned high status often see that status jeopardized by an innovation and for this reason, if no other, resist its adoption. The reason why a skilled craftsman should resist a machine that will displace him is obvious; less obvious but quite as reasonable was the resistance that physicians, whose status reflected their skill in more or less intuitive diagnosis of diseases, put up against such new diagnostic aids as the early x-ray, biochemical analyses, etc.

The way in which changing techniques, procedures, or organizational operations can jeopardize an individual's social status is dramatically illustrated by the career of Henry Ford. Having made his reputation and his vast wealth as a manufacturer of automobiles on the basis of the idea that the automobile should be a means of cheap and efficient transportation rather than a plaything, he was by 1925 the greatest figure in the automotive industry and one of the world's most wealthy men. At that time, however, changes began to occur in the organization of the automobile industry, such as the unionization of automobile workers and the development of management departmentalization. Ford stubbornly refused to adopt them and for as long as possible continued to be, as he had been, the individualistic ruler of the Ford Motor Company. Because he refused to change with the changing times, he became before his death one of the most hated men in the world; he represented antiunionism, employer paternalism, and industrial autocracy.[8] In effect, he lost his status as a great industrial leader because he refused to

[8] See K. Sward, *The Legend of Henry Ford*, Rinehart & Co., Inc., New York, 1948; and Allen Nevins and Frank E. Hill, *Ford: Decline and Rebirth 1933–1962*, Charles Scribner's Sons, New York, 1963.

relinquish his position as the individualistic master of the company that he had built.

The adoption of almost any innovation will adversely affect the status of some members of the society; and to the extent that those whose status is threatened consciously recognize the danger, they will resist adopting it. There is, moreover, another and more subtle possibility that may deter those who occupy valued status positions from adopting an innovation—the fact that it may turn out badly and its failure cast doubt upon the judgment of the adopter. There is no reason to suppose that the adoption of the steel moldboard plow directly jeopardized the status of competent and successful farmers of colonial America. Most did, however, refuse for a time to adopt it, as the peasants of India and other underdeveloped societies are now doing.[9] The rationalization was that metal would poison the soil; but the real reason must often have been a farmer's fear that if he adopted the new device and then suffered a crop failure—whether the failure was directly due to the effects of the plow or to some completely unrelated factor like the weather—he would lose his reputation as a sound man and be regarded instead as a fool. This same hazard has no doubt prevented many otherwise willing men from adopting new machines for their factories, from trying out new merchandising ideas, from installing new gadgets in their homes, from sending their sons to new kinds of schools, etc. No man, most particularly one who has earned and values the reputation of being wise and foresightful, wants to be thought a fool; and the early adopter of any innovation is always in some measure staking his reputation on the ability of the innovation to do what is expected of it. There was a period in the development of the modern automobile when a steam-powered car was technically better than that driven by an internal-combustion motor; but the failures of the former were considerably more spectacular (usually the boiler exploded) and drew more ridicule upon the driver. This more than any other factor

[9] And as modern American and other farmers have resisted for a time at least every innovation in agricultural technology, such as the tractor, contour plowing, chemical fertilizers, and disease-resistant seeds. As was indicated in the preceding chapter, advocacy and adoption of agricultural innovations have been much studied; and most of our knowledge about these processes is derived from agricultural rather than industrial and urban changes. For bibliographies and summaries of the research literature, other than those cited elsewhere, see The Rural Sociological Society, *Sociological Research on the Diffusion and Adoption of New Farm Practices,* Kentucky Agricultural Experiment Station, Lexington, Ky., 1952; and North Central Rural Sociology Committee, *Social Factors in the Adoption of Farm Practices,* Iowa State University Press, Ames, Iowa, 1959. A study made in Australia is reported by F. E. Emery and B. A. Oeser in *Information, Decision and Action: A Study of the Psychological Determinants of Changes in Farming Techniques,* Cambridge University Press, New York, 1958.

may have accounted for the rapid abandonment of efforts to perfect the steam-powered car.

ORGANIZED OPPOSITION AND COUNTEROPPOSITION

Widespread individual resistance to an innovation may become mobilized into organized opposition, of which the simplest form is that arising informally among the members of a residential community, an occupational grouping, or a social class. What usually happens here is that the latent resistance of individuals to an innovation becomes sharpened into hostility as the innovation gains adopters—as the device appears in use, as the idea gains currency, or as the proposed organizational form is translated into action. At such a time all that is needed to mobilize individual hostility toward the new is a self-appointed leader. Such a leader, who may be no more than the local gossip, can, by showing each individual that his hostility is shared by others, bring about a collective awareness that what is being advocated constitutes a threat to some valued aspect of the *status quo*. Once a local consensus of this sort has been reached, the group—those who have in common the hostile view—begins to exercise more or less effective social sanctions against any individual member of the community, profession, or class who has adopted or shows an inclination to adopt the innovation. Thus a small-town merchant who has introduced a new and more liberal credit system into his business may find that all the other merchants have turned against him and no longer greet him pleasantly on the street, no longer welcome him into Rotary meetings, no longer refer customers to his establishment, etc. If he does not, as it were, take the hint, he may then be subjected to more overt sanctions. He may find that the haulage company upon which he is dependent to bring his merchandise from freight yard to store has lost interest in his business; that his competitors, with whom, under normal conditions, he has a variety of symbiotic relations, are undercutting his prices; and that the local bank is no longer willing to extend him credit.

Every social grouping, formal or informal, exercises considerable control over its individual members.[10] Such control is one of the two methods—socialization is the other—by which group norms are maintained. There is no qualitative distinction between the application of sanctions to bring back into conformity an individual who deviates from a norm in a conventional manner, who, for example, commits a sin or a crime, and to bring back into conformity one who deviates by adopting some innovation. From the

[10] For an analysis of these groupings, their normative standards of conduct, and the ways they enforce them, see Richard T. LaPiere, *A Theory of Social Control*, McGraw-Hill Book Company, New York, 1954.

group's point of view, a deviation is a deviation; and any deviation is a threat to the continued existence of the group. When, however, any group brings sanctions against a member who has adopted or is about to adopt some innovation, it is ordinarily setting itself in opposition, not merely to a single individual, but to another, if very vague, group—to all those who have adopted the innovation and become interested in its use and preservation; and this group, through representatives, may in turn fight back in a way that no single individual could. A progressive small-town merchant may be brought back into conformity with the local merchandising norms by social sanctions, for there is not likely to develop support from outside merchants who have also adopted the credit device that brought him into local disfavor. A public school teacher who tries out some new teaching procedure and is promptly censured by parents and school officials, however, may be supported by the teaching profession (if it is their consensus that the new procedure is an improvement over the old), with the result that a more or less clear-cut group-versus-group conflict arises.

Social sanctions are everywhere and always brought to bear against the innovator, the advocate, and the adopter of anything new, with the result that some loss in social status—reputation, position, or acceptance—is at least temporarily incurred by anyone who is in any way progressive. In some instances it has been the effectiveness of control of this sort that, more than anything else, has retarded the development and adoption of an innovation. Although it is now acceptable for women to enter into almost all occupations, a half century ago the girl who took a position in business as bookkeeper or stenographer violated family and community norms and became the object (as might her employer also) of group sanctions; even the telephone girls of that time were considered, especially in the larger cities, as being little better than prostitutes. A half century ago the divorcee —now so commonplace that the role is hardly a distinguishing one—was an object of marked censure in all respectable middle-class communities; and the prospect of a woman's becoming in this way *déclassée* and the object of scorn no doubt retarded considerably the establishment of divorce as an acceptable resolution of marital discord.

It is evident, however, if only from the above examples, that the control that is normally exercised does not preclude the adoption of innovations. One reason for this is the organized counteropposition that may be generated by organized opposition. This counteropposition may be informal in organization, as it is when the members of a professional group rise to the defense of a progressive member or scholars rise to the defense of one who has advocated a new idea or theory that is publicly interpreted as being traitorous. It may, on the other hand, be or become formally organized, as was the advocacy of quarantine and other new public health measures toward the close of the last century. In this instance, local groups of medical practitioners became informally organized advocates for the new measures, met with violent resistance (some of it, such as the antivaccination society, formally organized), and then began the development of first local and ultimately national public health organizations.[11] A considerable number of organizations that are now established and conservative had their beginnings in this way. The college sorority started as a defensive organization, a home and a refuge from disapproval, in the days, the latter part of last century, when a college education was generally considered the prerogative of the male and the girl who ventured into a college was more or less overtly scorned and persecuted by male students and faculty alike.

Societies for the Prevention of Changes

In premodern societies, existing social organizations were probably strong enough and harmonious enough to delay if not prevent the adoption of innovations. Through much of the Middle Ages, for example, family, Church, guild, and state conspired to check the efforts, if not actually to destroy the persons, of advocates for anything new.[12] In modern societies, however, with their multiple and often conflicting informal and formal organizations, each of which has relatively limited power over the individual, formally organized resistance to innovations has often been embodied in an organization specifically developed to combat some one particular threat to the *status quo*. The Ku-Klux developed in opposition to the early efforts of reformers to bring to the Negroes of the South something of that equality with whites that was their constitutional right. The antivaccination society, still existent although dormant, emerged to give formal representation to the then general opposition to compulsory vaccination of school children. The antivivisection society, which was the parent organization of the now fully accredited local humane societies, arose in opposition to the use, then somewhat novel, of dogs and

[11] See Benjamin D. Paul (ed.), *Health, Culture and Community: Case Studies of Public Reactions to Health Programs*, Russell Sage Foundation, New York, 1955.

[12] The medieval Inquisition, for example, was an organization established by the Church to systematize and legalize the punishment for heresy. Heresy was, by the definition of the times, any suggestion that the existing social system could be improved by the adoption of something new, even so slight a change as that from one kind of hand tool to another. For centuries, more or less spontaneous local protests against heretics had been occurring—protests not unlike the lynchings by which Southern whites once endeavored to keep "upstart" Negroes in their place. The inquisitorial courts seem to have contributed to the expression of intolerance toward individual or group deviation of any kind rather than to have limited it; for popular protests continued to occur and occasionally led not just to the burning of one individual, but to the massacring of thousands.

other small animals in medical research. All such organizations, as well as their less militant companions, the historical and other societies for the preservation of everything from old buildings to even older customs, have resisted change that was under way; and while most of them have fought a losing battle, their delaying effects have often been considerable.

Formally organized resistance to change is by no means a thing of the past. Contemporary Americans may actively welcome minor modifications in the goods and devices that they use and even in the less important aspects of governmental and other organizations; but they tend to be almost as resistant to any significant social change as were their forefathers, and occasionally a very minor change will set off a wave of opposition that leads to the formation of an antichange society. When in 1962 the Bell Telephone Company announced that the two-letter prefix long used in dial phone listings would gradually be replaced by all-number calling, they did so with considerable caution and detailed explanation of the reasons why this change was necessary. The outcry against this proposal was prompt and widespread, and within weeks a large number of local societies for the preservation of letter calling made their appearance. These organizations conducted a brisk and noisy propaganda attack upon the telephone company and its proposal, threatened civil suit against the company if it persisted in advocating the change, and otherwise made a considerable mountain out of a molehill. For a month or two the newspapers treated the change as though it were one of the major social upheavals of the century; and much profound nonsense, some of it by scientists, was published on the subject before public attention shifted back to the more durable matter of baseball.

THE NATURE OF ADOPTERS

Individual willingness to adopt an innovation is, like innovation and advocacy, asocial; and willing individuals will be found in significant numbers only to the extent that the society is in a condition of dynamic incongruence. A society that is in a state of comparatively stable congruence or one that has become frozen in a condition of incongruence provides an advocate with very few if any members who are both willing and able to adopt the device, procedure, idea, or form of organization that he is advocating. Thus it was that the seventeenth-century Catholic missionaries to China, which was then in a relatively congruous condition, aroused the curiosity of Chinese scholars with their Western mechanical and scientific devices but made almost no headway in securing converts to Christian religious ideas and social practices. Two centuries later, when the old Chinese system had begun to weaken, Protestant missionaries found numbers of ready converts to Christianity; but, as became painfully evident to all except the missionaries themselves, these adopters of Christianity were mainly the socially dis-possessed and outcast, and in many instances criminals, who accepted Christianity, not as a means to eternal salvation, but as a way to food and the sanctuary from Chinese law that the extraterritorial jurisdiction of the mission compound provided.

Maladjustment and Marginality

Insofar as the individual members are concerned, a society that is in a condition of incongruence is fraught with conflicts and contradictions; and if the society is also dynamic, everything has a quality of uncertainty and instability. In such a society, of which our own is a striking example, the socialization of the individual proceeds in a markedly variable and erratic manner, with the result that he acquires an aggregation of rather hetero-geneous and often contradictory attributes of personality that fit him none too well for any social role and may mean that, whatever befalls him, he will be in some respects more or less discontented and disappointed. Moreover, the changes that occur within the society during the course of his lifetime will inevitably render antiquated many of the personality attributes that he has acquired. The result may be maladjustment of some kind and to some degree.

Maladjustment may arise because an individual has been so coddled and pampered in his parental home and, perhaps, also during his schooling that he is unprepared for the discipline of military life or the exacting demands of a job in business or industry; because he has acquired ambitions and expectations that are far beyond his abilities or opportunities; because he has acquired high ideals of domestic life but is faced with a marriage that will not work; because he has come to love the country, either because he was brought up there or because it has been idealized for him by his parents or books, but must live out his life in a city; because he has inadvertently acquired such normally incompatible desires as to want to be a man of letters and to live in luxury and ease. The maladjusting consequences of growing up and living in a dynamic and disorganized society are infinitely varied; but most individuals do manage in some fashion or other to resolve, or at least to keep under control, the stresses and conflicts within themselves and between themselves and the social circumstances in which they find themselves. Those who fail to do so make up that rather considerable body of misfits, malcontents, and psychotics to be found in any dynamic society.

The resolution or suppression of maladjustment, which is often de-scribed by psychologists as the "management of tensions," may be accomplished in a great variety of ways, only one of which is of interest in the study of social change: the individual rejects, insofar as he can, one of the conflicting elements of his universe—either an element of his own personality or an element of his environment—and adopts an element more in keeping with the remainder. This is what a conscience-stricken man attempts to do when he renounces the particular moral or other principle that precludes his fulfilling some desire or ambition and adopts, as best he can, the Machiavellian principle that the end justifies the means. It is what a discontented woman attempts when she divorces one man in order to marry another; and what an unhappy student attempts when he quits college to take what he hopes what will be a remunerative and undemanding job.

Those individuals who are seeking to resolve some sort of personal maladjustment, be it only discontent with their present brand of cigarettes, are marginal in this particular respect; they have a weakened attachment to whatever it is—a tool, a device, a value, a principle, an idea, or a form of human relationship—that is involved in their maladjustment. As was mentioned earlier, those whose attachment to anything is weakened are presumably more than normally susceptible to being persuaded to adopt an alternative.[13] In some instances marginality is a rather generalized condition.

[13] Perhaps the most controversial of all the problems of social change is the question of why some few members of a society are more susceptible than all others to persuasion by the advocate for a given innovation. These few, sometimes described as "initial adopters," are certainly distinct from their fellows either in their personal characteristics or in their situational circumstances, or both. Homer Barnett (*Innovation: The Basis of Cultural Change*, McGraw-Hill Book Company, New York, 1953, pp. 378–410, "Acceptors and Rejectors"), Everett M. Rogers (*Diffusion of Innovations*, The Free Press of Glencoe, New York, 1962, pp. 148–192, "Adopter Categories," and pp. 193–207, "Innovators as Deviants"), and most of the economists who are working on economic development believe that the susceptible person is usually one who has been made marginal in respect to the given innovation by empirical experience of an adverse nature or by status insecurity.

Herbert Menzel ("Innovation, Integration, and Marginality: A Survey of Physicians," *American Sociological Review*, vol. 25, pp. 704–713, October, 1960); James S. Coleman et al., "The Diffusion of an Innovation among Physicians," *Sociometry*, vol. 20, pp. 253–270, December, 1957); Snell Putney and Gladys J. Putney ("Radical Innovation and Prestige," *American Sociological Review*, vol. 27, pp. 548–551, August, 1962), and others have offered evidence which they believe indicates that it is the well-established individual, secure in his status, rather than the marginal one, who is most likely to adopt an innovation. In their view, leadership in any field of endeavor is a consequence of the possession of personal characteristics that are conducive to forward-looking, progressive action; and it is such leaders who are the most willing and able to try out new techniques, ideas, or forms of social organization.

The conflict between these two points of view is more apparent than real. Those who hold that it is established leaders who are most likely to adopt innovations tend to think of marginality as general rather than specific and to assume that the individual who occupies an established and respected position—

In our society adolescents tend to be marginal in regard to almost everything, except perhaps those particular values, sentiments, and forms of conduct that prevail among their peers. Most adolescents survive this period of general instability and grow to adulthood, which in this connection means to settle into those socially sanctioned roles that are appropriate to their particular stations in life, whether or not they covertly accept them. Some few, however, do not make this transition and remain throughout their lives marginal in many regards. They are what is often designated as the lunatic fringe, those individuals who are constantly flitting from cult to cult, doctrine to doctrine, diet to diet, and perhaps job to job. They are quick to adopt anything, old or new; but they contribute nothing to the establishment of new social elements, for they will drop the new just as quickly and irrationally as they took it on.

Usually, however, marginality is specific rather than general; and it is only those individuals, few or many, who are marginal in respect to the specific aspect of life involved who are the potential adopters of an innovation. Thus it is only the craftsman who is for whatever reason discontented with his hand tool or the product that he can produce with it—because, perhaps, he is less skilled than his fellows, has standards of a higher quality than they do, or is temperamentally unsuited to working with a hand tool— who is at all likely to adopt a power-driven substitute. It is only the businessman who is for some reason dissatisfied with the profits he is making— because, perhaps, he has an exceptionally extravagant wife, a desire to educate his children beyond their normal expectations, or an insatiable greed for money—who is at all likely to take on the merchandising of an entirely new kind of product or to adopt a new, untried merchandising technique. It is only the intellectual who has for some reason become bored or dis-

occupational or otherwise—cannot be marginal in the sense used by Barnett and others. They therefore equate the kind of marginality that is thought to lead to the adoption of innovations with generalized social marginality—i.e., with the socially dispossessed, the socially incompetent, and the socially unattached. But where a position of esteem is subject to constant competition, as among contemporary American physicians, the individual who occupies that position and is in most respects stable and responsible may be marginal in regard to the more dynamic aspects of medical technology; for if he fails to adopt the latest drug or other therapy, he may soon become known by his associates—and in time by his patients—as unprogressive and lose his position of leadership. Whether it is established leaders or lesser individuals striving to gain positions of leadership who are marginal toward the traditional depends, therefore, upon social circumstances. Where an elite, occupational or otherwise, is fairly free from competition, it will normally be the last, rather than the first, to adopt anything new. Where those who occupy elite positions are insecure, they may be the most, rather than the least, marginal in respect to those particular kinds of innovations that may aid them in preserving their status.

illusioned with the current ideas and beliefs in his particular field of interest who is at all likely to note, consider, and perhaps adopt some new intellectual offering.

Marginality of the Upward Mobile

There is a special and highly significant kind of marginality that occurs under conditions of dynamic, though not of static, incongruence. This is the marginality of those individuals who are ambitious to rise in the social scale—to gain entrance to a more lucrative and prestigious occupation, to secure acceptance as a member of a higher class stratum, to be in terms of status a social success. Ambition of this sort is characteristic of the socially mobile and is a function of an open class and occupational system.[14]

An individual who is striving to improve his social status is thereby demonstrating his discontent with the status into which he was born; he is, therefore, marginal in respect to many of the subcultural elements of that status. His striving to move upward may for the most part take rather conventional directions; he may, for example, work harder and longer at his job in the hope of promotion, he may sacrifice current satisfactions in order to secure an education that will lead to some higher occupational position, or he may in various ways emulate the morals and manners of the class to which he aspires. It is quite possible for an individual to rise in the social scale without in any way disturbing the social system; and in some open class systems, such as that of old China, upward mobility was a sort of musical chairs that led to a turnover in the personnel of the higher classes without in any way changing the subcultures of those classes.[15]

In all modern societies, however, and in those societies of the past in which a condition of dynamic incongruence has existed, one of the ways by which an individual has been able to improve his social position is through the adoption of innovations. The method is always fraught with risk, but to the successful large rewards may accrue. As has been pointed out, innovators themselves do not for the most part deliberately strive for

[14] It is the presence of significant numbers of such ambitious individuals in a society that, in the view of David C. McClelland (*The Achieving Society*, D. Van Nostrand Company, Inc., Princeton, N.J., 1961), distinguishes a dynamic from a stable society. He is not very clear, however, what social circumstances make for the presence or absence of achievement-motivated individuals in the society. For a valuable study of some of the correlates, psychological and social, of achievement motivation see Murray A. Straus, "Deferred Gratification, Social Class, and the Achievement Syndrome," *American Sociological Review*, vol. 27, pp. 326–335, June, 1962.

[15] See Robert M. Marsh, *The Mandarins: The Circulation of Elites in China, 1600–1900*, The Free Press of Glencoe, New York, 1961.

social success as conventionally defined. It is, rather, advocates who are more often, if not invariably, ambitious to gain wealth and recognition and who use the advocacy of innovations as a means of doing so. What they advocate may be adopted by ambitious individuals for the same reason. Thus Andrew Carnegie, contrary to the weight of established authority, adopted the open-hearth method of steelmaking and, because it turned out to be successful, became himself a famed steelmaker. Countless other men of industry and business have over the past two centuries built fortunes and reputations by adopting new technological processes, new modes of business organization or merchandising, or new financial procedures. Meanwhile countless others, equally ambitious, have failed, either because the particular innovation that they adopted was unsuccessful or because they applied it ineptly.

In the professions, as well as in business and industry, the adoption of an innovation is one of the ways, albeit uncertain, by which an ambitious individual may strive for rapid advancement in income and prestige. A young physician who is in a hurry to build a large practice and win the admiration of his fellows may to this end seize on the latest thing in diagnostic techniques or therapy. An eager young scholar or scientist may for the same reason become a specialist in the latest theory, the most recently developed field of interest, or the newest methodological gadget. A young educator may attempt to speed his rise to eminence as a public school administrator by putting into operation the very latest pedagogical or organizational concept. Those who are anxious to gain status in other than occupational fields may follow the same basic procedure and for the same reasons. A man who wishes to be looked up to as a social leader in the community may, for example, begin by building or remodeling his house in the very latest architectural fashion, have it decorated in the most advanced of styles, cram it with all the latest mechanical devices, and then proceed to join the newest club in the community and perhaps sponsor various new charitable and other community activities.

The Halo Effect

Although the initial response to any innovation, for reasons that have already been discussed, is resistance, the subsequent history of the innovation depends in considerable part upon what class of persons in the society begin to adopt it. Ideally, adoption should come from those who are in established positions of authority in the area of life that is affected by the innovation—by established manufacturers, if it is a new commercial product; by eminent surgeons, if it is an innovation in surgery; by respected scholars, if it is an innovation in ideas; by revered bishops, if it is a religious innovation. As has been pointed out, however, it is such people who are likely to be the last rather than the first to accept it. Those who are most likely to adopt it are those who are least likely to give the innovation a favorable test and most likely to bring it social discredit.

A highly ambitious young man who sees in some new mechanical device an opportunity to win wealth and position is not, for one thing, likely to have either the experience or the financial backing to develop, manufacture, and merchandise the device as effectively as would a large, established firm. He may fail and his failure may discredit the device itself. It has often happened that early and commercially unsuccessful adopters of new devices, materials, food products, etc., have done just this. Margarine, for example, was first put on the market by a number of small, new, and in many cases one-man firms. Many of these firms did so badly that in the United States at least margarine soon acquired a most unfavorable reputation, and it was years before reliable producers of this substitute for butter overcame the prejudice against it. New ideas frequently suffer a similar fate; those most likely to adopt a new idea, especially a philosophical concept or an idea for social reform, are college sophomores and capricious intellectuals, neither of whom are capable of giving the idea clear and effective representation. On the other hand, an intellectual doctrine or dogma that does happen to be adopted by men of established position and of a certain competence may be so effectively and persistently presented that it gains stature whether it has any intrinsic merit or not. Such was the case with the Freudian idea of man and his psychic troubles; as a dogma it may have had little to commend it, but it was initially adopted by medical men, who gave it the sanction of their position as medical scientists and dignified it as a science of man.

The fact that an innovation may be adopted by ambitious but unestablished individuals as a potential way to gain wealth and higher status does not, of course, preclude its becoming a functioning element of the society. It means, rather, that the particular innovation will go through a period of testing under somewhat unfavorable conditions; whether it survives the testing depends, presumably, upon its own intrinsic merits. A large and successful industrial organization can, through advertising and the halo effect of its prestige, furnish a new commercial product with a good deal of extrinsic value. If that product happens to have any intrinsic value—and a great many do not—the innovation will be tested under the most favorable conditions. Should the same product be put on the market by a new, inexperienced, and unrecognized firm, it will gain little if any extrinsic value (it may, in fact, be socially defined as substandard) and will win its way solely, if at all, on its intrinsic merits. Margarine finally proved itself in this way; and so, too, have a variety of other commercial products. The retreading of automobile tires was for many years considered a gyp operation, and the work was in fact generally poor; but retreads were so cheap in comparison with new tires that marginal motorists—and later truckers—patronized the retreaders. Eventually, retreading proved itself in spite of the adverse way in which it was adopted; and tire manufacturers were forced to assume retreading operations. Today a good retread is considered almost the equivalent of a new tire, and its use is socially sanctioned.

With an innovation that is not subject to the ultimate test of practicality, the character of its early adopters largely determines the social value that will be imputed to it. In late nineteenth-century England socialism was taken over mainly by intellectuals, men and women of recognized position, such as George Bernard Shaw. Consequently in England socialism became a respectable, if not widely popular, ideology. In America, on the other hand, the early socialists were almost to a man nonintellectuals without established position of any sort. They tended to be members of the Bohemian riffraff— the predecessors to the currently self-styled beatniks; and they brought discredit to the theory of Marx and to all other socialistic ideas.

In general, although not invariably, the diffusion of social elements, new or old, through the class ranks is downward. Since men tend to ape their superiors, what becomes established as a part of the subculture of an inferior class is likely to become class-bound; that is, members of the superior classes will associate the social element—device, idea, or whatever— with low-class position; thus for them it will have negative extrinsic value. Should an innovation of any sort be adopted first by members of a low class, most particularly by members of some such socially submarginal group as criminals, that innovation is not likely to become established in the general society. How frequently innovations have been lost for this reason is not, of course, on record; being lost, they are now unknown. The discrediting of innovations by their being adopted by members of a submarginal group, however, is easy to demonstrate when, as does sometimes happen, the innovation finally lives down its adverse beginnings. The cigarette as a new form of tobacco usage was, for reasons unknown, taken up in America by professional criminals, pimps, prostitutes, and that class of young hoodlums that was then known as "poolroom boys." The cigar, the pipe, and, for the workingman, chewing tobacco were respectable forms of tobacco usage. The smoking of cigarettes quickly became defined as an underworld custom in which no respectable man would indulge; and before long this definition of it was supported in various disparaging ways—for example, it came to be called a "coffin nail," and the "cigarette fiend" became a stock item in street fairs and carnivals. Not until World War I, when the sheer convenience of the cigarette led to its adoption by many American soldiers, did the prejudice against it begin to break down; and it was many years more before a woman could smoke a cigarette and still retain a reputation for respectability.

In academic circles in the United States today nothing is quite so certain to bring discredit to a new idea, educational procedure, or form of educational organization as to have it adopted initially by the professional educators. In the academic value system the educators are regarded as ir-responsible purveyors to the general public of any idea—educational or otherwise—that the public may for the moment desire. So it tends to be assumed that, if educators take up some new idea, that idea can have no value but that of expediency. The adoption by one or another of the other sub-groups within the academic world may also cast doubt on the value of new ideas, new theories, and even new research findings. Present-day American economists, psychologists, and sociologists are, for example, unlikely to con-sider worthy of serious attention a theory that has grown popular among political scientists; and sociologists will seldom turn to rural sociologists, and never to social workers, for their thoughts or findings on sociological matters.

Prestigious Adopters

Ordinarily those individuals whose positions are secure and also carry comparatively high prestige tend to be socially conservative and resistant to change of any sort. This is most clearly the case with those in hereditary positions, a matter of ascribed status; but it is also generally true of those who have achieved their positions by following socially prescribed proce-dures—who have, for example, won promotion up the ranks of an organiza-tional hierarchy by conforming exceptionally well to the organizational norms. In either case, the individual in a secure, prestigious position is presumably well-adjusted to it, emotionally and otherwise, and therefore dis-inclined to do anything that might jeopardize his retaining it. Through most of the history of the Catholic Church, bishops, archbishops, cardinals, and popes have been markedly conservative in theological matters; through much of the history of modern militarism generals, admirals, and others of high rank have tended to be content with traditional weapons and tactics and strategies and have strongly resisted any threat to the *status quo;* and in recent times, business entrepreneurs, once they have become established as successful, have usually endeavored to stabilize their operations and been reluctant to venture into new products or to try out new methods.[16] The reason is clear: if an individual's position is gratifyingly prestigious and

[16] A study of the rate at which large American corporate industrial enter-prises adopt proved technological innovations shows that "the diffusion of a new technique is often a fairly slow process. With few exceptions, it took 10 years or more for all the major firms in an industry to introduce the innovation" (Edwin Mansfield, "Diffusion of Technological Change," *Reviews of Data on Research & Development,* National Science Foundation, Washington, D.C., no. 31, October, 1961). See also a subsequent report on Mansfield's study, "Innovation in In-dividual Firms," *Reviews of Data on Research & Development,* National Science Foundation, Washington, D.C., no. 34, June, 1962.

is not in jeopardy, there is no incentive for his adopting something new. Prudence precludes his doing so, for his adopting of an innovation might simply bring him discredit; and at any event, adoption of the new would most likely add little if anything to his status gratifications. No doubt an occasional individual in a position of this sort will be sufficiently idiosyncratic to try out some minor variation on the established through curiosity or in the spirit of adventure, but he is not likely to risk his position by gambling on the value of some major innovation.

There are, however, certain social circumstances, organizational and ideological, that make occupancy of some prestigious positions—occupational and otherwise—insecure and that at the same time make the prestige that attaches to a position unstable. Where, for example, the class system is both ill-defined and very open, no man can for long take his class position for granted; by work or wile, another man may dispossess him or a new social class may emerge to take over the power and prestige of the class to which he belongs. Both these hazards have been somewhat characteristic of Western societies during the past two centuries or more, with the consequence that many prestigious positions of Western societies have been unstable and occupancy of them has been insecure.

It is both an oversimplification and an understatement to say that competition is the life of trade—an oversimplification in that the statement implies that competition is a unitary process, while in actuality it varies infinitely in form and degree; an understatement in that it restricts competition to trade, whereas competition stimulates not only trade but all forms of social activity. What is important in the present connection is that, whenever a person whose position is an established one with high prestige is subject to the competition of aspirants for it, or whenever the prestige of the position itself is subject to reduction by competition, there is an incentive for the person who occupies it to adopt innovations that would seem either to fortify his occupancy of the position or to strengthen the prestige of the position.

Under conditions of stable congruence, each established position, prestigious or otherwise, holds a monopoly of the particular rights and powers that are traditionally assigned to it. Thus, perhaps, a carpenter and only a carpenter has the right to work with wood for a profit; a landlord who has inherited his land and no one but a landlord who has inherited his land has the right to own land; a priest and only a priest has the right and power to speak God's will; and no one but the local barber-surgeon will dare to cut into human flesh. The antithetical circumstance, more or less characteristic of a condition of dynamic incongruence, yet never wholly so, is that in which each status position lacks total monopoly over its traditional rights and powers and those who occupy it must therefore compete to some extent with individuals or classes of individuals who are ambitious to obtain those rights and powers. Some, though far from all, of the competitive efforts will take the form, as has been seen, of adopting new devices, processes, forms of organization, or ideas. In the long run, perhaps, the advantage lies with aspirants for position, since in adopting innovations, they have everything to gain and little to lose, whereas the established person who is subjected to competition is generally in the disadvantageous position of having much to lose if he adopts an innovation that proves unsuccessful, yet being likely to lose what he does possess unless he is more progressive than any of his competitors.

Over the past century and more the general inability of families of high status to preserve that status through the generations, the brief day of fame that most business and industrial enterprises enjoy, and the constant rise of men of humble origins to positions of esteem and prestige in all walks of life suggest that most successful innovations have initially been adopted by ambitious individuals whose status is low. Of course not all those who have risen in the social scale have done so by adopting innovations; nor have all families and business firms who have lost eminence failed because they did not adopt innovations. In a great many instances, however, such has indeed been the case, as is demonstrated by data on the rise and decline of industrial and mercantile establishments. It is evidence of this sort that lends credence to the assumption that most social change is wrought by upward-mobile individuals. Some men of established position who are subjected to competition presumably do become aware of the need to change with the times—to adopt new devices, processes, organizational forms, or ideas in order to secure their positions against competition—and proceed to do so. Since adopters of this sort will, by contrast to marginal adopters, tend to give an innovation the best possible test and to bring to it the halo of their positions, an innovation that is adopted by persons of prestigious position is, therefore, likely to become an enduring element of the social system.

There are many specific instances in which innovations have, after an initial period of resistance, won over as adopters persons of prestigious position. The automobile was initially looked upon as a plaything or sporting device, and most of the early purchasers were young men about town who brought it more discredit than prestige. By the second decade of this century it began to be adopted by town and city physicians as a better means of transportation than the horse and buggy and by prospering businessmen as a symbol of their success. It thereby gained respectability; and as the device was improved and cheapened, more and more people came into the market. The initial response to the steel moldboard plow was general rejection. Fortunately, it was at the time such a costly device that a marginal farmer could not adopt it. Eventually prospering farmers, who it may be assumed felt the need to sustain their positions, began to adopt it; and within a short time it had all but replaced the wood plow. Earlier it was observed that the county agents of the United States Department of Agriculture discovered that it was easy to get a poor farmer to adopt anything new provided that it cost him nothing and that such a farmer usually brought discredit to the new because he was an incompetent worker and known for his foolishness. It was far harder, they learned, to find a competent and respected farmer who would try a new technique, seed, or device; but if such a farmer could be found and induced to try the new, he would not only give it a good test but also an aura of respectability.

The Adoption Cycle

In the previous chapter it was observed that advocates of innovations often make specious claims for them. These claims are factors in the persuasive process, and they are usually forgotten as an innovation becomes established as a social element. In the process of its being adopted, an innovation may, however, enter a boomlike cycle, during the rising phase of which it is widely acclaimed by its adopters as a revolutionary development that is bringing into being a new and unprecedented state of human affairs.

As was mentioned earlier, the advent of a new social element may cause more or less profound functional disturbances to other, related elements; for as the new resolves a preexisting incongruence, it often also produces new incongruencies by rendering dysfunctional parts of the complex in which it operates. Adaptive changes in these parts may then occur; and the process of change, once started in this way, may snowball. A half century after the development of the automobile as a fairly reliable means of transportation, its repercussions are still evident; and there is almost no aspect of modern society that has not in some way been affected by, and usually in turn has affected, the automobile. In the century or so since electric power was first put to use, the uses of electricity have constantly increased; and no end is yet in sight to its application.

The idea that an innovation will work a revolution in the entire social system and so bring into being a new era, however, is an illusion that is produced by the practice, common to the folk and all too frequently adopted by quasi scientists, of projecting any current trend indefinitely into the future. As an innovation gains more and more adopters, the growth curve in the rate of adoption runs sharply upward—usage increases geometrically. When all the members of the society to whom the innovation is relevant have adopted it, growth in the rate of adoption ceases (or, in some instances, the rate of adoption falls to a simple replacement level). There is, however, a tendency during the period of rapid adoption for people to project into infinity the rising growth in the rate of adoption, with the result that they impute to the new revolutionary consequences for the whole of the society. It is the same tendency that leads to excessive public alarm every time a rise is reported in such undesirable indexes of human conduct as crime or drug addiction or in some cause of death, such as lung cancer. The reported rise in rate may be real; but the public concern is excessive in that it involves the assumption that the rise will continue upward indefinitely, although it clearly will not; for if it were to do so, it would in these particular instances mean that in time everyone would be a drug-taking criminal and would die of lung cancer.

Men seem at times to be incapable of moderation, at least in respect to changes in their social system. They may for long staunchly resist pressures to change some dysfunctional technique, idea, or form of organization and grumblingly endure the consequences; and then, sometimes abruptly, they may become almost obsessed with some new replacement or supplement and leap to the conclusion that the new is going to resolve all the ills of mankind. Until well into the last century, no people in the whole history of mankind had discovered the fact that filth and certain diseases are causally correlated; nor had they come to define the sight and smell of the uncleansed human body as distasteful. A number of occurrences, including the discovery of bacterial cause of diseases, led to the development and establishment in Western societies of the idea and practice of both personal and public hygiene—to effective sewage disposal, pure water supplies, running water in habitations, flush toilets, soap and other detergents, etc. Up to some point or other all these changes were, perhaps, functional—i.e., they contributed to the health and comfort of the members of society; but if one is to judge by the amount of television time that is currently devoted to the advertising of chemical detergents, soaps, shampoos, deodorants, mouthwashes, bleaches, etc., that point has long since been passed. Personal cleanliness and rituals presumed to purify and make attractive the human animal have come to be something of a fetish; certainly they will not work the wonders claimed for them and, possibly, expected of them.

Somewhat similar excesses both in usage and in expectations have occurred with many new products—for example, the sulfa drugs, DDT, and penicillin; with many new technological devices—for example, the railroad, the automobile, the airplane, the telephone, the radio, the motion picture, and television; and with many new theories of society and forms and practices of social life—for example, socialism, welfarism, internationalism, public school education, social security, and consumer credit.

The motion picture, for example, went through a cycle of usage (as indicated by attendance at movies, interest in motion-picture stars, etc.) that reached its peak sometime in the mid-1930s. As the motion picture grew in popularity, the impression arose and gained currency that it was remaking our world—for good according to some, for ill according to others. It was thought that it was soon to replace the teacher in the classroom (as, two decades later, it was said that television was about to do);

that it was breaking down the barriers of regional and class isolation and would in due time produce an entirely homogeneous population throughout the world; and that it was, at the same time, undermining the family (completing, presumably, the task left undone by the automobile) and causing our high rates of juvenile delinquency (a problem that, a century earlier, was to have been solved by the establishment of public school education and that two decades later was to be blamed by many upon television). Meanwhile, there were hysterical publicists proclaiming that the very foundations of American democracy were being undermined, or at the very least revolutionized, by the development of radio; for, it was said, one man or a small clique of politicians could monopolize this new and vital means of communication with the public—as they could not do with the newspaper before it—and could and shortly would use it to control the public mind for their own personal interests. Two decades later much the same excessive concern was being expressed over the development of a pseudo innovation called "motivational research," through which advertisers and propagandists were supposed to be able to uncover and use to their own interests the unconscious forces that motivate human conduct. Still later the dubious discovery that visual images that were very briefly exposed and that would pass without consciously being noticed by the viewer (they would be subliminal) could have profound consequences to his unconscious was the basis for hailing television as the weapon by which tyrants would reduce us all to automatons unknowingly obedient to our master's face.

It should be observed that yesterday's revolutionary development is today's accepted commonplace, taken for granted, its newness largely forgotten, and the great expectations formerly held out for it transferred to something still newer. Countless times over the past hundred years the adoption of some new technique, new idea, or new form of organization has been widely defined as either the beginning of a new and wondrous era for mankind or the end of all that man values, if not the end of man himself. American society of today, however, is still recognizably an outgrowth of the society of a century ago, as is Western society in general. The actual changes in the course of the past hundred years have been many and various, and they may have come more rapidly and been of greater magnitude than the changes that occurred during any previous century in the history of man. Nevertheless, each has been specific and has come about by the prosaic and laborious processes of innovation, advocacy, and adoption; and no one of them has lived up to the passing expectation that it would revolutionize the affairs of man. The need for this historical perspective is apparent when one reflects upon the present prevailing assumption that recent technological developments in atomic fission and rocketry are ushering in still another "new age"—an age of total extermination or an age of new frontiers in the settlement in space, according to one's point of view.

chapter **7** *Physical, Biological, and Demographic Variables*

A social system operates in a context, even as do its parts, complexes, and assemblies; and the functional effectiveness of the system depends in part and in the long run upon how compatible it is with the particular context in which it operates. It is for this reason that the sociologist, most particularly the student of social change, must take into account factors and forces external to the society itself. In doing so, the sociologist becomes dependent for data, although not for the use he makes of them, upon some nonsociological fields of scientific endeavor; and his analysis is consequently limited by the availability of such data and his ability to interpret their relationship to sociological matters.

The context in which any social system operates is exceedingly complicated and consists of a large number of various kinds of elements, all subject to variation from place to place and from time to time, and most interdependent one with the others. For purposes of analysis these factors will here be classified into the physical and biological habitats, which are normally thought of as the environment upon which the society is dependent; the demographic characteristics of the social population; and the other social systems with which the system under consideration has symbiotic, competitive, or conflicting relations. This latter aspect of the context, insofar as it is of a different order from the preceding three, will be considered separately in subsequent chapters.

It is obvious that a social system does not operate in a vacuum or, alternatively, in some unspecified place in cosmic space. It operates on some specific part of the land surface of the earth and through the actions of men, women, and children who live by and are in turn affected by the other organisms with whom they share that specific part of the earth. It is also fairly obvious, although in fact frequently overlooked, that a social system that might serve well a few people living on a South Sea island would be totally inadequate for a few people living in the frozen arctic or for millions of people living on Manhattan Island. But what is by no means obvious is the actual relationship that exists between a social system and the various nonsocial aspects of its context. For one thing, the more that physicists, chemists, and biologists have discovered about the world in which man lives (and about man himself), the more complicated everything has turned out to be and the more, it has always appeared, there is still to be learned. For another, sociologists have been inclined to ignore the entire problem and to proceed on the assumption that, since as sociologists their concern is with society, they need not explore the relationship between society and its nonsocial context.[1] As a consequence, most of the attempts to trace this relationship have been made by physical and biological scientists who, however sophisticated in respect to their particular field of knowledge, have known little about society itself and have almost invariably viewed that little through a simple cause-and-effect frame of reference. The theories that they have advanced have, therefore, generally been more or less deterministic ones in which the physical or biological phenomena of their specialty are posited as the cause of social life or as the cause of changes in social life.

As Intervening Variables

One of the few things that may be said with confidence is that the environment in which a social system operates does not explain the existence of that system or even its character. A verdant piece of land may afford human beings an opportunity to maintain thereon an agricultural society; but the existence of a verdant piece of land does not ensure its being inhabited or, if it is, that it will be used for agriculture. It is men themselves, not physical

[1] John C. Harsanyi ("Explanations and Comparative Dynamics in Social Science," *Behavioral Science*, vol. 5, pp. 136–145, May, 1960) has ridiculed the tendency of sociologists to ignore factors external to the social system. He says, in part, "Among explanatory variables, special logical status belongs to variables *exogenous* to the social system, i.e., to the variables describing the natural environment of the society, and the biological properties of the population, in their aspects independent of human intervention. For if a social scientist suggests an explanation for a social fact in terms of other social facts, his explanation will be incomplete so long as he cannot offer explanation for these latter social facts themselves. But if he puts forward explanation for social fact in terms of variables genuinely exogenous to the social system his analytical task will be completed, as it will not be his business as a social scientist to find an explanation for these exogenous variables themselves" (p. 140). The trouble with this ironic argument is that few if any of the factors external to the social system are genuinely exogenous; for physical and biological factors are not exogenous but intervening variables.

or biological nature, who determine what uses they make of the environments that are offered to them. Men have often for long ignored, sometimes out of sheer ignorance, parts of the earth quite favorable to social life; they have also clung to arid and inherently inhospitable regions for centuries on end without any thought of seeking out a more favorable location for their society. On the other hand, different peoples have often fought long and disastrous wars for the possession of a particular piece of real estate; men have ventured on terrifying and dangerous voyages of discovery in the hopes of finding new lands favorable to their interests; and from time to time an entire people has been drawn or driven from its homeland into a wilderness settlement. All such movement, or lack of movement, of peoples and all the utilization, or lack of utilization, of the land surfaces of the earth are determined by social rather than natural forces.

Men cannot, of course, transcend the physical and biological potentialities of the particular part of the earth that they happen to inhabit. Their social system must provide them with a reasonably effective adjustment to their environment, or neither they nor their social system will survive. The potentialities do not function, however, as causes of the social system; rather, they operate to provide the *ultimate* limits within which men themselves may determine the characteristics of their social system. Although only through irrigation can considerable numbers of people support themselves through agriculture on arid land, the existence of arid land is not sufficient to explain the presence on it of a society using irrigation. Were it not for men these lands might be wholly unoccupied or only lightly populated by nomadic herdsmen. Arctic cold closely limits what men can do and still survive; but it does not determine what, if anything, men will do. Men have protected themselves against arctic cold by wearing heavy furs in the open and by huddling with their fellows in body-heated igloos; but although they can now build for themselves protective installations, artificially heated and as comfortable as any apartment house or office building in Manhattan, they have left much of the arctic unpopulated down to the present day.

Moreover, as will shortly be discussed, in their utilization of and adaptation to physical and biological nature men have never in the past even begun to approach the *ultimate* limits. Ignorance of nature has always set the operational limitations to social development. Men have, for example, herded goats on scanty grasses and lived on goat's milk when they might have brought water from the mountains to irrigate the soil; they have crouched around bits of glowing charcoal in the cold of winter when there was in the ground abundant coal with which they might have heated their habitations; and they have died of plague as it made its regular rounds when they might have done those things which, as is now known, would have prevented epidemics of plague.

Finally, not only do men determine what use is made of the environment, but they may also actively modify that environment in some respects and to a considerable degree. Men cannot transcend nature; but they can use or abuse what nature provides and, in the process, considerably change it. Clearly this is what happens when, in accordance with the imperatives and techniques of their society, men dig out a harbor where none was before, when they clear forest land to make fields and pastures, when they dig coal from the ground and drill miles into the earth for oil, and when, as in the modern world, they convert trees into paper, fibers, resins, and other materials not found in nature or fabricate plastics and rubber from petroleum. This is also what happens, for the most part quite inadvertently, when men overgraze the land and destroy its value to them, when they deforest the hills and cause the soils to erode away, and when they have so many babies that half or more must die of malnutrition or diseases fostered by malnutrition before they can reach maturity.

The role of the environment of a society in the determination of that society is perhaps most clearly seen when the various physical, biological, and demographic factors that constitute the environment are conceived as a complex of variables, each dependent upon others. Environments vary from place to place as well as from time to time; but although spatial variations are of interest to those sociologists who are engaged in a comparison of different social systems, such as South Sea islanders and Eskimos, it is temporal variations that are of interest in the study of social change. In respect to social change, physical, biological, and demographic factors operate as intervening variables, factors that intervene between one set of social circumstances and another.

The concept of intervening variables is entirely foreign to the folk mode of thinking, which is invariably in terms of cause and effect; it is not incorporated in any of the doctrines of social determinism, such as Marxism; and it has been ignored by some otherwise competent social thinkers, including not a few professional sociologists. It is, however, an indispensable concept in analyzing the role of environmental factors in the changes that occur in social life; for it often happens that changes in social life bring about changes in these factors that necessitate further changes in social life.

THE PHYSICAL HABITAT

Many of the elements of the technological component of a society and some of the elements of the ideological and organizational components are designed to provide the members of the society with methods of adjusting to or utilizing their physical habitat. Habitations, whether caves or modern skyscrapers, and clothing are designed to protect them from the weather;

footgear to protect their feet from injury; tools to aid them in cultivating the soil and working stone and other natural substances; and boats, carts, or other means of transportation to aid them in covering space. Some methods of adjusting to physical nature must exist if the society and its members are to survive. Those methods are certainly influenced by the specific characteristics of the physical environment—boats, for example, will hardly be developed in upland forests or carts on a small, rocky island—but they are not determined by it. Great cities have been built in a wide variety of physical settings—Paris and Berlin far inland from the sea, Venice and Amsterdam on stilts driven into tidal muds, New York on a firm base of granite, Rome on hills, and Chicago in a featureless plain.

The relationship between a society and its physical habitat, however, is exceedingly complex and cannot be summed up in a single law or principle. Men both modulate and modify their physical world—very little in the case of primitives, very much in modern societies. They modulate it when they construct buildings to protect them from heat, direct sunlight, wind, and cold. They modify it when they level hills, dig drainage ditches, or smelt metallic iron from natural oxides; but they may also modify it in ways far from intentional and in so doing create problems of adaptation that they may or may not in due course solve through the development of new techniques and related social devices. It is at such times that the role of physical nature as an intervening variable in the making of social change is most clear and pronounced.

The physical habitat is conventionally thought of as composed of climate, topography, and natural resources. These terms may be used to encompass the various components of the physical environment, but they do not begin to suggest the great complexity and variability of that environment. Climate, for example, is not an entity of itself. No matter what criteria are used, climates cannot be divided into good, bad, and indifferent; for the climate of any area is a function of a large number of interdependent variables. Thus the climatic significance of rainfall depends upon temperature, humidity, air composition and movement, land topography, and soil characteristics, as well as upon such related biological variables as forestation, the color, density, and texture of lesser vegetation, and the molds, funguses, etc., that live upon that vegetation. The precipitation in the arctic regions is exceedingly low, but there is never an absence of water. On the other hand, the rainfall in some of the higher altitudes of the tropics is great, but because of other factors there is little available water for man or plants.

Moreover, the climatic significance of rainfall varies also according to how and when the rainfall occurs. Other things being constant, a moderate annual rainfall that is spread more or less equally over the year makes for a far moister climate than does the same amount of rainfall concentrated during a few weeks of the year. Some desert areas receive 10 to 20 inches of rain a year; but the rain comes in a few heavy falls and is mostly lost through surface runoff. On the other hand, some fairly verdant regions are maintained by no more than 20 inches of rain that is spread lightly over the entire growing season. In a similar fashion, the daily and seasonal range of temperatures is far more important to man and his crops and domesticated animals than is the average or mean annual reading, which is what is usually given, as evidence of a pleasant climate, by chambers of commerce and tourist bureaus. The mean annual temperature of Death Valley in California is about 73 degrees; but there is hardly a spot on earth that is so uniformly uncomfortable; the range is far below freezing to well above 120 degrees, and one may be broiled at midday and yet frozen at midnight.

To say that any given area has a particular kind of climate is, therefore, to ignore the actualities. The climate of any area varies somewhat from hour to hour, from day to day, and from season to season. Moreover, at a given moment the climates of places within short distances of one another may vary widely as a consequence of topographical factors (and, indeed, of such social factors as land usage). The windward side of a tropical island may be comparatively moist and cool, while the lee side is at the same time arid and hot; the coastal fringe of such an island may be considerably less comfortable than lands of a few hundred feet elevation that are swept by trade winds. Within a 30-mile radius of San Francisco, the climates at a given moment may range from a foggy 60 degrees to a dry and sunny 110 degrees, with some sections within that radius enjoying a sunny, breeze-cooled 75 degrees.

Topography is, thus, one of the factors that contribute to the making of climate. It also affects the usage that men can make of space, and in earlier times it greatly restricted it; it provides, or fails to provide, natural harbors, access to the sea, rivers and streams, lakes and mountain barriers, valleys, etc. Some lands are level and well-watered and easy to traverse, settle, cultivate, or build cities upon; some, at the opposite extreme, are rugged and dry and inherently inhospitable to the uses of man. Men have sometimes ignored lands of the former sort and have sometimes struggled to survive on those of the latter; but whatever they have done, they have not been able to ignore the topography of the region in which they have done it.

Of vital importance to modern men, and only less so to their predecessors, are the natural resources that are available within a given region. What constitutes a natural resource is, of course, a matter of social definition. Three centuries ago coal was not so defined by any people in the world; a century ago petroleum was just beginning to be defined as useful; a generation ago uranium ore was no more than a geological curiosity. Historically,

Physical, biological, and demographic variables   **217**

the social definition of what constitutes natural resources has slowly enlarged, and it now includes the energy that can be released from atomic fission. Presumably this definition will continue to expand; and already, in fact, forward-looking scientists are dreaming of the useful materials that may someday be secured from the moon. As the social definition of what constitutes natural resources expands, the usable resources of the world enlarge. At the same time, any single resource is limited in quantity; hence, with the exception of the energy of the sun, use of that resource reduces the supply. Use of the energy of the sun has no effect upon the supply, for the sun is dissipating its energy at a rate unaffected by man.

An Intervening Variable

From the point of view of the geologist the physical world is undergoing constant change. Mountain ridges rise, are weathered, and recede; valleys fill with silt, are elevated to make plateaus, and are scoured in turn by rivers; the composition of the atmosphere changes as granite upthrusts release their carbon, and carbon is withdrawn from the atmosphere by rain and deposited in the seas. To the geologist, there is nothing stable about the physical world; but the geologist's temporal frame of reference is one that has no relevance whatever to social life. The record of civilization is but three or four millenniums long; the record of rocks is measured in hundreds of millions of years. Geological changes, excepting such rare occurrences as earthquakes and abrupt appearances of volcanic activity, have not significantly modified the physical characteristics of man's environment.

Certainly many climatic changes have occurred in certain parts of the earth within historic times, changes that were once taken to be geological. Thus within the past three thousand years the valley of the river Jordan, the region once known as Palestine, and the north central coastal regions of Africa have changed from semiarid to arid areas, from fertile plains and wooded mountain slopes to barren and eroded desert lands. Huntington and many other social geographers have assumed that these and other known changes in climate have been natural, i.e., that they have been local manifestations of those long-run geological changes that are unaffected by any human agency.[2] The drying up of the North African coast, for example, has been assumed to have been a consequence of the final ending of the latest glacial cycle, which may have lowered the levels of the seas, and brought an ice cap to much of Northern Europe some fifty thousand years ago.

It is the consensus of current scientific opinion, however, that most of the changes in climate and in topography and certainly those in physical resources that have occurred over the past two or three thousand years

[2] Ellsworth Huntington, *Mainsprings of Civilization*, John Wiley & Sons, Inc., New York, 1945.

have not been natural but have in fact been worked by man himself.[3] The annual rainfall of Palestine today is probably less than half of what it was in the time of Julius Caesar, when the hills of Palestine were forested, the slopes were green with grasses, and the valley lands were under cultivation. Today all this is changed; the forests were long ago leveled to build ships for Rome, the hillsides were gradually eroded to barren rock, and the valley lands then became parched and sandy. Today when rains fall, as they do at times, the water cascades down the mountains, flushes down the hills, and drains quickly through the valleys to the sea. Little water sinks into the soil, which is hard from the sun and almost devoid of vegetation. These great changes, it now appears, came about through man's own actions. The air above a region that is forested is cooler than it would be above the same region if the lands were barren. Thus deforestation meant for one thing that the thermal characteristics of the uplands were so changed as to cause moisture-bearing winds from the sea to ride high across the mountains rather than releasing the moisture as rain; for another, it meant that such rain as did fall was lost as runoff rather than conserved through percolation into the soil. Deforestation was, apparently, only the beginning of a chain of interdependent changes. As the trees were felled, the mountain slopes lost their ability to absorb and store ground waters; the grasses declined, mainly from lack of water but in part no doubt from persistent overgrazing of sheep and goats, which are exceedingly hard on pasturage, since they will, lacking grass, grub out the roots; and as the mountains and hills became incapable of storing water between rains, the irrigation system fell into disuse, so that valley lands, too, became barren and incapable of storing the day's heat for gradual release during the night, with the result that the days are now hotter and the nights colder than they once were.[4]

[3] A variety of historical illustrations of the ways in which man has both deliberately and inadvertently worked profound changes in his physical environment are provided by William J. Thomas (ed.) in *Man's Role in Changing the Face of the Earth*, University of California Press, Berkeley, Calif., 1956. More systematic analyses of the process are provided by Walter Firey, *Man, Mind and Land: A Theory of Resource Use*, The Free Press of Glencoe, New York, 1960; and Philip L. Wagner, *The Human Use of the Earth*, The Free Press of Glencoe, New York, 1960.

[4] The close interdependence of physical and biological factors is explored by Hadlow Leonard in *Climate, Vegetation and Man*, Philosophical Library, Inc., New York, 1953.

The domestication of sheep and goats was one of the early advances in social technology that led in many instances to most adverse long-run consequences. In reasonably moist regions sheep and goats do no appreciable harm to the land; but their special peculiarity is that they can forage on the rough grasses and brush of semiarid and even rocky lands, and here they are, in the long run, very

Halfway around the world and two millenniums later, Americans unwittingly began a process of rapid soil erosion that is still going on in what was, and perhaps still is, one of the most favorable pieces of agricultural land on earth, the Mississippi Valley.[5] By the time that settlers had moved into the plains west of the Mississippi, tributaries to that great river—the Missouri, the Red River, and the Arkansas—were flooding each spring as the snows in the Rocky Mountains melted and were taking vast quantities of silt down toward the Gulf. It was therefore assumed that such flooding and erosion was natural; and when conservationists began to decry the loss of topsoil, it was pointed out that the annual flood of silt-bearing waters had been going on since the beginning of time. Today it is known that that was not so and that men themselves, in the persons of the early beaver trappers, had actually started the process. Before the 1820s the eastern slopes of the Rocky Mountains were peppered with marshes and mountain meadows that had been produced by the damming of mountain streams by beaver; and these marshes and meadows served to catch and hold for gradual release the rapid runoff from melting snow fields. A decade or two of trapping practically exterminated the beaver, their dams rotted away, and the runoff water flowed swiftly down to the valley floor. Currently the beaver dams of more than a century ago are being replaced by man-made dams, at high cost and none too effectively.

---

destructive. Large areas of the Iberian Peninsula, of Greece, Palestine, etc., have been made progressively less productive of vegetation and more arid in considerable part through the practice of grazing sheep and goats on them.

It has been said that the most significant accomplishment of Dictator Tito's quasi-communistic government in Yugoslavia has been to force the peasants to keep their goats staked up. If true, this may not be so slight a change as the statement implies; for the barrenness of the hills of Yugoslavia and the aridity of the valley lands may have been brought about by overgrazing. Perhaps if the goats can be kept staked for a century or two, grasses and brush may again thrive on the hillsides and hold waters and erosion in check and so bring back some of the lost fertility of valley lands.

Deforestation and overgrazing are but two of many ways by which men have inadvertently destroyed the productive capacity of their lands. Irrigation, for example, by which inherently arid land has often been made fruitful, will in time destroy the fertility of the soil wherever temperatures are high and natural rainfall very low; for the surface evaporation of irrigation water leaves saline residues behind. It was, in part, the increasing salinity of the irrigated lands of the Euphrates Valley that brought an end to the great civilization that flourished there in antiquity; and many other irrigated areas have had to be abandoned in the Near East, India, and even in the modern American Southwest for the same reason.

[5] See Carl F. Kraenzel, *The Great Plains in Transition*, University of Oklahoma Press, Norman, Okla., 1955.

Until recent times, the ability of men to modify their physical environment, intentionally or otherwise, was limited by the slight physical power that they had at their command (that of their own bodies and of their domesticated animals). They could and often did deforest mountains and hillsides in securing fuel and timber for construction and, in some instances, by deliberate burning to clear lands for pasturage. They often used such exploitative means of cultivating their lands or so overgrazed their pasturages that the lands became in the end barren and unproductive. The process of such destruction was, however, slow and more or less imperceptible. Thus it took the Chinese more than a thousand years so to deforest the western mountains that many of the great rivers, such as the Yellow River, ran each spring in flood and in silt and had to be shored up with dikes to hold them in their course. The peoples of India have been more than a thousand years in reducing the fertility of their soil through poor tillage, deforestation, and consequent flooding and through the devious process of burning cow dung as their major fuel (the forests and woodlands having been exhausted) and so taking from the land and turning into the atmosphere the nitrogen and other elements that are essential to plant growth.

With the beginnings of the industrial revolution, however, Western peoples began to utilize and often to destroy natural resources at an unprecedented rate, a rate that even yet continues to rise. As was indicated earlier, the industrial revolution was first fueled by wood (in the smelting of iron); and within half a century most of Western Europe and Britain had been denuded of trees. Then came the discovery that coal could be coked, which led to the mining of coal, and this in turn to the invention and development of the steam engine. Through technological changes, coal came to be one of the most valued of natural resources, and the mining, transportation, and use of coal became a major economic activity. By 1850 most of the work of the Western world, except that in agriculture, was being done by coal-generated steam; and the transition to what Cottrell terms a "high energy" society was well under way.[6] The applications of steam power were rapidly extended, the steam engine grew in size, power, and efficiency; and for the first time man began to heat his habitations with coal and so to live in a temperate climate the year around. Meanwhile, the existence of pools of petroleum under the surface of the ground was discovered (oil seepages had long been known, and oil had been used in some places as a medicine); the technique of distillation was applied to secure kerosene from petroleum, and kerosene soon became the major fuel for the lamps of the entire world; the internal-combustion engine was invented to put to use the higher frac-

[6] W. Frederick Cottrell, *Energy and Society*, McGraw-Hill Book Company, New York, 1955. This work examines the historical relation between the energy usages of societies, social change, and economic development. It is one of the few major contributions made by sociologists to the study of social change.

tions (gasoline) that were produced by the distillation of petroleum; and the age of the automobile, the airplane, the Diesel-powered ship and railroad train, the farm tractor, and the powered lawn mower began. Then, a quarter century later, men began to pipe to industrial centers and put to use the natural gas that had theretofore been a useless by-product of the oil wells; and with this final development, the age of the fossil fuels came to maturity.

The social repercussions of all these developments in technology are many and varied and fairly self-evident, but the consequences to the physical environment are still somewhat uncertain. It is clear that there has already been withdrawn and burned a considerable proportion of the fossil fuels that were laid down by primitive forms of organic life, through their withdrawing carbon and hydrogen from the atmosphere, while the world was, geologically speaking, still young. The relatively stable hydrocarbons that were produced from this organic matter (coal, oil, and gas) lay for many millions of years beneath the ground; but within the last two centuries men have busily reversed the process that occurred during the long and distant Carboniferous age; they have at rapidly increasing rates been returning to the atmosphere the carbon and hydrogen that had been withdrawn from it and in the process fixing, as carbon dioxide, a great deal of the oxygen of the earth's atmosphere.

The Greenhouse Effect

The extent of man's current ability to change the world in which he lives, and thereby modify the conditions of his social survival, is exemplified in the potential consequences of the burning of the fossil fuels. The most obvious possible result is that eventually—a half century, a century, or two centuries from now—the available supply of such fuels will be exhausted, in which case the machinery of industrial society will come to a halt unless an adequate substitute for them is devised. Less evident, but quite as possible, a prospect is that in returning to the earth's atmosphere the elements that were withdrawn from it during the Carboniferous age, men will inadvertently return the earth to something of the climatic conditions that then obtained. During that geological period the carbon dioxide content of the atmosphere was far greater than it is at present; earth temperatures were apparently considerably higher than they are now; the atmosphere was very heavily laden with moisture; and plant growth was, as a consequence, far more rapid than any that is known of today.

There are some indications that the climates of the earth have become warmer by perhaps as much as 2 degrees over the last hundred years. Among these are the current recession of glaciers and the fact that certain regions of the earth now rarely experience such heavy frosts during the winter months as they normally did a century ago. Geophysicists and geographers at first interpreted this apparent change as evidence that the latest glacial age was only now coming to an end; later, they were inclined to explain it as the result of some long-term cyclical fluctuation in the sun's activity. Recently a hypothesis that was initially advanced in 1861 by J. Tyndall has been revived, refined, and bolstered with new data by a number of responsible geophysical scientists. The central idea of the hypothesis is that the critical factor that determines the temperature on the earth is the percentage of carbon dioxide in the atmosphere. Carbon dioxide, in combination with the moisture in the air, serves in much the same way as does the glass of a greenhouse to retard the radiation into space of the heat (the infrared rays) that is produced by the rays of the sun striking the earth. If there were no atmosphere, most of that heat would be dissipated, particularly during the night hours, and night temperatures on the earth would be exceedingly low. This theory holds that it was mainly variations in atmospheric carbon dioxide (resulting from the uplifting of indigenous rock which, exposed to weather, slowly forms carbonates) that brought on the various glacial periods; that it was the withdrawal of carbon dioxide from the atmosphere that ended the warmth and moisture of the distant Carboniferous age; and that in recent years men have rapidly been proceeding to restore the conditions of that age by building a carbon dioxide greenhouse over their heads.[7]

The greenhouse theory is still unproved; but if only because the consequences, should the theory prove to be valid, would be of such vast import, the theory cannot be ignored. The very idea that men can, however inad-

[7] J. Tyndall made his original suggestion of the greenhouse effect in "On the Absorption and Radiation of Heat by Gases and Vapours," *Philosophical Magazine*, vol. 22, pp. 169–194 and 273–285, September, 1861. Recent and more sophisticated discussions of the matter are provided by Harlow Shapley (ed.), *Climatic Change: Evidence, Causes, and Effects*, Harvard University Press, Cambridge, Mass., 1952; Gilbert N. Plass, "Carbon Dioxide and the Climate," *American Scientist*, vol. 44, pp. 302–316, July, 1956, and "The Carbon Dioxide Theory of Climatic Change," *Tellus*, vol. 8, pp. 140–154, May, 1956; D. R. Bates (ed.), *The Earth and Its Atmosphere*, Basic Books, Inc., Publishers, New York, 1958; and James L. Dyson, *The World of Ice*, Alfred A. Knopf, Inc., New York, 1962, pp. 247–274.

Some idea of the magnitudes of the changes that are being effected by the burning of the fossil fuels is given by the estimates of oceanographer Roger Revelle. He finds that the carbon dioxide in the earth's atmosphere at present is about three-tenths of 1 per cent. During the past hundred years we have returned to it some 360 billion tons; and at present rates we shall have added 1,700 billion tons more by the end of this century—an amount equal to 70 per cent of that now present in the atmosphere. Unless vegetation or the oceans absorb most of this addition, there will be a 20 per cent increase in the carbon dioxide in the atmosphere, which could raise the air temperature as much as 5 degrees (*Time*, July 6, 1959).

vertently, radically modify the climates of the world is frightening. Traditionally, such powers are divine; and although some individuals profess an ability to make rain fall and to sway the will of God, scientists are reluctant to find in human action the explanation for physical phenomena, if only because they fear that men may prove to be incapable of using such powers in ways conducive to their own ends. If the world as men now know it is doomed to extinction, better that this be the inescapable will of God than the error of men themselves. Certainly if the greenhouse theory should prove to be valid, the prospect for men would indeed be grim. As burning of the fossil fuels continued and the percentage of carbon dioxide rose, the temperature on the earth would rise; the percentage of moisture in the air would rise (by more rapid evaporation from the surface of the seas); the rate of vegetation growth would increase (as the result of more moisture, heat, and carbon dioxide to convert to plant tissue); and the increased vegetation would in turn further diminish the radiation from the earth of the heat absorbed from the sun. Once fairly under way this cycle would be progressive; and although tens of thousands of years were required for the locking up of carbon to bring an end to the heat and humidity of the Carboniferous age, modern society could very well get itself back into the climatic conditions of that age in another century.

Should this happen, men could no doubt survive; but societies as we now know them would become impossible. For one thing, most of the fertile lands and all the great cities would vanish under the seas. As world temperatures rose by as little as 4 or 5 degrees and as the atmosphere became heavy with moisture, the present icecaps would melt, releasing into the oceans the water that is presently stored as ice. It is an easy calculation, and a certain one, that the ocean levels would then rise a hundred feet or more. Scientists are currently worried, perhaps with some aid from laymen, over the possibility that men will make the earth uninhabitable in the event of an atomic war by the pollution of the atmosphere with fission products; but that, as can easily be seen, is not the only route to self-extermination. The new phenomenon of the industrial age, smog, is a recognizable disutility; and it is quite possible that men will do something to correct this particular form of atmospheric pollution before it poisons or suffocates the urban population. There is, however, no way that further release of carbon dioxide into the air can be prevented short of discontinuing the burning of the fossil fuels; and to do that would mean, lacking a cheap and effective alternative source of power, returning socially to the hard work and short life and material impoverishment which were the common lot of men two centuries ago. Although the rise of modern society cannot be accounted for in terms of the discovery of coal and oil and the invention of the steam and the internal-combustion engines, it is self-evident that the maintenance of modern life now depends upon energy from these sources.

Exhaustion of Natural Resources

Many peoples of times past have undoubtedly destroyed, in whole or in major part, elements of their physical environment that were essential to the welfare of their society. The usual ways of doing so in the premodern world have been deforestation, overgrazing of pastures, and exploitative cultivation of the soil. Whether the historic decline of any of the great civilizations of the past is to be accounted for in this way is simply not known. It is possible that inadvertent destruction of natural resources was a factor that contributed to the ultimate disappearance of Mesopotamian civilization, and it may have been one of the circumstances that weakened the people of Rome. There is, moreover, some evidence that even under conserving techniques of soil cultivation, those soils that have been cultivated for centuries lose the trace elements of rare minerals which seem necessary for good health. There are, however, so many other factors, biological and social, that may contribute to the decline of a civilization that it does seem unlikely that mismanagement of the physical environment should ever have been the only reason or even the major reason for a society's losing out in the struggle for survival.

The evidence is quite clear, however, that in times past men have not recognized the physically destructive consequences of their technologies or been guided by long-range considerations in their use of natural resources. They seem always and everywhere to have exploited their environments to the best of their technological capacity on a day-to-day or year-to-year basis, without thought of the distant future. Thus after more than two thousand years of recorded history, during which they deforested their entire lands, the Chinese had not learned that, if they were to have wood to burn, they must let trees grow to maturity; in 1935 a concerted effort by the Nationalist government to start a reforestation program failed because the peasants and villagers pulled up seedlings for fuel as fast as they were planted.

The first known program for the conservation of natural resources to be put into effect is that which developed in the countries of Western Europe early in the last century. (Britain, incidentally, did nothing of the sort and still does very little.) The destruction of forests to provide charcoal for the smelting of iron for some reason (historical data on this matter are lacking) impressed the people with the necessity of reforesting and maintaining forests as a timber crop; and in time their governments came to support programs of reforestation. Lands not suitable for cultivation or pasturage were set aside in perpetuity, sometimes, but not generally, in governmental ownership, as forest lands; standards of cultivation, cropping, and replanting evolved; and today there is more timber growing in Western Europe than there has been at any other time since the early Middle Ages. So embedded in the culture of these societies is regard for forest maintenance that even during the exigency of war and under military conquest no excessive cutting has occurred. The idea of the need to conserve essential natural resources has become an established element in the ideology of all Western peoples; but the actual practice of conservation, that of forests in Western Europe excepted, is almost unknown even today. Efforts to rehabilitate exhausted soils or to check water erosion after the damage has been done are not uncommon; but to exercise the social restraint and foresight to prevent soil erosion and to preserve the natural checks to water runoff are rare indeed.

The history of the semiarid lands on the western fringe of the Mississippi Valley is a case in point. First used as winter pasturage for cattle, these lands were put into cultivation late in the last century, mainly for dry farming of grains. With the coming of mechanized plowing, seeding, and harvesting, they were for a time a fruitful source of wheat; but the exceptionally dry years of the 1930s turned them into the dust bowl of Steinbeck's *Grapes of Wrath*, and they were left to the mercy of the winds. A rational program would have been to return the lands to grass, and there was at least talk of doing so; but the period of drought passed; and the advent of war in Europe, combined with governmental support prices for wheat, encouraged resettlement and replanting of these lands to grain. Now, a quarter century later, the stage is set for another disaster which could well ruin these lands forever. It is calculated that it takes nature about a thousand years to produce an inch of topsoil from bedrock, and there is no way by which man can speed this process; yet man can with modern machine tillage destroy an inch of topsoil in a single crop season. Soil conservationists claim that already fully one-third of the fertile soil of the Mississippi Valley is gone and that unless corrective measures are promptly taken—as is being done in a small way in some places—the great Mississippi Valley will be a barren waste before another century is out.[8]

The argument that is invariably brought against conservation measures is that their social cost is too high to be practical and that as one resource is actually exhausted, man finds an alternative—that there is no need, for example, to save the virgin forests when better structures can now be built of concrete. The American steel industry was built upon the fortunate happenstance that vast supplies of high-grade iron ore existed in the Mesabi Range in northern Minnesota, close to Lake Superior, and that these supplies could be brought by water transport to lakeside Indiana near to large deposits of coking coal. Seventy years of intensive mining have exhausted those high-grade ores; but human ingenuity has found substitutes—the discovery of a method of utilizing what low-grade ores are left, of a great deposit of high-grade ore in Venezuela, and of another in upper Nova Scotia. Means of mining and transporting these ores have been devised, and the American

[8] See William Vogt, *Road to Survival*, William Sloane Associates, 1948.

steel industry has not ground to a halt, as some pessimists had predicted it would.

It is true that through technological innovation a diminishing resource may be replaced by some substitute, and it is probably also true that there is no inherent limit to technological developments; but in every instance in which a new technique has produced a substitute for a diminishing natural resource, the energy cost, if not the social cost, has risen. Thus we are no longer dependent upon the metal copper—visible supplies of which have already shrunk alarmingly—for electrical wire and other usages where iron will not serve. Aluminum has begun to replace copper; and the supplies of bauxite mineral from which it is now derived are both widespread and seemingly inexhaustible. The energy cost of extracting metallic aluminum from ores is, however, many times that of smelting copper; so here, as in almost every other instance, as the shift is made from one natural resource to another or from one source of supply to another, somewhat greater reliance is placed on the fossil fuels. Consider, for example, the current efforts to devise an economical method of desalting sea water. That effort stems from the fact that in many parts of America, and to a lesser extent in other regions of the world, more water for irrigation of cultivated lands and for domestic and industrial purposes is currently being used than is supplied by rain. The deficit is at the present time being made up by drawing upon underground resources—by pumping water from the ground. The old-fashioned well of town or farmstead reached down 20 feet or so and drew upon subsurface waters that were replenished each rainy season; if there was little rain, then the well ran dry in midsummer. Modern techniques make possible very deep drilling (300 feet and more) into bedrock and pumping from great depths; and the water so obtained is geologic—i.e., it is water that has accumulated over the ages and that will not be replaced in a hundred or even a thousand years.[9]

In recognition of the fact that many localities are now relying on water supplies that will in time become exhausted, a substitute source is being sought in the inexhaustible oceans; but to make sea water usable, it must be demineralized; and so far the only workable method is distillation. There is nothing in the nature of things that would prevent men from making up the water deficit in this way; but the costs in energy would certainly be heroic.

One cannot fail, therefore, to come to the conclusion that the critical natural resource will be energy. Given an inexhaustible supply of energy, modern societies can replace any other diminished resource—theoretically,

[9] For the critical nature of our water problem and how it came about, see Ben Moreell, *Our Nation's Water Resources*, The University of Chicago Press, Chicago, 1956.

even fertile soil can be dispensed with and food can be grown in chemically nourished vats of water. Modern societies, however, are currently dependent for their major supplies of energy upon the fossil fuels; the total supply was determined by nature millions of years ago, and men cannot replace them. The known alternatives—direct use of sunlight on the one hand and atomic fission on the other—have at the moment very limited promise.[10] Estimates of how long the peoples of the world can continue to draw upon the available supplies of fossil fuels at current rates of consumption range from a pessimistic one generation to a most optimistic one century; but there is every reason to suppose that the rates of consumption will continue to rise, and to rise spectacularly, rather than remain constant. At present only a small pro-

[10] Nuclear-fission plants now in operation produce energy at economic costs about equal to that of coal and oil in Britain; and as our own supplies of fossil fuels run short, we might resort to this currently expensive source. But the long-run possibilities are still unclear, and the experts are divided between cautious pessimism and equally cautious optimism. On the former side are Walter Isard and Vincent Whitney, *Atomic Power: An Economic and Social Analysis*, McGraw-Hill Book Company, New York, 1952; and Hans Thirring, *Energy for Man*, Indiana University Press, Bloomington, Ind., 1959. Mildly hopeful that atomic fission may provide an economic and enduring substitute for the fossil fuels are Palmer C. Putnam, *Energy in the Future*, D. Van Nostrand Company, Inc., Princeton, N.J., 1953; and Norman Landsdell, *The Atom and the Energy Revolution*, Philosophical Library, Inc., New York, 1958.

The extent of the supplies of uranium and thorium ore, upon which the present technique of atomic energy depends, are unknown but undoubtedly limited. Moreover, the ashes of nuclear reactors pose a tremendous problem of disposal. Unlike the by-products of ore refining, they cannot be dumped into the sea or buried in casks in the ground, for they will continue to be highly dangerous to all organic life for tens of thousands of years. And should all the current energy needs of just the United States be supplied by nuclear fission, we should each year have to safely dispose of an amount of radioactive wastes equal to that which would be produced by the explosion of 200,000 atom bombs of the size dropped on Japan.

However, the problem of waste disposal, great though it would be, seems susceptible of solution. Already it has been found that the wastes can be chemically fixed in a special ceramic matrix which will remain stable for a hundred thousand years or more. In this form the dangerous wastes could be safely stored away in abandoned salt mines, natural caves, or other places far removed from human habitation.

Moreover, there is some prospect for an alternative to nuclear fission—fusion, a process in which energy is released as lighter elements are combined into atoms of heavier elements. Should a practical process be developed for the production of controlled fusion, the world's energy problem would, apparently, be solved forever. The material used would be deuterium derived from water, and there would be no radioactive wastes. See Richard F. Post, "Fusion Power," *Scientific American*, December, 1957, pp. 73 ff.

portion of the population of the world is included in high-energy societies—perhaps no more than 30 per cent; the United States, constituting less than 8 per cent of the population of the world, currently uses 60 per cent of the energy derived from the fossil fuels. Should the other peoples of the world begin, as they are tending to do, to use energy at this rate, consumption would mount at least sevenfold. At that rate, the world would have, taking the most optimistic estimate of the fossil-fuel resources, only a few decades' supply.

The social effects of local depletion of the fossil fuels can be seen in what has happened to Britain during the past thirty years. For a century and more Britain quite literally ruled the seas, in part because of her great navy, but also in part because Britain had established and maintained naval coal bunkers around the world. Most of the steamships of the world were dependent upon British coal and hence were to some extent under the control of the British. Coal was for many decades Britain's major export; but, as has now been belatedly realized, Britain was exporting an irreplaceable resource, and that resource is all but gone. The decline of Britain as a great world power is in some considerable part traceable to the fact that she has expended most of her energy resources. Moreover, the development of welfarism in Britain is also related, however indirectly, to the economic dislocations that have been induced by the loss of her chief source of external income.

Social Change and the Physical Environment

Changes in the physical environment of a society will produce incongruencies of some sort and to some degree within that society—for example, a decline in the food supply—that may in turn lead directly or indirectly to changes in that society. In the past such changes as have occurred in the physical environment have for the most part been produced by the society itself and have in the main been inadvertent; the kinds of social changes that have resulted seem to have been mainly atrophic. In the modern world men have at least the knowledge, stemming in considerable measure from the development of science, to forecast the physical consequences of techniques and be guided accordingly. They know the dangers of soil erosion; they can at least now sense the consequences of continued reliance upon the fossil fuels; they are aware of the hazards of large-scale use, especially military use, of atomic fission. Knowledge of men's dependence upon the physical world is not lacking; and where it is inadequate, it can be increased; but whether or not this knowledge will be applied to ensure a social future is quite another matter.[11] So far, the technological developments of the past two hundred

[11] The prospects that men will effectively apply scientific knowledge to the conservation of the physical resources and conditions upon which they are dependent are explored by Harrison Brown, *The Challenge of Man's Future*, The

years have led to increasing dependence upon and increasing exploitation of natural resources, and men are today destroying the physical basis of life more rapidly than ever before. For this reason, if no other, modern industrial societies must continue to change in order to survive. For the moment, however, old attitudes, old sentiments, and old values and modes of social organization stand in the way of men's using the resources of the earth in more foresightful ways. For the moment, it would seem, they prefer to dream of alternative worlds in space rather than adapting their societies to the limited physical potentials of the earth.

THE BIOLOGICAL HABITAT

Man is only one of the countless species of organisms that inhabit the earth and compete and conflict with one another for space and the means of sustaining life. The relations of man to the plants, animals, insects, bacteria, molds, funguses, and other organisms with which he shares his physical habitat is similar to his relations to physical nature but far more complex.[12] Man must be able to utilize effectively many of these organisms, for he is dependent on them for his food and for the fibers and other materials with which he clothes his body and in some instances from which he constructs his habitations and some of his tools. Man must also maintain sufficient control over competitive organisms—wolves that would live off his sheep, weeds that would choke his fields, birds and rats that would consume his grain, and bacteria that would destroy his body—that he may enjoy a man-made surplus of foods and other organic materials and himself live to consume them. Ways of accomplishing these ends are socially provided; but even as is the case with man's adjustment to physical nature, the particular ways that are used to control the biological habitat often determine in considerable measure the characteristics of that habitat.

The Ecological Balance

In the symbolism of agrarian societies, Nature is a bountiful agent who pours forth in abundance the foods and fibers by which men live. From the point of view of any organism, however, biological nature is a parsimonious

Viking Press, New York, 1954; Richard L. Meier, *Science and Economic Development: New Patterns of Living*, John Wiley & Sons, Inc., New York, 1956; and Raymond F. Dasmann, *Environmental Conservation*, John Wiley & Sons, Inc., New York, 1959.

[12] See Felix Marti-Ibañez, *Men, Molds, and History*, MD Publications, Inc., New York, 1958.

witch forever engaged in maintaining scarcity. There is no abundance in nature for any organism; and if man enjoys the fruits of the field, the forest, and the seas, it is because he has won them by his own efforts from the greedy and insatiable mouths of a multitude of competitors. As a consequence, the relations of man and his society to the biological habitat are considerably more dynamic than are those of man and his society to the physical environment. The latter submits to his use and abuse passively; should he level a hill, it stays level, and should he mine and burn coal, it is gone forever—although there may of course be some physical by-products of this action. The biological habitat, on the other hand, is inherently unstable, and it responds rather than submits to man's uses and abuses. As a complex of intervening variables, the biological habitat is, therefore, more sensitive to social influences than is the physical, and changes in it are far less subject to prediction.

In only one respect is the biological habitat of a society constant. This is the normal tendency for the many subhuman species of organisms that inhabit a given area of the earth to maintain a natural, ecological balance— that is, a balance between species and between the numbers of each species to the end that all the means for sustaining organic life are fully utilized. In nature there is no surplus of space, sunlight, soil nutrients, or anything else, and there is no waste. The voracious appetites and high reproductive powers of the organisms of each species assure that all are constantly competing with one another for the means of maintaining life and that the species as a whole is, as it were, constantly trying to increase its numbers at the expense of some other competing species. A mountain meadow, for example, may be inhabited by a considerable number of grasses, each with its special organic characteristics and each occupying to the fullest those areas of the meadow in which, because of soil and other factors, it has a competitive advantage over the other species of grasses. Birds, field mice, mildews, and molds will consume and live on the surplus seeds produced by these grasses; some grazing animals will feed on the grasses themselves; predators of one sort or another will hunt birds, mice, and grazing animals; etc. Other plant species, other animals, and countless varieties of insects, bacteria, and other lower forms of life will be busily living on one another and so keeping the numbers of each species down to some normative level, or else living on the by-products of plant and animal life (dead vegetation, animal wastes, etc.) and ultimately returning to the soil the nitrogen and minerals that make continued plant growth possible.

In a hypothetically closed ecological system the various species of plants, animals, insects, and simpler organisms would remain constant and the numbers of each species would vary only with seasonal cycles; the grasses, for example, would die out in the fall, to be replaced by seedling grasses the following spring. Organic life on some small islands does actually

Physical, biological, and demographic variables 231

approach this ideal ecological balance; but elsewhere there is always some change occurring in species and in the position of the various species vis-à-vis one another. Thus a new plant or animal species may invade an area and upset the prior balance, as is the case when wolves move down to the valley from their mountain habitations because of a scarcity of game or when a disease sweeps through a stand of timber. Or the balance may be disturbed by the fact that a dominant species (one that is unusually successful in the area) adversely changes the conditions on which it has thrived. Deer, which eat the bark and the soft tips of trees and shrubs, may, for example, through overgrazing prevent both trees and shrubs from growing. All such disturbances to the ecological balance tend, however, to be self-correcting; and through time there is total utilization of the means of sustaining organic life.

The Social Balance

In a sense man is always and everywhere an intruder in nature; although himself an animal, in his competition with the lower organisms he has the advantage of being able to augment his biological equipment with cultural aids. No doubt very early man had nothing but his bare hands and slow wits to aid him in competition with other predators; but in time man devised tools and strategies, and since then he has been the dominant animal wherever he has gone. The degree of man's dominance over the lower organisms has varied widely over the ages and from society to society, depending in major part upon the complexity and effectiveness of his technology; but his dominance has never been total; it has always been, and still is, precarious.

At the most primitive level of technology, the collection culture, in which man lives by hunting, by fishing, or on such edible vegetation as nature happens to provide, the organic surplus on which he lives is obtained simply by his outcompeting other animals. The hunter kills the game that otherwise the fox or the wolf or some other predator would get, with the net result that there are men in place of foxes, wolves, or other predators. Where agriculture and animal domestication exist, the relation of man to his biological environment is far more complex, far more fruitful for man, and somewhat less precarious. Both the herder and the farmer secure their livelihood by maintaining a socially established—as distinct from a spontaneous— ecological balance. Thus a farmer begins by removing from the land the plant species that grow there naturally and planting in their place plant species that are useful to him; for example, he tears out the fine grasses and plants a coarse grain, such as wheat, from the seed of which he can make his daily bread. In so doing he totally upsets the natural balance and establishes an artificial, a social, one. To maintain this social balance, he must continually resist the natural tendencies for the ecological balance to revert to its former state. Thus he must keep weeds from his fields, keep down the numbers of mice and rats, birds and rabbits, and other small animals that would rob him of his harvest or destroy his growing grain; he must fence his fields to keep off deer or other large animals that might graze on his grain; and then, if the weather is favorable and no disease strikes, he will, come fall, have a harvest of food far greater than uncontrolled nature would provide.

The history of culture is in considerable part the story of man's development of methods of dominating his biological environment. Slowly, and very erratically, man's techniques have improved through the invention of new cultivation methods, new means of destroying competitive organisms, and new and more fruitful plant and animal species. Particularly over the last two hundred years, the techniques of agriculture and animal husbandry have improved with great rapidity; and today, in the United States at least, the production of food and natural fibers is a remarkably rational and highly organized operation. On the whole Western societies do far better in the systematic and long-range exploitation of biological resources than they do in the use of those which are distinctly physical. Whereas there is a considerable possibility that we may run out of top soil, exhaust the supplies of fossil fuels, or adversely affect world climates, there is almost no possibility that we shall lose our current dominance over the lower organisms and be overwhelmed by rats, destroyed by wolves, or killed off by bacteria. Just why Western peoples have exercised more ingenuity and more foresight in the biological than in the physical realm is not clear. Perhaps it is the immediacy of the biological in comparison with the physical: an invasion of rats is an immediate and evident threat to men, whereas the erosion of soil is slow and its effects on man may seem distant; the destructive consequences of cancer are apparent, and many scientists are engaged in studying it, whereas the possibility of upsetting our climates through the burning of coal and oil seems very remote, and only a handful of scientists are interested in studying this danger.

Biological Theories of Social Change

In many historical instances the social life of a people has been disastrously upset by their failure to control biological nature—usually either because some epidemic disease has decimated the people themselves or because some disease has destroyed their crops or their herds. From such instances has come the theory, usually advanced by biologists or epidemiologists, that it is the disturbances of the biological habitat of man that induce social change. Frequently cited in support of this theory is the presumed rise in the incidence of malaria in the later days of Rome, which is thought to account for the incompetence that the Roman legions developed and the general corruption that came to pervade Roman society. Cited also are the great plagues which swept over medieval Europe shortly before the Renaissance, which undoubtedly disturbed social life as well as sharply reduced the population; and the prevalence of syphilis during the Renaissance, which is thought by some medical historians to have had the effect of stimulating men to unusually energetic action.[13]

That changes in the biological environment have in times past often had violent social repercussions is not difficult to demonstrate. In the fourteenth century rat-borne plague (the Black Death) swept out of Asia into Europe, and for nearly a century plague was a major cause of death. Estimates vary; but before the epidemic ran out, the population of Western Europe had been reduced by perhaps one-third. Panic was pandemic, and many towns and cities were deserted and often not resettled for years or even decades after the plague struck. There was a great unsettling of peoples, much migration, desertion and fragmentation of family units, etc. Economic historians often cite the plague as the cause of a general breakdown of the quasi serf system that had obtained in agriculture and of the traditional barriers between the laboring and other economic classes. The decline in population led, they hold, to a general scarcity of labor and, in time, to a consequent rise in the position of the worker. Some technological innovations are thought to have sprung directly from this labor scarcity. Thus the invention of the horse collar, which made possible the use of the horse as a draft animal, came not long after the plague; and it did greatly improve the productive ability of the worker in agriculture. The horse had long been used, of course, as a beast of burden; but it could not be linked to wagon or plow by the traditional yoke, which was usable only with oxen, which have high and heavy shoulders. With the development of the horse collar, the horse quickly became the major source of traction power in agriculture, displacing the lumbering ox and the weakling human for plowing and similar heavy tasks. It is calculated that this development alone enabled the peasants of Europe to double agricultural production within a century and without additional manpower.

Many of the characteristics of contemporary Irish society, such as the frequency with which the Irish indefinitely postpone marriage, are at least indirectly traceable to the potato famine of the 1840s; and some of the attributes of American political organization might perhaps be traced,

[13] A deterministic view of the role of disease on human affairs is presented by H. Zinsser in *Rats, Lice, and History*, Little, Brown and Company, Boston, 1935. The actual role of disease as an intervening variable is explored and illustrated by H. E. Sigerist in *Civilization and Disease*, Cornell University Press, Ithaca, N.Y., 1943; and Ronald Hare in *Pomp and Pestilence; Infectious Disease, Its Origins and Conquest*, Philosophical Library, Inc., New York, 1955.

still more indirectly, to the same disaster. The potato famine was brought about by the near destruction for a number of years in succession of the potato crop by fungus. Within ten years the population of Ireland fell, through excessive deaths from starvation and through migration to the United States, from more than eight million to less than four million. The disaster so impressed the Irish people with the economic disutility of too many children that, although their strong Catholicism has precluded general resort to birth control, their numbers have remained more or less constant in the century and more since. And the impact of some two or three million Irish immigrants on pre-Civil War America is beyond estimate; the existence of Catholicism in America today, for example, is but one of the long-range results. It was the Irish immigrants who constituted the bulk of American Catholics, and it is the descendants of Irish immigrants who do so today.

As an Intervening Variable

A very considerable proportion of modern technology and not a little of modern ideology and organization has to do with the control of the biological environment. In a general way, it may be said that problems of biological control have brought these new social elements into being or at least have been the occasion for their invention and development. Had not yellow fever defeated the French in their efforts to cut a canal across the Isthmus of Panama, man might never have discovered that this grave disease is transmitted by a mosquito and that the control of this insect is desirable for this reason and some others. Had not gray wolves been too clever to come within gun range, the cowmen of the Rocky Mountain regions might never have discovered that strychnine (the *nux vomica* of the ancients) is an excellent means of killing these predators; and strychnine might not now be used to keep down the number of rodents that eat our crops and stored grains and birds that would live off our fields. Had it not been that typhoid bacilli can be water-borne, it might never have been discovered that a pure supply of water is essential to life in congested cities. And so on.

It would, however, be more exact to say that the role of biological factors in the development of new techniques, new organizations (such as mosquito-abatement districts, sewage districts, etc.), and new ideas has for the most part been that of an intervening rather than a determining variable. The problems that have been solved by these developments have usually been precipitated by man himself. Thus "society" is the "causative" agent; and wolves, bacteria, or whatever are biological factors that simply intervene between one set of social circumstances and the emergence of another.

The complexity of the processes by which organisms live with and upon one another has been briefly noted. When man breaks into the natural balance to establish a social balance fruitful to him, he thwarts or frustrates nature; and, in a manner of speaking, nature never forgets or forgives. If he leaves his garden untended for but one summer, it will become a jungle of weeds, rich with insect and animal life; if he pauses but briefly in his war with the common housefly, houseflies will appear in vast and dangerous numbers. Moreover, it has often happened that man himself has quite inadvertently provided conditions favorable to the invasion of plants, animals, insects, or bacteria inimical to his own welfare. In such cases the "problems" posed were clearly of man's own making.

To some extent the history of the last six centuries in the West has been that of a continuing race with biological disaster; man has solved one problem of biological control only to produce, meanwhile, two or more others. Bubonic plague is a case in point: plague was certainly a biological phenomenon, but Western man had himself set the stage for it by building towns and cities and storing food (mainly grains) in urban establishments. The rats of Western Europe prior to the thirteenth century were unsociable, timid creatures of forest and field. With the growth through the Middle Ages of trade and urban communities, conditions favorable to invasion by two other species, first the black rat and later the great gray rat, were established. Both these rats, presumably native to urban Asia, are bold and vicious and prefer to live close to and upon the unintended bounty of man; they are experts at robbing granaries and other stores of human food. The black rat with its infected fleas first came into Europe early in the fourteenth century and shortly killed off the indigenous rats. By the time of the plagues of the fifteenth, sixteenth, and seventeenth centuries, the gray rat had all but displaced the black. Gray rats with their fleas came in by ship, and gray rat communities linked Asia with Western Europe. Thus whenever plague reached epidemic level in Asia (where it had long been endemic), conditions were favorable to its fairly rapid spread to Europe.[14] The rats brought the fleas that transmitted the disease to the humans with whom they came in contact.

The rise of cities posed many new problems of biological control, some of which were not solved until very recently, and a few of which are still unsolved. Under the conditions of life, technological and organizational, that had obtained under the feudal system, when men had lived together in small numbers and had seldom moved from manor to manor, epidemic diseases had been of slight consequence. When typhus or typhoid, smallpox or scarlet fever,

[14] There is some evidence that the spread of the black rat, if not the plague, to Western Europe was facilitated by the movements and butchery of Tamerlane and his military horde. During the latter half of the thirteenth century this poor man's Genghis Khan descended from the central Asian plateau to kill all the native peoples he could lay hand on; and their corpses, left piled in town or city streets, must have fed countless rats. It is possible, therefore, that as Tamerlane moved westward, a rat migration followed in his wake.

malaria or syphilis, or any other of the many contagious diseases (a great number of which were no doubt endemic during the feudal period) broke out in one feudal unit, the disease had little chance of spreading to other units. These diseases are disseminated by direct contact, by fleas, by flies, by mosquitoes, by lice, or by body filth in water or on food. As men came to congregate in towns and to travel with some frequency from town to town, the hazards of death from a contagious disease were immeasurably increased; and many diseases, plague among others, became epidemic in towns and cities. It was, in fact, the frequency with which urban populations were decimated by epidemics that first gave the city the reputation of being a destroyer of life, a reputation that even now is not entirely gone. Disease had always, of course, been a problem of man, usually ignored by him; but it was man's own actions which in one or another of various ways raised the problem of disease to the stature of a crisis and which, in the long run, made solution imperative.

The social provision of conditions favorable to the invasion of man by disease has increased rather than diminished since the rise of the early cities. Less than a century ago in the towns and cities of America typhoid fever became one of the major causes of death—and for social rather than natural reasons. In rural America, as in feudal Europe, farms were generally scattered—in contradistinction to the postfeudal European village system—and each farm family lived in its own somewhat isolated and closed economic and social unit. It was the common practice for each farm unit to draw its domestic water from a fairly shallow well and to dispose of body wastes in a nearby latrine. Should *Eberthella typhi* be introduced into this system—by, say, an infected passer-by's using the family's outhouse—the entire family might succumb to typhoid fever; but nearby farm families would not necessarily be affected. Typhoid fever was, under these social circumstances, endemic and occasionally epidemic within a small locality. With the growth of urbanism during the nineteenth century, however, it became a critical problem that led to technological and organizational changes of considerable magnitude. In the making of these changes typhoid fever operated as an intervening variable, not as a determinant.

Briefly what had happened was this: In moving to town or growing city, the farm families had frequently brought with them their practice of using shallow wells and outhouses. Under the new form of organization—that is, many adjacent households—these family practices encouraged the spread of typhoid fever; for if one family became infected, the wells of other families would become contaminated. As a result, widespread epidemics of typhoid fever became common, and what had been a relatively minor problem grew into a major one. In due time a variety of social changes, technological and organizational, were effected that sharply reduced the possibility of a general epidemic—the development of urban water-supply systems and sewage-disposal systems and the legal prohibition of both household wells and outhouses. Note that in this sequence an organizational change—urbanization—had brought about a rise in the incidence of a disease that in turn fostered changes in social technology and organization. Typhoid fever intervened between the first and second series of social changes; and the change in this biological factor—i.e., the rise in its incidence—was brought about, not by a whim of nature, but by man himself.

A similar sequence of changes has frequently been involved in the rise of diseases that affect man's domesticated plants and animals. As will later be noted, one of the most significant of the quantitative changes that have occurred over recent centuries has been the rapid rise in human numbers. In considerable measure, this increase has been made possible by the diffusion from place to place and from continent to continent of plant species that are exceptionally productive from the human point of view. The potato, now a staple of Western societies, was indigenous to North America; and its introduction to Europe (circa 1600) gave a tremendous boost to food production there. The starch root manioc, indigenous to South America, was at about the same time introduced to Africa; its cultivation accounts in considerable measure for the subsequent growth of African populations. Since both plants thrive on sour soils that are not useful for the growing of grains and the other traditional food plants of Europe and Africa, their introduction meant in effect the addition of new agricultural lands.[15] During recent times what was a more or less casual diffusion of food plants has been rationalized by agronomists, and the world has been scoured in a search for those plants which will be most productive in this region or that and for this purpose or that. As a consequence modern Americans rather literally have the whole world at their door.

The diffusion of plants, combined with the human mobility that has made that diffusion possible, has, however, had many adverse biological consequences; for as the plants of the world were brought to Europe and America, so, too, and quite incidentally, were the insects, molds, funguses, and soil and other bacteria of the world.[16] As a result, man's problems in maintaining a favorable social balance in his gardens and fields and in forests and pastures have been infinitely increased. Hardly a plant that modern man would grow is free from attack by a host of imported destructive insects, molds, funguses, bacteria, or virus infections. It is therefore probable that, if modern people were forced to resume the agricultural techniques of just a century ago, their

[15] See Redcliffe N. Salaman, *The History and Social Influence of the Potato*, Cambridge University Press, New York, 1949; and William O. Jones, *Manioc in Africa*, Stanford University Press, Stanford, Calif., 1959.

[16] See A. Standen, *Insect Invaders*, Houghton Mifflin Company, Boston, 1943; and L. O. Howard, *The Insect Menace*, Appleton-Century-Crofts, Inc., New York, 1931.

food and fiber production would promptly fall toward zero; for until very recently there were no direct defenses against insects, aside from actually picking worms and bugs from growing plants, and none whatever against soil worms, of which there are many varieties, or against the molds, funguses, and bacteria that uncontrolled will destroy many plants. Man has himself been responsible for the progressive invasion of such organisms, and it has only been through great innovative endeavor that he has been able to devise means of counterattack.[17] The discovery that the juices of certain plants—e.g., derris—contain substances that are poisonous to many of the sucking and chewing insects was the first major step; subsequently various synthetic chemicals, of which the famous DDT is but one, were developed; and for the moment it is possible for a sophisticated farmer to hold his own against the lower organisms.

Those organisms have not, however, passively submitted to man's control. Through the mechanism of evolution, they have often become immune to the particular chemical that has been used against them. Moreover, when one bug or other organism is eliminated, there is often another species ready to take its place. Chemical control of the lower organisms has, therefore, turned out to be a never-ending process. Today's insecticides, fungicides, microbicides, etc., may be sufficient to the task today; but by next year or the year after they are likely to be impotent. Consequently, modern man is dependent upon the chemists to discover or devise a constant series of new poisons; and the question does arise where this continually stepped-up juggling with nature is leading. One of the dangers is that in their efforts to keep down the bugs, men will succeed only in poisoning themselves.[18]

[17] Organizational changes in agriculture, particularly in the United States, have aggravated the problem of plant disease and insect control. Under the older diversified type of farming, the small area devoted to each crop and crop rotation for each area retarded the spread of an insect or disease, each of which specializes on one particular plant species. The large area with a single crop that is characteristic of modern industrial farming, on the other hand, gives an almost unlimited opportunity for any disease or insect that thrives on the particular plant—wheat, corn, soybeans, or the like—that is being cultivated in this manner.

[18] The danger arises from the fact that most of the modern pesticides are highly stable and do not disintegrate after serving their purpose; rather, they accumulate in plant tissue and then in the organs of grazing animals and appear in high concentrations in the milk and meat used for human consumption. They also pollute streams, where they kill fish and other life; and they may appear—as the equally durable detergents are doing—in domestic water supplies. Moreover, they frequently kill birds and other natural agencies of insect control and may in this way increase rather than diminish the problem they were intended to solve.

These and other dangers and difficulties in the use of modern pesticides have been dramatically reported by Rachel Carson in *Silent Spring*, Houghton Mifflin

DEMOGRAPHIC FACTORS

Man is very poorly equipped by nature to survive in competition and conflict with other organisms. He is no match for the lions, tigers, wolves, and other large predators with one or another of which he would in nature presumably compete for game. He has little natural protection against the elements; his nails are a poor substitute for claws; his teeth can neither slash nor tear; he can neither run like the wolf nor climb like the monkey; and worst of all, his young take a most unconscionable time to grow to maturity. Without culturally provided weapons and tools and without the advantages of social organization, the human species would quickly disappear. Man, of all the animals, is totally dependent upon the existence of society; and of all the animals, only man is capable of developing and maintaining a society. The question has, at times, been asked: Did man lose the biological capacity to survive in nature because he evolved society and made such equipment unnecessary? or did he become social because, lacking such equipment, he could not otherwise survive?

This is, of course, the kind of question to which no answer can be found, but it does lead to a somewhat more realistic one—to the question of what role man the animal plays in the making of social change. It is at least obvious that the biological characteristics of man, including his superior capacity to learn, are inseparably bound up with the existence of society per se. There is no evidence, however, that the marked differences between various societies or that the changes which occur within a given society can be accounted for in terms of biological differences in men. The evidence and arguments that have been advanced by generations of racial determinists have failed to show any relation between the "racial stock"—itself a very dubious concept—of a people and their culture. So far as can be ascertained, there are no significant differences in the average innate abilities of different peoples to learn or to be creative; nor are there any demonstrable differences between them in average inherited sense perceptions, temperament, or other elusive qualities that might aid in explaining their different cultures. That different peoples have had quite different cultural histories would seem self-evident; but the factors responsible would all seem to lie outside the biology of man himself.

It is of course perfectly obvious that men vary, for genetic reasons, in such matters as skin color, skin texture, hair color and texture, eye color, etc. Any one of these differences, most especially that of skin color, may be socially defined as significant; and if there were no such differences, there

---

Company, Boston, 1962. A more balanced account of the same dangers and difficulties is provided by J. W. Day in *Poison on the Land*, Philosophical Library, Inc., New York, 1957.

could be none of the particular kind of racial prejudice and segregation that obtains in the modern world. The fact that men often explain social differences in racial terms does not make their explanations valid; but it may aid in the perpetuation of social differences, as it has no doubt in the case of the Negro in the United States.

The idea that certain peoples, conceived of as races, as biologically distinct entities, have a special and inherent genius for technological, military, political, religious, or general cultural development is easily disposed of. During the fifteenth and sixteenth centuries the Spanish were the dominant naval power of the world; since then they have been militarily, as well as otherwise, of no international significance. The Italians fathered the Renaissance, reviving the learning, architecture, and some of the lost technologies of the ancients, and developing commerce to an unprecedented level. For a century and more Italy from Florence to Venice was a center of cultural ferment; here were the beginnings of world exploration, of international trade, of the arts and of the sciences. But what the Italians fathered, others, fully as ingenious in their turn, were to develop. South Germans gave birth to Protestantism; and they, the Swiss, and the peoples of the Low Countries, to the technological and organizational developments to which Protestantism gave ideological support. Meanwhile, the Italians resumed their neomedieval life. France, now struggling to preserve the illusion that it is still a great power, was for two centuries and more the center of European political life; she set the fashions in clothing, morals, and manners for the elites of all the Western world; and she gave birth to those political ideologies that colonial America was to borrow and use as the ideological basis for a new political order.

Similar, even more striking, instances of shifts in the roles of various peoples can be drawn from the history of world culture. The dark-skinned peoples of darkest Africa discovered the technique of smelting iron and were using this metal for tools and weapons at a time when the ancestors of contemporary Europeans were clothing themselves in raw furs and arming their spears with stone. Indeed, ages later, African primitives supplied much of the iron that was used by the early Crusaders. The Chinese, who have contributed little that is new to world culture during the past few centuries, were nevertheless highly civilized at the time when Western Europeans were living a rather primitive, feudal life.

The biological potentialities of peoples would seem to be everywhere much the same and to have been more or less constant over the known history of human society; and the extent to which and the particular directions in which these potentialities, mental and physical, have been developed seem to be matters that have been socially determined or at the least socially mediated. The people of northern China are, on the whole, considerably larger than those of the southern provinces, those of northern Japan larger than those of the southern islands, those of contemporary America much larger than were those of colonial America, etc.; but these differences in body size would seem to be due in considerable part to differences in food habits and food sources. Observable differences between peoples and in the same people at different times in general level of health, length of life, and, most varied of all, average level of activity would also seem to be biological consequences of social rather than genetic factors.

Population Numbers and Social Change

Although no biological differences of a qualitative order (i.e., genetic) would seem to have played much if any part in the differential development of cultures, those of a quantitative order, on the other hand, have most certainly been significant. The size of a human population is, in fact, an important variable in the making of social change.[19] Clearly, a human community of two or three hundred members cannot possibly devise and put into operation a complex division of labor, a mighty military machine, or a system of urban life. Moreover, the fact that they are few in numbers means that, in comparison with a society that encompasses a million or more persons, the total number of elements in the social heritage will be relatively few and the possibilities of innovation through the synthesis of existing elements will also be limited. For these reasons alone, small societies tend to be stable. Primitive societies, usually small, have been characteristically unproductive of innovations, as have isolated agricultural communities. The small, isolated units of European feudalism, for example, produced nothing of note except the moat and the drawbridge.

The fact that a small population precludes much change does not, however, mean that the reverse is true. There is a definite relation between population *growth* and social change; but the existence of a large population does not necessarily result in change and may actually preclude rather than facilitate change. The standard of living of a population depends in part upon its density (here used in the sense of the ratio of the number of persons to their means of maintaining life) ; and in respect to social change the density of the population is quite as important as is its size; for there is a direct relation, apparently universal, between the standard of living of a people and their propensity to work changes in their society. The relationship is complex and interactive; but it might be summed up in the statement that only those peo-

[19] Some of the relations between population size and the forms of social life are examined by Maurice Halbwachs in *Population and Society: An Introduction to Social Morphology*, Otis D. Duncan and Harold W. Pfautz (trans.), The Free Press of Glencoe, New York, 1960. For the most part, however, demographers have been so much engrossed in examining the ways in which social factors determine population size and characteristics that they have made little study of the ways in which the latter affect the former.

ple who have a high standard of living can work changes in their society, and only those who do work changes in their society can for long enjoy a high standard of living.

The Saturated Population

Until very recently all the peoples of the world have lived at or perilously close to the subsistence level. In times past there have been some brief and limited periods during which given peoples, for example, the Athenians, have managed to keep their numbers under control; but although man has of necessity maintained some sort of social balance over his biological habitat, adapting nature to his own ends, he has rarely escaped from the consequences of the fact that he, like other organisms, is capable of producing many offspring. The reproductive capacity of man is low in comparison with ants, oysters, dogs, and most other organisms; but it is sufficiently high that man, like other organisms, has over time usually achieved a saturated population—i.e., one that consists of so many persons that all the available means for the support of life are absorbed in maintaining life. It is at this point that natural controls, high infant mortality and a short life span, come into operation to offset the high birth rate and keep the population numbers constant.

The mechanics of natural controls on population are much the same with man as with the lower animals. Malnutrition is chronic in a saturated population; and any temporary decline in food supplies (such as crop failure, failure in the hunt, or poor fishing) results in famine. Undernourished and, as is typically the case, overworked mothers bear a high proportion of stillborn infants and of ill-formed infants destined to die from undernourishment or disease before they have hardly begun to live. Since the per capita supply of food is barely adequate and the struggle for existence harsh, the general level of health is low and the entire population vulnerable to disease. A saturated population is usually afflicted with some endemic disorder—malaria, yaws, hookworm, etc.—and periodically decimated by a disease of epidemic character. As a result, the average life span is very short.

A saturated population may support a small social elite at a standard of living that is considerably above that of subsistence, and those who constitute such an elite may be sufficiently free from the daily struggle to survive to apply themselves to creative endeavors that might work eufunctional changes in the culture. But they seldom make the attempt, if only because any improvement in social productivity—such as that which might come from a technological innovation—is promptly absorbed by increased numbers. In such a society if there is more food, there soon will be more mouths to eat it; for if there is a bit more food, then the death rates, infant and otherwise, will fall slightly until the increased numbers of living take up the slack and the natural checks to further growth come back into operation.

Through most of human history most of the peoples of the world have apparently been unable to escape this biological cycle of adversity; and that adversity has led in turn to social incentives to procreation that operate to perpetuate the cycle. Where the death rate is very high, it is only by maintaining a very high birth rate that a given family, tribe, or other social unit can assure its own survival. The fact that societies of the past have usually had saturated populations in considerable measure explains the slowness with which world culture has evolved. For if there is one valid generalization about social change, it is that those societies that are most in need of change (i.e., those that are most impoverished) are least likely to bring about changes, other than changes of an atrophic order, in their social systems.

The Affluent Society

In times past periods of rapid social development seem always to have been associated with territorial expansion, which has enabled the population to rise for a time above the level of subsistence. No doubt the enlargement of habitable territory is a quantitative consequence of qualitative changes in the social system; but once under way, territorial expansion has enabled the people to increase their means of subsistence somewhat more rapidly than their numbers increased. Thus it was when the Chinese left their feudal units to settle new lands, in the period following 400 B.C., that they also began to develop the classical Chinese social system; and it was while the Romans were conquering and exploiting Western Europe and North Africa that they evolved their technology and their military-political system of organization. In each instance the end of expansion and the maturation of the system coincided.

The development of modern Western society followed the same pattern up to a point. The gradual decline of feudal isolation, accelerated by and reflected in the medieval Crusades, led to the settlement and cultivation of lands that had lain fallow since the withdrawal of the Roman legions. The result was, apparently, a somewhat better than subsistence level of living; and socially implemented events—such as the almost constant warfare that accompanied the gradual consolidation of postfeudal peoples into national units and the great plagues previously referred to—kept the rate of population growth considerably below the biological maximum.[20] Subsequently the social changes that were achieved—technological improvements in agriculture, world exploration and exploitation, the introduction of new food plants, and many others —kept social productivity increasing somewhat faster than the population increased. The gap between human numbers and means of subsistence was

[20] For estimates of the size of medieval populations and an analysis of some of the factors that entered into their determination, see J. C. Russell, *Late Ancient and Medieval Populations,* American Philosophical Society, Philadelphia, 1958.

never very great; the majority of people lived, then as in earlier times, at a subsistence level. It did, however, become economically possible for a sizable and constantly growing class of persons—the rising *bourgeoisie*—to live in comparative affluence; and it was this class that for the most part provided the ingenuity and enterprise that kept the ball of change rolling. From this class came the traders, the early factory owners, and the early scientists and physicians, who gradually broke the bonds of medieval thought and organization and eventually introduced those changes that inaugurated the industrial revolution and all that has occurred since.

In the emergence of modern Western society the North American continent played a crucial role. By its settlement and by its production of food for export to Europe, first rice from the plantations of the Southern seaboard, later sugar from the Deep South and grains and meat from the Middle West, European populations were enabled to maintain a somewhat better than subsistence standard of living in the face of rising population numbers. Moreover, agricultural techniques were improving in America, as they earlier had in Western Europe, with consequent increases in the per acre production of food and fibers.

The possibilities of territorial expansion have historically diminished as the empty spaces—those occupied by primitives with little ability to control the biological habitat—have been brought under Western-type settlement and cultivation. Today the possibilities of territorial expansion for any people in the world are decidedly small. For the most part the uncultivated lands—such as those of the Amazon Valley, those of the central plateau of Africa, and those of the higher latitudes—are in terms of current Western values mainly submarginal. And the hope, once high, that man could exploit the food resources of the oceans to an extent never before realized and thereby triple or more the production of the necessities of life has recently been tempered by the discovery that the oceans are, from the biological point of view, mostly desert.

There are no doubt many ways in which Western society can improve its present techniques of agricultural production; and in the long run it may be that its current techniques can be successfully introduced to the so-called underdeveloped peoples of the world. Assuming that men do not in the meanwhile irrevocably destroy the present physical resources of the world, the agricultural production of the world can no doubt be steadily increased. That this will bring a higher than subsistence standard of living to those peoples who are currently living at or near subsistence levels does not, however, follow; for unless all the peoples of the world bring their numbers under strict and continuing control, the population of the world will certainly increase to absorb any increases in production.

In the West, and only in the West, deliberate control of numbers began in a small way during the eighteenth century, and possibly somewhat before, among the *bourgeoisie*. The members of this class seem to have recognized that as family units they could preserve their comfortable economic status only if they kept the number of their children within bounds. To do so was, of course, contrary to traditional ideology, including religious sanctions and personal pride in virility. Yet this new class did come to recognize what had been ignored by man everywhere else—that nature is opposed to surpluses, social as well as otherwise. This discovery may justly be described as the most important one that has been made in historical times in that it makes possible the preservation of the social advantages that accrue from innovations that bring about increases in productivity.

For a century or so, the members of the *bourgeoisie* restricted the size of the family mainly by delaying marriage. Theretofore marriage had followed promptly after physical maturation, in the middle class as in all other classes. In most times and places the average age of boys at first marriage had been about sixteen, that of girls a year or two lower. Toward the end of the nineteenth century (by which time vital statistics were being kept in most Western countries) the average age at first marriage had risen seven years or so; that of men of the bourgeois class, however, had risen to thirty or more, and that of women of this class to twenty-six or more.[21] Meanwhile the technique of chemical prevention of conception had appeared, first in France about 1850, and had been widely adopted by the *bourgeoisie* of England, France, Germany, and the United States in spite of religious and medical resistance to it. As a consequence of birth control, the birth rates of the *bourgeoisie* have at times (for example, during the 1920s and 1930s) fallen to as low as fifteen per thousand, as compared with general rates of twenty-five or more per thousand. In time the lower classes began to adopt birth control, although the effects on their birth rates have been less spectacular.

The general decline in birth rates from about 1850 on, however, was more than offset by an even more marked decline in the death rates. The latter came as a consequence of the rising standard of material welfare, of the decline—with mechanization—of the rigors of work, of the virtual conquest of such endemic diseases as typhoid, typhus, malaria, smallpox, scarlet fever, etc., of the improvements in maternity and infant care, and of the growing ability of the medical profession to correct for or at least modulate the effects of degenerative diseases. Western populations, France excepted, have therefore increased rapidly over the past hundred years, but far less rapidly than they would have had not some control been exercised over the birth rates. Moreover, the productivity of Western societies has increased during the same period even more rapidly, with the general consequence that living standards of all classes, not excepting the unproductive, have risen far above that of subsistence.

[21] See Benjamin Kidd, *Social Evolution*, Macmillan and Co., New York, 1894, appendix I, "Marriage Ages of Various Sections of the Population in England," pp. 331–334.

Affluence and Change

Both quantitative and qualitative social changes have, it is evident, been responsible for the historic growth of Western populations (and, in fact, of those of Asia, Africa, and elsewhere); for the fact that this growth has not kept pace with social productivity; and for the consequent fact that Western peoples have been enjoying, as no others in history have done, a constantly rising standard of living. This increasingly high standard of living has, in turn, been one of the important factors in the furthering of social changes. Thus here as elsewhere population size and density have operated as an intervening variable—changes in social circumstances have by way of changes in population brought about a higher than subsistence standard of living which has in turn fostered still other changes in the society.

Social affluence will not of itself lead to innovative, advocatory, and adoptive actions.[22] A prospering people may, like a rich elite, do no more than enjoy the fruits of their prosperity and thereby assure a rapid return to adversity. Although affluence provides an opportunity for a people to work adaptive changes in their social system, whether or not they will do so depends upon other circumstances, most particularly those of an organizational character. Affluence can, perhaps, best be characterized as a prerequisite to social change; for only those individuals who are free from immediate want are able to devote themselves to innovative endeavor (i.e., they must be socially subsidized in order to engage in currently unfruitful activity), and only those people who can afford to postpone current consumption in the prospect of higher subsequent return are in a position to develop and adopt innovations.[23] Those who live from hand to mouth, or from harvest to harvest, as

[22] Such, however, is the view of Shepard B. Clough (*The Rise and Fall of Civilization: An Inquiry into the Relationship between Economic Development and Civilization*, Columbia University Press, New York, 1957). His historical evidence does seem to indicate that an economic surplus, however achieved, has been essential to innovative endeavor and the adoption of new social elements. But his assumption that an economic surplus acts as an imperative to social change is contravened by other historical evidences that he has not examined. Classical Chinese society, for example, was for many centuries able to maintain a large court and an even larger political bureaucracy on a luxurious scale; it did not, however, produce much in the way of significant social change. The surplus—extracted, it is true, from the populace by taxation—went mainly into pomp and ceremony.

[23] And even in a generally affluent society only those few who, according to the findings of Murray A. Straus ("Deferred Gratification, Social Class, and the Achievement Syndrome," *American Sociological Review*, vol. 27, pp. 326–335, June, 1962), have the foresight to use a present surplus for future gains will be willing and able to gamble with innovations. The majority of the members of an affluent society, like those of a subsistence society, live a hand-to-mouth existence, the difference being that their hands are full rather than empty.

have most of the peoples of the world, are inherently and understandably conservative. For them, survival depends upon the current fruits of the existing social system; there is no surplus with which to gamble that a change in the system will ultimately be rewarding.

Historically, as has been noted, affluence has been associated with growth both of the means of production and of the social population. A growing population, whether the growth comes from a declining death rate in the society or from in-migrations from other societies, will have an atypically high proportion of members in the younger age levels—a growing population is in terms of age composition a youthful rather than mature society. Other conditions being favorable, the higher the proportion of young members in the population, the more dynamic the society will be; for the young have been less thoroughly socialized into the existing social elements than have mature members and have yet to achieve and establish themselves in occupational and other positions. For these reasons, the young are more amenable to adopting new techniques, ideas, and modes of organization. Whether they are also more likely than are mature and socially established individuals to engage in innovative endeavor, however, is not clear. One would suspect that they are; and some evidence indicates that many if not most of the critical innovations of the past century and more, notably those in technology, have been made by men in their early rather than late maturity.[24] The young not only are somewhat less habituated to the established practices and ways of thinking of the society, but are also generally less constrained by familial and other responsibilities and have less of a vested interest in the *status quo*.

There is at least one further way in which social affluence fosters social change. In an impoverished, saturated population there is always a surplus of labor—economically marginal individuals, of whom there are many, compete for the opportunity to earn a livelihood, or, alternatively, slaves or indentured laborers work for their keep; hence, no incentive exists either for organizational efficiency in the use of labor or for the development of labor-saving devices. In an affluent society, on the other hand, labor is always in short supply and is therefore costly. Its high cost encourages the invention and adoption of labor-saving devices (which historically have ranged from the use of horses in agriculture to the automatization of machine production of goods) and of organizational procedures that assure the maximum return from labor (such as the division of a productive process into highly specialized tasks). Later there will be occasion to observe that industrial technology and organization arose in part in response to labor scarcity and that they have gone farthest and fastest in those countries, such as the United States, where the demand for labor has persistently outrun the supply. The almost total absence of domestic labor in contemporary America, for example, has been

[24] See Harvey C. Lehman, *Age and Achievement*, Princeton University Press, Princeton, N.J., 1953.

an encouragement to the mechanization of the American home and the industrialization of food preparation.

There is more than a general relationship between the size and density of a population and the dynamism of a social system. Specific changes in a society may sometimes be related directly to socially induced antecedent changes in the population, particularly in the sex and age composition of the population. Thus at least in respect to the United States it is necessary to qualify the assumption that it has been the industrialization of the means of production that, by weakening the family and offering new economic opportunities to women, has been responsible for the progressive liberation of women in Western societies from their traditional bonds to the domestic sphere. For in America, where that liberation has gone much farther than it has in England, France, Germany, and other highly industrialized European nations, the sex composition of the population, which was for long atypical, was undoubtedly a factor involved in that liberation. Women, especially in the early-maturity age group, were in short supply; and their value was correspondingly higher than in Europe, where there was generally a slight surplus of women of marriageable age. The scarcity in America was a consequence of a number of unusual social circumstances: Frontier settlement was preponderately male, and frontier communities were chronically short of marriageable women. At times this meant that there was an effective surplus of women in the older, more settled regions of the East, from which the males migrated. With the beginnings, about 1830, of heavy immigration from Europe, even the eastern areas tended to have a somewhat higher proportion of marriageable males than females, since the immigrants were mostly young males come to make their fortune in the land of opportunity; and although they may have intended to return to their homeland once that fortune had been made, most of them in fact never did so. As they settled down to live out their lives in America, some obtained brides from home; but the more ambitious of them were likely to enter the local marriage market, since taking a native American wife was one way of gaining status in American society.

In a rapidly growing population, such as that of the United States during most of the past century, there is an unusually high proportion of young married adults and of children; and this, too, has had considerable bearing on the nature of some of the changes worked in the society. Thus American preoccupation with public school education, with the provision of playgrounds and other facilities for children, and with the development of special organizations for children and youths, such as Boy Scouts and Girl Scouts, may have been stimulated by the atypical age composition of the population. It is certain, at any event, that a variety of other recent changes in American society are directly related to the rapid rise in the proportion of elderly persons in the population. This latter development, very much pronounced during the past few decades, has come about mainly as a consequence of an increasing life span; and it has in turn fostered both ideological and organizational concern with the problems of old age. One aspect of this development has been the emergence of the special field of geriatrics in medicine; others are the establishment, both publicly and through commercial agencies, of various facilities for the aged—rest homes, retirement centers, old-age pensions, retirement annuities, etc.

THE INSTABILITY OF INDUSTRIAL SOCIETY

Man's age-old dream of a utopia has in part been achieved by modern industrial society, since for the first time in human history the majority of the members of a society can live in physical comfort and enjoy material plenty. The means by which these ends are now achieved, however, preclude the achievement of the other aspect of the utopian dream—a self-maintaining, stable social system; for industrial society has established, to a greater degree than have societies in the past, unstable relations with the physical and biological habitats in which it operates. Just to hold its own—i.e., to continue the current levels of production and the current domination of the lower organisms—modern society must remain dynamic, constantly improving the techniques of production, finding alternatives to diminishing natural resources, and discovering new controls over biological nature to replace those which lose, as all do in time, their effectiveness.

There is probably nothing in the nature of things that precludes modern society from constantly changing to meet new physical and biological circumstances; but there are various current changes in Western society that, should they be perpetuated, may bring an end to the extraordinary dynamism that brought industrial society into being and that is essential to its continued existence. Among these is the recent rise in the rates of the population growth among the various peoples of the world. Affluence, it has been noted, is a prerequisite to social change, even as it may be a consequence of social change; and it was an extraordinary combination of circumstances that lifted the Western world from the historically normal cycles of adversity and set it off on the road to affluence. It now seems likely that one of those circumstances—the unusual demographic conditions—which facilitated the rise of industrial society is already on the wane. The hope of demographers during the 1930s that Western population numbers would become more or less stabilized about 1960 at levels which would not impose too great a strain on natural resources and agricultural potentials has not been realized. The sharp rise in the birth rates of Western peoples that began with the outbreak of World War II has not, as was then expected, declined; already these high birth rates, combined with a further increase in the average life span, have pushed our numbers far above the anticipated maximum; and there is at present no reason to suppose that stringent control over births will reappear.

It seems evident that Western societies can in the short run support our present population numbers at a high, even a constantly rising, standard of living. It is quite possible that continuing improvements in technology, combined with foresightful conservation of exhaustible resources and well-organized maintenance of controls over biological nature, might enable Western societies to maintain a very much larger number of people at high levels. There are limits, however; and there is always the danger that, in the endeavor to satisfy growing social needs, modern men will destroy one or more of the physical resources or biological circumstances that are necessary for the maintenance of the industrial way of life.

Moreover, many of the non-Western peoples of the world are struggling for the first time to industrialize and to share the material wealth and social freedoms that Western peoples now enjoy. Their efforts to do so are probably foredoomed to failure, if only because their numbers are so great. Non-Western populations have been growing steadily since the seventeenth century, mainly as a consequence of new food plants that have been brought to them by Westerners, of some improvement in agricultural and other technology (such as the irrigation systems built in India by the British), and of foods supplied through trade from Western sources. For the most part there has been no general rise in the standard of living; population growth has tended to keep pace with increases in the means of subsistence. Within the past few decades, and most strikingly since World War II, two developments have occurred in many non-Western societies that seem to preclude Western peoples' continuing for very long to live as rich nations in a world of impoverishment: the first is the growing desire on the part of an emerging middle class in Asia, India, Africa, and Latin America to enjoy the material standards of Western societies; the second, which precludes achievement of the first, is the population explosion that has occurred in most of the non-Western societies of the world.[25]

[25] It has been predicted that ". . . barring either a catastrophe, or a deterioration of social conditions for progress in health of global proportions," the population of the world will climb to between six and seven billion by the end of the century (United Nations Department of Economic and Social Affairs, *The Future Growth of World Population,* United Nations, Department of Public Information, New York, 1958, p. 132).

The unprecedented rate at which the population of the world has been increasing in the years since World War II has occasioned considerable alarm among demographers and food economists, an alarm which the present agricultural surplus of the United States does nothing to mitigate. Whether it will be physically and socially possible to increase the world's production of food as rapidly as the world's mothers bear babies is hotly debated. The alternative, that

The population explosion in non-Western societies seems to have been a consequence of falling death rates; in these societies the birth rates are close to maximum, and natural checks are the only checks that have been and still are operative. The checks of chronic malnutrition and occasional famine have probably not been lessened; but the introduction of Western medicine and especially some crucial public health measures have, within recent years, reduced deaths from the more common endemic and epidemic diseases. Pressure on the food supply has therefore been intensified rather than reduced; and the clamor for political freedom and the demands for economic and other aid from Western societies stem in part from an actual decline in the material standard of living. It has now become evident that, if Western societies are to preserve some sort of balance in the international power structure, they must try to purchase the support of Indian, African, and Latin-American peoples through a sharing with them of Western wealth. The material needs of these peoples, who constitute about one-third of the population of the world, are, however, presently insatiable and, barring the improbable miracle of sharp and enduring decline in native birth rates, will continue to mount. There exists, therefore, the unpleasant prospect that in the years to come Western peoples may find themselves exhausting already contracting resources—especially fossil fuels and soil fertility—in the endeavor to feed and equip a constantly enlarging mass of dependents. Should that come to pass, the rich would grow poorer while the poor would grow only more numerous; and, one may suspect, the current period of rapid social change would thereby be brought to a close.

the natural checks of starvation and chronic malnutrition will again become operative in all the underdeveloped countries of the world and so cancel out the effects of public health and related measures, is one seldom contemplated; and hardly anyone has been so foolhardy as to suggest that widespread and effective adoption of birth control will check the impending increase in world population before starvation intervenes.

For a few of the many studies and speculations about the population explosion and its probable consequences, see the following: W. S. Woytensky and E. S. Woytensky, *World Population and Production: Trends and Outlook*, The Twentieth Century Fund, New York, 1953; E. John Russell, *World Population and World Food Supplies*, George Allen & Unwin, Ltd., London, 1954; Warren S. Thompson, *Population and Progress in the Far East*, The University of Chicago Press, Chicago, 1959; and Philip M. Hauser, *Population Perspectives*, Rutgers University Press, New Brunswick, N.J., 1961.

chapter 8 *The Technological Variable*

One of the common intellectual errors of our age is to treat the social components of a social system, both conceptually and operationally, as distinct and quasi-independent entities, i.e., to take literally the abstractions "technology," "ideology," and "organization." The division of the totality of a social system into components is a useful heuristic device, and it is intellectually justified in that the elements of each component have some things in common that distinguish them from elements of the other components; but a component is not an entity, nor is it an operational unit. The operational units of a society are the assemblies, complexes, and subsystems, each of which involves parts or elements from all three components.

The technology of a society is *conceptually* distinguishable from all else in that it consists of the devices, knowledges, and skills by which men control and utilize physical and biological phenomena, including their own bodies. The technology of prehistoric man is known only indirectly, through inferences from such surviving artifacts as stone tools, pieces of pottery, and earthen works or other remains of structures; but it is evident that until close to the beginnings of the historic period, man's technology was never more than just sufficient to enable him to survive in competition with the lower animals. Until man became a herdsman, by discovering the art of domesticating some of the lower animals, or became an agriculturalist, by discovering the art of domesticating food plants, he lived from hand to mouth on what he could collect from field, forest, lake, or ocean. His numbers were few and his life uncertain; and while he was undoubtedly social, he had no surplus above that which was necessary for sheer survival to devote to improvements in his technology. At any event, he did not gain much in his power over nature for thousands of years.

It is generally believed that the first critical development in technology came with the domestication of plants, although where and when this first occurred is unknown. Other things being equal, a herding people are more numerous and secure than are those who live by hunting; but like the latter, they must be migratory, following the grasses on which their horses or cattle feed. They do not, therefore, develop much in the way of physical accouterments; and they are, for evident reasons, organized into comparatively small, self-sufficient groups. An agricultural people, on the other hand, from opportunity and necessity lead a settled life. They acquire a vested interest in territory from the labor that has gone into the clearing and breaking of their fields; they come to have a body of use rights in that territory; and they develop fixed habitations. It is thought that in order to preserve these interests and rights and to protect their habitations, early agriculturalists must have developed some sort of complex and fairly large-scale forms of organization, some sort of government; that in time they must have evolved some of the arts of trade, through which they could exchange some of the products of their fields for desired products of other peoples; and that because they were settled, they had time to devote to the improvement of their arts and crafts and to the devising of systems of writing and computing, and thus were able to inaugurate the historical period of man's existence.

All this is, of course, speculative; but the historical record does begin with settled, agricultural peoples, and it is only through their accounts that we have any evidence regarding the many migratory and preliterate peoples of early times. From about 3000 B.C. until the end of the Roman era there appears to have occurred a very slow and erratic enlargement and improvement in world technology, to which many peoples made their special contributions. During this period some plant and animal species (agricultural peoples are usually also domesticators of animals, either for food or power or both) were shaped to conform closer to man's needs, possibly, but not certainly, by deliberate crossbreeding and selection. The arts of irrigation came to be quite highly developed, especially in the Near East and the more arid parts of China. The water lift, powered either by foot or by draft animal, was invented, enabling farmers to irrigate their fields from shallow wells or surface streams and pools. The wheel was invented and variously applied. Sailing barges were developed both in the East and in Europe (but, strangely, not in the Americas) by maritime peoples who took to the sea both to explore and conquer and to engage in trade. All the fabricative arts, such as textile manufacturing, were through this period considerably improved, as were the techniques of construction. Nevertheless, by the fifteenth century of the Christian era, the most efficient of the technologies that had come into existence—that of China—was by modern standards primitive and ineffectual.

In that century, as in the thirtieth century B.C., most of man's control and use of nature was accomplished by the direct hand of man himself. Man might use horses or oxen to pull his plow and donkeys or ships to carry his burdens and, less often, himself, and he did use tools to supplement his hands; but his hands guided the plow and beat the donkey and held and manipulated the tools with which he seeded his field and harvested his grain, cut down the trees and reduced them to lumber, cut the stone to make his buildings, dug and smelted the ores to get the iron from which his tools were made, etc. Moreover, man's control of his biological habitat had during this long period increased only in respect to his domestication of plants and animals. He had learned almost nothing about the various diseases that attacked them or his own body, and he was quite as ineffectual in dealing with an endemic or epidemic disease as he had been forty-five centuries earlier.

The technology of modern Western societies is largely, therefore, the product of the last few centuries. About four centuries ago the rate of change in technology began to accelerate and it has since continued to accelerate. With it have come other spectacular changes: a rapid increase in the number of people in the world, with a rising standard of material well-being for those of Western societies; a lessening of territorial and social isolation, both mental and physical; a great enlargement of the units of economic interdependence with a concomitant decline in local self-sufficiency; a profound change in what are socially valued as natural resources; and the emergence, together with many other ideas, of the doctrine of technological determinism.

Technological Determinism

It has now come to be commonly assumed that technology is the base upon which the remainder of society—the ideological and organizational components—rests. Men may not, so this view goes, live by bread alone; but without bread there can be no life; and since it is the technology of a people that provides their bread, their means of subsistence, great or small, the nature of the technology of a people is the key to an understanding of their entire society.

That the technology of a social system is one of its vital aspects cannot be denied; but the idea that it is the base for society leads irresistibly to the theory that it determines society. Thus the sociologist Ogburn, like many thinkers before him, held that the normal pattern of social change is first innovation in technology, then disparity between the newly innovated technique and preexisting ideological and organizational elements (what he called social lag), which leads eventually to adaptive changes in these latter aspects of the society.[1] The idea of technological determinism, to-

[1] Two recent contributions to the thesis that technological change is prior to change in the other components are Jean Fourastié's *The Causes of Wealth*, Theo-

gether with its comrade-in-arms economic determinism, is a highly significant element of the ideological component of all modern societies. As such it has provided a rationale for a variety of economic and political activities, it has served to justify wars and revolutions, and it has often facilitated technological and organizational changes of considerable magnitude. It is a theory that may encourage change, but as a theory *of* change it is no more scientifically valid than is geographic or any other determinism and should have no better standing.

The prevalence of the idea of technological determinism in modern Western society (and now in Russian and Chinese society) both reflects and implements the considerable preoccupation of Western society in recent years with the technological component, a mental orientation that has by no means been the historical normal. Many societies, including Western society during the Middle Ages, have evidenced far more concern with developing or maintaining their ideological or organizational system, or both, than with their technological. Classical China, for example, was by the seventh century highly developed ideologically and organizationally—the developments had come mainly during the preceding two or three centuries—although the arts of agriculture, construction, fabrication, and medicine were but little changed from what they had been in the time of Confucius. The high value that was placed upon ideological and organizational aspects of life is indicated by the prestige that was accorded to the scholar, the political bureaucrat, and, on a more general scale, the filial son. Conversely, the craftsman, the peasant, and the tradesman were tolerated as necessities rather than respected for their social worth. In medieval Europe somewhat similar conditions obtained. During the early Middle Ages considerable effort and ingenuity went into the development of religious ideology and the organization of the Church system, into the evolution of urban forms of life, and into the development of political, military, and craft-guild systems. No comparable changes occurred in either the agricultural or industrial arts, although later in this period major developments occurred in the techniques of construction, in the building of cathedrals. And throughout the Middle Ages it was, by and

---

dore Caplow (trans.), The Free Press of Glencoe, New York, 1960; and Lynn White's *Medieval Technology and Social Change,* Oxford University Press, Fair Lawn, N.J., 1962. Fourastié has attempted to demonstrate that technical progress based upon scientific knowledge made progress in all other regards possible. White, a historian, attempts to explain some of the major changes in the life of European peoples in terms of specific technological innovations. Thus it was, in his view, the invention of the stirrup, which enabled the mounted warrior to attack with lance in hand, making of his horse, himself, and his lance a powerful projectile, that led, through a series of historical events, to the rise of the feudal system. The work contains, nevertheless, a wealth of material on medieval technology.

large, the priest, the politician, the military strategist, and the guild master whose social roles were most honored.

Among primitives, too, the stress has often been on the ideological and organizational aspects of life to the neglect of the technological. Many primitives have had exceedingly complex beliefs and social practices, while their technology has not been developed to a comparable degree. The Australian aborigines, for example, had almost no tools and lived a very simple hand-to-mouth existence; yet they had a tribal organization that was quite complex and functionally effective, and they had a system of beliefs and magical practices that was most elaborate and devious. The Iroquois Indians had a large-scale, intricate, and remarkably effective political and military organization; yet they lived mainly by hunting and fishing and never evolved much in the way of tools, military or otherwise. Indicative of the rather general tendency of primitive peoples to live together in complex ways while living by very simple means is the fact that anthropological reports on primitive peoples seldom devote much space to their technologies, not, one may judge, simply because anthropologists are biased toward the organizational and ideological, but, rather, because they find the few and characteristically crude tools and techniques of primitive peoples inherently uninteresting in comparison with their often unique and always complex systems of beliefs, magic procedures, and forms of organization.

A fairly strong case could no doubt be made for the view that in the course of history men have on the whole tended to devote whatever talents for innovation they may have possessed to the ideological and organizational components of their society rather than to the technological. From this point of view, the great stress on technology in our society at present and in the immediate past is historically atypical, and the idea of technological determinism is but an aspect of this atypical concern with technology. That stress has made for an unprecedented amount of change in the technological component of Western societies, a change which has in turn impressed upon the minds of men the importance of the technological. The physical manifestations of technology make changes in it visible—the contrast is obvious between sailing ship and steamship, between horse and buggy and automobile, between cobbler's shop and shoe factory, and between brick and plaster structure and steel and concrete skyscraper, whereas changes in ideology and organization are less evident. Moreover, recent changes in technology have involved the growth of a variety of highly specialized occupational groups that are engaged in developing and applying new techniques—engineers, agronomists, physicians, and physical and biological scientists. These technicians and scientists have acquired considerable social prestige, and with it economic and political support. Their occupational preoccupation with technology has understandably led them to stress the priority of technology in the changes that are occurring in our society. They see the world in terms of their special occupational concerns; and since as a class they occupy something of the place once reserved for priests, from their ranks come many of the commentators on and interpreters of the contemporary social scene. Developments in technology and in science on which technology is based are reported and discussed in countless professional journals, and a good deal of what is so recorded seeps down in simplified form to the popular press. By contrast, the significant changes that are occurring in the ideological and organizational components of our society often go unremarked, unless, indeed, their cumulative effects become manifest in political or other events.

The sheer weight of attention that is given to technological changes in modern societies fosters the view that technological change is primary, both in importance and in time, and that all other change is somewhat incidental to or follows on it. Furthermore, there is a long-standing assumption, not without its factual basis, that rational procedures can be and often are applied in the development of technology, whereas changes in ideology and organization come, if at all, in an unsystematic, hit-and-miss fashion. In contrast to the physical and biological sciences, those that deal with society are still struggling to get out from under the age-old accumulation of theological and metaphysical concepts of social life; and although social scientists proceed upon the hopeful assumption that eventually man will be able to apply to his social arrangements something of the rational control that he now exercises over biological and physical nature, few of them would assert that that time is yet in sight. Child psychologists, educators, family counselors, personnel officials in industry, criminologists, social workers, etc., do often claim that they provide "scientific" guidance in interpersonal and organizational affairs; and the fact that such functionaries have considerable status and are respected in modern societies may perhaps be taken as an indication that the hopes of social scientists may ultimately be fulfilled. At the moment, however, contributions to changes in technology are ordinarily made by those who have been trained in some field of the sciences and who proceed in their innovative or developmental endeavors in a somewhat systematic manner, whereas contributions to change in ideology or organization are more often made by politicians, businessmen, philosophers, or reformers, who with slight knowledge of the actual nature of social life must proceed, if at all, in a haphazard and unsystematic way.

The Magnitude of Technological versus Other Changes

The magnitude of the changes that have been worked in Western technology over the past two centuries is often considered unique and is in fact as great quantitatively and qualitatively as in the change from the technology of primitive hunters to that of early modern Europe. In some respects, Western technological development since 1750 surpasses that which had been achieved by all the peoples of the world up to that time.[2] At mid-eighteenth century the best agricultural techniques that had been developed could produce only a very small surplus above that which was necessary to maintain a farmer and his family, and it then took perhaps eight or nine workers in agriculture to support one person in town or city. The industrialized techniques of today are, by contrast, so productive that one agriculturist can and often does produce enough to feed fifteen or more nonagricultural persons.[3] From the invention of the wheel until well into the nineteenth century, transport by land never transcended the limitations of the draft animal. Once the railway was invented, development of transport by land came very rapidly. Such was the case with most, if not all, developments of a technological order; they evolved slowly and erratically for the first few thousand years and then changed more in the last century or so than in the whole of their preceding history.

It does not follow, however, that the technology of Western society has necessarily been changing more rapidly than have its other components. There are no objective scales by which to measure the magnitude of changes in these other components; there are no such criteria as bushels per acre or miles per hour by which to gauge the extent of ideological or organizational changes. A comparison of current social ideas, beliefs, values, and modes of social organization with those of two centuries ago, however, readily reveals that these intangible aspects of our culture have changed quite as rapidly and as radically as have the technological.

[2] For historical materials on eighteenth- and nineteenth-century technological development see Charles Singer et al. (eds.), *A History of Technology,* Oxford University Press, Fair Lawn, N.J., vol. IV, 1958, and vol. V, 1959. This five-volume work is descriptive rather than analytical, and it does not include the technological developments of the twentieth century. It is, nevertheless, the major work on the history of technology; and it provides, albeit incidentally, much material on the processes of innovation and development, suggestions of the ideological and organizational circumstances that have fostered technological innovations, and the repercussions on the former of the latter.

[3] In the United States, one working farmer now produces the food and fibers necessary—at current standards of living—for twenty-six people. As a consequence, only 8 per cent of the American people are now directly dependent upon agriculture, whereas in spite of heroic political efforts to force industrialization of the productive processes, in the Soviet Union about 55 per cent of the population is directly dependent on agriculture. One measure of how highly agriculture is industrialized in the United States is the fact that 90 per cent of our agricultural production is accounted for by one-half of the farm establishments. For accounts of the technological and organizational changes that have released men from agriculture for urban industrial work, see Norman S. Gras, *A History of Agriculture in Europe and America,* Harper & Row, Publishers, Incorporated, New York, 1940; and Theodore W. Schultz, *The Economic Organization of Agriculture,* McGraw-Hill Book Company, New York, 1953.

Consider, for example, the contrast between the modern Western view and the eighteenth-century Western view of man and the universe; these views differ quite as much from each other as the automobile does from the oxcart or the airplane does from the sailing ship. In the time of the oxcart and sailing ship man was generally considered to be the *raison d'être* of the earth and all that exists upon and around it, and the whole of the universe was conceived as fixed and finite. Philosophers may not all have accepted the theological doctrine of the divine origin of man; but they could conceive of no point or purpose to the universe except that of providing habitation for man—the highest form of life. Within the past century the universe as astrophysicists define it has expanded a millionfold. Our sun, not long since the center of the universe, has become just one of the millions of stars that make up our own galaxy, and our galaxy but one of countless galaxies; and no star or galaxy is now considered stable. As man's perception of space and the materials in space has been expanding, so, too, has man's view of time. The geologists have constantly and sometimes substantially lengthened their estimates of the age of the earth, and the astronomers have come to think in terms of millions of light-years. Meanwhile, the biologists, with considerable help from the physical anthropologists, have reduced man to one of nature's creatures, deprived him of divinity, and made him subject to the same basic organic laws as are the ape, the dog, and the angleworm. Moreover, as the universe has enlarged, man's stature has contracted; he is but a speck on a speck, and he may well be a very inferior sort of speck at that. Elsewhere in our own galaxy and also in many of the multitude of other galaxies that exist, far higher forms of life may have evolved.

The modern scientific view of man and the universe may have little direct effect upon the conduct of modern men (aside, perhaps, from their current endeavors to venture out into space); but it is clearly evident that this modern scientific view is as different from that of two centuries ago as the spinning wheel is from the modern textile factory or the oxcart from the automobile. Here, at least, ideological change has come quite as rapidly as has technological. The same degree of change can be seen in many other aspects of our ideological heritage, in some instances reflecting and effecting comparable degrees of change in actual conduct. The traditional idea of the nature and role of women, in the West as elsewhere, was that women are inherently inferior, physically, emotionally, and mentally, to men and must be held in bondage to the domestic sphere of life. The status of women was for the most part that of chattel and although there were minor exceptions, the roles of women were those of servants, mothers, housewives, and prostitutes. The past century has brought a radical change in both the idea of the nature and roles of women and in their actual status and conduct. Within that century the idea that women are inherently inferior to men has been largely replaced by a more or less equalitarian view of the sexes. In some times and places, indeed, the idea has gained currency that the female is the superior sex; this idea, it will be recalled, was basic to one of the arguments advanced for the extension of the franchise to women—that the woman voter, being more rational and of purer motives, would work toward the elimination of corruption from politics. Today only the most unenlightened psychologist will claim that the female is by inherent nature either emotionally or mentally different from the male; femininity as well as masculinity are by most psychologists (the major exception being those of Freudian leanings) considered to be acquired attributes. Even the layman is unlikely to hold to the old notion that women are more emotional and less rational than men; and although men may fight to preserve some of the old social prerogatives of the male, if only in token form, they are not likely to do so on the ground that their mothers, wives, and daughters are by nature inferior.

female

The social status of the female in modern society is not in all respects, perhaps not in most respects, the same as that of the male; but it is certainly approaching a state of equality. Even in the eyes of the law, usually the slowest aspect of a society to adapt to changing ideas and organizational procedures, modern women, especially in America, have rights that would have been unthinkable as little as a century ago. Women may vote and may even hold political offices; they may own and control property, and in many of our states they have equal rights with their husbands in property accumulated during the course of marriage; they have as much right in law and in fact to an education as have their brothers; and in many instances (for example, in regard to marital responsibility) they are actually favored by the law over men.

The magnitude of the change in the position of women that has come in both ideology and actual social status during the course of a hundred years is certainly as great as that which has been wrought in any aspect of technology during the same period. Only one blinded to the actual facts of recent changes by the dogma of technological determinism could seriously hold to the thesis that change has come first and mainly in technology and that the "social" changes have lagged far behind.

Nevertheless, the idea is an important part of our current ideology; and it has had a considerable influence on social conduct, especially political, thereby demonstrating that ideas may at times be father to social actions. It was, for example, mainly to foster the adoption of more efficient technological devices and procedures (later to some extent to encourage their innovation) that the United States Department of Agriculture was established; and until it was given new directions during the 1930s, the Department served primarily as an agency of technological advocacy. The idea of technological determinism has been, likewise, the justification for, if not the motivation behind, the various attempts that have been made since World War II to aid the peoples of nonindustrial societies by bringing to them the benefits of

Western technology, agricultural as well as industrial. The operational assumption has been that both the high standard of living and the political freedom of Western peoples stem directly from their advanced technology and that primitives and the nonindustrialized peoples of the Near East, India, and Asia can achieve similar standards of well-being and comparable political freedom if only they can be induced to adopt Western technology. The fact is, however, that social change does not come about in such a simple manner. Giving the Indian farmer a metal plow, better seed, and instructions on modern means of cultivation will not break the cultural cycle of adversity which has over the centuries kept him, and will for the foreseeable future continue to keep him, at the level of bare subsistence.[4] An increase in agricultural productivity, assuming that it can be forced into being, would bring about only an increase in the numbers of Indians living at the subsistence level. Other changes, far more difficult to achieve, would have to be worked in Indian society before the people of India could profit qualitatively from Western technology; they would have to learn, counter to all the ideals, sentiments, and imperatives of familism, to control their birth rate, to eat rather than worship their cows, to put to useful labor the multitude of beggar-priests who have for centuries lived parasitically upon the productive, etc. The pre-industrial peoples of the world are underdeveloped in all respects, not just in the technological; and only those who subscribe to the doctrine of technological determinism could imagine that the introduction of modern technology into these societies would set these societies on the road to material prosperity and political freedom.

TECHNOLOGY AS AN INTERDEPENDENT VARIABLE

The social function of technology is, as has been observed, to control and put to service in man's interests physical and biological phenomena. Its role in social change is not that of a determinant—i.e., not that of antecedent cause—but, rather, of what may for convenience be termed an interdependent variable. In many respects, the technology operates within the social system as the physical and biological habitats do outside that system. Changes in ideology or organization or both may work changes in the technology that in turn implement further changes in the former. When such is the case, the technology, abstractly conceived, is a passive agent, much as the physical environment can be the passive object of changes that are brought about by society and that in turn pose new problems of social adaptation.

[4] The futility of what might be described as technological bootstrap lifting is well documented by A. F. A. Husain in *Human and Social Impact of Technological Change in Pakistan,* 2 vols., Oxford University Press, Fair Lawn, N.J., 1957.

The established techniques of a society are in the nature of enabling powers rather than imperatives to action. The skills of a shoemaker, like the tools of his trade, permit the making of shoes, but do not impel it. If, when, and where a shoemaker makes shoes, a carpenter builds a building, an engineer directs the construction of a new steel mill, or a primitive hunter takes bow and arrow in quest of game are matters determined by nontechnological forces that emanate from the ideological and organizational components of society. A workman works, not just because he is skilled and has the knowledge to do that work, but also because he is the father of a family, accepts responsibility for their welfare, and has, under the particular conditions of his society, no alternative but to make shoes, build buildings, hunt game, or do whatever it is that he is skilled at doing. These and the many other possible conditions that impel the application of a technique are ideological and organizational.

Changes in technology, like the application of an existing technique, are also impelled by nontechnological forces. Moreover, the processes by which technological changes may be accomplished are ideological and organizational. A technique does not change itself; even where, as is often the case, the incongruence that is resolved by a change in technology is an incongruence of various elements of the technology, the change is accomplished by ideological and organizational means. Innovation is, it will be recalled, a symbolic process; advocacy proceeds symbolically and, in the end, organizationally; adoption comes first through symbolic acceptance (as a result of decision making) of the advantage of the new over the old.

Technological Congruence

The persistence and widespread popularity of the idea of technological determinism has obscured the fact that very little is actually known about the relations of the various social components to one another and that the degree of functional interdependence between various elements of a given component cannot at present be specified. It is almost self-evident, however, that the functional efficiency of any given technique depends in part upon other and related techniques. The art of constructing fishhooks will come to nought unless it is combined with the art of making fishing lines and the art of fishing itself. The finest of mechanical skills will be unfruitful apart from machinery and materials to work on; a tractor will be useless without fuel and oil and a competent operator; an automobile assembly line will come to a halt unless countless other aspects of the technique of making automobiles continue in operation. Thus it is that the functional effectiveness of a given technique may range, depending upon its technological context, from zero toward perfection. In the context of a modern cabinetmaker's shop, the technique of machine routing greatly facilitates the fashioning and ornamentation of furniture; in the shop of a Chinese cabinetmaker, its functional value would be nil, for in this context wood is worked by simple hand tools that require quite different and perhaps more complex manual skills.

Consider, by way of a more realistic example, what effects the introduction of the steel moldboard plow into India would have. The farmers of India currently plow shallow furrows through very moist land, hardly more than grooves in the soil, by means of an ox-drawn wooden device. This ancient means of plowing is from the Western point of view exceedingly inefficient; but a modern plow would not of itself be an aid to the Indian farmer in the breaking of his land. Give it to him as a gift, and he would soon relegate it to the storeroom, if he had a storeroom; for his bullock would be unable to pull it and he himself could not guide it. A modern plow cuts deep, turns the soil over, and works well only on semidry land and at a fairly fast clip. In wet soil or at slow speeds it becomes fouled; so either the plow would have to be redesigned to suit the lumbering pace of the bullock, or the bullock would have to be replaced by a more agile beast, a horse or a mule. In the latter case, the farmer would need to learn to care for and provide for a new kind of domesticated animal, and the entire economy of his farm would be considerably disturbed in the process. Once he had acquired a horse, disposed of his beloved bullock, learned to handle and care for the horse, and modified his cropping to conform with the fodder needs of a horse, he would still have other adaptations to make before the new plow became an efficient tool. Since his high-shouldered bullock had pulled against a yoke, but his new horse or mule would be unable to, he would have to acquire and learn to use an entirely different kind of traction harness; since the new plow would go far deeper than did its predecessor, he would turn up hidden stones in his fields which he would have to dispose of; since it leaves the land rough and scarified, he would have to acquire and learn to use a harrow to break the clods and level the field; since iron will rust, he would have to learn to keep his plow under cover when it was not in use; and since iron cannot be shaped by a knife or stone rasp, he would have to have available the services of a blacksmith able to heat, shape, and retemper the point of his new plow.

When the closely interdependent items of a technological complex are relevant, each to all the others, that complex is in a state of congruence; and a change in any one item is more likely to reduce than to increase the functional efficiency of the complex. Even a quantitative change in an item may reduce the effectiveness of the whole. Thus if larger than normal wheels are put on an automobile, maximum speed and fuel efficiency may be somewhat increased; but at the same time the effectiveness of the braking system and the life span of the engine will be sharply reduced. In a similar way, the addition of more stories to a building may render the entire structure unsafe and decrease its usefulness. Thus not until a great many antecedent developments had occurred in building technology (steel frames, elevators, pressure pumps to lift water to upper floors, and a stage system to bring down sewage, etc.)

did it become technologically feasible to construct multistoried office and apartment buildings.

A qualitative change in a technological item is even more likely than a quantitative change to reduce the functional effectiveness of a complex that has been in a state of relative congruence. By 1950 commercial aviation had arrived at a fairly mature stage of development: the four-motored piston plane had become safe and comfortable, its performance was quite predictable, its operators and maintenance men were highly skilled, the problems of servicing it—fuel, oil, food for passengers, etc.—had been worked out, and airports had been designed and constructed for its use; and the airlines might have settled down organizationally to the routine type of operations that the railroads had achieved within a half century after the invention of the railway. But, as everyone knows, they were not permitted to do so.

Eighteen years earlier, an English ex-aviator, impatient with the inherent limitation of piston engines, had begun experimenting with an entirely different method of converting burning fuel into forward motion—the thrust provided by a jet of hot gases. By the end of World War II, the jet engine had become a workable device, although so inefficient in its use of fuel that it was practical only for military fighter planes, where speed counted more than cost or range. Improvements in the jet engine soon led to efforts to develop economical and safe, long-range jet transport planes. That in itself took a great deal of doing, for the existing types of airplane frames were designed for piston engines and were inappropriate to the very much higher speed, heavier fuel loads, and other conditions imposed by jet engines. Reliable and fairly economical jet-engined transport planes finally became available; but before they could be put into operation, a great many changes had to be made in the technology of aircraft usage. Airport facilities had to be remodeled to accommodate the new planes—runways had to be lengthened, loading facilities modified, landing and takeoff guidance techniques improved, etc.; what had been good enough for planes with a maximum speed of 250 miles per hour could not meet the needs of planes with twice that speed. Pilots and maintenance men had to learn a new and quite different body of skills, and the older pilots, often unable to make the transition, were retired. Because of the much higher speed and range of the jet transports, new navigational, visual (radar), and other guidance techniques had to be developed. Before all these changes in technology were accomplished, operating jet planes was considerably less efficient and, indeed, less safe than operating piston planes; but as these changes were worked out, the efficiency of operating the jet plane improved; and within a few years a new congruence had been achieved.

Technological Incongruence

Men have long devised and adopted technological devices that have had no immediate, or even foreseeable, practical function. There was a good deal of this sort of thing during the later Middle Ages, when ingenious mechanics were experimenting with the application of gears and cogs in the transmission of power; they built intricate machines to act, in very limited ways, like human beings—for example, to write a signature, to make a move or two in a game, or to dance at high noon around a clock tower.[5] Currently many of the gadgets that are offered on the market are short-lived conversation pieces of no real use value. For the most part, however, any innovation in technology or the adoption of an innovation occurs in a technological complex that has been adversely affected by changes in its context and has become functionally ineffective, at least by social definition. Incongruence is thus the normal antecedent to change in any technological element. It may, of course, persist for long, even for centuries in some cases, without corrective changes occurring; but when and where change in a technological element does occur, it is usually an effort to resolve an existing incongruence.

Incongruence in the context of a technological complex can arise in a variety of ways. An agricultural or industrial technique may, as has been observed, destroy or seriously damage a natural resource upon which it is dependent, with the result that a modification in the technique becomes necessary in order to maintain the flow of valued goods or services. As will shortly be seen, changes in organization or ideology may lessen the functional effectiveness of a given technique and require the development of a new technique for congruence to be reestablished between the technology and the other social component. Once external disturbances to the functional value of a technological complex have appeared, that complex itself loses something of its internal congruence; and changes both within it and external to it may then become self-perpetuating—as has so clearly happened with transport technology, disturbances in which have had repercussions that continue to be felt more than a half century after the appearance of the automobile.

Although the early automobile was functionally far less effective than the horse and buggy as a means of personal transportation, its development was an effort to resolve a growing incongruence between transport technology and changes in forms of social organization that had occasioned this incongruence. Throughout the nineteenth century there had been occurring, for a variety of antecedent reasons, some of which were technological, a growing specialization in labor, a decline in family size and unity, progressive separa-

---

[5] It was probably, however, such relatively pointless application of gears, levers, shafts, etc., to the transmission of power that led to an improvement of techniques in the design and fabrication of gears, etc., and paved the way for their subsequent application to such useful devices as the early steam engine. Mechanical gadgets have often become in time the basis for, or incorporated into, socially valuable technological developments. See Shelby T. McCloy, *French Inventions of the Eighteenth Century*, University of Kentucky Press, Lexington, Ky., 1952, for many such instances.

tion of work and recreation, rising standards of material welfare, etc., that fostered a demand for personal, as distinct from public, means of transportation. The only available technique aside from the bicycle, which was widely adopted by the working classes, was the horse and buggy; but concomitant changes in social life were making this means of personal transport increasingly disadvantageous. Cities and towns were growing larger and becoming more congested; and partially for that very reason, new ideas and values of public health and sanitation were emerging. As a result of all these changes, the horse and buggy was increasingly becoming a disutility. A horse requires considerable space for its maintenance; it cannot be housed close to the owner's residence unless he and his family are willing to put up with stable smell and filth, hay and grain must be stored near at hand, space must be available for stable wastes, and there must be facilities for their ultimate disposal. Moreover, horses and houseflies go hand in hand—or did so in pre-DDT times; horse traffic, especially under conditions of urban congestion, means dung-polluted air; and dung-littered streets, so it turned out, provide food for vast numbers of noisy, dirty English sparrows.

In public transportation the horse-drawn omnibus and rail car had long since been replaced with the more convenient, sanitary, and rapid electric tram; but the growing numbers of urban people who felt the need for private transportation had no alternative to the horse and buggy, the disutility of which increased as did their numbers. It was this acute and constantly growing incongruence between transport technology and social organization which was eventually to be resolved by the invention of the internal-combustion motor and its application in the development of the automobile.

That the internal-combustion motor was applied to the problem of private transportation, rather than to some alternative problem, seems to have been implemented by an existing incongruence within the technological component itself. At the time, the major useful product of the petroleum industry was kerosene, used to fuel lamps; and the higher fractions—gasoline—were a waste product that was becoming increasingly difficult to dispose of. It had been found, for example, that gasoline polluted rivers and created a serious fire hazard when it was returned to the ground. The existence of large quantities of unwanted gasoline led to various attempts to find a use for it; and one such endeavor culminated in the invention of the internal-combustion engine. Here, then, was a new and tempting source of power. The gasoline engine was inadequate, however, for the needs of factories and other traditional areas of power application, including the railroad and the streetcar. Its "logical" use was, in view of the need for a replacement for the horse and buggy, in the provision of motive power for private transportation; and the incongruence within the technological component was in this way resolved.

As has been indicated, however, the early automobile was not functionally effective, because it operated in a horse and buggy context. Gradually brought into use in spite of its disadvantages, the automobile was soon producing more technological incongruencies than it had resolved. It frightened horses, it distracted blacksmiths from their traditional function, and it resulted in demands for new and better road systems.

The resolution of an existing incongruence, technological or otherwise, by the invention and adoption of a new element commonly does produce a variety of new incongruencies—sometimes described sociologically as the "unanticipated consequences" of a social change. In the case of the automobile, the disturbing effects of this new means of transportation spread like ripples on a pond, until almost every aspect of society was in some way or other affected. Moreover, these disturbances to the function of existing elements have grown rather than diminished over the years. Today, for example, cities and even towns are losing some of their functional value as the suburban form of organization gains dominance, a change made possible if not fostered by the automobile. The suburban shopping center, with its vast parking areas, has to a considerable extent replaced the congested urban retail district. Even such a traditional establishment as the hotel, which evolved in fairly recent times from the ancient inn to meet the needs of railroad transportation, has been rendered more or less obsolete; and in its place has emerged by various states, including that of the rustic motor camp, the modern motel, a hotel on the ground located outside the urban center for easy access by automobile.

IDEOLOGY AND TECHNOLOGICAL CHANGE

The role of technology as an interdependent variable is perhaps most clearly seen in the way in which changing ideological elements may lead to technological changes that in turn require ideological adaptations. The uses to which an existing technique are put, it will be recalled, are determined in considerable part by beliefs, values, and other aspects of the ideological component; thus today the surgeon's skill with the knife is applied to the saving of life, while in some times and places skill with the knife was devoted to ornamenting the body by scarification and in others to dismembering people as punishment for crime. It will also be recalled that all social changes, including those in technology, are effected through symbolic processes and depend upon the body of symbolic elements—the knowledge—that is available to innovators, advocates, and adopters.

There are, however, other and more indirect ways in which ideological elements may affect the technology; and there are at least some instances when a change in technology leads to a subsequent change in ideology. Thus the tendency for modern societies to be preoccupied with technology, by contrast to societies of other times, is, as has been indicated, largely a function of modern ideology. In most times and places men have sought in prayer or in war or in the powers of a charismatic leader relief from even such obviously physical and biological disasters as famine, flood, and plague. Modern men, on the other hand, are prone to believe that through change in or application of technology almost any anticipated problem can be solved and any impending disaster averted. This belief is the culmination of a series of interwoven ideological changes and actions that were predicated on them that began in the later Middle Ages and that, four centuries later, are still going on. They include the slow decay of religious fatalism, the increasing value attributed to this life as against the life hereafter, the decline of respect for the authority of tradition and of faith in the infallibility of traditional authorities, and the rise of science as the accepted means of ascertaining the true nature of the world in which man lives and upon which he is dependent.

It has been these various ideological changes, in combination with related changes in social organization, that on the one hand released individuals from ideological constraints and on the other encouraged them to explore in increasingly systematic ways the world about them. Their discoveries provided a growing body of scientific, as distinct from mythological and superstitious, knowledge of physical and biological phenomena; and in due course this knowledge was used, as it still is being used, as the basis for innovations in technology.[6] The development of modern medical technology can be taken as representative of what has happened also in metallurgy, industrial chemistry, electronics, and almost every other aspect of Western technology.

The premodern medicine of Western, as of other, peoples was a mixture of magical procedures and empirical practices that were handed down in a casual way from generation to generation. A competent practitioner could, no doubt, set a broken bone and staunch a bleeding wound, but he had very little valid knowledge of the human body and no understanding of or power over the infectious diseases; most of his treatments for organic disabilities were ineffective, and the remainder were probably dangerous. Under the circumstances, the status of physician was low, his numbers few, and the majority of people no doubt lived and died without professional aid. In the sixteenth century Andreas Vesalius published a great treatise on anatomy, much of the data for which had been derived—in accordance with the burgeoning scientific spirit—from actual investigation of cadavers; and around him at the University of Padua, where he worked, there began to emerge a school of nontraditional, scientific medicine. The accumulation of knowledge about the human body, its processes, and its ills was for long painfully slow. It was more than a century, for example, before William Harvey discovered

[6] That all the major technological innovations of the last century and a half have been based upon scientific discoveries is one of the significant findings of the case studies reported by John Jewkes et al., in *The Sources of Invention*, St. Martin's Press, Inc., New York, 1958. A good deal of other data indicating the close relations between science and technology is to be gleaned from the *McGraw-Hill Encyclopedia of Science and Technology*, McGraw-Hill Book Company, New York, 1960.

the circulation of the blood, and another two centuries and more before the bacterial cause of infectious diseases was understood. Men were, however, perhaps for the first time in history, actively investigating the life processes rather than accepting the word of authority—that of ancient documents or that of priests, princes, elderly physicians, or old wives.[7]

The application of the growing body of scientific knowledge about anatomy, physiology, biology, etc., to the improvement of medical technology was slow in coming. The medical techniques of the eighteenth century were in few respects better and in some respects far worse than were those that had been relied on during the Middle Ages. The popular practices of bleeding and physicking, for example, undoubtedly killed far more patients than they cured. As late as the Crimean War, military surgeons achieved an unblemished record of failure; every patient on whom they worked died of septicemia. Nevertheless, by the late eighteenth century the new ideological orientation toward medical practice began to bear practical fruit in various discoveries, such as Edward Jenner's discovery that the serum of cowpox gave immunity to humans against smallpox. Thereafter, innovations in medicine came with increasing frequency; and the ability of the medical practitioner to prevent disease, to influence the course of diseases, to speed recovery from injury, and otherwise to aid the ill and postpone death has constantly increased. Each such gain has further encouraged the belief that there is no problem, in medicine or elsewhere, that man cannot solve by the invention and development of a new technique.

The current strength of this belief is evidenced by the complacence with which most modern men, including not a few scientists, view the post-World War II population explosion. The alarmists, mainly sociologists, are in a decided minority. The dominant opinion is a new version of the old thesis that the Lord will provide; namely, that however rapidly world population may increase—and current predictions are that it will increase to at least six billion by the end of the century—technologists will find ways to increase world production of the necessities of life even more rapidly. Perhaps they will, but the assumption that they will rests on faith alone; and should they do so, faith in their ability to do so will have played a vital role in their achievement; for obviously, if men now believed that the potentials of the world were fully utilized, they would make no effort to find new resources.

A dramatic example, exceptional only in its magnitude, of the way in which ideology may foster technological development is provided by the massive, costly, and unprecedented efforts to venture out into space that have been undertaken by Russia and the United States in recent years. The scien-

[7] For an account of the transition from folk to scientific medicine see Lester S. King, *The Growth of Medical Thought,* The University of Chicago Press, Chicago, 1963.

tific rationale for these endeavors—itself an ideology—is that anything that is unknown deserves exploration; that is, scientific curiosity needs no further justification. What has made possible the tremendous expenditures of social resources, however, has been still another ideology, one with more crass and emotional appeal—the belief that whoever (in this case either Russia or the United States) first gets into space will have gained a major victory in the struggle for national survival. It is not clear just how it came about in the years immediately following World War II that the peoples of the West or their political leaders on the one hand and those of Russia on the other decided that they were locked in a struggle from which only one would emerge. But the idea did emerge, grew into the dominant ideological drama of our times, and led to various political and military antics, of which the struggle to conquer space is only one.

The political and military advantages that will accrue to whichever side wins in the struggle for space have never been clearly specified. On the whole the advantages that will obtain from success in this endeavor are as vague as were those of the medieval Crusades and those of the more recent endeavors to Christianize the heathen of Asia. Some advocates of the American effort have claimed that we may find one or another of the planets of our solar system, or some planet in another solar system of our galaxy, habitable and thus be able (they imagine) to solve the problem of excess population by migration to another world. Others have been less imaginative and have claimed only that the moon, once occupied, might provide a new source of minerals that are in short supply here on earth and would in any event serve as a platform from which we could spy on our enemies and from which, in time of war, we could launch missiles. Objections based upon practicality are brushed aside by the claim that science will find a way, or by the more devious and rather impressive observation that such early world explorers as Columbus were also in their day generally thought to be engaged on fool's errands.

Whatever time may prove, it is evident that the current efforts to get men into space and safely back again stem from beliefs that are peculiar to our times and without which no such endeavors would be undertaken, and that these beliefs are essential to the actions, if not always prior in point of time. Most, if not all, technological developments have comparable ideological bases. As will be seen, the ideological component of any society functions mainly to preserve the social *status quo;* and it is only when and where, for whatever reasons, new beliefs, values, and ideas emerge and gain some currency that change in technology is likely to occur.

In most societies of the past, as was so clearly the case in Western society during the Middle Ages, ideology has tended to reconcile the members of society to a passive acceptance of the *status quo,* including the impoverishment and hardships that are consequent upon a limited control of nature. The emergence in Western Europe of a more active, self-confident orientation toward the world is one of the major ideological developments of social history, and it set under way the great burst of individual enterprise that has culminated in modern industrial society. The forces and conditions that gave rise to this body of new ideas, attitudes, and values will be explored in the following chapter. What is pertinent here is that technological changes were fostered by the new ideology and that the success of these changes has, in turn, reinforced modern man's faith in his ability to dominate the world about him.

In some instances the repercussions of technological changes have had quite direct and specific effects. In the Middle Ages and well down toward the present day, craft techniques were enmeshed in magic and ritual, were looked upon with a considerable amount of awe, and were often monopolized by the members of closed guilds; secrecy was a higher value. These ideological and organizational conditions operated to discourage technological innovation. Many factors were involved in the ultimate modification of the cult of secrecy regarding techniques; and perhaps one of the most important of them was a technological development—the invention of printing from movable metal types. With the advent of printing, knowledge of the technology, as well as of other aspects of Western society, and ultimately knowledge of the world were gradually made available to all who were literate; and literacy in time became almost universal. Subsequent innovations in communication technology —the rotary press, cheap paper, typesetting machines, the telegraph, the telephone, radio, and television—all in turn furthered what that invention had begun; and many of the ideological changes that have occurred in recent times have been facilitated by the technological changes that have increased man's ability to communicate through time and space.

ORGANIZATION AND TECHNOLOGY

Marked incongruence may arise and persist between functionally interdependent elements of technology and organization, as is the case when an established small-plot land-use system precludes the application of mechanization to agriculture or when guildlike work regulations discourage the use of newly developed tools and procedures. Contrary to the belief of the technological determinists, such incongruence is not invariably the result of changes in technology; it may be, and perhaps just as often has been, the result of a change in organization that has disturbed the functional effectiveness of some element of the traditional technology.[8]

The occurrence of social lag, i.e., the delay of organization to make

[8] Although the doctrine of historical materialism as developed by Marx and Engels has been popular with European scholars, two recent books on technology —one historical and the other theoretical—suggest that Europeans may be less

adaptive changes to a change in technology, is easy to document. Existing forms of work organization, political organization, or family or other organization or specific values, sentiments, or customs that are an integral part of any such organization have often precluded or at least retarded the application of new technologies. For a long time the knowledge that malaria is transmitted by mosquitoes could not be put to practical use in a program of malaria prevention because traditional political jurisdictions often made it legally impossible for the residents of one area to protect themselves from mosquitoes that bred in an adjacent area. Public health officials were prone to remark that mosquitoes are indifferent to political boundaries; but for a quarter century and more political organization lagged, in this respect at least, behind technological possibilities. Something of the same sort obtained in respect to road building to meet the needs of the automobile and to water supply and sewage disposal, problems that had been produced by the growth of cities and that could have been solved, had it not been for political considerations, by the then existing technology.

Such examples, however, do not validate the idea that it is a sort of law of social life, that is, the social normal, for technology to change more rapidly than does organization; for it is quite as easy to document the claim that organization changes more rapidly than, or in advance of, technology. The following illustrations of this latter sequence of developments are presented not to prove the latter claim, but rather to indicate that there is, in fact, no normal sequence of change—that there is the same complex interdependence between technology and organization as there is between ideology and organization.

Urbanization and Food Technology[9]

The cities of premodern Asia, while they relied heavily on grains, maintained a complex symbiotic relation with their immediate rural hinterland; the wastes of the city, the night soil, fertilized the peasant's fields; the peasant in

---

inclined than Americans to view technology as an independent variable. In *Social, Economic, and Technological Change: A Theoretical Approach* (International Social Science Council, Paris, 1958) Georges Balandier and others stress the interdependence of technology and social organization. In *A History of Western Technology* [Dorothea W. Singer (trans.), Charles Scribner's Sons, New York, 1959] Friedrich Klemm traces the growth of technology as but one manifestation of general cultural change.

[9] An excellent brief analysis of the factors that precluded large-scale urbanization in prehistoric, ancient, and medieval societies and of the developments that gave rise to great metropolitan cities in the nineteenth century is provided by Kingsley Davis in "The Origin and Growth of Urbanization in the World," *American Journal of Sociology*, vol. 60, pp. 429–437, March, 1955. Extensive studies of city life and the growth of modern cities include Adna F. Weber, *The Growth of Cities in the Nineteenth Century*, Columbia University Press, New York, 1899;

turn provided the city with fresh vegetables, with fish (often cultivated in rice paddies), and with meat, mainly pork and poultry. By modern standards these cities were not very large, and by modern standards the urban diet was exceedingly poor; but in comparison with the diet of European cities in the Middle Ages, it was very good indeed; for the peoples of Asia had evolved storage and other techniques, which, with intensive cultivation of the hinterland, made it possible for them to supply their cities with a varied diet. These techniques were unknown to the West and were in fact never adopted in the West.

European towns of the later Middle Ages were comparatively small; and except for those that were located on the sea, where fish played a large role in the diet, the food supply consisted mainly of meat and grains, as it had in ancient Rome. Population density was so low that much land could be devoted to pasturage, and meat animals could be driven to the urban markets from considerable distances. As populations grew and the cities of the West enlarged, the meat-and-grain pattern was more or less preserved by the importation of grains from abroad—of rice from colonial America, wheat from Australia, etc. Relieved of the necessity of producing all their own grains, Europeans began to devote an even larger proportion of their agricultural lands to pasturage; and dairying came to supplement and complement meat production (e.g., skim milk from buttermaking was used to feed pigs). The arts of food preservation, especially of meats, developed little; to the old techniques of smoking, salting, and drying, there was added only that of corning with sodium nitrate. In early modern times the winter diet of urban people of Northern Europe and Britain was, therefore, particularly monotonous and lacking in vitamins and other dietary necessities, although this was not recognized at the time. The excessively high mortality rates in the cities of this period were in most part due to poor sanitation, the prevalence of disease-bearing rats, and sheer congestion; but they were in some part attributable to the fact that urban health levels were far lower than those in the rural hinterlands. The farmers, unlike the urban dwellers, could supplement their preserved meat-and-grain diet with milk, eggs, and stored vegetables.

The initial impact of industrialization, in Britain and in some parts of Europe, was to draw people away from the cities to the scattered factory sites that were located where water power was available. With the introduction of steam power, however, great factory towns, such as Birmingham, began to emerge; and the old port cities, such as London and Antwerp, began to grow with unprecedented rapidity. One of the many consequences of this organizational change, which was both qualitative and quantitative and which itself

V. Gordon Childe, *What Happened in History,* Penguin Books, Inc., Baltimore, 1946; Henri Pirenne, *Economic and Social History of Medieval Europe,* Routledge & Kegan Paul, Ltd., London, 1926; and Henri Pirenne, *Medieval Cities,* Princeton University Press, Princeton, N.J., 1939.

followed as an adaptation to technological changes, was marked technological incongruence of many kinds. Old water-supply systems were unable to meet the needs of industry and the rising population; old sewage-disposal methods were ineffective, even in the judgment of people who knew nothing of bacteria; old means of transportation, of both persons and goods, soon became ineffective; and, of immediate interest, the existing techniques of supplying food to the cities were inadequate, especially so in that, as the urban populations prospered, they came to demand better and more varied foods.

The provision of food for a city is accomplished as much through organizational as through technological means; and at no point in time is it really possible to separate the one aspect from the other.[10] Nevertheless, in the actual course of historical developments there are many instances in which technological developments obviously came as a response to organizational needs. (No doubt there are quite as many instances in which organizational changes followed technological developments, as a way to apply those developments efficiently.) The growth of cities, the emergence of a large middle class with rising standards of living, and other related organizational changes in Western society created food needs that were not met, and that for long were not to be met, by changes in food technology. Most of the dietary changes that did come about were produced through organizational rather than technological means—i.e., through the importation of such luxuries as tea, coffee, spices, nuts, and other stable products of other lands. Thus until well into the last century, urban populations, even those of the larger American cities, were poorly fed.

One of the first important developments in food technology was not so much an innovation as an adaption to new conditions of an old innovation—the rural icehouse of people of the north. In regions of heavy frost it had long been the practice for farmers to cut natural pond or river ice during the winter and keep it in earth burrows where butter, eggs, meat, and root vegetables could be stored during the productive months. Eventually this cold-storage technique was transferred to ships, where it made possible not only a better diet for sailors, but also the transportation over long distances of such perishables as meat, cheese, and animal fats. Soon ice itself was being shipped about by sea as a commodity, and the cold storage of foods in port cities became possible. In time the practice developed of moving ice by railway to land-bound cities; and it was then but a step (first taken in the shipment of meat from Middle Western cattle centers) to the refrigerated freight car.[11]

[10] See W. P. Hedden, *How Great Cities Are Fed*, D. C. Heath and Company, Boston, 1929.

[11] See Oscar E. Anderson, Jr., *Refrigeration in America: A History of a New Technology and Its Development*, Princeton University Press, Princeton, N.J., 1953.

By the opening of this century every prospering townsman in America had his own domestic icebox. Ice-protected fresh meats, vegetables, and even fruits were being delivered in quantity to all the larger cities of America and, in due course, came to be delivered to those of Europe and Britain. The great demand for ice—combined, one may suspect, with the growing pollution of ice-supplying rivers and lakes and the rising standards of hygiene—led in time to the invention of the mechanical refrigerator, first used on a large scale to produce ice for sale and for commercial use. It was then but a step, albeit a considerable one, to the electric-powered domestic refrigerator, which in turn made possible the development of the frozen-food industry, a development that was itself of great complexity. Finally, if that term can be used in connection with an evolving technology, the freezing machinery used by food processors was miniatured and offered for home use, both for the deep freezing of home-processed food and for the storage of commercially frozen foods.

Meanwhile, the discovery, initiated by Pasteur's work for the French wine industry, that bacteria and funguses are the agents of food spoilage, had led to perfection of the technique of heat sterilization.[12] By the end of the last century, a thriving food-canning industry had evolved; and housewives throughout the Western world had learned how to preserve in a fairly acceptable state various kinds of fruits and vegetables. The demand for containers had led to new, mechanical methods of manufacturing cans and glass jars and various kinds of effective closures. As commercial techniques improved, the initial prejudice against tinned products, often warranted, diminished; and the canning industry was given a tremendous boost by the invention of a method of reducing the water content of milk under vacuum and preserving it in tins. World War I precipitated a large-scale tinning of meats and meat products for the supplying of troops, and with the end of the war a civilian market for these evolved.

Meanwhile, also, the practice of packaging in small lots dry cereals, flavored cornstarch for puddings, and other stable foods and food supplements was evolving. Many factors no doubt contributed to this particular development; but of these perhaps the most important was the desire on the part of the early mail-order houses—which were then a very recent organizational innovation—to add food to the items that they could supply to their customers. In fact, a number of mail-order houses that dealt in food specialties soon appeared; and the packaging of dry foods in handy household lots rapidly extended to include such materials as tea, coffee, sugar, and dried fruits, which had previously been sold in bulk.

[12] Empirical discovery of the preservation of foods by heat sterilization was reported as early as 1810 by the French scientist Nicolas Appert; but neither he nor subsequent experimenters could perfect the process, and practical applications were few, mainly because the true nature of the process was not understood. This is but one of many instances in which technological advance has had to await upon scientific discovery.

Once they are well under way, changes in food technology have tended to be self-perpetuating; i.e., a given development has often produced incongruencies that could be resolved only by other technological changes, as was the case when the availability of canned fruits undermined the market for sun-dried fruits, then available only in bulk, and thus forced improvements in fruit drying and packaging. But organizational changes, too, have frequently been involved in keeping food technology dynamic. Recently, for example, marketing procedures of the large chains of markets, together with sharply rising labor costs (a result, as will be shown later, of other organizational changes), have led to the packaging of such perishables as fresh meats, fruits, and vegetables. The development of the self-service market was made feasible by packaged, tinned, and, later, frozen foods; it was an organizational change that was implemented by technological developments. For long, however, meat and fresh produce had been sold in such markets as bulk commodities. This practice was, of course, something of an anomaly, and the labor costs of handling meats and fresh produce on an individual basis eventually became prohibitive. The solution, now fairly widespread, was to prepackage both fresh as well as stable products. The prepackaging of meats and natural cheeses was not difficult; but the prepackaging of fresh produce necessitated a variety of changes in production techniques. Thus, for one thing, if fresh fruits and vegetables were to be mechanically packaged in plastic bags and in this form held in storage for considerable periods before sale—and if costly repackaging of them to eliminate spoiled pieces was to be avoided—it meant that they would have to be harvested far before maturity and, in some instances, that new and more durable varieties would have to be developed. Here, clearly, technological changes were fostered by antecedent organizational developments.

Urbanization and Lighting Technology

The rise of industrial food processing and new storage methods is but one of the many series of technological changes that have been fostered by the growth of cities and related organizational changes. Transportation, communication, and various other technological complexes also were similarly affected. The development of modern artificial lighting, for example, was intimately bound up with the change in the cycle of daily life of urban peoples, with the separation of work and play, and with the increase in individual mobility.

Medieval and early modern Europe used as lighting devices the candle, made from mutton tallow, the lamp, fueled with vegetable oil, and the pitch-pine fagot. During this period the daily time cycle of the people of European, as well as Asiatic, cities tended to be the same as that of rural peoples—up at dawn and to bed shortly after dark. In the temperate zones this pattern means that the waking day is long in spring and summer, shorter in fall and winter;

and in these climatic zones this pattern has inherent advantages even today, for in the city as well as in the countryside, artificial heating aside, it is pleasanter to work and play in the warmer months than in those of winter. There are, thus, no very obvious reasons, except convention, why modern urban dwellers in the temperate zones should for much of the year sleep during the hours after dawn and depend upon artificial lighting for five or six hours after sunset. Why, then, do they do so?

Perhaps one of the basic reasons for this practice is that with the growth of factories and mechanized forms of production, work was geared to the power source and had to begin and end on a time schedule. All the workers had to be assembled when the power was turned on, and the activities of many individuals had to be coordinated. Thus the life of the factory workers necessarily followed a fixed time cycle; and since it did, that of merchants, households, public transport, etc., had to follow suit. When the life of the whole urban population became time-geared in this way, convenience dictated that the daily cycle be held constant throughout the year.

Until fairly recently the usual urban workday was twelve hours or more; and this was usually interrupted, as it still is in much of France and Italy, by a two-hour midday dinner interval. At least in the late fall and winter months, therefore, factories were operated and shops were open during many hours of darkness. Artificial lighting became, in this way, a vital social necessity that was poorly met by the traditional devices. Quantitative changes of one sort and another evolved—the many-candled chandelier with reflecting prisms, the large oil lamp with metal reflector, etc.; and in time, fostered by the need for better lighting, a series of qualitative changes in technology occurred.

Toward the close of the eighteenth century, the traditional and never very satisfactory flaxen candlewick was replaced by one of cotton; later, someone discovered that a wick braided of three or four separate yarns and impregnated with chemicals would curl over in the flame of the candle and burn down as the fat was consumed, thereby eliminating the nuisance of frequent wick trimming. About 1820 the idea of using the waste gas from coking ovens (carbon monoxide) for lighting appeared; and shortly thereafter began the slow, trial-and-error developments which were to culminate in the gaslight era of urban illumination. The first actual application seems to have been made in London and to have involved the welding, end to end, of the barrels of war-surplus rifles to form pipes through which gas could be conveyed from coking house to public street lights. The use of gas in homes, however, was considerably delayed by the appearance shortly after the middle of the century of the kerosene lamp, which displaced both the candle and the whale-oil lamp.

With gaslit streets and kerosene-lamplit homes, shops, and factories, the people of mid-nineteenth-century Western cities were able to extend their waking day further and further into the hours of darkness. They began to get up later and later and go back to bed later and later, as time is measured by the sun; and the life of the city became more and more geared to the hours of darkness. One organizational development that was no doubt in some measure responsible was the progressive separation of work and play. In the older social systems, work and play had been more or less entwined; even festival days had usually had some occupational significance, as, for example, did the harvest festival. The mechanization of work made it difficult for the worker to gossip and otherwise enjoy himself while at work; and as mechanization progressed, the worker came to be increasingly isolated from his fellows and his work to be paced by the machine rather than his own inclinations. In urban office and mercantile establishments a similar purification of work occurred, although for different reasons—essentially the progressive depersonalization of the relations between members of working staffs and of the relations between clerk and customer. At the same time, opportunities for, or at least interest in, participant forms of recreation in home and neighborhood were declining as these two modes of organization, the one formal and the other informal, lost much of their functional integrity.

For a variety of organizational reasons, therefore, urban people began to seek their recreational satisfactions more and more in such commercially provided recreational facilities as the public house, the dance hall, and the theater. None of these agencies was new, but use of them increased rapidly during the later half of the nineteenth century. Gas lighting was gradually extended into private dwellings and commercial establishments; and a major advance in gas-lighting technology occurred when the Austrian chemist Welsbach invented the mantle, still used in gasoline lanterns and lamps, that bears his name. With it, the first true incandescent light was produced—the light comes from a hot ceramic mesh rather than from the bare flame itself. Candles and oil lamps more or less disappeared from the cities, and the gasworks with its huge and smelly tank became an integral part of the urban capital plant.

Gas lighting had, however, one serious disadvantage that became increasingly evident as use of it increased and especially as mass entertainment in gaslit buildings became the normal. The gas lamp was a potential fire hazard; and a series of disastrous theater fires and attendant panics finally dramatized the need for some less dangerous source of light. It was this need, combined with a desire to find new uses for electricity, that led Edison to the protracted series of experiments that finally culminated in the incandescent electric light bulb. Since that time, the uses made of artificial light and lighting technology have continued a development in which the one factor—the organizational—has fostered changes in the other, and the other—the technological—has made possible changes in the one. Thus, for example, the use of electric advertising signs fostered the invention of the fluorescent light—which is far more economical than the light bulb—and cheap fluorescent lighting has in turn led to the floodlighting of highways and sports stadiums. At present, this developmental process shows no signs of abating.

Urbanization and Transportation[13]

The development of urban transportation offers what is perhaps the clearest and most undebatable example of organizational changes that are antecedent to technological change. In the cities of today, as in the cities of London, Paris, New York, and Boston in the early nineteenth century, the demand for efficient transportation, a function of the urban style of life, rather than of mere numbers of persons, far exceeds the ability of the technology to supply it. During the past century and a half, a series of new transport devices have appeared and been put to use; but organizational changes in urban life, as well as sheer growth in unit size, have invariably outrun urban transportation facilities, with the result that congestion has been chronic.

In premodern times it was the transportation of goods, rather than of persons, that was critical for town and city life; and for this reason most urban aggregations had been located on the sea or on other waterways. In some cities, such as Paris, elaborate canal systems had evolved by which goods were moved into and about the city; others, such as London and New York, depended on wagon and pushcart transport between dock and land-bound markets. Since at this time work and residence were closely related, spatial mobility of persons was comparatively rare; and each street and cross-roads tended, in terms of the inhabitants, to be a self-sufficient living area. The city was, in effect, a composite of occupationally specialized villages. The urban dweller, at least the commoner, could walk to his various destinations had he wish or need to do so.

As cities became industrialized and grew in size, place of work and place of habitation (and, later, place of recreation) became increasingly discrete and separated. The physical plant of the city, like the work of its inhabitants, was in effect becoming differentiated and specialized. The rise of the factory

[13] Most studies of the relation between changes in transportation technology and urbanization have centered upon transportation between urban centers and their hinterland, rather than upon transportation within the urban complex itself. A popular account of the history of trolleys, horsecars, streetcars, buses, elevated railways, and subways is provided, however, by John A. Miller in *Fares, Please!* reprint ed., Dover Publications, Inc., New York, 1961. Some materials on transportation within cities will also be found in the following: Harlan W. Gilmore, *Transportation and the Growth of Cities*, The Free Press of Glencoe, New York, 1953; George W. Hilton and John F. Due, *The Electric Interurban Railways in America*, Stanford University Press, Stanford, Calif., 1960; and George R. Taylor, *The Transportation Revolution: 1815–1860*, Holt, Rinehart and Winston, Inc., New York, 1951.

no doubt began this separation of place of work from place of habitation; but once having begun, the process has continued until the city itself is now for many persons only a place in which to work, and their habitations have moved outside the confines of the city to suburban, and often quite distant, areas.

As places of work, residence, and recreation became separated and increasingly distant from one another, transportation of persons became a critical problem. The narrow, often winding, and seldom paved city streets became jammed with people walking to and from work, to and from market, etc.; and the time that people spent in such going and coming eventually became inordinate. The first technological adjustment to the need for personal transportation was the commercial provision of passenger-carrying wagons, which slowly evolved into buses that rumbled down the major thoroughfares. The carriers, initially operated on an individual basis, were gradually integrated for economy of operation and public convenience into transportation systems; in due course they either came under some sort of public regulation or were absorbed by municipal government.

In some places in America horsecars, as they were called here, persisted until late in the nineteenth century; but in such cities as London and Paris, they very soon became a major contribution to the congestion of the more heavily traveled streets. They were slow, they often became bogged down in the muddy roads, and under the best of conditions they raised clouds of dust and filth; and after the development of the railroad for long haulage, numerous attempts were made to replace them by adapting the steam train to urban passenger transport. Of these attempts, the London experiment was perhaps the most fruitful and significant. The city of London is situated on heavy chalk soil which overlies bedrock to a depth of a hundred feet and more. Chalk is easily tunneled, and relatively little support is needed to prevent cave-in. In the early 1840s railroad builders began boring rail routes beneath the heavily congested streets of central London, first cutting just below the surface (sometimes through the basements of buildings), later burrowing deep into the chalk and even passing under the Thames. The initial result was far from satisfactory; accidents were frequent, the smoke from the engines was suffocating, and the service was erratic and undependable; but since almost anything was preferable to trying to get across the city by surface means, these lines prospered. With the eventual substitution of electric power for steam power, an entirely new and satisfactory mode of urban transportation was achieved. Paris, almost as congested as London had been, achieved something of the same result in a different way. Ancient and early modern Paris had been traversed with many waterways which served as lines of transportation. As the city grew and land values rose, these had often been bridged over to make streets, and they themselves had become subsurface barge canals (what have often been referred to by dramatists, including Victor Hugo, as the sewers of Paris). These canals served well in transporting heavy freight to the center of the city; but as the demand for passenger transportation grew acute, and as horse-drawn surface vehicles proved to increase rather than relieve street congestion, many of the canals were drained, lined, and converted to electric-railroad use. Such was the beginning of what is now the large, complex, and relatively effective Paris Metro.

Boston eventually developed one subway line, but in most American cities a variety of factors tended to discourage underground transportation. New York, for example, is situated on granite; Chicago on spongy ground that was formerly swampland. Moreover, American cities had less tortuous street systems than did those of Europe; and once the electric streetcar, an American innovation, was developed, the surface transport problem was to some extent eased. Eventually, however, in both New York and Chicago the time came when the congestion of the central districts became intolerable, and in both cities, the solution to the problem, long delayed and soon antiquated, was the overhead electric line.

In both Europe and America the horsecar had, meanwhile, been provided with rails on which to travel, thus eliminating the problems of chuckholes, mud, and dust. It was therefore but a step to the electrification of these lines; and since the electric streetcar was faster and more reliable than its horse-drawn predecessor, the change-over went a long way toward relieving surface congestion. But meanwhile also, the demand for transport had been increasing, and not only because the cities were growing in size and the density of their populations increasing. As the industrialization of urban life progressed, work and living and play continued to be more and more differentiated, both as to place and as to time. In spite of all the developments in transportation—surface, subsurface, and elevated—that had occurred since the opening of the century, the larger cities were even more congested by the end of the century than they had been at the beginning. Organizational changes in social life, qualitative as well as quantitative, had continued to outrun technological provisions for passenger transportation.

So far in the twentieth century no enduring solution to urban transportation needs has been achieved. The bicycle was for a time hailed as the solution, particularly in Europe, where it was for a while a favored means of personal transportation, particularly by members of the working class. The automobile and the paved street systems that grew up in time to serve it helped, but only for a time. The development after World War II of suburban residential communities, especially marked in America, together with the inadequacy of railroad commuter services, soon led to an unprecedented congestion of roads into the cities, of city streets, and of parking lots, a congestion that the building of freeways, overhead interchanges, urban overpasses, and multistoried parking facilities has modulated but has never eliminated. A hundred years and more ago the centers of our great cities were clogged with pedestrians, horse-drawn carriages and wagons, and pushcarts. Today they are clogged with pedestrians looking for transportation, electric and gasoline buses trying to find room to maneuver, and trucks and automobiles jammed bumper to bumper, unable to move and unable to park. Each of the many technological developments that have occurred between these two points in time has had its effects on human conduct and social organization; but in each instance organizational changes, technologically and otherwise implemented, have soon rendered inadequate the latest development in urban transportation and set the stage for a subsequent one.

Labor Organization and Technology

One of the clearest examples of organizational implementation of technological change is provided by the circumstances surrounding the invention, circa 1400, of the keeled sailing ship. The ancients, most notably the Romans, had evolved sailing barges of considerable size and seaworthiness, but their ships could sail only with the wind and had to depend upon oars, manned by slaves, to go crosswind or upwind. Slavery was an organizational necessity for the operation of the early galleys, for only forced labor would submit to the exceedingly hard conditions and the very short life of a galley oarsman. During the early Middle Ages the sailing barge was rediscovered and put to use, first in Italy, in the development of commerce; but slavery, at least that forthright form of slavery that was necessary to keep the galleys supplied with oarsmen, was not a part of medieval culture.[14] A limited supply of forced labor was secured through enslavement of African natives, who proved, however, to be physically and psychologically inadequate to the work, and by covert enslavement of Europeans, especially of convicted criminals who were often "bought" from their jailers. Manpower for the early period of the commercial revival was obtained in these ways, but the need for galley oarsmen soon ran far ahead of the supply. The result was an incongruence between organizational inability to supply oarsmen and technological inability to do without them, an incongruence that led to the invention of the keeled sailing ship.

That invention consisted, in essence, of a synthesis of the design of the traditional Norse sailing boat and the shipbuilding arts of Southern Europe. The Norsemen had developed a boat with a deep keel that could sail across the wind and so tack upwind, but their boats were too small to be used in commerce; the shipbuilding arts derived from the Romans enabled Europeans to construct large, sturdy craft. When the two were combined, there began to emerge the sort of large, dependable, and maneuverable craft with which

[14] See C. W. W. Greenidge, *Slavery*, The Macmillan Company, New York, 1958.

Columbus was to discover the New World.[15] This craft, unlike its European predecessor which needed large numbers of oarsmen, needed only a small crew; and needing only a small crew, it could roam far from supplies of food and fresh water.

The foregoing may suggest something of the historical interdependence between labor supply, which is basically a matter of social organization, and technology. The existence of large-scale slavery seems everywhere and always to have been associated with a little developed and unchanging technology, although the absence of slavery has not necessarily assured technological progress. It was perhaps the existence of slaves in ancient Egypt that discouraged technological development; for the Egyptians seem to have been quite ingenious in political, religious, and artistic realms, and yet to have built their pyramids with the crudest of tools and to have relied more on brute force than on engineering skills to move and pile up the stones of these grandiose burial vaults. The cultivation techniques employed on the rice and, later, on the sugar and cotton plantations of the pre-Civil War South involved the use of simple hand tools and labor that was no more efficiently used in 1850 than it had been a century before. Here, as in other places where slaves have been used in agriculture, the pattern of land usage and landownership and the kinds of crops grown and the methods of cultivating them were adapted to the limitations of unskilled, undependable, gang labor. The existence of such a labor supply seems everywhere to have precluded, in industry as well as agriculture, the development of efficient, complex, and skill-requiring tools.

On the other hand, a felt scarcity of labor, the product of various ideological and organizational factors, has often provided the incentive to improvements in technology and, hence, to an increase in labor productivity. As was indicated earlier, it is the conclusion of many economic historians that the technological and commercial developments of the Renaissance period in Europe were fostered by the scarcity of both rural and urban labor that followed the great plague of the fourteenth century. The chronic scarcity of labor in the settled regions of America following the Revolution, a consequence of a variety of factors, most important of which was the availability of free lands westward, seems to have been one of the conditions that contributed to the zest that Americans showed for mechanical and other labor-saving devices of all sorts. Many such devices were indigenous to America; many others were borrowed from Europe and put to far more intensive use here than in their native lands.

The artificial, organizationally maintained, scarcity of craft workers that was produced by the medieval guild system was not to any extent offset by

[15] See S. C. Gilfillan, *Inventing the Ship,* Follett Publishing Company, Chicago, 1935.

increased efficiency in the use of labor. In fact, the guilds were on the whole able to stabilize productive techniques, as well as the hours and conditions of labor and the price of goods. When in the nineteenth century industrial workers began to form into guildlike unions and clamor for higher wages, it was generally assumed by economists that, should the unions succeed, they would, like the guilds of old, bring technological development to a halt; and in fact the craft unions did and still do strive to retard, if not totally prevent, the introduction of labor-saving devices. In some instances they have been fairly successful in stabilizing their productive techniques; but in the long run and for the most part, the effect of union organization has been to foster, rather than discourage, the development and adoption of new labor-saving devices and procedures. The unions achieved an artificial scarcity of skilled labor and demanded and secured an artificially maintained high wage for it; but they did not at the same time capture control, as had the old guilds, of the productive organizations in which they worked. These organizations, individual firms, were often highly competitive with one another, and their owners or managers were as a consequence constantly under pressure to lower productive costs, increase quality, or both, if they were to survive. One way that they were able to do so was by increasing the man-hour productivity of skilled workers through the use of more efficient tools, which was often a matter of powering hand tools; another was by replacing skilled, unionized workers with cheaper unskilled labor through the subdivision and simplification of work tasks. Both ways meant innovation in technology, and the sum of that innovation was the progressive mechanization of industrial production. The scarcity and high cost of skilled labor has never, of course, been *the* determinant of technological development; and once highly efficient productive techniques are developed, they can be adopted, as has been the case in Japan, for use where labor is cheap and plentiful. Through the nineteenth and well into the twentieth century, however, union-produced scarcity of skilled labor was one of the factors that contributed to the rapid mechanization of production in America, Western Europe, and Britain. Over the past few decades, changes in the character and operation of organized labor, together with other factors, have tended to reverse the consequences to technology of this particular organizational system.[16]

[16] As long as the major concern of organized labor was to raise wages, the general effect was to provide an incentive for progressive mechanization of the productive processes. As the goal of unions shifted increasingly toward the stabilization of employment, success in this endeavor has tended, as it did so markedly in the railway and shipping industries, to discourage further mechanization. Nevertheless, some very recent advances in production technology, notably the automatization of machine production, have been fostered by union-created labor scarcity and high wages. For the growth of automatization in industry, its ante-

The amount of labor that is apportioned to each of the various categories—rural, urban, unskilled, skilled, white-collar, administrative, etc.—of any society is in part a function of the class system. In a relatively closed class system, where there are strong ideological and organizational barriers to individual movement out of and into class positions, the relative inflexibility of the supply of labor in any one category serves to discourage technological development. On the one hand, labor-saving devices cannot be introduced because the labor so displaced would be unable to shift into new work functions; on the other hand, any new device that requires new skills or more skilled workers would strain the existing, inflexible supply of workers. In such a class system technological change is further discouraged by the class-linked attitudes and biases of the members of each class. It was, for example, the high value placed on pastures and woodlands by the early modern English landlords who wanted to preserve their riding-to-hounds style of life that for long prevented, and to some extent still does prevent, a more intensive cultivation of the English countryside. In medieval Europe both technological and commercial development was inhibited by, among other things, the fact that one of the most honored occupations was that of priest, and many bright and ambitious lads who might otherwise have contributed to technological and related changes entered the Church and were thereby removed from mundane matters.

By contrast, in a class system that is relatively open and that permits the individual to move into a higher category than that into which he was born, or alternatively to slip downward in the class hierarchy, technological change is, other factors being equal, encouraged. For one thing, individuals may be able to secure advancement in the class hierarchy by innovating or adopting some new devices or procedures. For another, workers tend to leave the less rewarding occupations and crowd into those that are more rewarding, if only in terms of prestige, thereby producing a scarcity in the former that may lead to the development of labor-saving changes in technology. A striking example of this technological consequence has been American industrialization and mechanization of household labor. Since colonial times, domestic labor has been scarce in all but the Southern states. In the American system of class values the status of domestics was

<hr/>

cedents, and some of its consequences see Robert A. Brady, *Organization, Automatization, and Society,* University of California Press, Berkeley, Calif., 1961; Georges Friedmann, *Industrial Society: The Emergence of the Human Problems of Automation,* The Free Press of Glencoe, New York, 1955; and Floyd C. Mann and L. Richard Hoffman, *Automation and the Worker,* Holt, Rinehart and Winston, Inc., New York, 1960. An interesting account of the way in which rising labor costs fostered the mechanization of cotton growing is provided by James H. Street in *The New Revolution in the Cotton Economy,* The University of North Carolina Press, Chapel Hill, N.C., 1957.

then, as it still is, very low, however well such workers were paid. Since, for the most part, it was possible for a domestic—almost invariably, by the way, a female—to improve her status if not her income by entering factory, office, or clerical work or by marrying, the supply of domestic labor tended to be small and to be composed of incompetents or girl novices on their way to better things. Even during periods of heavy immigration, the supply of domestic labor was never for long adequate to meet the demand.

The chronic American undersupply of domestic labor, together with such other factors as rising standards of living, new spheres of activity for women of the middle classes, and progressive urbanization of the population, created a continuing need for improvement in household technology. This undersupply of domestic labor was one of the factors, previously unmentioned, that contributed to the progressive industrialization of our food technology. It also forced some, if never sufficient, change in home design and some, if long delayed, simplification in household decor. American domestic establishments have never become the engineered structures that some avant-garde architects have advocated, for the persistence of conventional values and tastes has precluded the development and adoption of "machines for living." The typical modern home is, however, certainly a far more efficient structure than was the multistoried, furbelowed hodge-podge of rooms, passages, and useless spaces that was the middle-class standard and ideal a century ago. Moreover, it was no doubt the chronic undersupply of domestic labor that was in considerable measure responsible for the rapid and ceaseless substitution of mechanical for manual labor in the home; first plumbing, automatic heating, gas and electric cooking appliances, and powered cleaning equipment and, more recently, powered lawn mowers and other mechanical servants.

In this connection, the post-World War II vogue in America for the householder to become his own plumber, electrician, cabinetmaker, painter, and appliance repairman should be cited as an example of the way in which a scarcity of labor may affect technology. A good many factors, organizational and otherwise, have been basic to this development; but the immediate antecedent was and still is the very high cost and inefficiency in home maintenance and repair of craft labor, one reason for which has been the rigid work jurisdictions that have been maintained by the unions. The Jack-of-all-trades who could remodel a kitchen, install a new window, and build on a porch may not have been particularly efficient at any one of the many specific tasks involved; but the series of superspecialists who are now required to do these jobs, although each is very efficient in accomplishing his special task, have a collective efficiency that is incredibly low.

As the cost and difficulty of maintaining, repairing, and remodeling homes rose during the years following World War II, more and more householders took to doing their own work. Many of them evidently found such work not only a great saving of money but also a fairly pleasant leisure-time activity; and thus began the do-it-yourself vogue. Long since it has become socially acceptable for anyone—doctor, lawyer, teacher, or preacher, as well as carpenter, mason, plumber, or mechanic—to turn himself into a week-end handy man. The progressive invasion of the crafts by amateurs fostered the emergence of retail establishments to cater to their needs; and soon manufacturers of paints, plumbing and heating materials and equipment, electrical appliances and supplies, etc., developed materials, tools, parts and prefabricated units especially designed for the limited skills of the amateur craftsman. As a result of such technological changes, it has become possible for an amateur craftsman in many instances to get results comparable to those of a skilled worker and at a fraction of the money cost.

The Division of Labor and Technology

The progressive division of work tasks into a host of highly specialized activities is one of the commonly recognized consequences of the mechanization of production. What is not so evident is the fact that a division of labor has in turn sometimes fostered technological change. A classic example of this latter phenomenon is the way in which the development of cottage industry in England led to the mechanization of textile production, which economic historians often consider to be the beginning of the industrial revolution.[17] Mechanization of textile production may not have been the actual beginning, but it was certainly one of the major strides on the long route to modern industrial procedures.

In early eighteenth-century England textile production was still a handicraft industry, in which the spinning wheel and the hand loom were the major tools. Goods for sale were mainly guild-produced, and marketing of them was guild-controlled. Characteristically, the guilds held production down and prices up; and the supply of commercial textiles was never sufficient to meet the demand, especially the growing demand in British-controlled India. Enterprising free-lance merchants were gradually able to develop a new source of supply by using the labor of cottagers—small farmers and their families who lived on the outskirts of such port cities as London. In this procedure the merchant, working outside guild regulations and, frequently, in violation of laws regulating the production and marketing of goods, served as an entrepreneur; he obtained bulk fibers

[17] For some subsequent developments in textile technology, their organizational backgrounds, and their social repercussions see Neil J. Smelser, *Social Change in the Industrial Revolution*, The University of Chicago Press, Chicago, 1959.

(linen or wool), had them spun into yarn by a cottager (who usually received, as compensation for his labor, a portion of the yarn that his household had produced), had the dyeing done by another cottager, the weaving by still another, etc. As this system grew, cottagers came to specialize in one or another of the phases of textile production; and there developed a crude, but in terms of the times effective, division of productive labors. In time, however, the first of a series of technological incongruencies in textile production made itself felt. One weaver could consume the yarn produced by many spinners; and, for reasons unknown, cottagers tended to prefer weaving to spinning. Spinning was, in modern terms, the bottleneck in textile production. It was to break this bottleneck, which was a direct consequence of the cottage-industry form of division of labor, that the spinning jenny (consisting of a number of spindles, each with a fiber-feed mechanism, ganged together and driven first by horsepower and later by waterpower) was invented.

It is possible that in this instance, as may have been the case in many since, the concentration of labor on one single phase of the productive process was itself an important factor in the invention of a more efficient tool. A worker who does a single task over and over may be somewhat more likely to perceive the possibility of mechanizing his work—e.g., of substituting a powered tool for the repetitious motion of hand and fingers— than is one who shifts from task to task as the productive process proceeds. Moreover, as a work task is progressively broken into a series of specialized activities, each activity in effect grows simpler and increasingly more susceptible to mechanization. Another example from early textile technology illustrates this circumstance: The spinning jenny soon made weaving the bottleneck in textile production, a bottleneck that was eventually broken by the mechanization of the loom. As textile production increased, the demand for flax began to exceed the supply, and manufacturers cast about for a cheaper fiber. The decline of rice production in America had led some plantation owners to find profitable alternative crops, among the more promising of which was cotton. Since the fibers of cotton are firmly attached to the cotton seed, separation of fibers from seed by hand was a slow and tedious task. Nevertheless, a small cotton-producing industry grew up in America, and hand ginning by slaves became common. To get any significant quantity of cotton ginned required a massing of workers; and the cost of labor, even when slaves were used, was excessive. It is thought that it was the sight of a large number of workers sitting at a long table patiently pulling cotton fibers from the seeds with their fingernails that inspired Eli Whitney to invent the simple device (a wooden drum with spikes that swing through slots in a grid and pull the fibers free from the seeds) that was the first mechanical gin, a device that enabled the spinners of England to shift from reliance on flax to reliance on cotton.

Technology and Social Change

The techniques by which men control natural phenomena and put them to their own ends do not operate and are not changed irrespective of ideological and organizational factors. Contrary to the belief of the technological determinists, techniques are not independent variables. But there is perhaps one sense in which the role of technology in social change is distinct from that of both ideology and organization. The more complex and effective the technology becomes, the greater are the opportunities for still further changes in technology. Whether or not these opportunities will be realized depends, of course, largely upon factors external to the technological component. Increasing complexity and efficiency in ideology and organization, on the other hand, seem generally to decrease the possibilities for subsequent changes, technological, ideological, or organizational. For whereas an efficient technology helps to liberate the individual members of society, releasing them from the need to labor constantly in order to survive, the more efficient the ideological and organizational components of the society, the more effectively the individual members are constrained by the established elements of the social system, including the technological, and the less they are free to engage in those deviant forms of conduct that might bring changes to the society. Thus a major, and possibly fatal, error in the doctrine of historical materialism and in the current attempts by Communist Russia and China to realize the mandate of this doctrine is the assumption that it is possible for a society to stabilize its ideology and organization and yet remain dynamic in its technology.

chapter 9 *The Ideological Variable*

Men may devise, develop, and adopt new techniques, and those new techniques may in turn pose new problems of technological, ideological, or organizational adaption. A technique, however, is never the activating force in social change. That force is, rather, a mental construct—an idea, the perception of a problem to be solved, the conviction that that problem can be solved. The idea that mountains can and should be moved will not alone move mountains; but the idea that moving mountains is possible and desirable must exist before men can or will apply themselves to devising means for doing so.

The activating role of ideas in the making of any social change has been recognized by most social philosophers and many sociologists. Most of them, however, have ignored or failed to recognize its complex, variable, and limited nature; for most have blindly adhered to some dogma of ideological determinism. Intellectuals are no doubt occupationally predisposed to stress the function of the intellect in social life; and when they turn their attention to social change, their occupational bias tends to lead them to presume that change is caused by intellectual forces, if not by intellectuals like themselves.[1]

There have been many versions of the thesis that the key to an understanding of both the stability of society and changes in society lies in the ideological aspect of the social system. Plato conceived himself as the architect of the good society, and in his grand design philosophers like himself were to be the guides to and guardians of social welfare. Comte, two millenniums later, saw in the evolution of the human mind the cause of social progress; and he, too, placed the achievement and maintenance of the good society in the hands of intellectuals like himself. Marx had little use for

[1] This bias is clearly evident, for example, in one of the most recent works on social change—Don Martindale's *Social Life and Cultural Change*, D. Van Nostrand Company, Inc., Princeton, N.J., 1962.

291

intellectuals as a class; in his general theory he was a technological, an economic (organizational), and an ideological determinist in turn. In this latter role, he held that it was class consciousness—a mental awareness on the part of the members of the downtrodden proletariat of their common interests—that would eventually give rise to the revolution out of which the good society was to emerge. Durkheim believed that "collective representations"—mystic and mystifying mental constructs—were what makes for social cohesion and hence for social stability. Sombart held that the appearance of a new and unique "spirit," an energizing body of ideas that made acquisition of wealth the major goal of life, was what instigated the changes that constituted the rise of modern society. And Sorokin holds that it is a slow cyclical shift in social values and sentiments from those of a sensate to those of an ideational (idealistic) character and vice versa that is the essence of social change.

All these and the many other forms of ideological determinism evince a considerable amount of social sophistication and cannot be brushed aside in the same cursory way as can technological, biological, or geographic interpretations of social change. Max Weber's theory that it was the rise of the Protestant ethic that brought into being modern industrial and capitalistic forms of economic life, although a form of ideological determinism, is still the most acceptable of the various attempts that have so far been made to explain the rapid changes that have occurred in Western societies during the few centuries past. It does, however, incorporate the same conceptual error that appears in all forms of determinism, ideological or otherwise. Whereas the historical evidences that are used to substantiate a deterministic theory may be reasonably valid and, perhaps, even fairly representative—certainly such is the case with the data offered by Weber —the frame of reference is the prescientific one of simple cause and effect. As a consequence the particular ideological factors that are singled out for examination in any theory of ideological determinism are treated as an independent variable.[2]

No idea, belief, system of values, ideal of character, ethical code, or

[2] Inspired by Karl Mannheim's *Ideology and Utopia: An Introduction to the Sociology of Knowledge* (Louis Wirth and Edward Shils (trans.), Harcourt, Brace & World, Inc., New York, 1936), American sociologists began during the 1930s what was hoped would prove to be systematic investigation of the nature and role of ideology in society. The field did not prosper, however; and a quarter century of desultory effort has not contributed much to our understanding of the ideological component of society. For a bibliography and evaluation of the field, see Kurt H. Wolff, "The Sociology of Knowledge and Sociological Theory," in Llewellyn Gross (ed.), *Symposium on Sociological Theory*, Harper & Row, Publishers, Incorporated, New York, 1959; and Norman Birnbaum (ed.), *The Sociological Study of Ideology, 1940–1960*, Basil Blackwell, Oxford, 1962.

other ideological element ever operates as a wholly independent factor either in the maintenance of the social *status quo* or in the making of social changes. Like other elements of the social system, most ideological elements function only in interaction with other elements, with the result that the social consequences of any given ideological element may vary from context to context and a change in an ideological element may be canceled out by a change in its context. The same idea that may, where hypermotivation and other necessary personal-social qualities exist, lead to innovative endeavor may lead to nothing more significant than daydreaming in a less favorable social context. The same faith that may inspire men in one society to industry and enterprise may lead to nothing more fruitful than prayer in another. The recognition of the bacterial cause of disease has led in our time and place to the invention of effective means of control; where different values and different organizational circumstances existed, the same recognition could have been buried in priestly documents. The religious beliefs of southern Italians and Sicilians are no doubt one of the factors that keep their birth rate impoverishingly high; yet the people of northern Italy, who share the same beliefs and are no less religious, have reduced their birth rate over the past fifty years to close to the European average.

To insist that ideological factors are not independent variables is not, however, to deny their importance in the making and maintaining of society. They cannot be regarded either as causative forces or as constants; for they do not arise from nothing to produce their effects and their effects vary with varying contexts. They are, however, a vital part of social life; and in combination with other factors, most particularly organizational, they operate either to foster and facilitate changes in the social system or to discourage or channelize them.

LANGUAGE AND SYSTEMS OF SYMBOLIZATION

Symbols—verbal, gestural, and graphic—have often been described as the *modus operandi* of social life; and it is certainly true that a considerable part of social life is symbolic. The whole of culture is embodied in symbols; it is mainly by symbols that the social heritage is transmitted from generation to generation; through symbols the members of a society are guided into their various social roles; by means of symbols men secure many of their gratifications and are upon occasion punished for their errors; and by the manipulation of symbols men arrange their personal affairs and come to collective decisions. Moreover, and what is most pertinent to social change, it is through the synthesis of symbols into unique combinations that innovations occur, by symbolic methods that innovations are promoted, and as a consequence of symbolic processes that they are adopted and social changes thereby accomplished.

Not only is a considerable part of social life symbolic, but the rest, the nonsymbolic aspects that lead to the production of food and the maintenance of life, is dependent upon symbols. As a consequence, the distinction between what is symbolic and what is not is not always clear. Men frequently mistake symbols for things, as they do when they people their world with ghosts of their own imagining; and they sometimes mistake the symbol of a quality for the quality itself, as they do when they judge a man to be kind because he speaks in a kindly fashion. Moreover, many symbols represent other symbols, rather than things. Philosophers, cultists, and even politicians often bemuse themselves with the manipulation of symbols that are so many times removed from anything nonsymbolic that the symbols have no other referents than symbolic ones; and although scientists attempt to test the symbols that they use against their sense perceptions, they are not always certain of the success of this endeavor. Ultimately, of course, it is the ability, always facilitated by symbols, of men to relate themselves nonsymbolically to their fellows and jointly with their fellows to the physical and biological habitats that determines their ability to survive; and a society in which the population is preoccupied with symbolic constructs, rites, and rituals is most likely a society that is going to seed.

The relationship between the symbolic and the nonsymbolic is by no means simple and by no means constant. A man who speaks in a kindly way may indeed conduct himself in similar fashion. He may be a kind neighbor, a kind husband and father. He may, on the other hand, be quite the opposite or kind in some respects but not in others; he may exploit his wife and be mean to his children, while treating his neighbors in the kindliest fashion. The same complex and inconstant relationship between the symbolic and the nonsymbolic obtains in a society as a whole. As a consequence, the symbolic constructs of a society—the beliefs, values, attitudes, knowledge, and ideological systems—are no certain index to the technological and organizational components of that society. It is in part for this reason that historical data, always symbolic, must be used with great caution and that the student of social change cannot assume that a change on the symbolic level—for example, the enactment of a new law, the acceptance of a new social philosophy, or the announcement of newly discovered knowledge—necessarily means a comparable and equivalent change in the nonsymbolic aspects of social life.

Spoken and Written Languages

Whether the language that a people speak—their basic system of symbols—is considered to be a part of the ideological or technological component of their society is a matter of definition. It is here included within the ideological component only as a matter of convenience, for there is little reason to believe that the particular character of the language that is spoken has any direct or constant bearing upon the ideas and other mental constructs that are fashioned from it. Languages do vary widely, as, for example, Chinese does from English, and so, too, of course, do ideas, beliefs, knowledge, and other symbolic constructs; but to explain Confucian ideology, say, as a consequence of spoken Chinese or early Christian beliefs as the result of Latin is patently absurd; it is to mistake the tool for the arts of the craftsman.

Undoubtedly the words of a given language are a sort of catalog of the things and processes known to and important to those who speak that language. What is not verbally symbolized does not, in the social sense, exist; and anything so symbolized has at least symbolic existence. The languages of primitives do not contain many terms for abstractions (nor do the subcultural languages of children, the uneducated, and some special groups in complex modern societies); and the speech and thinking of primitives is correspondingly pragmatic. The spoken language can, however, be very rapidly elaborated; it is perhaps the most elastic aspect of any culture, for new words can be added without disturbing existing words and their usages. Thus by simple addition to their language, the Japanese were able to keep up *linguistically* with their transition from a feudal type of society to an industrial one.

On the whole, the form of the spoken language of a society seems more to reflect the society than to limit or determine what usages are made of the language or what ideas, beliefs, concepts, values, etc., are embodied in linguistic form. The same is not true of the written language, which may impose strong constraints on usage.[3] The earlier forms of writing were pictographic and ideographic; and although the remains—such as cave writings—provide some clues to the life of the times, the primary significance at the time of use was probably more aesthetic than communicative, more supernaturalistic than pragmatic in intent. In pictographic and ideographic writing ideas or objects are represented by designs; thus to

[3] The constraints that a particular method of representing symbols may have on the usages of those symbols are even more evident in methods of notating quantities. The Roman system of representing numbers, and the same is true for some other systems, including the Chinese, was cumbersome and lacked any means of representing zero. Although the Romans were competent engineers and could make the necessary calculations for the successful construction of large buildings, aqueducts, etc., they developed nothing in the way of pure mathematics. Modern mathematics, so essential to science, stems from the Arabs, and its development by them seems to have been facilitated by their way of recording numbers and, quite as important, by their invention of zero. See A. Hooper, *The River Mathematics,* Holt, Rinehart and Winston, Inc., New York, 1945.

represent an army, a number of pictures of soldiers might be used. Such writing is necessarily cumbersome, vague, and little suited to the recording of abstract ideas, such as time and space.

The development of systems of writing in which speech sounds rather than ideas and objects are represented came considerably later, the earliest known examples dating from about 2000 B.C. The advantages of writing of this sort are the same as those of the spoken language itself—flexibility and specificity. Babylonian, Egyptian, Chinese, and—halfway around the world and centuries later—Mayan society were able to record historical events, to keep records of legal and economic transactions, to control the actions of political and other agents who were not under the direct supervision of king or court, to publicize legal edicts, etc. The character of the written language undoubtedly facilitated the development of each of these great civilizations—as of other and later ones, including our own—although it did not, of course, determine the specific usages to which the language was put in each time and place.

Monopoly of the Written Language

In many societies the technique of writing has become the monopoly of a small class of persons who have used the written word as an instrument of resistance to change. Although the priests of ancient Babylon and Egypt no doubt monopolized the written word to some extent, the classic examples are the scholars of old China and the churchmen of the Middle Ages. In the Chinese form of writing, each word, idea, and object, rather than syllable, is represented by a written character, with the result that there are thousands of separate characters (phonograms, ideograms, and pictograms) in the written language. Characters can be added or compounded but they cannot be modified in accordance with changes in speech. Once it became established, the Chinese written language tended to remain stable, however much the spoken language changed over the centuries. By the beginning of the Christian era, written Chinese had come to represent a dead language, perhaps because learning to read and write it meant learning the meanings of some thousands of characters, many of which represented words that were no longer spoken. Writing was, thus, a skill quite distinct from speaking, and it may be assumed that those who were taught to read and write were taught also to think in terms of the recorded ideas. At any event, successive generations of those who were literate did their thinking in terms of the ideas that had been set down by Confucius about 400 B.C. Perhaps because the written language was so complex and so few persons could read and write and because for the same reason very little was recorded, the ideas that had been put into writing by the ancients, of whom Confucius left the most behind, came to be considered by scholars the source of all social wisdom; and for somewhat the same reasons the scholars became recognized as the living agents of that wisdom. In time there emerged an elaborate bureaucratic system, manned by scholars and dedicated to the preservation of the social principles, of which filiality was the foremost, that had been enunciated by Confucius. Confucius's writings had become sacred; his interpreters, who held a monopoly over those writings, priests; and their function the maintenance of social stability.

Neither in ancient Greece nor later in Rome was writing ever monopolized by a single class of persons, in part, perhaps, because both the Greeks and the Romans used an alphabetical form of writing, which is far simpler and more flexible than is the character writing of the Chinese. Writing, particularly in Greece, was used to record many things—mental speculations of one sort or another, philosophies, and even observations about the nature of the world, the heavens, and various other societies. With the decline of Rome, writing in general fell into disuse throughout Western Europe; and although here and there the written records of Roman times were preserved as a sort of sacred duty, literacy all but disappeared. When in time feudal isolation began to break down, the old Greek and Roman writings were gradually rediscovered and monopolized by churchmen, who in due course, and mainly through the efforts of St. Thomas Aquinas, reconciled Roman legalistic writings and Greek philosophy and protoscience with the Christian Bible. The maintenance of the monopoly of the churchmen over the records of the past was facilitated by the fact that the Greek and Latin in which they were written had by then become dead languages. During the Middle Ages a variety of written vernaculars evolved; but their use was limited to pragmatic matters, such as the recording of business contracts, the sending of messages to distant persons, etc. The records of the past, monopolized by the churchmen, had by then become sacred; consequently, although Western peoples gradually became literate, they had no access to the knowledge of the past; and churchmen, like the scholars of old China, were able to use their monopoly of this knowledge as a means of preserving the social *status quo.*

To a very remarkable extent the minds of Western men were held in bondage to the Church by this means for some centuries. In spite of organized efforts to prevent it, however, change was occurring; and the world of the European was being rapidly expanded by explorers who brought back from other societies doubts about the claims of the churchmen (for example, the claim of the universal value of Christian morals). As the gap between what the Church sanctioned and what men did grew ever wider (for example, the gap between the principle of the brotherhood of man and the actual slaughtering of native peoples and between the Church prohibition of usury and the actual borrowing in order to engage in trade), the authority of the Church became suspect; but until nonchurchmen were able to gain access to the records of the past and prove to their own satisfaction that the Church was fallible, the authority and integrity of the Church were not openly questioned. The break came with the invention of printing, which soon led to the multiplication of copies of the written records—first, of course, the Bible—and then to the translation of them from the Greek and the Latin into various vernaculars. In a very real sense, the invention of printing was the ideological turning point in the history of the Western world. It inaugurated and facilitated the mental ferment that was in time to give rise to science and to new philosophies.

IDEOLOGY AND SOCIAL STABILITY

Under conditions of complete stability, the beliefs, superstitions, ideals, and other symbolic constructs of a society would be in concordance with one another and with the various technological and organizational elements of that society. What the members of the society would say and think would parallel what they did. Under such conditions, the ideological component would simply be the symbolic embodiment of the other components and would function to provide a rationalization for them, to aid in transmitting them from generation to generation, and to discourage any modification of them.

Although few societies have approached stability, there has been in all societies, past and current, a marked and persistent tendency to cling to existing symbolic constructs, however irrelevant those constructs may be to the operational aspects of the society. Since beliefs, superstitions, ideals, and the like are *de facto* no more than man-devised symbolic constructs, one might suppose that they could readily be discarded for others more in accord with nonsymbolic realities. Such is not, however, the case. The ideology of a society, its body of symbolic constructs, is often more resistant to change than is its technology or organization, in spite of the fact that any change must come via symbolic means. In modern, highly industrialized societies a great many of the prevailing ideas and ideals are those that were appropriate to and derived from agrarian social life. Familism is still the normative ideal, although the actualities of kinship relations may be quite otherwise; concepts regarding sex and other moral concepts are those of the old patriarchal family and the small, isolated agricultural community; and in the midst of war and preparation for war, modern men cling to the belief that they are dedicated to the maintenance of peace.

The fact is that everywhere and always men tend to look upon their symbolic constructs with a degree of awe. Even as they may create from symbols gods who, once established, dominate their minds and even their conduct, so they may impute to their various symbolic constructs sacrosanct qualities that give those constructs an importance far greater than the realities of life.[4] The folklore may have it that actions speak louder than words, that it is not what one says but what one does that counts; but in actuality it is usually what a man says that determines in large measure the opinion that his fellows have of him. The social test of loyalty—to church, family, class, race, or nation—is invariably a verbal test. What marks a man as a heretic or traitor is usually his rejecting or expressing doubt about some cherished concept, not his acting in ways contrary to it. Thus a Southern politician might, if he chose, work diligently to undermine the legal dominance of whites in the South; but should he dare openly to criticize the concept of white supremacy, his constituents would certainly not vote for him again. A racketeering labor leader might with considerable impunity rule his organization with ruthless self-interest, violating in practice every principle of the democratic process; but should he publicly express the view that democracy is but an illusion, he would by current definition be proving himself subversive and be classified as a Communist. A man might seduce a woman and be considered reprehensible; but he would be regarded as far more reprehensible and dangerous to society should he disparage the concept of the virtuous nature of all womankind.

Folklore

The heritage of every society includes a considerable body of beliefs, assumptions, and concepts that define the nature of the world in which the members live and through which they perceive the events, both natural and social, that occur around them. These symbolic constructs are a sort of précis of the empirical experiences of the people over the past and provide interpretations of the causes of those experiences. Thus a fishing people may come to believe, from the fact that fishing boats have from time to time been swamped in a given area, that a sea god has decreed the area taboo, that a vicious monster dwells there, or something of the sort. An agricultural people may come to conclude, from vague and random evidences, that seeds will not germinate unless planted when the moon is in its first quarter; and a modern, industrial people may come to believe, from no better evidence, that a rise in stock-market prices is a certain indication of economic well-being.

Everything in and surrounding a society is provided by the folklore with some sort of symbolic representation, and a great deal of what the individual growing up in society learns is via the symbols rather than through direct experience. He may learn, for example, that such and such a

[4] See Guy E. Swanson, *The Birth of the Gods*, The University of Michigan Press, Ann Arbor, Mich., 1960.

plant is poisonous—as, indeed, it may be—not by eating the plant and becoming ill, but by indoctrination into the belief of its poisonous character. Many of the beliefs, superstitions, concepts, etc., of the folklore are functional, in that they protect the individual, and in turn the society, from misadventure; but they are also, individually and *in toto*, forces of social conservatism that tend to preclude individual and collective experimentation—experimentation that might prove disastrous, but that might also turn out to be socially rewarding. If the members of a primitive society have learned through the folklore to believe that the world beyond the valley in which they live is filled with evil spirits, they may thereby be precluded from venturing over the hills into what may well be fruitful new territory. If the folklore has it that the light of the full moon induces madness, people will be unlikely to venture forth in the full of the moon and discover for themselves how beautiful its light can make the world. Subservience to the folklore operates, therefore, as a strong deterrent to innovation, to the advocacy of innovations, and to their adoption. It may be said that in general and with few exceptions the folklore binds the members of a society mentally to the *status quo* and inhibits change.

In addition to beliefs, superstitions, assumptions, concepts, etc., the folklore includes various bits of social wisdom, embodied in precepts, maxims, adages, sayings, proverbs, and other rule-of-thumb guides, in accordance with which the folklore would have the individual conduct himself. It also includes a variety of myths and legends, such as children's stories and adult folk tales, which serve for the most part as demonstrations of the validity of other elements of the folklore. The various elements of the folklore, however, are more or less discrete; for example, there is little relationship between the belief that moonlight induces madness and the assumption that the earth ends just over the horizon or between the idea that one should let sleeping dogs lie and that a stitch in time saves nine. Moreover, the folklore is not represented in or monopolized by some organization; everyone has access to it, and everyone can be, if he wishes to be, an authority on it. As a consequence, the folklore can change piecemeal to adapt, however slowly, to changing empirical experience. Furthermore, an individual may violate one part of the folklore without, in the view of his fellows, jeopardizing the whole; he may be decried as a fool, but he will not be subjected to more serious sanctions.

Religious Ideology

Superimposed on the folklore there is in every society a body of symbolic constructs that are more or less interdependent and that provide explanations for what is outside the range of empirical experience—explanations for the origins of the world, of man, of man's society, of whence man comes and of where he goes upon death, of man's purpose in life, etc. Such explanations are invariably based upon the idea of a supernatural being or beings; systematized and related, they constitute a religious ideology. Associated with a religious ideology there is always some organizational system, more or less highly institutionalized, that claims a monopoly on the right to represent the supernatural to the members of society.

Operationally a religious ideology is never distinct from its associated religious organization; the latter derives much of its power from the former, and the former is perpetuated over time by the latter. The ideological and organizational aspects of religion may, however, become incongruent, as did Christianity and the Roman Church during the later Middle Ages, with the result that the religious system functions poorly. Moreover, in some times and places numbers of religions or sects adhering to the same religious ideology have competed with one another for social acceptance, with the result that no one of them has exercised any great influence in the society. Such was the case in Rome at the beginning of the Christian era, and such has been to some extent the case in the Protestant parts of the Western world over the past few centuries. The role of religious ideology has, therefore, varied from time to time and from place to place.[5]

Under conditions of comparatively stable congruence, such as existed in old China and in the middle period of medieval Europe, religious ideology and its associated organization are the most powerful forces that operate to maintain social stability. Even under conditions of marked incongruence, religion may staunchly and quite effectively resist adaptive changes in the society. It is, for example, in considerable part because Spanish Catholicism remains medieval and the position of the Church unassailable that contemporary Spain is the most laggard of the countries of Western Europe. It is true that neither in Spain nor elsewhere is religion an independent variable; a marked change in political organization could, it must be assumed, break the hold of the Church. The current hold of the Church over the minds of the Spanish people is, however, a major reason why marked political or economic changes have not occurred.

The reasons why highly integrated organizations, religious and otherwise, serve as stabilizers of the entire society will be analyzed in later chapters. The stabilizing effects of religious ideology itself stem from the fact that

[5] The most useful single work on the variable role of religion in society, with special reference to recent and contemporary American society, is J. Milton Yinger's *Religion, Society and the Individual*, The Macmillan Company, New York, 1957. Especially useful are his Chapters 10 and 11, both titled "Religious Change and Social Change." See also David O. Moberg, *The Church as a Social Institution*, Prentice-Hall, Inc., Englewood Cliffs, N.J., 1962.

it is impervious to modification on the basis of empirical experience. Acceptance of it is a matter of faith; and once it is accepted as true, its validity thereafter stands. A belief about the size or shape of the earth can be tested by empirical experience, as one such belief ultimately was; the belief may long preclude a test being made, and it will certainly give way slowly to evidence that contradicts it. But any explanation that man has devised for the origin or existence of the earth cannot be tested; to those who have been inducted into it, it is the true explanation, and there is no evidence that can be gathered to advance against it.

A religious ideology serves a variety of functions for the individual members of society; to the extent that it is congruent with the other aspects of the social system, it comforts, it reassures, it provides point and purpose to life, and it rationalizes the misadventures of life. The individual members of society have, therefore, a self-interest in preserving the ideology—to doubt its validity weakens their confidence in themselves. Because the members of society value it, an accepted religious ideology may be used by the associated religious organization as a means of social control. The same will of God that gives purpose to life and explains the existence of the earth and of all things of concern to man can be and always is used to coerce the individual members of society into conformity to social standards and, as is often the case, to the standards that the religious organization imposes upon the society.

Religious idealists will hold that the control over the individual that is exercised by religion is of a different order from that exercised by political or economic factors. It is, they think, spiritual, rather than crass and sensate; it appeals to "higher" values, to altruism and other nonselfish qualities of man. If such were in fact the case, then there would be no heaven or hell, nor any ideological promises of reward for virtue and punishment for infraction of religious codes. The real and significant difference between religious and other modes of social control is that religious rewards and punishments are accepted (or, conversely, rejected) on faith and are never, because they cannot be, subjected to test. A legal system that does not over the long run demonstrate that crime does not pay will lose its power; an economic system that does not for the most part reward the industrious with economic goods will in the long run cease to function. No one, however, can test a priest's threat that, unless his version of supernaturalistic will is followed, one's spirit will be punished throughout eternity; for no one returns from the land of the spirits to give evidence as to what does happen.

The untestability of religious controls means that, as long as faith endures, those controls will be effective and that faith itself will tend to be self-perpetuating. Religious faith, the acceptance of a religious ideology, is never an independent social variable; but it has often been the least dependent of the various aspects of a social system, and it has commonly been used by a religious organization to perpetuate the *status quo* and to discourage social change.[6]

Secular Ideologies

In some times and places, most strikingly in Western societies of today, supernaturalistic explanations for certain things, such as the origins of society, the mechanism of life, and the physical nature of the cosmos, have been displaced and replaced by naturalistic ones. Naturalistic explanations cannot replace supernaturalistic ones in answer to such man-posed questions as the purpose of life or in regard to such man-made assumptions as that there is life after death. Moreover, the distinction between supernaturalistic and naturalistic explanations is never quite clear; concepts usually range by degrees from supernaturalistic through metaphysical to naturalistic; and even modern scientists may become confused in trying to draw lines between their mode of thought, that of metaphysicians, and that of theologians.

Nevertheless, there has been at times a striving toward secular as distinct from sacred interpretations; and that striving has given rise to ideologies that are at least more naturalistic than supernaturalistic, more secular than sacred. There is certainly a difference in degree that operationally amounts to a difference in kind between explaining death as God's will (or, alternatively, as the will of some evil spirit) and explaining it as the consequence of natural processes. On the basis of the former explanation, all that man can do about his reluctance to die is to express it in an appeal to God (in prayer), whereas the naturalistic explanation permits man to gain—as he has now done—knowledge about the life processes which may in turn give him some control over them. There is an equivalent distinction between explaining the origin and existence of the going political order as God's will (as in the concept of the divine right of kings of the later Middle Ages) and explaining government naturalistically as a creation of man for the fulfillment of human ends (as in the concept of contract, which arose to displace that of the divine right of kings and which served as

[6] For a historical account of the role of the medieval Church in discouraging changes in medieval society, see Will Durant, *The Age of Faith: A History of Medieval Civilization*, Simon and Schuster, Inc., New York, 1950. The conservative role of Confucian ideology and the scholarly class in China is described by C. K. Yang in *Religion in Chinese Society*, University of California Press, Berkeley, Calif., 1961. Specialized studies of the way in which religious organizations endeavor to constrain both the minds and the conduct of the members of society include Robert J. Miller, *Monasteries and Cultural Change in Inner Mongolia*, Otto Harrossowitz, Wiesbaden, Germany, 1959; E. O. James, *The Nature and Function of Priesthood: A Comparative and Anthropological Study*, Vanguard Press, Inc., New York, 1955; and Alvak W. Sulloway, *Birth Control and Catholic Doctrine*, Beacon Press, Boston, 1959.

the rationale for the invention and adoption of parliamentary forms of government).

A critical development in the social history of Western society, one that greatly facilitated the technological, organizational, and other ideological changes which distinguish modern from medieval society, was a gradual contraction in the role of religious ideology and an increase in that of secular ideologies.[7] Unlike a religious ideology, a secular ideology includes concepts that are ultimately testable, and hence a secular ideology can change as a consequence of empirical experience. As long as men really believe that their king is king by divine will and, being divinely designated, can do no wrong, they will be unwilling to rebel from his rule, whatever evidence is provided by their personal experiences with his governing. But when men come to believe that their government was created for reasons of convenience by themselves or their forefathers, they will no longer hold it in superstitious awe and may, with provocation, act against it.

THE PROTESTANT ETHIC

No other of the many changes which brought about a new and liberating mental climate of secular rather than sacred concepts in Western society was quite so important as Luther's idea that every individual is empowered by God to determine for himself the will of God. In the ideology of Christianity as it was developed and interpreted by the Roman Church, the individual was supposed to be entirely free to choose the path of righteousness or to give way to the temptations of the devil. Free will of this sort was a logical necessity if the Church—with God above it—was to mete out rewards and punishments; it placed the responsibility for what the Church might do to the individual on the individual's choice. Since the Church held a monopoly on the ability to read God's will, it could lay down for the individual, to choose or not as he saw fit, what conduct was righteous. It was upon the ideological premise that the Church and only the Church was empowered to determine God's will that the whole authority of the Church rested.

For some centuries before the Reformation, social change of considerable magnitude had been taking place here and there in Western society. The Crusades, themselves expressive of the social tensions that had been produced by incongruencies within the feudal system, had enlarged the known world of Western Europeans; they had brought about some blending of various ele-

[7] For a detailed history of the transition in Western society from sacred to secular modes of thought, with special reference to thought about social life, see Howard Becker and Harry E. Barnes, *Social Thought from Lore to Science*, 3 vols., new ed., Dover Publications, Inc., New York, 1961 (first published in 1938).

ments of European culture; they had posed new problems of food preservation, transportation, weapons, etc., that led directly to the development of some new techniques; and they had brought about considerable cultural borrowing from the peoples of the Near East.[8] With the gradual disintegration of feudal isolation, trade developed between various regions of Western Europe; and regional specialization in production evolved, first in agricultural production. Trade led to the emergence of trade centers, which often became in time also centers for the production of metal, wood, textile, and leather products. A new class of workers, craftsmen, grew up; and in time they organized themselves into local craft guilds.[9] With the decline of feudal sovereignty, the Roman Church became a major unifying force for all Western European peoples, who were otherwise divided by language, customs, and loyalties into a multitude of local groups. Rome, as the seat of the Church, came to be the ideological center of Western Europe; and the Pope, the titular ruler of all Western peoples. Had the Church been reasonably adaptive, the long-standing goal of a new-day Holy Roman Empire might conceivably have been achieved; but medieval churchmen became instead staunch defenders of the unstable, malfunctioning *status quo* and individually and as an organization resisted most of the changes, such as the growth of trade, that were already under way.

There were a number of specific ways in which the churchmen, using religious ideology as their primary source of power, succeeded in retarding changes throughout the Middle Ages. Church prohibition of usury discouraged, although in the long run it did not prevent, the accumulation of venture capital, the development of an effective monetary system, and the financing of trade. In part, perhaps, because of this prohibition, surplus wealth tended to be immobilized in the form of jewels and articles made of the precious metals or to be dissipated by the wealthier churchmen and the secular princes in the building of palaces and in courtly pomp and ceremony. Even more impeditive to change, especially that of a technological character, was the diversion of attention, materials, and manpower into the building of religious edifices—cathedrals, basilicas, and other monuments to God, to personal pride, or to superstitious fear of the hereafter.[10] Churchmen encouraged, and indeed

[8] See Aziz S. Atiya, *Crusade, Commerce and Culture,* Indiana University Press, Bloomington, Ind., 1962.

[9] See M. Postan and E. E. Rich (eds.), *The Cambridge Economic History of Europe, Vol. II: Trade and Industry in the Middle Ages,* Cambridge University Press, New York, 1952.

[10] A further drain on the human resources of medieval society was the large number of saint's days and other religious holidays that were celebrated during the year. Such holidays tended, apparently, to accumulate over the centuries, new ones being added from time to time while none of the old ones fell into disfavor. By the later Middle Ages the work week had as a consequence been reduced in

themselves participated in, the practice of investing wealth that had been acquired by trade or other means in religious structures, both as a means of achieving note and repute in this life and as atonement for the sins committed in acquiring that wealth; for it was the prevailing belief that divine favor could be purchased in this way.

Much of what enterprise did emerge through the Middle Ages was thus channeled off into the building of religious monuments. The techniques of constructing them were gradually improved; and by the sixteenth century the arts of stoneworking, cathedral architecture, and religious ornamentation had been highly developed. But the concentration upon religious structures largely precluded efforts of a more practical and fruitful character. Throughout the period there was a growing need, largely the result of increasing trade and commerce, for roads, bridges, port facilities, housing, etc., that everywhere in Europe went unsatisfied. Towns did increase in size and number, but the problems that their growth imposed were seldom solved. Even late in the Middle Ages the water supply and sanitary techniques that had been developed by the Romans were still not put into use; and towns and cities, while liberally provided with religious edifices, were filthy rabbit warrens of meandering, unpaved streets and haphazard, inconvenient buildings that set the stage for the recurrent plagues of the period.

The role of the medieval Inquisition in preserving the stability of medieval society has perhaps been exaggerated. There is no doubt, however, that it was the most massive effort at thought control in recorded history prior to that undertaken by the government of Communist Russia. During the eleventh and twelfth centuries the social tensions that resulted from the acute and ever-growing incongruencies of medieval society were frequently expressed in mob attack upon individuals who were accused of heresy—i.e., with being advocates of change of some sort or other, all change being popularly defined as a violation of God's will. The Church eventually set up special courts and procedures to regularize the suppression of heretics. Those charged with the crime of heresy—a very elastic term at best—were given a formal trial and, if found guilty in accordance with the accepted concepts of proof, were subjected to punishment. The power of the Inquisitors was no doubt very great, and throughout the period of the Inquisition a miasma of fear undoubtedly hung over all the peoples of Western Europe. The constant danger that he might be accused of heresy by his fellow townsmen must have had a constraining effect upon every individual and been a strong deterrent to innovative, advocatory, or adoptive conduct.

Nevertheless, medieval society did change slowly and segmentally; and in the long run the gap between what the Church represented and ideolog-

---

many instances to as little as three days. Such a heavy allocation of time to nonproductive activities must have gone a long way toward absorbing the gains in man-hour productivity brought about by improvements in technology.

ically held to and what the members of medieval society were actually doing became unbridgeable. Perhaps only because they were waging a losing battle against social changes, churchmen grew cynical and corrupt. Marked and atrophic changes occurred within the Church organization itself; and many churchmen came to use the sacred powers bestowed upon them for personal aggrandizement rather than for maintaining the power of the Church. Meanwhile, the need—unsatisfied by the Church—for physical protection for the towns, for security along the trade routes, etc., constituted a social vacuum into which strong individuals could and did move—a foresightful brigand might become guardian, guaranteeing for a fee the safe passage of goods in transit; an ambitious but unemployed ex-feudal lord might build himself an army and forcibly consolidate and pacify an area over which he could rule. In these and other ways, political unification of the peoples of Western Europe under secular, rather than religious, leadership evolved; and as their position solidified, secular rulers came increasingly to challenge the right of the Church to exercise authority over economic and political matters. Since these secular leaders tended to be oriented toward change rather than stability —perhaps only because change had given them their opportunity to gain power—they were supported in the struggle against the Church by the members of the newly rising class of independent (i.e., nonguild) merchants, manufacturers, and bankers, and by the functionaries, such as scribes, lawyers, and physicians, who ministered to the needs of this class.

The Reformation

Such was, in brief, the social climate that gave rise to Luther and the Reformation that he led.[11] A churchman more idealistic than the majority of his fellows, Luther struggled for a time to reform the Church from within; but, as he eventually discovered, a venal organization is easier to replace than to rectify, especially when there are on hand powerful if latent forces ready to support a rebellion. Luther's major charge against the Church was that the Church sold indulgences—i.e., that the Church absolved wealthy sinners from the religious consequences of their sins—a practice that was in effect a means of reconciling the disparity that existed between Church principles and social

[11] See Charles Beard, *The Reformation of the 16th Century*, The University of Michigan Press, Ann Arbor, Mich., 1962.

The conditions that gave rise to Luther's rebellion from the Church had evidently been long-standing and widespread, and Luther was not the first priest to advocate reformation of Christianity. A generation before Luther there arose in Italy a Florentine priest who preached Church reform in almost the same words that Luther later used. He was hanged and burned for his heresy in 1498 by order of the Borgia pope, Alexander VI, an exceedingly corrupt man. For an account of this prelude to the Reformation, see Roberto Ridolfi, *The Life of Girolamo Savonarola*, Cecil Grayson (trans.), Alfred A. Knopf, Inc., New York, 1959.

practices. Luther's break with the established church was, however, far more than a protest against organizational corruption; it expressed such latent, and Church-repressed, ideological developments as that of nationalism and that of distrust of the Pope and his representatives, and it reflected such practical needs as strong local political authority and freedom from antiquated religious constraints on trade and finance.

In 1517 Luther published his ninety-seven theses repudiating the medieval sacrament of penitence and the sale of indulgences as practiced by the representatives of the Pope. Two years later he specifically denied the *jus divinum* of the Papacy; and the following year he sketched a program for the establishment of a new church that would be directed, locally and nationally, by laymen rather than a hierarchy of priests. This latter provision stemmed ideologically from Luther's belief that every individual is equipped by God with a conscience which enables him to determine for himself God's will and makes it unnecessary for him to turn to an established religious authority— a priest—for guidance. The new church would be maintained of, by, and for the laity, who, in Luther's terms, constituted the universal priesthood of all true believers.

In making his Protestant churches what would now be termed "democratic," Luther undoubtedly achieved a major religious innovation. Nonreligious precedents for democratically organized groups were not lacking; the early guilds, for example, had been run more or less democratically by their members. But it was Luther who perceived local and lay autonomy to be the correction for the organizational venality that developed in a centralized church and who established the practice, since followed by most Protestant sects, of a lay board empowered to select and, when dissatisfied, to dismiss its pastor and to deal with financial and other practical church affairs.

As Protestantism spread through the Germanic countries, it was for the most part the local citizens of independence and means who staffed the lay boards of the churches. Such being the case, it is quite understandable that the appointed pastors should have been inclined to identify the values and sentiments of citizens of this sort with Christian theology. The ultimate result was the emergence of religious support for a system of values and sentiments which has since come to be called, perhaps unfortunately, the Protestant ethic.

The Protestant Ethic and the Spirit of Enterprise

Earlier it was observed that the most useful theory of social change that has so far been advanced was Max Weber's idea that the major force for change in the Western world, the force which, he thought, accounted for the rapid development of modern society, was a distinctive ethic that was embodied in Protestantism.[12] Although his theory is overly particularistic and makes ide-

[12] Max Weber, *The Protestant Ethic and the Spirit of Capitalism,* Talcott Parsons (trans.), George Allen & Unwin, Ltd., London, 1930. R. H. Tawney (*Re-*

ology the determinant of change, it has much to commend it, and in modulated and much qualified form may be taken as a working hypothesis. Weber came to his theory by the method of historical comparison. He observed, in considerable detail, that there had been little change in Western society through the Middle Ages, and almost none in such non-Western societies as those of India and China for many centuries. Comparing medieval, Indian, and Chinese societies with European societies of the seventeenth and eighteenth centuries, during which the industrial revolution occurred, he came to the conclusion that the variable had been religion. Whereas the religions of medieval Europe and India and China had operated as stabilizing factors, that of the recent West—Protestantism—had operated to foster change. The energizing factor in Protestantism was, he concluded, its emphasis on the ability and the desirability of the individual's assuming responsibility for his own welfare. The ethic—the character of the ideal man—that was embodied in Protestantism was thus one of individual self-reliance, personal integrity, and enterprise in the satisfaction of personal needs and interests.

The ideal man of Confucian China was above all else filial; he was guided in all things by regard for the welfare of his ascendants, living and dead, and for the good name of his family. His personal goal was to join, in good time, the spiritual company of his ancestors and be honored among them; and in accordance with Confucian ideology the means to this end was meticulous adherence to the precepts of Confucianism—which covered such practical matters as how to raise filial sons, choose their wives, and bury dead elders. The ideal man of China was not an idealist; he was, rather, a willing social conformist, who lived as well as his station in life permitted, and with one eye on heavenly reward for good conduct. This ethic no doubt contributed in some measure to the prolonged stability of Chinese society, for it left no scope for individual enterprise.

The ideal man of Buddhist India was, and to a considerable extent still is, an ascetic. His sole concern was with spiritual matters, his only goal the attainment of divine grace. For him living was just a means to spiritual ends, and all worldly conditions were accepted passively and with resignation. The ideal man of China was exemplified by the scholar, who was authority on, exponent of, and adherent to Confucian philosophy; that of India, by the saintly, and very unsanitary, Buddhist beggar.

The ethic of medieval Europe stemmed in theory from the Christian concept of the fall of man. Because man—in the person of Adam—had failed his Maker, mankind was on trial; life in this world was punishment for origi-

ligion and the Rise of Capitalism, Harcourt, Brace & World, Inc., New York, 1926) was among the first to criticize the Weber thesis, mainly on the historical grounds that economic enterprise had appeared here and there in Western Europe prior to the Reformation. A critical evaluation, largely justified, has recently been made of the thesis by Kurt Samuelson in Religion and Economic Action, Basic Books, Inc., Publishers, New York, 1961.

nal sin, nothing should be expected of it but tribulation, and a good man would patiently and passively endure the indignities which God in his infinite wisdom had seen fit to inflict. This ethic was exemplified in the cloistered monk; and there were in fact a very considerable number of monks. The cloistered monk lived in poverty and isolation from worldly affairs, cultivating his garden and fields from the necessity of having to eat, but devoting himself to prayer and meditation. Insofar as matters of this world were concerned, he was apathetic, without enterprise, and entirely reconciled to whatever might come his way. Should plague sweep across the land, he waited for it to strike him down; should his crops fail, he simply endured hunger; should his roof leak, that, too, was the will of God.

In contrast to these three social ideals, the Protestant ethic made individual self-reliance, individual enterprise, and individual endeavor desirable qualities. In terms of the Protestant ethic, the passive and unenterprising characteristics of the medieval ideal were in truth but laziness, indifference, and incompetence. The medieval ideal was, again in these terms, simply a craven coward who was afraid to meet and conquer the world about him; he took refuge in his monastery, hiding from life and excusing his ineffectuality under a cloak of saintly humility; he was a social weakling, making no contribution to the welfare of society. The ideal represented by the Protestant ethic, on the other hand, had courage and confidence in his own abilities; he met the world about him actively and with intent to subordinate it to his own ends and interests; he recognized that what happened to him here on earth was largely of his own making; he assumed responsibility for his own welfare; and he was guided in all matters by his own conscience.

Qualifications

There is no doubt that the various ethics as perceived by Weber and briefly described here had a factual basis; but what is not known is the extent to which any one of these ethics actually prevailed within the society or the extent to which it affected the conduct of the members of that society.[13] An

13 Many of the attempts to test the Weberian hypothesis have produced supportive evidence. Robert K. Merton ("Science, Technology, and Society in Seventeenth-Century England," *Osiris*, vol. 4, pp. 36–362, 1938) and Isidor Thorner ("Ascetic Protestantism and the Development of Science and Technology," *American Journal of Sociology*, vol. 58, pp. 25–33, July, 1952) have shown that most of the contributors to postmedieval science and technology have been Protestants or closely associated with Protestant culture. Edward Hughes (*North Country Life in the Eighteenth Century*, Oxford University Press, Fair Lawn, N.J., 1952) has traced the rise of a new and Protestant elite, both mercantile and industrial, in England during the early phases of the industrial revolution. This new elite displaced a Catholic landed gentry. Gerhard Lenski (*The Religious Factor: A Sociological Study of Religion's Impact on Politics, Economics and Family Life,*

ideal is often only that—a symbolic construct, mouthed by the populace, but otherwise ignored. Moreover, even where an ideal is fulfilled in conduct—as it tended to be by the Confucian scholars and the medieval monks—the numbers of those who fulfill it may be too small to have significance or their status may be too low or too isolative to have any real effect on the society. There is some evidence to suggest that the Confucian ethic was widely honored in conduct and was an integral part of Chinese society; but it may be doubted that the medieval ethic was much more than a rationalizing device. There were many cloistered monks, and these monks did tend to live in accordance with the medieval ethic; but, unlike the Confucian scholars, they were isolated from the larger society, took no part in maintaining it, and did not provide living examples for others to follow. They seem to have been tolerated rather than emulated; and it could hardly have been otherwise—a society of cloistered monks would last at most a single generation. Most of the churchmen and all of the peasants and townsmen no doubt conducted themselves in ways that fell short of, if not in direct contrast to, the medieval ethic.

Medieval society was, however, lethargic and unenterprising in those areas that were to be so actively developed during the postmedieval period. By current standards the tempo of life was unbelievably slow. The building of a cathedral, one of the most enterprising activities of the period, might take a century or more; and in this field of endeavor, in which medieval peoples displayed their greatest creativity, only two major architectural innovations occurred—the ribbed vault and the flying buttress, technological developments that made possible the Gothic form of construction. Medieval peoples did engage in almost constant warfare and slowly improved the tools of this particular activity; they built towns, however badly; they developed trade; and they evolved the guild as a basic form of social organization. Thus some change occurred, and some enterprise existed.

It may perhaps be said that stability was the ideological motif of the Middle Ages, that the ideal man was passive and apathetic, and that most Europeans were in fact unenterprising adherents to convention and tradition; but the relation between these three aspects of medieval ideology is uncertain. The ethic that secured its highest expression and representation in the cloistered monk can hardly have been the direct cause of the general passivity that pervaded European populations; it is quite likely that the ethic was more

Doubleday & Company, Garden City, N.Y., 1961) finds that even in contemporary America religious affiliation is correlated with the values placed on work, education, individual freedom, and the like; that Protestants, and to an almost equal extent Jews, value these much more highly than do Catholics, who are inclined to put high on their scale of values leisure time and economic security. His findings are contrary to those reported by R. W. Mack et al., in "The Protestant Ethic, Level of Aspiration, and Social Mobility," *American Sociological Review*, vol. 21, pp. 295–300, June, 1956.

a reflection of that passivity than a determining force. Moreover, in addition to the ethic there were many other ideological elements that were conducive to a passive, unenterprising orientation toward life. Medieval man was ridden with countless and often contradictory superstitions about his world; his faith in the powers of magic—good and bad, and religious and secular—seems to have been inexhaustible; and his life was in fact as well as fancy short, hard, and uncertain. There was, thus, empirical experience to substantiate the ideological view that life on this earth was an ordeal to be borne in patience and in the hope of heavenly reward.

Quite as important as medieval ideology in retarding social change was medieval social organization. The Church was strong and powerful; and, as was mentioned earlier, it drew into its ranks and there immobilized many of the ambitious and clever men who appeared in medieval society. It was in this and other ways an organizational bulwark against change of any sort. The towns, too, as they grew in size and importance, tended to put organizational restraints on change. They often became quasi-independent political entities that were ruled by leaders who were more interested in the consumption than the production of wealth; they placed tax and other constraints on trade; and they discouraged personal mobility by setting up rigorous qualifications of citizenship. In due course the guilds became the basic and almost universal units of production and distribution; and as they acquired local monopoly on craft production of goods and on trade, they brought all development, technological and otherwise, to a standstill. It was, therefore, in an organizational as well as ideological context of stability that the individual grew up and lived out his life during the Middle Ages. Enterprise, other than that of the most conventional sort, was not rewarded; it was both ideologically and organizationally punished. An ambitious lad would therefore tend to satisfy his ambitions in a religious, political, or military career; and only a rare individual would venture, against the entire weight of the society, to strike out in new directions.

The social circumstances that attended and followed the Reformation were in many respects quite different from those of the Middle Ages. The Renaissance in Italy had weakened if not broken the hold of tradition; the emergence of such great and recognized artists and artificers as Da Vinci provided a new example—that of a man of action—for others to follow; the new mode in the field of letters had somewhat weakened the hold of Scholastic ideology; and the beginnings of world exploration and discovery had already lessened the ethnocentrism of European peoples. First in the Germanic countries and later in Britain, the religious centralism of the Roman Church was being replaced by a considerable measure of religious self-determinism; and the Protestant and Anglican Churches began to foster rather than to hamper individual endeavor by advocacy of the ethic of enterprise. Since it was a codification of personal values and sentiments that were already being honored by an increasing number of the members of Western society and since it was concordant with changes that were already taking place, changes that offered opportunity and reward to men of enterprise, the ethic contributed, along with many other circumstances, to the emergence of comparatively large numbers of enterprising men. Had those other circumstances been different, the ethic, assuming that it had merged, might well have come to nought.

There has been a tendency in all the discussions of the role of Protestantism in relation to enterprise, both by proponents of Weber's theory and by dissenters from it, to assume that during the early modern period Protestants as a class were enterprising, while non-Protestants were unenterprising. Two errors are here involved. In the first place, the Protestant ethic is not theological, and its identification with and support by Protestantism was a historical accident. The idea that men can and should be individually independent, self-reliant, and creative in their adjustment to the world is a secular, not a sacred, concept. Moreover, in its stress on this life, the ethic implicitly depreciates the afterlife and, hence, the importance of religion. In fact, the ethic was soon being advocated by secular leaders who appealed solely to material and other self-interests and gave it no sacred implications.

Since the Protestant ethic was not a necessary part of Protestant theology but was only associated with it by being sanctioned by Protestant pastors, it could be and was adopted and acted upon by members of other religions. The Catholic Church for long fought against some of the consequences of individual enterprise among Catholics, most notably the enterprise of the early scientists; and on the whole the Catholic peoples of Western Europe (as of the Americas) became industrialized later and less extensively than did those of the dominantly Protestant countries. But Catholics and other non-Protestants, most particularly Jews, have been enterprising and have made many and often major contributions to the development of modern society. As far as can be ascertained, the Protestant ethic was not advocated by the Church of England, which is theologically much closer to Catholicism than to Protestantism, or, for that matter, in the public schools or universities of England. Nevertheless, an effective number of seventeenth- and eighteenth-century Englishmen were enterprising, whether they had been officially inducted into the ethic or not; and it was in England that the industrial revolution and associated changes came first and developed most rapidly.

The second error in the assumption that Protestants as a class were enterprising while non-Protestants were not is the fact that at no time were more than a small proportion of the members of any Protestant society really enterprising. A number of Protestant sects actually did not subscribe to the ethic; they stressed, not the power of the individual over his worldly fate, but the fall of man and his eternal sin, sin that consigned him to a life on earth of trial and tribulation. In this they reflected, if anything, the medieval ethic. Moreover, where the Protestant ethic was sanctioned, its effects on the majority of the members of the working classes were no doubt slight; as will be shown later, individual enterprise was characteristic mainly of the middle classes.

Elements of the Protestant ethic did no doubt creep into American folklore, to reach and perhaps occasionally influence the conduct of lower-class individuals. Thus Benjamin Franklin, one of the early American advocates of the ethic, reduced elements of it to simple precepts that became popular sayings—to wit, "early to bed and early to rise, makes a man healthy, wealthy, and wise." A century ago probably every literate boy in America had learned, via McGuffey's readers, that a penny saved is a penny earned, that a rolling stone gathers no moss, and that honesty is the best policy.[14] The great popularity of the folktale of the lad who wins success through industry and enterprise, most industriously if not enterprisingly exploited by Horatio Alger, suggests that the ideal of getting ahead in the world by adherence to the Protestant ethic was widely accepted.[15] Possibly nineteenth-century Americans, exclusive of those of the somnolent South, were as enterprising as any people have ever been. Nevertheless, the history of innovations and their acceptance clearly demonstrates that only a very small proportion of the American people were actually enterprising. Moreover, in America, as in Europe, the majority of these enterprising individuals were concentrated in one class category—the *bourgeoisie*; and the ideological and organizational peculiarities of this class were fully as important to the emergence of modern society as was the Protestant ethic.

IDEOLOGY AND SCIENCE

The Protestant ethic was but one of the new ideological elements that began to emerge in the later Middle Ages and that reflected and in turn stimulated the technological and organizational changes that are still under way in Western societies. Of these other ideological elements none has perhaps been quite so important to technology as the idea that the evidence of one's senses is superior to the word of traditional authority and none quite so significant for organization as the discovery that society is made by man, not decreed by God. Both these ideas, as well as such related and subsidiary concepts as the idea that men are inherently equal, are contrary to medieval ideology and yet have their roots in medieval European society; and it is to particular characteristics of that society that these ideas that aided in changing it are to be traced.

[14] See Richard D. Mosier, *Making the American Mind: Social and Moral Ideas in the McGuffey Readers*, King's Crown Press, New York, 1947.

[15] See Irvin G. Wyllie, *The Self-made Man in America: The Myth of Rags to Riches*, Rutgers University Press, New Brunswick, N.J., 1954.

One of the distinguishing characteristics of the medieval Church was its claim to secular as well as sacred authority. As has been pointed out, the Church for long held an effective monopoly, not only on the Bible, but also on the rediscovered writings, mainly secular, of the ancients. Scholasticism rationalized this inclusion of secular with sacred ideas; and the Scholastic rationale was easily extended to include the whole of medieval folklore—the prevailing folk beliefs about the earth and sun, the processes of life, the causes of disease, etc. Thus in theory at least, all of human knowledge was contained within the Church and churchmen were the source of all wisdom. Just how this organizational monopoly of the entire ideological component of medieval society actually affected daily life is not clear; but that it stultified innovation in this component is evident, for it made any expression of doubt regarding established and Church-sanctioned folk ideas and beliefs a crime against God and Church.

The incongruence that developed as empirical experience became increasingly contradictory to established ideological authority was not resolved. On the contrary, it was furthered by the refusal of the Church to relinquish its hold on secular matters. For example, the Church's persistence in holding to the dogma that usury—a secular matter—was sinful, even while the need for venture capital was constantly increasing, weakened and strained the already diminishing religious faith of those who needed credit and those who had the means of granting it. Although the need for venture capital was for a while more or less effectively met by Jewish moneylenders, by the time of the Renaissance Italian banking houses had begun to make their appearance and were loaning money in competition with the Jews and in violation of Church sanctions. In this and countless other ways, the disparity between what the world appeared to be and what it was ideologically asserted to be grew ever greater.

A belief, ideal, or other symbolic construct can be held *in vacuo*; and, as was mentioned earlier, there is in any society considerable difference and even contrast between reality and symbolic representations of that reality. During the later Middle Ages, however, the entire ideological component was at odds with nonsymbolic realities, and the disparity became intolerable. A great variety of intellectual cults and movements made their appearance. Some of them had as their objective bringing conduct into conformity with Church law and dogma, but others were attempts to adjust ideology to empirical experience. Among the latter were such heretical endeavors as alchemy, cabalism, and Satanism. These were attempts, however ridiculous they may seem from a modern perspective, to gain a better understanding of the world or to exercise more effective control over it. Behind the cult of Satanism, for example, was the idea that since God was doing so very badly for his children —inflicting them with plague, with famine, with disasters of every sort—a wise man might do well to align himself with the devil. From these and many other such attempts to find alternatives to Church dogma about secular matters no gains were made; but the need that these antics reflected was what in due course gave rise to early science.

The medieval method of controlling nature, used by both the churchmen and their heretical opponents, was the manipulating of symbols. The alchemist might burn his sulphur and boil the messes that he brewed; but like priest and cabalist, astrologer and witch, diviner and sorcerer, he placed his primary reliance on the magic to be worked through signs and words or spells and incantations. During the fifteenth century there appeared here and there men who turned their attention from symbols to things. Encouraged no doubt by the writings of the ancients—especially of Aristotle—such adventurous and ingenious men began to test against the evidences of their senses some of the prevailing and Church-sanctioned beliefs about the world. The existence of God, the Church's claim to divinity, and other sacred ideas were not, of course, testable by empirical means; but secular ideas were, and thus in claiming authority over secular matters, the Church had inadvertently laid itself open to proof of fallibility.

One of the earliest demonstrations of the erroneousness of a Church dogma regarding the world was provided by Marco Polo, whose eyewitness report (early in the fourteenth century) of the glories of China cast doubt on the belief that Rome, center of Christendom, was also the center of civilization. Perhaps the first critical blow to the prestige of the Church came with the discovery of the New World. Columbus undertook his westward journey on the basis of a theory of the shape of the earth that had been advanced, and to a degree proved, by the Roman Pliny and that had gained some currency among literate nonchurchmen during the fifteenth century. The Church, however, had committed itself to the belief that the earth is a sort of platform, centering around Rome, about which moved the sun and the moon and the stars. Consequently, Columbus's discovery of the Americas (which were thought, for a time, to be Cathay) demonstrated that at least in the idea that the earth is a platform the Church was fallible. Copernicus then ventured the hypothesis that, far from being stationary, the earth moved on an axis and through the firmament—an interpretation which fitted observable facts far better than did the view that the heavens moved about the earth.

Meanwhile, precursors of the experimental scientists were exploring some of the more obvious physical and biological phenomena—dissecting organisms to ascertain their anatomical structures, measuring the flow of heat with crude thermometers, exploring the properties of air through vacuum and pressure, and testing in various ways the force of gravity. By modern standards their equipment, procedures, and problems were all exceedingly primitive; but what they were doing was a remarkable advance over reliance on traditional authority to ascertain the processes of nature and resort to spells and incantations to affect it, and what they discovered about nature was invariably at odds with the established view of things.[16] Thus late in the sixteenth century Galileo demonstrated, by dropping spheres of equal size but different weights, possibly from the tower of Pisa, the falsity of the belief, current at the time, that a heavy body falls faster than a light one.

The Philosophy of Science

The resistance of the Church to the evidences and interpretations that were being advanced by the early empiricists may have been an important factor in the development of a rationale in support of the empirical method of gaining an understanding of the world in which men lived. Those who sought to test belief against the evidences of their senses were necessarily on the defensive, since the weight of authority was against them. They therefore proceeded in their quest for knowledge self-consciously and aware that they were violating the principle that all Church doctrine was sacrosanct. Since what they were doing was contrary to an institutionalized faith and was being done in an age of faith, they were impelled to find a faith to justify their empirical endeavors. Aristotle had provided them with a historical precedent, and almost from the beginning they turned to him for authority. Thus he became the ideological father of the emerging philosophy of science.

It is probably impossible and certainly difficult for those who live in a society in which science is an integral and honored part to appreciate how radical was the idea that men could rely on their own sense perceptions and only on their own sense perceptions to inform them about the nature of the world in which they lived. In all societies, empirically derived knowledge had existed, for such knowledge was the basis for the technology by which men earned their livelihood. Invariably, however, empirical knowledge had been mixed with folk beliefs of a nonempirical character; and often it had also been blended with sacred concepts. Moreover, with very rare exceptions, men did not distinguish between the method by which empirical knowledge was derived and that by which folk beliefs and religious concepts were produced. As a result, technological practices, such as agriculture and medicine, had always been compounded of fact and social fancy, and no effort had been or could be made to distinguish between the two.

Aristotle had, it is true, laid down the dictum that there is order—natural order—in the universe and that man could discover this order by careful and unbiased observation and the application of logic to the analysis of the data thus obtained. What Aristotle had begun, however, was lost to Western peoples for more than sixteen centuries, and it was not until many men had individually struggled free from bondage to medieval mental dominance and struck out to observe the world for themselves that their endeavors gained

[16] See George Sarton, *Six Wings: Men of Science in the Renaissance*, Indiana University Press, Bloomington, Ind., 1957.

ideological sanction. Early in the thirteenth century friar Roger Bacon had written in defense of empirical investigation and had unsuccessfully endeavored to convince Pope Clement IV that there was substance to the findings of the early scientists; but a good three centuries passed before anything like a true philosophy of science began to emerge to provide the empiricists with ideological sanction, if not prompt social acceptance. (Francis Bacon's *New Atlantis* may be taken as the turning point in this development.)

Rationality

The conceptual base for the new philosophy was the very secular belief that man is a creature of reason and that through the full and free application of reason he can come to understand the laws of nature and in turn to manipulate nature to his own ends. This rational concept of man was perhaps only a secularized version of Luther's idea that every individual has within him the ability to ascertain the will of God; but it gave scientists a justification for ignoring all prior authority and determining truth for themselves, even as Luther's concept provided a justification for the religious break with the sacred authority. It also symbolized what scientists had been attempting to do and provided them with an increasingly refined ideal of the observational methods to be followed and the logic by which inferences might be drawn from their data.

The idea that man is a rational animal gained currency slowly and was often put to contrascientific ends. Some of those who accepted the ideal of rational man maintained that man's rationality gave him the power to perceive truth without need to rely on his sense perceptions—that it gave him power to find truth in his own mind; and since it was much easier to meditate on the world than to explore it, the development of science was hampered by metaphysical speculations that from time to time were accepted as scientifically valid. Even today, metaphysical concepts, such as Freudianism, dominate some fields of inquiry. Eventually, however, the philosophy of science became an established part of Western ideology; and the idea that man is capable of rational use of his sense perceptions and is not dependent on some higher authority, religious or political, for knowledge of the world in which he lives became embodied in Western culture.

The philosophy of science is an ideological construct that, unlike most such constructs, facilitates social change; and its social role is thus the antithesis to that of religious ideology.[17] It involves the assumption that

[17] For somewhat varied interpretations of the relations between science and other aspects of society see Alistair Crombie (ed.), *Scientific Change: Studies of the Conditions for Scientific Discovery and Technological Invention from Antiquity to the Present*, Basic Books, Inc., Publishers, New York, 1963; W. Dampier, *A History of Science*, 2d ed., The Macmillan Company, New York, 1942;

there is law and order in the universe and that the laws of the universe can be ascertained by rational procedures; but it does not, as do most ideologies, designate the nature of the universe. That nature is, in the philosophy of science, what scientists must discover; and so far, what they have discovered has almost invariably run counter to both the folklore and the dogmas of religious and other organizations. It may be assumed that as long as scientists continue to proceed in accordance with the philosophy of science, new knowledge will continue to be discovered and, when applied to practical purposes, to bring about changes in society.

Much of early scientific endeavor was undoubtedly motivated by resentment of Church authority, which rather precluded any but those within the Church organization from gaining stature as men of knowledge. Even in the universities, many of which had been established by political leaders, priests or at least theological concerns tended to dominate; and when theological concerns in time gave way to secular matters, most of the universities came to stress classics—ancient languages and the philosophies of the ancients—rather than science. Scientific discoveries in astronomy, physics, mechanics, and later biology, however, were gradually applied to problems of navigation, construction, etc.; and with the application of science to practical problems, the social status of scientists improved. Moreover, once it had been demonstrated that science could contribute to human welfare, the emphasis in science shifted from criticism of the *status quo* toward improvement of it. This shift in emphasis was in time codified for scientists in what came to be called "positive philosophy."

There had long been, and there still is to some extent, a tendency for dedicated scientists to claim that their interest was in enlarging knowledge for the sake of knowledge. Their problems were invariably incomprehensible to laymen, and their endeavors just as invariably seemed devoid of practical significance to the man of practical affairs. With the demonstration that scientific findings could have very useful applications, there began to emerge among scientists a new rationale for their labors—that any scientific finding, however impractical it might seem at the moment, might in the end prove of benefit to mankind. Knowledge, scientific knowledge, thus became defined as a means to social change and to many as *the* means to social change.

As so often happens with new ideas, and in fact with anything new, positive philosophy was advocated as the great cure-all for man's troubles, material and social. By the end of the eighteenth century the intellectuals of Western Europe had convinced themselves that a scientific utopia was about to be realized. It was this conviction, together with a number of

Bernard Barber, *Science and the Social Order*, The Free Press of Glencoe, New York, 1952; and Lewis S. Feuer, *The Scientific Intellectual*, Basic Books, Inc., Publishers, New York, 1963.

other ideas, that led to the belief that progress in human affairs was not only possible but inevitable.

THE SECULAR CONCEPT OF SOCIETY

In most times and places the existence and nature of social elements have been attributed to some supernatural or at least superhuman agency. Even the pragmatic Romans sanctified their legal enactments by which they endeavored to determine social practices on the grounds that man-made law is a manifestation of natural law. Contemporary Russian ideologists, with considerable difficulty it is true, hold to the thesis that whatever is done in the name of communism is in accordance with the Great Design—it is a step toward the fulfillment of man's destiny as outlined by Marx, with addenda and deletions by Lenin. Ideological sanctification of social practices forces individual adherence to them, precludes critical evaluation of them, and discourages deliberate modification of them. Such sanctification is, therefore, one of the means by which a social system stabilizes itself.

Throughout the Middle Ages, the Church held staunchly to the thesis that the existing forms of social organization had been established by God and that any variance from them was sinful and would invoke God's wrath. To constrain those individuals who had little faith or who were subjected to overpowering temptation, the Church supplemented this purely ideological control with Church courts that were empowered to use direct coercion and with such other means of control as excommunication—all, of course, in the name of God. When the Protestant Reformation brought a major break with the tradition that the Church was the final arbiter in secular as well as sacred matters and men began to think of their society as a secular agency, rather than as something divinely decreed, it became ideologically permissible for them to change social practices as need or fancy dictated. The fact that they did not always do so can be variously explained. Secular substitutes for the sacred interpretation of social life were soon devised, and these provided rationales for preserving the *status quo* even as the sacred had done. Geographic determinism was one of the earlier of these. Biological determinism was another and more persistent one; it served in particular to rationalize such aspects of the *status quo* as class and ethnic differences and differential status. What were probably the major deterrents to more rapid change, however, were the limited ability of men to invent new and more functionally effective forms of social life and the difficulties inherent in gaining acceptance for any such new form and functionally integrating it into the existing system.

By the seventeenth century the idea that society is secular had become firmly established in Protestant countries, was gaining social sanction elsewhere, and was being used to justify social experiments of considerable

Social change **320**

magnitude, such as that of the Puritans' Mayflower Compact.[18] These experiments invariably fell far short of expectations for them; and the dislocations that prefaced the industrial revolution, as well as those that followed upon the introduction of industrial techniques of production, cast considerable doubt on the idea that man could design for himself a more fruitful social system than the one he had inherited from his forefathers. When, however, the idea that society is a man-made thing came to be fused with scientific positivism, all doubt regarding the social future was dissipated by faith in the certainty of progress.

The idea of social progress was, as was earlier noted, one of the vital ideological elements of early modern society. It took various forms, of which the evolutionary version for long enjoyed the greatest academic standing. Operationally, however, it was the idea that man can apply the same rational procedures to the development of human relations as he can apply to his relations with nature that was, and perhaps still is, of major social significance. It was this idea which underlay the Puritan rebellion to the corruption of Elizabethan England and the attempt of the Puritans to establish via a contract or collective agreement a utopian society in America; it was this idea that fathered the American Revolution and was manifest in the Constitution of the United States; and it was this idea that was presented systematically in Comte's *Positive Philosophy*, which in turn came to serve as the rationale for the social sciences.

Enterprise and Social Progress

Since the idea of social progress through deliberate human action, scientific or otherwise, was developed by adherents to the Protestant ethic, who honored individual enterprise, and since action taken in accordance with this ethic invariably encountered resistance by established organizations, notably governmental, individual enterprise was generally considered to be the agency of desirable social change.[19] Such being the case, it was held that governmental and other forms of organization should act only as representatives of the individuals who together constituted the organizational membership and that organizational action should not exceed that which was necessary to assure equality of opportunity for those whom the organization represented. The most doctrinaire statement of this thesis was that

[18] A detailed history of the gradual shift in England from sacred to secular ideas and values and of some of the consequences to social action of that shift is provided by W. K. Jordan in *The Charities of London, 1480–1660: The Aspirations and Achievements of the Urban Society*, Russell Sage Foundation, New York, 1960, and *The Charities of Rural England, 1480–1660: The Aspirations and the Achievements of the Rural Society*, Russell Sage Foundation, New York, 1962.

[19] See R. V. Sampson, *Progress in the Age of Reason: The Seventeenth Century to the Present Day*, Harvard University Press, Cambridge, Mass., 1956.

made by the English classical economists, who were extreme advocates of *laissez faire* in all economic matters. Actual implementation of the idea that social progress can come through, and only through, individual enterprise was perhaps most marked in the United States, probably for reasons not directly related to the idea itself; but the idea did permeate the thinking of many of the intellectuals and even of some of the political leaders of all Western countries during the nineteenth century.

It is of course impossible to ascertain the extent to which the changes that occurred through the actions of enterprising individuals during the later eighteenth and nineteenth centuries were implemented by the idea of social progress. About all that can be said with confidence is that the rather wide acceptance of this idea provided a climate that was favorable to individual enterprise and that on the whole the constraints on individual freedom by political and other forms of organization, including the family, tended to give way. Thus governmental support of the old trade and craft guilds, which were contraindividualistic, was gradually replaced by legal sanctioning of freedom of contract and what came to be called free trade. By the middle of the nineteenth century most of the governments of the Western world were officially committed to the free mobility of persons, to a general hands-off policy in regard to economic activities, and to the protection of the rights (variously defined, of course) of the individual to property and to use of it for personal gain. Possibly the clearest indication of this commitment was the establishment, both in the United States and abroad, of governmental agencies that granted patent rights to inventors— an attempt to provide economic incentives to innovative endeavors.

The conditions that tended to obtain in Western societies during the later eighteenth and the nineteenth centuries can perhaps be summed up in the statement that change was more rapid during this period than it had ever been in human history and that the ideological component of Western societies during this period contained unprecedented encouragements to change by providing both a rationale for and incentives to individual enterprise. The relation of the latter to the former is certainly not that of simple cause and effect; but that the prevalence of faith in the idea of progress through individual enterprise facilitated the making of those changes seems beyond doubt. It remains to be seen whether comparable social changes can be accomplished in societies in which quite different ideas tend to dominate the minds of men.

SOCIALISTIC IDEOLOGY

The idea of progress through individual enterprise is historically atypical and operationally asocial; for society is organization, and organization is contraindividualistic. Society exists by subordinating the individual to the behavioral standards of groups, both formally and informally organized. The idea that society can be improved by freeing the individual from social constraints to engage in activities of his own determination is, therefore, in opposition to what is socially normal. It violates the general tendency of society to approach a condition of stability, and its appearance and acceptance may be taken as a sort of social aberration.

The idea of progress through individual enterprise did not go unchallenged, and its intellectual dominance as an idea was comparatively short-lived. Metaphysicians put their faith in some abstraction such as social destiny; racial determinists clung to the belief that the past, present, and future of man were simply a matter of the inherent racial characteristics of peoples; many of the social evolutionists held to the comforting view that social progress was inevitable in any event and that nothing that man deliberately did could affect its course. Moreover, even in the midst of change, the political and economic elites of the moment preferred to believe that the changes which had brought them to the apex of the social hierarchy were now complete and that society would, or at any event should, become stable and their own status enduring.[20]

It was the ideology of socialism, however, that gradually displaced and largely replaced the idea of progress through individual enterprise. The roots of the ideology go very deep. Plato was a socialist of sorts, and ever since his day social philosophers had from time to time advanced various elements of socialistic ideology. The synthesis of these elements into a doctrine, however, was accomplished by Karl Marx, who, although now unacknowledged outside Communist countries, was at least the grandfather of all contemporary socialistic thought.

Marx was one of the nineteenth-century social evolutionists who took the metaphysical position that change is a historical imperative which man himself cannot evade. Marx believed, it will be recalled, that the changes that were then being worked by individuals constituted a transitory phase in the evolution of the good society; these were the changes in the techniques of production that the inventive genius of individuals was producing. These changes in technology had so far brought a tremendous increase in the production of the necessities of life; but the same genius that was making them possible had not been, was not being, and could not be applied to improving the distribution of what was produced better to serve the interests and welfare of the members of society. It was leading, on the contrary, to a

---

[20] For a detailed analysis of the many conservative and even reactionary ideologies that have been advanced in Europe during the present century—ranging in character from Agrarianism to Zionism—see Feliks Gross (ed.), *European Ideologies: A Survey of 20th Century Political Ideas*, Philosophical Library, Inc., New York, 1948.

systematic (capitalistic) exploitation of the masses who, under industrialized productive techniques, were becoming wage slaves entirely dependent upon economic forces beyond their control, forces that currently were working against their collective interests.

The individualistic phase of social evolution, Marx granted, had played a significant role in the historical movement toward the good society; but that phase was drawing toward a close (this was in 1848); the working classes in industrial societies were beginning (all in accordance with the historical imperatives) to realize that they had a bond of common interest and that they were being exploited by their capitalistic masters. With the emergence of class consciousness, the next phase of the evolutionary process would begin; the united working classes would throw off their bondage to the capitalistic exploiters and set up a government which represented themselves, and that government would then put into effect a new social order based upon the communal ideal of to each according to his need. In time, this new order would become so much traditionalized that governmental enforcement of it would no longer be necessary—it would be self-maintaining; and the evolution of the good, the ultimate, society would have been completed.

Marx's thesis soon became the ideological base for a variety of political movements, revolutionary and otherwise, in Western Europe, in England, and in czarist Russia. Each of these interpreted Marx in whatever way best suited its own interests; but all of them and all subsequent variants of socialistic ideology to some extent incorporated the assumptions that individual enterprise is inimical to the welfare of society as a whole and that the valid way to bring about socially desirable changes is through governmental organization. Socialistic ideology, whatever its form, is thus opposed to the idea of progress through individual enterprise; to the constituent elements of this idea—the Protestant ethic and the idea of man as a rational creature; and even, though never explicitly, to the scientific method. It substitutes government for the individual, the political process for individual enterprise, the authority of political leaders for science.

Communist ideologists, now as much an established part of Russian and Chinese society as theologians were of medieval European society, hold to the view that it was the adoption of socialistic ideology that caused their revolutions and that the Communist governments are guided in all that they do by this ideology. The new societies that are being created by political fiat are, in this view, simply a realization of the grand historical plan that was first discerned by Marx and that was outlined in *Das Kapital*. Communist ideologists are, it will be evident, ideological determinists.[21]

[21] Barrington Moore, Jr. (*Soviet Politics—The Dilemma of Power: The Role of Ideas in Social Change*, Harvard University Press, Cambridge, Mass., 1950) finds that Marxian ideology is in actuality but one of many factors that determine

The actual role of socialistic ideology in the changes that have been occurring in both East and West over the past half century is far from clear. The effects of revolution and of ideology in revolution will be considered later; at this point it may be observed that there has been a growing acceptance of socialistic practices, by whatever name they may be known, in all the countries of the world and that this acceptance has been accompanied by an ever-increasing reliance on government and a diminishing scope for individual initiative. Today in Western societies, as in those that are avowedly communistic, collectivism rather than individualism is the dominant motif.[22] Laissez-faire economists have all but disappeared; and in all the countries of the West economic theory now ranges from post-Keynesian reliance on government as the provider of incentives for a high level of economic activity to outright social welfarism, the modern euphemism for state socialism. Political scientists are no longer primarily concerned with political preservation of individual freedom of action and have turned their major attention to political provision of security, material and otherwise. Nowhere in the academic world is there a discipline that is dedicated to the thesis that freedom of individual action must be preserved; and nowhere outside the universities is there a respected political party or admired intellectual cadre committed to the idea that dominated men's minds through the last century— the idea that social progress comes through individual enterprise.[23] There is, rather, very considerable agreement that the agency of social improvement is government or organizations of a nonpolitical sort, such as labor unions, that operate under the shelter of government.

That government, quasi-governmental agencies, and organizations eco-

---

the course of the communistic government of Russia and that if all the other relevant forces are in balance, then, and only then, will the Russian leaders formulate their policy in terms of the ideology which is, in theory, the *raison d'être* for their position as leaders.

[22] For histories of the ideological trend in Western societies from individualism toward collectivism see Friedrich A. Hayek, *The Constitution of Liberty*, The University of Chicago Press, Chicago, 1960; Carl A. Landauer, *European Socialism: A History of Ideas and Movements*, 2 vols., University of California Press, Berkeley, Calif., 1960; and Joseph A. Schumpeter, *Capitalism, Socialism and Democracy*, Harper & Row, Publishers, Incorporated, New York, 1942. These books are all critical of the trend; but for more pointed attacks on the rise of socialistic ideology and practices see Friedrich A. Hayek, *Individualism and Economic Order*, The University of Chicago Press, Chicago, 1948; Walter Gellhorn, *Individual Freedom and Governmental Restraints*, Louisiana State University Press, Baton Rouge, La., 1956; and Felix Morley (ed.), *Essays on Individuality*, University of Pennsylvania Press, Philadelphia, 1958.

[23] Indeed, such defenses of individualism as the John Birch Society have brought only discredit to individualistic philosophy.

nomically and otherwise protected by government have grown tremendously in power and scope in Western countries over the past half century and that this growth has constantly and severely reduced the range of individual enterprise will be demonstrated shortly. The present trend and its consequence to individual endeavor reverses the ideological and organizational developments that took three centuries and more to produce the industrial revolution and that then obtained for a century or so. The return to organizational authoritarianism is still far from complete; but should the trend of the past half century continue, Western societies will have arrived at the political goal of socialism long before the century is out. Whether, having achieved political hegemony, Western societies will also have achieved the socialistic goal of a high level of human welfare depends in considerable part upon the validity of the socialistic idea that government can and will produce the kinds of adaptive social changes that heretofore have been forthcoming only where and when men have been individually free to innovate, advocate, and adopt them. At least one thing seems certain: social survival now depends upon constant change, and today a society that moves toward stability moves also toward extinction.

chapter 10 Family and Community Organization

The various organizational elements of a society, like the technological and ideological, may be the object of change, as is the case when an existing form of organization is supplemented or replaced by a new form; they may produce an incongruence in some aspect of the society, whether organizational, technological, or ideological, that is corrected by change in that aspect; or they may operate to discourage change per se, as is most frequently the case. Like other social elements, those that go to make up the organizational component are devised by men and are maintained or abandoned by men; but the relationship of men to the organizational is considerably more intimate and personal than is their relationship to the technological or ideological. By and large it is through organizational means that men are socialized into the culture of their society and through organizational means that the technology is applied and the ideology instilled. As a consequence, the ability of men to devise and adopt changes in any aspect of social life depends in considerable measure on the degree to which their forms of organization hold and restrict them to organizational standards of conduct.

In the broadest sense, the function of organization qua organization is to coordinate the activities of the members of a society in ways that will enable the social system, as distinct from the people who at any moment constitute the social membership, to survive. More specifically, organization assures the perpetuation of the social population; the preservation and effective application of the technology; the protection of the social population where and when necessary from human and other predators; and the maintenance and fulfillment of ideological elements, including those ceremonial and ritualistic devices that function specifically to bind the individual members to their particular forms of organization. How effectively a given system of organization or of any one of its constituent

327

elements serves these functions depends not upon the form of that system or element but upon its relevance to the technological, ideological, physical, and biological context in which it operates. The functional efficiency of any particular form of organization may, therefore, range from near zero toward perfection.

No matter how inefficient in terms of its context, however, every organization is everywhere and always highly resistant to change; for no matter how much incongruence may exist between it and other organizations, or between it and related elements of the technology or ideology, every organization, even one that is ostensibly dedicated to the working of change, as many in our own society are, operates to preserve its structure and its context, organizational and otherwise.[1] A given organization may not succeed in preventing changes that ultimately destroy it; but to the extent that it is internally integrated, i.e., to the exent that its own elements are functionally congruent the one with the others, it resists being changed and it discourages changes in its context. Survival is, in a manner of speaking, the motif of any organization, and stability is the *sine qua non* of organizational survival. All

[1] A social organization operates to discourage changes in much the same way as does the established capital plant—roads, buildings, etc.—the stabilizing effects of which are clear and obvious. People tend to value aesthetically and sentimentally those structures and other man-made additions to the natural terrain; and often the older they are—and hence the less functional they are likely to be —the more they are valued. Ancient graveyards, remains of ancient civilizations, or stones left behind by Neanderthal man have often acquired an almost sacred value. The very idea of dispossessing the bones of the long dead in order to build a convenient roadway for the living may seem sacrilegious; and certainly any such proposal as that of removing the Colosseum at Rome, or any other old Roman ruins, for that matter, wherever located, would raise cries of protest not only from antiquarians but from the general publics of all Western countries.

Medieval cathedrals, basilicas, fortresses, monasteries, palaces, and walled towns clutter the lands of Europe and operate as a very tangible dead hand to restrain those living from adopting many of the modern techniques of construction. Their value as habitations, as workshops, or as places of recreation and assembly is small; but they have been preserved for aesthetic and sentimental reasons for centuries, and now they have acquired in addition considerable economic and prestige value. Many such old relics have been taken over by government and are maintained, in part, for purposes of national prestige—tangible evidence of the age and the past glories of the nation. Many have also become tourist attractions and thus acquired considerable economic value to the nation, if not to the local inhabitants. The hill towns of Italy, for example, were perhaps functionally appropriate in both their site and their structure to the early Middle Ages, when security from wandering bands of warriors was a condition for survival. Today these hill towns are little better as habitations than museums; but many of them have been made national monuments, and their abandonment is discouraged, while any modernization that would be apparent is prohibited by law.

the processes of social change—innovation, advocacy, and adoption—are, thus, contraorganizational.

The stabilizing effects of organization are not a consequence of calculated endeavor on the part of a member or members, although calculation does, of course, occur, particularly when an organization or its context is jeopardized by advocated change. Under such circumstances the members—or at least the leaders—may divert the organization in whole or in part from its usual activities to defensive efforts. This is what happens when the members of a primitive tribe abandon their normal pursuits to ward off the inroads of settlers; when a corporation unites with its competitors in an effort to break the powers of unionized labor; when a Southern white community riots and otherwise resists legal attempts to desegregate its schools; and when a political bureaucracy shifts from its routine activities to battle the legislative forces that would liquidate it. These and comparable organizational activities, however, are crisis phenomena. An organization that is required to defend itself in such violent or obvious ways is already on the defensive; it is already failing in that it has not prevented the change that is threatening it. Normally the ways in which any integrated organization assures its own continuation are inherent in the processes of organizational operation; they are the very means by which organization is effected and operates. Thus whatever its manifest function, the latent function of an organization is to perpetuate the *status quo*.

Social organizations vary tremendously in structure, size, and form and in a number of other dimensions. Some are loose and informal associations, as are peer groups, neighborhood groups, friendship cliques, and temporary alliances formed for some political or other reason. Others are highly institutionalized with established structures and fairly explicit membership, as are family and tribal units and many religious, political, military, and business organizations. A social organization may be highly specialized in function and may involve only one particular aspect of the lives of its members, as is the case with many modern work and recreational organizations; or it may have many functions and exercise a more or less total jurisdiction over the lives of its members, as did the medieval monastic orders, as does the Roman Church vis-à-vis its priests, and as the old extended family and most forms of tribal organization have tended to do. A social organization may encompass only a few persons or as many as millions; and it may have a very brief life or, as is more common, a very long one that transcends the lives of its individual members.

Organization and Individuality

All organizations, irrespective of their size, form, and manifest function, have some characteristics in common—a delimited membership, with a more or less categorical distinction between members and all nonmembers; some established criteria for selecting new members and a procedure for applying these criteria; some method by which new members are inducted into the special values, sentiments, ideas, and practices of the organization; some ways of rewarding individual members for good conduct and punishing them for bad; and some division of the membership into organizational roles, some of which are offices that bear various organizational powers and responsibilities. Each of these organizational characteristics operates to subordinate the individual members to the organizational whole and thus to discourage, if not entirely preclude, the development and expression of individuality. Thus the more functionally integrated the various organizations of a society, the less likely it is that any one of its members will develop those personal characteristics which lead to innovative, advocatory, or adoptive behavior.

It is impossible for any human being to live apart from his fellows or to live with them without being a member of some, if not many, organizations. Individual independence is always segmental and always limited in degree; individual freedom is the absence of some specific restraint, not a carte blanche to do as one pleases; and whenever they exist, individual independence and freedom are made possible by society. In the absence of society, the only "right" that an individual has is that of dying.

Every organization provides each of its individual members with a variety of rights that constitute rewards for fulfilling obligations to the organization; and the rights that any particular member enjoys vary quantitatively and qualitatively according to his role or office. In some instances these rights include the grant of certain more or less specified degrees of freedom—for example, the right to be absent on occasion from organizational activities; the right to violate organizational rules under certain conditions; and the right to make decisions concerning organizational problems (a normal right of the member who occupies the office of leader). Many organizations, moreover, include one or a number of deviant roles, such as the cherished black sheep of the family, the village slut, the country-club drunk, etc., that give the individual who occupies them some freedom from the normal organizational obligations. Furthermore, within the membership of any organization there is always a good deal of interpersonal give-and-take which tempers and modulates the organizational structure of rights and obligations.

All such individual variations are in a sense organizationally sanctioned. They are kinds of individual actions that have been shown by experience to aid, often in some vague and devious way, the survival of the organization itself; and sanction of them is a sort of organizational recognition that men are human, hence variable and fallible, however well trained and regulated they may be. Thus a village community may tolerate its habitual drunkard as a bad example, as a source of amusing gossip, or as someone with whom the respectable men may upon occasion vicariously identify themselves; and a community in which the husband is normally head of the family unit may covertly sanction the rule of a wife in a particular family on the unstated but possibly quite expedient principle that any husband so weak-willed as to submit to domination by his wife is too much a weakling to provide able guidance to a family.

Wherever there is any scope within an organization for individuality, some individuals will no doubt find ways to usurp organizational rights for their own personal benefit; and whenever there is scope for personal judgment in the determining of organizational affairs, error cannot fail to be frequent. But with any established, well-integrated organization the safety factor is high, and the organization can survive considerable exploitation by some of its members and many errors in direction. As a religious organization, the Roman Catholic Church remained more or less intact through hundreds of years during which many of its members, including not a few popes, exploited their organizationally provided powers for personal ends and still more made what are seen in the perspective of time to have been monumental blunders. Similarly, the Chinese family system persisted in a relatively unchanged form for a period of fifteen hundred years during which specific family units were continually rising through personal exploitation of the system and falling through misadventure or personal incompetence. The heads of family units were not uniformly wise and well-intentioned, wives were not universally submissive and diligent, and sons were not invariably filial; but the family as a system of organization survived because it fulfilled its functions more often than it failed and because the kinds of deviations that arose within it, like those which arose within the Church organization, were not conducive to change in the organizational system itself.

Deviations from the standards of society at large—what are locally and socially defined as crime—are violations of organizational rules, formal or informal, political or nonpolitical, that are beyond the limits of social toleration. A criminal act may stem from ignorance, foolishness, or accident; or it may be and for the most part is a calculated effort on the part of an individual to exploit the larger social organization for personal benefits. A criminal is, thus, an exaggerated parallel to a selfish father who exploits his family or a worldly bishop who exploits his diocese. He harms the larger social organization by violating its rules and procedures; he tries to secure more values from it than is his organizationally defined right; and when he succeeds, he deprives someone else of values—of life, property, or happiness. But he does not in this way jeopardize the survival of the larger social organization itself or threaten it with change. The vital threat to the survival of the larger social organization comes not from such conventional deviants as thieves, rapists, murderers, and their like, but from members who are by mishap so poorly socialized and so ineffectively constrained that they come to question the validity of the organizational system itself or the validity of the ideology and technology to which that system is functionally attached.

Similarly, a dominating wife, an exploitative father, a wayward son, and a greedy bishop do not question the validity of the organization that they exploit; it is the very existence of that organization that affords them their opportunity for personal gain. But a disgruntled son who has been so ineffectually socialized into familism that he questions not only the wisdom and justice of his father but of fathers in general, a priest who has so little faith in and loyalty to the church that he cannot accept the venality of churchmen, or a cavalryman who has been so poorly inducted into the thesis that the man on horse rules the world that he sees in cannon the source of victory may set off a revolt against the organization itself—as did, respectively, Hu Shih, Martin Luther, and Napoleon Bonaparte.

Not even in theory can an organization prevent, or for that matter survive without, some deviant conduct on the part of its members; always and everywhere the individual has and must have some personal freedom. A well-integrated, functionally effective organization can and does, however, discourage the appearance of those special kinds of deviations that may result in innovation, advocacy for an innovation, or adoption of what has been innovated and advocated. The various and mainly subtle ways in which this end is achieved can be summarized by saying that organizational membership binds the individual to the roles that he occupies and in the process blinds him to the possibility that there might be alternatives to the particular forms of conduct that the organization demands.

Since in some times and some places individuals have come to innovate, advocate, and adopt new techniques, new ideas, and new forms of organization, it is evident that individuals can under some conditions and in some respects act as individuals rather than as members of organizations. No organization qua organization grants this contraorganizational freedom; but when, for whatever reasons, an organization loses its functional effectiveness, its structure may become so much weakened and its operational processes so much disorganized that it fails to fulfill its latent as well as its manifest function. It has then begun to disintegrate, and it is the disintegration of an organization that is the organizational antecedent to social change.

THE FAMILY AND SOCIAL CHANGE

The basic unit of social organization in most societies, past and present, is a kinship group—a clan, a tribe, or a family. A kinship relationship among its members gives an organization exceptional powers over them; and for this and other reasons the clan, the tribe, or the family has usually been the primary organizational defense against change of any sort. In a general way it may be said that only when and where the clan, the tribe, or the family has become markedly disorganized has change of any magnitude occurred within a social system and conversely that where the basic unit has been stable and integrated, the social system has remained unchanged, however marked its malfunctioning.

The Feudal System

The feudal form of organization, which prevailed throughout Europe at the beginning of the Middle Ages (parallel forms of which existed in pre-Confucian China, in Japan prior to the nineteenth century, and elsewhere), subordinated the family to the manorial unit.[2] Membership in the manorial unit was hereditary, however; and the members, whatever their status, constituted a closed group into which individuals could not move at will and from which they could not escape. The members of feudal society were bound by ties of birth to place, to their organizational unit, and to position within the unit. At the height of the feudal system, there was almost no individual mobility, either spatial or social, in Western society. There were some small bands of roving thieves who lived parasitically on the fringes of the manors; here and there family units struggled to survive in independence and isolation; in the remnants of the old Roman towns some squatters eked out a precarious existence; and priests who were without a church would wander from manor to manor. But for the most part, the people of Europe were incorporated into and immobilized by feudal organization.

The feudal unit was isolated in both the physical and the social sense. It was spatially separated from other units; serfs seldom ventured beyond the protection of their lord; and a lord and his soldiers seldom left their stronghold except to engage in war with neighboring lords. Feudal people lived in a little, self-centered, and insulated world, the cultural content of which was small and primitive. Moreover, since feudal organization had evolved under conditions of social chaos and was oriented toward defense against military attack, the keynote of life was security; and the first requirement for membership, in addition to birth, was uncritical loyalty to the group, symbolized

[2] Feudalism has everywhere been associated with militarism, rigid stratification, social isolation, and marked subordination of both the individual and family units to the feudal organization. In other respects, however, feudal systems have differed considerably from one another. For comparisons and contrasts see Rushton Coulborn (ed.), *Feudalism in History*, Princeton University Press, Princeton, N.J., 1956. For a detailed analysis of European feudalism, with special emphasis on the closed and isolative character of life on the feudal manor, see Marc Block, *Feudal Society*, L. A. Manyon (trans.), The University of Chicago Press, Chicago, 1960.

by loyalty to the lord. In such a small, monolithic society each manor was in most respects self-sufficient as well as isolated; there was little possibility of any individual's developing qualities of originality; and were any to have done so, he would promptly have been dropped into the dungeon as a threat to the security of the manor.

Feudal organizations were not entirely self-contained. Some small trade in iron did exist; between allied manorial units there was an interchange of women as wives for the sons of lords; and the wandering priests no doubt brought some vision of the larger world to the manor. Nonetheless, over the course of some hundreds of years, feudal technology, ideology, and organization seem to have changed very little. Feudal society had grown up as a fusion of Roman, Germanic, and other social elements, all debased and simplified. Agriculture was of the primitive hoe type, and little was cultivated except grains. The textile arts had all but disappeared; most garments were made from leather, usually obtained from wild game. For hand tools there was little beyond the wood hoe, a metal hand scythe, hammers, and crude knives; pots and cooking dishes were made locally of hearth-baked clay; the huts of the serfs were made of field stone, wattle, and mud; sanitation was unknown; and there seems to have been very little even of the magic with which primitive and other premodern peoples have consoled themselves for their ignorance of nature and inability to control it. The literacy of the Romans had been lost, and history was composed of local myths and legends.

The Decline of Feudalism

What broke the isolation and organizational integrity of the people of feudal Europe is a matter of conjecture. It was certainly not some single event— a more than normally disturbing war, the invention of some new tool or weapon, an invasion by tribal barbarians, or the like. One hypothesis, as satisfying if no more valid than any other, is that a series of bad crop years intensified the normal insecurity of feudal life and inaugurated a progressive cycle of adversity—hunger in the manors, war on neighboring manors, neglect of crops, greater hunger, and so on. At any event, something brought about a general lowering of the welfare of feudal people; and this in turn gave rise to the greatest mass movement of recorded history—the First Crusade. Evidence that acute social discontent developed among feudal people was the emergence early in the eleventh century of a spirit of asceticism—a new ideology that provided an escape from social realities and produced a wave of salvation seeking through retreat to monkish life, through fasting, through self-abasement, and through long pilgrimages, of which that to Jerusalem was the most demanding and in time became the most popular.

Originally individual expeditions by discontented feudal lords, pilgrimages to Jerusalem, possibly with the encouragement of Urban II for religiopolitical reasons, became a mass phenomenon by the end of the eleventh century. The idea that social salvation—and, no doubt, personal profit—lay in the freeing of the Holy Land from Moslem rule became the dominant and highly activating ideology of Western European peoples; and it encouraged them to break from their feudal isolation, band together in military assaults on the Holy Land, conquer and lose, and try again and again. Crusades were undertaken throughout the twelfth and thirteenth centuries and, less frequently, for another two centuries more.[3]

The Crusades did not bring social salvation to the people of Western Europe, although many individuals, especially members of the rising body of merchants, no doubt profited by the chaos that the Crusades created. But they occurred during the period of declining feudal isolation, declining power of the feudal form of organization to constrain the individual, and of increasing individual mobility, both spatial and social. The mingling of people from various manors into crusading masses and their exposure to the nonfeudal culture of the Moslems fostered cultural exchanges and fusions. Thus in time the West came to borrow back from the East some of the lost cultural devices and ideas of the ancients. Moreover, the movement of masses of people to and from the Holy Land created the need for and stimulated the emergence of transport and trade in goods and services. Some of the old Roman towns revived; new trading and craft centers developed; and new political units—nonfeudal in form—were fashioned through the forcible consolidation of manorial estates.

There is no satisfactory way in which to measure the rates of social change in Western societies since the feudal system began to decline. Clearly, change has not been constant, nor has it accelerated at a fixed pace. Nor has it followed any perceptible, fixed sequence, such as from technology to organization to ideology. In some times, and usually also in some special places, change has been comparatively rapid; in other and longer periods, various social systems, whether in a condition of relative congruence or one of incongruence, have remained relatively unchanged. Where change has occurred, it has often been quite segmental—there would, for example, be a burst of innovation in military technology, in building construction, or in religious organization; but in some instances, as in Florentine society during the fifteenth century, change has occurred simultaneously in many aspects of society.

The great complexity, the unpatterned variability, and the regional character of the change that has occurred in Western societies are considerably obscured by the practice of historical stereotyping. That practice has the

[3] The best general account of this period of Western history is provided by Will Durant in *The Age of Faith: A History of Medieval Civilization,* Simon and Schuster, Inc., New York, 1950.

justification of convenience; and it may be argued that modal or ideal-type concepts are necessary tools for sociohistorical analysis. As long as any such designation for a historical period as "the Middle Ages," "the Renaissance," or "the industrial revolution" is recognized as simply a label that is applied to a vaguely delimited period of social history and that has been chosen in terms of only one of many possible criteria to suggest something of the character of life during that period, there is no objection to using it. The danger is that many are inclined to infer from the label that the period designated by it is clear and distinct and that life during that period was uniform, stable, and dominantly of such and such a character. "The age of chivalry," a phrase that is sometimes used by historians to characterize certain trends in social life during the eleventh and twelfth centuries, might, for example, lead the unsophisticated to suppose that during a given period Western Europeans were mainly knights who were primarily engaged in such lofty and honorable endeavors as rescuing maidens from distress and jousting with equally honorable competitors. In fact, however, an exceedingly small proportion of the population were knights; and those of the knights who were not expending themselves in pilgrimage to the Holy Land were busily grabbing lands and trying to build personal empires for themselves. During this period military combat did become a well-defined way of life for some of the people of Europe; and there did emerge various rules and standards of military combat. It was developments of this sort that led to the concept of the "age of chivalry." Then, as always, however, combat was a means to very crass ends; and while combat may have been rife among knights and their followers, it was certainly not normal—it was far from characteristic of the populace at large.

The dangers of typifying periods of social history are perhaps most apparent when one considers how unrealistic it would be to designate the twentieth century as the "age of science." It is true that the ideology of science is currently in ascendancy and that many of the changes that are occurring in contemporary societies stem at least indirectly from scientific discoveries. Science did not begin, however, with the opening of this century; it has roots far back into the past; and in certain respects the eighteenth or the nineteenth century would be more deserving of the title. Moreover, even today only a very small proportion of the population are scientists, are seriously interested in scientific developments, or are directly affected by them. Furthermore, much, perhaps most, of the change that is occurring in our society is wrought by nonscientists—by social reformers, business leaders, politicians, and individual members of the general public. Science, or perhaps more accurately pseudo science, is an important motif of modern life, one that somewhat distinguishes this period in social time from others, so that the designation "age of science" has a certain poetic justification. But to apply it would be quite unscientific, for the lives of modern people do not revolve around and consist of scientific pursuits. Like those of many other people of many other times, the lives of modern people are exceedingly variable and variably constituted.

Revival of Familism

Among the many interdependent factors that have affected and continue to affect the rates of change in Western societies has been the form and integrity of family life. The relationship between the family as a form of social organization and social change has not, of course, been one of simple cause and effect; but in general it may be said that when and where the family in the extended form has prevailed, social changes of any sort have been few and of minor character; and, again in general, where change has been rapid and significant, the family has been more or less nuclear in form and unstable and unsubstantial in character. The extended family is a kinship unit that encompasses as an integrated and working whole all males who are directly related by birth, together with their wives and unmarried daughters—i.e., males whose relation to one another is that of father, uncle, brother, nephew, or son. In this system marriage is contractual, and the individual is in all respects ideologically and organizationally subordinated to the perpetuation of the family line. Although the extended family system obtained in China for nearly two thousand years, in Roman society for some centuries, and in other times and places for considerable periods of time, it is an inherently unstable form of organization. It can be maintained only when it is functionally integrated; and it tends to break down into its constituent nuclear units of husband, wife, and children when subjected to stress. The nuclear form, on the other hand, being a minimum kinship unit, can persist over long periods of time, whether functionally integrated or not.

As the feudal system of organization disintegrated, the family in its extended form again became the basic unit of social life. It never achieved the position that it had held in Roman society or the dominance that it had enjoyed in premodern China; but, like the manorial unit which it came to replace, it was the first line of defense against change; and such it remained, with varying degrees of effectiveness, until very recent times. The extended family emerged, sporadically and at various rates in different regions, classes, and occupations, as an organizational adaptation to the chaos of postfeudal life. On the one hand, it was for the individual a small island of comparative security in a world of uncertainty; on the other, it assumed the functions of regulating procreation, of physical maintenance, of socialization, and of social control, without which the species cannot survive. Other forms of organization were concurrently beginning to develop—new political units, towns, and trade organizations and, in time, the guilds;

and some of these in due course came to supplement and in some respects to substitute for the family; but in many places and for considerable periods the extended family was the organizational agency in which and through which some semblance of social order was achieved. The people of Western Europe during the postfeudal period were often in a position comparable to that of the American settlers in the wilderness two centuries ago—surrounded by hostile forces, dependent upon their own resources, and faced with constant uncertainty. Alone, a man could not survive; with his wife, his sons, and the sons of his sons, he and they might protect themselves from adversity. Moreover, with a few minor and local exceptions, the postfeudal family was also patriarchal; and both Church law and secular law as they developed tended to represent and reinforce patriarchal values, sentiments, and procedures—property rights, for example, were vested in the father, and the legal status of women was that of chattel. Thus for a number of related reasons the social system that evolved out of the remnants of feudalism come to be functionally geared to familism and, to that extent, oriented toward social stability.[4]

As a form of organization the extended family was exceptionally well designed to defend itself against change. As a socializing agency it had the advantage, over such modern alternatives as the public school, of having total jurisdiction over its members; they were born into the family, they spent the whole of their early years within it, and they were entirely dependent on it during those years. It was an intimate unit of organization, and the training of incoming members was subject to constant and knowledgeable direction. Moreover, it was a control as well as training agency, and errors in socialization could be promptly perceived and quickly corrected by group constraints. Under these circumstances, the various items of family culture tended to be incorporated in the personality of the individual as he grew to maturity and thus to become, insofar as he was concerned, self-maintaining. Quite commonly, the result was that the values, sentiments, motivations, tastes, etc., of the family system were so well instilled and were so much a part of the individual that he was incapable of deviating from them or from what they required of him.

[4] Just one of a great many ways in which the emerging medieval social system discouraged change was the custom and legal practice of *retrait lignager*, in which a man could redeem and regain possession of property that had been owned by and sold by one of his kin by repayment of the price that had been paid for it. Since this right, which was vaguely derived from the feudal system of property ownership, was in theory without time limitations, the purchaser of property, especially land, could never be certain that he would retain possession year after year or generation after generation. This uncertainty seems to have discouraged the exchange of land, investment for its improvement, and changes in land usages. See Marc Block, *Feudal Society*, L. A. Manyon (trans.), The University of Chicago Press, Chicago, 1960, pp. 131–133.

The extended family also had various organizational devices and procedures which indirectly operated to circumscribe the individual and to preclude his having varied and conflicting experiences. Contractual marriage, either acknowledged or in covert form, was one such device; it discouraged sexual experimentation, made marriage irrevocable, and assured that women would be tied to the families of their husbands in a subordinate status. For women any position other than that of wife and mother was made more or less intolerable, the only exception being that of nun, who became wedded to Christ and subordinated to the rules and regulations of her order. Since men were expected to accept passively the wives chosen for them by their elders, and since the immediate object of marriage was the provision of sons, men, too, were prevented from venturing out on their own; and by the time they were out of their teens, they were usually weighed down with responsibility for a wife and a growing number of children. In the extended family, as in tribal and other forms of basic organization, there were many cultural incentives and sentiments that fostered early marriage and a high birth rate. The primary function of these incentives may have been to maintain the social population against normal odds; but an important, if incidental, consequence was that they discouraged social change by preventing venturesome conduct on the part of individuals. A father—or, for that matter, a mother—who was engaged in an unending struggle to maintain his growing family and to care for his aging parents in accordance with the established social practices was unlikely to have either the time, the energy, or the inclination to devise or to try out something new. The power of the dead hand of the past was thus augmented by the grasping hands of the present.

In other ways, too, the organizational devices and procedures of the extended family operated to preoccupy the individual and to preclude his straying from the tried and true. The usually elaborate ceremonials and rites surrounding births, deaths, and marriages were demanding and time-consuming, as were family anniversaries of one sort and another. It is perhaps difficult for modern people to realize how much time was devoted to group activities of this sort; actually such activities probably absorbed most of the time that an individual had free from the grim business of making a livelihood.

For these and related reasons, the extended family tended to discourage and at times to preclude individual mobility, both spatial and social.[5] Under

---

[5] Familism, and perhaps to an equal extent also tribalism, precludes the development of such individual qualities as independence and self-reliance and assures that the individual will be psychologically group-bound and as dependent upon the group for reassurance and ego support as he is for his material welfare. Where strong traditions of familism or tribalism still persist, it is, for example, almost impossible to establish and operate modern, Western-type hospital facilities. The sick and injured cannot be treated in hospitals as individuals; for if they

it, the individual usually lived out his life in the place in which he was born and in the particular class and occupational status of his father. Since, as will be shown, spatial and social mobility are positively correlated with social change, their being discouraged by the extended family was in effect a discouraging of social change. Even where an individual did manage in some way to break away from his place of birth and his status at birth, the effect of the extended family system was to return him—or, more probably, his sons—to his original status, if not also to his place of birth. In the Confucian system of China, it was possible for even a peasant's son to climb to high estate via the ladder of scholarship; and in this endeavor a boy's family—indeed, his entire clan—might aid him. If he did succeed and was in due course appointed to some official position by the central government, he carried along with him a considerable band of relatives. His parents, most certainly, had a rightful share in his prosperity; and along with them came improvident uncles and their families, his brothers and their families, unmarriageable aunts, sisters, etc. To reduce the dangers of political nepotism, the governmental practice was to place an official in some province other than that of his birth; but this practice did not relieve the individual of his family obligations. Wherever he might be located, an official soon found himself surrounded by kith and kin, who, in accordance with custom, proceeded to do him the honor of living on his bounty. However great his wealth, it would be shared by many and soon reduced; and upon his death his sons would be hardly better off than he had been at birth. Thus did Chinese familism assure that none could for long enjoy the fruits of exceptional endeavor.

In Western Europe familism operated, although in a less direct and consistent way, to keep the individual tied to place and status and to divide and dissipate rewards for exceptional endeavor. A peasant boy might leave home to make his fortune in the town, and a town boy might migrate to a larger and more prosperous center; but if either accomplished anything, it was likely to be divided among so many relatives that his personal reward for achievement would hardly be worth the effort. Even today there are vestiges of this consequence of Western European familism. Many Italian villages, especially those of the south, are supported entirely by remittances from young men working abroad or in industrial centers. Their prospect is bleak and discouraging; for unless they can break the ties of sentiment, loyalty, and filiality to their relatives back home, they have little chance to improve their personal lot. The more they earn, the more is demanded of them; for the numbers of their relatives simply multiply to absorb all surplus. Less marked

---

were to be detached from their kin, they would be deprived of the group support that is essential to their mental welfare, however desirable it might be from a physical point of view. In a wry sense, therefore, the practice of medicine under these conditions is group medicine.

but at times almost equally deterrent to individual initiative is the common parental expectation that a son will follow in his father's footsteps—for example, enter the parental business and take over when the father retires.

The Decline of Familism

Familism is still comparatively strong in Italy and Spain, somewhat less so in parts of Germany and in Scandinavia. In eighteenth-century America it was dominant among the ruling class in the Southern colonies—i.e., among the plantation owners; it was strong among the upper class in the Northern colonies, especially the New England; and the tradition of familism has tended to linger on in both regions. Familism has persisted in somewhat modified form among the peasants of Europe; and its influence has waxed and waned since the fifteenth century in various places, at various times, and according to various circumstances. As a form of organization, however, the extended family probably passed its apex, at least so far as townsmen were concerned, during the fifteenth century. The general historical drift was toward a gradual and fragmentary shifting of the functions that were fulfilled by the extended family to other, nonkinship organizations; and this change in time reduced the family to a sort of residual unit composed of husband, wife, and children, a unit with limited and tenuous relations with other blood relatives, with restricted authority over its own members, and with a marked tendency to be a discrete unit.[6]

[6] Sociologists and social historians have tended to assume that the turning point in this process was the industrial revolution, that prior to the eighteenth century the prevailing family system in Western Europe was of the extended type, that the rise of machine production destroyed the economic base for the extended family, and that the new productive techniques gave rise to the nuclear family. Sidney M. Greenfield ("Industrialization and the Family in Sociological Theory," *American Journal of Sociology*, vol. 67, pp. 312–322, November, 1961) has correctly pointed out the error in this assumption and has advanced the thesis that it was in fact the existence of the nuclear family that fostered the industrial revolution. What he has failed to take into account is that the nuclear family can vary and has varied widely both in its character and in its consequences. The fact that it is small does not necessarily mean that it is also weak; nor does the fact that it is weak necessarily mean that it is conducive to social change, for it never operates as an independent variable.

It is generally true, however, that the modern family is both nuclear and unstable, although due account must be taken of ethnic, national, class, regional, and individual differences in family life; and the contrasts are sometimes quite marked. The Southern Negro lower-class family is characteristically an unstable and ineffectual unit, whereas the middle-class Negro family tends to be strong and durable, although distinctly nuclear in character. The Southern white middle-class family, which is also highly integrated, has, on the other hand, many of the

The decline of the extended family was brought about by a wide variety of changes in the context in which it operated—all of which were, obviously, worked by individuals who were members of some sort of family unit. Many of these changes were technological, many were organizational, and some of them were changes in ideology, or at least led to modifications of ideology. As a system of organization the extended family resisted these changes; but as individuals broke through the organization's defenses against change and by their individual efforts began bringing changes of one sort and another about, those changes weakened the family and so made escape from bondage to it ever easier.

Something of the way in which developments in other organizations had deleterious effects on family integrity is indicated in the history of the Church and of the towns of medieval Europe. As the Roman Church extended its influence, both theological and political, over European peoples, it offered among other things an expanding organizational opportunity for girls and boys to escape from the jurisdiction of their parents. They could enter a Church order, transferring filiality from home to convent, monastery, or the lay priesthood; and they could do so with ideological and social sanction. In actuality they simply escaped one set of constraints to be subjected to another; so for the most part, all that those who left the family for the Church did was contribute to the growth of the Church as an organization. That growth, however, was one of the factors that in due time led to the corruption of the Church; and this corruption was in turn one of the conditions that gave rise to new religious ideology and organization—to Protestantism and all that it implied for individual endeavor. Moreover, the fact that a boy could enter the Church meant also that there were open to him opportunities for social advancement far greater than those afforded by any family unit. He might, and some few did, become in time bishop, cardinal, or even pope.

The rise of the Church as an important organization in Western Europe was paralleled by the rise of towns and of the trade—itself conducted through new forms of organization—that made towns possible. Town life did not of itself weaken familism; for the extended family could be and often

---

residual qualities of the old extended family—for example, pride in family lineage, considerable loyalty to kin, however distant, and a strong sense of family unity.

Among the many studies and discussions of the modern family, the factors that have changed it, and the ways in which it has in turn affected other aspects of American society are the following: Eli Ginzberg (ed.), *The Family and Social Change*, Columbia University Press, New York, 1960; Arthur E. Glick et al., *American Families*, John Wiley & Sons, Inc., New York, 1957; John R. Seeley et al., *Crestwoods Heights*, Basic Books, Inc., Publishers, New York, 1956; John Sirjamaki, *The American Family in the Twentieth Century*, Harvard University Press, Cambridge, Mass., 1953; and Bernard J. Stern, *The Family: Past and Present*, D. Appleton-Century-Crofts, Inc., New York, 1938.

was maintained within the urban context. The town was always in some measure, however, a cosmopolitan place—to it came traders, through it wandered vagabonds of one sort and another, and from it went residents who traveled to distant places. Moreover, the population of a town was itself occupationally differentiated. Thus the town, unlike the family, provided variations and contrasts in both thought and action; and a perceptive individual could discover for himself that the ways of home were not the only or the universal ways of man. As a boy grew to maturity in the cosmopolitan atmosphere of a town, he might, therefore, be ideologically if not physically and organizationally drawn away from his family.

In town life, even during the Middle Ages, a family unit was not able to maintain economic self-sufficiency; it had of necessity to enter into symbiotic relations with various nonfamily organizations—to buy its bread from the baker, its meat from the butcher, and its cloth from the weaver. Thus the family as such lost its independence to a considerable extent. Work came more and more to be done in a shop rather than in the home, and where work was men had to go. Men, young and old, tended to be away from their homes for a large part of the day and merged with the members of other families in some nonfamily organization. The separation of family and work life is almost total in the modern world, but it began early in the Middle Ages; and wherever the guild form of organization obtained, it was sharp and marked.

In recent times, the development of public school education has been one of the many changes in organization that have reduced the importance of the family, given the individual opportunity for nonfamily experiences, and lessened his reliance on the family. Some of these changes in organization began, as the school system did, as supplements to the family; but many came to be replacements for the family, and all contributed to its decline.

Many kinds of technological developments have had adverse effects on the family, first in its extended form, and later and currently in its nuclear form. Every improvement in transportation and in communication technology has in some measure weakened the bonds of family life in that it has lessened the isolation of the family unit and enlarged the individual's world. One need only contrast life in a rural hamlet or in a single isolated farm family in America a century ago with life in their counterparts today to see the effects of technological developments on the size of the farm family's world. A century ago the road away from home was two ruts that wandered into the local trading center and lost themselves; and transportation down the road was by foot, by horseback, or by horse-drawn wagon. A railroad line might run through the village or a steamboat tie up occasionally at the river wharf; in either case, travel away from the locality was rare and a major adventure; visitors to the locality were few and consisted mainly of drummers who called on the village merchants, of new, usually transient,

Family and community organization   343

teachers for the local school, if, indeed, there was a school, and about once a generation of a new parson for the church. Aside from word-of-mouth news brought by the occasional visitor or returning traveler, communication with the outer world was limited to the weekly paper from the nearest large town, such bulletins as the *Farmer's Almanac,* and an occasional letter from some friend or relative who had gone to settle elsewhere. Today, however, even a relatively self-sufficient and comparatively isolated farm family lives close to the larger world; not far off is a highway jammed with cars, trucks, and buses, and it is only a matter of minutes to the nearest town via the family car or pickup truck. From that town the member of the farm family can go by train, bus, or airline almost anywhere in the world that he might wish to go. Through the miracles of modern communication technology he can, moreover, learn something about what is happening almost everywhere in the world—not, of course, that it is necessarily valid; he can hear the finest music via record or radio; he can hear and see everything from Madison Square Garden prize fights to Hollywood's stock westerns via television; he can call up any one of millions of fellow Americans via long-distance dial telephone; etc. With all these technological aids at his command, it is today almost impossible to preserve even a modicum of social isolation.

Technological inroads on the physical and social isolation of the family began, perhaps, with the rise of medieval towns, which being dependent upon trade, were dependent upon the transportation of goods from regions of production to centers of consumption. Major strides in the development of transportation were, successively, the invention of the keeled sailing ship, which eventually brought products and persons to port towns from the far corners of the world; the development of inland canals, which made ports of a sort of land-bound towns; the invention of the railroad, the steamship, the interurban electric car, the automobile, and the airplane, which made transportation of goods and persons progressively easier and faster. Meanwhile, developments in communication were opening up the world of the individual in another dimension. First came the evolution of writing the live and local language, rather than the dead language Latin; then the invention of printing, which multiplied things to be read; the invention of wood-pulp paper, which made possible popular newspapers and journals of various sorts; the invention of the telegraph; and so on.

As new means of transportation and communication were invading the privacy of the family and drawing off its individual members, other technological changes were gradually depriving the family of many of its productive functions. As has already been mentioned, town life led the family to depend upon nonfamily organizations for many of its goods and services. Toward the close of the eighteenth century innovations in productive technology, including mechanization of work activities, began to take from the home and put into the factory and shop most of what productive functions were left to the family.[7] The industrialization of food processing and mass distribution, described earlier, were one strand of this development; the industrialization of household lighting was another.

As the family was stripped more and more of its productive functions and the home ceased to be a center of work, the economic dependence of the individual on the family declined, and with it one of the major incentives for family unity. In the old extended family system, a young man who did not live in a family context was without normal and visible means of support; and even when he was able to find some way of earning a livelihood, the habitation, meals, and services that he could obtain were shabby substitutes for those that a family would provide. Today, on the other hand, a prospering independent can buy all the good things of life—all, that is, except love and companionship.

Ideological support for independence from family membership has generally been slow in coming. Even today men honor home, mother, wife, and children ideologically, with slight regard for the actualities of modern life. Even today they give token observance to such ideas and concepts of the extended family as virginity, the inherent desirability of children, and the inviolability of the home, although in point of fact teen-age chastity is rare, children are often a burden, and a man's home is subject to invasion by building inspectors, process servers, agents of mortgage holders, solicitors for countless so-called charities, and the omnipotent tax collectors.

The idea that dedication to the religious life was even more worthy than adherence to family evolved fairly early. The more limited idea, an ideological product of the period of world exploration, that a boy, especially an extra son, might go adventuring evolved somewhat later. Later still some ideological sanction was given to migration to the New World and, subsequently, to migration from farm to town. Usually, however, the migrant was expected either to return to the bosom of his family laden with riches or else in due course to call to him the family he had left behind. Not until quite recently has the idea that a son might justifiably leave his parental roof to establish himself in independence become at all general, and it is still subject to many qualifications.

[7] For a detailed description of how a change in textile technology in early industrial England gave an economic advantage to women and children and thus lowered the prestige of the father as head of the family, reduced his economic importance to his wife and children, and so undermined his authority, see Neil Smelser, *Social Change in the Industrial Revolution*, University of California Press, Berkeley, Calif., 1959, chap. IX, "Pressures on the Family Division of Labor."

For a general, if not very discerning, analysis of how recent technological developments have affected family life, see W. F. Ogburn and M. F. Nimkoff, *Technology and the Changing Family*, Houghton Mifflin Company, Boston, 1955.

On the whole, ideological sanctioning of release from family membership came first and most fully to sons. Until just a few decades ago it was generally assumed, and often no doubt with good reason, that a girl who left her home to work in the city or to migrate to some distant land would probably come to some bad end. Aside from working in a city factory, with all that that implied, from being a nun, or from taking a job as schoolmarm, there was little in the way of respectable economic opportunities for an independent woman. Not until well toward the close of the last century, when the idea that the female is inherently weak, emotional, and irrational—a part of the ideology of the extended family—was sufficiently dispelled, were women granted some rights for a formal education; and it was decades later before the franchise was extended to them. Women were, and still are to some extent, encumbered by the values and sentiments of the old double standard of morality; a girl's brother might be a gay blade, but she would, by social definition, be only a fallen woman.

Today it is possible in Northern Europe, Britain, and the United States for a woman to live and work independent of close family attachments without being suspect; but the normal role of a woman is still that of wife, housewife, and mother; and while a woman is far less circumscribed by family life than was her sister of a century ago, her acceptance in the larger world is always somewhat conditional and somewhat constrained by ideological survivals from the time when she was more servant to than equal of the male.[8] It is in considerable measure this semisubordinated status which accounts for the fact that even today very few women make recognized contributions to social change, even in such traditionally feminine fields of endeavor as dress designing.

THE BOURGEOIS AND OTHER ATYPICAL FAMILY SYSTEMS

The relationship between the size and integrity of the family and the dynamism of the social system is by no means constant, for in any society the family is but one of a number of interdependent forms of organization. Although in general the extended family is concordant with and conducive to social stability and in general the nuclear type is both reflective of and favorable to social change, the particular organizational and ideological context in which the family operates may either augment or offset the effects of either form of the family.[9] In many primitive societies, for example, the fam-

[8] Mirra Komarovsky, *Women in the Modern World,* Little, Brown and Company, Boston, 1953.

[9] Failure to realize that the family unit always operates in conjunction with other forms of organization was one of the errors of the culture and personality

ily has been an unstable nuclear unit of secondary rather than primary importance; marriage has been, from the Western point of view, a rather casual association, and the authority of parents over their children has been weak and ineffectual. Nevertheless, these societies have been comparatively stable because tribal organization in some instances and village organization in others has provided strong defenses against change.

In Western society since the Middle Ages the general relationship between the form of the family and social dynamism has been qualified in a number of ways. In the first place, it has usually been the urban working-class family that has been most disorganized by technological and other change and that has, therefore, had the least control over its individual members. Working-class families have not, however, contributed proportionately to the making of social changes; and, indeed, the working class has on the whole been more resistant to change, both ideological and technological, than have the middle and upper classes. In the second place, there have emerged several

---

school of psychologists and anthropologists, who enjoyed a considerable vogue during the 1940s. The other was the assumption, derived from such neo-Freudians as Karen Horney (*The Neurotic Personality of Our Times*, W. W. Norton & Company, Inc., New York, 1937), that the human being is inherently insecure and must be constantly reassured, from birth to death, that those about him love and want him. These two errors, synthesized, provided the basis for the theory that the personality structure of the individual is formed in infancy and early childhood and that the character of the individual is determined by the manner in which parents, especially the mother, manage such vital matters as infant feeding and bowel evacuation. If the infant is treated in these and other respects permissively, it was believed, it will develop a sturdy, self-confident personality; if, on the other hand, it is subjected to discipline, it will feel itself rejected and grow up to be an insecure, neurotic adult. This theory gave rise to a considerable literature of protest against the induction of children into the cultural practices of society and against the authoritarian parent who endeavored so to induct his children. See Ralph Linton, *The Cultural Backgrounds of Personality*, Appleton-Century-Crofts, Inc., New York, 1945; Abram Kardiner et al., *The Psychological Frontiers of Society*, Columbia University Press, New York, 1945; W. A. Davis and R. J. Havighurst, *Father of the Man*, Houghton Mifflin Company, Boston, 1947; and T. W. Adorno et al., *The Authoritarian Personality*, Harper & Row, Publishers, Incorporated, New York, 1950. The myth that the modern American family tends to be authoritarian gave way in the face of overwhelming evidence to the contrary, but the idea that the individual's personality is wholly determined in the family and during the first few years of life persists. It runs counter to the evidence, such as that advanced by William H. Sewell ("Infant Training and the Personality of the Child," *American Journal of Sociology*, vol. 58, pp. 150–159, September, 1952). Nonetheless it has been borrowed by such students of social change as Everett E. Hagen (*On the Theory of Social Change*, The Dorsey Press, Inc., Homewood, Ill., 1962) in an attempt to explain the resistance of most member of most societies to innnovations of any sort.

atypical systems of family organization that have violated the general rule that the large, integrated family is conducive to stability and the small, weak family conducive to change.

The Bourgeois Family

The most striking of these exceptions was the family system that developed, during the period that gave rise to the Reformation, among the growing numbers of merchants, bankers, lawyers, and other enterprising men who were undermining the foundations of medieval society and inaugurating those technological, ideological, and organizational changes which have continued to the present day. These men no doubt came initially from extended, highly integrated family units; and their initiative and enterprise must have violated many familistic values and sentiments. It may be presumed that in order to undertake his venturesome career, each must have had to some extent to sever his identification with his kin and that his kin probably considered him foolish, if not perfidious.

As the numbers of enterprising men increased, particularly in Northwestern Europe, and won position and recognition, they came to form something of a class of their own, with their own special subculture. Their values and sentiments became, as has been seen, incorporated into an ethic; Protestantism evolved to give them an appropriate religion and religious sanction; and they developed a unique family system.

The family organization of this new class, which came in time to be designated as the *bourgeoisie,* had much of the integrity of the extended family; but normally only the members of the immediate family—father, wife, and immature children—lived under the same roof. Usually the family maintained close relations with parents and siblings throughout their lives, and the father of a family watched over and was held responsible for the welfare, psychological as well as material, of his elders and his dependent siblings, such as his unmarried or widowed sisters. What was primarily expected of him, however, was that he maintain his own wife and children in comfort and security and that he be fully responsible to the larger society for their conduct. At the same time he was granted the right, as were his sons after him, to venture far afield in the pursuit of means to maintain his family and was held personally responsible should he fail to be successful in this quest. The bourgeois family system has been derided for its rigid subscription to the moral codes of familism, its ethnocentrism, its stress on respectability, and its authoritarianism. It was, in fact, a bulwark of stability in a universe of change; but in contrast to the old extended family, the bourgeois family system permitted—and possibly even encouraged—the changes which ultimately destroyed it.

The bourgeois family system operated in terms of a dual set of values. On the one hand, and in accordance with some of the elements of the Protestant ethic, family stability and security, both economic and psychological, were a major value. It was incumbent on the father of the family to rule the family members in terms of their own collective interests (he had to see to it, for example, that his children married well) and to make certain that they would never know adversity. It was this obligation that, in time, led the members of the *bourgeoisie* to delay marriage and, later, to resort to birth control in the effort to achieve and then preserve a high standard of living. This same obligation made for very high standards of financial integrity and such foresightful domestic practices as the avoidance of debt. Thus it was that a sound bourgeois son would not assume the responsibilities of marriage and then of children until and unless he had reasonable cause to believe that he could at the time and in the foreseeable future support a wife and children in the relatively high standards of his class and that he could provide his children with the education and standing that would enable them to marry well and to maintain, if not improve, the status to which they had been born. On the other hand, the bourgeois family system also sanctioned those elements of the Protestant ethic that foster individual enterprise; thus the system encouraged the individual to be venturesome—in business, in a profession, or in whatever field of endeavor—provided that the risks involved did not jeopardize the security of the family. Operationally, this meant that a bourgeois son could undertake an uncertain but potentially rewarding career—he could go adventuring occupationally—provided that he delayed assuming the responsibilities of family life until he had achieved success and that thereafter he might continue to embark on ventures of a business or other sort provided that failure in them would not jeopardize the welfare of his family. He therefore operated in two distinct realms and in terms of two distinct, although not mutually exclusive, sets of values and sentiments.

There can be little doubt that the bourgeois family system was an important factor in the technological and other changes that occurred with such great and such increasing frequency from the fifteenth century onward. The family did constrain the individual, even its titular head; but the constraints that it imposed did not deny the individual freedom to engage outside the family sphere in enterprising endeavors. No doubt the responsibility for family welfare was often a hampering burden and a check on enterprising endeavor. On the other hand, the existence of a reasonably secure base—the family—from which to work and to which to return no doubt contributed, psychologically at least, to the individual's freedom to engage in enterprising endeavors; for fear of adversity, personal and collective, can be quite as inhibiting as is a sense of duty, honor, or some other organizational sentiment. At any event, it was for the most part members of the *bourgeoisie* and of bourgeois families who made the innovations, who served as advocates, and who first became adopters of the changes that *in toto* distinguish social life today from that of three hundred years ago.

The bourgeois family system was as a form of organization functionally appropriate to a period of rapid social change and as such no doubt contributed considerably to the making of the changes that did occur. In its basic characteristics it persisted for four centuries and more, during which every other aspect of Western society underwent profound and almost constant modification. In later years it, too, however, became the object of change. Its stability was progressively weakened by divorce; the authority of the father over family members was undermined by various changes external to the bourgeois family system itself—for example, by such changes as the freeing of women from the legal and other bonds that tied them to the domestic sphere; and the integrity of the unit declined as more liberal and less demanding economic values came to prevail.

The bourgeois family system no longer obtains among members of the middle class, and the family of the middle class today does not provide the stable organizational base that the bourgeois system did. As a rule the middle-class family today is weak and insecure, and often it is transitory; and the modern middle-class individual is more likely to seek and find in some organization other than the family—usually a political or occupational organization—assurance that he will be protected from adversity and provided for in times of personal incapacity. The effects on social change of this shift in individual dependence from family to other kinds of organizations is at present incalculable; but it is possible that the decline of the bourgeois family system is directly related to the growth of political and economic bureaucracy, which tends to provide, in the short run at least, something of the psychological and economic security that is no longer obtainable through family membership.

The Petty Bourgeois Family

Concurrent with the development of the bourgeois family system was the emergence of a secondary type of atypical family organization, nuclear in form, but nonetheless strongly resistant to change. It embodied and maintained the values and sentiments of the small, cautious, and unenterprising shopkeepers, independent craftsmen, and guild masters who gradually formed into a distinct socioeconomic class—the petty *bourgeoisie.* This family system required its members to be industrious, responsible, and self-reliant; and in these respects family life was like that of the grand *bourgeoisie;* but unlike the bourgeois family system, that of the petty *bourgeoisie* did not distinguish categorically between family life and occupational endeavor. Very often, in fact, the two realms were inseparably interwoven, as was so commonly the case with the small shopkeeper. As a result, the family system of the petty *bourgeoisie* did not sanction the taking of occupational risks any more than the taking of risks in the choosing of wives for their sons. Security and continuity were the primary concern, both for the family and for the small business upon which it was dependent.

The petty bourgeois family system trained its members into rigorous family morality, into an exceedingly cautious outlook on life, and into acceptance of the idea that a bird in the hand is worth two in the bush. From petty bourgeois backgrounds came many of the individuals who through exceptional endeavor and initiative contributed to the dynamism of Western society and thereby moved into the class of grand bourgeois. But since the petty bourgeois family system did not sanction the risk that such endeavor inevitably entailed, the European lower middle class was for the most part as resistant to change as was the lower laboring class.[10]

The French Peasant Family

With one notable exception the family system of the peasants of Western Europe was, and to a considerable extent still is, semiextended in form, highly integrated, and staunchly resistant to change of any sort. The exception is that of the peasants of France since the Revolution, an exception that clearly demonstrates the interdependence of family and other forms of organization.

[10] C. Wright Mills developed the thesis in *White Collar: The American Middle Classes* (Oxford University Press, Fair Lawn, N.J., 1951) that a new kind of petty bourgeois class is currently developing in America, one composed, not of small shopkeepers and independent craftsmen, but of clerical employees in large and bureaucratically organized industrial and commercial establishments. Like their European predecessors, they are, according to Mills, security-oriented and therefore very conservative and resistant to change. Daniel R. Miller and Guy E. Swanson have presented substantive evidence in support of this thesis in *The Changing American Parent*, John Wiley & Sons, Inc., New York, 1958. They find that the progressive bureaucratization of American business—a matter that will be examined in a later chapter—has given rise to a class of fathers who are themselves so well adjusted to the routine, unenterprising work and style of life of the bureaucrat that they instill in their children the personal attributes of rule-abiding dependence rather than those of individual self-reliance and independence.

A number of other sociologists have reported a fairly consistent relation between the structural integrity of the family background and the individual's tendency to resist social change. See, for example, Bernard C. Rosen, "Family Structure and Achievement Motivation," *American Sociological Review*, vol. 26, pp. 547–585, August, 1961, and "Socialization and Achievement Motivation in Brazil," *American Sociological Review*, vol. 27, pp. 612–624, October, 1962; Eugene A. Wilkening, "A Sociopsychological Approach to the Study of Acceptance of Innovations in Farming," *Rural Sociology*, vol. 15, pp. 352–364, December, 1950, and "Changes in Farm Technology as Related to Familism, Family Decision-making, and Family Integration," *American Sociological Review*, vol. 19, pp. 29–37, February, 1954; and Harald A. Pedersen, "Cultural Differences in the Acceptance of Recommended Practices," *Rural Sociology*, vol. 16, pp. 37–49, March, 1951.

During the last century and this the French peasant family has been nuclear in form; rarely has it included more than father, mother, and immature children. In this respect and in others the French peasant family resembles that of the lower-middle-class American urban workers—marriage usually occurs in the early twenties rather than, as is the case with most agricultural people, in the teens; the birth rate is very low; and family authority is weak. Nevertheless, the French peasants of today are hardly less resistant to change of any sort than are their Italian, German, Dutch, and other Western European counterparts.

The small size and the weak ties of the French peasant family are rather easily explained. The equalitarian ideals that prevailed immediately after the French Revolution led, among other things, to national legislation that revoked primogeniture—that is, the right of the eldest son to the family properties—that had been a traditional part of the extended family system. Primogeniture, derived from Roman times, had prevented properties, most especially land, from being morcellated, from being divided down the generations into smaller and smaller parcels. It was one of the mechanisms by which large estates were accumulated and then preserved; and in modified form primogeniture still obtains among all the agricultural peoples of Europe (and the royal houses), with the exception of the French.

In France equal distribution of family property to all the children upon the death of parents became a legal mandate, and before long the agricultural lands of the peasants were being morcellated into units too small to maintain an ordinary peasant family. About 1850 the effects of morcellation were to some extent arrested by the adoption and rigorous use of birth control by the French, including the peasants, a consequence quite contrary to the expectations of those who had devised the law revoking primogeniture. The peasant family became small; and because it was a small unit that lacked self-sufficiency, it also became weak. Moreover, the fact that frequently a wife owned land that she had inherited from her father tended to lessen the authority of the husband; and where power is divided it is usually lost. At any event, the French peasant family has little of the unity and integrity that are characteristic of peasant family life elsewhere. Nevertheless, for reasons external to the family system itself, the French peasant is characteristically conservative and prefers to till his fields, to make his wine, and to do almost everything that he does in the manner of his *grand-père*.

COMMUNITY AND STATUS-GROUP ORGANIZATION

A community of families that forms on the basis of residential propinquity—whether it be a village, a town, or a looser aggregation of scattered rural families—ordinarily serves as a supplement to the family and functions as the second line of defense against change. But where the family is weak, as it is among the French peasants, a residential community may serve in lieu of the family as the first line of defense against change. The French peasant family is small and loosely knit and has little jurisdiction over its individual members; but the French peasant is not free to follow his personal inclinations, if any, for he lives in a tight little village, a community that imposes rigorous social constraints.

The rural village—primitive, peasant, or "modern"—has characteristically consisted of a handful of families who have lived in close proximity for generations and who have developed strong ties and a considerable body of community culture—local myths and legends, local prides and prejudices, perhaps even something of a local dialect (as was invariably the case in the Middle Ages). Communities of this sort have been highly if informally organized, and membership in them has been almost as tightly controlled as membership in the family and has been determined by the same mechanisms —birth or marriage. In many respects, this type of community has been a family of families. The values, sentiments, etc., have for the most part been extensions of those of the family and at any event have not conflicted with them. The various family units of which such a community has been composed have been arranged in some sort of hierarchy, according to respectability, wealth, time of residence in the area, or some other such criterion. Those of high position have normally striven to preserve their status; those of inferior position to rise in station. The community has been further divided, even as the members of each family, into subgroups on the basis of sex, age, and, in some instances, occupation.

An urban counterpart to the tight little village is to be found in many modern cities, especially those of Europe, and in contemporary suburbia. Since membership is mainly a matter of residence, the modern urban community is a rather tenuous organization and tends to be transitory; and the culture of such a community is limited in scope and is fairly fluid. It can, nonetheless, exercise strong, if segmental, control over its individual members.[11]

Somewhat different in character and usually considerably more constraining on the individual are associations of families that arise in urban populations on the basis of a community of interests rather than of residence. In some times and places, associations of family units, particularly those based on common class interests, have been highly and somewhat formally organized. In the towns and cities of old China, for example, class position was frequently the basis for an association of families, especially families of

[11] For an analysis of the nature of community relationships and of the power of the community to exercise control over its individual members in contemporary America, see Roland L. Warren, *The Community in America*, Rand McNally & Company, Chicago, 1963.

high position, who tended to close ranks against members of less notable families. Associations of the same sort have occurred and still do occur in American and European towns and cities—the proper Bostonians are a classic example; and bourgeois families have always tended to associate with one another and to isolate themselves from their status inferiors. Associations of family units have also been formed on the basis of common ethnic identity (such as the Anglo-Saxons versus the Irish and the French in New England); on the basis of equivalent seniority (the old families versus the new); and on the basis of a mixture of these and class or other interests.

In modern urban communities, associations of family units are generally less important for the maintenance of the *status quo* than are those of a non-family character; for the same conditions that have weakened the ties of family life have also, with some exceptions such as that of the French peasants, weakened both the residential basis and the common-interest basis for associations of family units. Modern people still form into communities; and where there is little in the way of residential propinquity or class or other interests to bring and hold families together, people form associations on other bases, as individuals rather than as members of families.

Peer Groups and Other Status Groups

The major bases for the formation of associations of individuals are age, sex, occupation, and leisure-time activities. Associations on these bases range in form from the tight-knit little band of hoodlums to the prestigious and formally organized clique of socially prominent young matrons, from the informal group of journalists who gather at some favorite bar to talk shop to the exclusive club of prospering business executives, from the grubby lot of Bohemians who haunt the jazz and jive joints to the rich and gracious patrons of the opera.

Since those who form into associations on these bases come together in terms of some interest that they hold in common, they tend to be of about the same social status; hence they are often designated "peer groups." Peer groups form in all societies; but in modern societies they are more substitutes for than supplements to the family and other traditional forms of organization. Each such group has something of its own norms to which the individual members must conform in order to maintain membership; these norms do not, however, necessarily coincide with the cultural standards of the society at large or with those of the family and other organizations to which each of the several members also belongs. They do, however, represent the *status quo*. Thus while the norms of an urban street gang are by general social definition antisocial and may encourage gang theft, vandalism, and intergang warfare, they are not asocial; they are relatively standardized and stable, and the activities that they encourage are all traditional street-gang activities, the forms of which have hardly changed since Roman times. Occasionally street hood-lums have been organized toward more efficient achievement of one or another of their traditional activities, as were those of Germany by the Nazis for more effective persecution of Jews. The norms of a peer group, whether those of a street gang or those of the highly respectable members of the local Junior League, are not, however, designed to encourage change of a socially signifi-cant kind.

Membership in a peer group is not mandatory as is membership in a family or in a family-based residential community. It is within some limits voluntary and stems from the individual's need for status. In modern urban-ized society there are always a great variety of peer groupings to which an individual may seek admission, and he can often pick and choose from among those that are open to him that one whose norms are most congenial to him. Thus a slum boy may join the Boy Scouts rather than the local street gang, and a society matron may join a garden club rather than the Junior League. Because of the great variety of peer groups in modern society, modern peer-group constraints do not result in the social homogeneity that has been char-acteristic of most societies of the past; and the resulting diversity of sub-cultures may indirectly undermine the stability of the social system. More-over, if he chooses, an individual can wander rather freely from group to group; and should he find none entirely to his liking, he may hold himself independent of all of them. Freedom from the constraints of a peer group or other primary group organization may lead to innovative, advocatory, or adoptive behavior. It is more likely, of course, to result in some such con-ventional deviation from the normal as alcoholism or schizophrenia.

Parents Surrogate

One of the ways through which communities, particularly residential com-munities, exercise constraint over the individual is through the provision of parental surrogates. In the peasant village and the small town community, and even to some extent in modern urban and suburban residential communities, every adult may upon occasion assume quasi-parental supervision of any child. The adult may, thus, protect a child from misadventure, correct the child for misbehavior, or complement the child for exemplary conduct. Where the community is small and its membership stable, each adult knows per-sonally every child and tends to regard deviant conduct by any child as a threat to the welfare of the community; the adult is, moreover, encouraged by social sanctions to assume responsibility for every child's conduct. As a con-sequence, the community tends to supplement family training and to correct for errors in that training.

To the extent that every adult is inclined to assume the role of parent surrogate, no child is free from familistic constraints. Although his own parents may be lax, indulgent, or even antisocial, the child will be more or less effectively socialized into the accepted norms of family life by more responsible and demanding adults. A child growing up in any such community is surrounded by repressive adults. There is no escaping them; for wherever he goes, he carries with him the forbidding image of a parent surrogate, an image which no doubt often merges with that of omniscient God or the local evil spirits.

The effectiveness of control through parents surrogate is well illustrated in the operation of the Chinese community of San Francisco a generation or two ago. At that time San Francisco's Chinatown was in most respects comparable to a slum-ghetto, which normally has very high crime and delinquency rates, as, for example, does New York's Harlem. The population was immigrant and ethnically distinct from the larger society; it was economically ill-favored; it was subject to a great deal of prejudice. Moreover, inadequate housing and poverty made integrated family life next to impossible; most mothers worked in sweatshops, and of necessity children lived much in the streets. Nonetheless, the Chinese of San Francisco had then, as they still have, atypically low crime and delinquency rates. The reason lies in the fact that, although a family unit could exercise little effective control over its members, including small children, the Chinatown community as a whole maintained family morality by making every respectable adult a parent surrogate. Every adult tended to treat every child and youth he encountered as his own, holding them to the standards of conduct he would demand of his own and rewarding and punishing them in a similar manner. Though a Chinatown child hardly saw his own father and mother from dawn until dark, he never lacked mothering; and a Chinatown youth was never free from parental supervision.

Status-group Control

A system of parents surrogate aids in socializing the younger members of a community into the standards of conduct to which the families of the community subscribe. Its effectiveness, like that of the family itself, is based on the extent to which the individual is directly dependent upon membership in the community for his material and social welfare and is attached to the community—by bonds of loyalty, because he has no inclination to go elsewhere, or because he has no opportunity to escape. Peer groups and other groups that are based on the individual's need for status, on the other hand, attract and hold their individual members only by the status satisfactions that they provide; they have no other rewards to offer. Thus peer groups and other status groups have relatively little power to socialize, although they may have considerable effect as agencies of social control. Membership in a play gang or similar group does, of course, influence personality development; through street-gang associations a youth may be inducted into the arts and mores of the adult gangster; through her participation in the Junior League a young matron may learn to adhere to the values and sentiments of the social elite, as well as to behave as they do. Whatever socializing influence a status group exerts is, however, incidental to its avowed and momentarily rewarding activities; and any really demanding long-term and all-encompassing training or educational program would probably result in the dissolution of the group itself.

A status group can and does, however, demand individual conformity to its own norms; and conformity is largely a matter of the subordination of the momentary interests and impulses of the individual members to collective goals. In return the group provides each of its members with companionship of a sort, with activities that are more an end in themselves than a means to ends, and above all with status, with recognition as one who belongs. Since most individuals have a strong need for social acceptance and are highly sensitive to slights and other signs of rejection, most are willing to conform to the norms of the status groups to which they wish to belong; and since these norms are group rather than individually determined, they operate as constraints on individual initiative.[12] To the extent that they constrain the initiative of the individual who is subject to them, they preclude him from contributing to social changes of any sort.

A modern urban community, as will shortly be seen, offers far greater opportunity for idiosyncratic behavior than does a peasant village; and most social change has been generated in an urban context. The anonymity of life in modern cities and the freedom of the individual to behave as an individual can, however, be exaggerated. In the cities and in such urban extensions as the suburban community, the family and family-linked organizations may have comparatively little hold on the individual; and he may, should he be so inclined, detach himself from their influence. But the great variety of status groups that result from the very presence of large numbers of people and the characteristic congestion of urban life means that wherever he may go and whatever kind of life he may lead, the individual is unable to avoid members of more or less organized groups. Far from being an isolate wandering in a lonely crowd and free within limits to struggle against the built-in barriers to creative endeavor, he cannot fail to encounter some friends, acquaintances,

[12] For a general analysis of the nature of status groups, the character of their norms, and of the processes by which the individual is induced to adhere to those norms, see Richard T. LaPiere, *A Theory of Social Control*, McGraw-Hill Book Company, New York, 1954. Other works that deal in one way or another with the social controls exercised by status groups include G. C. Homans, *The Human Group*, Harcourt, Brace & World, Inc., New York, 1950; W. F. Whyte, *Street Corner Society*, The University of Chicago Press, Chicago, 1943; and S. N. Eisenstadt, *From Generation to Generation: Age Groups and Social Structure*, The Free Press of Glencoe, New York, 1956.

or casual associates, without whom few men can get along, and all of whom constrain the individual and in one way or another strive to normalize his conduct.

In modern society there are some status groups that make change their *raison d'être*. Ideologically they are in one way or another dedicated to the proposition that the *status quo* is antiquated and must be replaced by something else. Youthful radicals, such as those who may be found on most university campuses, invariably take this stance and form little cliques that discuss the needs for social reform, write petitions, or advocate this or that social change. Similar groupings, both in and out of student circles, fix their attention on one or another of the arts or on philosophy of a sophomoric sort. They are the avant-garde who pose as contratraditionalists and talk far into the night about the new movement in poetry, music, literature, or the graphic arts. Even the more adult, sedate, and respectable clubs and informal associations that consist of urban women, businessmen, journalists, bureaucrats, teachers, and scholars may upon occasion talk about and listen to lectures on some daring new proposal for political, economic, or other reform. Such talk and the slight actions that sometimes follow from it no doubt reflect the dynamism and resulting diversities of contemporary social life and may possibly contribute a little to the changes that are already being worked in society.

For the most part, however, even status groupings that make change their *raison d'être* are a part of the social apparatus for maintaining the *status quo*. They provide harmless channels for the dispersal of individual discontent; their function is cathartic, not creative. Groups of this sort normalize rather than liberate the individual's vague desire to do something about a society which he finds in some respect distasteful and unrewarding; they provide the individual with an audience that is safe and at the same time reassuring and with unconventional but also usually impracticable solutions to the social problems that disturb him. Thus in a complex and subtle manner radical, reformistic, or avant-garde groups may serve as a third line of defense against actual social change.

Social Isolation and Social Change

The degree of social isolation or detachment that is necessary if any individual is to strive toward innovative, advocatory, or adoptive conduct is as asocial as the change that it would produce. Organized society everywhere and always operates to maintain its established forms; and to this end it everywhere and always, although in varied ways and with variable success, subordinates the individual to it and discourages him from working changes that might, depending on the circumstances, either improve or reduce its functional effectiveness. Only when and where and for whatever antecedent reasons there are interstices in or between the organizations of the society is there any considerable possibility that an individual will achieve the degree of social isolation, of freedom from the constraints that organizational membership imposes, that is necessary for initiative to emerge and be exercised in any walk of life.

The subtleties and complexities of the operations of organized society in preventing the emergence of individual initiative, and thus of change, are well illustrated in the varied ways in which agriculture developed in America. Most of the key developments in technology and organization in Western agriculture over the past century and a half are of American origin and have been most fully exploited by Middle Western American farmers. The relative conservatism of European and British farmers can in considerable measure be traced to the fact that they have tended to be family-oriented and to live in family-linked village communities. A farmer who was tempted to try out some new tool, procedure, or seed would, under these social circumstances, be a rarity; and under these circumstances he would quickly be brought back into conformity to local practices by social controls. The members of his family would most likely be appalled by the thought of his taking a chance with their economic security or, at the very least, jeopardizing the reputation of the family by making a fool of himself. His village peers would attempt to talk him out of his foolish idea; and failing this, they would soon be poking sly fun at him for thinking that he knew better than everyone else. Meanwhile, no doubt, rumors would generate, exaggerating what he proposed to do; he might become the butt of rather vicious jokes; and overt antagonism might soon become manifest. In the end the community might well become alarmed for its safety and mobilize against him—its priest appealing to God and the village elders to reason and the weight of secular authority. Only a very stubborn man with exceptional faith in his own judgment would be able for long to resist such pressures to conform.

In America the village system prevailed through most of the New England colonies, and agricultural technology in New England was much the same as that of England and the Continent and about as resistant to change. In the coastal regions of the Southern colonies a different kind of agricultural system—plantations worked by slaves—evolved very early in the cultivation of rice. In the development of this system, the English settlers displayed considerable ingenuity; they imported Dutch hydraulic engineers, for example, to devise complex and effective water-control methods; and they brought in slave labor and adopted methods of marketing slaves and of housing, breeding, and working them. Meanwhile, they borrowed the arts of rice cultivation from Asia and adapted them to the particular climatic and other physical circumstances of their delta lands. At the same time they also developed a form of social organization that in due course brought an end to incentive and opportunity for further change.

The plantation system of the Old South was centered on the extended family unit; there was great pride in family lineage and family honor, and the status of the family became the major motif. Although each family was comparatively self-sufficient and spatially isolated, social isolation was precluded by the existence of a castelike interfamily organization—a community of families from neighboring plantations who had comparable economic and social position and who on the one hand held themselves aloof from all social inferiors and on the other visited back and forth and intermarried among themselves. This social elite had informal but rigid rules of membership and norms of conduct, and it imposed strong control over each constituent family unit and every individual member. In this social context it was at the least unseemly for a plantation owner to think of deviating from the traditional ways, technological as well as organizational; and one who dared to undertake some new method of cultivating the soil or of handling his slaves would have fared no better than would the humbler farmer of a European or British village. In fact, few seem to have ventured anything new; for between 1750 and the advent of the Civil War the agriculture of the region changed in only one salient respect—from major dependence upon rice cultivation to major dependence on cotton, with such attendant shifts as that in the location of plantations from river mouths to upriver situations.

What happened in the Middle Western states was very different. There a unique pattern of land usage evolved, mainly as a consequence of governmental control of the settlement of the land. Surveyors laid out the public lands, mainly unbroken plains, in a checkerboard fashion, into sections of a square mile each. Each of the early settlers, who usually claimed a section, and often in time gained ownership of it, built his homestead on one of the section sides, since roads, such as they were, followed section lines. As the better of the lands filled up with settlers and as cultivation became more intensive, sections were gradually broken up into quarters of 160 acres. By this time the practice of living in an isolated home had become traditional; and as the sections were quartered, each new farmer set up his establishment about as far away from his neighbors as he could. The result is that Middle Western farmers never have lived in village clusters, a fact that disturbs some rural sociologists who feel that isolated farm homesteads preclude the development of wholesome community feelings and activities. Perhaps they do, but they have certainly provided the individual farmer with an unusual degree of social isolation and, hence, freedom to follow his own inclinations, as distinct from community practices.

The residential isolation of the Middle Western farmer has been at least one of the factors, perhaps one of the most important, that have made for his technological progressiveness. The Middle Western farmer developed and put to general use the cradle scythe (its inventor is unknown), which has not even yet been accepted by the peasants of Europe; he rapidly adopted the McCormick reaper, the first mechanical one; and he was, as he still is, generally receptive to new seed strains, new crop plants, new breeding and feeding procedures, and the latest mechanical devices. In the course of half a century he converted the vast grasslands of the Mississippi Valley into the greatest breadbasket of the entire world; and in the half century since, his constant increasing of the productivity of this area has been a source of embarrassment to the American economy and the Congress of the United States.

The flat and fertile land of the Middle West made it possible for the new agricultural techniques to be used, but the ability of the farmer to adopt them as they became available to him was mainly due to an accident of residential distribution. Isolated both spatially and socially from his fellows, a farmer could try out something new without arousing community resistance. Should he wish to, he could even experiment secretly with a new seed or a new type of plowing and reveal his venture only if it proved to be effective. Moreover, the fact that he did not gather daily with his peers and compare experiences meant that he was not continually being reeducated in traditional agricultural practices and that he was comparatively free from community discouragements to experimentation. No doubt freedom of this order had its disadvantages for the individual, and many ventures must have been ill-fated. There was constant risk that the individual might fail through ignorance and the lack of wise counsel, and his life was no doubt to some extent a lonely one. The long-run social advantage, however, was enormous. Whereas the Southern plantation system began to stagnate almost as soon as it reached its full development, Middle Western agriculture continued to be and has continued to be about as enterprising, as technologically progressive, as it was during the first years that the area was settled. There have come first and most extensively the many changes that constitute the really great agricultural revolution, a revolution that has liberated the majority of the American people from bondage to the soil and has enabled them to contribute to the urbanization and industrialization of American society.

11 *Stratification, Mobility, and Urbanization*

In a completely stable society, every individual would live out his life and die in the place of his birth—village, farm, town, or city; and at birth he would inherit not only his family membership but also the class, occupational, and other social positions that he would occupy throughout his life. In the course of time he would progress from one age role to another—from infant to child to youth to adult, and, should he live long enough, to elder; but in all other respects his life would be as stable as the society of which he was a part. No actual society has ever achieved complete stability, which has been regarded as the ideal social condition by countless utopians from Confucius to Marx; yet every society, including our own, has evidenced constant tendencies to move in the direction of stability.

One of the stabilizing factors in a society, one that is often in concordance with family and community organization, is a rigid stratification of the social population into the sexes and into differentiated classes, differentiated occupations, and in some instances differentiated ethnic or religious categories. Such stratification tends to tie the individual to the various categories in which he finds himself at birth and to prevent him, or at the very least discourage him, from changing his position by his own efforts. Rigid stratification discourages social mobility in much the same way that familism discourages spatial mobility, with the indirect but sociologically significant consequence of resisting and retarding social change.

SOCIAL STRATIFICATION

Literal-minded adherents to democratic ideology (and, ironically, those remaining idealists who subscribe to Marxian philosophy) profess to believe that in the good society all men are equal. A social system can, no doubt, assure equality of *oppor-*

tunity in some few respects—it can, for example, assure all adults the right to vote and all children the right to attend public school; but it cannot be—or at least no known social system ever has been—in any general way equalitarian. Any kind of social organization involves differentiation of some sort, if only that of distinguishing between those who belong and those who do not and that of separating those who belong into such functional categories as leaders and followers.

Although differentiation of the population into social strata exists in all societies, systems of stratification vary widely in form and may also change through time, as do the bases for differentiation and the degree to which strata are functionally integrated. Perhaps the most general basis for differentiation is sex; everywhere societies divide the members on the basis of sex, and each sex has a distinctive subculture, a more or less clearly defined place in the social system, special economic and other functions, and special role relationships with others of that sex and with those of the opposite sex. In no society is there ever any real doubt as to which sex category an individual belongs or is it ever difficult to determine whether a man or a woman is adhering to the norms of the appropriate sex subculture or behaving in accordance with the proper sex role. By so little as a single feminine gesture, a feminized male can reveal himself as belonging to the despised third sex category and thereby damn himself in the eyes of his society. The differentiation of the members of a society into occupational, class, religious, or ethnic strata may be less obvious; but it is often quite as categorical. In a rigid class system, for example, no one can fail to know and keep to the particular class position—whether high or low—that he occupies; and no one can fail to recognize him as one who belongs in that position.

The system of stratification of a society is a more or less fundamental and essential aspect of its organizational component, its central function being that of providing a workable division of labor—the term "labor" being used in a very broad sense of the word.[1] How well it serves this central func-

[1] The universality and functional bases for sex, age, and occupational differentiation are seldom questioned by sociologists; but the idea that the division of the members of a society into socioeconomic classes is also universal and has its functional bases offends those, including sociologists, who have a strong equalitarian bias. A clear and unequivocal statement of the functional view by K. Davis in 1949 (*Human Society*, The Macmillan Company, New York, pp. 366–377) inaugurated a debate over the matter that is still in progress. For a summary of this controversy see Egon E. Bergel, *Social Stratification*, McGraw-Hill Book Company, New York, 1962, pp. 25–32. The most recent contributions to the controversy are Wilbert E. Moore, "But Some Are More Equal than Others," *American Sociological Review*, vol. 28, pp. 13–18, February, 1963; and Melvin Tumin, "On Inequality," *American Sociological Review*, vol. 28, pp. 19–26, February, 1963.

tion, however, is dependent upon how appropriate the system is to its particular context; and changes in the context have often made a given class or other stratum, or indeed the entire system of stratification, dysfunctional. The landed aristocracy of eighteenth-century France may have been, as French revolutionaries claimed, useless social parasites; but in earlier times and under different conditions they had served as the managerial class of French society with an important function to fulfill.

Those who belong to a given social stratum do not constitute a group in the same sense that the members of a family, tribe, village, labor union, or even political party do. Who can belong may be rigorously defined; yet no definite limits may be set on how many can belong. All the male members of the society belong to the masculine segment of the society, although they never operate as an organizational entity and their belonging consists mainly in their sharing certain recognizably masculine cultural characteristics. Groups, formal or informal, may be formed among those who belong to a stratum, as is the case when the socially elite families of a locality close ranks against commoners by living in an exclusive residential section, when members of a professional class establish an association, when workers form a union, or when college girls join into a sorority. But a stratum as a whole may seldom if ever act in concert; and those who belong to it are invariably members of a number of specific groups—family, community, religious, corporate, etc.— that may conflict one with another. Attachment to a given stratum can, however, be exceedingly important to the individual, as a Negro will find when he enters any association of whites, as a man will be painfully aware when he visits a women's dress shop, as a civilian realizes when he loses his way on a military reservation, and as a workingman will be made to understand should he dare to take a short cut through the lobby of the Waldorf Hotel.

Whatever the bases for its particular strata—sex, age, position at birth, occupation, etc.—and whatever its particular form, a system of stratification is the most general and the least specific kind of social organization. Nevertheless, the subcultural norms of each of the various strata may be as compelling as are those of any established group—such as the family—and may, therefore, operate as an effective barrier to social change. Generally speaking, it may be said that, other things being equal, the more clearly and rigidly stratified the social population, the less likelihood there is that individuals will innovate, advocate, or adopt changes in the existing technology, ideology, or organization.

Ascription to Strata

The most rigid system of stratification is that which results when every individual is ascribed to a particular stratum at birth in terms of his ethnic identity, the occupation of his father, or the class position of his family and his status or position cannot be changed by any action of the individual himself.

The ascribing of individuals to particular strata has perhaps most commonly occurred on the basis of class. A hereditary class system existed in many ancient societies, for example, Egyptian and Greek, where it was usually associated with political and economic slavery; it has been an integral part of all feudalistic societies; it seems to have reached maximal development in the caste system of premodern India; and elements of it have persisted into modern times in the form of hereditary titles.

Ascription of individuals to occupational strata, with of course class implications, has been very common in primitive societies, where magical powers, military skills and techniques, and tribal chieftainship have often been passed down the family line from father to son. Ascription to a special stratum within a society on the basis of religious or ethnic identity has been even more common. In old China, for example, the majority of the people were Confucians and traced their lineage, validly or not, back to the time of the Middle Kingdom; but there were also a number of distinct minorities, of which the Mohammedans, raisers of beef and tanners of leather, were over the centuries most effectively kept in their place. Whether they represented a different ethnic strain or were simply Chinese converts to Mohammedanism is not clear; but they constituted a definite stratum and had a subculture that was in some salient respects different from that of the true sons of Han. The Jews have constituted a somewhat comparable and equally unenviable stratum in Western societies since the early Middle Ages; and even today the status of Jew, like that of American Negro, once ascribed, is exceedingly difficult to evade.

Monopolization

Systems of stratification in which the status of the individual is a matter of ascription are usually considered to be closed, whereas those in which status is the result of individual endeavor are regarded as open. In actuality, however, no system is every wholly open; for with rare and limited exceptions, those who constitute any particular stratum tend always to close their ranks against outsiders and to strive to monopolize their position. This is especially true of strata which are, in terms of the values of the society, highly rewarding; but those who constitute any stratum above that of the very lowest also struggle to protect themselves from invasion from below. Thus the domestic slaves of the South, those who worked in plantation households, were often very jealous of their position; low though it was, it was considerably better, in terms of status, work conditions, and material rewards, than was that of the field slaves.

The methods by which those who constitute a given stratum endeavor to secure and hold a monopoly over the special rights and privileges and distinctive characteristics of their position have varied with time and circumstance; but in all instances the effort to restrict admission to the stratum has led to the establishment and maintenance of strict selective criteria. The result, when successful, is the negation of the principle of achievement and the institution of a quasi-ascription procedure in the admission of individuals to the stratum. Currently members of the upper classes of Western societies work toward closing their ranks and monopolizing their privileges by such means as the establishment of trusts for family wealth to protect the financial status of their descendants, and by such informal and not very effective devices as sending their children to presumably exclusive schools and universities. Some of the labor unions have achieved what amounts to a system of ascription to occupational position by rigorous limitation of membership and a tacit understanding that the sons of members are to be given priority for admission as apprentices; and there is some tendency, especially in England and European countries, for the medical profession to recruit its new members from medical families. The same tendency toward monopoly and the closing of ranks against outsiders exists to greater or lesser degree in all modern occupations, within some, but not all, classes, within ethnic and religious majorities, and in the whole of the male stratum of the population. Although the profound change in the status of women that has been occurring over the past century in all Western societies, and most markedly in America, has given women a growing freedom from economic dependence upon their fathers and husbands, and with it considerable liberation from the constraints that were imposed by the old sex subculture and the subordinate position in law and in personal relations, men in general, if not husbands in particular, have staunchly resisted the invasion by women into their occupations. They have tried, with modest success, to keep women occupationally segregated in business and industry and to keep them out of the more rewarding and prestigious professions or at least to hold their numbers to a token. Thus a woman may teach primary and even secondary school, and she may work in scientific or other research positions; but she is rather effectively excluded from the professorial ranks of colleges and universities. A woman may sing in a choir or even become an operatic star; but she has almost no opportunity to become a successful composer, concertmaster, or jazz musician—these are still male prerogatives. A woman may, against considerable resistance, become a successful dermatologist or psychiatrist; but there is little chance for her to achieve note as a surgeon or diagnostician—such prestigious roles are almost all reserved for men by men.[2]

[2] That there has occurred over the past century a profound change in the status of women in America, but that women are still far from the economic equal of men, is demonstrated by Robert W. Smuts in *Women and Work in America,* Columbia University Press, New York, 1959. For comparative purposes see also Takashi Koyama, *The Changing Social Position of Women in Japan,* UNESCO Publishing Center, New York, 1961.

Stratum Isolation

To the extent that those who constitute a class, occupational, or other stratum succeed in closing their ranks against outsiders and in monopolizing the distinctive subculture of their position, they isolate themselves socially from the members and the subcultures of other strata. Social isolation of this sort is almost as effective a barrier to social change as is spatial isolation; for it means that those who belong to the isolated stratum live and move mainly among their own kind and gain slight, if any, understanding of the problems of those of other strata and hence have little ability to solve those problems, should they wish to do so, which is rarely the case. Moreover, such isolation tends to preclude their adopting into the norms of their own stratum cultural elements that are operative elsewhere.[3]

Numerous factors, some of which have been indicated, have contributed to the technological conservatism of English and European agriculture. In England one of the more important of these has been the tenant-farmer system, which, like that which has prevailed in our Southern states since the Civil War, has created a hiatus between the owners and managers of agricultural land and those who actually work on it. Since the industrial revolution, many English landowners have been men who were reasonably progressive as industrialists but who, however progressive they might have been in their management of business or industry, once having adopted the prestigious role of landed gentry, have shown slight inclination to apply their ingenuity to the improvement of the tools and procedures by which their land is cultivated. In part, at least, this disinclination has stemmed from their ignorance of and general disinterest in the problems of their tenants.

Most social elites, whose presumed function has been that of political, economic, or other management, have probably known little and understood even less of the life and circumstances of the lower classes. What au-

---

[3] Sociologists have made little effort to analyze the ways in which social stratification isolates the members of one stratum from those of the other strata, but there is no dearth of descriptive material upon which to base such analysis. In *The Analysis of Social Change* (Cambridge University Press, New York, 1945), for example, Godfrey Wilson and Monica Wilson show how tribalism produces a kind of stratifying isolation among the people of modern Africa; Stanley Elkins describes in *Slavery: A Problem in American Institutional and Intellectual Life* (The University of Chicago Press, Chicago, 1959) the isolation of white and Negro society in the pre-Civil War South and how it provided a basis for the ethnic stratification which has persisted, with only slight modification, down to the present day; and Simone de Beauvoir provides in *The Second Sex* [M. M. Parshley (trans.), Alfred A. Knopf, Inc., New York, 1953] a detailed description of the segregation of the sexes in France and of the resulting isolation of women in a special and narrow world apart from that of men.

thority they have actually exercised over the lower classes has therefore probably been exercised mainly in terms of traditional preconceptions rather than the actual needs of those classes. The novels of an earlier day, when the gap between the elite and the commoners was sharp and unbridgeable, abound with descriptions of misguided good intentions on the part of members of the elite—of the Lady Bountifuls who assumed that a basket of food would solve the problems of poverty; of the idealistic gentlemen who imagined that a helping hand would save a slum girl from a life of sin; etc.[4] For the most part, social elites have lived a life apart from and indifferent to that of their social inferiors; and wherever those of a social elite have made an effort to improve the lot of a lower class, they have generally done so with profound ignorance of the realities of lower-class life. It is for this reason that so many of the reformistic movements, political and otherwise, of the eighteenth and nineteenth centuries, most of which were initiated by members of the upper class, were so fantastically unrealistic.

Social isolation of occupational strata has probably been an even more effective barrier to change, especially technological change, than that of class strata. The ability and willingness of the producers of goods to adapt to the interests and needs of merchants, and hence indirectly of consumers, has always been considerably less than perfect and has at times approached zero. The unwillingness, in part the result of ignorance, of the textile guilds of preindustrial England to supply in quantity the kinds of cloth salable in the Indian market has already been described; and although the textile industry of Lancaster evolved to provide what the guilds could not, it in turn came to be insensitive for long periods to changing market demands. Even today, the ability of industrial producers to adjust to the market is far from perfect; for a good ten years (from 1950 to 1960), for example, the American automobile industry ignored the growing evidences that the

[4] Of the nineteenth-century novelists who wrote about the lower classes for the entertainment and edification of the middle and upper classes, Charles Dickens had the greatest success in England and Victor Hugo in France. Dickens was especially given to long and detailed descriptions of the appearance, manners, and mode of life of his lower-class characters. This seems to reflect his unwillingness to assume that his readers would have any knowledge and understanding of the kind of people about whom he was writing. In this he was no doubt entirely correct; for although an interest in the lower classes had developed, the English middle and upper classes probably knew more about tribal life in Africa than about that of their serving girls and plumbers. The very considerable attention that was aroused by the detailed descriptions of lower-class life in Charles Booth's *Life and Labour of the People of London* (1891) indicates both that interest and the extent to which the upper classes, including intellectuals, were isolated from the lower classes.

American market wanted smaller and less expensive rather than larger and more expensive automobiles.

In recent times social isolation of occupational strata has been very marked in certain professions, especially law, medicine, and the military. Since at least the time of the flintlock gun, professional military men have been dependent upon industry for arms; and yet they have seldom taken full advantage of industrial technology and have repeatedly frustrated the efforts of inventors and manufacturers to improve the efficiency of arms production by simplifying design, standardizing parts, etc. To some extent, this resistance to change on the part of the professional military has come from their traditional isolation from the larger society.[5] The almost categorical estrangement of the officer class from those who do the actual fighting has had somewhat similar consequences, consequences that are reflected in the military saying that sergeants win battles and generals lose wars. Medical practitioners have often long remained aloof from and ignorant of the findings of biological scientists; and in many instances a scientific discovery that might have been applied to practice was ignored because the discoverer was a Ph.D. rather than an M.D. An equal and equally inhibiting social isolation of medical practitioners from nurses, technicians, and others who deal directly with the ill exists today, as it did a hundred years ago and five hundred years ago. Medical schools are currently trying to lessen the social isolation of physicians from those with whom and on whom they practice by the introduction into their curricula of such broadening courses as medical sociology; but against these and related efforts is the long-run trend toward the differentiation of hospital nursing personnel into three or more grades of nurses.

One of the clearer historical evidences of the way in which social isolation of occupational strata may retard technological change is the effect that occupational differentiation of the sexes has had in delaying changes in domestic technology. For a variety of reasons, the homes in which women have had to do their work have been designed as well as constructed by men, and to some extent they still are; and since men were until recently excused from domestic labor and somewhat contemptuous of it, they seem seldom to have applied themselves to the rationalization of the house and its usages. At any event, domestic architecture and kitchen and other domestic appliances changed slowly, far more slowly than did the techniques of factory, shop, and office. For example, in 1940 as in 1840, the standard height of kitchen sinks, work surfaces, and washbowls in America was 36 inches, although during that century the average height of adult American

[5] For material on the isolation of the military officer corps from other segments of American society see Morris Janowitz, *Sociology and the Military Establishment*, Russell Sage Foundation, New York, 1959; and C. Wright Mills, *The Power Elite*, Oxford University Press, Fair Lawn, N.J., 1956.

women had increased by about 5 inches. In recent years American architects have endeavored to design functionally efficient kitchens, and industry has provided the American housewife with a battery of well-designed tools. But in Britain and Europe, where the division of labor between the sexes, with a consequent occupational estrangement of the sexes, has been slower to break down, even the more modern house is a monument to domestic inefficiency; and what effective appliances a housewife does have available to her are mostly American inventions and are often produced by European subsidiaries of American industry.

Stratum Centricity

The tendency for any stratum to isolate itself from the life of those of other strata is fostered by, and at the same time leads to, a stratumcentric contentment with its own subculture. Social isolation of a stratum tends to insulate it from criticism from without—to keep it unaware of contrasts and contradictions; and stratum centricity tends to protect it from criticism from within. The respective roles of these two factors in preserving subcultural stability varies from case to case; thus the comparative stability of criminal culture seems to result mainly from the stratumcentric regard of criminals for their style of life, for the criminal class can hardly fail to be aware that its activities are adversely regarded by most noncriminals. On the other hand, an established social elite has often been quite unaware that it was not being accepted at its own value by the other classes until some overt action of rebellion has breached its smug complacence.

The ways in which a stratum may achieve and maintain stratumcentric qualities are well illustrated by the professions in contemporary America. Every one of our professions, not excluding the scientists, tends to generate stratumcentric attributes—to consider that what those of the profession do and what they represent is of primary social importance; to believe that the theories, techniques, devices, etc., that have currency in the profession are the best, if not the ultimate; and those who belong support one another in so believing, however much they may quarrel about minutiae. Such beliefs are perhaps essential to the maintenance of *esprit de corps* within the profession. They may even be necessary for the recruitment of new members; for example, unless the teachers of sociology believe in the achievements of sociology, they will not encourage bright young men to undertake the study of this discipline.

One of the most ingrown of the current professions is that of the professional educators. In the course of half a century they have developed a monolithic system of recruitment and training and a subculture that is as distinctive and integrated as are those that have evolved over a number of centuries among physicians and lawyers. Through it the professional educators make reasonably certain that no one who has not been effectively indoctrinated into the educationist subculture will gain admission to their ranks, that any member who deviates from the approved values and standards can be shuttled into some harmless provincial post, and that they themselves can be kept insulated from the criticisms of outsiders, including scholars and scientists. The various schools of education are not formally integrated; the relationship between the profession and the political agencies which in fact enforce professional standards, such as state accrediting bureaus, is more covert than overt; and the standards of the profession are implicit rather than explicit. Nevertheless, the educationists (as they prefer to be called) of the United States are almost as isolated, almost as closed and self-validating a stratum, and, consequently, almost as resistant to significant changes in educational philosophy or pedagogical techniques as is the Roman Catholic Church to changes in theological doctrine. Those who actually administer and teach in the public schools are usually forced by local circumstances and the demands of expediency to deviate somewhat from the educationist party line, even as parish priests must often bend Church dogma and rule to parish needs. Those who teach education in the schools of education, however, operate largely in a social vacuum and in terms of their own subcultural values, sentiments, and professional interests. They have, necessarily, their own closed-circle literature; and if any of them read what noneducationists write, it does not show in their own writings. They have, inevitably, their own societies and associations; and what transpires in them has no discernible relation to the world outside. And they have a profound and reassuring contempt for the substantive scholarly disciplines; for they firmly believe that if a teacher knows how to teach, she can teach what she does not know.

Strata Rites and Ceremonials

A part of the apparatus of an established and more or less closed stratum, whether class, occupational, or otherwise, is a complex of rites and ceremonials that engage the attention of those who constitute the stratum, draw off their surplus energies, and provide harmless channels of intrastratum rivalry. The basic function of these rites and ceremonials is, perhaps, that of maintaining cohesion and fostering high morale; but they also serve to discourage the individual from innovative endeavor of any sort, for they keep him preoccupied with the minutiae of such activities and preempt his time. There is probably an inverse relationship between the truly functional work demanded of those who belong to a given stratum and the amount of time and effort that they are required to devote to rites and ceremonials. Thus a modern physician devotes a high proportion of his day to the treatment of the ill and very little to ceremonial activities, while a modern priest does just the reverse; most of his time is absorbed in prayer and other religious rites and a very small part of it goes into direct labors with his parishioners. A leisure class, such as the so-called idle rich, may actually have little leisure; for the norms of the class may require those who belong to it to participate in a constant round of activities, all of which are supposed to be essential to the maintenance of class position.

Since free time and freedom from social responsibilities are prerequisite to innovative endeavor and only slightly less essential to advocacy and adoption, the rites and ceremonials of a stratum contribute in an indirect way to the maintenance of the *status quo*. A man who is fully occupied with attending and giving parties, with participating in pseudocharitable activities, with sports competitions, with attending the marriage and other rites of his friends and acquaintances in full formal regalia or, in the more modern manner, with participating in conferences, conventions, and committees will hardly have time to contemplate the state of his class or occupation; and should he attempt to do so, he will quickly be distracted by the urgencies of some more immediate demands on his attention.

Stratum Position and Individual Motivation

Moreover, to the extent that a stratum is closed and its subculture stable, those who belong to it will not be motivated to inaugurate or to adopt changes of any sort. Just as the extended family produced in its members those kinds of motivations and degrees of motivation that were appropriate to family membership, so does a class or other stratum generate in those who belong to it only those motivations and associated interests and other personality attributes that are appropriate to the position of the stratum in the system of stratification. Even the subculture of an established slave class may be fairly successful in reconciling each slave to his humble and arduous position. Certainly habitual thieves consider theft the proper means of securing a livelihood and for the most part have none of the hopes and aspirations common to more honest men. At the most, the ambitions of a thief do not extend beyond becoming recognized among his own kind as an exceptionally skillful and successful thief; he is hardly likely to consider as enviable the status of the successful novelist, the recognized scientist, the acknowledged inventor, or the noted reformer. Any such status achievement is, in his eyes, petty, foolish, and unrewarding, a foible of those who are not smart enough to live by their wits. For much the same reasons a modern woman is sometimes unsympathetic toward her husband's preoccupation with getting ahead in his business or profession, since even today most women are motivated toward family and domestic activities in accordance with the sex subculture of times past.

To the extent that the individual's position is ascribed, or even quasi-ascribed, there is, furthermore, no incentive for that individual, should he be so motivated, either to exceed the stratum norms or to digress from them. Should he do so, should he venture to advocate some change in the activities or practices of the stratum, he would be subjected to pressures toward conformity; he would be punished, in either subtle or crass ways, and thereby discouraged in his endeavors to disturb the *status quo*. On the other hand, there would be no prospect for rewards, either psychological or material, for success in his deviant endeavors.

A closed system of stratification puts a premium on conformity to the established organizational, ideological, and technological norms of the class, occupation, sex, ethnic, or other stratum in much the same ways as did the extended family. It makes individual achievement a matter of superiority in conforming; and it precludes competition with those who belong to higher strata and eliminates the need for competition with those of lower strata. The lord of a medieval manor might take pride in the excellence of his pseudofeudal castle, in the superiority of the horses which he rode, etc., as some lords of the late medieval period certainly did; and he might perhaps have the ambition to become renowned among his fellow aristocrats as a deadly swordsman, an inexhaustible drinker, or something of the sort. But his class position bound him to the role of lord of the manor and made it quite unthinkable that he should devote his energies to such unconventional goals as the improvement of his vineyards or his pastures or the development of a more profitable way of merchandising the products of his land; and the fact that his peasants were bound by birth to their own humble class position meant that none could rise to compete with him for the position that he occupied.

Today there are few if any class or other positions that are equally secure and devoid of incentives to endeavor of an individual sort. Nevertheless, as will be shown in detail later, the drive toward stability is everywhere present; and in limited spheres it has made for at least a partial closure of strata, especially occupational strata. Thus a modern American plumber has little incentive and less opportunity to exert himself; his union and the informal norms of his craft set minimum standards of work and reward, and these are for the most part also the maximum. A plumber can work himself into the position of a plumbing contractor; but the incentive to do so is rather slight, if only because he would then have to employ and worry about those whom he hired. Because membership in the union is rigorously controlled and the jurisdiction of plumber jealously guarded, he need not compete with the members of other crafts or with ambitious upstarts. As a consequence, modern plumbers, like the lords and peasants of another day, go about their affairs in conventional ways and in no hurry, conforming to, rather than attempting to deviate from, the techniques, production norms, and other subcultural characteristics of the plumbers of America.

Channelized Mobility

No system of stratification has operated so effectively that it has been able to prevent the rise of occasional individuals who are ambitious to transcend the limits of the class and other strata to which they have been ascribed or to preclude them from disturbing the *status quo*. The various strata of the more stable social systems seem, in fact, to have included organizational mechanisms for dealing with such potentially disturbing individuals, some more or less traditionalized procedures for diverting their attention and efforts into noncreative, socially acceptable channels.

During the Middle Ages, for example, the Church provided channelized occupational opportunities for ambitious men in the monastic life and in advancement up the ranks of the Church hierarchy. A man who entered a monastery might rise to the position of abbot, but in the process he would do nothing to change either the nature of monastic life or the society at large. The more ambitious of churchmen could, and many did, become bishops, and a few could even become cardinals; but they advanced up the Church hierarchy by exceptional conformity to organizational norms rather than by creative endeavor. Later the Church added the opportunity for advancement via missionary work in foreign lands. But although a missionary might disturb the culture of the natives whom he tried to convert, he was removed as a potential irritant from the home scene; thus any effects that he might have on the Church in Rome were indirect and unforeseen.

Religious channels of upward mobility clearly did not draw off all the ambitious men that medieval society produced; some turned their efforts to political achievement, some to the making of war, and a few to the development of commerce, the arts, and the beginnings of science. It is safe, however, to infer that if the Church had not provided such socially undisturbing opportunities to advancement as the monastic life, cathedral building, and other channelized ways to success, medieval society would have been far more dynamic than it was. Old Chinese society well illustrates how effective fixed channels of mobility can be in absorbing the energies of enterprising men. In that society there were two main ways, both highly traditionalized, by which an ambitious individual could improve his status without disturbance to the *status quo*. One way, the one that was most approved, was via the examination system.[6] Through scholarship, which was defined as ability to

[6] See Chang Chung-Li, *The Chinese Gentry: Studies on Their Role in Nineteenth-Century Chinese Society*, University of Washington Press, Seattle, Wash., 1955.

perform intellectually in conformity with Confucian ideology, a man might rise from the humble position of peasant to the exalted one of mandarin in the government service. The examination system operated to assure that only the most conventional and intellectually disciplined men would enter government service; hence governmental bureaucracy was by and large internally efficient, stable, and uncorruptible. Government service was a channel of upward mobility; through it ambitious and hypermotivated men could satisfy their ambitions, and by it they were prevented from exercising initiative and so disturbing the *status quo*. As a system of law and order, however, it evidently failed upon occasion; for in some times and places another, quite unofficial, channel of social advancement existed—brigandage. When and where the local representatives of the government exceeded social tolerances—when too many of their legal judgments ran counter to local opinion, when their tax levies were too far in excess of the people's ability to pay, etc—some bright and ruthless young man might muster a gang of his own and set about plundering the governmental officials and their soldiers and perhaps in the end murdering them. If he could then win the tacit support of the local citizens—if, that is to say, his extralegal rule cost the community less than had that of the official government—he was well on his way to becoming a war lord. It was through the rise of bandits to unofficial rule of municipalities, regions, and even provinces that the official government was kept in check and overly ambitious—i.e., too greedy or too adventurous—governmental officials were disposed of. Depending upon the circumstances, the official government would in time either make peace with a successful bandit or send in sufficient troops to restore its own authority. In the long run, this dual and mutually offsetting system of channelized mobility seems to have discouraged any persistent individual violation of the political principles sanctioned by Confucian ideology; at any event, the politics of China remained almost unchanged from the ninth to the nineteenth century.

OPEN STRATA AND SOCIAL CHANGE

The system of stratification that existed during the Middle Ages was in all respects—in terms of class, sex, occupational, and other strata—more closed than open. Some few individuals did through their own efforts change their class, their occupational, their regional, and even at times their religious positions. Social mobility was not, therefore, unknown; and the efforts of individuals to improve their status no doubt sometimes took forms that made for minor changes in the social system. Until the fifteenth century, however, both social mobility and social change would seem to have been rare. At least on a comparative basis, the rise in the rates of change that began in that century was rapid and significant, a number of key innovations and discoveries occurred, and a number of enterprising men made their appearance. Gutenberg invented printing from movable types, Luther revolted from the Church, Columbus discovered the Americas, Galileo charted the heavens, Machiavelli wrote the first realistic analysis of the political process, etc. The period of the Renaissance, as well as that of the Reformation which overlapped it, was one of great social ferment; during this time came the invention of the large sailing ship and the world explorations that followed on it, the breakdown of the monopoly of the Church on the written word, the secularization of the rediscovered knowledge of the ancients, the beginnings of science, the emergence of peaceful trade as an important economic phenomenon, and new impetus to and directions in architecture, graphic art, and music.

To some extent, no doubt, this apparent burst of enterprise was the culmination of changes that had long been under way and that had been overlooked or ignored by the historians of the time. But it is clear from the historical record that the mobility of persons, both social and spatial, which accompanied the rapid changes of the fifteenth and sixteenth centuries was unprecedented. Many of the known contributors to the changes that were being worked in Western society, such as Gutenberg and Luther, were men of comparatively humble origins; and many of them had migrated, as had Columbus, from the regions of their birth. Moreover, descriptions of life in the centers of change, such as Florence and Venice, leave no doubt that the attachments of individuals to family, class, and other organizations and strata were blurred and conflicting and that high status was frequently achieved by individual enterprise, the forms of which ranged, apparently, from fratricide to excellence in trade or the arts.

Although the relation between the openness of the system of stratification and social change is not a direct one of cause and effect, a partial correlation exists between social mobility and social change. Social change presupposes social mobility and at the same time produces mobility. Thus the development of the large sailing ship provided the means for Columbus and the other world explorers to gain esteem, if not wealth, by venturing out over the seas; and the discovery of new lands provided the opportunity for venturesome soldiers to become conquistadors and for equally venturesome merchants to become merchant princes.

There is reason to think, however, that an entirely fortuitous factor— the sharp decline in population and displacement of persons that came about as the result of recurrent plagues, particularly those of the fifteenth century—helped during the later Middle Ages to break down class and other strata barriers and to weaken the bonds of family and community life, thus facilitating both social and spatial mobility. The Black Death was, as has been mentioned, a consequence of antecedent changes in the technology and social organization of Western peoples. In turn, it disturbed the existing social order by destroying noble families, by leaving many individuals without family attachments, by causing many towns and cities to be evacuated, by increasing the cost of labor because of its scarcity value, etc. The chaos that followed on the plagues—the breakdown of normal life, the decline in productivity, the migrations of people away from and then back to their homes—must also have provided the more vigorous and ambitious of the survivors with unprecedented opportunities for personal advancement in political, economic, or other walks of life. It constituted a break in the continuity of medieval society; and while it may not have made all men equal, it did in many instances reduce the importance of preplague ascription of individuals to strata. Thus as the survivors returned to a town or city that had been more or less completely evacuated for a decade or two, a baker's apprentice might step into the occupational role left vacant by the baker's death, a former servant might claim the estate left vacant by the death of his master and his master's family, and a municipal clerk might proclaim himself successor to the mayor, long deceased. In these and in countless other ways, ambitious and ingenious individuals may well have broken from their traditional class and occupational positions to achieve new and higher ones and in the process, perhaps, work some small changes in their society. The possibility of upward social mobility often, perhaps always, exists in times of social chaos, whether that chaos be produced by war or revolution or some act of nature.

The Rise of the Bourgeois Class

Fostered by change, which was accelerated perhaps by the plagues that in turn facilitated further social change, there began during the fifteenth century, particularly in the non-Mediterranean parts of Europe, the gradual emergence of a new class of persons. These were men who were not attached either by birth or by cultural ties to any of the traditional class strata; they were the men, or the descendants of the men, who had been taking advantage of the opportunities for individual advancement that the change and chaos of the fifteenth century afforded, and who were, in their turn, through their individual enterprise working further changes in their society.[7]

[7] Where a bourgeois class did not emerge, as in Italy and Spain, there was little change in other aspects of social organization, of technology, and of ideology. In *The Forgotten Class: The Russian Bourgeoisie from the Earliest Beginnings to 1900* (Frederick A. Praeger, Inc., New York, 1959) Valentine T. Brill describes the conditions in premodern Russia that discouraged the rise of a class of enterprising men and thereby delayed the adoption of Western industrial techniques and forms of political and social organization. For various aspects of the historical emergence of the bourgeois class in Western societies see Elinor G. Barber, *The Bourgeoisie in Eighteenth Century France*, Princeton University

The roots of this newly emerging class no doubt went deep; and precursors must have made their appearance occasionally in the centuries preceding. It was not until the fifteenth century, however, that their numbers became sufficient to give them any collective power in Western society; and it was not until then that there emerged the ideology, the Protestant ethic, that provided the rationale for what they represented and the system of organization, the Protestant churches, that gave them some semblance of class cohesion and an agency through which they could as a class exercise influence on social affairs.

The rise and historical role of the Protestant ethic as a codification of the values and sentiments of the men who were, by violating tradition and through independence and self-reliance, making piecemeal changes in the culture of Western society has already been discussed. The historical happenstance that these values and sentiments came to be associated with a revitalized version of Christian theology is no more than that; they might more logically have come to be identified with Judaism, for through much of the Middle Ages many of the enterprising men—traders, moneylenders, and early men of science—were Jews.[8] But the Jews were an alien people, set

---

Press, Princeton, N.J., 1955; Sylvia L. Thrupp, *The Merchant Class of Medieval London,* The University of Chicago Press, Chicago, 1948; and Bernard Bailyn, *The New England Merchants in the Seventeenth Century,* Harvard University Press, Cambridge, Mass., 1955. The latter describes the way in which a new class of enterprising merchants—including those who engaged in the slave trade—rose to displace and replace the established elite of Puritanical New England society.

[8] The role of the Jews in the recent history of Western society has been much debated. One theory has it that they brought from Arab lands to the West the intellectual heritage of antiquity and were responsible for the intellectual awakening that eventually undermined the authority of the Roman Church; another is that they introduced to the West the arts of trade, of a money economy, and of individual economic endeavor. The first theory is based upon the fact that among the Arabs Jews were for a time granted special privileges as scribes and scholars and that the tradition of scholarship became deeply embedded in Jewish culture. But this theory overlooks the fact that, although there were exceptions, such as the subordination of theology to mathematics, astronomy, medicine, and philosophy by the Spanish Jews of the tenth century, Jewish scholarship tended to mean mastery of Talmudic law and that most Jewish intellectuals were until late in the Middle Ages preoccupied with the rituals of Jewish theology.

The idea that it was the Jews who introduced to the West the trading and other economic arts that were prerequisite to the emergence of modern Western society has been elaborately developed by Werner Sombart in *The Jews and Modern Capitalism* [M. Epstein (trans.), The Free Press of Glencoe, New York, 1951]. His central thesis is that the Jews are, presumably for biological reasons, more rational than the ordinary run of men and that it was by the application of

apart culturally and held apart politically from the body of European society. What they were and what as enterprising men they represented could not, therefore, gain social sanction, most particularly ideological sanction. Thus it was that the values and sentiments of individual enterprise became officially attached to Protestantism rather than Judaism and that organizational and ideological support was accorded to non-Jews—to those individual Christians who found in the Protestant rebellion from the established Church a religious justification for furthering their personal interests.

Just how important a role Protestantism and the Protestant churches played in the formation of a class out of the discrete individuals who were engaged in enterprising endeavors is impossible to ascertain. Protestantism did lend ideological sanction to individual enterprise and thus provided a sort of ideological bond between the various men who were engaged in enterprising endeavors; and the churches offered them a place for gathering together and a tangible symbol of their shared values and sentiments. At the same time Protestantism provided a religious justification, as Judaism did for the Jews, for their being persecuted as a group by the guildsmen and others who found their own interests jeopardized by the changes that enterprising men were working in medieval society. The religious affinity of those who were engaged in enterprising endeavors made them collectively responsible for what each one did; and in France it was as Protestants, not as individual entrepreneurs, that they were massacred, legislated against, and even driven from the land.

In part, perhaps, because in France and to a lesser extent elsewhere they were subjected to religious persecution, it was not until the seventeenth century that the numbers of enterprising men were sufficient and their position in the social structure sufficiently strong for them to be specifically designated as a class, as the *bourgeoisie*. The term "bourgeois" originally denoted any member of a medieval borough—i.e., a townsman; but it came to be applied by French nonguild workingmen to their employers and was then gradually extended to include the entire class of persons who secured their livelihood by independent endeavor rather than, on the one hand, as hired workers or, on the other, as members of the landed aristocracy or one of the traditional occupational organizations—i.e., the craft and trade guilds, the Church, and the political and military organizations. The class therefore included, often no doubt in a rather tangential way, the growing numbers of physicians and lawyers, scribes, independent traders and manufacturers,

---

rational procedures to the production and distribution of economic values that they brought about the industrialization of Western society. An implied criticism of this single-factor, dogmatic view is provided by Max Weber in *General Economic History* [Frank H. Knight (trans.), The Free Press of Glencoe, New York, 1951].

bankers, scholars, and, no doubt, successful rogues of one sort and another.

Although the class acquired a name, and although most of its members were of the Protestant faith, it never did develop class consciousness in the Marxian sense of this term; and although the members developed something of their own style of life, including, as has been discussed, a special type of family organization, and took great pride in their status, they never succeeded in effectively closing their ranks and solidifying their membership. The reason is obvious—those of this class were highly individualistic, and their most distinctive quality was independence from organizational constraints.

The bourgeois class was from the outset an open class; and although cliques and communities of bourgeois often formed into closed enclaves within the larger society, their attempts to be exclusive were in the long run self-defeating; for as bourgeois persons insulated themselves from competition with those of other classes, they lost the incentives to individual achievement that had made them individually independent and enterprising. Thus their children, or their children's children, either graduated into one of the elites or sank into a lower-class position. Status as a member of the class was, by very definition of who constituted the *bourgeoisie,* mainly achieved, and achieved by enterprise rather than by advancement *up* an organizational hierarchy.

For some centuries the existence of a rewarding class position, vague and varied as it was, which individuals could attain by personal endeavor of an enterprising sort was one of the incentives to such endeavor; and through these centuries this was the one aspect of the system of social stratification of Western societies that encouraged rather than discouraged the working of social changes. Not all of the enterprise by which men gained and held membership in the class made for changes in the society; much of it consisted of excessive rather than innovative endeavor—of working harder, more skillfully, or more enduringly than normal; and some of it no doubt consisted only of taking credit for what others had done, together with the profits of their labors. But under these circumstances the chances that changes would occur were high, since at least one of the ways to success was through the invention or adoption of a more efficient method of production, a new product, a more efficient mode of organization, a new procedure for treating the ill, a new idea about nature, or anything else that was new and salable.

The Bourgeois Revolutions

The political revolutions of the eighteenth and nineteenth centuries were, as will be shown in detail later, a protest against the great body of legal constraints on individual enterprise, particularly in economic matters. That body of legal constraints adversely affected the *bourgeoisie*, for it gave legal support to the traditional and by then dysfunctional rights of the aristocrats and the landed gentry and to the monopolistic practices of the various craft and trade guilds. Bourgeois discontent with a governmental orientation that represented the aristocrats, guildsmen, and peasants had been long-standing; and that discontent had given rise to a variety of new political ideologies, including the Lockian contention that the king rules by consent, not divine right—that government is designed by man and can be remodeled when the need arises.

What may have precipitated the bourgeois revolt against the political *status quo* was the sharpening of social incongruencies that came with the technological developments that ushered in the industrial revolution. Particularly in England, but also in France and the American Colonies, those enterprising men who were endeavoring to apply industrial techniques to the productive processes found themselves hampered by the maze of legal controls over trade and productive activities, even as do their contemporary counterparts. The revolts that followed led to the establishment of new forms of government that more or less represented the *bourgeoisie* rather than tradition, and to the elevation of the *bourgeoisie* to a position of political dominance. For much of the nineteenth century most of the governments of Western Europe, France being the major exception, and those of North America were bourgeois in ideology and were more or less laissez-faire in practice. As a result, political support of closed classes—and, indeed, of closed sex and other strata—largely disappeared; and although the removal of legal and other reinforcement of custom did not mean the prompt or total disappearance of barriers to mobility, it did facilitate a gradual decline in the strength of the traditional system of stratification.

The long-run consequence was a general, if perhaps rather temporary, opening of the entire system of stratification. The traditional elites were opened for competition from below (even the British began to grant nonhereditary titles); and prospering industrialists began to buy and barge their way into the ranks of the pseudo aristocracy. The ancient tradition that a person of humble origin should stay in his humble place was eventually replaced by the ideal of the self-made man; and a variety of organizational devices, such as publicly supported schools, evolved to encourage and enable an ambitious and industrious lad to shake off the shackles of a low class and occupational status and achieve higher and more rewarding position. In effect, then, the open class ideals and practices of the *bourgeoisie* became the model for the entire system of stratification. Even the age-old distinction between the social role and personality characteristics of the sexes was in time disrupted; eventually women became in many respects equal to men before the law, eventually they were granted the right to a formal education, and eventually they gained some access to politics, business, and the professions.

Achievement of Status and the Principle of Reciprocity

The idea that status, occupational and otherwise, should be achieved rather than ascribed is historically atypical. In most times and places status has been a matter of birth or some other fixed criterion, and it still is in many places; and, as has been seen, the ascription of status is an important factor in the maintenance of social stability. Conversely, to the extent that status is a matter of achievement, social change rather than social stability will obtain, except in those instances where achievement is socially channelized into noncreative activities.

Where status is a matter of achievement, all individuals are subject to more or less constant stress; and those who fail to accomplish what is socially rewarding become, to some degree or other, social outcasts. Family and other group membership may cushion the personal consequences of failure; but there is no doubt that in a relatively open system of stratification personal insecurity is rather general throughout the society. Rather than automatically receiving social support in accordance with a traditional system, the individual is responsible for his own personal welfare; and what he gets from society is more or less in proportion to what he contributes to it. For where status is a matter of achievement, the principle of reciprocity operates.

In every social system there is a good deal of reciprocity; for it is impossible for any individual to get anything unless another gives it—whether what he gets is maternal care, prestige, wealth, or an elaborate headstone on his grave.[9] In a closed system of stratification, however, what is given in return for what and by whom is fixed; it is a matter of tradition, rather than of personal give-and-take. Thus a slave will be fed in return for his labors; and where slavery is institutionalized, a master will feel that the food which keeps his slave alive is a fair reward for the labor. That a master grows rich and lives in luxury and leisure will, under the slave system, seem no more than just; a master was born to rule and to reap the rewards of his position. Equally fixed are the exchanges between the individuals of different strata—class, sex, occupational, or otherwise—in any closed system of stratification. In general and over the long run, systems of this sort have functioned effectively; for if the contributions of the various strata of a society to the society had not been equal to what all the strata jointly had received from the society, the system would not have survived. But in par-

[9] The reciprocal nature of most social relationships is explored by George C. Homans in *Social Behavior: Its Elementary Forms*, Harcourt, Brace & World, Inc., New York, 1961.

ticular instances and in the short run, most generally when other aspects of the social system are undergoing change, reciprocity between classes or other strata tends to be replaced by exploitation—those who belong to one stratum may continue to secure the rights of their position without adequately fulfilling their obligations.

The comparatively open nature of the system of stratification that existed in Western societies during the nineteenth century tended to keep fluid what was exchanged (goods, services, etc.) between the various strata and the values of what was exchanged; for the openness of the system enabled most individuals to exercise some choice regarding what they would give in order to get. For example, a worker might decide, and many workers in fact did, that the wages offered were not commensurate with the labor demanded; an employer might conclude that a worker was not worth his hire; and a wife might come to feel that anything—even the degrading status of being divorced—was better than enduring the unsympathetic rule and harsh demands of her husband. Undoubtedly many of the choices so made were misguided, many led to personal disaster, and many were the consequence of irresponsible whim; but the fact that an individual was able to make some choice—to choose which candidate he would vote for, to quit his job, to change his occupation, or to set out after an elusive million dollars—meant that there would be some adjustment, if gradual and perhaps only partial, of stratum rights and obligations to changing conditions; it meant that any exploitation of one class by another, of one occupation by another, etc., would be gradually resolved by a withdrawal of individuals from the exploited stratum, and, conversely, that any stratum that was obviously receiving more than it contributed to society would be invaded by individuals from other strata. Thus under the conditions of constant technological and other change of this period the openness of the system of stratification tended to result in reciprocity, in a more or less equable exchange of values.

Change and the System of Stratification

That a relatively open system of stratification facilitates change in the other aspects of the society would seem fairly clear, but how change in these other aspects affects the system of stratification is much less apparent. There is undoubtedly a considerable degree of functional interdependence between the technology and the form of occupational stratification and some degree of functional interdependence between both and the form of class stratification. Slavery may have worked fairly well under conditions of hoe cultivation of single crops, such as rice, sugar, and cotton; and slave labor was effective in building pyramids and in rowing barges. But because it was so very inefficient and unreliable, it was uneconomic in the operation of small, diversified agricultural units; and it became both unnecessary and inexpedient when the galley gave way to the sailing ship. As has been intimated, the guild form of work organization, which appeared in such otherwise diverse civilizations as those of medieval Europe and old China, may have functioned fairly well in the production of handicraft goods; but it was rendered obsolete by changes in the techniques of production.

The emergence of machine methods of production eventually brought about the dissolution of the old craft guilds; their political power waned and with it their ability to monopolize production and markets; and since they produced at the highest rather than the lowest possible cost, they failed in competition with industrial producers. The individual entrepreneurs who eventually came to replace the guilds were dependent on a free labor market, which although it was not formally organized, involved considerable informal organization—the workers in each trade or craft in a locality had a kind of subcultural unity. As the industrial process became ever more complex and for technological and economic reasons the small factory, shop, or mine gave way to the great industrial complex, the effectiveness of the loosely organized free labor market seems to have declined; for with the growth in the size of productive enterprises, and later distributive enterprises, the buyers of labor, the employers, gained a local monopoly over workers; and in an effort to reestablish a balance, the workers eventually formed defensive units of formally organized workers—the early trade unions. The growth of these formal organizations in size, power, and aggressiveness over the past century was implemented by the technological and other changes that over the same period were fostering an ever-increasing concentration of economic powers in the hands of corporate employers.

Meanwhile, the same changes in technology, together with related changes in ideology and organization, progressively disturbed the functional effectiveness of all forms of occupational and class stratification and gave rise to new or modified forms. Within two centuries, the traditional elite, composed of the landed gentry and the remnants of the feudal aristocracy, was all but dispossessed by a new elite, consisting of the more successful business and industrial leaders—the capitalists of the Marxians. Recently this new elite has been joined, in a manner of speaking, by a neo-elite consisting of the more successful of the leaders of organized labor, and by a peripheral class composed of wealthy ex-gangsters, stars of the entertainment world (who were once considered as belonging to the demimonde, no matter how successful they were), etc. The formal organization of labor has in many instances raised the social status and the income of workers and at the same time helped to lower that of the small shopkeepers, self-employed craftsmen, and free-lance functionaries who were once independent and self-reliant petty bourgeois.[10] Changes in medical technology, including the growth of hospital

[10] Other, but related, factors have been changes in technology, in modes of both production and distribution—e.g., the development of self-service merchan-

care for the ill, have considerably devaluated independent general practitioners; and the medical profession has become increasingly professionalized, increasingly specialized, and increasingly organized into formal operational units—into clinics, hospital staffs, governmental teams, etc. The same trend toward specialization and the extension of formal organization has existed, in one way or another, in all the professions and indeed in all occupations. A lawyer is no longer a lawyer but is instead a corporation, estate, tax, criminal, patent, or other specialist in some aspect of the law; and he is no longer a man practicing the law but is more likely one who works, often for a salary, for some legal organization. A teacher is no longer a man endeavoring to transmit the intellectual heritage to his juniors; he, too, is a specialist in primary, secondary, or college teaching and in history, economics, physics, or some other subject, working for a vast and highly organized educational bureaucracy.

Functional and Dysfunctional Consequences

From one point of view, the many and the continuing changes that have been and are occurring in the system of stratification of Western societies are functional. They are organizational adjustments, often long delayed and never wholly effective, to the changing technological and other aspects of the social system. Thus the progressive liberation of women from the home, from segregation from men, and from the inferior status that was their traditional lot was an adaptation to ideological and organizational changes that followed on the industrialization of productive processes. Had modern women remained bound in the old manner to their homes, their present status would be that of parasite; for the work that was once done at home has been taken from it by factory, field, shop, school, hospital, and other external agencies. Only the most stalwart archconservative would seriously question the functional necessity in modern industrial society for labor unions, for group medical practice, for the accrediting of public school teachers, for public regulation in the public interests of transportation and communications, or for most if not all of the changes that have come about in occupational, class, and other forms of stratification.

---

dising, the growth of governmental constraints on economic activity, etc. For an analysis of the way in which all these factors hamper the small, independent producer and distributor, see John H. Bunzel, *The American Small Businessman*, Alfred A. Knopf, Inc., New York, 1962. In *White Collar: The American Middle Class* (Oxford University Press, Fair Lawn, N.J., 1951) C. Wright Mills has dramatically portrayed the decline of the petty bourgeois; and in *The Crisis of the Middle Class* (Holt, Rinehart and Winston, Inc., New York, 1955) Henry Grayson analyzes the recent changes in American society that have reduced the role and modified the character of the upper middle class.

As old forms of stratification have disintegrated and new forms gradually emerged, the new forms have, however, at some point in their development invariably become resistant, as do all modes of organization, to further change; and at that point they have begun to evidence qualities that are dysfunctional from the point of view of society as a whole. Perhaps the clearest and most striking example of a functional adaptation to change that has become a dysfunctional resistance to change is provided by labor unionism, although much the same thing has happened in somewhat more subtle ways in medicine, law, teaching, and even scientific endeavors as professionalization has increased. The efforts of the early labor unions were directed, with ultimate success, toward raising the wages of workers in business and industry through collective bargaining with employers. As the unions became more highly organized, however, and hence more bureaucratic in structure, stability of employment emerged as a secondary goal; and in the effort to achieve this end, the unions resorted to the same practices that had made the medieval guilds a factor in technological and economic stability—e.g., monopolization of occupational jurisdiction, limitations on membership (by such means as elaborate and often unnecessary training and by setting other qualifications for union members), constraints on the efficient use of labor, prohibitions on the adoption of labor-saving devices, etc. In some instances, particularly in railroad operation and the construction industry, the unions were successful in preserving old techniques and in maximizing the labor costs of production or other accomplishment. Moreover, like the medieval guilds, the unions were often successful in securing legal sanction of their restrictive regulations. Thus today legally maintained standards of safety in building construction more often reflect the interests of the craft unions—of carpenters, electricians, plumbers, etc.—than those of the owners and future users of buildings.

The effects of labor organization on our technology, however, have been quite varied. In some instances, most notably in the construction industry, the organization of labor has aided in stabilizing technology; in others, especially in the factory production of goods, it has provided an incentive to the further mechanization of productive processes by maintaining an artificially high price for labor. Occasionally, in fact, unionized labor has effectively priced itself out of the market, forcing entrepreneurs to move their establishments to an area where the cost of labor was lower, to replace workers with machines, or to find a substitute for a commodity with an artificially maintained high cost. (The shift in the United States from coal to oil and natural gas as industrial fuels, for example, was at least hastened by labor union resistance to the mechanization of the soft-coal mines.)

The evolution of guild-like constraints on the use of labor has of recent years had some stabilizing consequences for the class structure. To the extent that unions have established a monopoly over their particular work function and thus been able to achieve some stability of employment, they have at the same time erected barriers to individual mobility out of the laboring class into an economically superior class position. The devices—seniority in hiring and promotion, pension programs, unemployment insurance, production quotas, etc—that have been evolved to protect the individual worker from adversity and from competition with his fellows all operate to tie the worker to his craft or trade and, often, to the firm by which he is employed. Formally and informally maintained work quotas together with the seniority system, for example, prevent the individual worker from applying himself, should he wish to do so and be capable of doing so, to the improvement of the technical processes with which he works and thereby lifting himself, should he be successful, out of the class of employed workers. Health insurance, unemployment insurance, pension programs, and the like give the individual worker a strong vested interest in staying on his particular job and thus deter him from trying to better his personal position by seeking an administrative post or by moving into another occupation. For the majority of workers, the freedom from the strains of competition and the comparative security that have been brought by such devices may be more highly valued than the lost opportunity to rise in the class and occupational hierarchy. This same freedom and security mean, however, that the working class is becoming closed; and since the same sort of thing is happening, in one way or another and to some degree or other, with most class and occupational strata, it may very well be that the period of high rates of individual mobility are coming to a close.[11]

[11] It is frequently assumed that the more highly industrialized a society, the higher will be the rates of social mobility, a view elaborated by Seymour M. Lipset and Reinhard Bendix in *Social Mobility in Industrial Society*, University of California Press, Berkeley, Calif., 1959. There is a good deal of evidence, however, that beyond some indefinite point industrialization brings a decline rather than an increase in social mobility. Many sociologists and social economists have concluded, often on the basis of considerable research data, that this point has been passed in such Western societies as Britain and the United States. See, for example, D. V. Glass (ed.), *Social Mobility in Britain*, The Free Press of Glencoe, New York, 1955; Ely Chinoy, "Social Mobility Trends in the United States," *American Sociological Review*, vol. 20, pp. 180–186, April, 1955; R. K. Merton, *Social Theory and Social Structure*, The Free Press of Glencoe, New York, 1949, p. 380; Natalie Rogoff, *Recent Trends in Occupational Mobility*, The Free Press of Glencoe, New York, 1953; W. L. Warner, *Structure of American Life*, The University Press, Edinburgh, 1952, pp. 76 ff.; and Joseph A. Kahl, *The American Class Structure*, Holt, Rinehart and Winston, Inc., New York, 1957.

Uncertainty regarding the rates of social mobility in modern societies is paralleled by equal uncertainty concerning how individuals do achieve upward movement in modern societies. For example, in *Social Class and Social Change in Puerto Rico* (Princeton University Press, Princeton, N.J., 1961) Melvin M. Tumin holds that formal education is the most significant ladder to individual advance-

MOBILITY AND SOCIAL CHANGE

No matter how stable a society, there is always some opportunity, however slight, for individual movement through space and up or down the social hierarchy. Even under feudalism, an exceptional serf might gain acceptance into the household of the lord as servant, craftsman, or warrior; or he might, and evidently some few did, break from his bondage to the manor and join some marauding gang of independents. Historically, however, individual mobility, both spatial and social, seems to have been the exception; and periods of high mobility seem to have been both rare and brief. Those periods have, apparently, been times not only of high individual mobility but also of rapid change in the social system itself. The one cannot be explained by the other, or the other by the one; but each may facilitate changes in the other—individual mobility, for example, may foster technological changes and technological changes may implement individual mobility.

The various forces that may lead to the detachment of an individual from his normal context and his moving to some new place or into some new social stratum may be roughly classified into two sorts—those that operate to drive him out of his homeland or out of his class, occupational, or other position and those that serve to attract him to another place or position. It might be hypothesized that movement which stems from forces of the first sort is mainly an adjustment to antecedent social changes and is not likely to lead in turn to other changes, whereas movement which stems from forces of the second sort is a reflection of those qualities of independence and enterprise that are essential to and are sometimes manifest in innovative, advocatory, or adoptive endeavor. It has sometimes happened, however, that persons have been driven from their homeland because they were advocates or adopters of new ideas or practices; and it has often happened that persons who have been driven from their homelands or positions have found new opportunities in new lands or new occupational or other positions and have taken advantage of them. The relation between the occasion for movement and the social consequences of movement are not, therefore, by any means constant.

Most movement of persons away from their homelands seems to have been a consequence of their having been displaced rather than attracted to new places. There have been some exceptions, such as the migration of persons to California in search of gold and the more recent waves of migration to this same state of persons from other states in search of better jobs and a temperate climate; and some of the immigrants to America, such as the Italians who came in large numbers in the two decades prior to World War I,

---

ment up the socioeconomic scale; but in "A Skeptical Note on the Relation of Vertical Mobility to Education" (*American Journal of Sociology*, vol. 66, pp. 560–570, May, 1961) C. Arnold Anderson advances impressive evidence that such is not in fact the case.

came in search of wealth and with the intention of returning home once that wealth had been won. But most of the immigrants to America, including those early arrivals who came on the *Mayflower,* had in one way or another been driven out of their homeland; and most of the people who moved westward individually or, like the Mormons, en masse had left home because they were no longer wanted or because they could not endure their condition there.

Expulsion, for political or other reasons, is the most forthright way in which persons have been driven out of their homelands; and although expulsion is relatively rare, a number of people, including the criminals who first settled Australia, have been displaced in this way. Far more common, however, has been economic displacement of persons following upon crop failure, war, revolution, or technological change. The two or three million Irish peasants who came to the United States in the 1840s were refugees from the disastrous famine that was induced by a series of crop failures; much of the movement of New Englanders westward during the same period stemmed from the fact that the lands of New England were losing their fertility; and the more recent dust-bowl migration of the mid-1930s into California of farm families who were displaced from their Oklahoma and Texas Panhandle lands by a series of severe drought years was a more dramatic instance of the same sort of thing. Wars and revolutions always lead to some displacement of persons or classes of persons, either because the victors drive out the vanquished or, and perhaps more commonly, because economic disturbances wrought by the war or revolution have effects much like those of crop failure. Thus it was the economic chaos that followed the Civil War that drove many Southerners from their homeland and led them to settle the Southwest.

Technological changes can have and often have had similar consequences, displacing people from their traditional context and driving them to seek economic opportunities elsewhere. The migration of Western peoples from farm to city over the past two centuries has in considerable part been the consequence of technological changes in agriculture which have reduced the need for manual workers. The attraction of the city has, of course, played a part in this movement; but the city would not have been so attractive if opportunities on the farm had not been declining. The northward and cityward movement of Negroes during this century has also been in considerable measure the consequence of their being displaced by technological changes, in this case the gradual mechanization of cotton growing and its transference from the Old South and the Deep South to Texas and the Southwest.

Persecution has been one of the most frequent conditions and, in that it involves so very many different factors, one of the more complex that have led to a displacement of persons and their movement away from their homeland. In many times and places a minority of the social population, usually for a variety of reasons, has been subjected to such general political, economic, and social devaluation by the majority that it has found its position intolerable. Such was the case with the Puritans in Elizabethan England, the Huguenots in seventeenth-century France, the Mormons in nineteenth-century Illinois, and the Jews in Nazi Germany. In these instances, as in countless others, persecution led to either individual or mass exodus from the homeland and settlement elsewhere.

Displacement of persons from class or occupational position, with resulting movement into another position, has no doubt been fully as common although less spectacular. The devaluation of an established elite by technological, ideological, or organizational changes has already been mentioned; devaluation of this sort has been a more or less continuous process in Western societies for some hundreds of years. Occupational displacement, which is usually brought about by technological changes, has also been more or less continuous; almost every technological development has devaluated the skills and techniques of those of some occupational stratum and driven them to a reluctant search for new occupational positions. Ideological changes may work to the same end, although more subtly. Thus with the decline of religious ideology and the related rise in the importance of secular ideology, there has occurred a marked devaluation of the occupation of priest and preacher; and many men who a century ago might have entered the ministry now find their way into such other fields of endeavor as social work.

As a rule, those who are displaced from their homeland or from a class, occupational, or other position are stripped of most of their usual rights and possessions and must begin anew, often with many circumstances against them, to gain social acceptance and an established position. Under some conditions and for some few individuals this plight may serve as an activating challenge. Thus some of the multitude of impoverished immigrants who came to America worked and fought their way to wealth and high estate, and in the process some of those who did no doubt contributed to the dynamism of American society. The effect on American society of the majority, however, was indirect and grew out of their numbers rather than their personal characteristics and personal endeavors.[12] By contrast, those who voluntarily move from place to place or stratum to stratum in order to improve their personal position usually enter the new context aggressively and with personal attributes favorable to their succeeding. Unlike persons who are displaced, they have not been deprived of all that they value and do not begin their endeavors with a background of failure.

[12] For attempts to assess the effects on American society of the great waves of immigrants who came to America during the latter half of the nineteenth century and the early decades of this, see Charlotte Erickson, *American Industry and the European Immigrant, 1860–1885*, Harvard University Press, Cambridge, Mass., 1957; and E. P. Hutchinson, *Immigrants and Their Children, 1850–1950*, John Wiley & Sons, Inc., New York, 1956.

Invasion and Social Change

In terms of their effects on those who are already established in an area (or in a class or occupation), those who move in, individually or collectively, are invaders. They may or may not be welcomed; but they are at any event representatives of another culture or subculture who are recognizably distinct from the natives and who with rare exception disturb the social life of the natives in some way and to some degree.

The long-run consequences of any invasion depend upon a multitude of factors—the number of invaders versus natives; the extent to which their cultures, and hence their interests, values, and attitudes, differ; etc.[13] The European invaders of North America more or less destroyed the native population and built for themselves a somewhat new social system; those who invaded Central and South America, on the other hand, tended to reestablish in the New World the social system of the Iberian Peninsula, subordinating the natives to a position of peonage. Some immigrants have endeavored to create a new, utopian society in the new land, as the early New Englanders,

[13] The effects on a society of out-migration would also seem to be quite varied, depending presumably upon the character of those who migrate, their numbers, and the condition of the society from which they migrate. The idea, frequently advanced, that it was the expulsion of the Jews from Spain that brought that society to stagnation is hardly tenable; nevertheless, it was probably the eviction, by popular demand, of the Moslem and Jewish minorities by James I of Aragon in 1247 that ended the prosperity of this particular Iberian kingdom; for within a year or two Aragon had lost 100,000 Jews and Moslems, who comprised most of the craftsmen, merchants, and traders. It is possible, also, that the elimination, by massacre and migration, of most of the Protestants from France during the Huguenot wars retarded the technological and economic development of French society, since it was mainly the Protestants who were through their enterprise disturbing the old system.

Nevertheless, there have been other instances in which heavy out-migration has had little enduring consequence to the social system. In pre-World War II Germany a considerable proportion of the physicians, scientists, technicians, and business entrepreneurs were Jews. Their extermination and dispersal may have had marked short-run consequences—it is said, for example, that German medical practice during the war was adversely affected by the shortage of qualified medical men; but Germany, which had through the persecution of the Jews lost a great many of its enterprising men (and through war casualties lost many of the remainder), was the first of the countries of Europe to recover economically and otherwise from the war. The massive migration of the young men from Sicily and southern Italy in the decade preceding World War I must have had many immediate consequences, such as producing a surplus of women of marriageable age. The long-run result seems to have been only the provision of some financial support for the families of those who went abroad and to that extent the preservation of the social conditions that had fostered the migration in the first place.

the Amish, and the Arcadians tried to do in North America and as the Jews are currently trying to do in Palestine. More, however, have endeavored to re-create on a large or small scale the physical and social conditions of home and have formed into colonies, often in an urban setting but in some instances in rural ones, such as those of the Scandinavians in Minnesota and the Italians in California. In some instances invaders have remained culturally distinct for centuries, as have the Moslems of China and the Jews of Western Europe. More often, perhaps, they have gradually been assimilated into the native population, as were the Huguenots in England and the Irish in the United States.

Invasions of classes by ambitious newcomers have equally varied long-run consequences. As English industrialists pushed their way into the landed gentry, they did little more than displace former members of this class; and the invasion of the elite of the post-Civil War South by enterprising Northerners (the carpetbaggers) had very temporary effects, for the newcomers were soon absorbed into the apathy and social ceremonialism of the elite whom they came to displace. On the other hand, the more recent invasion of New York and New England society by self-made industrialists and businessmen has brought about a radical change in the manners and values of the recognized elite; and the still more recent invasion of American academic life by bright and ambitious men from nonacademic backgrounds has done much to shatter the calm and break the tradition of humanistic scholarship in American institutions of higher learning.

In many instances invaders have brought with them cultural items that the natives have borrowed and found useful, thus adding to their cultural stock. It was in this way, to cite but one example, that American labor learned the art of collective bargaining. Welsh coal miners, who had come to California to work in the quartz mines of the Sierras, brought with them knowledge of the technique of organizing and striking as a means of collectively bargaining for higher wages. Workers in the cigar-making industry of San Francisco borrowed this technique, initially with the goal of driving cheap Chinese labor out of the industry; their use of it was so successful that it rapidly spread eastward. Invaders may also bring cultural items that can be synthesized with native items into innovations; thus American jazz music is the end product of a blending of many musical elements—African rhythms, Scotch-Irish ballads, Baptist hymns, French band music, etc. The introduction into England by Huguenot refugees of various craft skills and processes from the Continent was one of the important antecedents to the industrial revolution in England.[14] In France these skills and processes had been largely

[14] See Margaret T. Hodgen, *Change and History: A Study of the Dated Distributions of Technological Innovation in England*, Wenner-Gren Foundation for Anthropological Research, Inc., New York, 1952. Hodgen has plotted the locations of Huguenot settlement in England and those in which innovations, mainly

monopolized by the guilds; brought to England by individual craftsmen who could not maintain a monopoly over them, they tended to enter into the public domain and to become fused with one another and with the English technology.

Because they have left their normal social context and are strangers in the society or subsociety in which they settle, invaders are often free from normal social constraints. If they do not reestablish social constraints by banding together in a colony, they may enjoy—or, as they may see it, suffer —a period of comparative social isolation that is conducive to individual experimentation. They may become culturally marginal—somewhat detached from the culture of their homeland or subculture of their original position and inadequately socialized into the culture or subculture of the new place or position—and at the same time insensitive or not subject to local social controls. It is the possibility that newcomers to a society or to an occupation or class may produce fruitful innovations that is the basis for the idea that "new blood" rejuvenates a decadent society, a hidebound class, or a decrepit business; and it is the same possibility that is responsible for the persistent prejudice against foreigners, the *nouveau riche,* and amateurs.

The fact that an invader is not socialized into the norms of the new place or position and is insensitive to local controls often means, among other things, that he becomes competitive with members of the society, class, or occupation in which he is striving to gain acceptance in a way which they regard as unfair or abhorrent. Thus he may become an irritating stimulant, forcing established members to exceptional effort and even to endeavor of an enterprising sort. The Jewish intellectuals who came to America as refugees from Nazi Germany not only brought ideas to merge with those already here, but also violated, if only through desperation, some of the constraints on interpersonal competition and thus brought about some enduring changes in academic practices. The currently accepted practice of overtly seeking academic placement—of applying for jobs in colleges and universities by send-

---

technological, appeared in the years following and finds what she considers to be a significant correlation between the settlement in England of the Huguenot immigrants, who had been skilled craftsmen and business entrepreneurs in France, and the occurrence of innovations in England. That immigrants often stimulate change in the society in which they settle is demonstrated by Margaret Stacey in *Tradition and Change: A Study of Banbury,* Oxford University Press, Fair Lawn, N.J., 1960; and Oscar Handlin (ed.), *The Positive Contributions by Immigrants,* UNESCO, Paris, 1955. The Banbury study is that of a community in which a new industry has been located and to which migrants come from other parts of the country in response to the demand for workers. Stacey finds that it is these immigrants, outside the preexisting social structure, who act in progressive and enterprising ways, while the natives resist rather than implement the changes that are occurring in the life of the community.

ing out a vita—came about in this way. Before 1940 or thereabouts a young Ph.D. or a mature man who wished a better post would no more have thought of announcing his candidacy for a job than a physician would think of advertising for patients; but Jewish refugees, having no academic sponsors to speak for them, engaged in various forms of self-advertising; and in time what had been unthinkable became an accepted practice.

URBANIZATION, MOBILITY, AND CHANGE

In the folklore of many peoples urbanization has been associated with sinfulness and corruption. In the Old Testament the cities of Babel and Sodom and Gomorrah symbolize the evil in man, whereas good is represented by shepherds and the pastoral peoples of the hills; in American folk drama villainy is often personified by a man from the city, with his opponent, the hero, a sturdy and sterling country man. The capital city of many ancient civilizations is often depicted in the records, presumably written by men who were urban, as crass, venal, immoral, and as living parasitically on the rural hinterland. Plato considered Athens dissolute; Confucius held up for emulation familistic, rural values and practices; and even in Roman law, made by and for the citizens of Rome, the patriarchal, rural idea of *patria potestas*, the rights of a father over his wife and children, was a fundamental and continuing part. During the later Middle Ages, the city came to be looked upon, at least by country men, as a center of vice and a consumer of sons and daughters; and with considerable reason the belief prevailed that those who migrated to the city were doomed to an early death. Then and on down to the present day, the city has frequently been characterized, always in contrast to the healthy and virtuous bucolic life, as a place of disease and drunkenness, licentiousness and improbity—as is evidenced in Shakespeare, Voltaire, Dickens, and the latest play on Broadway.

The persistence of the idea that urban life is per se sinful and corrupt would seem to be a reflection of the fact that when social changes have occurred, their point of origin has been urban and their adoption has come most rapidly in an urban context. Conditions favorable to individual mobility, both spatial and social, and thus to innovative endeavor and the advocacy and adoption of innovations, have most often appeared in urban aggregations and least often in rural hamlets, villages, or the open countryside. Known contributors to social change—i.e., known inventors, discoverers, and advocates of social and other kinds of reform—have almost invariably worked in or from an urban base; and a considerable proportion of them have been also city-bred. Pastoral and agricultural peoples have no doubt produced many enterprising individuals; but since pastoral and agricultural peoples have, at least until modern times, lived together in small and closely knit communities of families and their systems of class and other stratification have always been far more closed than open, the only way that an enterprising individual could escape organizational constraints was by leaving his home and migrating to a town or city, where opportunities for achievement were greater and the conditions of life both more stimulating and more liberating.

The Structured and Stratified City

The fact that people live together in large, compact aggregates, that they earn their livelihood through specialized craft and other nonagricultural techniques, and that those of diverse class and other strata rub elbows in the streets does not of itself mean that urban society will be dynamic. The population of a town or a city can be and often has been structured—highly organized and differentiated into numerous small, integrated, and socially isolated groups. In modern societies, urban life has been inimical to the maintenance of familism; but such has not always been the case. The great cities of premodern China were aggregates, not of individuals, but of extended families; and although an individual could and presumably did wander freely through the city, he did so, not as an independent entity, but as the son of such and such a family; his attachment to his family unit, both ideologically and in terms of economic and other forms of dependence, was almost as great in the city as in the small town or village. If, as was the case with craftsmen, an individual worked outside the family context, it was as a member of a guild; and the ties of guild membership were almost as strong and enduring as those of a kin grouping. Moreover, the families and guilds of these great cities were organized into communities to a degree unknown in the modern world; and a neighborhood that consisted of a number of families who had lived in close physical proximity over many generations had social relations as close and restraining as those of any village. Under these circumstances, class position, and, with it, occupational status, tended to be self-perpetuating; a boy followed his father's occupational footsteps, he was normally affianced at birth to the daughter of a neighboring and socially similar family, etc. Undoubtedly there was social mobility of a sort in these cities; but it was the family unit, not the isolated individual, who gained or lost in wealth and social position. Undoubtedly, too, there was some spatial mobility; but again it was the family unit that upon occasion moved from town to city or from city to city or, if it fell on evil days, returned to the land from which some early ancestor had lifted it.

A high degree and somewhat comparable kind of organization of urban society seems to have obtained in many times and places.[15] The great cities

[15] See Gideon Sjoberg, *The Preindustrial City: Past and Present*, The Free Press of Glencoe, New York, 1960, for varied historical examples of cities that

and the many towns of premodern India must have been highly structured; at any event they were not centers of social ferment. The cities of antiquity, such as Cairo, Alexandria, Constantinople, Carthage, and Rome, had each in its turn a period or periods of rapid development; but each was for centuries socially stable, if not free from such events as war; and it may be assumed that during the periods of stability these cities were highly structured and their populations spatially and socially immobilized. The relation between urban society and social change has not, therefore, been constant. The towns of medieval Europe were produced by change and no doubt for a time contributed to change; but they also became, each in its own time, staunch, if in the long run unsuccessful, defenders of the *status quo*.

The Open City

It is urbanization as a process, rather than the city as an established entity, that seems most conducive to and expressive of social change. A town or city can be as unproductive of individual enterprise and as discouraging to it as can an agricultural village; but a growing town or a town that is growing into a city is *pari passu* conducive to innovation and the adoption of innovations. Growth of a town or city is itself, of course, a consequence of antecedent changes, changes that have released or driven people from their native, usually rural, context and drawn them to the town or city. The population of a city can be increased by internal reproduction, and population increase of this sort has been an important factor in the growth of modern urban centers. In times past, however, towns and cities had relatively high death rates and tended to have comparatively low birth rates, with the consequence that rapid growth invariably involved heavy in-migration from the rural hinterland, from abroad, or from both. It is the movement of outlanders into the town or city which, once inaugurated, produces conditions favorable to the emergence and adoption of social changes.

There are a number of ways in which a considerable influx of new members may disturb the existing organizations of urban society and produce a condition of openness. Migrants to a town or city are for the most part men and women of early maturity, since it is normally the sons and daughters of a family, rather than their parents, who can and will respond to the attractions of some place other than home. Even migration that results from displace-

---

were highly structured. In a reversal of the view advanced above, Lewis Mumford, who has never become reconciled to modern modes of social life, argues that the modern city imprisons the individual, deprives him of any opportunity to express his unique qualities, and destroys his spirit (*The City in History: Its Origins, Its Transformations, and Its Prospects*, Harcourt, Brace & World, Inc., New York, 1961).

ment, such as the movement into the Southwest from the South after the Civil War, is movement of preponderately young people; for the fully mature and the aged are on the one hand better established in their native context than their children are and, on the other hand, less adventurous and less capable of surmounting the difficulties and hardships of moving to another place and way of life. The population of a town or city that is growing through in-migration has, therefore, an abnormal age distribution that is more than normally favorable to change; for, as has been seen, innovative endeavor is more characteristic of the young than the old; and the young, being less habituated to the *status quo*, are somewhat more susceptible than are their elders to adopting new things.

Moreover, the relatively high proportion of young people in the population of a growing town or city, many of whom are new arrivals who are freed to a degree from parental and other organizational constraints, makes for more than normal competition between all the maturing members of the urban community. The new arrivals have at the outset no established occupational, familial, or class position; they must make their way in all respects; and their efforts to do so, largely, of course, unfruitful, disturb the existing organization and put on the defensive those who hold by right of birth or seniority occupational, class, and other positions. Thus there is injected into the life of a growing town or city a kind and intensity of interpersonal competition that formerly did not exist. The scion of an old, established family can perhaps no longer be confident, as his father was before him, that his social credentials will secure for him a comfortable position in trade or politics, the debutante of his choice, and a mansion in the proper section of the city. He may, rather, discover that he has numerous energetic, and from his point of view unscrupulous, competitors for all these things.

A growing town or city provides, furthermore, new opportunities of all sorts for the more ambitious and enterprising of both the established and the newly arrived citizens. Congestion brings rising land and property values and new usages for existing buildings; new housing is needed; and in modern cities all the elaborate public and private services and facilities must be expanded and ramified. This enlargement of economic opportunities of itself tends to open the way to individual mobility up the occupational and class hierarchy; however resistant the traditional elite may be to acknowledging successful newcomers, they are much less likely to reject the sons and daughters, or at least the grandsons and granddaughters, of a newcomer who has made a fortune constructing jerry-built housing, paving streets under favorable contracts, or building a great industry from a one-man shop.

As the organization of urban society is disturbed by new arrivals, most particularly by their sons and daughters, all the conditions previously discussed as most favorable to innovative, advocatory, and adoptive endeavor emerge. Preexisting family unity is weakened; the newcomers, mainly without family ties in the city, marry through choice and build their family life with less than normal regard for the traditional family ideals and practices, while the old families may be considerably weakened by both the example and the competition of the newcomers. The old residential and occupational segregation, which tended to make the town or city an aggregation of closely knit communities of interests and values, each exercising considerable constraint on the individual, is at the same time and in much the same ways disrupted—a prized and prestigious residential section may be invaded by newcomers and so devaluated. These and related changes tend in turn to open the class system (the son of an old family may, for example, marry across the tracks), to modify and weaken symbols of status, and to bring a general quality of individualization to the life of the city.

In a rigidly structured and stratified town or city everyone—or almost everyone—is a native and has his fixed and recognized positions. Not everyone will know everyone else personally, as in a small town or village; but everyone will be known within the communities of persons among whom he circulates, works, and lives. In the open city, on the other hand, there is a high degree of impersonality in many of the relations of citizen to citizen; and it is always possible for an individual, should he desire to do so, to shift his membership in the more or less transitory and changing communities of persons that form under these conditions. He may, therefore, mingle with and learn from different kinds of persons and to a degree cross class and other barriers; thus although he be born and reared in a slum ghetto, a modern urban child can, and some few children do, get a formal education, acquire at least the veneer of manners of a higher class, and thereafter pass himself off as a member of that class, or indeed in time earn the right to claim membership in it.

It is in the open city, moreover, that the greatest possibility exists for the individual to achieve a degree of anonymity and some freedom from the demands and constraints of social membership. Here, if anywhere, he can to some extent follow his personal inclinations, evade filial, marital, and other obligations, and devote himself to those activities which he himself considers most desirable—to a life of crime, to self-indulgence, or perhaps to some creative endeavor.

Urbanization in Recent Social History

The variety of changes that were antecedent to the revival of town life during the early Middle Ages—the breaking up of feudal estates, the opening of new lands for cultivation, and the development in time of new agricultural techniques—both released and drove ex-serfs from the shelter of feudal organization. Some of them took refuge in the remnants of the old Roman towns, where in due time they or their descendants established themselves as craftsmen or traders; and for a century or two these towns seem to have been centers of change—most especially those, such as Bruges, that were the locale of the annual trade fairs to which came merchants from all of Western Europe. In time, however, the organization of the towns became crystallized. The guild form of organization stabilized both production and commerce, and both technological and organizational change came to an end. The political organization of the towns grew rigid and efficient; and with this rigidity the rates of individual mobility, both spatial and social, declined. One indication of the decline of social mobility was the fact that power over municipal affairs, which had for long been held by semipopular councils, became concentrated in the hands of a hereditary elite—in such cities as Venice and Florence, in the hands of noble families, and in Northern European towns, in those of the guild masters. In many instances citizenship in a town was a matter of birth, and to go from town to town, one needed a kind of passport. Each town tended, moreover, to isolate itself economically from all others by the imposition of heavy import and export taxes and by the granting of monopolies on specific economic functions to the local guilds. So isolated and independent, and consequently so closed, were these towns that they even fought wars with one another.

Conditions other than the character of town life contributed, it will be recalled, to the stability of medieval life—the ideological and organizational constraints of the Church, the diversion of enterprise and social resources into the construction of religious edifices, the frequency with which medieval people held religious and other festivals, the losses from recurrent war, etc. The character of town life was, thus, concordant with the ideological and other organizational circumstances of the times.

The closure of medieval towns probably reached its peak during the late fourteenth and early fifteenth centuries; thereafter disruptive forces began to manifest themselves—the epidemics of plague; the beginnings of political unification; the decline of both ideological and organizational control by the Church; the discovery of the Americas, which in time brought an influx of new capital, mainly gold, and later new sources of food, thus releasing men from the land and sending them into the towns. It was the disturbance to the organized life of such towns as Florence that made for the social ferment of the Italian Renaissance, and of such towns as Worms, Strasbourg, and Bern that gave rise to the many religious and other changes of the Reformation. The Renaissance was short-lived, and Southern European towns and cities soon relapsed into a condition of comparatively static incongruence in which they remained for some centuries. The Reformation, however, as has been pointed out, signaled the rise of a new and effective ideological complex and of a new and open class system. These and related technological and organizational changes arose in towns and had their main effects on town life.

Individual towns and even cities of Western Europe rose and declined in importance and in dynamism. Bruges, for example, was for a century or so one of the liveliest trade and cultural centers; eventually, however, it became hidebound, its harbor silted up, and Antwerp, Brussels, and other cities superseded it. During the heyday of Spanish power and activity, Madrid, Barcelona, Santiago, and other Iberian towns and cities grew and in growing became open and dynamic; but as Spain sank into apathetic obscurity, Paris, London, Amsterdam, and other Northern European cities became the meccas for adventurous individuals and the new centers of social change.

The process of urbanization—the movement of people into cities and the consequent opening of urban society—has continued unabated down to the present time. At the end of the fifteenth century probably not more than 5 per cent of the population of Western Europe resided in towns or cities; the remainder lived in small, tightly knit agricultural villages or, in some instances, isolated rural establishments. Through the sixteenth and seventeenth centuries the proportion that was urban steadily if rather slowly increased; and then, with the beginning of those technological and related organizational changes that are encompassed by the term "industrial revolution," the shift of people to the city began to be increasingly rapid. By the opening of the nineteenth century, perhaps 15 per cent of Northern Europeans were urban (in North America the proportion was, at this time, far less); and through the nineteenth century and on into this century the rate of movement into cities has continued to increase. Today the majority of Europeans and Americans are urban residents; and in America at least, the urban way of life has in many respects been adopted by those who live in small towns and even rural hamlets.

If only because they have continued to grow, modern cities and towns are for the most part more open than closed, more dynamic than static. They are therefore centers of high mobility, of considerable and continuing disorganization, and of social change. Many of the changes that have come about in recent decades, especially changes in organization, would seem, however, to be leading toward a stabilization of urban life; and should this trend long continue, the process of urbanization may come to an end and the modern city, like the city of many other times and places, become structured and rigidly stratified. The pronounced trend in America after World War II toward the development of suburban residental and shopping communities around the great urban centers has some such stabilizing potentiality, for the suburban community is somewhat more conventionalizing and constraining than is the metropolitan area itself. Far more significant, however, in the view of many sociologists, is the progressive bureaucratization of economic, political, and social life.

chapter 12 Economic and Professional Bureaucratization

Small, socially isolated societies such as primitive villages and tribes may function effectively on the basis of the family or the community form of organization and a two- or three-dimensional system of stratification. But in all the larger societies, those that are conventionally described as civilizations, where the activities of any considerable number of people have had to be coordinated under the directive authority of a leader, another form of organization—bureaucracy—has invariably existed. In any small organization personal loyalty, if not affection, is a major factor in the acceptance of authority. The father of a family, for example, can exercise strong and effective leadership over the members of his family, guiding his sons in the cultivation of their fields, etc.; for they have been trained into accepting him as their leader, not only because he is *the* father of the family, but because he is *their* father. As the organizational unit enlarges, however, there comes a point at which the relations of leader to led can no longer be personal—at which it is impossible for a leader to know, by name, by personal idiosyncrasies, etc., those over whom he exercises authority and at which those who are led cease to know their leader as a person. It is at that point that the organization of the unit begins to take on the characteristics of bureaucracy.

In family, tribal, and other intimate forms of organization, leadership is personal; in class and other systems of stratification, relationships are impersonal and do not involve centralized authority. In that it provides for directive leadership over numbers of individuals who are impersonally related, bureaucracy is thus a form of organization that combines some attributes of both. It differs from both, however, in that its manifest function is clearly defined and its operating rules and procedures are recognizedly man-made—characteristics that have led modern sociologists to describe bureaucracy as a rational rather than institutional form of organization. Whereas the existence of government may be accepted by the members of society as divinely ordained or as, at the very least, an expression of natural law, the various bureaucratic arms of government are apparently always recognized, however vaguely, for what they are—human agencies devised by human beings to accomplish some fairly specific aims.

It is often assumed that since their origins and functions are secular rather than sacred—i.e., not entirely lost in the mists of tradition—bureaucratic organizations are by nature dynamic rather than resistant to change. In this view, the fact that those who are included in or subject to a bureaucratic organization recognize its purpose and its human origins means that they are willing and able to make whatever adaptive changes are necessary in either the structure of the organization or its operational rules and regulations. Certainly most of the bureaucratic organizations of modern society were established in a calculated way to solve recognized problems and in origin were thus adaptations to emerging social needs; but it does not follow that, once established, a bureaucratic organization will make adaptive changes to new contextual circumstances. Or, to put the same matter another way, the fact that the bureaucratic form of organization begins as a tool devised by man to serve some human need does not mean that it necessarily continues to be a tool subject to human control. On the contrary, as will be shown, bureaucracy is as inherently resistant to change as is any other form of organization.

Bureaucratic Structure and Procedure[1]

Like any other form of organization, bureaucracy places limits on membership and distinguishes members categorically from nonmembers, often by distinctive dress, as in the Catholic priesthood and in military organizations, or by other obvious symbols, such as the badges and numbers which may be worn as organizational identification by the workers in a modern industry.

[1] There is general agreement among social scientists concerning the structure of bureaucratic organizations, but considerable difference of opinion regarding the social consequences, especially the effects on the dynamism of society, of bureaucratization. At the one extreme are those who, like Max Weber, exalt the mechanical efficiency that is possible in bureaucracy (see H. H. Gerth and C. W. Mills, *From Max Weber*, Oxford University Press, Fair Lawn, N.J., 1946, chap. 8, "Bureaucracy"). At the other extreme are those who stress the rigidity and lack of adaptability that is inherent in the bureaucratic form of organization. For a strong statement of the latter view see L. von Mises, *Bureaucracy*, Yale University Press, New Haven, Conn., 1945.

More recent and more tempered analyses of bureaucracy include Robert K. Merton et al. (eds.), *Reader in Bureaucracy*, The Free Press of Glencoe, New York, 1952; Peter M. Blau, *Bureaucracy in Modern Society*, Random House, Inc., New York, 1956; and Peter M. Blau and W. Richard Scott, *Formal Organizations*, Chandler Publishing Co., San Francisco, 1962.

Membership even in a mature bureaucratic organization is not normally a matter of ascription, although in some instances, as in the case of the medieval guilds, it has tended to become so. Ordinarily admission to membership is achieved by an individual's meeting some more or less elaborate and taxing standards that have been established by the organization and that are designed to assure that a newly recruited member will possess the specific personality attributes and skills that are essential to effective performance within the organization.

Most bureaucratic organizations provide for the training of their neophytes into the particular duties to which they will be assigned and, most especially, into an acceptance of the values and assumptions upon which the organization operates. At the same time a bureaucratic organization tends to detach its neophytes, both by rule and by training, from their dependence upon and loyalty to other organizations, such as the family, that might conflict with their loyalty to the bureaucratic organization. Professional soldiers, for example, have often been discouraged from having families of their own; and almost from its inception the Roman Catholic Church prohibited its priests from marrying and restricted their association with parents and siblings. Modern political and economic bureaucratic organizations achieve something of the same end—undivided loyalty—by incorporating a member's family rather than detaching him from it.

Since the membership of a bureaucratic organization is not self-perpetuating, as is that of a family or tribe, but must continually be replenished by recruitment, rewards for membership are of necessity fairly obvious and attractive. The rewards for being a member in good standing of such an institutional organization as the family are seldom thought of as such; the individual who is born into a family, for example, and socialized by it simply takes his membership for granted. Although the designated rewards of membership in a bureaucratic organization may range from simple maintenance and payment of a wage, as is the case in mercenary military forces, to such spiritual boons as assurance of acceptance into the kingdom of heaven, they normally consist of some combination of material and psychological values. Of the latter, the most characteristic are prestige in the eyes of nonmembers, freedom from personal adversity (the organization ordinarily provides assurance that the individual will be taken care of in sickness and old age), and the prospect of promotion up the organizational hierarchy in accordance with some explicit schedule. Together, these organizationally provided values tend to relieve the individual member from the necessity of competing with his fellows and to give him a sense of security.

A bureaucratic organization may be very large, encompassing thousands of members, or comparatively small, as were the local guilds of the Middle Ages; and it may operate as a single bureaucratic system or a vast system of bureaucratic systems, as do the Catholic Church and such corporate organizations as General Motors. However large or small and however simple or complex, all mature bureaucratic organizations have certain structural characteristics in common. Each has a table of organization, which may or may not be embodied in a formal document or chart, that provides for the division of the membership in two distinct, but operationally interrelated, dimensions—work functions and authority.

The extent to which there is a division of labor among the members depends in considerable part upon the kind of work that is undertaken by the organization. In an army of foot soldiers the division of labor may be simple, whereas in a modern industry it is ordinarily exceedingly complex and extensive. Whatever the division of labor, it is effected by departmentalization within the total system, with each department and often each subdepartment assigned a special work function and a defined relationship to all the other departments, so that in theory, and usually to a considerable extent in practice, each subdepartment contributes to the effectiveness of its department and each department to that of the bureaucracy as a whole. This departmentalization of work functions makes for a differentiation of the members of the bureaucracy in terms of their work specialization—for example, of a differentiation of the soldiers of an army into infantrymen and artillerymen, of the priests of a priesthood into parish priests and teaching priests, etc.

Whatever their work specialty, members are also ranked into some sort of hierarchy of authority, which, again, may be either simple or complex. In any one of the medieval guilds there were but three grades of authority—master, journeyman, and apprentice; in military bureaucracy it is traditional to divide the total membership into two mutually exclusive classes, officers and men, and each class into half a dozen or more ranks. Whether many or few, each rank, grade, class, or level has its assigned position within the hierarchy, from highest to lowest; and each position is under the direct authority of the one above and in direct authority over the one below. Normally, the number of members who occupy a given position increases at a more or less geometric ratio from the highest to the lowest; the typical structure of the old guild, for example, was two apprentices to every journeyman and two journeymen to every master.

The particular office which a member of a bureaucratic organization occupies embodies both the rights and obligations that pertain to its work functions and those that result from its hierarchal position. An officer with the rank of captain, for example, is in most respects the status equal of all captains (seniority influences promotion and has some bearing on the personal status of the individual) and as such shares with them common obligations and common rights; but he is also captain of a specific command and as such has obligations and rights that are limited to that particular command. In somewhat the same way, all civil servants of a given grade may receive the same income, have the same car-parking rights, and be expected to perform at the same level of competence; but they may belong to such different bureaucratic organizations as the Post Office Department and the Department of Agriculture and, further, serve in a specialized subdepartment of the one or the other.

Each of the many offices of a bureaucratic system is established and maintained by the authority of the system itself. In premodern bureaucracies these rules and regulations were generally more a matter of understanding, of tradition, than of overt, written statement; today they are mostly codified in writing, although the explicit rules and regulations will be supplemented and at times qualified by tacit understandings between the person who occupies a particular office and those who occupy offices above and below him. The rules and regulations are supposed to provide the person who occupies the office with detailed guidance in his obligations to the organization—to what work he is to do, how, when, and under what conditions he is to do it—and with almost equally detailed guidance in the protocol of his office—the kind and nature of his relations to other officeholders. Rules pertaining to work are intended to assure that what an officeholder does is done in the most efficient manner possible and that it neither overlaps nor conflicts with that of other officeholders but is functionally articulated with it. Rules pertaining to protocol are designed to assure that orders issued by those in positions of command will flow downward in a systematic and effective fashion.

Each office is thus a functional cog in the organizational whole; and each officeholder is necessarily deprived of the right to exercise personal judgment in the conduct of the affairs of his office, except where the rules and regulations specifically grant a degree of freedom to his office. As a consequence bureaucracy is an impersonal system of organization in two distinct senses: the members of a bureaucratic organization are not related by bonds of intimacy and sentiment; and the office is prior to the man who occupies it—officially, he is not a person but a functionary. In theory at least it matters little who occupies what office; from the organizational point of view men are interchangeable parts.

But men, even well-trained bureaucrats, have their human prides and vanities, insist in developing some intimacy with those with whom they associate, and cannot be wholly prevented from occasionally exercising initiative. A fully developed bureaucracy will provide many official sops to petty personal pride and vanity—special little privileges, symbols of special status, etc.; and bureaucrats are often exceedingly jealous of their petty rights. No bureaucracy can, however, abolish the human need to be liked as well as respected, to be a person as well as an official, and to relate oneself to others in terms of intimacy. Since the rules of office preclude their being overtly expressed, personal interests and concerns are manifest in covert ways. Friends may exchange personal favors, cover up for each other's deficiencies, supplement official communications with gossip, etc.; and within a bureaucratic organization there are always unofficial friendship cliques, which are tied together into one or a number of loosely federated covert systems of organization.

The covert structure or structures give a modest semblance of intimacy to what is essentially an impersonal organization, thus fulfilling the needs of the members to be persons as well as officeholders. They also operate, particularly in times of crisis, to supplement the formal structure, either by circumventing its inadequacies or by tempering those official commands that are deemed, in the judgment of the persons involved, to be inexpedient or unjust. Thus through its covert structure a bureaucratic organization can act with dispatch in an emergency—it can cut red tape—and officially rationalize its action at leisure; and it can also, in the same informal manner, so dilute a command from high authority that by the time that it reaches those functionaries who are directly affected by it the command has no effect at all.

Many of those who are fully aware of the inherently stabilizing character of bureaucracy as a system of organization are nonetheless inclined to think that a bureaucratic organization is able to achieve dynamic adaptability through the mechanism of its covert structure.[2] But, as will be seen, the character of bureaucracy is such that it tends to make the members of a bureaucratic organization as cautious and unventuresome in their personal relations as they are in their official ones. When a bureaucrat does exercise initiative within the covert structure of the organization, it is usually because he regards the personal risk of doing so to be less than is the risk of remaining within his official role. A particular officeholder may, of course, be a less than perfect bureaucrat; but bureaucracy as a system is designed to assure a high level of conformity to the rules and regulations and to discourage, by failing to promote them or by actually removing them from office, those individuals who are tempted for personal or idealistic reasons to transcend or violate their assigned duties. Moreover, since it is generally those individuals who conform most fully to the rules and regulations of office who gain promotion, the leaders of a bureaucratic organization, like the rank and file, tend to be ultraconformists, rather than enterprising individualists.

BUREAUCRACY IN MODERN SOCIETY

In the small societies of the past, bureaucracy seems never to have been more than a supplement to intimate, institutional forms of organization,

[2] The thesis that the covert structure of a bureaucratic organization gives to it considerable flexibility, although the formal structure tends to rigidity, is developed by Peter M. Blau in *The Dynamics of Bureaucracy: A Study of Interpersonal Relations in Two Governmental Agencies*, The University of Chicago Press, Chicago, 1955.

such as the extended family. Governing was in many times and places accomplished through fairly personal means, a prince ruling his small company of subjects directly and without the aid of many functionaries; and premodern military forces, such as those of feudal times, were often merely a band of personal followers of the chief or lord. Apparently both political and military leaders resorted to a bureaucratic form of organization only when the numbers of their subjects or followers became too numerous to be dealt with on a personal basis—as might happen, for example, when a prince extended his domain through conquest of neighboring peoples.

The Egyptians, Babylonians, and other early civilizations no doubt had political, military, and religious bureaucracies of some sort; it would be difficult to imagine how they could have maintained political order and fought their large-scale wars without this kind of organization. It is known that the genius of the Romans—what made it possible for them to conquer, rule, and exploit much of Western Europe—was their development of political and military bureaucracies and at a later time of bureaucratic organizations that engaged in large-scale economic activities—the *universitates* which, many centuries later, were to serve as the prototype of modern business corporations. The Chinese, too, developed an elaborate political bureaucracy which enabled a succession of emperors to rule after a fashion millions of citizens who were scattered over a vast territory, a bureaucracy that survived a succession of military conquests by foreign invaders.

The decline of the Roman Empire, wrought by a variety of factors, was evidenced in the progressive deterioration of the political and military bureaucracies through which Rome had maintained its power. Eventually familism and feudalism became the dominant forms of organization in the West; and for long the Church was the only organization with a bureaucratic structure, and that a weak and diffuse one. The armies of the Crusades seem to have been aggregations of small, personally commanded bands of soldiers rather than bureaucratic machines of disciplined, mechanically obedient, professional fighters; this would in part account for their very uncertain performance. At any event, it was not until well into the Middle Ages that bureaucracy as a form of organization regained importance. It then gradually came to be used in limited ways in economic organization, specifically in the organization of the guilds, which as small economic units were held together by a mixture of personal ties and impersonal bureaucratic rules and regulations. Bureaucracy in political organization developed as princes and overlords—wishing to free themselves, either because the task was too great or because they were otherwise engaged, from the necessity of ruling their subjects directly—established permanent officials to perform their various duties for them. These permanent representatives of the princes and overlords quickly secured assistants, the assistants secured subassistants, etc.; and in time the whole group was organized in a more or less bureaucratic fashion. As principalities were united into nations and as nations developed large armed forces, the role of bureaucracy in Western society necessarily increased. By the opening of the modern era, government, military operations, both on land and on sea, and religion, with the exception of Protestantism, were organized in a more or less bureaucratic fashion.

The technological and other changes that ushered in the industrial revolution were, for the most part, staunchly resisted by all existing bureaucracies—economic, political, military, and religious. (Since the Protestant churches had never achieved the organizational integration of the Roman and English Churches, resistance was less in countries that were dominantly Protestant.) Where technological changes were adopted and became effective, as in Britain and Northwestern Europe, many of the old bureaucracies were gradually weakened and, in many instances, eventually liquidated. The guilds were slowly crushed by competition with new forms of production and distribution; the establishment of parliamentary governments tended to break the hold, not only of the hereditary aristocracy, but also of the traditional political bureaucracies; and although military bureaucracy persisted, especially in Europe, by and large the old bureaucracies, and hence the role of the bureaucratic form of organization, declined sharply during and following the later eighteenth century.

So, too, it will be recalled, did the extended family, the community, and the traditional systems of stratification. What tended to take the place of these disintegrating forms of organization was a great variety of voluntary associations, large and small, that were formed by their participants to achieve jointly some goal beyond the abilities of any one of them alone or to solve some problem, such as the building of a bridge over a stream or the provision of fresh water to a town, that was of concern to all of them. Many of our present forms of organization, such as municipal government, have at least a historical relationship to the developments of this period. It was a time of organizational experimentation; and although most of the voluntary associations that were formed proved to be ineffectual and short-lived, the period was one that was organizationally conducive to innovation of all sorts. None of the traditional forms of organization—neither the family, the community, the class and other systems of stratification, nor the existing bureaucracies—was able to exercise effective authority over individuals or to prevent the adoption of changes that were initiated by individuals.

Bureaucracy and Social Change

In time, however, the many technological and other developments that followed the decline of traditional forms of organization led to a resurgence of bureaucracy; for they posed problems of organization that could be solved only, or at least most effectively, through this form of organization.

On the whole, the family in Western societies remained rather weak as a first line of defense against change, even as did the community. Today the family is generally nuclear rather than extended; and its authority over its members is reduced by competition with other agencies, such as the school, and by the high rates of individual mobility. The class system remains more open than closed, with the lines between strata both vague and variable. But over the past century there has been a notable increase in the number, size, and powers of bureaucratic organizations—economic, political, academic, and otherwise—that operate to constrain individual enterprise and inhibit social change. Thus although it is still possible and even permissible for an individual to work his way out of working-class origins, the bureaucratization of labor (unionization) has reduced the incentives for his doing so, while the bureaucratization of business and industry has made it increasingly difficult for him to do so.

The rise of bureaucracy as a dominant form of organization in modern industrial society is a change which has on the whole been an organizational adjustment to problems that were posed by antecedent changes, especially those of a technological nature. Through bureaucratic organization Western peoples have over and over met one specific problem after another. Thus, to cite but one example, when a city or a town abandoned its volunteer fire brigade and set up a corps of professional fire fighters, organized somewhat in the military manner, it sharply reduced the danger of an uncontained fire wiping out the entire community.

Each advance in efficiency thus secured has, however, quite incidentally erected a barrier, although not necessarily an unbreachable one, to further changes, technological or otherwise; for bureaucracy, like other forms of organization, discourages the emergence of changes from within and resists the impact of changes imposed from without.[3] The elaborate and highly efficient systems of fire-fighting agencies that have evolved over the past century—local fire departments, suppliers of fire-fighting equipment, etc.—have made extensive fires a thing of the past; but they have also, with considerable help from the trade unions and other bureaucratic organizations, tended to prevent experimentation in materials and in design for homes and larger structures; and the fire-prevention building codes of many communities are today an unrevised heritage from the last century.

Bureaucracy achieves efficiency through reducing the various activities

[3] The danger that the progressive bureaucratization of modern society will bring to an end the period of social dynamism is presented, in rather exaggerated form and without due regard for the other and equally significant changes that have been occurring to the social organization of modern society, by Joseph Bensman in *Mass, Class, and Bureaucracy* (Prentice-Hall, Inc., Englewood Cliffs, N.J., 1963); and by Robert Presthus in *The Organizational Society: An Analysis and a Theory* (Alfred A. Knopf, Inc., New York, 1962).

of the members of the organization to rule and routine. Each rule and procedure has, presumably, been determined by calculation and test to be the most expeditious way of accomplishing some end—the most efficient sequence by which to assemble an automobile motor, the safest way to land a jet plane (under specified conditions), the quickest way to route a letter from New York to San Francisco, etc. Scrupulous adherence to the relevant rules and procedures is thus the *sine qua non* of bureaucratic life. But anyone who year after year can and will follow the rules of a bureaucratic office without doubt or deviation is *ipso facto* demonstrating a lack of imagination, initiative, and courage to innovate anything whatever or to adopt the innovation of another, unless, indeed, it comes to him by way of an order from above. Even then, his adoption of the new will be qualified and tentative, and the new will be abandoned at first opportunity in favor of that which has been validated by the test of time.[4]

Bureaucracy no doubt maximizes the productivity of those individuals who, left to their own devices, would dissipate their time and energies in futility. Quite likely most men, even those of a dynamic society, need the protective shelter and systematic direction that bureaucracy provides. And it is undoubtedly true that many modern technologies can be efficiently applied and many nonmaterial social values, such as public health, provided only through bureaucracy. Nevertheless, the fact that bureaucracy makes for efficiency in many specific aspects of life does not mean that the increasing bureaucratization of modern society will in the long run make for greater social efficiency, for it is also true that bureaucracy does much to discourage the emergence of innovative individuals and even more to retard the adoption of whatever innovations do appear.

In the first place, potentially innovative individuals may be drawn into a bureaucratic organization and reduced to bureaucratic conformity by the system; rewards for bureaucratic conformity are often high, especially when compared with the uncertainty of any reward, material or prestigious, for innovative endeavor. In the second place, a bureaucracy almost always exercises direct or indirect control over some nonmembers, forcing them to conform to some extent to rule and regulation by the bureaucracy. This is most clearly evident with political and religious bureaucracies; but modern economic, scientific, and academic bureaucracies also commonly extend their influence to nonmembers. Thus American farmers must often produce what is specified for them by the great food-processing companies, subcontractors for automobile parts must conform to the needs of one or another of the three major motor companies, and scientists often find themselves con-

[4] For an analysis of some of the techniques by which bureaucrats resist changes that have been ordered by administrative leaders, see Richard T. LaPiere, *A Theory of Social Control*, McGraw-Hill Book Company, New York, 1954, pp. 405–415.

strained to design their research projects in accordance with the rules and prejudices of fund-granting foundations or other bureaucratic organizations.

There is a third and somewhat more subtle way in which bureaucracy operates to discourage change. It is a way that is dramatized, but hardly illustrated, by the apocryphal tale of the inventor who finds it impossible to market his automobile carburetor, which greatly increases gasoline mileage, because Such and Such Oil Company is against him. The grain of truth that this folk tale reflects is the inherent tendency for any mature bureaucratic organization to resist change from without—i.e., to be reluctant to adapt itself to changed external conditions or to adopt innovations that are available to it. A bureaucratic organization that is under duress, as industrial and business organizations that are subject to competition tend to be, may have changes forced on it by administrative leadership; but one that enjoys a monopoly over its particular function, as do most political bureaucracies and most public utilities and other protected economic organizations, can simply ignore changes in context and refuse to adopt innovations or even to test them out.

Isolation and Closure

A bureaucratic organization tends in the foregoing ways to isolate itself from the context in which it operates and to move toward a condition of internal stability. As it approaches stability, it becomes a self-maintaining and self-validating system, more complex than but not unlike a traditionalized social elite or a proud and ingrown family. At some point in this process, the function of the organization becomes the maintenance of its own structure and operations rather than the provision of the social values that it was designed to supply. In effect, the survival of the organization qua organization becomes the paramount concern of those who occupy the offices of the organization, including its highest administrative offices; but since each officeholder sees survival in terms of his particular office, rather than in terms of the system as a whole, organizational struggle for survival takes the direction of preserving the organizational *status quo*.

Isolation and its companion, self-validation, are accomplished by means of censorship, in crass or subtle ways, of communications that originate outside the organization and the provision of substitutes for them that are favorable to the system itself. Military bureaucracies usually achieve almost total isolation of their forces during times of war; the cloistered monasteries of the later Middle Ages were islands of ignorance about the world outside their walls, and no doubt Russian bureaucrats read little that has not been officially sanctioned and depend upon rumor for the actual facts of life. In modern democratic countries, where the free flow of news and views is considered vital to social welfare, bureaucrats—political or otherwise—

have easy access to criticisms of bureaucracy in general and their own organization in particular. Nevertheless, they usually either generate among themselves, or through official channels are provided with, rationalizations of news and opinions that are unfavorable and counterevidence and opinions that are favorable to the organization of which they are functioning parts. The memorandums which flow unceasingly through bureaucratic channels, house organs (common in business and industry), articles and editorials in journals that cater to special occupational groups, etc., all aid in giving the individual bureaucrat reassurance that the bureaucracy in which he serves is right and all critics of it wrong. Thus, as has been noted, even professional educators, who are only loosely integrated and not yet fully bureaucratized, have demonstrated their almost total isolation and their almost total dependence upon communications that originate with fellow educators. Apparently they are immune to the constant criticism that is voiced by the scientists and humanists on the other side of the campus, indifferent to the books and articles that batter at their professional complacence, and undaunted by the many movements for pedagogical reform which outsiders originate. Evidently they listen only to fellow educators and then hear only that which validates their presumption that what is should be.

Isolation and self-validation may not, however, entirely protect a bureaucratic organization from the threat of change. A political or military bureaucracy, particularly in the modern world, may be called to account by higher authority or by public outcry; the stability of any kind of bureaucratic organization may be jeopardized by an administrator who—perhaps because he has been brought in from outside or perhaps because his position is itself threatened by external pressures—calls for reorganization, the adoption of some new technique, or a modification of organizational goals. A political appointee may be assigned the task of revitalizing a torpid governmental agency, a new manager hired by the stockholders to modernize a dying business, or an energetic scholar brought in as president of a moss-encrusted college. If the circumstances are or can be made to seem sufficiently critical, some changes may in fact be effected. But it is always possible for a bureaucratic organization to block a drive for change and thus avoid the necessity of actually making changes. The procedures are varied, and all are familiar to professional bureaucrats. One device is to bring discredit upon the person of an administrator who has, however unwillingly, become the advocate for change. Another is to bring discredit upon the change that is so advocated—i.e., to test out or apply the new technique, procedure, or whatever in such a way as to demonstrate its inferiority to the old. Both devices are easy for the members of a bureaucratic organization to apply, for the success of an administrator or of what he advocates depends upon the actions of a large number of individuals, only a few of whom are subject to his immediate personal supervision.

Every mature bureaucratic organization has, furthermore, a variety of built-in and continually operating defenses against change. One of these is the bureaucratic preference for group, rather than individual, decisions. In all matters that affect the activities of two or more divisions, subdivisions, or sub-subdivisions of a bureaucratic organization, the committee or conference method is the procedure that is ordinarily used in reaching decisions. No doubt the procedure has its functional basis; it aids in the pooling of information, and it contributes to the *esprit de corps* of those who have to work together to put a decision into effect; but it also assures that matters which threaten bureaucratic complacence will be ignored just as long as possible and that any decision eventually taken regarding such a matter will be in the nature of a compromise. The effect of the group method of making decisions is so to divide responsibility that no single individual is responsible for decisions that are made; and division of responsibility often leads to negation of responsibility and hence frequently to failure to take effective action.

Another standard bureaucratic procedure which retards the making of adaptive changes is the avoidance of making decisions by denial of authority to do so. Each bureaucrat within the organization may say of a given problem that it is outside his department. Since the rules and regulations of a given bureaucratic office, even one that involves considerable administrative responsibility, deal with established procedures, techniques, etc., anything new falls, or can be made to seem to fall, beyond the jurisdiction of any office. Anything new—a problem that is not already covered by rules, a technique that is not already incorporated into the system, etc.—can be referred from office to office until the threat of change dies out or until the problem or proposal finally gets lost in someone's files.

THE BUREAUCRATIZATION OF ECONOMIC LIFE

By current standards the economic life of the peoples of medieval Europe was exceedingly sluggish. New productive techniques evolved slowly, were adopted even more slowly, and were often applied with great inefficiency. There were some major, but relatively local, periods of development in trade, such as those which centered, at different times, about Venice and Genoa. The productivity of labor, although far higher than it had been during the feudal period, was low; the standard of living was consequently only slightly above that of bare subsistence; and since total productivity of the necessities of life rose both slowly and erratically, it never far outran the pressure of population.

Many factors were jointly responsible for the economic impoverishment and comparative stability of the economic life of medieval peoples. As has already been mentioned, the Church cast its constraining shadow over everything, including the work that men did. Both organizationally and ideologically it discouraged ventures of all sorts, in technology as elsewhere. It drew off into its shelter large numbers of men of promise and directed those whom it could not subdue into such socially undisturbing forms of enterprise as cathedral building and missionary work among the heathens. It channeled communications, and it endeavored with considerable success to prevent both spatial and social mobility. The official doctrine of the Church was, moreover, conducive to a passive acceptance of things as they were and inimical to the view that men could of their own volition make them anything else.

The political organization of medieval peoples was perhaps less discouraging to social change than the religious. Many princes were endeavoring, in their fumbling way, to work change of a sort—mainly to extend their principalities into kingdoms and thus to unite politically the diverse peoples of Europe; but their efforts to bring about political unification operated to retard rather than accelerate change in the economic aspects of life; for wars, which were almost constant, impeded the production and distribution of goods. In the long run the consolidation of principalities into kingdoms proved favorable to economic life; but in the short run, political fragmentation and the struggles for power inhibited the growth of markets, specialization in production, and efforts to improve productive and distributive techniques.

The economic organization of the later Middle Ages was of mixed character. In rural areas, where the extended family was the basic unit of both production and consumption and as such was commonly hampered and constrained by old landownership and land usage practices inherited from feudalism, there was little incentive to increase production, and few improvements were made in agricultural technology. In the towns, where the guild form of organization tended to dominate in both production and trade, guild masters usually maintained a strong hold over local political as well as economic affairs. The power of the guilds waxed and waned both locally and over Europe in general; and although their control over the economy was never absolute, the guilds did by and large exercise a constraining force. Their quasi-bureaucratic form made them highly conservative, technologically and otherwise; and to preserve their position without making adaptive changes they had, perforce, to maintain as much of a monopoly as they could over the production and distribution of goods. They were not, it will be recalled, reluctant to resort to force to punish an individual guildsman who dared to violate price and other regulations or to drive out any upstart outsider who thought to set up in competition with them. Moreover, the guilds were profit- (or wage-) oriented rather than production-oriented; and as a result they contrived to maintain an artificial scarcity of goods, they were slow to increase production even in the face of rising demand, and they were disinclined to adopt any sort of labor-saving device or procedure. It was in part at least because of the influence of the guilds on medieval economic life that so few changes occurred over the course of many centuries in productive and distributive technology.[5]

Individual enterprise, however, was not entirely lacking. It was individual enterprise that led to the development of sea-borne commerce during the fifteenth century; and although world exploration during this and the following century was often given encouragement by governments, especially those of Portugal and Spain, the ventures were undertaken by individuals rather than some preexisting organization. By the time of the Reformation individual enterprise was represented in Northern Europe by the small class of independent bankers, independent merchants, and independent factory owners. The latter, the prototype of the capitalists who were to become dominant during the eighteenth and nineteenth centuries, were no doubt the dynamic factor in the economic life of Western Europe and Britain; it was they who brought about the gradual emergence of a new and open class system and who eventually revolted from the dead hand of both the Church and monarchial government. For some centuries, however, they were few in number; and their endeavors were staunchly resisted by all the older forms of organization—most effectively by the guilds.

The Entrepreneurial System

Particularly in France and Britain, the balance of economic power—and, hence, indirectly of political power—slowly shifted in favor of the individual entrepreneur. The demand for finished goods, especially textiles, was growing both at home and abroad, and the rule-bound guilds were incapable of increasing their production to satisfy the growing needs; and since the population of the towns was rising and the guilds refused to enlarge their operations, there was a considerable body of available and unattached

[5] The guild form of work and trade organization seems always to have been associated with technological and economic stability, although the extent to which it is stability that fosters the emergence of the guild form of organization and the latter that produces stability is never ascertainable. A development not unlike that which occurred during the Middle Ages in the West produced guildlike monopolization of crafts and trades in the Byzantine Empire during the tenth century. In the interests of consumers, governmental regulation of the medieval guilds evolved; and between the guilds and government, individual enterprise was all but eliminated in Western Europe and the period of innovation in the production and distribution of goods came to a close. See P. Boissonnade, *Life and Work in Medieval Europe*, The Macmillan Company, New York, 1927, pp. 46–47.

labor. The system that evolved was one in which enterprising individuals hired labor and provided materials, and subsequently the means of production, in producing goods that could be profitably disposed of outside the channels of guild-controlled trade. Cottage industry, one consequence of this system, has already been described. More common on the Continent was small-factory production—workshops in which hired labor was employed in working raw materials into finished goods, initially by simple craft techniques.

Until well toward the close of the eighteenth century, individual entrepreneurs operated against many handicaps. The local guilds and the municipal laws that the guilds sponsored were against them; the mercantilist policy of national governments, which encouraged exports but restricted imports of all except specie, made it difficult for them to obtain raw materials from abroad and to sell finished goods to countries that did not have gold for payment; and they lacked any systematic procedure for the marketing of their goods. All these conditions made any economic venture both difficult and hazardous; but since the rewards for success were great, individual enterprise was ideologically encouraged during this period.

As the gap between the desire for goods and technological and organizational ability to produce them widened, men applied themselves in increasing numbers to the mechanization of productive techniques. The first major advance toward mechanization was the invention, by James Hargreaves about 1765, of the spinning jenny, a device driven by water wheel which could spin simultaneously a considerable number of threads. Its success inaugurated the vogue that still obtains for the replacement of human hands and muscles by power-driven machines in the processing of raw materials into finished products. The spinning jenny and the many other inventions which soon followed gave a tremendous advantage to individual entrepreneurs. They could and did exploit the new mechanized means of production, while the guilds remained loyal to the old craft techniques. By the close of the eighteenth century, the individually operated economic establishment was well on its way to becoming the dominant type of nonagricultural productive and distributive unit in Britain and Northern Europe.

The individually operated economic establishment was organized, although it did not constitute an organization in the full sense. The only permanent member was the entrepreneur himself; all the others, the employees, had no claim to organizational membership other than that in the judgment of the entrepreneur they contributed more in economic value than they cost in wage or salary. Each one was, therefore, subject to constant economic coercion; and by such coercion, qualified only by whatever alternatives the labor market offered the worker, the entrepreneur could secure obedience to his will. If he wished to install new and more efficient machines, he could do so without regard for the feelings of his employees; if he decided that it was for the moment unprofitable to continue operations, he could simply discharge his staff and close up shop; if he was prospering, he need only enlarge his plant and hire more workers to increase production.

The entrepreneurial system thus gave great flexibility to the enterprising individual in that he was not bound to the past by an organizational apparatus; but as time proved, it was very hard not only on the hired worker but on the employer as well. The system not only made it possible for an employer to adapt his operations to changing market conditions, technological developments, and kinds and sources of raw materials, but in the long run forced him to do so; for the system made it comparatively easy for any ambitious, shrewd, and industrious man to become an entrepreneur. An individual might start with as little as one employee and expand his operation through reinvestment of his profits. Such being the case, an established entrepreneur was always subject to competition from young upstarts; and while he might have some competitive advantages over newcomers, such as his good reputation in the industry, these could easily be canceled out if a competitive newcomer could, through the adoption of labor-saving devices, more effective use of labor, etc., produce or distribute goods more efficiently.

The ideal establishment was, no doubt, just that—an ideal. Actual establishments included many staid one-man or one-family businesses or shops, so beloved by the petty bourgeois, and some equally staid large industrial or mercantile firms that were living on their reputations. Under the direction of an atypically ambitious and venturesome man, the former kind of establishment might in fact become enterprising; under the indifferent management of the son or grandson of its founder and developer, a once-enterprising firm might become lethargic and unprogressive. What made the system highly dynamic, however, was the fact that aging and ingrown firms tended to be pushed out by those that were, in marketplace terms, more efficient and that, as the latter in turn developed hardening of the organizational arteries, new firms rose to displace them.

The typical establishment was, at least at the outset, owned and operated by one man. If it prospered, its owner might make it a family firm by forming in due course a partnership with his son or sons—hence the frequency with which nineteenth-century firms were designated "So-and-So and Sons," "Such and Such Brothers," etc. A common alternative was the formation of a partnership between two or more individuals who were not related, each of whom contributed his financial share to the capital plant and, in theory, his share in directing the firm. Both kinds of partnerships operated on the trust and mutual respect of each partner for the others, and each partner was legally responsible for contractual obligations undertaken by the others. Where mutual trust was valid, a two- or three-headed firm could direct a much larger operation than could a one-man unit; and since direction of the firm would still be highly personal, it could also achieve the same dynamic quality as could a one-man firm.

The Rise of the Corporation

The entrepreneurial system has persisted down to the present day, but it has long since ceased to be the dominant form of organization in the economies of Western peoples. In the place it formerly held has come the corporation, a legal entity that is in legal theory devoid of persons—i.e., an organization that is prior to and independent of the persons who establish and maintain it. It is the rise of the corporate form of organization in business that has brought about the increasing bureaucratization of economic life, and it is the extent to which this form of organization prevails that is the effective measure of that bureaucratization.

Corporate organizations of a semiprivate character were evolved by the Romans to supplement their many governmental and military bureaucracies. Frequently they were formed for some specific venture—such as the importation of grain from Carthage—and were dissolved upon the completion of that venture. Their advantage over political and military bureaucracies for such purposes lay, presumably, in the fact that the task would be completed before the organization achieved bureaucratic stagnation. In the later Middle Ages, a rather primitive form of the corporation was devised—or, more probably, borrowed from the ancients—to enable monarchs to extend their economic power, especially over parts of Asia and the New World, without actually taking political jurisdiction over foreign lands.[6] In this procedure, the sovereign gave an individual or group letters patent that granted monopoly rights over some proposed venture and did not hold the person or persons so privileged personally or legally responsible for their actions on behalf of the venture. Ventures ranged from the settlement of new lands

---

[6] Previously, according to Will Durant (*The Age of Faith,* vol. IV of *The Story of Civilization,* Simon and Schuster, Inc., New York, 1950, p. 627) the Church prohibition of usury had been evaded by a somewhat similar organizational device, which may have been the immediate antecedent to the letters patent. Of this he says, in part, "Commercial credit began when an individual or a family, by what Latin Christendom called *commenda,* commended or entrusted money to a merchant for a specific voyage or enterprise, and received a share of the profits. Such silent or 'sleeping' partnership was an ancient Roman device, probably relearned by the Christian West from the Byzantine East. So useful a way of sharing in profits without directly contravening the ecclesiastical prohibition of interest was bound to spread, and the 'company' (*com-panis,* bread-sharer) or family investment became a *societas,* a partnership in which several persons, not necessarily kin, financed a group or series of ventures rather than one. Such financial organizations appeared in Genoa and Venice toward the end of the tenth century, reached a high development in the twelfth, and largely accounted for the rapid growth of Italian trade." In colonial America much the same device was often used to spread the high risks of whaling and of ventures in the tea trade.

to the establishment of trade with a specified people. The granting of monopoly rights with exoneration from liability led, perhaps inevitably, to serious abuses, but it did, no doubt, accelerate the development of world trade and the settlement of the New World.

Perhaps the most extensive and enduring organization that evolved out of the issuance of letters patent was the East India Company. At first, trade with India was conducted by independent merchants of various nationalities; but in 1600 Queen Elizabeth granted a charter of monopoly to "The Governor and Company of Merchants of London" for a period of fifteen years. By the end of this period, the London merchants had evolved an elaborate and efficient organization which maintained trade with India until the Company was taken over by the British government in 1858. The original company was financed by over one hundred shareholders, and centuries later it was used as the model for the modern joint-stock or corporate form of economic organization.

The trend toward the corporate form of organization, which became pronounced in Britain by the middle of the nineteenth century, came as an adaptation to changing technological and marketing conditions. The development and exploitation of such early innovations in machine technology as the spinning jenny and the steam engine had called for a great deal of enterprise but fairly small amounts of capital. There came a time, however, when the investment of materials and labor that was required for the development and exploitation of innovations often was too great for any one man or partnership of two or three men to undertake. Large quantities of venture capital were needed, for example, to build and operate steamships and to build and operate railroads; moreover, both the building and operating required a larger number of workers than could be directed personally by an individual entrepreneur.

Toward the close of the eighteenth century, it will be recalled, pessimists had been freely predicting the end of the iron age, since the smelters were running out of timber to make into charcoal. Two generations later, many were thinking that the machine age had run its course and was about to flounder through the inability of men to finance such great and uncertain ventures as that of the steamship and the railroad. But even as the discovery of coking coal had saved the iron age, the adoption of the corporate form of organization came to the rescue of the machine age. Through this form of organization, which quickly won public and political acceptance, an entrepreneur or group of entrepreneurs (usually described as "promoters") could form a company and sell shares which did not obligate those who purchased them beyond the amount of their investments. Thus it became possible for a large number of individuals to pool such sums as they could reasonably afford to lose without jeopardizing the remainder of their holdings and without becoming in any way personally responsible for commitments made by the company. If the company failed, they lost what they had invested in its stock, but nothing else; if it succeeded, they shared in the profits earned. Moreover, since the company was, in law, an entity in its own right, the founders and operators of the company as well as the shareholders were exempt from being held personally responsible and thus risked only the time and effort that they expended on company affairs.

By its very nature, the corporation brought about a partial if not total separation between the owners of the company and those who operated it and to that extent depersonalized the organization; and in time the managers of companies were almost as much hirelings of the corporation as were the common laborers. It was, however, mainly the growing size of corporate operations and the problems posed by the use of new techniques that were responsible for their developing bureaucratic characteristics. How both these factors contributed to the bureaucratization of economic life is well illustrated in the transition from sailing ship to steamship. A sailing ship could be and usually was owned by a merchant or chartered to him by the owner. The merchant directed each of its voyages to some particular market or source of raw materials; but from the moment it left land, it was in effect an individual undertaking; for until the ship returned or reached an agent of the merchant, the captain was in absolute command. He was subject, of course, to a large body of rules that had evolved over the centuries; but these rules were rules of prudence, not specifications of proper procedure. He therefore sailed fast or slow, this route or that, in accordance with his personal judgment of what was expedient. He might, as did the clipper captains in the China tea trade, endeavor to reach port ahead of competing captains; and should he lose the ship in such an endeavor, he was held personally responsible—he was ruined, assuming that he himself had survived.

With the advent of the steamship it became possible for the first time to schedule the arrival and departure of ships; and it also became impossible for the first time for a captain to retain full personal responsibility for the operation of his ship. A scheduled ship operation required a more complex land-based organization, which in itself reduced the personal role of the captain of a ship and subordinated him to the schedule laid out for him. A captain could no longer plot his route in terms of his personal judgment but instead had to set his course according to the book and to endeavor to maintain the designated speeds. Moreover, with the advent of wireless communications, the captain of a ship became subject to orders from his company office while en route from port to port. Meanwhile, his personal authority on shipboard was in fact, if not in theory, weakened by his dependence on the judgment of his chief engineer, who was the final authority in mechanical matters. As ship operations became more and more complex and mechanized, the structure of authority on shipboard also became more complex and ramified, until the captain of a great ship was no longer the personal director of the affairs of his ship but became instead the chief administrator of a mobile and highly impersonal bureaucratic organization.

The impact of the problems posed by railroad technology on the organization of land transport was even more profound; for although a steamship can go its independent way from port to port, a freight or passenger train must for safety proceed from mile to mile on a predetermined schedule that is coordinated with the schedules of all the other trains that operate along the same line or on intersecting lines. In the early days of the railroad each train did operate with something of the freedom of a ship at sea; but as traffic increased, it became imperative that the movement of each train be determined in accordance with that of all the others; and from this necessity came a very rapid adoption of the bureaucratic form of organization. Once inaugurated, the bureaucratization of railroad operation spread throughout the entire system, until every activity was encased in its change-resisting body of rules and regulations. By the end of the nineteenth century, the railroad companies of both Europe and America had become so thoroughly bureaucratic in organization that they were almost incapable of adopting new technological developments or of shifting their operational procedures; and it was therefore possible for them to be taken over by governments or brought under the jurisdiction of governmental agencies without loss of their operating efficiency. The measure of their organizational unprogressiveness is the fact that in no country did the railroads assume responsibility for the operation of such new means of transportation as the motor truck and bus and the airplane. They left the development and exploitation of these new technologies to the enterprise of others and continued as organizations to be dedicated to the proposition that their task was to keep the trains running on schedule, come what may, refusing to recognize the functional idea that their business was supposed to be that of providing transportation of goods and persons by the fastest and cheapest means available.[7]

[7] The railroads probably represent an extreme of corporate conservatism, although Henry W. Ehrmann has shown that in modern France business organizations of all kinds, whether large or small, tend to be monopolistic and technologically and organizationally inert (*Organized Business in France*, Princeton University Press, Princeton, N.J., 1957). For other views and findings see Alvin W. Gouldner, *Patterns of Industrial Bureaucracy*, The Free Press of Glencoe, New York., 1954; A. D. H. Kaplan et al., *Pricing in Big Business: A Case Approach*, The Brookings Institution, Washington, D.C., 1958; Wilbert E. Moore, *The Conduct of the Corporation*, Random House, Inc., New York, 1962; and W. Lloyd Warner, *The Corporation in the Emergent American Society*, Harper & Row, Publishers, Incorporated, New York, 1962.

The Bureaucratization of Production

The utilization of many technological innovations in addition to those of the steamship and the railroad has necessarily required organization of a bureaucratic sort—the telegraph, the telephone, the commercial airplane, the radio, coal gas, and more recently natural gas and electricity for power and heat, etc. In the application of other technological innovations bureaucracy has developed in the interests of efficiency, rather than as the result of necessity. Thus it was to increase productive efficiency that Henry Ford adopted, adapted, and developed the principle of interchangeable parts and the routinized assembly line in the manufacture of automobiles. According to legend, the principle of interchangeable parts was conceived first by Paul Revere in the making of muskets; if legend be true, he must also have devised an assembly line of sorts. But not even in the machine industries was this principle strictly and systematically applied until Ford undertook the mass production of his famous Model T automobile in 1914 and thereby began a development which has gradually spread to the production of all but the more esoteric of art goods.

The technique of mass production is but a special application of the bureaucratic form of organization. It reduces each of the many actions, human and mechanical, that are involved in the total productive procedure to rule and coordinates each with all the others. Under this system workingmen, as well as all those involved in the control of workingmen, in the supply of raw materials, in the disposition of the finished product, etc., become functionaries. Thus although a workingman may still be a skilled worker, he is no longer a craftsman; for he can no longer exercise personal judgment in the performance of his task. Moreover, as productive operations are subdivided and routinized, they become susceptible to increasing mechanization until, as is so often the case today, a workingman no longer does the work—he starts and stops the machine that does the work for him. Even the control of machines has, of recent years, been increasingly turned over to machines—to electronic devices that permit automatization of many productive procedures.

The gains in productive efficiency that have been brought about by the progressive bureaucratization of productive procedures account in considerable measure for the currently high standard of living of Western peoples. These gains, however, have been achieved at a price; for mass-production methods mean on the one hand standardized products and, on the other, technological inflexibility. The American automobile industry, for example, has done a great deal to extend and refine the technique of mass production; but the farther it has gone in this direction, the less it has contributed to the improvement of the automobile as a transportation device. The existence of a vast and productively efficient plant with a human organization to operate that plant discourages both the innovation and the adoption of new kinds of automobile forms. European manufacturers of automobiles, who have been and still are to some extent less efficient in production, have been far less reluctant to adopt new devices and test them out; and over the past three decades and more all the major innovations in automobile technology except power steering and the automatic transmission have come from England and Europe.[8]

The Bureaucratization of Distribution

Mass production of goods presupposes a large market for goods, since mechanized production is economic only when the machines are used at full capacity. The development of methods of mass production has, therefore, been predicated upon the existence of large and continuing markets; and large markets became possible only with the organization, along bureaucratic lines, of the distribution of goods. Where, as tends to be the case in peasant and primitive societies, the production and consumption unit are the same, distribution is simply a matter of allocating the food and other goods available to the various members of the group. But where producer and consumer belong to different basic organizations, some system of exchange of values is necessary; and if producer and consumer are separated by considerable distances, some mode of transporting goods and whatever is used in repayment for goods also is necessary.

The simplest form of trade, that in which the producer himself offers directly to the consumer the goods he has produced, has existed in many societies and still exists today. Agriculturists have usually sold their produce this way by holding periodic market days in town or village; and the fabricators of goods—the baker, the candlestick maker, etc.—have frequently sold their products in the shops in which they were made. Where the producer has been unable to go to the consumer, or vice versa, trade has been conducted by intermediaries, by merchants and traders, many or few, who have dealt in one special kind of goods or in many varieties.

In general the merchant guilds of the Middle Ages either dealt in local products for local markets, as, for example, did fishmongers, or exported a local product, such as swords, and imported a foreign product, such as leather. Exchanges of the latter sort could often be accomplished without the medium of money, which until fairly recent times had uncertain and

[8] Once the device had been perfected, the automatic transmission was rapidly adopted by American automobile manufacturers. For some reason they delayed a quarter of a century before adopting power steering. The device was invented by F. W. Davis in 1926, but manufacturers were almost totally indifferent to its potentialities. Not until 1951, when the Chrysler Corporation first made power steering optional equipment, was its utility generally recognized.

variable value, and were thus a sort of barter between two guilds in different towns. The transportation and actual exchange of goods was often a difficult and hazardous matter and might be effected by one guild or the other or by representatives of each who met, goods in hand, at a central point, initially a trade fair, and there effected the exchange. It was from such meeting places that the great trade centers of the later Middle Ages evolved.

In time sea-borne commerce, which, as has been indicated, had been developed by individual entrepreneurs, also came into the hands of the merchant guilds. Their operations were highly organized, and hence efficient and reliable, but they tended to become fixed and costly to the consumer.[9] Eventually changing market demands, to which the merchant guilds could not adapt themselves, new kinds of goods, and the mercantilistic policies of Western nations led to the emergence of a new form of trade, one that was based mainly on money and conducted mainly by individual entrepreneurs. In this system, which was for long illicit, a merchant assembled from individual producers a body of merchandise which he paid for either in cash or, in the cottage-industry system of England, in kind, and which he disposed of, either for money or goods, in some foreign market. In the simplest of many procedures, a merchant himself took the goods to the foreign land, smuggled it past customs, and peddled it to consumers. Alternatively, he might send his goods through intermediaries to an opposite number in the foreign market.

What is interesting and significant about the emergence of this mode of distribution is that it established a pattern for distribution which, once it had become legitimatized and systematized, served very well through the nineteenth century and has only now begun to be displaced by a still newer procedure. As it evolved, the free-lance merchant who dealt in quantity became a sort of merchant's merchant—a wholesaler—who purchased from various producers, by then become factory owners, and assembled at a central distribution point goods of some common kind—shoes, clothing, packaged foods, hardware, etc.—which he sold to retailers in the area that he served. A wholesaler could purchase from producers in larger quantities,

[9] Costly, because the merchant guilds held monopoly powers and therefore operated on the principle of high unit profit and low turnover. To extend monopoly control, merchant guilds often banded together in restrictive associations. The greatest of these associations was the Hanseatic League, formed in the thirteenth century by a number of commercial towns to protect their trade from feudal tolls, thieves, and competitors. For a time the League effectively promoted trade by clearing the Baltic and North Seas of pirates, dredging and improving waterways, charting currents, and developing maritime law. Within a century, however, it had turned from the promotion of trade to the maintenance of a monopoly over trade, squeezing the consumers on the one hand and the artisan producers of goods on the other. So exploitative was the League that in 1381 English workers revolted and murdered all identifiable members of it.

and hence at lower prices, than could any single merchant; and since a wholesaler stocked for many retailers, each retailer could operate with a comparatively small inventory of goods and replenish his stock as quickly as he needed to.

Distribution through wholesalers proved to be especially valuable and was widely adopted in America, where the great distances made direct buying from producers especially difficult. In Britain and Europe retail merchants tended to rely somewhat more upon direct purchase from producers, either from the producers' catalogs or by way of traveling representatives of producers. It may well be because of the elaborate development of the wholesale house in America that most of the subsequent developments in distribution have been of American origin. These subsequent developments, which have culminated in such marketing devices as the chain store and the supermarket, seem to have begun with two separate innovations—the mail-order house and Woolworth's five-and-ten-cent store.[10]

The mail-order house was a rather logical development from the wholesale house; it was simply a wholesale house that circumvented the local retailer and sent goods ordered by mail from a catalog to the consumer by freight or parcel post. The savings to the consumer were considerable, and the mail-order house could offer a much wider variety of goods than could small-town merchants. Farm families located far from major trading centers came in time to do a considerable proportion of their buying of consumers' hard goods and even of such capital goods as plows, furniture, windmills, etc., from such establishments. The development of mail-order merchandising was one of the important factors responsible for the decline during the early decades of this century of rural trade centers—i.e., rural crossroads towns. It also helped to establish the principle of large unit sales at small profit per unit, a principle that English and European merchants are only now discovering. It was this principle, quite new to merchandising, that Woolworth applied to urban retailing; and it was the success of Woolworth's first five-and-ten-cent store that led him to establish a chain of such stores and which did much to inaugurate the now widespread practice of operating a number of scattered retail outlets through a wholesale-like central agency. It is not clear just where the idea of letting the customer serve himself, which is now a part of the supermarket system, originated. Woolworth did adopt the practice of displaying his merchandise on open counters and letting the buyer select what he wanted; it may be that the self-service idea was derived from this practice.

In recent decades mercantile practices have made many radical adaptations to the American penchant for considering an automobile a necessity and

[10] See Boris Emmet and John E. Jeuck, *Catalogues and Counters: A History of Sears, Roebuck and Company*, The University of Chicago Press, Chicago, 1950.

finding every possible excuse for using it. Since the American farmer now has motor transport and thinks nothing of driving 50 miles or more to do his shopping, the mail-order house has tended to become a wholesale department store, with a chain of retail outlets in all fair-sized and large towns. Since urban shoppers can seldom find a place to park their cars in the business center of a town or city, merchants—chain and individual—have tended to move out to the semiopen spaces of the suburbs and create shopping centers. And since labor costs have risen rapidly during the post-World War II years, the self-service principle has been adopted wherever it has been physically feasible.

On the whole, therefore, the bureaucratization of the distribution of goods does not seem so far to have had as stabilizing effects as has the bureaucratization of the production of the goods so distributed. Just why is not evident; perhaps it is because it is still easier to establish a merchandising firm than a producing one and for a small independent merchant to grow into a large one than for a small producer to become a major producer. At any event, the efficiencies of large-scale merchandising have not yet enabled large mercantile firms to ignore the competition, actual or potential, of small, dynamic units; and large firms have by and large changed techniques and procedures with changing market demands.

The Bureaucratization of Labor

The entrepreneurial system required a relatively free labor market; for if an entrepreneur was to adjust his operations to shifts in market demands, to adopt new techniques, and to refine productive procedures, he had to be able to determine the size and character of his labor force and what his workers did and how they did it. As gradually became evident during the nineteenth century, the power of an entrepreneur to hire and fire at will invariably meant that the worker was uncertain of gainful employment and often meant also that the hours and conditions of his work were markedly deleterious to his physical welfare. And as corporate organization became dominant in business and industry and the size of establishments increased while their relative number diminished, workers often found that, although the labor market might be free for employers, it was anything but free for workers—i.e., an employer could hire and fire at will, but an individual worker often had no immediate alternative to working for a particular employer at the wage and under the conditions that the employer determined.

The practice of workers' banding together against their superiors had evolved in various places during the later Middle Ages. Peasants had learned the value of joint action—such as refusal to work and rioting—against landlords; and journeyman members of craft guilds had sometimes banded together on a town-wide basis to fight what they considered to be unjust treatment by the guild masters. Such efforts on the part of workers had, however, been sporadic and generally ineffective; and the only durable result had been the incorporation into common law in England and fiat law in some European countries of prohibitions against combinations of working people. In the early phases of the industrial revolution, factory workers, especially those of the rural factory towns of England, frequently rioted against reduction of the work force, reduction of wages, or total closing of the establishments in which they had been employed; and the laws against combinations of working people were as a consequence in many instances made more severe. Nevertheless, craftsmen from the rapidly disintegrating craft guilds, who were accustomed to being organized and thereby protected in their employment, tended to form, under the new employer-employee system, into informal clubs wherein each worker agreed with his fellows upon such matters as the wage to be accepted, the amount of work to be accorded, etc. The effectiveness of such informal organization and agreements was limited by the ability of the club to exert sanctions on digressors and to prevent nonmembers from working in the craft or trade that the club represented.

The informal club was not notably successful in the crafts, nor was it adopted by industrial or commercial workers. It seems, however, to have provided, in England at least, the seed from which the trade union movement grew during the second quarter of the nineteenth century; and at any event, it provided the idea that in union there is strength, an idea that was to become a movement slogan. In England and elsewhere the laws against combinations of workers were in time either repealed or relaxed; and by midcentury most English skilled workers were organized into trade unions. Although the power of the unions waxed and waned in accordance with the general demand for labor, by the end of the century trade unionism was firmly established—i.e., it was widely practiced and given general social and legal sanction—in all Western countries.

Where and at such times as trade unions exerted strong power, the effect was, depending upon other factors, either to freeze economic operations or to further the mechanization of productive procedures. The classic example of the former effect is that provided by the railroads, where the organizational sluggishness induced by bureaucratization was aggravated by a rapid and total unionization of railroad workers, with the result that the many rules and regulations of the operational system were augmented by fully as many rules and regulations established and maintained by the various trade unions to which the workers belonged. A good example of the latter consequence of union-created scarcity of labor has been the shoe industry, where the high wages demanded by unionized workers led manufacturers to adopt machine substitutes for hand labor. Today, even the lasting of a shoe is accomplished by machinery.

Until well into the present century, union organization retained its trade character; and neither the unskilled or semiskilled worker in industry nor the worker in commerce was protected by union membership. However, as the progressive consolidation and bureaucratization of industrial and commercial operations gave corporate managers intolerably great power over workers, a corrective arose in the form of a movement toward industrial unionism. In this new movement the goal was the organization of all the workers—skilled, unskilled, white-collar, and blue-collar—in a given industry. The movement made great headway in England and on the Continent in the years immediately following World War I and in the United States during the 1930s.[11] Today most of the employees of all the major industrial and commercial establishments in Western societies belong either to an industry-wide union or to a trade-type union; and in many instances trade unions covering related crafts are integrated in some way or other, as into the AFL in the United States.

The growth of union organization, especially industrial union organization, which includes semiskilled and unskilled workers, has undoubtedly tended to bring about an uneasy equilibrium to the labor market. Representatives of the unions now come to the bargaining table with an economic coercive power over business and industry that is often equal and sometimes superior to that which corporation managers can exert over labor. As the organization of labor came to balance off the organization of management, labor was enabled to claim a share of the gains in production that were brought about by improved techniques and increased efficiency in the use of labor. Whether labor has also been able in the course of time to increase its share of what is produced is a matter for labor economists to debate.[12] On the whole, it seems likely that labor's share has not changed significantly over the past century and that the rising standard of living enjoyed by labor has been brought about, not by labor itself, but by the increases in industrial and business productivity that have followed upon the introduction by enterprising management of more effective techniques and more efficient modes of organization.

In the struggle to maintain its old share labor has, however, become increasingly bureaucratized; and today there is very little freedom in the

[11] For various aspects of this development see Walter Galenson, *The CIO Challenge to the AFL: A History of the Labor Movement, 1935–1941*, Cambridge University Press, New York, 1960; Lewis L. Lorwin, *The International Labor Movement: History, Policies, and Outlook*, Harper & Row, Publishers, Incorporated, New York, 1953; and C. Wright Mills, *The New Men of Power: America's Labor Leaders*, Harcourt, Brace & World, Inc., New York, 1948.

[12] George H. Hildebrand, for example, holds that the major consequence of the organization of labor has been to reduce occupational mobility and so intensify class stratification ("American Unionism, Social Stratification, and Power," *American Journal of Sociology*, vol. 58, pp. 381–390, January, 1953).

labor market. Today most workingmen belong to a union, which is now a large and elaborate bureaucratic organization that specifies the kind of work that they may do, the conditions under which they may do such work, and the minimum wage they may accept for doing that work. Frequently the union even designates the kinds of tools that workers may use, sets maximum standards of production for them, and determines on the basis of seniority in the union rather than proficiency in work which of those available for employment will be sent to an employer who is in need of workers. One consequence of the bureaucratization of labor—its discouraging effects on efforts to move upward in the occupational and class systems of stratification—has already been discussed. Another, and in the long run perhaps more significant, is its encouraging management to stabilize its operations.

The bureaucratization of labor may be seen as a counter to the growth of corporate organization in industry and business. It has tended, however, to accelerate this growth; for the stability of employment and the security that organized labor demands can be provided only if business and industrial establishments are themselves stable and, hence, secure; and it is only through bureaucratic caution, technological and otherwise, that such establishments can avoid the risks of failure that invariably accompany change of any kind. Neither the bureaucratization of business and industry nor that of labor has as yet brought anything approaching stability to the economic life of Western peoples; but both have certainly reduced both the opportunity and the scope for individual enterprise; and bureaucracy has come to be the dominant form of organization today, even as the entrepreneurial system was dominant through the nineteenth century.

BUREAUCRATIZATION OF THE PROFESSIONS

All the older societies, primitive and civilized, had their priests or magic men who by social definition served as middlemen between supernaturalistic forces and the population. In some societies their powers were inherited, and the priests formed a closed class with an organizational monopoly over magic or religious powers. In others, ability to interpret or influence the supernatural was acquired through training or occasionally through purchase of magical powers. In either case the priesthood functioned for the individual as a source of consolation and confidence and for the social system as a supplement to other forms of social control, and in both roles it was invariably an important factor in stabilizing the social system. The status of a priesthood depended upon a continued acceptance by the population of the supernaturalistic beliefs from which its powers were derived; and in order to ensure a continued acceptance, a priesthood was of necessity oriented toward the preservation of the institutional, class, technological, and other aspects of the system of which those beliefs were a functioning part.

In neither primitive societies nor in the societies of antiquity were practitioners of the applied arts, such as law and medicine, held in great esteem. In primitive societies magic and the applied arts were often intermixed; a magic man might drive off evil spirits by spells and incantations and, almost as a side line, serve as the local bonesetter. In the civilizations of antiquity some separation of magic and the practical arts existed; and where it did, the status of the practitioners of the practical arts—the bonesetters, the designers of buildings, the keepers of records, the pedagogues, etc.—was always markedly inferior to that of the seers, the temple priests, the oracles, the necromancers, and other claimants to extrasensory powers. Practitioners of the practical arts were often held as slaves in the households of rich and powerful men; they were sometimes tolerated for their curiosity value, as were the scholars and pedants of Athens; and in a few instances they were supported by patrons along with artists and musicians, as were the learned Jews among the Moslems.

The lowly estate of practitioners of the practical arts no doubt reflected the low quality of the arts they practiced and, hence, their relative unimportance to the social system. It also resulted in their being unorganized, either in formal or informal ways. Not until the Middle Ages did practitioners of the practical arts begin to be organized into what are now known as the professions. There was no parallel to the professions either in the societies of antiquity or in the premodern civilizations of India and China. In China, for example, the practice of medicine was open to anyone who was able to read and had access to the rather small and highly traditional body of medical literature; and anyone usually meant a student who had failed in the first examination of the official system and was not even qualified to serve as tutor to young scholars.

The Professional Form of Organization

As a form of organization, a profession combines some characteristics of a class and some of an occupational stratum, although it operates in a way distinct from both and unique to itself. Like those who belong to a class, those who belong to a profession may be and usually are dispersed and unrelated to one another by formal organizational ties; a professional man belongs to his profession in somewhat the same sense that a nobleman belongs to the nobility, rather than as a member of a specific organization, such as a family or a guild. The unity of those who belong, again in a manner somewhat akin to that of the nobility or of those of any other clearly defined stratum, is a by-product of their sharing a fairly common set of techniques and knowledges and a more or less honored code of member-to-member and member-to-nonmember conduct and their placing a high value on membership in the profession. In these respects, a profession is very much like a class or an occupational stratum; but a profession differs from these in that membership is never ascribed and can be achieved only after completion of a lengthy and elaborate training program. Membership is open, in theory at least, to all; but to become accepted as a recognized member of a profession, an individual must proceed first to apply for training, then to be trained in a specialized field of knowledge, and finally to be accredited by some sort of agency that represents the profession and reflects and maintains its standards for performance.

Except for the accrediting agency (one of the earliest of which was the English Royal College of Physicians), a profession is not a formal organization. Once accredited, a member of a profession is about as free to sell or otherwise dispense his services as a member of society can be. He is, moreover, equally free to use his personal judgment in the application of professional knowledge and techniques to the fulfillment of professionally sanctioned goals. Since he is neither tightly constrained by rules nor directly controlled by fellow members nor bound as is a priest or magic man to a specific set of practices and interpretations, he may, should he be so inclined, engage in innovative endeavor or experiment with innovations made by others. The professional form of organization would seem, therefore, to permit a fair balance between the efficient and responsible practice of an applied art and individual freedom to extend and improve that art.

Ideally, and to a considerable extent in actuality, the member of a profession is self-motivated and self-confident regarding his competence within his particular specialty. Motivation and self-confidence make him strongly individualistic, disinclined to subordinate his personal judgment to rule and regulation, and prone to apply his knowledge and skill in an enterprising manner. In these respects the member of a profession represents the values and sentiments of the Protestant ethic. Regard for his reputation among his fellow professionals and for the prestige of the profession itself, together no doubt with professional concern for the welfare of those whom he serves, tends, however, to constrain him and to limit his enterprise to those kinds of endeavors, quantitative and qualitative, that are sanctioned by the profession as a whole—e.g., to the improving of medical techniques, as distinct from simply exploiting some particular technique to his own personal advantage.

Perhaps the distinctive characteristics of a profession can best be suggested by the contrast between the values of the member of a profession and those of a bureaucrat. The member of a profession is more concerned with ends than with means—with saving the lives of patients, with transmitting knowledge to students, or with seeing that justice is done. A bureaucrat is engrossed in means—with fulfilling the letter of the law, with compliance with the rules and regulations, and with satisfying the obligations of his designated office, no matter what the social consequences may be.

Origins of the Professions

Professionalization began to emerge during the fifteenth century, first in the fields of medicine and law. In the preceding two centuries, there had evolved from guildlike organizations of teachers and students the university system of training in theology and, initially as a sort of incidental matter, of simultaneous training in these two applied arts. In time, and as a reflection of the declining power of the Church, university students and faculty came to specialize in one or the other of these arts; and theology, as it ceased to be a field of study prerequisite to any other, tended to lose its dominant position. At the same time the status of those trained in medicine or law or some other of the applied arts, whether together with or apart from training in theology, was rising as a consequence of new social needs. The plagues and their aftermath stressed the social importance of physicians; world exploration gave new value to the mathematical skills of navigators and map makers; the growth of commerce increased the importance of men skilled in the law, in finance, and in accounting (double-entry bookkeeping was devised in Italy during the period of the commercial revival); and in due course various factors demonstrated the social value first of engineers and finally of scientists.

As the social demand for trained and accredited practitioners rose, a number of interrelated changes began to come about. For one thing, the faculties of universities gained power and prestige, and pedagogy itself acquired some of the attributes of a profession. For another, the graduates of a university college came to have, not only a bond of unity in their common training, but, since the prestige of each was in part determined by the status of the college from which he had come, pride in and loyalty to that college. It was from interrelated changes of this sort that in time came the professionalization of medicine, law, accounting, engineering, etc. Moreover, the rising demand for professional services, together with a somewhat declining faith in the efficiency of magic, the progressive secularization of social life, and the growth of humanistic values, stimulated both practitioners and teachers to a search for more knowledge and more efficacious techniques. It was this search, facilitated by the comparatively loose organization of each of the several professions, that led to many of the inventions and discoveries in medicine, engineering, etc., and to many of the innovations in legal, criminological, and penal practice.

The rise of modern medicine well illustrates the relationship between the development of professionalization and advances in professional knowledge.[13] The physicians of the early Middle Ages were practitioners of folk

[13] For the early history of the medical profession in America see Richard H. Shryock, *Medicine and Society in America, 1600–1860*, New York University Press, New York, 1960. For background materials on some of the other profes-

arts, and they were mostly organized into local guilds. For centuries no significant gains were made in either knowledge about biological processes or in ability to control disease. The emergence of medicine as a profession, with medical training centers at universities, did not lead directly to increases in knowledge or improvement of techniques. New ideas, such as the surge theory of blood movement, did develop in some of the medical colleges, but the medical faculties tended to be doctrinaire and their students to cling tenaciously to the ideas and procedures that they had been taught. Nevertheless, these faculties—or at least the more imaginative members of them—did not entirely isolate themselves; and they eventually caught something of the spirit of the scientific movement that was evolving. In due time, astronomy, then physics and chemistry, and later anatomy and biology were recognized as worthy fields of endeavor by many universities, and scientists themselves became more or less professionalized. The full acceptance by medical men of the value to them of scientific findings did not come until well on in the nineteenth century. Meanwhile, however, practicing physicians, inspired by the idea of scientific investigation, attempted here and there to extend their knowledge of disease by empirical means; and by these means some crucial discoveries were made—vaccination against smallpox, antiseptic procedures in surgery, anesthesia, etc.

The discovery of bacteria as the agent of contagious disease by the chemist Pasteur no doubt did much to open the doors of the medical schools to pure scientists (i.e., men not accredited as physicians) and to convince the medical profession that the practice of medicine should be based upon scientific knowledge of biological structures and processes. By the end of the nineteenth century, the major medical schools of Europe were training their students in the biological and biochemical sciences as a prelude to study of medical treatment and therapy, and in due time this practice spread to the United States and elsewhere. The overall result was a tremendous increase in knowledge about biological processes, in ability to prevent the spread of contagious diseases, and in ability to influence the course of many diseases. One hundred years ago a practicing physician probably killed as many patients as he cured; today he can save many of those who would have died, with or without medical aid, a century ago.

The development of the other professions has been roughly parallel to that of medicine, with the notable exceptions of law and pedagogy, which

---

sions see Edward Kremers and George Urdang, *History of Pharmacy*, J. B. Lippincott Company, Philadelphia, 1951; Roscoe Pound, *The Lawyer from Antiquity to Modern Times*, West Publishing Company, St. Paul, Minn., 1953; Robert Robinson, *The Attorney in Eighteenth-Century England*, Cambridge University Press, New York, 1959; and Nicholas Stacy, *English Accountancy, 1800–1954*, Gee & Company (Publishers) Ltd., London, 1954.

have been little affected by the rise of science. Social scientists proceed on the assumption that eventually their findings will serve practitioners in such applied social arts as politics, the law, education, etc., in much the same way as biological findings have served medicine and the findings of physics have served engineering; but so far developments in law and pedagogy have come via empirical rather than scientific means.

Bureaucratization of Education

The universities of the later Middle Ages were the major centers of intellectual activity, and their relatively loose organizational structure enabled exceptionally original men as well as traditionalists to flourish on their faculties. It was because they did that most of the men who contributed to the developing sciences were either members of university faculties or had been trained by university faculties. Nevertheless, the universities were for the most part dedicated to a form of scholarship that derived from their theological origins—i.e., the sterile, rationalistic thinking of the Scholastics—and that in time came to be called a classical education. It stressed the classical languages and the writings of the ancient Greeks and Romans; it had no practical application, aside from archeological studies, which, in turn, provided more material for classical study.

By the nineteenth century, when the social demands for trained physicians, engineers, etc., had become critical, the old universities had more or less sorted themselves out into those that catered to the upper classes—e.g., Oxford, Cambridge, Heidelberg, and Harvard—and those that were responding, if only in a random way, to the need for creative scientists and trained technicians. The former, together with the preparatory schools which grew up to feed them selected and indoctrinated students, justified their providing a classical education (and knowledge of the classics) on the grounds that, while it might have no practical value, it produced men of wisdom and principle, the sort of men society needed to guide and direct the activities of scientifically informed but otherwise unerudite technicians. (Were not the leaders of Plato's Republic to be philosophers rather than doctors, lawyers, or scientists?) The medical, legal, and other technically oriented schools and universities represented the professions rather than the upper classes and tended, therefore, to be considerably more receptive to innovations in subject matter and in pedagogical procedures and to encourage pure-science endeavors on the part of both faculty and students.[14]

[14] During the nineteenth century a disproportionate number of the innovations in medicine occurred in Germany and America, while British and French medicine was relatively unprogressive. Joseph Ben-David has related this difference to the character of the academic systems that prevailed in these four countries. In Germany and America the universities were highly competitive, both internally and with one another. In Britain and France, on the other hand, medicine

The idea of publicly supported education as an instrument of political power (as a means of assuring loyal and effective citizens) goes back to antiquity; but the effective provision of free secular schools emerged fairly recently as a corollary to the representative form of government. In Europe, the systems of public education that evolved were from the outset centrally controlled by the national governments, and they quickly became bureaucratized. Moreover, they were on the whole oriented toward a trade school type of training. As a consequence, European public schools, whatever their merits, have not generally provided channels for upward mobility or served as feeders of students to the universities. Their major role has been that of preparing the children of peasants and urban workers and of the petty *bourgeoisie* to follow in their parents' footsteps; they have not, that is to say, been a major factor in facilitating individual mobility and, hence, in fostering social changes. In the United States, on the other hand, the public schools that began to develop in the 1830s were creations of local political action and for long remained subject to local support and control, thus following the organizational principle laid down by Luther in founding the Protestant churches. As a result, they tended to reflect the aspirations of parents for their children, rather than some principle of state or national educational policy. Their outstanding characteristic was, perhaps, diversity; each school was in a sense an experiment in formal education; and what sort and how much formal training a child would secure depended on the luck he had had in his birthplace.

The critics of contemporary American public education are inclined to use as their base line a highly romantic idea of the kind of education with which school children were provided in the good old days. As a matter of fact, that education was often little more than routine training in reading, writing, and arithmetic. With the growth of high schools and a prolongation of the period of compulsory attendance, the school curriculum tended to become an uneasy mixture of low-level trade school courses and equally low-level classics borrowed from the private school system of England. Nevertheless, as long as the schools were under the direct jurisdiction of local authorities, they were highly varied; and as long as they were varied, there was some possibility that some of them would serve their students well.

During the course of the present century, the public schools and to a somewhat lesser degree the publicly supported universities of the United States have become progressively bureaucratized and centralized. Many factors have been responsible for this change. The professionalization of educators, which began with the establishment of normal schools to supply trained

was centralized and monopolized by a few institutions, and these few did not engage in competition for dominance (Joseph Ben-David, "Scientific Productivity and Academic Organization in Nineteenth Century Medicine," *American Sociological Review*, vol. 25, pp. 828–843, December, 1960).

teachers to local school boards, was one such factor. The pressure of numbers of students, with a consequent rise in cost of public education, led, among other things, to a consolidation of one-room schoolhouses; and as the size of the school unit grew, so did the need for systematization of the educational program. The new means of transportation, which, together with the shifting demands for labor, made the American people more mobile, made it apparent that school offerings would have to be standardized at a state, if not national, level so that a student could transfer from school to school without too much loss of standing. Because of these and related factors the university schools of education have become bureaucratic agencies for the selection and training of educational bureaucrats; and state political agencies have evolved to maintain minimum standards of school administration and instruction. Inevitably, these bureaucracies have come to exercise strong authority over the character and the quality of school offerings.

The general consequence of the progressive bureaucratization of public-school education has been to reduce the qualitative and quantitative differences between schools and in the process to orient the entire system toward the provision of a standard and minimal educational diet that is designed to meet the abilities and needs of the run-of-the-mill student. To the extent, unascertainable, that the school system achieves this objective, it ceases, of course, to provide an avenue of social advancement for exceptional individuals and tends, not only to freeze educational offerings and standards, but to discourage individuals from exercising initiative.[15]

The Bureaucratization of Science

The same forces that have brought a progressive bureaucratization of primary and secondary public schools have worked, usually in more subtle ways, to

[15] Two studies which indicate that the contemporary college student is highly conformist in comparison with the student of some unstated prior period are Paul F. Lazarsfeld and Wagner Thielens, Jr., *The Academic Mind*, The Free Press of Glencoe, New York, 1958; and Philip E. Jacob, *Changing Values in College*, Harper and Row, Publishers, Incorporated, New York, 1957. Whatever the truth of the matter, it is commonly assumed outside the ranks of professional educators that our public school systems are functioning badly and that formal education tends to stultify rather than liberate, to discourage rather than foster individual achievement, and to provide the student with a diet of predigested pap rather than an intellectual comprehension of the world in which he lives. The following are examples of the almost continuous protest against the present educational system: Hilda Neatby, *So Little for the Mind*, Clarke, Irwin & Co., Ltd., Toronto, 1953; Lydia Stout, "What Strangles American Teaching: The Certification Racket," *Atlantic Monthly*, April, 1958, pp. 59 ff.; and Mortimer Smith, "How to Teach the California Child: Notes from the Never-Never Land," *Atlantic Monthly*, September, 1958, pp. 32 ff.

foster the bureaucratization of our universities, both public and private. How vital it has become for a university to provide its undergraduates with what is now defined as the standard educational fare is demonstrated by the fate of the educational experiment that was undertaken at the University of Chicago under former President Robert Hutchins. This experiment was an ingenious undergraduate program designed to encourage exceptional students to unconventional scholarship; but, if nothing else did, the untransferability to other universities of units earned in the program doomed it to failure. American universities do vary considerably, both in their qualitative standards and in the details of their offerings; but they are all under constant pressures, economic and otherwise, to adapt their undergraduate curriculums to the interests and abilities of students who have grown up under a highly bureaucratized primary and secondary school system—e.g., to offer the students advanced versions of the social adjustment and other nonintellectual courses that are so common in modern high schools and of the synthetic or so-called survey courses that in the high schools often serve in lieu of substantive courses on special topics. Moreover, the universities are constantly under pressure to dilute the college curriculum with whatever elementary courses the high schools have failed to provide—such as beginning mathematics and English composition.

It is possible that the increasingly onerous and intellectually stultifying undergraduate educational functions of our universities will in time be absorbed by state, county, and municipal colleges, the number and quality of which have increased greatly in recent years. The universities might then become, as they were a century or so ago, institutions of higher learning devoted to professional training. But their release from the burden of teaching hordes of indifferent college students will not necessarily reproduce in the universities that climate of intellectual freedom which, in another day, encouraged invention and discovery of a scientific and technological character. For the professional schools of the universities have, like the professions themselves, become highly bureaucratic and have thus lost much of their former adaptability; and scientific endeavor has of recent decades become financially dependent upon and thus to a degree subservient to such bureaucratic organizations as the private foundations, corporate businesses, and military and political agencies.[16]

[16] The result has been, apparently, a general shift of attention from the extension of scientific knowledge to its application to practical problems. Of the 150,000 scientifically trained men employed by American industry in 1957, only 3 per cent were engaged in basic research (*Scientific and Technical Personnel in American Industry*, National Science Foundation, Washington, D.C., 1960). For an analysis of the way in which the scientist in industry loses his freedom and is subjugated to bureaucratic rule and routine, see Simon Marcson, *The Scientist in American Industry*, Harper & Row, Publishers, Incorporated, New York, 1960.

The early scientists needed little in the way of equipment and usually worked alone. For them it was sufficient that they were relieved, as members of a university faculty tended to be, of the need to earn their livelihood through practical and profitable employment. The theorists, who need mainly time, may still be able to develop their concepts; but the experimentalists, who test out and refine conceptual innovations, now frequently need in addition to time very costly apparatus and the aid of many assistants. Of recent years very considerable amounts of money have been made available for research, especially in the physical and biological sciences, on the assumption that through scientific discoveries society can solve its most pressing problems—including those of national defense—and so achieve progress.

That assumption is no doubt valid within limits; but the agencies that have developed to provide financial support to scientific research have rarely been content to give money to scientists and let the scientists go their unpredictable ways. As responsible organizations, they have, rather, been inclined to dictate, usually in a subtle and indirect fashion, what problems should be attacked and even how they should be attacked. With characteristic bureaucratic caution these agencies have tended to favor large-group projects, thereby avoiding any possibility of personal responsibility should the project produce nothing of scientific value, in fields and on problems that are sanctioned either by tradition or by the fact that they are currently fashion-

---

For an analysis of the adjustment, personal and collective, of scientists to their status under industrial organization, see William Kornhouser, *Scientists in Industry: Conflict and Accommodation,* University of California Press, Berkeley, Calif., 1962.

Industrial leaders may argue that it is the task of industry to develop and apply scientific knowledge to practical ends and that the extension of that knowledge is the responsibility of such nonprofit organizations as the universities. But even as more and more scientists are being drawn into industrial work, the scientists in universities have become dependent upon and hence subordinated to fund-granting agencies, especially governmental, which are far more interested in the solution of practical problems than in the extension of basic knowledge. Illustrating the current dependence of universities upon outside agencies and hence the subordination of scientific endeavor to outside agencies is the fact that in the academic year 1961–1962 Stanford University, a private institution, secured nearly one-half of its operating income from governmental grants for research, mostly in military and space-age projects ($27\frac{3}{4}$ million of a total income of $59\frac{4}{5}$ million). Prior to World War II, the university had been completely independent of government sources of income. The developments since World War II that have had the general effect of reducing the research scientist to a bureaucrat are analyzed by Leonard S. Silk in *The Research Revolution,* McGraw-Hill Book Company, New York, 1960. See also James L. McCamy, *Science and Public Administration,* University of Alabama Press, University, Ala., 1960.

able. Projects of this sort may have value in developing innovations, but they fall mainly in the field of technology rather than basic science. Basic science is not subject to programming or certain to produce results; it is a venture into the unknown, and what, if anything, will be found there is entirely unpredictable.

To what extent the current means of financing research discourage scientists from truly creative endeavor is unknown. Perhaps those scientists who are attracted to the comparatively safe and clearly rewarding role of industrial, governmental contract, or foundation researcher would not be creative scientists under any circumstances. The fact that such researchers can and do escape the tribulations and avoid the personal sacrifices of creative endeavor, however, may discourage many who would otherwise do so from assuming the risks and personal costs of creative endeavor. At any event, it is clear that, while many men are currently engaged in research of one sort or another, most of them operate within the confines of bureaucratic roles and that science, like other aspects of our society, has become progressively bureaucratized over the past several decades.

Bureaucratization of the Applied Arts

The forces that have tended to encourage bureaucratic organization of education and of science have also affected, perhaps to an even greater degree, practitioners of the applied arts. The medical profession may again be taken as an example of what has happened, in one way or another, to all the professions, including engineering, architecture, law, etc.[17] Bureaucratization of medicine has progressed fastest and farthest in Britain, where the private practice of medicine has become, under the National Insurance Act, subsidiary to politically organized, financed, and controlled provision of medical services. Even in the United States, where organized medicine—i.e., the American Medical Association—maintains a very active campaign against socialized medicine, a variety of organizational developments has reduced the scope of individual enterprise and individual self-determination in the practice of medicine. Most of these developments have come as attempts to improve the quality of medical service, to ease the practitioner's labors, or to enable the sick to secure care that would not otherwise be forthcoming. Nevertheless, they have all contributed to the establishment of rules and regulations con-

[17] One of the consequences of this trend seems to be the social devaluation of the individual practitioner. Jerome E. Carlin has found, for example, that lawyers who practice on their own are by and large inferior, both in terms of income and professional reputation, to those who work as members of legal firms (*Lawyers on Their Own: A Study of Individual Practitioners in Chicago*, Rutgers University Press, New Brunswick, N.J., 1962).

straining the individual practitioner, for they have invariably assumed a bureaucratic or partially bureaucratic form.[18]

The physicians' own voluntary organizations, local and national, are the oldest and least constraining. Their value in fostering higher standards of training, in diffusing new techniques among practicing physicians, in discouraging the excesses of fads and fashions in medicine, in purging their ranks of irresponsible and dishonest members, etc., cannot be doubted. Even these associations, however, by setting informal and formal standards, tend to discourage some of that kind of experimentation which, however disadvantageous in the short run, is essential to progress in medical therapy. Moreover, they encourage the practitioner to be a conservative conformist, since his status, if not his survival as a member of the profession, often depends upon his treating his patients in the currently approved manner.

As knowledge of the human body and its disorders increased and as such techniques as surgery became refined, specialization in one or another area of medicine became necessary. No man could know the entire field of medicine, and no man could be highly skilled in all its many arts and techniques. In time, therefore, a complex division of labor evolved in medical practice, as it had in law, business, industry, and other occupations. With this division of labor there came new problems of organization. For a time, the services of specialists were secured for a patient by his general practitioner; but the procedure was far from satisfactory, from both the patient's and the physician's point of view. Early in this century there arose, especially in the United States, a movement toward the formation of clinics—working associations of general practitioners and various specialists. At first these clinics were no more than a group of medical men who shared an office building and referred patients to one another on an informal basis. Over the years the clinic has become both widely accepted and highly organized. It has proved to be economically efficient and, on the whole, advantageous to both physician and patient. Efficiency and improved standards of practice, however, have been achieved at some loss of independence by both practitioner and patient and by a growing tendency—strongly resisted by some medical men—to treat the disease rather than the person—i.e., to ignore the fact that the patient is not an assembly of discrete body parts but a complex whole in which his state of mind is often as important as are such objectively measurable phenomena as white blood cells and blood pressure. Even more

[18] The bureaucratization of the professions under a welfare state is described by Roy Lewis and Angus Maude in *Professional People in England,* Harvard University Press, Cambridge, Mass., 1953. For an analysis of the tendency of the professions in America to develop guildlike closure and isolation, specifically psychology, sociology, and medicine, see William J. Goode, "Encroachment, Charlatanism, and the Emerging Profession," *American Sociological Review,* vol. 25, pp. 902–914, December, 1960.

important is the fact that a large clinic is necessarily organized along bureaucratic lines and tends to some extent to force the individual practitioner to conform to the rules and routine of a bureaucratic organization.

The bureaucratization of medical practice is most marked, however, where a practitioner operates under the jurisdiction of a political or commercial, as distinct from medical, organization. The growth of medical insurance—health, accident, hospital, etc.—means, among other things, that even a private practitioner is frequently compelled in the financial interests of insured patients to proceed in accordance with rules laid down by insuring agencies; sometimes this means his conforming, whatever his personal judgment, to prescribed procedures, and invariably it means burdensome paper work. Even more constraining to a practitioner is employment in one of the many semicommercial, usually corporation-sponsored, hospitals or health centers, in one of the growing number of Veterans' hospitals that are operated by the Veterans' Bureau, or as a medical officer in one of the armed services. In any such organization the professional man is necessarily subordinated to the bureaucrat, and the practice of medicine becomes, for good or for ill, systematized and standardized by rule and routine.

chapter 13 *Government and Political Bureaucratization*

The progressive bureaucratization of the economic life of Western peoples has been accompanied by an even more rapid bureaucratization and extension of government. Through the nineteenth century Western peoples were inclined to consider government to be at best a necessary evil, and every proposal for enlargement of the scope of government and improvement of its organizational efficiency was strongly resisted. During the present century, however, Western peoples have progressively allocated to government functions that were formerly the province of such nonpolitical forms of organization as family, community, church, and business enterprise. It is now the general assumption that government should take major responsibility for the welfare of the members of society, protecting them from adversity, both individual and collective, and working such changes in the nonpolitical aspects of society as would seem to be necessary in the preservation of political sovereignty or in the interests of social welfare.

Within the past hundred years there has thus occurred a radical change in political ideology and a profound, if not yet quite so radical, change in both the role and the nature of government. These changes can be analyzed in considerable detail, and the forces and circumstances that brought them about are fairly evident; but their effects, actual and potential, on change per se are difficult to ascertain. Even among social scientists, the tendency is to accept the validity of current political ideology and to see government as the normal and, indeed, the only effective agency of social change.

The special kind of organization that is government is no doubt as old as human society; but except perhaps in the Greek city-states and in Rome during the Republic, reliance on this kind of organization has never before been so extensive as it is in most of the social systems of the world today. The emergence of the idea that through government man can

442

achieve his greatest desires and the concomitant expansion, proliferation, and bureaucratization of governmental agencies are developments of great complexity, both ideologically and organizationally. Moreover, they are developments in which the ideological aspect commonly obscures the actual nature and functions of existing governmental agencies, with the consequence that it is exceedingly difficult to distinguish in any given instance between what is ideological and what is real. Thus, to take a striking example, the political ideologists of Communist Russia assign credit for all the desirable changes that have occurred in Russian society since the Revolution to the political direction of Russian economic and social life; and they blame other kinds of organizations, such as religion, for all recognized inadequacies. Thus, too, it has now become the general practice in Western societies to attempt to solve every recognized malfunctioning of society by the establishment of a new governmental agency, the enactment of a new law, or the repeal of an old law. The ability of government to work desired social changes is not, however, unlimited; government may embody in legislation the will of a tyrant or the aspirations of a people, but the extent to which actual changes in the society can be credited to political efforts is never certain. No one, least of all, perhaps, Russian political ideologists, really knows whether the government of post-Revolutionary Russia has fostered or, alternatively, hampered the industrialization and other changes for which the ideologists give government full credit.

The Nature of Government

The layman, at least the modern layman, has no difficulty in distinguishing governmental from nongovernmental kinds of organizations. Government collects taxes, makes and enforces laws, and provides military protection from enemies. But it is far from easy to analyze the distinction between organizations that are thought of as government and those of another kind, for what distinguishes government is neither its size nor its organizational structure. Tribal government may encompass as few as a hundred or two hundred members; modern governments may include within their jurisdiction a hundred million or more citizens. Governmental organization may be inseparably interwoven with other kinds of organizations, as is usually the case with tribal, clan, and other primitive societies, and as becomes the case even in modern societies when industrial, labor, and other bureaucracies resort to force in an effort to achieve their organizational ends. On the other hand, government may be, and in most large and complex societies always has been, organizationally distinct from such other kinds of organizations as the family, the community, and business.

In some times and places, government has been informal in structure and even covert in nature, as has often been the case with the rule of the elders in tribal and village societies. In the main, however, government is formally organized, operates in accordance with formally designated procedures and in terms of explicit laws, and is legitimatized in one or another of several standard ways. When such is the case, the personnel of governmental agencies —e.g., politicians in office, policemen on duty, and soldiers in uniform—is categorically distinguished from ordinary citizens; and the scope and jurisdiction of organizational authority are quite clearly defined and may not, as a rule, be exceeded. Thus our Federal Interstate Commerce Commission is empowered to regulate the railroads, but it cannot enact or enforce motor-vehicle laws.

In many societies, notably those of times past, governing has been, in theory at least, a personal prerogative that was inherited through the family line; and in these societies the governmental organization has usually consisted of a whimsically devised coterie of the friends, relatives, and acquaintances of the chief, prince, or king. An extension of this system, if such it may be termed, has been government through a special, hereditary class—such as the Brahmans of India and the aristocracy of postfeudal Europe. The polar extreme to hereditary government—and every degree in between has been operative in some times and places—is that which is ideologically preferred in modern Western societies, i.e., government of a parliamentary type, which is supposed to be, and to some extent actually is, representative of the people who are subject to it. Under both extremes—viz., monarchy and democracy—there may be greater or lesser use of the bureaucratic form of organization in the actual administration of governmental functions. Clearly, then, government cannot be distinguished from nongovernment on the basis of the criteria that are used to differentiate family from class or either of these forms of organization from bureaucracy.

What most clearly distinguishes government from other *kinds* of social organization is its dependence upon coercion as its primary means of control. Whatever the form a government may take, however traditionalized or socially sanctioned, it exists and achieves its effects, whatever they may be, by virtue of the fact that it can and if necessary will forcibly exact obedience to its dictates; and herein lies both its special qualities as a distinct kind of social organization and its peculiar limitations as a factor in the making of social change.

The agencies of government, especially those of modern societies, may operate in many ways. With the exception of conscripted soldiers, the members of a modern governmental agency, whether elected, selected, or employed, participate voluntarily, although this has not always been the case. Modern governmental agencies, both military and civil, usually purchase the goods and services that they need on the open market, just as a business corporation or a private householder does, although, again, such has not always been the case. Governmental agencies, at least those of Western societies, whether legislative, regulatory, or military, may proceed with as cautious a regard for public sentiment as does a politician up for election or a business that is trying to win a market for its products. Nevertheless, government is and always has been organized coercion. Under conditions of political or military tyranny this fact is self-evident; under the conditions of life in contemporary Western societies it may be somewhat obscured. But it is as true today as in times past that no operation of government is possible without coercion; no law, whether legislative enactment or administrative ruling, has social significance unless it is equipped with teeth—i.e., with physically enforceable penalties for failure to obey.

The primary function of government may therefore be described as the maintenance within its jurisdiction of a monopoly over the right to use coercion. The jurisdiction of government may be narrow or wide; whatever it is, unless government maintains a monopoly on coercion within its jurisdiction, its existence is threatened, as it is, for example, when peasants take up cudgels against the king's taxgatherer or when criminals intimidate citizens whom the police are supposed to protect from unauthorized coercion. In most premodern societies the jurisdiction of government was traditionally restricted to the making of war, the collection of taxes, and the gross protection of citizens from loss of property or life through violence. Under such circumstances it was not a violation of the governmental monopoly of coercion when husbands beat wives, flogged sons, and brawled with neighbors in the local tavern. In modern societies, on the other hand, the jurisdiction of government is so extensive that about the only occasion on which the individual citizen can legally use force to achieve his ends is in the killing of wild game—and even this right is hedged about with a maze of legal restrictions.

From one point of view, coercion is the most effective means of controlling the conduct of human beings. Slaves chained in a galley can be lashed into totally exhausting themselves at the oars; tributes and taxes can be extracted through coercion and in no other way; and through coercion people may even be induced to violate their customs, traditions, and other cultural imperatives. Fear of pain, of physical deprivation, or of death may surmount all other considerations. Nevertheless, the ability of government to maintain within its jurisdiction a monopoly over the use of force has always been limited. In many times and places, perhaps in most times and places, government has been considered an unmitigated evil by the majority of the people, inevitable, but to be evaded at almost any cost short of life itself; and sometimes even loss of life has been deemed preferable to subservience to a particular government. Said Patrick Henry, "Give me liberty, or give me death."

Even when and where, as in most modern Western societies, the legitimacy of the established government is unquestioned and government is considered the major means to social welfare, government can preserve its monopoly over the use of force only by constant and unremitting effort; and its success is never more than partial. Always there are counterclaimants to this right to extract by force what cannot be otherwise acquired; the criminal, young or old and operating as an individual or as a member of a gang, is even today almost as commonplace as is the policeman who represents law and order; in many places rioting citizens are a constant threat to the power and stability of the existing government; the recurrent resort by organized labor or organized industry to outright force or some more subtle means of coercing their opponents is a direct infringement of government's monopoly on force. Moreover, the propensity of ordinary citizens to break certain kinds of laws, especially those governing the use of motor vehicles, public sanitation, building construction and usage, moral conduct, payment of taxes, etc., indicates that, however much people may accept the desirability of government in principle, they do not submit voluntarily to any law that runs counter to their own personal interests or desires. Plato's ideal, self-maintaining government, has never been realized—for the very simple reason that the rule of government is rule by force.

Civil versus Military Agencies

A theoretical distinction exists between the civil and the military functions of government. The civil, the primary, function is to determine and enforce the laws that are applicable within the governmental jurisdiction, whereas the military is to provide physical protection from attack by outside forces or to endeavor to extend the jurisdiction of government—i.e., to conquer other peoples. These functions have not, however, always been separate and exercised by organizationally distinct agencies. In ancient Rome, as in many premodern societies, civil and military functions were fulfilled by different organizations, the leadership of each (senators and generals) was distinct, and separate tribunals existed for the dispensing of civil and of military justice. At the same time, the actual enforcement of civil law—arrest, imprisonment, and execution—was left to garrison soldiers who acted on behalf of the civil authorities.

The development of distinctly civil law-enforcing agencies is fairly recent and is one of the changes that are associated with the extension and bureaucratization of civil government in Western societies. In times of either political or military crisis, military forces may be called upon to exercise the civil function of maintaining domestic peace, and in the less modernized of contemporary societies they may at times supersede the civil authorities. Modern governments do, however, make an organizational distinction between the police, whether local or national, and the military; and organizationally, if not always operationally, there are categorical distinctions between civil agencies, such as the local sheriff's office and the Federal Bureau of Investigation, and military agencies, such as the shore patrol and the United States Army.

THE EXTENSION AND BUREAUCRATIZATION
OF GOVERNMENT

The need for government to monopolize coercion, to exercise what are usually described as police powers, seems to arise from the fact that group survival depends upon personal attributes of a different order from those that enable individuals to survive under presocial conditions. In the animal world, physical strength and prowess determine survival; and the physically weak, the injured, and the aged either fail in the quest for food or are brought down by predators. In society, on the other hand, the value of an individual to the welfare and survival of the group may depend upon psychological rather than physical attributes. The brute strength of a stupid young man may be of some social value in battle and in the fields during harvest; but over time the social value of his weakling brother or his aged and enfeebled father may, by virtue of wisdom or willingness to subordinate personal interests to those of the group, be far greater. Apparently, it has been to assure that the socially most desirable, rather than just the physically strongest, members of society could survive and contribute to group welfare that government of some form or other has been operative in every social system of which there is knowledge.

Within any social system, primitive or civilized, ancient or modern, both the ascribed status and the achieved status of an individual are determined by factors other than mere brute strength. Thus in accordance with the established system, upon the death of the father the eldest son of a family might assume authority even though the youngest were stronger; a family of six members might possess a large plot of land, although a numerically stronger family had only a small one; and the lord of the manor would be the lord although his serfs were many and collectively far stronger. In the long run it is presumably to the benefit of all that differences in status and authority be socially determined and maintained rather than that land and other means of production and authority be assumed by those individuals who happen to possess superior strength and the willingness to use it. Yet in any society the temptation for individuals to resort to force is always great; and in all societies there are at least a few members who are not constrained by moral sentiments or consideration of the rights of others from resorting to force. It is, presumably, to prevent the rule of all by such individuals and thus preserve the social system that government has everywhere exercised a monopoly on coercion.

The extent of the jurisdiction of government over coercion has varied widely, as has been noted. During the course of some centuries, the government of Rome seems to have monopolized most forms of coercion within Rome and in all the well-established areas of the Empire. No one knows how safe it was to venture down a city street in the dark of night, but it is known that property and other traditional rights were quite effectively protected and that the public roads were reasonably safe for travelers. On the other hand, in China during the same and subsequent periods, property rights were none too well maintained by the magistrates and soldiers of the central government; and as a consequence, men with considerable wealth felt impelled to keep little armies of their own and most householders to keep a vicious dog chained in the courtyard.

The present extent of the jurisdiction of government—its inclusion of almost all aspects of social life—has, however, no historical precedent; and the extension of government and the development of efficient, bureaucratic means for the enforcement of its police powers constitute one of the more significant of the social changes that have occurred in Western societies during the past century or two. Symbolic of this change has been the abandonment within the present century of the custom of carrying a cane, a custom that came from the time, not so far distant, when no man felt safe on street or highway without a cudgel with which to drive off thieves and other ill-intentioned fellows. The growing ability of government to assure its citizens reasonable safety from physical attack and their properties safety from theft reflects a rising standard of respect for life and property and, by freeing the members of society from the constraints of fear, has in turn fostered other changes in the social system. Where, as in many times and places, an individual had to be constantly on his guard against violence to his person or his property, he no doubt became security-minded; and constant fear of attack no doubt extended to fear of anything unknown—of any change. At any event, there appears to have been a rough relation between periods of physical insecurity and periods of cultural stagnation. This does not mean, however, that secure societies have necessarily also been innovative ones; for while a social climate of peace and security may favor innovative and adoptive behavior, it does not assure it.

It is perhaps difficult for the member of a modern Western society to appreciate the character of life in a society that lacked extensive and effective civil control. Conditions can hardly ever have been as constantly tense and dramatic, or as deadly, as they are represented to have been in the American West by modern dramatists; but in many times and places they were certainly confining and restraining. Home, boarded and shuttered at night, was often the only truly safe place; travel was invariably fraught with dangers; strangers had always to be looked upon with suspicion; and for the physically weak, having strong and loyal supporters, such as a number of stalwart young sons, was often requisite to personal survival.

At the height of their power the Romans maintained a remarkable degree of peace among the people whom they conquered; this may well have been one of the reasons why the natives became so fully Romanized. With the decline of Roman power, Roman garrison soldiers and other Roman functionaries were gradually withdrawn from most of Western Europe; and ultimately Rome itself was conquered by tribal invaders. For nearly a thousand years, from about 500 to 1500, the peoples of Western Europe were unable to re-create for themselves the comparative security that the Romans had provided. Tribal wars were frequent; the extermination of conquered peoples was a common practice; and the possession of land, the basis of subsistence, was determined mainly by superior might, individual and collective. It is perhaps significant that through most of this long period the cultures of the peoples of Western Europe changed little and that that little was in the direction of greater rather than lesser malfunctioning; even military technology did not begin to improve until the twelfth century. Gross evidence of the cultural effects of the prevailing insecurity of the period is to be found in the fact that, following the disruption of Roman authority, the population of Western Europe seems to have declined by more than half and that an upturn in population did not begin until the twelfth century.

It was apparently in an attempt to achieve at least a modicum of physical security that Western peoples gradually developed the feudal system. The system of fiefs, defensively organized against physical attack under the leadership of a hereditary lord, constituted a revival and synthesis of two Roman legal relationships—the precarium, a landlord-tenant relationship, and the patrocinium, a patron-client relationship—that had been common in Roman society. Under feudalism these two relationships became fused and permanent and lost their voluntary character. The position of client-tenant became hereditary and subservient to that of the also hereditary position of landlord-patron; the serfs, who occupied the former, worked the land in return for protection provided by the lord, who occupied the latter and who functioned in both a military and civil capacity.

The effectiveness of the feudal system is commonly exaggerated. No doubt the feudal lords were able to maintain comparative peace within the manorial population; but since the lords were almost constantly at war with one another, death by violence, either in attack upon another feudal castle or in defense against attack, was not uncommon. Even in the tenth century, by which time the feudal system had reached its fullest development, the scope and duration of physical security were so much limited that only a small proportion of the fertile lands of Western Europe could be cultivated—only those immediately adjacent to a feudal castle, and even there crops were often destroyed by enemies before they could be harvested. Life was therefore very hard; and this circumstance, in conjunction with the fact that the feudal system was isolative, that it made for categorical stratification of the population, etc., precluded improvements in technology as well as in social organization.

The laws that were enforced by the feudal lords are not on record, for the period is one of almost universal illiteracy. Presumably they were a mixture of personal whimsy and local custom, with some elements of ancient Roman law that had been preserved by word of mouth through the centuries. It is known, however, that even at the climax of its development, feudalism was anything but systematic; each fief, apparently, had a somewhat distinctive character and was in some respects subject to modification in accordance with the personal inclinations of successive lords. Law as the term is understood today—a body of fairly stable, recorded, and more or less impartial rules of conduct—did not exist.

With the beginning of the Crusades, the isolation of feudal fiefs and the authority of the feudal lords began to decline; and in time a new if only slightly more effective system of government emerged. By the thirteenth century there existed in many parts of Western Europe multiple systems of civil rule, different in form but somewhat allied in principle to those that today result in such overlapping political jurisdictions as municipal, county, state, and national governments.

One of these systems of civil rule stemmed from and was administered by the Church. Throughout the Middle Ages, the Church claimed and in some measure exercised jurisdiction over all of Western Europe in matters of moral conduct; and since through much of the Middle Ages the Church was trying to extend its powers over those of secular authority, there was a tendency for the Church courts to include within the concept of moral conduct an ever-increasing variety of actions. Moreover, Church law as it affected laymen was implicit rather than explicit; anything that could be labeled "heresy" became contrary to Church law. The administration of Church law was accomplished by varied and varying organizations and procedures. In some times and places, the bishop ran his own police and judicial system; in others, the secular government, either local or national, was used on occasion to enforce what the bishop or some other Church functionary deemed the law to be. It was during the thirteenth century that the court procedure known as the Inquisition began to emerge. The Inquisition was no doubt the most systematic and effective of the attempts of the Church to enforce Church law, and it persisted in Spain until well into the nineteenth century.

Feudal authority of diminished scope survived the decline of the feudal system itself, and remnants of it lingered on until modern times. The lords became attached to the king and in return for their loyalty were in time granted such local powers as maintaining the peace among their tenants, enforcing local customs regarding property, etc. To some extent they were predecessors of local civil authorities as they are known today. The character and effectiveness of their rule, however, was dependent largely upon their own personal qualities; and if the evidences of dissatisfaction and disloyalty among the commoners are any indication, their rule must have been for the most part exploitative. Certainly it did not provide the peasants with much in the way of physical security, for the peasants everywhere banded together in tight and sometimes fortified little villages as a defense against roving thieves and bands of marauders. In the growing towns, on the other hand, the need for effective, if limited, civil rule led to the development of various forms of municipal government. In some times and places, as, for example, in Florence under the Medici, responsibility for the maintenance of peace gravitated into the hands of the head of a strong, patrician family—a prince, if in origins only a merchant prince. Elsewhere, as in Venice during its domination of trade with the East, a quasi-democratic system of councils evolved that served legislative, judicial, and administrative functions. In many of the towns the craft and merchant guilds were in part devices for the preservation of the peace—or, at least, preservation of law that was favorable to the activities of the guilds. In their maturity, the guilds came to rule the entire life of town or city through the burgomaster, who was their representative; and while this system did much to make towns and cities physically safe for citizens and their property, it also aided in bringing the economic and social life of the Middle Ages to a standstill.

Over both town and country and in considerable conflict with the Church for dominance were the king and court. The jurisdiction and powers of king and court grew and contracted with the fortunes of war, with the success or failure of alliances, and with the personal character of the king himself. The efforts of churchmen to establish religious dominance over the whole of Western Europe stemmed, on the one hand, from the usual crass desire of those in positions of power to enlarge it and, on the other hand, from the idea, which centuries earlier had been given some tangible basis by Charlemagne, of a Holy Roman Empire. The efforts of ambitious kings and courts during this period to carve out political empires had a somewhat more substantial basis; for the growth of trade with the Orient, the beginnings of regional specialization in both agriculture and in the fabricative arts, the emergence of interregional trade, and later the discovery of the New World made for economic interdependence that ran counter to the existing political differentiation. Since only the most primitive forms of commerce, such as chain trading, can be conducted under conditions of physical insecurity, one of the great needs through the Middle Ages was safety for goods and persons in transit; another was the need for some legal basis for the trust, without which large-scale commerce is almost impossible, that both producers and merchants had to have in one another.

Neither secular nor sacred political unification of Western Europe was ever accomplished, but there was a gradual and very costly consolidation of its many peoples into national units; and meanwhile and thereafter various devices were evolved to make the best of unfavorable circumstances. Highways of the king, intermittently patrolled by troops, were established in some places and gave some slight assurance of safety in passage; eventually the seas adjacent to each nation were claimed as sovereign territory; and national navies developed which often offered safe passage to merchant ships. An effective standard of interregional and international exchange evolved on the basis of the gold florin, originally coined in 1252 in Florence;

and Jewish bankers, who were free from the Church prohibition on usury, developed a fairly effective international financial system, the first of its kind. Concurrent with the development of productive specialization and trade was the rediscovery of the knowledge and legal practices of the ancients— a revival of learning that culminated in the emergence of a literate, and in a sense educated, class of scholars, scribes, and legalists, who were attached to secular rather than sacred authority. One complex and significant result of this revival was the glorification, in theory if not always in practice, of Roman political and legal principles; and thus began the procedure, honored to this day by lawyers and jurists, of seeking a precedent in the past for a problem of today. The effect of the glorification of Roman law was, in the long run, to regularize, standardize, and stabilize civil law and to give to its administration some quality of impartiality; for lawyers and jurists came to identify justice with the Justinian Code of the Romans.[1]

The Bureaucratization of Police Forces

The emergence of law as a profession, with the establishment of schools of law in the universities, was the first major step toward a systematic maintenance of the peace in post-Roman Western history. By the eighteenth century European and British citizens were fairly safe from bodily attack and their property from expropriation by fellow citizens, and they had some legal rights vis-à-vis government itself. By then churchmen had lost almost all coercive power over individuals, although religious persecution of minorities was far from uncommon. By then, too, the conduct of local civil affairs had in most places been systematized, brought under the general jurisdiction of the monarch, and given a democratic cast—i.e., made somewhat responsive to local needs and desires—that was still lacking on the national level.

The systematization of the courts of law had, however, far outrun that of the procedures by which law violators were identified, apprehended, and, if found guilty, fined or imprisoned. The functionaries of the courts were by and large professionals with some standards of integrity and grounded in a common understanding of the law and its administration. But the

[1] Except in Britain, where the courts tended to rely for their precedents upon common law—i.e., local traditions, customs, sentiments, etc. This practice made for considerable flexibility in legal interpretations over time and permitted wide regional variation in legal practices. The Justinian Code, which acquired almost sacred stature among jurists on the Continent, was fiat law and tended to foster the centralization and stabilization of legal authority. It is possible that the common-law basis of British justice contributed somewhat to the social diversity of the British people, and so indirectly to the changes that culminated in the industrial revolution.

police, bailiffs, prison keepers, etc., were either political appointees or petty business entrepreneurs; and in either case they tended to use the coercive powers of the law for personal profit rather than in the interests of abstract legal justice. Prisons were usually operated as a municipal or royal concession, at so much per head; and in them the wealthy prisoners could live in comparative luxury, while the poor ones died of malnutrition and disease. For these and related reasons the law itself was generally held in low esteem; and although such safety as existed was dependent upon the law, every man's hand was inclined to be turned against it.

Effective reform came slowly, impelled in part by the emergence of the idea of the right and dignity of the individual, an idea which played such a vital ideological role in the revolutions that ushered in parliamentary government, and in part by the rising level of material well-being that followed the industrial revolution. In time jails and prisons were made public institutions, and during the nineteenth century an entirely new philosophy evolved regarding their function.[2] The standards of prison care became at least tolerable; and such ameliorative practices as the mark system of reducing sentences for good behavior, parole, and the suspended sentence developed in England and America and eventually spread to European countries. Equally important, there was established in London a systematically organized police force, one which was patterned on the military, and hence bureaucratic in form, and which in time became the model for police forces of all Western societies.[3] In London, as elsewhere, the identification

[2] For a detailed history of one aspect of this development see Negley K. Teeters, *The Cradle of the Penitentiary: The Walnut Street Jail at Philadelphia, 1773–1835*, The Pennsylvania Prison Society, Philadelphia, Pa., 1955. For some recent developments in penology see Donald R. Cressey, *The Prison: Studies in Institutional and Organizational Change*, Holt, Rinehart and Winston, Inc., New York, 1961.

[3] Prior to the development of such police forces, the major responsibility for the detection and apprehension of one who committed a crime against a person or personal property lay with the victim. If he could catch and bring that person to court, he could then level criminal charges against him. Simply reporting a crime would not, however, result in action, unless the victim happened to be a person of power and prestige, in which case court officials could easily and quickly produce a scapegoat.

The established practice had been to maintain hired watchmen to patrol city streets, particularly at night. They were poorly paid and seem to have done little to protect the honest citizens against criminals, who, according to some estimates, then constituted a good 20 per cent of the urban population. During the eighteenth century the more honorable of the criminal-court magistrates began to employ agents to seek out the perpetrators of reported crimes, a practice almost identical to that which had developed more than a thousand years earlier in China. These

and arrest of violators of criminal law had been haphazard procedures. The police, such as they were, were a heritage from the days of the king's men, spies and informers hired by the king. They were hated and despised, usually corrupt, and hardly distinguishable from the criminals whom they were supposed to keep under control. Although employed by the city, they were often paid on a bounty basis, with the result that their interest was in feeding the courts with victims, rather than in the enforcement of the law. Sir Robert Peel, then Prime Minister, is generally credited with the idea of making police work respectable by making the police of London responsible, and with doing this by organizing them in a military manner. The task was accomplished during the 1820s under the direction of Colonel Charles Rowan, who recruited sturdy young men of good social background, put them into distinctive uniforms, drilled them in a semimilitary manner, established a rank hierarchy and appropriate pay scales, etc. For some years the term "bobby," derived from Sir Robert, carried much the same contempt as "peeler" did in Ireland, where Peel had set up an effective constabulary; but in time, and in part through such practices as never going armed and providing such auxiliary services as directing road traffic, then, as now, highly congested, the Metropolitan police won the grudging admiration of the respectable element of London; and "bobby" came to be a somewhat affectionate term.

The bureaucratization of local police forces has been but one of a

---

court agents, or "runners" as they came to be called, were the prototype of the modern detective force rather than of the uniformed police. The London police force was a true innovation with little in the way of historical antecedents. A system of national constabulary had been established in France in the fourteenth century and a municipal one in Paris late in the seventeenth century by De la Reynie. But these forces, and those developed in Italy, Spain, and some other Western European countries, were repressive agents of political authority rather than police in the modern sense.

The innovation contributed by Peel was the idea that a police force should represent citizens, rather than the authority of the king, and should serve in their interest by protecting them from those of their fellows who would harm their person or steal their goods; and it was to this end that the London police force that was formed under his jurisdiction set out to patrol the streets as representatives of law-abiding citizens.

For the history of this remarkable development see Gilbert Armitage, *History of Scotland Yard*, Wishart, London, 1932; George Dilnot, *The Story of Scotland Yard*, Geoffrey Bles, Ltd., London, 1929; Douglas G. Brown, *The Rise of Scotland Yard: A History of the Metropolitan Police*, George G. Harrap & Co., Ltd., London, 1956; and Leon Radzinowicy, *A History of English Criminal Law and Its Administration from 1750*, The Macmillan Company, New York, 1948, vol. 1. For a discussion of modern police organization see O. W. Wilson, *Police Administration*, 2d ed., McGraw-Hill Book Company, New York, 1963.

series of related developments in attempts to solve the problems of maintaining the peace, problems which have in the course of time grown more rather than less difficult. For one thing, there has been a considerable extension of the jurisdiction of police powers into areas of life that were once considered outside the scope of government. To preservation of the physical safety of the individual, for example, has been added protection of the public against diseases of a contagious order. This has meant such things as legal constraints on freedom of movement (e.g., quarantine), regulation of property usages (e.g., prohibition in towns and cities of household privies and of conditions that favor the breeding of rats), and in some instances enforcement of compulsory vaccination against smallpox. Protection of property has come to include protection against fire and has taken, in addition to the development of fire-fighting bureaucracies, the form of laws regulating both the construction and use of buildings—laws which, ultimately, the police must enforce. The London bobbies may initially have assumed responsibility for the regulation of road traffic as a public relations measure; but regulation of traffic soon became a regular police function and is today in London as elsewhere one of the major police tasks. The concept of what constitutes protection of the individual has, moreover, been constantly extended. As a consumer the individual is more or less effectively protected from adulterated or poisoned commodities, from many of the sharp practices that were once traditional in the marketplace, and from loss of goods or wealth through confidence games, stock swindles, etc.[4] As a businessman the individual is protected to some extent from absconding employees, dishonest associates, and irresponsible customers. And as a citizen everyone is today protected by law not only from physical assault but from libel, from verbal defamation of character.

The expansion and elaboration of police jurisdiction has increased the number of police needed for law enforcement and has led to a multiplication of police agencies—i.e., to the establishment of special traffic, vice, and other police bureaus. At the same time, the conditions of law enforcement have been complicated by such social changes as the increasing size and greater depersonalization of urban communities, increased personal mobility, and the growing ability of law violators to escape from the locality in which they have committed crimes that has come with improved means of transportation. To offset insofar as possible the advantages to the lawbreaker of such changes, a variety of new police practices and organizations have evolved. The identification of persons, for example, has developed into

[4] For one example of the gradual extension of police powers as a result of adverse experience with unrestricted free enterprise, see James H. Young, *The Toadstool Millionaires: A Social History of Patent Medicines in America before Federal Regulation*, Princeton University Press, Princeton, N.J., 1961.

a science-based technique in which fingerprints, blood type, and other physical criteria may be used to detect a criminal or identify a corpse. Local police forces have been supplemented by regional, national, and recently international organizations (e.g., Interpol); and the development of electronic communication methods, first the telegraph and now radio, television, and teletype messages and pictures, has made possible quick transmission between individual police and between various police agencies of information, queries, etc.

Police Powers and Social Change

The many changes that have occurred over the past two hundred years or so in the arts and organizations for maintaining the peace and in the scope of police powers constitute adaptations to many antecedent changes—to the changing standards of individual welfare and human relationships, to the declining integrity of such traditional social agencies of training and control as the family and the community, to the growth of cities, and so on. Many of the former changes have done no more than cancel out the adverse effects of the latter on the maintenance of the peace; and in some respects the crime problem is as acute today as it was in Elizabethan England. Nevertheless, it is now possible for a law-abiding citizen of any Western society to conduct his affairs and live out his life without more than casual, and that usually momentary, concern about his personal safety or the physical preservation of his property rights. Today he is far more likely to be injured or killed in a highway accident than through personal assault and far more likely to lose money through his own mismanagement than through theft or the chicanery of others. The law of the jungle has not been repealed; but it is to a remarkable extent kept under restraint through the policing powers of modern government.

The extent to which a high level of peaceableness within a social population contributes to social stability depends, no doubt, upon related factors. Effective policing may for a considerable time repress conflicts, especially those between minority and majority groupings, that might otherwise be expressed in violence which might in turn lead to an adaptive resolution of the bases for the conflict. The violence that attended the emergence of organized labor, for example, was in part responsible for labor's success. Social changes often intensify policing problems; and if prompt and effective action could be taken to repress the unpeaceable consequences of those changes, change might be retarded if not actually prevented. If, for example, the police had been able to enforce the early motor traffic laws, which usually made 35 or 40 miles per hour the maximum speed permissible, we might still be driving automobiles incapable of going any faster.

There is, however, some reason to think that, other things being equal, freedom from the law of the jungle facilitates innovative and adoptive behavior. Freedom from worry about extraneous matters, including that of personal safety, certainly favors creative endeavor; science in particular has been advanced mainly by men of peace and under conditions of personal security. A society that gives considerable scope to brute force also gives honor to it; and such a society provides a poor social climate for a man of innovative inclination.[5] A farmer or craftsman who must do his work with one eye out for enemies (Indians, thugs, or whatever) and one hand on a gun or other weapon is not likely to have either the time, the patience, or the margin of safety necessary for trying out some new crop or some new tool. Many of the notably peaceable communities of the past, such as monastic priests, the Amish, and many island primitives, have also been socially stable; and in some periods and places of cultural ferment, as in Florence during the Renaissance, life has been distinctly insecure. Nevertheless, peace and "progress" are at least somewhat related; and it seems likely that the emerging police powers of government have on the whole encouraged rather than discouraged the changes in science and technology, and perhaps those in economic and some other forms of organization, that have been occurring in Western societies these past hundred years and more. The same cannot, however, be said of the use of the powers of government to effect social changes.

GOVERNMENT AS AN AGENCY OF SOCIAL CHANGE

Although the powers of government are in the first instance directed toward maintaining the peace, they may also be directed toward shaping or modifying the character of the society. Conquered peoples have often been

[5] The hazing of freshmen and the general rowdiness that was characteristic of student life in American colleges and universities fifty years ago cannot have been conducive to intellectual endeavors, if only because the stress was thrown on physical activities. The long-standing academic prejudice against college football stems from the belief that an institution that makes much of the game and the men who play it will also tend to depreciate scholarship and the student who excels in his studies; it is not, as football enthusiasts have sometimes claimed, based on the assumption that there is necessarily an inverse relation between brawn and brains.

One of the gross historical evidences suggesting that where brute force is honored, significant social changes will not be forthcoming, is the fact that it was Northern Europe, most especially England, where feudalism was weakest and declined most rapidly, which made the major contributions to the emergence of modern society. After the short-lived Renaissance, Italy, where elements of feudal disunity and respect for the values of feudalism lingered on for centuries, produced few innovations and was exceedingly slow to adopt those of other peoples. See Marc Block, *Feudal Society*, L. A. Manyon (trans.), The University of Chicago Press, Chicago, 1961, pp. 282–312.

forced to pay tribute to the government of their conquerors and thus indirectly have had to modify their own economic life. Conquered peoples have sometimes been induced, through force where necessary, to adopt new techniques and new forms of social organization that were favorable to the interests of their conquerors. It was in such ways that the Romans built their empire and that, two thousand years later, the British endeavored to make India and their other possessions economically profitable. Very often in the history of mankind a government, ordinarily through its military, has been perverted from its civil function in the interests and aims of political tyranny. Kings, princes, and chieftains have frequently ruled for a time in accordance with their personal whims or personal ambitions. Such a state of affairs is not limited to premodern, hereditary forms of government. Napoleon turned France into an armed camp and in his vain desire to become Emperor of all Europe brought French society to ruin; Hitler aroused Germany to a similar endeavor; and the political rulers of Russia have for two generations applied all the powers of government, civil and military, to realizing the Communist ideology, or at any event, to keeping the ruling clique in power while endeavoring to force the industrialization of Russian life.

Political tyranny cannot for long exist without considerable support from those who are governed, but revolt from tyrannical rule is always delayed; for tradition—often sheer habit—gives an established government powers that transcend its coercive strength. Moreover, a political tyrant can always secure the support of some elements of the social population through bribery and the promise of benefits to come. Like many tyrants before them, both Napoleon and Hitler secured the support of the military class, and of industrialists who produced military equipment and supplies, by enlarging the military establishments and elevating them to high estate; and both at the same time promised every greedy citizen the profits, material and otherwise, of military conquest. Furthermore, the promises of a tyrant may be considerably reinforced by widespread wishful thinking among those who are governed—they may impute charismatic, supernaturalistic powers to the tyrant, as the French did to Napoleon and the Germans to Hitler.

Political tyranny has often had a profound short-run effect upon the direction and intensity of social action; and during the short run some changes of long-run significance may sometimes have occurred. By sharply reducing the ratio of men to women in postwar France, the Napoleonic Wars may have fostered, as they are commonly believed to have done, that matrilinear quality that is to be observed in French family and economic life today. The Nazi extermination of the Jews clearly resolved, at least for a generation or two, the centuries-old problem of the Jewish minority in Germany. Effects of this sort and probably most of the long-run effects upon society, however, have been incidental ones rather than those intended, or at least promised, by tyrannical government; and the main stream of cultural development seems to have been little affected by politically created and directed flurries of social activity. Too much tyranny may, perhaps, sap the vigor of a people and contribute to their decline as a nation, as the Inquisition did in Spain; but it seems seldom to have brought about eufunctional changes of significance in the social system. For one thing, the force of government has, as will be seen, limited ability to induce its citizens to develop or adopt new cultural devices; for another, the personal insecurity that is characteristic during times of tyranny discourages innovation and the adoption of innovations; and, for a third, a milieu of tyranny invariably honors brute strength and animal cunning and depreciates those human qualities that are essential to creativity of any sort.

Nowhere is there a clear line between government as an agency for the maintenance of the peace and government as an agency of social determination.[6] Nor is there a clear line between the use of governmental powers to gratify the whims, fancies, and ambitions of a tyrant and his cohorts and their antithetical use—what may be crudely described as the tyranny of the many over the few. Thus in maintaining the peace, government does in a sense force upon the few—those who would violate the law—the standards of conduct desired by and favorable to the interests of the many; and in trying to achieve his ends, a tyrant may in some instances actually act on behalf of some interests of the many, as the Fascists did in destroying the power of the Mafia in Sicily.

A distinction of sorts, vague and uncertain though it may be at times, does exist, however, between the use of governmental powers to protect each individual from the rule of force by others—to maintain the peace—and the use of governmental powers to protect all members of society from adversity. To the extent that it is successful, the former use of governmental powers frees each of the members of the society to live in accordance with cultural imperatives and, as long as his doing so does not jeopardize the freedom of others, to follow his personal inclinations. The latter use, on the other hand, is an attempt to assure that, whatever the culture and whatever his individual performance, no member of the society will suffer from want; and it operates on the assumption, an assumption that has not yet been validated, that through proper political manipulation a society can effectively provide for the welfare of every one of its members.

In times of stress governments have in the past often assumed some welfare functions, presumably in an attempt to prevent popular uprising. When, for example, the Roman economic system, a complex mixture of governmental, corporate, and private endeavors, faltered, the hungry of

[6] A variety of attempts to make this distinction clear are offered in Claude R. Sowle (ed.), *Police Power and Individual Freedom: The Quest for Balance*, Aldine Publishing Co., Chicago, 1962.

Rome (not, of course, those of the provinces) were fed by the public treasury. In times of war, particularly during the course of a siege, governments have often been impelled by military necessity to ration food and otherwise attempt to minimize the adversity to the population. Governments in the past have also at times endeavored, ostensibly in the public interest, to enforce codes of morality, in some instances because the government was the secular arm of organized religion, more often because the government represented a social class with a moral standard higher than, or at least different from, that of the majority of the people. During the Middle Ages, for example, town governments often regulated and occasionally tried to prevent prostitution. These endeavors may have stemmed from recognition that venereal diseases are transmitted by prostitutes; more likely, they reflected the family morality of the guild masters who controlled the town government.

Ideologists have often proposed utopian societies in which every individual would live out his life free from want and from the necessity to labor at hard and unrewarding tasks; but concerted effort to achieve such a society through political means is, with a few exceptions (the most striking of which was the attempt of Emperor Wang during the third century to establish a socialistic state in China), distinctly modern. In the West at least, it reflects the tendency for representative government to become, in Aristotle's terminology, demagogic—i.e., for those who offer the most and demand the least to be elected to office by the citizens of republican states. It also is a reflection of the rising standard of living that has been wrought by technological and other changes in Western societies; to an extent far greater than in times past, modern society can at least in the short run afford to protect the weak, the incompetent, and the unfortunate from hardship. And perhaps the fact that politicians have repeatedly claimed credit for the economic and other gains over the past two hundred years has helped in creating the illusion that political action is the *modus operandi* of social progress.

Political Preservation of the Status Quo

Most of the law of the past and a good deal of the law of modern societies has been legal reinforcement of traditional aspects of the social system. The rights of persons and property that are preserved through the police powers of government are established rights; the peaceable relations that are enforced are for the most part those of the basic organizations of the society; and so on. Much of the law that was enforced by municipalities and other governmental agencies during the later Middle Ages, for example, was directed toward the preservation of the established rights of the old aristocracy and those of the guilds. All such law—i.e., all law that represents the traditional—whatever its indirect consequences, has the direct effect of helping to preserve the *status quo*.

So, too, does much legislation that superficially seems intended to work changes in the society—laws that are often classified as welfare legislation. Although contemporary welfare legislation is usually thought to have had its origins in the Elizabethan poor laws, in point of fact these poor laws were devised in an effort to check popular unrest and thus to ensure the preservation of the *status quo*. They were at most a minimal political concession to the many strong forces of social change that were then at work in English society; they did not prevent profound changes from occurring, but they may very well have helped to delay them. The mercantilistic legislation of the late Middle Ages has also been viewed as social welfare in character. At least in theory it was intended to increase the national wealth and thus, by implication, the welfare of the people of the nation. But the practical basis for it was the need at that time for liquid wealth in the king's treasury for the prosecution of military affairs; and the major social consequence of mercantilistic legislation was to more or less freeze the economic activities of peasants, craftsmen, and merchants. Indirectly, it may have fostered some changes; for it led to the popularization of smuggling and eventually to such *sub rosa* and contraguild methods of goods fabrication as the cottage-industry system that was a prelude to the industrial revolution in England.

The political revolutions that toward the close of the eighteenth century ushered in the parliamentary form of government were in considerable part a delayed adjustment to the changes that had been occurring in productive technology, economic organization, and class structure. Most particularly in England and the United States, they served to free individuals from the overburden of accumulated governmental constraints on economic enterprise—from the "welfare" legislation of the seventeenth and eighteenth centuries—thus eliminating legal support of the monopolistic rules and regulations of the guilds and governmental controls over the export and import of goods. As legal restraints on individual enterprise were repealed or lost their effectiveness through nonenforcement, the constraints of custom and tradition gradually lost much of their hold on economic life; and the doctrine of *laissez faire*, most effectively enunciated by Adam Smith, emerged as one of the dominant ideologies of the nineteenth century.

The extent to which freedom from political restraints on economic endeavors contributed to the flowering of the industrial revolution has been hotly debated for a century and more. That the profound technological and organizational changes that have occurred since the beginning of the nineteenth century have been rather closely associated with freedom from political controls is obvious. Some recent evidences, notably the differential rates of economic recovery following World War II in West Germany on the one hand and in France and Britain on the other, seem to indicate that political regulation of economic activities is more likely to deter than to accelerate changes in technology and economic organization and activity.[7] But just what the relation is between the political and the economic is far from clear; certainly it is not a simple causal one. Political freedom could of itself lead to anarchy and technological and economic retrogression; and the conditions that foster change, in that they involve a great variety of interdependent factors, are perhaps as much a cause of political freedom as a consequence of it. When a significant proportion of the members of a society are for ideological and other reasons inclined to be enterprising in technological and other respects, they may be hampered by legal enforcements of the dead hand of the past; but they may also apply their enterprise to breaching the laws that constrain them (to black marketing, smuggling, etc.), thus in time bringing discredit to governmental regulation, and eventually producing a political climate of freedom.[8] Conversely, when the prevailing concern of the members of a society is with security, with preserving existing rights and positions, however unfruitful, government will no doubt be used as an instrument to maintain the technological, ideological, and organizational *status quo*. Government is not, in sum, an independent variable; however vital, it is but one of the organizational elements that together determine both the extent to which the individual members of society adhere to predetermined forms of conduct and the extent to which

[7] In both France and Britain wartime controls, such as the rationing of food, heavy taxation on luxury goods, and stringent regulation of money, were continued for some years following the war in the effort to assure that what little wealth was being produced would be more or less equably shared by all. In West Germany, on the other hand, the government adopted a policy of economic *laissez faire* as soon as it was free to do so; and although economic and other conditions were far worse at the end of the war in West Germany than in France or Britain, West Germany was the first to recover economically. There is reason to think that it was in some part the freeing of men of enterprise from political constraints that made for the rapid rise in West German production and that it was the discouragement to enterprise by political constraints in France and Britain that was in good measure responsible for their slow recovery.

[8] Harry Schwartz ("The Organization Man, Soviet Style," *The New York Times Magazine*, June 2, 1957) has suggested that even in Soviet Russia, where the government is ostensibly devoted to the working of social changes, political bureaucracy is a dead weight; that a special class of individuals has arisen outside the political system who are highly skilled at circumventing that system and who serve, for a price, as the advocates for changes wanted or needed by various individuals or segments of the population; and that the Russian economy operates, as a consequence, on two levels—the sluggish official one, and the dynamic illegal, unofficial one.

they are culturally free to devise, advocate, and adopt new techniques, new ideologies, and new forms of organization.

The only statement that can be made with confidence about the role of governmental controls, above and beyond those that are concerned with the simple maintenance of the peace, is the broad generalization that the larger the role of government, the smaller the role of the individual in the determination of the social future. Whether this means that wide and effective governmental control over economic and other nonpolitical aspects of social life makes for or reflects a condition of social stability is one of the major ideological controversies of the twentieth century.[9]

The Growth of Political Constraints

The nineteenth-century socialists—Marxian, Fabian, and otherwise—generally conceded that political *laissez faire* was in major measure responsible for the individual enterprise that had brought about the industrial revolution. Marx, it will be recalled, explicitly credited the *bourgeoisie,* the class that represented enterprise, with the inventions and the organizational developments that had brought about industrialization and the rapid rise in social productivity; but, he argued, the industrial revolution had been accomplished, the production of material goods was as a consequence no longer a problem, and what remained to be done was to improve the distribution of what could now be so easily produced. In his version of socialism it was to secure equable distribution of material wealth that the exploited producers of goods would revolt from the capitalistic owners of the means of production and then communalize those means.

The central goal of all socialists has been national, i.e., governmental, ownership and operation of the means of production. They would have private lands become public property, private businesses become public businesses, and both agricultural and industrial production be conducted of, by, and for the people through government agencies. They assume that government agencies can direct the productive processes more efficiently and distribute the products more equably than is or can be done under any system of private ownership. The socialistic proposal is, in fact, but an extension to all forms of production of the empirical discovery that some kinds of social values can be provided more effectively through government

[9] For evidence and argument that it is governmental control that is the active variable—i.e., that it is government that induces stability, rather than stability that leads to an extension of government—see Fritz M. Marx, *The Administrative State: An Introduction to Bureaucracy,* The University of Chicago Press, Chicago, 1957. For historical support of this thesis see Hans Rosenberg, *Bureaucracy, Aristocracy, and Autocracy: The Prussian Experience, 1660–1815,* Harvard University Press, Cambridge, Mass., 1958.

agencies or governmentally regulated private enterprise than through socially uncontrolled private enterprise. Socialist ideologists have not invented the practice that they advocate; they have simply projected into infinity what has been learned in specific circumstances.

As early as the seventeenth century some municipalities began to undertake such public works as the development of a sewage system, the building and maintenance of public streets, and the provision of street lighting. Even then the idea of public ownership and operation was not new; long since the Roman art of supplying water as a public service had been rediscovered and put into use; but the extension of this idea to new realms came very slowly and only after private enterprise, usually individual enterprise, had proved unable to satisfy public needs.

The industrialization of productive processes during the later part of the eighteenth century and throughout the nineteenth was in every instance accomplished through private enterprise; and, as has been pointed out, the prevailing principle at that time was for government to prevent the use of force by individuals or groups but otherwise to give free scope to individual initiative. This principle was gradually compromised in all Western societies as experience demonstrated that first this and then that technological device could not operate in the public interest through unregulated private enterprise. The experience with railway transportation was typical: the invention, development, and exploitation of the steam-powered, rail-routed train was everywhere accomplished through private enterprise. From about 1840 the growth of railroads was rapid and chaotic; and Europe, Britain, and to a lesser extent the United States were soon webbed with numbers of competing lines. In laissez-faire economic theory, competition is the life of trade—i.e., the stimulus to productive efficiency; and in actuality it is no doubt in many cases just that. But competition between the parallel and intersecting lines of numbers of railroad companies proved in the course of time to be contrary to the public interest. Rather than leading to the provision of the best and cheapest possible transportation, it led, rather, toward the worst. Once a railroad company had made its very heavy capital investment in a railroad line, its tendency was to try to undersell its competitors, regardless of actual costs; but since the effort of each to undersell all others could only end in bankruptcy, competing lines were driven to consolidation, thereby achieving a monopoly on transportation between the various points on their combined routes; and monopoly, it soon became evident, led directly to high rates and poor service for the public. So neither free competition nor monopoly was satisfactory from the public point of view.

In Europe the railroads were eventually nationalized, taken under governmental ownership and management. In Britain and the United States the railroads came to be publicly regulated in the public interest (although in Britain they were subsequently nationalized in the European manner). In the system that evolved in the United States, first state and then Federal agencies were established by law to govern the operation of the private railroad corporations, to fix rates, to determine schedules, and to set minimum standards of service. Integration of lines into operating systems was encouraged, but consolidation into monopolies was and still is discouraged.

It was experience with the railroads that more than any other single factor led in the United States to the emergence of the concept of public utilities—the concept of extending governmental police powers to include regulation of those economic facilities that are vital to the public welfare and that are, for technological or other reasons, inherently incapable of operating to the public interest on the basis of free competition. The concept of public utilities, once socially sanctioned, has proved subject to almost indefinite extension; and during this present century governmental regulation of a wide variety of products and services has been undertaken on the grounds that it is in the public interest, with the result that unregulated private enterprise is almost unknown today.[10] Meanwhile, in the United States as elsewhere, the idea of public works was slowly, and at first against the greatest resistance, extended to cover an increasing variety of properties —harbors, river dikes, public parks, canals, etc. With public works as with public utilities, it was prolonged social adversity with private enterprise that forced responsibility for their provision onto government. The development of public highways is as good an illustration as any of the general process.

Until the advent of the automobile, road systems outside the cities had been local, casual both in structure and route, and privately maintained. Two kinds of private roads had evolved in the United States—and developments in Europe were for long not greatly different—the privately owned and operated toll road, usually a major route between a port and some important inland city, and the rural road that connected farmsteads to the local trading center, which was the responsibility of the property holders who used it. By the close of the century, when townships had developed, most of the rural roads were given some tax money support by local government, although the actual work of maintaining the roads usually devolved on individual farmers; i.e., the farmers were paid a small sum from public funds by the township for filling in potholes in the road adjacent to their own property.

The railroad made most of the old toll roads obsolete, and most of

[10] For the early phase of this change in the United States see Harold U. Faulkner, *The Decline of Laissez Faire: 1897–1917*, Holt, Rinehart and Winston, Inc., New York, 1951; and for some of the more recent developments see John D. Hogan and Francis A. Ianni, *American Social Legislation*, Harper & Row, Publishers, Incorporated, New York, 1956.

them fell into disuse; for it was far easier, cheaper, and quicker to move goods or persons by railroad than by freight wagon or stagecoach. By the time that the automobile became a reasonably reliable means of transportation, there were therefore no roads outside the city itself on which to travel except those used by farmers. Adequate, perhaps, for slow-moving horse-drawn vehicles going to the local market town, these roads were most unsuited to the automobile; they were dusty and muddy by turns and deeply rutted, and they wound hither and yon and ended almost invariably in some farmer's barnyard. Determined and adventurous motorists worked out cross-country routes of a sort.[11] It was not, however, until effective public demand for good through roads—for example, effective political lobbying by the automobile associations—forced various agencies of government to assume responsibility for road construction and road maintenance that regional and then national road systems could in fact be built. Private enterprise could not, or at any event did not, rise to meet this growing social demand for roads.

POLITICAL WELFARISM

That governmental regulation of private enterprise and governmental ownership of social facilities has in many specific instances been a historical necessity is evident; but it does not follow, as the early socialists held, that what is necessary or at least advantageous in some instances has universal value. No doubt the railroads and now the airlines must be governmentally regulated in the interests of public convenience and social efficiency; but the case for similar regulation of milk distribution, for example, especially minimum-price maintenance, is far less certain. Public provision of highways, and even of irrigation systems and flood-control devices, may be a necessity, if only because such provisions are not forthcoming under private enterprise; but the case for public housing and for many of the other public works of modern society cannot be justified in the same way.

---

[11] And enterprising publishers developed handbooks for their guidance. Of these the most successful was known as the *Blue Book*, which gave detailed instructions on how to get from town to town. The nature of those instructions indicates the character of the roads at this time. The motorist would be told, for example: Set speedometer at zero at the county courthouse. Proceed north along Main Street for 1.3 miles; turn right at the schoolhouse and after crossing the bridge, turn sharply left. Thereafter the road winds. At 3.2 miles take right fork. Watch out for RR crossing! At 8.5 miles . . . etc.

In 1915 the first attempt was made to plot out a motor route across the country, and the result was called the Lincoln Highway. The "highway" consisted of local roads, none paved except in towns and cities, that more or less connected with one another, the route being indicated by painted bands on trees and telegraph poles.

Doctrine of the Mature Society

At some indefinable point in the extension of governmental regulation and public ownership of productive properties, the function of government ceases to be that of serving the public necessity and convenience and becomes that of providing for the welfare, material and otherwise, of the individual members and various self-interest groups of the society. Invariably the justification for making government responsible for social welfare is the assumption, basic to socialistic theory, that Western societies have achieved a technological, demographical, and organizational maturity and that the remaining problem for modern industrial society is to assure efficient utilization of the technology and the productive plant and an equable distribution of the social wealth. Such was the assumption upon which Marx built his revolutionary ideology in the 1860s; it was also the assumption upon which the Labor government of Britain nationalized much of the country's capital plant in the 1920s and upon which the United States began the development of national welfare programs in the 1930s.[12]

The thesis that Western societies had achieved maturity became a popular and persuasive doctrine during the 1930s; it held, as had Marx nearly a century earlier, that man had at long last achieved total conquest of his environments, physical and biological, and that his various organizational arrangements had come close to ultimate perfection. The need, once great, for innovation and the individual initiative that is necessary to innovation had, therefore, all but passed; with one more stride, the socialization of the means of production, the utopian system so long envisioned by idealists would become a reality, and men could then settle down to enjoy the fruits of past endeavor in peace and quietude. That final stride would be the effective assumption by government, through a wide variety of specific agencies, of responsibility for the production and distribution of the more important of the social values—all those that are essential to the health, happiness, and material well-being of the members of society.

There may be some doubt as to whether governmental agencies of regulation or operation are better fitted than family, corporate, and other non-political forms of organization to maintain the production of social values—whether, for example, socialized medicine is more efficient in the utilization of medical technology than is a system of private practitioners. There can be

---

[12] Said President Franklin Delano Roosevelt in justification of the New Deal program: "Our industrial plant is built . . . our last frontier has long since been reached. . . . Our task now is not necessarily producing more goods. . . . It is distributing wealth and products more equitably" (quoted by Max Ways in "Growth: A New Mask for Big Government," *Fortune*, April, 1960, p. 112).

For a historical survey of the emergence of this idea in the United States see Richard Hofstadter, *The Age of Reform: From Bryan to F.D.R.*, Alfred A. Knopf, Inc., New York, 1955.

little doubt, however, that governmental regulation and ownership of the means of producing social values, material and otherwise, exercises a generally stabilizing effect upon society. In this respect, at least, socialism—or "welfarism," as is the currently preferred term—is appropriate to and contributes to social stability; and in this respect it is inappropriate to conditions of ideological, technological, and organizational incongruence—the actual condition of all the societies of the modern world.

The very rapid technological and organizational changes that have occurred in Western societies during the postwar years and, most particularly, the intense economic and military rivalry that has grown up between the United States (representing what we like to think of as the free world) and Russia have forced a revision of welfare theory. Most contemporary advocates of welfarism, including most of our practical politicians, have abandoned the goal of the stable society and have identified their program of political encroachment upon individual and other forms of endeavor with the need for continuing social change. Such change, they now claim, can be most rapidly and effectively accomplished by political means; for only through government can the processes of change be systematized and guided toward socially desirable ends. In this claim they make an error quite different from but fully as great as that made by the socialists of another day. The earlier socialists were correct in their view that governmental controls and operations lead to stability; but they were incorrect in their assumption that stability can be maintained and is desirable. The modern advocates of welfarism accept the now self-evident fact that modern societies must continually change if they are to survive; and then they assume, contrary to historical evidence, that change can be best achieved through governmental means.

Political Bureaucratization

The tendency, analyzed elsewhere, for organizations, corporate, academic, etc., initially in the interests of operational efficiency, to become bureaucratic in structure is most pronounced in government; for the agencies of government have a more or less effective monopoly over what comes within their jurisdiction. They are not forced by competition with comparable agencies, as nongovernmental organizations may be, to make constant adaptations to changing external conditions. Usually the only way in which they compete with one another is in securing continued financial support from legislative or other tax-distributing arms of the government; and in their competition with other agencies for such support, operating efficiency is not a determining factor.

The bureaucratization of governmental agencies has proved functionally advantageous in the exercising of police powers and in the performance of such routine tasks as the distribution of mail, the maintenance of sanitary services, etc. But in the regulation or operation of any technique-based organization—a hospital, an industrial plant, a farm, etc.—the unchecked bureaucratic nature of a governmental agency tends to prevent changes in the technical base and in the ways through which the technique is utilized. Nationalization or, as in the United States, regulation of railroads was no doubt inescapable; but the long-run result was to more or less freeze railroad technology, railroad routes, and railroad operating procedures. Under governmental auspices the railroads were enabled, since they were free from the spur of competition, to become totally bureaucratic; moreover, they were forced to this end by the bureaucratic regulations under which they existed. So in time railroad organization became a monolithic system of interdependent bureaucracies—governmental, administrative, operative, and labor organizations—in the context of which technological changes were almost precluded.[13] Over the course of the past half century, during which the automobile, airplane, truck, and pipeline have become major means of conveyance, the railroads of the Western world have remained essentially unchanging; and a considerable part of the responsibility for their static character devolves upon governmental regulation or ownership.

As more and more governmental agencies have been established during the course of this century and charged with one welfare function or another—with regulating the production and distribution of electricity, with protecting the farmer from the risks of competition in the marketplace, with operating old-age-pension, unemployment, and other programs of a charitable sort, etc. —an entirely new structure of authority (or "power system," as it is sometimes termed) has gradually emerged.[14] As this has come about, the individual as such has steadily lost in his powers of self-determination, in his ability to make free choices; for in every area of life that has been touched by government bureaucracy, the demand for conformity has become irresistible. At the same time, the scope and authority of many traditional social roles

[13] It is the thesis of Robert E. Lane (*The Regulation of Businessmen: Social Conditions of Government Economic Control,* Yale University Press, New Haven, Conn., 1954) that political regulation is gradually bringing about the same condition in all aspects of our economy.

[14] In such absolute terms as tax money collected and spent and the numbers of persons employed directly by government—national, state, and local—government in the United States in the nineteenth century grew at about the same rate as the national income and the numbers of the population.

During this century, however, every index—absolute or relative—of the role of government in our social life has risen progressively. A detailed and carefully documented study of the changes in the scope, character, and costs of government in America between 1900 and 1949 is provided by Solomon Fabricant in *The Trend of Government Activity in the United States since 1900,* National Bureau of Economic Research, Inc., New York, 1950.

have been reduced: a father has lost most of his authority over his children; a small businessman has become a part-time functionary, without pay, for tax and other governmental agencies; a corporation president has become a prisoner not only of his own organization but of the many governmental agencies (municipal, state, and Federal; taxational, regulatory, and directive) that together set the metes and bounds within which a corporation can operate. Moreover, the general public has lost much of its former power to influence the direction of governmental action; for as public welfare agencies have been created, they have been delegated administrative powers that have quickly become self-maintaining and largely beyond the reach of the voter. Today in all Western societies (and it must be even greater in Communist countries) the social impact of governmental bureaus, commissions, and other regulative and operative bureaucratic agencies is as a consequence far greater than that of the laws made by duly elected legislatures.[15] It is only a slight exaggeration of the actualities to say of modern governments that they are by, for, and of the bureaucrats.

The extension of government into welfare functions has, moreover, led of necessity to an increasing reliance upon trained, semiprofessional administrators in place of elected or appointed politicians. The administration of a modern town or city requires men of technical competence in a variety of highly specialized fields—accounting, business tactics and strategy, engineering, etc.; and so, to an almost equal degree, does government at all levels—county, state, and Federal. As experts have been brought into government service, the role of the politician has diminished. The mayor of a city and the President may be duly elected politicians; but both mayor and President are, like chief executives of modern corporations, dependent upon the many regulative and operational bureaucracies which actually administer government and upon the host of technical specialists without whom no town, city, state, or national government could long keep operating.

The rising importance of government technicians, like the concomitant growth of regulative and operative bureaucracies, has tended to increase the distance between the general public and the government agencies that are supposed to serve it; for the government technicians constitute an occupational class or system of occupational classes that are self-maintaining and largely independent of the citizens whom they govern. A municipality may discharge its city manager through its political machinery; but if he has good standing among those of his occupational group, he will quickly be placed in an equivalent job elsewhere; and his successor will be a man of very

[15] For an analysis of the ways in which, and the great degree to which, governmental agencies extend their regulative powers, see Lowell B. Mason, "The Unauthorized Growth of Bureaucratic Powers," in Helmut Schoeck and James W. Wiggins (eds.), *The New Argument in Economics*, D. Van Nostrand Company, Inc., Princeton, N.J., 1963, pp. 201–215.

similar values, skills, and administrative outlook. The days when king and court ruled under the monarchial system have long since gone; but as governments assume welfare functions, they tend to be taken over by bodies of men almost as clearly defined and as closed as were the aristocrats of an earlier time.

The decline of the old-line politician is hard to regret; he was, and those of his sort who remain still are, without principles other than to stay in power. Modern administrative technicians, on the other hand, are generally men with strong principles and, certainly, with considerable knowledge and skill in their special field. They, like the bureaucracies that they administer or influence, tend to be uncorruptible; but, like the members of any highly integrated occupational group, they tend also to be dedicated to the *status quo*—to that body of existing ideas, values, knowledges, and skills that is honored within the occupation of which they are members. The very qualities that make them uncorruptible, including the social controls that operate within the occupation itself, also make them resistant to changes; and under conditions of incongruence their undoubted efficiency may be more than canceled out by their tendency to keep things as they are. The old-line politicians were wasteful of the social values over which they had control, and they administered government with a maximum of inefficiency; but they were also highly adaptable; hence the government over which they reigned moved with the times—i.e., it responded to every fluctuation in political pressures, many of which reflected underlying changes that were occurring in the technology, the ideology, or the nongovernmental organizations of the society.

Governmentally Programmed Change

The idea, now quite dominant, that one of the major tasks of government is to produce desired changes in society reverses, as has been shown, the old socialistic goal of social stability through governmental management. Attempts by government to work specific changes have not been lacking in the past; but they have been confined to organized application of existing technology, such as slum clearance and low-cost public housing. The current goal, however, is far larger and far more generalized; it is to increase the material prosperity of the people, to improve their nongovernmental forms of organization, to provide them with better housing and recreational facilities, even to give them, through some as yet undiscovered means, peace of mind. All these are, no doubt, worthy objectives; and where the program for change involves no more than the organized application of already existing technology, a modicum of success is no doubt possible. Attempts to produce new techniques or any other qualitative as distinct from quantitative changes through governmental planning and management are, however, quite another thing.

Government and political bureaucratization **471**

As has already been discussed, innovation is an entirely unpredictable and individual achievement; it may be fostered but it cannot be planned. Moreover, the functional consequences of the adoption of any innovation are at present unpredictable, since the ways and the extents to which various elements of the social system are functionally interdependent are not yet known. Thus when social planners, governmental or otherwise, venture from the tried and true (as they must if they venture to advocate an innovation), they do so without much ability to forecast the consequences. Even when the government has tried to preserve some aspect of the *status quo* that has been threatened, the results have usually been quite different from those that were anticipated.[16] When, for example, in one of the many efforts to keep France

[16] The most costly and total failure has been the effort, in the United States as elsewhere, to protect farmers from the changes that were occurring in other aspects of the economy. Initially and until the mid-1930s the United States Department of Agriculture was, by congressional mandate and its own orientation, engaged mainly in helping farmers increase production by advocating the newest in cropping techniques, land usages, etc. Under the New Deal it was given a new goal, that of preserving the small family farm that was being threatened by the very techniques that the Department had been advocating; and to this end Congress has since enacted program after program to be administered by the Department. Each such program has in time turned out to have had exactly the opposite effect of that intended; it has hastened the shift from family-farm agriculture to large-scale, corporate farming, with the result that today 9 per cent of the farms in the United States produce 50 per cent of the total agricultural product.

For the rationale behind the effort to preserve the family-farm system see Joseph Ackerman and Marshall Harris (eds.), *Family Farm Policy*, The University of Chicago Press, Chicago, 1947; for the history of governmental efforts to influence agriculture see Murray R. Benedict, *Farm Policies of the United States, 1790–1950*, The Twentieth Century Fund, New York, 1953; and for the failure to preserve by political action the family-farm system see Edward C. Banfield, *Government Project: An Account of Big Government in Action*, The Free Press of Glencoe, New York, 1951, and Edward Higbee, *Farms and Farmers in an Urban Age*, The Twentieth Century Fund, New York, 1963.

A minor but illuminating example of the inability of government to predict the social consequences of political action is provided by one of the side effects of the income tax laws in Britain. The British economy has been sorely in need of new venture capital for decades, since its industrial plant is for the most part antiquated. Political efforts to improve Britain's position in international trade have been hampered by this fact; but at the same time British tax laws discourage investment in industry and encourage those who have venture capital to "invest" it at the race tracks rather than in industrial stocks; for capital gains are heavily taxed, while what is won at betting is tax-free. See W. F. F. Kemsley and David Ginsburg, *Betting in Britain: A Report on Betting Habits and Spending in 1949–1950*, Central Office of Information, London, 1951.

agriculturally self-sufficient, the government of Napoleon established subsidies for the production of sugar beets, no one anticipated or could have anticipated that this legislation would in the course of time help to make France the heaviest per capita consumer of alcoholic beverages in the world. Nor did the New Deal ideologists who designed the agricultural parity price system during the 1930s foresee that the long-run effects would be to speed the growth of large-scale, industrial agriculture and so hasten the doom of the small, one-family, diversified agricultural unit that they were in fact attempting to save.

The inability of governmental agencies to predetermine the consequences of politically sponsored changes is accompanied by another inability—the impossibility of inducing significant qualitative changes by coercive measures. Men may be deterred by coercion from doing some things that they might like to do; and they may be bribed through tax monies or relief from taxation into doing what they want to do anyway—i.e., they may be encouraged by government to work at their trade, pursue their scientific investigations, treat sick patients, etc. They cannot, however, in the same ways be induced either to want to be creative or to act for long in ways that are contrary to their established cultural attributes and so repugnant to them.[17] It is for this reason that every instance in which governments have tried to increase the national birth rate through legal means have failed; that attempts to legislate into existence equality for a racial or other subordinated minority have failed; and that political efforts to make a people religious or to deprive them of an established religion, to change their sex morals (e.g., to eliminate homosexuality), and to improve domestic harmony have been entirely futile. Government may sanction changes that have occurred, and in the long run it does; but it does not directly and in a predetermined fashion fix the course of social changes. In an effort to do so, government is far more likely to dampen the individual enterprise through which changes of a qualitative character come into being.

Political Homogenization

As was observed earlier, governmental regulations inevitably reduce the scope of individual freedom, including freedom to try to find some unprecedented solution to a problem. Like the informal social controls that are exercised by the family, the community, and other groups, governmental regulations are normalizing. But whereas the informal social controls of groups give some

[17] This fact, persistently ignored by legislators, was first brought to the attention of sociologists by William Graham Sumner in *Folkways*, Ginn and Company, Boston, 1907. For a recent analysis and reaffirmation of the validity of Sumner's position see Harry V. Ball et al., "Law and Social Change: Sumner Reconsidered," *American Journal of Sociology*, vol. 67, pp. 532–540, March, 1962.

scope for individual variation and sanction status differentiation within group membership, law and the regulations of governmental agencies are absolute; and enforcement demands, although it seldom secures, absolute conformity to them. Moreover, whereas the informal norms of group life are based upon some concept of the average ability and willingness of the members of the group to conform to them, and a subaverage individual is induced by social controls to exert himself, law and the regulations of governmental agencies are formulated in terms of some concept of the least capable and least willing of the many individuals who are to be covered by a particular law or regulation. As a consequence, law and regulations tend to reduce the performance of all to that of the lowest common denominator.

Thus in the formulation of a tax law or a tax-bureau regulation it is assumed, and for the most part quite correctly, that those affected will not willingly pay the full tax due, that they will report on income or other matters dishonestly unless coerced to do otherwise, etc. In modern societies, where taxes are heavy and many agencies are engaged in taxation, an individual must keep elaborate records and preserve all evidences bearing upon his claims to honesty in his dealing with tax agencies, even though he be one of the rare individuals who are actually honest; i.e., every individual is required to behave as though he would, if he safely could, evade his tax obligations. Similarly, in other more complex and socially significant ways, exceptional individuals are forced by all the laws and regulations that affect them to perform in the manner required of the least competent, least responsible, and least willing of those for whom the law or regulation was devised. Law and regulation do not coerce an inferior individual to strive to excel; rather, they lower the performance of all to, or at least toward, the standard set for the inferior. It is for this reason that it has been said with considerable validity that government secures from man not the best that is possible but the least that is tolerable. The minimum standards set by any governmental agency—e.g., the minimum permissible butterfat content in milk sold at retail, the minimum wage to be paid a given class of workers, the minimum standards of construction in the building of a house, the minimum amount and quality of work to be performed for a given fee—tend always and everywhere to become also the maximum. To the extent therefore that government regulates the conduct of men and groups, it discourages exceptional performance, including those kinds of exceptional action—innovation, advocacy, and the adoption of new devices, ideas, and forms of organizations—that lead to social change.

Welfarism and the Spur to Accomplishment

As government assumes responsibility for the material and psychological well-being of individuals and categories of individuals, it also fosters apathy.

Men may not be inherently lazy, as some philosophers have held; but although there are always some exceptions, some self-driven men, the extent to which they will exert themselves usually depends on the one hand upon the nature and extent of their unfulfilled needs and desires and on the other upon the rewards for endeavor. If a man is hungry or if he wants social approval, some luxury, or just the satisfaction of success, and if the social circumstances are such that the rewards for this or that kind of endeavor will enable him to fulfill his needs or desires, he will be inclined to undertake it. But if he has no urgent needs or unfulfilled desires, or if the prospect of reward for endeavor is slight, he will be inclined to lie abed and make the best of things as they are.

Every attempt by government to relieve the individual of responsibility for his own welfare reduces the social spurs to individual accomplishment, for it lessens to some degree the unfulfilled needs and desires of the members of society; indeed, it is the ultimate goal of welfarism to leave no needs and desires unfulfilled. If, for example, an individual is relieved by old-age pensions and other governmental devices from the need to prepare financially for his later years, he will have no incentive to do so; he will tend, that is to say, to live from hand to mouth without thought of the future.

Moreover, every attempt by government to assure individual welfare also reduces in some way and to some degree the social rewards for individual endeavor.[18] For except where government itself produces social values through public works of one sort or another, what is given by government to those who need must be taken from those who have produced a surplus of values—from those who, for example, have been trying to store up wealth for their own old age. In contemporary systems of welfarism the actual process of taking from some to give to others is exceedingly complex, elaborately disguised, and shot through with contradictions; but the end result is to penalize those individuals and categories of individuals who excel

[18] The following are some of the specific ways in which political welfarism reduces individual enterprise and thus discourages social change: Every man who is drawn into governmental service is bureaucratized and is, therefore, one less man in the social population who might otherwise be innovative or at least the adopter of something new. In each of the many and steadily increasing areas of conduct that are subject to governmental regulation, the individual is discouraged from innovative and adoptive endeavor; for all such endeavor is politically penalized, while conformity is in one way or another politically rewarded. As the monetary costs of government increase, the monetary incentives to individual and corporate enterprise are reduced; thus tax losses may, in many instances, be preferable to gross profits. And as the social role of government increases, the expert on law and bureaucratic regulations becomes more highly regarded, and with good reason, than the technician, scientist, or producing and marketing expert.

in any respect in order that the unproductive and improvident shall not suffer what in prewelfare days were the normal consequences of their incompetence.[19]

No contemporary government has as yet achieved the goals of welfare ideologists; but every contemporary government has moved in this direction with increasing rapidity during the past half century. The result to date has not been effective stabilization of modern life or the reduction of modern populations to a condition of general apathy; for government has inherently limited powers over society, and it never operates as an independent variable. So far, at any event, the stabilizing and initiative-discouraging consequences of the extension of government into welfare realms have in most societies been more than canceled out by counterchanges in other aspects of social organization. Thus while the modern individual is far more a captive to his government than was the individual of a century ago, he is also far less subservient to family, class, and related forms of organization. Whether he is in the end more or less free, and hence more or less likely to contribute in some way to future social changes, will become evident only as the future becomes the present.

[19] As the advantage shifts under welfare programs from those who give—i.e., from the productive members of society—to those who get, social parasitism becomes a fruitful way of life. How to live without working in modern American society is ironically described by Wyatt Marrs in *The Man on Your Back: A Preface to the Art of Living without Producing in Modern Society*, University of Oklahoma Press, Norman, Okla., 1958.

chapter 14 *Conflict and Change*

A number of the nineteenth-century social theories involved the idea that all change is and can be accomplished only through conflict, through a head-on, violent clash between those who represent the new and those who have a vested interest in the old—between downtrodden workers and their capitalistic exploiters, a submerged ethnic minority and the dominant majority, a progressive society and one that is decadent. This idea appears to have developed as a purely ideological adjustment to the disappointments that followed upon the French Revolution. The destructive and bitter conflicts of that revolution and the counterrevolution that followed it had led only to the Napoleonic Wars, wars that gave France a brief period of glory, but ended in defeat and near-total exhaustion. Logically, perhaps, the social philosophers of the late nineteenth century should have deduced from the disaster of the French experience that conflict, both internal and external, is detrimental to social progress; but the focus of attention on such concepts as Darwin's idea that the struggle for survival is a part of the mechanism of biological evolution led many of them to regard conflict as the means to social improvement.

Of the various, and mostly conflicting, theories which embodied the idea that social change is accomplished through social conflict, that advanced by Marx gained the most extensive and enduring following. As was noted earlier, this aspect of Marx's theory was time- and place-bound. Marx applied the idea of change through conflict only to industrial societies in their early maturity, specifically to the revolt on the part of the industrial workers against their capitalistic exploiters that was to bring about the transition to the good society. Marx did not glorify conflict per se. In the century since, however, the prestige of Marx has often been invoked to justify, in the name of progress, conflicts of widely varied sorts—first and most notably, revolution in preindustrial

477

Russia, subsequently revolution in also preindustrial China, and later the ideological break between Russia and China over the need to destroy the capitalistic-imperialistic nations by force in order that world communism might prevail. Moreover, a sort of neo-Marxian thesis has been adopted when occasion has seemed to warrant by non-Communist advocates of freedom from real or imagined political, economic, and social persecution. No analysis of social change would, therefore, be complete without a consideration of the role that social conflict plays in the making of social change.[1]

Definitions of Conflict

By conflict Marx and other nineteenth-century theorists meant a violent, physical clash of people who have unalterably opposed and irreconcilable interests, values, sentiments, and loyalties. Today, on the other hand, conflict is often used as a blanket term to encompass all kinds of contrasts, oppositions, and contradictions—between various elements within the personality of the individual, between individuals, and between social groups—irrespective of the nature of the conduct that they produce. In this usage, an individual who is both ambitious and indolent suffers from an internalized conflict; a husband and wife who disagree regarding the proper method of raising their children are in conflict; and the opposition between the desire of workers to maximize their wages and that of their employer to increase his profits is conflict, although it may result in nothing more violent than a haggling over wage scales.

That conflict in this general and now most frequently used sense is involved in the working of social changes cannot be denied. Any change always involves considerable stress, both individual and collective. Once accomplished, a change may reduce an antecedent incongruence and the strains that it imposed upon the members of society; but in the process of being accomplished, the change produces its own stress and strains—discontents, frustrations, dissensions, and disappointments. In this general sense, it is a conflict within his own personality that incites an innovator to his innovative endeavors; a conflict of ambitions and opportunities that leads an advocate to seek personal success in a socially atypical manner; and a conflict of values, interests, and status prospects that induces an

[1] Other and more extensive attempts to analyze the relationship between social conflict and social change are Oliver C. Cox, *Caste, Class, and Race: A Study in Social Dynamics*, Doubleday and Company, Inc., Garden City, N.Y., 1948; Lewis A. Coser, *The Functions of Social Conflict*, The Free Press of Glencoe, New York, 1956; Ralf Dahrendorf, *Class and Class Conflict in Industrial Society*, Stanford University Press, Stanford, Calif., 1959; and Peter A. Munch, *A Study of Cultural Change: Rural-Urban Conflicts in Norway*, H. Aschehoug & Company, Oslo, 1956.

adopter to venture to use something new. Moreover, the resistance that both advocates and adopters encounter from those who resent the appearance of the new may be regarded as conflict. But such internalized, interpersonal, or intergroup stresses and strains appear in all societies, in stable as well as dynamic ones; only in the ideal society of the utopian dreamers is there freedom from conflicts of interests, values, sentiments, etc. The extent of personal, interpersonal, and intergroup conflicts may vary considerably from society to society and may change over time within any given society; but at no time or place has social life been free from stress and strain, from contrast and dissension, from opposition between individual and individual and between group and group. Even in a highly integrated society of isolated primitives, there is at the very minimum a constant struggle of individuals and subgroupings for sheer survival, which means that the individual is always under some duress and that there is a covert conflict between his desire to continue living and the fact that he can do so only if someone else, perhaps an elder or an infant, is denied a share of the food. Conflict in this general and sweeping sense is, thus, a normal aspect of all societies and hence cannot be used to explain the comparatively rare instances in which significant changes occur within some societies.

Nor, as a matter of fact, can conflict in the more restricted sense of overt violence between protagonists. Occasionally the advocates of a change and those who adopt it may encounter overt and violent opposition; and they may themselves resort to forcible means to achieve their ends. In such instances the normally peaceful and characteristically imperceptible processes by which social changes are achieved take on some of the characteristics of social events: that which is being changed becomes an issue widely noted and discussed, the protagonists become for the moment heroes and villains in a popular social drama, and the struggle between the old and the new becomes a conflict in which words and ideas give way to physical violence. In the process of becoming established, the union form of labor organization, for example, was accompanied both here and in Europe by recurrent resort to force. Union organizers used thugs—goons—in the attempt to intimidate reluctant workers into joining the union; employers retaliated by hiring other thugs to drive off the organizers; established unions used the strike— a coercive device—to force employers to give way to their demands, while employers countered with the lockout and, at times, the strong arm of established political authority. Even the eventual enfranchisement of women, the presumably weaker and gentle sex, involved a good deal of militant action on the part of both those who worked toward this goal and those who fought against it.

Conflict of this sort is not, however, a necessary accompaniment to change. Only a very small proportion of the radical changes that have oc-curred in Western societies over the past two hundred years have been accompanied by violence of any sort, although they undoubtedly involved much stress and strain. Moreover, violent as well as other kinds of conflicts may occur where change does not. Hence conflict of a violent sort is no more the cause, method, or process by which social changes are achieved than is conflict in the more general sense of stress and strains and oppositions. Like the latter, it is a normal and well-nigh universal social phenomenon.

That violent conflict between individuals or groups in the effort of each to satisfy some mutually exclusive interest or value is normal has commonly been deplored by idealists and has often been denied, or at least ignored, by sociologists. The latter have not closed their eyes to the frequency with which men, in our society and in other societies, resort to force—to murder, rape, strikes, riots, wars, and the many more subtle but even more commonplace uses of coercion. But they and other students of social life have frequently considered the outbreak of conflict a failure of organization—evidence that the society is in a disorganized condition. Insofar as social change is concerned, the implication of this view is that conflict is not the *modus operandi* of change, but that, on the contrary, change, at least change in social organization, is the way to eliminate conflict.

The idea that conflict stems from disorganization has, however, limited validity. Some conflict, such as clashes between juvenile gangs, may express a functional ineffectiveness of the organizational systems involved, in this instance of the family and community systems. But social organization of itself provides a condition that may make for conflict. Whatever its specific character, social organization always differentiates those who are included within its scope—it sets the members of the Jones family apart from the Browns, the upper class from the lower, townsmen from countrymen, Protestants from Catholics, both from Jews, etc.; and whatever the society, however stable or dynamic, the various organizational units will have somewhat different group interests and values, some of which will be mutually exclusive and may upon occasion lead to violence. Family feuds, peasant riots, religious persecution, etc., stem not from disorganization but from differences resulting from organization; and conflicts between organizational units of this sort are as much a part of an unchanging social system as they are of a dynamic one. Moreover, as will shortly be shown, organizations of a militant sort exist for the sole purpose of engaging in conflict, and such organizations are an integral part of almost all social systems.

Since social change is asocial and the historical exception rather than the rule, its occurrence is not to be explained by factors or processes, such as conflict, which are common to all societies at all times. A particular conflict, interpersonal or intergroup, may pose a problem that becomes resolved by a change. The prolonged conflict between Indians and white settlers in North America, for example, was more or less resolved by the establishment of reservations on which the Indians could, if they wished, continue their premodern way of life. A particular conflict may perhaps somewhat accelerate a change in process. The battles over unionism during the last half of the last century, for example, may have speeded the acceptance of the union form of labor organization; and the passive resistance of militant Negro organizations may be weakening the barriers between Negro and white in the United States. But a particular conflict between the advocates of a change and resisters to it may have no bearing whatsoever on the outcome. Such was evidently the case with the violent clash between the Irish immigrants and native Americans in Pennsylvania during the 1850s and 1860s and with the almost equally bitter struggle between cattlemen and nesters, farmers, over the fencing of the Western Plains; in both cases it was change—the gradual assimilation of the Irish and the economic decline of cattle raising on the plains—that brought an end to conflict, rather than conflict that brought about change. Moreover, as has been mentioned, conflict in the sense of a violent clash between individuals or groups may be absent from the area of social life in which rapid change is effected. There is, thus, a variable and uncertain relationship between social conflict of the violent kind and social change, a relationship that will be most clearly evident when such specific forms of conflict as war and revolution are subjected to detailed analysis.

WAR AND SOCIAL CHANGE

No event looms larger in the mythology of primitives and in the recorded history of civilized men than that of war. In most societies, past and present, the making of war has been among the most honored of occupations; and to preparation for war and warfare itself most societies have devoted a very considerable proportion of their social resources. Currently the United States is diverting upwards of 15 per cent of the gross national product to paying for past wars and for what are euphemistically termed defensive preparations to prevent future war. Perhaps one-half of the scientists and the more highly skilled technicians in the United States are directly or indirectly working on military projects; and so much of our industry is engaged in the development and manufacture of military devices that any considerable reduction in military expenditures would have profound effects upon the economic life of the nation. All the major governments of the world are involved in comparable if not equivalent expenditures of their national resources for military purposes; and for the peoples of Russia and China and some other countries this means a shortage and even lack of the necessities of life.

In view of the great importance that war has had and continues to have in human affairs, it may seem odd that almost nothing at all is known about the antecedents and the social consequences of war. Ideological justifications for maintaining military forces, for entering into a state of war with some specified enemy, and for resort to military force in the effort of one side to overthrow and the other to preserve an established political order are not lacking. Military historians have always been able to devise *post hoc* explanations for the advent, course, and outcome of a military event; and at least in recent times the literary aftermath of each military event— documents, fiction, military biographies, explanations, justifications, apologies, etc.—has been immense. World War II produced one scientific investigation of men at war, and in the years since a few studies of military organization have appeared; but only two studies have attempted to ascertain in an objective manner the social conditions and forces that make for war per se, and their findings are inconclusive.[2] During the formative period of the United Nations a research section was established to conduct studies into the causes of international tension and conflict; but nothing of value came of the project, and it soon languished from lack of both scientific and political support.[3]

The indifference of sociologists to the phenomenon of military conflict is especially puzzling. Sociologists have devoted a good deal of attention, both theoretical and empirical, to the study of class conflict and, in the United States, of conflict between ethnic groups. They have applied themselves with considerable diligence to trying to ascertain the antecedents

[2] The first of these was made by Quincy Wright, an international lawyer, and reported in *Causes of War and Conditions of Peace*, Longmans, Green & Co., Inc., New York, 1935, an enlarged version of which was subsequently published as *A Study of War*, 2 vols., The University of Chicago Press, Chicago, 1942. The second was a quantitative analysis by Lewis F. Richardson of the wars that have occurred in recent times. In his *Statistics of Deadly Quarrels* (The Boxwood Press, Pittsburgh, Pa., 1960) he offers evidence to indicate that most of the wars of the past have been preceded by a period of military preparation on the part of one or all of those who became belligerents, from which he concludes that an arms race is an unstable system that can end only in war.

[3] After ten years of more or less systematic research, the tensional project under UNESCO came up with little but doubts that psychological tensions, such as those produced by the frustration of personal ambitions, are an independent determinant of international conflict. See International Sociological Association, *The Nature of Conflict*, UNESCO, Paris, 1957.

Nevertheless, a number of authors have offered psychological explanations for war, of which the following are representative: E. F. M. Durbin and John Bowlby, *Personal Aggression and War*, Routledge & Kegan Paul, Ltd., London, 1950; Otto Klineberg, *Tensions Affecting International Understanding*, Social Science Research Council, New York, 1950; and T. H. Pear (ed.), *Psychological Factors of Peace and War*, Philosophical Library, Inc., New York, 1950.

Since 1957 there has been published by the University of Chicago Press a quarterly *Journal of Conflict Resolution*, devoted to articles by social scientists on international stresses and the phenomenon of war.

of such comparatively minor social irritants as juvenile delinquency, marital discord, and adult crime. Much attention, some of it fruitful, has been devoted to studying and theorizing about the normative characteristics of social life in modern societies during times of peace; but little effort has been made to gain an understanding of why men go to war and what happens when they do. Indeed, sociologists and other social scientists have proceeded for the most part as though military violence were a momentary social aberration, rather than one of the major activities of man. One can only conclude, therefore, that the deliberate and systematic destruction of men and their properties is ignored simply because it is the most inexplicable of all the organized endeavors of man.

War and the Military Establishment

What most clearly distinguishes war from other forms of conflict is the fact that it is a highly organized, calculated undertaking on the part of at least one, and usually all, of the belligerents. There is nothing spontaneous or fortuitous in the making of war, as there usually is in outbreaks of ethnic and class conflict. The combatants in war are professionals, or at the very least are led by professionals, who are trained in the existing arts of warfare; and the entire operation is traditionalized and conducted in accordance with culturally determined rules and procedures. In many respects war is, therefore, an occupational activity distinct only in form and consequences from such other occupations as tilling the soil or hunting for game; and in these respects the search for its causes leads to the study of the social system of which the military establishment and the making of war are functional aspects. The function that war serves is never clear and has no doubt varied; but the existence of a military establishment has invariably been the immediate cultural imperative for the making of war.

A few peoples have been so much isolated by geographic and other factors from contact with other peoples that they have had no occasion or opportunity to go to war and have therefore not developed a military establishment. A few others have faced the threat of assault and met assault by others passively. Most peoples, however, have included in their social system, whether simple or complex and whether large or small, a military subsystem that is represented by a more or less occupationally specialized segment of the population; and many social systems, such as the feudal, have made the military subsystem the central one to which all other aspects of the society are but supplementary. The frequency with which societies have gone to war or been drawn into war and the duration and consequences of wars have been varied; but being at war has been just as normal for most peoples during most periods of human history as being at peace. Indeed, in some times and places a condition of peace seems to have been the quantitatively atypical, to have been a period of cessation from warfare induced by exhaustion and devoted mainly to recuperating from one war and preparing for another.

It is the current Western view, a view that is echoed propagandistically by Communist leaders, that war is an atypical and abnormal phenomenon, that it constitutes a breakdown or failure of social relationships somewhat analogous to the breakdown of the normal psychological processes that is involved in individual psychopathology. In this view war stems, not from the social systems of the peoples who engage in it, but from the evil intent of vicious political leaders—i.e., the leaders of the enemy. Thus from the American point of view, our recent wars were caused by the Kaiser, Hitler, etc.; and our current heavy preparations for war are purported to be defensive attempts to make the cost of any future war so great that not even the leaders of Communist Russia or China will be so mad as to instigate a military attack upon us. This view of war is, however, no more than a rationalization of the contradiction between two coexistent systems of values, sentiments, and interests, the one relevant to peacetime social life, the other operative during times of war and in preparation for war.[4]

No doubt men have always placed a fairly high value on peace, most especially while they were recovering from the adversities of war. At the same time they have also and even during times of peace given honor to those personal and social qualities that are functionally appropriate to war—to personal valor; to the subordination of individual interests, including life itself, to the military success of the group; and to willingness and ability to kill in battle, even though no one is permitted to kill elsewhere. In most of the societies of the past and present, the heroes of mythology have almost always been warriors; much folk legend deals with war; a good deal of modern drama and fiction either portrays war and its making or uses war as a background for personal adventure; and a major part of recorded history, and of historical analysis of recorded history, is concerned with war. Conversely, many of the greatest villains of mythology, of modern drama, and of history have been men who lacked the courage or the integrity to die for their tribe or country; and in all complex societies the worst crime with which a man could be charged has been treason.

[4] The peacetime and wartime systems of values and sentiments are in many respects not only different but also incompatible. Thus a man who abandoned a promising and profitable career and his wife and children for a dangerous and personally unprofitable adventure during peacetime would be defined as an irresponsible fool; but if he does the same thing when his country is at war, he is acclaimed a hero. During peacetime the violent death of an overage slut may be reported in the press as though it were social disaster; but in time of war the violent death of a thousand young men will be proclaimed a victory for mankind, provided only that at the time of their death they were wearing the uniform of the enemy.

Ideological sanctioning of war does not of itself make war a socially normal rather than abnormal state of affairs; for, as has been noted, an ideology can exist *in vacuo*. But in most societies of the past as well as of the present general ideological sanctioning of war has had a substantial base in the existence of a military establishment with its own ideological, technological, and organizational complexes. Although the immediate antecedent to war is the existence of a military establishment and only those peoples who have military establishments go to war, the ultimate forces that make for war cannot any more be traced to the existence of a military establishment than the high crime rates of all modern societies can be traced to the large and complex policing forces that they maintain. One might argue whimsically that if there were no police, no criminals would be caught and identified as such; but even as it is the prevalence of criminals that has given rise to police forces, it is the prevalence of war that has made for military establishments. A society without a military establishment could easily be conquered by one so equipped, and it is this danger that in part explains the near-universality of military establishments.

About all that can be said about war in general is that it is socially normal and commonplace and invariably involves military establishments. Forms of warfare, the size and character of the social groups that engage in war, and the functions of war have been infinitely varied. In some qualitative as well as quantitative respects modern wars are distinct from those of the past; and to the extent that this is the case, data on past wars do not apply to an analysis of recent and prospective wars, although they may provide a perspective for such analysis.

PREMODERN WAR

All recent wars have been justified, by one combatant or the other or both, on the grounds that enlarging the physical territory under the political jurisdiction of the nation would bring material profit and a gain in national power to its people. As a prelude to World War II, the Nazis camouflaged this crass appeal to the avarice and pride of the German people with profound nonsense about Destiny and the imperatives of geopolitics; for their part, the Japanese ideologists turned to a quasi-Malthusian theory of population pressure and discourse about optimum population as a justification for attack upon the Chinese mainland and, later, adopted an Asiatic version of geopolitics and Aryan racism to explain their assault upon the United States.

The appeal to long-run economic self-interest and national pride has no doubt helped to reconcile civilian populations to the sacrifices required by their involvement, either as aggressors or defenders, in recent wars. It is quite possible that political and military leaders have themselves been somewhat motivated by the same considerations; for it has been truly said that men learn from history only that men do not learn from history. No war of recent times, however, has paid for its cost through the acquisition of new territories by one belligerent at the loss of the other. In the past century and a half there have been four major wars in Western Europe; yet the national boundaries of Western nations have been changed but little. World War I cost Germany its territories in Africa, but the nations that assumed jurisdiction over them acquired an economic and political burden, not a profit. The various peoples of the world have now become so interdependent that military conquest of one by another cannot be made to produce a material profit. Thus it is that following both world wars the victors, far from occupying and taking over the territories of the defeated, have in their own economic and political interests undertaken to reestablish the economies of the vanquished.

Wars of Conquest

There were times, however, when war could result in profitable extension of territory, and in such times true wars of conquest occurred. When the earth was lightly populated and the various peoples of the world were economically self-sufficient, a people with a superior military technology and effective political organization could, and often did, channel their energies into profitable territorial expansion. Often, no doubt, this was the easy way to increase their wealth; for the alternative, improvement in productive technology and intensified productive endeavor, was a slow and laborious process that could not be accomplished by directive political leadership or be made dramatically appealing. Wars of conquest may thus have aided in dispelling internal tensions—manifest as general discontent, individual restiveness, etc.—without changing the system itself, since territorial conquests would expand the social system without greatly modifying it.

The extension of a social system to include and gradually assimilate native peoples has not always involved war. Over the centuries the culture and political authority of the Chinese Middle Kingdom spread until it encompassed most of Eastern Asia; yet the process was, on the whole, peaceful. On the other hand, the empires of the Romans, the Bantus of Africa, and, later, the Spanish, the British, and other Europeans were built through military conquest, and in each instance, conquest was materially and otherwise profitable to the conquerors. In the long run peoples who have been conquered have often profited by acquiring from their conquerors new and fruitful technologies and forms of organization, as did those of Western Europe under the Romans. Where this has happened, the ultimate result of conquest has been the diffusion of culture from conqueror to conquered with, somewhat incidentally, an enlargement and perhaps development of the military subsystem of the conquering society. The Roman social system, for example, became a great military as well as commercial system; and during the period when Britain more or less ruled the seas, England was a great center of naval technology and organization.

The results of successful conquest, however, have varied considerably. The Chinese were conquered a number of times by militarily superior but in all other respects—technologically, organizationally, and ideologically—inferior peoples, of whom the Mongols of the late twelfth century were the most recent and best remembered. In each instance the invading conquerors were absorbed into Chinese society without affecting the Chinese social system in more than token ways. On the other hand, the European conquest of North America, where culturally inferior tribal peoples were in possession, led to the virtual extinction of the natives.

In many instances wars of conquest have had few significant or enduring consequences. For centuries following the decline of Roman power, the tribal peoples who occupied much of Western Europe were engaged in almost incessant wars of conquest. The common sequence was for one tribe or petty kingdom to go to war with a neighboring one and, if victorious, to more or less exterminate the losers and occupy their territory, only to become, in due course, the object of conquest by some other tribe. Through the centuries the fortunes of specific tribal groups rose and fell; but tribal culture, and even the military subsystem of tribal culture, changed but little.[5] The origins of the feudal system that eventually evolved, first and most markedly in Southwestern Europe, are usually attributed to the insecurity that prevailed following the decline of Roman power and during this period of intertribal warfare. Feudalism was, in fact, a system that centered around the provision of security from military attack; but it had historical roots in Roman law, Roman forms of status relations, and Roman techniques of construction; and it was highly structured, isolative and self-sufficient, and militarily as well as otherwise devoted to the preservation of the *status quo*. Thus the social changes that were fostered by the insecurity of intertribal warfare led only to a new but equally static social order.

Predatory Wars

Most peoples have been productive and have created either directly, as have agriculturalists, or indirectly, as have traders, the values they have consumed.

[5] Nor have much more recent conquests by Europeans of Europeans had very significant and enduring effects on the culture of the conquered. The people of the Po Valley, for example, were conquered and ruled at one time and another by Germany, Austria, and France; but their social life remained in all salient respects Italian. The Spanish ruled Naples intermittently from the fourteenth century until the French took over, briefly, early in the nineteenth century; yet the Neapolitans would not even adopt as their own the Spanish language.

Even those who have conquered and subjugated other peoples have often contributed to the welfare of the conquered about as much as, and sometimes even more than, they have taken from them. Thus over the long run, the Romans probably brought about, through the physical security that they maintained and the technology and organization that they provided for those they conquered, an increase in productivity that was greater than what they demanded as tribute to Rome. Thus, too, the British gave to India more than they took, for undoubtedly they increased the productivity, as is evidenced by the rapid increase in the population of India under British rule.

A few societies, however, characteristically small, have lived off the productivity of others by preying on them in a manner somewhat analogous to that of wolves; they have taken the necessities of life or their equivalent in precious metals and jewels and have given nothing in return. The wars or raids that they have instigated are distinguishable from attacks by ordinary bandits, common to most societies of the past, by their scope and by the fact that they have been made by a people with a distinct culture rather than, as is the case with bandits, by members of a subcultural group of the society itself. In some few instances a predatory society has been able to maintain itself over long periods. The Carib Indians lived almost entirely by preying on productive tribes, but they ranged so far that each tribe that became their victim had time to recover between attacks. Through some centuries the Bedouin Arabs were able to maintain an essentially predatory life by judicious but not excessive robbing of trade caravans and sufficiently infrequent raids on non-Bedouin peoples.[6] There is, however, a self-evident limitation to the number of people who can live by predatory means, a sort of natural check on the growth of predatism analogous to that which, in natural conditions, keeps down the number of wolves.

Moreover, predatory societies have frequently destroyed the sources of their plunder. Although Tamerlane during the later fourteenth century posed as a conqueror on the model of Genghis Khan, his warrior horde was in fact only a predatory band which, having plundered and massacred the people of an area, had to move on to find new sources of wealth. In a more complex way, the Spanish conquistadors of the sixteenth century did the same thing. Their subjugation and occupation of foreign lands was secondary to their search for liquid wealth; because they found much gold, especially in Peru, Spain came to depend upon this source of wealth, and it was when the supply ran out that Spain sank as a nation into obscurity.

[6] For a description of this predatory practice see G. P. Murdock, *Africa*, McGraw-Hill Book Company, New York, 1959, pp. 397–405. It was, apparently, a fusion of the predatory culture of the tribal Bedouins and the political organization of the Arabs that led to the conversion of many of the ports of North Africa during the sixteenth century into piratical principalities; for the Barbary pirates were for the most part Arabized Berbers.

The effects of predatory warfare on culture in general would seem to have been both temporary and insignificant. Undoubtedly the military arts of predatory societies have been adapted to the kind of warfare—to attack upon defenseless peoples—in which those societies have engaged; and no doubt the social organization of predatory societies has been appropriate to living off the productivity of others. But since predatory societies have been few and their life cycle has generally been short and since the arts of predatory war and the predatory way of life are inappropriate to a normally productive society, little of durable value has survived. Predatory warfare can therefore be ignored as a significant factor in social change.

Ceremonial Wars

Much the same can be said of warfare of a ritualistic or ceremonial character; it is colorful and hence interesting and can, of course, be studied for itself alone. But for the societies involved, ceremonial warfare has always been an end in itself, similiar to burial rites, harvest festivals, and other such traditionalized activities. It serves its function for the participants, but it does not foster change of any sort. On the contrary, it seems to be one of the devices for directing the discharge of social tensions into socially undisturbing, however bloody, channels and thus aiding in the preservation of the *status quo*.

Wars between primitive peoples have often been of this character; they have occurred more or less regularly, have followed ritualistic procedures (such as body painting, war dancing, and attack in ceremonial manner and in accordance with a rigid code of proper military conduct), and have led to the victor's gaining some prized token of victory (such as scalps to wear as evidences of personal prowess, heads to shrink, and body parts to eat). The Romans, once their military conquests had extended as far as the means of transportation and communication permitted, shifted to some extent from the making of war to the staging of gladiatorial contests—ceremonial combats between individual warriors. During the feudal period conflict would seem at times to have been little more than a military tour de force; and during the early Middle Ages, when feudal units were being united into larger political systems, kings and princes appear to have encouraged the postfeudal knights to engage in tournaments as a ceremonial outlet for their military skills and aspirations.[7]

[7] The war-impelling powers of a military establishment, including the traditions of warfare, the value placed upon valor in combat, and the lack of occupational and status alternatives for the professional military man, are perhaps most clearly illustrated by what happened in postfeudal Europe. As trade and other factors fostered social integration, the feudal knights and their henchmen became increasingly anachronistic. They were an embarrassment to the Church, to kings and princes, and to the traders and the growing urban popula-

Medieval Wars of Consolidation

Wars of conquest, when successful, have led to the politicomilitary subordination of native peoples and their territories to the conquerors. Rather different in both instigation and consequence were the European wars of political unification that began in the ninth century with Charlemagne's attempt to re-create the Holy Roman Empire, got well under way during the thirteenth century, and continued intermittently until the late eighteenth century, when the present lines of nationality became fairly well defined and stabilized. These wars were for the most part instigated and conducted by the political aristocracy—by feudal lords become dukes, overlords, princes, and kings—and, again for the most part, were matters of indifference to the common people who, with considerable reason, tended to consider all political authority an unescapable but unmitigated evil. What loyalties the common people had were loyalties to the locality of their birth and to their traditional liege lord whose powers were being gradually subordinated to distant authority. Only as the peoples who were being forcibly united politically became economically interdependent and came to share a common language, a common history, etc., did anything like national sentiment and loyalty emerge. Meanwhile, the general populace of Western Europe considered the making of war the private preserve of dukes and princes and kings and would-be emperors.[8]

For their part, the politicomilitary leaders of Western Europe proceeded to treat subject peoples and their territories as pawns in the game of power politics. They formed alliances to coerce other leaders into abdicating their rule; they used interfamily marriages as a means of binding kingdoms together; they bought and sold and traded as well as stole territories; and, when all else failed, they called upon their knights to do battle on their behalf. As political consolidation proceeded, erratically and most slowly, and as traditions of feudalism faded, wars became a kingly prerogative and warriors

---

tions; for they were agents of disunity and conflict. They could neither be ignored nor endured; and they and what they represented were eventually neutralized in two interrelated ways: the cult of chivalry directed their militancy into ceremonial mock combat; and the Crusades removed their persons from the European scene. For an analysis of this and other historical periods during which the presence of a body of fighting men has been an incitement to warfare, see L. Montrose, *War through the Ages*, Harper & Row, Publishers, Incorporated, New York, 1944.

[8] According to Alfred A. Vagts (*A History of Militarism*, W. W. Norton & Company, Inc., New York, 1937), war during this period was quite literally the sport of kings and aroused neither popular interest nor support. Fighting men were mostly mercenary professionals, and perhaps for this reason fighting itself was conducted in accordance with restraining rules not unlike those that are enforced on modern workers by their unions.

mostly hired mercenaries. It is quite likely that during this period the most important role of war was to keep rulers preoccupied with enlarging their powers and so distracted from attempting to intensify their domestic rule; for the period was one of considerable technological, ideological, and organizational change which would have been retarded had strong governmental controls existed.

The high costs of war, which had to be borne directly by the king's treasury, however, did lead to the development of the mercantilistic theory of wealth and of the role of government in the making of wealth. It was in accordance with this new theory that all the governments of Western Europe began to impose constraints on international trade by discouraging the import of goods and raw materials and encouraging their export. As has been mentioned, governmentally imposed constraints on international exchange of goods had various, significant consequences for the economic life and technologies of European peoples. For one thing, they retarded specialization in production; for another, they fostered the search for non-European markets for goods, especially manufactured goods, such as cloth. To some extent, the colonial ambitions of the nations of Europe stemmed from the fact that for two centuries and more each nation could engage freely in trade only with its own colonial outposts.[9]

Moreover, it was during this period that most of the sentiments and attitudes of nationalism were evolved and many of the international antagonisms that still prevail were generated. Certain practices, still current, were also developed during these centuries—e.g., national subsidy of food production to assure self-sufficiency during war; economic embargo of the enemy; levy of import duties to discourage the outward flow of specie; and, of course, perfection of the fine art of smuggling.

The gradual, erratic consolidation of feudal peoples into modern nations is usually interpreted as a political adjustment to the growth of towns and the concomitant decline of feudal organization, to the specialization in production and trade that fostered the rise of towns, and to associated changes in transportation and communication. In this view European peoples were at that

[9] Colonialism was, therefore, a cumbersome alternative to the economic integration of European peoples. The colonial system made it possible for England, France, Belgium, Holland, and Germany to industrialize without uniting; for each was able to market its industrial surplus in its colonial lands. With the collapse of the colonial system after World War II the nations of Europe became *de facto* economically interdependent; political recognition of that fact has come about, reluctantly and in limited degree, during the decades since. See Louis Lister, *Europe's Coal and Steel Community: An Experiment in Economic Union*, The Twentieth Century Fund, New York, 1960; and Ernst B. Hoas, *The Uniting of Europe: Political, Social, and Economic Forces, 1950–1957*, Stanford University Press, Stanford, Calif., 1958.

time becoming united into blocs by technological and economic changes, and political consolidation simply gave legitimacy to what was occurring. To the extent that this interpretation is valid, the wars of the period were products of antecedent changes and led in turn to political changes of significance. There is some doubt, however, that this interpretation is altogether valid; for, although the tempo of technological and economic changes increased and economic interdependence grew ever greater, the process of political consolidation came to an end and national boundaries became fixed about 1800. Only now, after nearly two centuries of stalemate warfare, have any very effective measures been taken to reduce the economic isolationism that was long imposed by traditional nationalism.

MODERN WAR

During the eighteenth century profound changes in the political and economic organization of European nations gave rise to various forms and degrees of revolutionary violence and at the same time more or less brought to an end both the period of empire building by wars of conquest and that of political consolidation via the quasi-private warfare of kings. As has been mentioned, the emergence of parliamentary forms of government reduced the power and role of the hereditary elites and gave the rising middle class representation in governmental affairs. Since their interests, economic and otherwise, were jeopardized by war, they were inclined to throw their influence on the side of peace and against the king, his aristocratic supporters, and the military establishment, all of whom had a vested interest in the making of war.

With some notable exceptions, the major function of the military establishments of the more advanced European nations was for a century or more that of maintaining control of colonial territories; for it was only in this role that the military received the support of the middle class, who were interested, not in territorial expansion, the prestige of the royal court, or ancient insults to the nation's honor, but in the extension and preservation of commerce.[10] It was, thus, to this special middle-class end that Britain fought to hold North America, India, and South Africa, and to maintain its right to sell opium in

[10] It was in part to reconcile the economic values and sentiments of the middle class with the old sentiments of nationalism that English economists devised the concept of the economic man, an abstraction not unlike that of the corporation. In his role as an economic man, an individual was supposed to be motivated solely by economic concerns and untroubled by filial, humanitarian, or nationalistic sentiments. As a demonstration of the validity of the concept, English businessmen bought and sold Russian government bonds on the London market while their sons were fighting and dying in the Crimean War.

China; and it was mainly for the same end that Britain gained and for long held dominance over the sea lanes of the world.[11]

A distinctly new kind of warfare emerged in France after the Revolution under the leadership of Napoleon. It involved most of the attitudes and sentiments and the interests and presumptions that had been operative during the old wars of political consolidation; but for the first time the interests of government—of king or of parliament—were identified with those of the people. Also for the first time in centuries the mass of the people were called upon directly to man and otherwise support the military establishment. Napoleon, for example, established the principle of the conscript army; and his Grand Army was both a people's army and a popular one. (Impressment and other devices for securing soldiers and sailors had long been used, but the practice was quasi-legal and very unpopular and had led mainly to the debasement of the military forces—i.e., induction of criminals, etc.) Moreover, Napoleon's efforts, initially successful, to build a great European empire received such general support from the French people that even in defeat Napoleon remained a popular symbol of French unity and military ambitions, so much so that after his escape from Elba he was widely welcomed as the savior of France and again, if briefly, given popular support.

The avowed and obvious purpose of the Napoleonic Wars—to unite Europe under French political leadership—was an old and traditional one. But just as the character of war itself had changed—from a clash of ambitious political leaders and their mercenary fighters to attack by a more or less ideologically and organizationally united nation upon other nations, with the military establishment operating only as an agency of the nation—so, too, had the forces that led to this new kind of war. Something of the nature of these forces can be inferred from the fact that for the French people the Napoleonic Wars were in the nature of a great crusade and Napoleon himself far more than a military leader; he was the Messiah, endowed with charismatic powers, who would lead history's chosen people in the fulfilling of their destiny.

All extensive and prolonged wars have no doubt developed a *mystique*, a complex of assumptions and expectations that have no empirical basis; for presumably even crass, professional, mercenary soldiers must have faith in the ability of their commanders or they will desert to the enemy. What was distinctive about the *mystique* of the Napoleonic Wars was its intensity and wide-

[11] This dominance was won by British ships and cannon and the ability of British sailors to stay long at sea without falling ill of scurvy, an ability for long limited to them. With the advent of the steamship, Britain was able to maintain her dominance of the seas by her economic coercive powers that derived from control of the major coaling stations along the sea lanes. Thus British coal powered a good deal of sea-borne commerce and gave Britain the power to maintain her version of freedom of the seas.

spread acceptance by the people as well as the military establishment. Moreover, the *mystique* of the Napoleonic Wars extended beyond faith in the invincibility of the military commander; it encompassed a pseudo-rational justification for the wars themselves and assurance that, the wars well ended, France as a whole would automatically profit and prosper. The medieval Crusades had involved a vague, nonnationalistic *mystique* of a somewhat similar sort; but in the intervening centuries the wars in Europe were, with the partial exception of the Thirty Years' War, unpopular conflicts between ruling cliques rather than between peoples.

The Napoleonic Wars would appear to be in salient respects the prototype of the Franco-Prussian War, of the two world wars of the present century, and, presumably, of any major international war that may in the future occur. As were the Napoleonic Wars, each world war was inaugurated under the direction, real or nominal, of a popular leader with imputed charismatic powers (the Kaiser, Hitler, Mussolini, the Japanese Emperor) and on the popularly accepted presumption that the war was a historical imperative and that victory would lead by unspecified magic to an era of great material prosperity. It might be held that such a *mystique* is necessary to secure popular support for a war; that no modern war can be undertaken without popular support; and that, therefore, the *mystique* is a creation of war makers rather than an active agent in the making of war. Even so, the question then arises of why it is possible by propagandistic and other means to develop the *mystique*; and in the answer to this question lies in considerable part the explanation for the outbreak of the great wars of modern times.

Social Crisis and Political Alternatives

When incongruencies within a society result in acute malfunctioning, the rule of the established leadership—religious, economic, and political—is jeopardized. Under a condition of static incongruence the traditional elites may hold their positions by a careful balancing one against another of the various dissident elements that the crisis has produced; but when effective forces for rectifying the incongruence are emerging within the population—i.e., where energetic and ambitious men are advocating changes of one sort and another and are, incidentally, bidding for the powers held by the traditional elites—only one or another of three general resolutions is possible. The first of these is the incorporation, individually, of the advocates of change into the established elites and a testing in practice of the changes that they propose, in the process of which the traditional leaders necessarily lose some of their power and must accept social changes that violate their own values and sentiments. (This was what happened in the United States during the Great Depression of the 1930s, when through normal political processes a great variety of organizational changes were sponsored by the Federal government, by various state governments, and by many private establishments.) The second possibility is revolution, an outburst of violence directed by long-frustrated advocates of change against the traditional elites and the system that they represent. The third possibility, and the one that is relevant here, is the distraction of the attention of the dissident elements in the population by channeling social anger and aggression into the making of war and, at the same time, offering conquest of the enemy as a quick and easy solution to domestic problems.

The resort to war as a social pacifier is probably as old as tribal society; ceremonial wars and warlike ceremonials have no doubt always served to distract people from real to politically created troubles and to leave them, the war ended, emotionally if not physically exhausted. The great wars of modern times have served something of the same function but have not been conducted in a restricted ceremonial manner. They have, rather, been unlimited in scope and character, large-scale, and ruthless; for they have been to a remarkable degree people's wars—wars initiated for the people and conducted for the most part by the people who, unschooled in military tradition and ritual, have been rather indifferent to military etiquette and so have fought with an unprofessional vigor and a total disregard for the niceties of traditional warfare.

That it was malfunctioning sufficiently acute to constitute a crisis for the established leadership that gave rise to the Napoleonic Wars seems fairly evident. Napoleon was thrust into the political leadership of postrevolutionary France by the frantic and dissentious revolutionary rulers who had been unable to bring any order out of almost total chaos. As First Consul he was expected to establish through a kind of limited dictatorship the systematic political reforms that the Directory, the agency that was intended to provide democratic leadership, was unable to institute, reforms that were necessary to forestall a counterrevolution that would bring the Bourbons back into power. Acting incisively and with considerable political skill, Napoleon did much to restore domestic order and to rationalize the political system; but nothing that he or any political agency could accomplish could bring real order to the malfunctioning social system that was then and has ever since continued to be characteristic of France. Within a few years he was, therefore, faced with loss of power. There were many contenders for his position, many radical and reactionary political factions plotting against him, and much restlessness and disillusionment among the common people. It was at this point that he chose, or was forced by circumstances, to found a dynasty. Perhaps it was only because the title "King" was associated with the postrevolutionary Bourbons that he proclaimed himself Emperor; but at any event that title invoked memories of Charlemagne and the Holy Roman Empire, and Napoleon had himself crowned in Rome rather than in Paris. He soon turned the attention of France toward the building of an empire over which he could rule, and he was shortly being popularly acclaimed as the savior of a France that was in dire need of salvation.

Somewhat comparable social conditions—incongruencies within the organizational component, the established elites in jeopardy, and a political figure who could assume or be made to assume the discarded mantle of Napoleon as messianic savior—have been the bases from which the two world wars emerged. Pre-World War I Germany, like pre-World War II Italy and Japan, was an explosive combination of a preindustrial political and class system and an industrial technology; and the social chaos of Germany under the Nazis is so well remembered that it need only be called to mind. In each of these instances going to war was an attempt to preserve the power of the existing military, economic, and political elites; and it was, therefore, an alternative, however uncalculated, to the institution of changes in the existing social system.

It is impossible to assess the extent to which the great wars of modern times have retarded social changes. They affected the nations that were attacked almost as much as the nations that were instigators of attack; they all ended in military disaster for the latter; and yet at the same time the victors gained nothing except a cessation of hostilities. Indeed, after the two world wars it became incumbent upon the victors to aid in the rehabilitation of the vanquished, a demonstration of the extent to which modern nations are economically and otherwise interdependent. The social cost of these wars—in capital plant, in irreplaceable physical resources, in man-hours, in casualties, and, most importantly but unmeasurably, in strain on the social structures—has been variously calculated. Translated, however cautiously, into positive social values, that cost is far greater than the total expenditure over two centuries of all Western societies for publicly provided education and far greater than the total expenditure for public welfare—for poor relief, modern social security programs, etc. Had the effort and materials expended in warfare been put to constructive enterprises, the entire housing plant of Western peoples, a plant which as it exists leaves very much to be desired, could have been completely rebuilt in accordance with modern standards. It does not follow, of course, that if these great wars had not occurred, the efforts and materials devoted to them would have been forthcoming or, if forthcoming, applied to these or comparable social purposes; but it is self-evident that the great wars of modern times have been destructive of vast social and material resources that might have been applied, in accordance with peacetime values, to the welfare of men.

Conservative Influence of the Military Establishment

Moreover, each of these great wars has in turn contributed to the perpetuation and, perhaps, the intensification of the military tradition in Western societies and has provided new justification for maintaining large military establishments. Thus after the Napoleonic Wars all the Western nations adopted compulsory military service in one form or another; it was as an outgrowth of these wars that the Prussian military caste gained ascendancy in Germany; and the effectiveness of the British navy during these wars in maintaining an embargo on France hardened British resolve to maintain a great naval force by which to preserve freedom of the seas, for Britain, at least. At the termination of World War I, France promptly resumed defensive preparations against Germany; and although there was much talk about disarmament and various projects were proposed to enable and encourage reduction in military establishments, the United States was the only modern nation actually to reduce its forces. After World War II the military of even the traditionally nonmilitant United States promptly embarked upon the greatest and most costly military program of history.[12] At this writing the world is, quite literally, an armed camp; and probably for the first time in recent centuries, and certainly for the first time in American history, peacetime expenditures for war, past and future, are borne by the general publics of the various nations with passive resignation. Moreover, for the first time in American history our peacetime military establishment has high prestige and takes precedence over other, traditionally valued, aspects of social life. Thus there is meaning of a sort in the statement that war breeds preparation for war and that preparation for war makes war an imperative.

The existence of a large military establishment has in the past operated toward the preservation of the ideological, technological, and organizational *status quo*. Military forces are of functional necessity highly bureaucratic in organization. They are, or at least they have been in the past, incapable of generating even technological changes from within and almost impervious to pressure for changes from without.[13] As a consequence, in all wars of record

[12] For an account of the growth of the American military establishment during and following World War II, see Walter Millis, *Arms and Men,* G. P. Putnam's Sons, New York, 1956.

[13] The characteristic conservatism of the professional military is a standard and often dominant theme in the writings of military historians, who often make the heroes of a war, not its military leaders, but civilians who have overridden the resistance of the military to changes in weapons and tactics and have thereby saved their country from certain defeat. The following works are representative of the very large literature that is critical of the military and in which are recounted many specific instances in which the unwillingness of military leaders to adopt new weapons or adapt their tactics to new weapons used by the enemy has resulted in heavy casualties if not loss of the war itself: B. H. Liddell-Hart, *Strategy,* George Allen & Unwin, Ltd., London, 1941; Theodore Ropp, *War in the Modern World,* The Duke University Press, Durham, N.C., 1959; Stanislaw Andrzejewski, *Military Organization and the State,* Routledge & Kegan Paul, Ltd.,

one side or the other, and usually both of them, have fought with the tools, tactics, and strategy of the preceding war; and victory has often gone to that force, however inferior in men and weapons, that has inadvertently or through extraordinary leadership applied some new technique or procedure. At the battle of Agincourt, for example, a small force of English archers slaughtered a great assemblage of French knights and men-at-arms who unwisely relied on the arts of warfare that had evolved during the Crusades—on heavy body armor, the mace and the sword, and person-to-person combat. This marked the beginning of the end of medieval military tools and tactics; but every change came slowly and was staunchly resisted by the professional military. When the crossbow replaced the longbow, the musket the crossbow, the cartridge rifle the musket, and the machine gun and automatic rifle the single-shot rifle, each was for a time treated in the manner of its predecessor. The British army, for example, had developed a formation—the close-order square —that was very effective in overwhelming an enemy equipped with slow-firing, hand-charged muskets. With the advent of the cartridge rifle, which could be reloaded much more quickly, this attack tactic was outmoded; but the British continued to rely upon it for another generation. It was eventually discovered that the way to charge a firing line equipped with rifles was by a rapid and massive advance of men; many would fall, but because the firing power of the enemy was limited by the time required to reload, the size of the attacking force and rate of advance necessary to get a sufficient number of men safely through the field of fire were easy to calculate.

In World War I the machine gun came into its own; and when the German advance through France was finally checked, the Germans stabilized their lines by mounting these guns at such short intervals that they could cover the entire field by cross fire. The Allies repeatedly attempted to breach

London, 1954; and Tom Wintringham, *The Story of Weapons and Tactics*, Little, Brown and Company, Boston, 1943.

J. I. Green (*Infantry Journal Reader*, John Wiley & Sons, Inc., New York, 1943, p. 62) reports that the following argument was advanced by a British general after World War I against the mechanization of fighting forces: "The longer we can keep horses for artillery and cavalry, the better it will be for the Army, because thereby you keep up the high standard of intelligence in the man from his association with the horses."

Morris Janowitz (*The Professional Soldier: A Social and Political Portrait*, The Free Press of Glencoe, New York, 1960) finds some reason to think that modern military technology has somewhat lessened the traditional isolation and stability of military elites. The heroic-leader type of military man, long on courage and short on enterprise, that has been dominant in military forces in times past is, Janowitz believes, now augmented and to some extent subordinated by what he terms "military managers" and "military technologists," both of whom are by training and inclination more closely allied to civilian business and industry than to the military establishment itself.

these lines by the massive attacks that had proved effective against rifles; in the course of one year they suffered upwards of a million casualties in what proved to be futile attacks of this sort. Eventually some unknown genius realized that the firing power of a machine gun is many times that of a rifle and that the only way by which a line of machine-gun posts can be overwhelmed is by the infiltration of single men who slip through the interstices between the sweeps of machine-gun fire and attack each machine-gun post from behind with grenades. This and related tactics were then highly developed and reduced to routine procedures; and the next time that the Germans swept into France, in World War II, the British and French were prepared to resume the kind of warfare that had been interrupted by the Armistice of 1918. Unfortunately, the Germans had mounted their machine guns, together with small, rapid-fire cannon, on tanks and troop carriers and equipped them with two-way radio; and they refused to fight in the manner that had by then become traditional.

The military establishment may impose its conservatism on the society at large in several ways. For one thing, it withdraws from the civilian population numbers of young men, often of superior ability, as are those who enter the nation's war colleges, who might otherwise contribute in some degree to the dynamism of the society and reduces them to bureaucratic functionaries. For another, to the extent that it is honored by the society, the military establishment also provides an organizational and individual ideal that is in all respects conservative and opposed to change. Moreover, as an agency of government, it characteristically casts its organizational weight on the side of the traditional in governmental procedure; and to the extent that it draws upon the civilian economic system, its influence is strongly and often effectively conservative.

Under exceptional provocation and in an effort to save itself, a military establishment has occasionally joined in whole or in part with revolutionaries; but the existence of a strong military establishment is in all modern nations a deterrent to rebellious action on the part of civilians, and hence a check on the kinds of changes that might be inaugurated by such action. Moreover, the maintenance of a military establishment, like the making of war itself, directs social effort and material resources into unproductive channels, effort and resources that might otherwise be applied to the working of changes of one sort or another—to the rebuilding of slums, the enlarging and improving of road systems, the reclaiming of land, reforesting, etc. As will be indicated later, there may be some incidental profit to the civilian society in our current vast expenditures for war; but they are surely slight compared to what could be accomplished if they were applied directly to the solution of current civilian problems. Thus had the hundreds of billions of dollars that the United States spent in the decade 1950–1960 for military preparations been applied to the development of urban-suburban rapid transport, the irksome problems of highway congestion and of smog—twin problems that have adversely affected the lives of a good many of the American people—might now be solved.

The fact that prior to and during World War II military needs were the immediate incentive to the development of radar, atomic fission, and some other devices useful to peacetime life has been cited as evidence that war and preparation for war are stimulators of technological change. It is held that the development of atomic fission was the direct outcome of war, that it could not have been accomplished by private or even corporate initiative, and that peacetime applications of atomic energy have been made possible by military use and subsequent testing of bombs. It is further held that military needs were the incentive that led to the rapid development of jet motors for aircraft; and that rapid development of space vehicles has been sponsored by the military establishments of the United States and Russia and would have occurred very slowly if at all under private or even civil governmental jurisdiction. It is also noted that the military establishment both of the United States and of Russia, and of other modern nations to a lesser degree, is employing directly or indirectly a very considerable proportion of the country's physical and engineering scientists and technicians, especially those in electrical engineering, aircraft engineering, and related fields. Each military establishment is, moreover, subsidizing from public funds the education of large numbers of scientists and technicians; and it seems obvious that the post-World War II boom in the physical and engineering sciences and technologies is closely related to the cold-war endeavors of the various military establishments of the world.

Prior to World War II wars and preparations for war had never provided any direct incentive to scientific and technological development; yet the growth of science and technology had proceeded at a constantly increasing tempo for a century and a half. It is highly probable that the crisis of World War II and the subsequent cold-war technological competition between the West and Russia may have speeded the *development* of atomic energy, of certain areas of electronics, and of jet motors and rockets. There is no reason to assume, however, that development would not have come, more slowly and undoubtedly at lower social cost, without the military incentive; and it is certain that the innovations thus developed were not sponsored or in any way fostered by war needs or fear of war. The scientific bases of atomic fission were all at hand before World War II; the jet motor had been conceived, devised, and brought toward practicality in prewar England; the rocket had been conceived and all its basic ingredients invented in prewar America.[14] Moreover, so far as can be ascertained, no major scientific discoveries or

[14] The possibility of developing atomic fission for military purposes was recognized long before World War II. As early as 1927, Stanton A. Coblentz (*Marching Men*, The Unicorn Press, New York, 1927, p. 467) suggested that such bombs would be used in the next great war, and he foresaw something of the hazards of atomic radiation to noncombatants.

technological innovations were brought about by direct military promotion of scientific and technological endeavor.[15] Military establishments, our own and those of our presumed future enemy, are understandably concerned with the perfecting of established weapons and the refining and application of proved techniques, not with pure science exploration into the unknown. There are, in fact, some reasons, vague and slight and untestable, to suspect that in a frenzied effort to exploit to the fullest the military potential of present scientific knowledge, pure scientists in numbers have been distracted from the pursuit of knowledge to the application of knowledge and that the high rewards offered to young men for developmental work has reduced the number of those who have entered into a career of basic scientific exploration.

Moreover, it is very certain that the elaborate, costly, and in the long run probably ineffectual programs of military security which were instituted during World War II and which have been maintained ever since have retarded the growth of scientific knowledge and technological innovation.[16] A potential innovator is not likely to endure with equanimity the personal indignity of a governmental security clearance or, at any event, to do his best work under the scrutiny of suspicious and often officious nonscientists. For him personal freedom, which any project sponsored by the military precludes, and free access to the body of existing knowledge, which the military security program denies, are essential to his labors. There is no knowing how many hunches, half-formed concepts, half-seen facts, momentarily irrelevant discoveries, etc., have been buried in the classified files of military organizations during recent years. What can be said with confidence is that the hoarding of the materials of science and technology by the military violates one of the major requirements for an open and changing society—that of the free interchange of ideas.

War-produced Chaos and Social Change

Apologists for war per se, as distinct from ideologists who justify a particular war, have occasionally put forth the comforting idea that war is one of the

[15] On the contrary, according to Vannevar Bush (*Modern Arms and Free Men*, Simon and Schuster, Inc., New York, 1949), it has been scientists and nonmilitary technicians who have provided the incentive for the development of all the new military techniques.

[16] For an analysis of the program of military security and its effects upon science see Edward A. Shils, *The Torment of Secrecy: The Background and Consequences of American Security Policies*, The Free Press of Glencoe, New York, 1956. Military security procedures have no doubt somewhat deterred the growth of scientific knowledge in certain fields and have not accomplished anything much of practical value. The effort to protect the nation from treachery from within is, in the words of Robert A. Horn (*Groups and the Constitution*, Stanford University Press, Stanford, Calif., 1956, p. 177), "A great symbolic rite rather than . . . a practical policy."

important checks on the natural increase of human populations. War may have been such a check in some times and places. The tribal wars of Europe, where the victors usually massacred the vanquished, may possibly have helped to keep down the total population of Western Europe during the Dark Ages. During the Middle Ages, on the other hand, when fighting was a professional job and the civilian populations were not directly affected, war casualties can have had little effect. Those who died were, for the most part, males; and as wildlife conservationists have finally discovered, it is the number of females of childbearing age, rather than adult males, that determines the birth rate—assuming in the case of human populations that effective moral checks on intercourse do not operate or, alternatively, that birth-control procedures are not in effect.

At any event, recent experience lends no support to the hope that war reduces or checks the growth of a population and so, in the long run, enables men to maintain a higher than subsistence standard of living. On the contrary, the two world wars had no perceptible long-run effect on population growth. There was in both instances a war-fostered rise in birth rates, which was offset by an abnormal decline in the birth rate after World War I but not after World War II. The military casualties that occurred during these wars were more than canceled out by a wartime decline in civilian death rates, such as resulted during World War II from the decline in casualties from motor accidents and the rise in the general level of health. On the other hand, there would seem to be little if any validity in the fear that our recent great wars have reduced the vigor of the involved populations, and hence their productivity and proclivity to work social changes, by bleeding them white. Many have assumed that the Napoleonic Wars resulted in a breeding down of the French population, since it sharply reduced the proportion of young, physically sturdy males, leaving behind mostly old, undersized, and physically inferior younger males to reproduce. The British were inclined to blame their slow economic recovery after World War I and their general social apathy upon the loss of the better part of a whole generation of young men—the very men who, in the normal course of events, would have constituted the most energetic if not the most creative segment of the population. French politicians likewise often saw in World War I casualties the reason why France responded so sluggishly to the problems of peace; and the same reason was advanced for the political and economic incompetence of post-World War I Germany.

The idea that our recent major wars have reduced the social energies of the societies involved by depleting the ranks of young men in their physical prime ignores, however, the fact that the sex and age composition of a population is only one of the many interdependent variables that together determine the course and intensity of social action. During World War II Germany and Japan each lost a major part of its young manpower—a far greater proportion than was lost by either France or Britain; nevertheless, both West Germany and Japan recuperated from that war much more rapidly than did either France or Britain.[17] The consequences of heavy war casualties to Germany and Japan were apparently more than offset by other, nondemographic factors; evidently these same factors did not become operative or at least not operative to the same degree in France and Britain.

Some may find some slight consolation for the huge costs of recent wars in the possibility—and it is hardly more than that—that in some instances and some places war has indirectly and quite incidentally produced or heightened conditions favorable to change. Some economic historians have thought that the American Civil War stimulated the rapid industrialization of North America during the decades following it in part by enabling men to amass great fortunes, and hence venture capital, through war profiteering; and it is possible that both world wars affected the United States, but hardly European countries, in somewhat the same way. Certainly during each world war a number of very enterprising men emerged in the industrial world, men such as Henry Kaiser; and some of them continued after the war to invest and engage in large business ventures. But it should also be observed that the war-fathered fortunes and men of enterprise constituted an exceedingly small proportion of the nation's invested capital and enterprising men.

World War II involved heavy destruction of the capital plant of Britain, of most of the countries of Europe, and of two major cities of Japan. West Germany and Japan seem to have profited somewhat from this destruction, for they rebuilt their destroyed plants and cities with regard for functional utility. The net result, marked in the case of West Germany, has been a sort of forced slum clearance. The new German cities are for the most part built on the satellite pattern, with industry located outside the metropolitan centers and provided with efficient, if rather bleak, housing for workers. The English, on the other hand, took little advantage of the war-wrought opportunity to increase the efficiency of their urban plants; and the French, inevitably, restored the bomb-scattered stones to their original positions.

Modern wars have uprooted a large proportion of the men in the populations of the belligerents, especially the younger and more impressionable men, who make the best and most durable soldiers. These men have been removed from the normal context of family and community, admixed with others from different regions and walks of life, and exposed to some extent or other to the culture of the civilians among whom they have been stationed, who have lived where they have done their fighting, or over whom they have maintained military control. It might be assumed that the survivors of such an experience would thereby be liberated from the bonds of their home culture and that they

[17] For an account of what happened in Germany, see Alistair Horne, *Return to Power: A Report on the New Germany*, Frederick A. Praeger, Inc., New York, 1956.

would return to civilian life with a far more cosmopolitan outlook than they had before the war. One might suppose, further, that they would be inclined to introduce, if not originate, changes into their home society; that, for example, German soldiers who had been stationed for years in occupied France might have acquired some taste for French cuisine and might desire to have it at home. The gross evidence, however, is that at least in Europe, war-determined spatial mobility has done little to lessen cultural provincialism. For a thousand years and more the various peoples of Europe have warred over one another's territories; but in 1950 as in 950, the various peoples of Europe were speaking a great variety of distinctive languages and a multitude of regional dialects; and they still had markedly different national and regional food tastes, family organizations, agricultural techniques, prides and prejudices, etc., just as they had had a thousand years before.

In the United States, on the other hand, war-occasioned uprooting and mixing of people has helped somewhat to reduce regional differences and has done a great deal to stimulate population redistribution, probably because distances are great in comparison with those in Europe and there are no national and linguistic barriers to individual mobility or settlement in a new region. At any event, after the Civil War many Southerners scattered westward; and during and after both world wars there was a considerable shift in the American population both to the West and from farm to city. Such movements of people are, as has been seen, one of the conditions that make for qualitative social changes. Whether the uprooting, admixing, and transportation of large numbers of young men to foreign lands has tended to cosmopolitanize them is, however, not evident; but it has certainly disrupted what would have been the normal course of their lives, and it has given them an opportunity that would not otherwise have been provided to explore and learn from the larger world. It may be granted that travel and life under military auspices during wartime is not the ideal way in which to acquire an education (it was once said, "Join the Navy and see the world through a porthole"); and there is very little in the military culture itself that the civilian-soldier will find valuable when he returns to civilian life. Nevertheless, such forced spatial mobility has no doubt often led to social mobility and may in this way have contributed to the dynamism of American society.

War, it has been observed, makes strange bedfellows. Most particularly in the American military forces during wartime, where the stress on preserving democratic principles has frequently led to extravagant waste of trained manpower, a civilian-soldier is thrown into association with men from all class strata and almost all occupational strata. Thus a country boy can, if he is alert and so inclined, learn at least indirectly something of urban life, a boy from the Bronx something about America west of the Hudson, a laborer's son something of the attitudes and sentiments of college students, etc. In such ways an individual's stratum isolation may be broken to some extent and his universe enlarged. Moreover, during the recent wars many of the normal constraints on interclass marriage were abrogated, parental control of girls was weakened, middle- and upper-class girls were encouraged to associate with soldiers stationed locally as a patriotic duty, etc., with the result that many young men were able to marry into a higher-class position.[18] Although it may be generally true, as sociologists hold, that in interclass or interracial marriages a girl assumes the status of her husband, association through marriage with a family of higher status does give an exceptional young man an unprecedented opportunity to prove himself. Thus, although wartime marriages may on the whole be bad risks, the conditions that foster them temporarily open the marital avenue to social advancement.

The extent to which war-accelerated spatial and social mobility has contributed to the dynamism of American society cannot be ascertained; but there is certainly good reason to suspect that a general loosening of the social structure during and immediately following war may be taken to be change that is favorable to the generation of further change. Such disturbance to the organizational system releases individuals to a degree from bondage to the *status quo*—to their own particular position in the society; and it is most likely that of the many so released some few will become, if only in modest ways, innovators, advocates, or adopters of new techniques, new ideas, and new forms of organization. Against this possible but by no means certain effect of our recent wars must be set the tremendous growth in size, power, and pervasive influence of our peacetime military establishments after World War II. The United States has not become a fully developed garrison state, tied by fear and by subservience to military minds to a stable if unrewarding way of life, as many predicted during the early postwar years would happen.[19] But the people of the United States, as well as those of the other major nations of the world, are profoundly and for

[18] David McClelland (*The Achieving Society*, D. Van Nostrand Company, Inc., Princeton, N.J., 1961, pp. 410–412) has suggested still another way in which the social circumstances that are incidental to war may foster social change. War service takes men from their homes and prevents them from exercising their normal parental authority over their children; these children will, McClelland thinks, develop a more than normal desire to achieve success and as adults be more highly motivated and enterprising than children brought up under normal, peacetime family conditions. He assumes, as have many before him, that fathers tend to be autocratic and that it is autocratic family life that makes for social conformity and resistance to change of any sort.

[19] And, as some hold, has in fact happened. For this view see C. Wright Mills, *The Causes of World War Three*, Simon and Schuster, Inc., New York, 1958; and Fred J. Cook, *The Warfare State*, The Macmillan Company, New York, 1962.

the most part adversely affected by preparation for a war that is still to come.

REVOLUTION AND SOCIAL CHANGE

In the Marxian theory, it will be recalled, the depressed and progressively exploited masses of a society eventually generate an awareness of the collective nature of their plight and, aroused by an especially atrocious example of the ruthlessness of their masters, rise in wrath against them. By destroying the persons of those in positions of traditional leadership, the masses destroy the traditional power system itself; and out of the resulting chaos there then emerge new leaders, children of the masses, dedicated to the establishment of a just, equalitarian social order. This theory of revolution as the mechanism of social change has the admirable virtues of being simple, categorical, and hence understandable; but it has also the serious defect of having no perceptible relation to actual social experience. It provides for the believer an ideological system by which some of the varied, unclear, and indefinite conflicts that have occurred within societies may be interpreted and by which the uncertain future of societies may be predicted. Many who consider themselves scientists have adopted and elaborated this theory in one way or another, but they have had to impose it on the facts of social history, for it is not derived from those facts.[20]

Rebellion versus Revolution

The first thing to be observed about mass uprisings against authority—political, religious, or economic—is how rarely evidence of such uprisings appears in the historical record. Wars of the sorts previously discussed have been so frequent and so much rooted in the cultures of those involved that they can only be described as a normal part of social life. Aside from small, tribal societies, the division of social populations into an impoverished, depressed mass and one or a number of small elites—into slaves and free men, serfs and lords, peasants and landlords, etc.—seems also to have been the normal rather than the exception. The power of numbers has always been on the side of slave and worker; and since police and military establishments have usually been staffed mainly with commoners, so, too, have

[20] For a scholarly version of the idea that revolution is a major factor in social change, see Alfred Meusel, "Revolution and Counter-revolution," *Encyclopedia of the Social Sciences*. For a more realistic appraisal of the nature of revolution and of its role in bringing about an improvement in the social system, see Hannah Arendt, *On Revolution*, The Viking Press, Inc., New York, 1963.

been the instruments of coercion. Nevertheless, the masses of the great civilizations of antiquity seem never to have risen against their rulers; neither the history of premodern India nor that of premodern China provides any example of violent and widespread revolution; and through all the turmoil of the Middle Ages kings and princes rose and fell through victory or defeat in war with other kings and princes, never through the action of those over whom they ruled.

Rebellion, local and specific, against a person or persons in a position of authority has, on the other hand, been comparatively frequent. Galley slaves and other slaves who were worked on a gang basis probably had slight opportunity, and little energy, to rebel against their masters; but domestic slaves and those used in craft and field labor sometimes did so, individually if not collectively. Both Athenian and Roman law had provision for the treatment of a slave who had killed his master; and in both Athens and Rome, and in China as well, legal procedures existed for the capture and punishment of escaped slaves. In more recent times, slaves of African origin occasionally attacked overseers; and a few short-lived and small-scale slave uprisings occurred during the seventeenth and eighteenth centuries.

If European serfs ever rebelled from their lords, that fact is not of record. With the decline of the feudal system serfs did, however, break individually from their traditional bondage and seek shelter and freedom either in the towns or in wilderness areas; but their movement was hardly rebellious, since it was only a personal adaptation to changing social organization. During the Middle Ages peasants sometimes became enraged over new tax levies or harsh treatment and attacked the local taxgatherer or the steward of their landlord; and in the towns there was one period when journeymen formed bands to resist with violence the tendency of guild masters to close their ranks to admission from below—i.e., to make the status of guild master hereditary. As large and long-range sailing ships came into use, a new and evidently fairly common form of rebellion— mutiny—made its appearance; and in early industrial England factory workers sometimes rioted in protest against low wages, lack of employment, etc.

The emergence during the eighteenth century of parliamentary forms of government in the West and of the correlate idea that government is an agency of the governed, rather than a divine or natural establishment, gave rebellious behavior a certain social sanction. Particularly in France and the United States, mob and other riotous action became a recognized and acceptable extralegal means of protesting against authority and, more commonly, of assuming authority whenever no authority existed or of usurping authority whenever there arose a general consensus that the person in authority had failed to fulfill his obligations, had violated his rights, or had exercised his rights in an unjust manner. In some instances the forms of rebellion became traditionalized, as, for example, did the French custom of sabotaging public property and the American practice of lynching.

It is doubtful, however, that rebellion has been a significant factor in the making of social changes. Most rebellion, ancient, medieval, and modern, seems to have been occasioned by peculiarly local and atypical circumstances—often, no doubt, by excessive (in terms of the social norms) zeal, greed, or ruthlessness of the person in the position of authority—and to have been directed against a person or clique of persons rather than against the social system that the person or clique represented. Rebellion does not, in other words, seem often to have arisen from or to have reflected deep-seated discontent with the social structure itself. Very often, in fact, it has been a protest against the attempt by those in positions of authority to change, in however small measure, some aspect of traditional organization—to change a status right or obligation, the scope of a social role, etc. It was to preserve their rights of eventual entry into the role of guild master that medieval journeymen rioted; it has been to keep Negroes in their traditional position that Southern whites have resorted to lynchings and other mob actions; it was to preserve the sanctity of monogamous marriages and their own version of Christianity that the citizens of Missouri and then Illinois drove out the Mormons.

The major long-run effect of rebellion, potential as well as actual, has probably been to intimidate those in positions of leadership and in this way to constrain their initiative. For the most part, perhaps, constraint has operated to keep leaders from too blatantly exploiting their powers for personal gain; but it must also have discouraged many well-meaning and enterprising leaders from attempting to introduce changes that might have proved functionally advantageous. Thus the riotous protests of Southern whites against attempts to integrate Southern public schools is no doubt one of the reasons why public officials have been reluctant to do so. Thus, too, it was local and spontaneous rioting that nearly a century ago prevented Western engineers from laying out the railroad lines of China in an efficient and rational manner. In China graves were scattered about individually, and the attempt to move graves in order to obtain straight and low-level rights of way provoked intense friction with local inhabitants; as a result railroad lines were actually laid to prevent disturbance to existing burial sites rather than to get from point to point in the most expedient manner.

Civil War

Closer to true revolution in character and playing a more significant role in social change than rebellion is that form of armed conflict that historians designate as "civil war." The category is by no means clear; for conflicts so labeled have varied widely in scope, in the nature and proportion of the social population that has instigated them, in the occasions for the uprising, and in outcome. They may, however, be distinguished from simple rebellion in that the authority that is challenged is always political and in that it is the jurisdiction of the system of authority, rather than the integrity of the person who occupies a position of authority, that is under attack. The ostensible reason for the conflict may be religious, economic, or political; and the dissentious faction may be differentiated regionally, as it was in the Boer War and the American Civil War; religiously, as it was in the Huguenot wars; or politically, as it has been in the wars that have of late occurred in Southwestern Asia.

Civil war implies a greater degree of political unity and a closer rapport between government and people than ever existed in premodern times. In the ancient civilizations, conquered peoples frequently tested by force the authority of their conquerors; and in the Middle Ages dukes and princes often challenged the authority of their king. But in the former case the revolt was not against a traditionally accepted authority, but against an authority that was maintained by coercion; and in the latter case the conflict was not between a people and their government but between a subordinate authority and his superior. Not until the later Middle Ages had the process of political consolidation in Western Europe and the integration of people and government progressed to the point where true civil war was a possibility.

The earliest of the civil wars were religious in motif and were occasioned by the development and spread of Protestantism and the rise of the bourgeois class that found in Protestantism ideological sanction of their individualism and enterprise. Of these the Thirty Years' War in Germany, the Huguenot wars in France, and the Scottish revolt were the most extensive and significant. Those in Germany and Britain resolved to the advantage of the Protestant factions; the almost century-long Huguenot wars, on the other hand, ended in the dispersal of those Huguenots who had managed to survive. The American Civil War centered on the controversy over slavery and was in this respect unique, for nowhere else did the issue of slavery lead to civil war. The civil wars in India and Southwestern Asia that followed upon the withdrawal of European political control have been of highly mixed character: in some the war has been a simple struggle for power between political cliques; others have reflected regional differences in interests and cultural attachments; and still others have stemmed from opposed political philosophies and social outlooks—e.g., "democratic capitalism" versus "communism."

As with other kinds of wars, the ideological justifications that have been advanced for civil strife have had rationalizing value in the given time and place but have not furthered an understanding of the social circumstances that give rise to civil strife. With the wisdom of hindsight, social historians have usually discovered a considerable variety of mutually exclusive explanations for each civil war; but a general theory of civil war has not yet been formulated.[21] Unlike most kinds of wars, civil wars do seem to be directly related to social change. Apparently the dissident faction, that region or segment within the general population that declares its independence of the traditional political authority, attempts through violence either to legitimatize change that is in process or to prevent its legitimatization.

Two quite different civil wars, the Huguenot wars in France and the American Civil War, would seem to substantiate this interpretation.[22] Protestantism began to gain converts in France early in the sixteenth century, although from the first the converts were subjected to vigorous persecution; and by midcentury the French Protestants had evolved a number of strong and economically aggressive craft and trade centers, sociocultural islands that competed economically with the traditional guild-bound towns. Their success led to a rapid spread of Protestantism, if not of the socioeconomic organization of the Protestant centers, and seemed likely to jeopardize both Church and State. Moreover, the guild-bound towns became resentful of the unregulated competition by the Huguenots in both production and trade. Local rebellions against the Huguenots, in which many of the latter were slaughtered, led in 1562 to the first of a succession of civil wars in which Huguenots were ranged against government forces. The conflict dragged on for over a century; indeed, as late as 1815 the Huguenots, by then few in number, were still being persecuted.

On the face of it, the conflict between the Catholics, represented by the established government of France, and the Huguenots was over religious authority; but religious differences were hardly more than a symbol of the incompatibility of these two social subsystems. The dominant one, that of traditional French society, was monarchistic, highly stratified, basically rural, and, in the towns, ordered and held constant by the guild form of occupational organization. That of the Huguenots, who were for the most part craftsmen, traders, and professional men, members of the emerging bourgeois class, was dedicated to the principle of individual freedom rather than

[21] For examples of such varied interpretations of one civil war see Howard K. Beale, "What Historians Have Said about the Causes of the Civil War," in *Theory and Practice in Historical Study*, Social Science Research Council, New York, 1946.

[22] There are many recent and current civil conflicts in non-Western parts of the world, such as the struggle of the Algerian Arabs to gain political freedom from France, which may have been somewhat comparable to the Huguenot wars; and the Korean conflict had at least a slight resemblance to the American Civil War. But in the modern world no society is permitted to resolve its domestic conflicts free from outside interference, for every such conflict is currently defined as a localized manifestation of the cold war between the free West and the totalitarian governments of Russia and China.

political and religious authoritarianism. From the point of view of the peasants, landlords, guildsmen, and burghers, as well as of the political aristocracy, the Huguenots were dangerous upstarts who violated tradition and traditional rights and prerogatives and jeopardized the *status quo*. From a broader viewpoint, the Huguenots represented the forces of social change that were ultimately to revolutionize the culture of Europe and, incidentally, bring revolution to France.

Whereas in the Huguenot wars the established government, since it represented the aristocracy and was interwoven with the Church, was the defender of the *status quo*, in the American Civil War the established government fought for change against a section of the nation that was in opposition to that change. The immediate issue, of course, was the proposed abolition of slavery, a change that would affect the Southern slave states but not, at least not immediately and directly, the Northern nonslave states. Behind this issue, however, was a growing industrialization and urbanization of the North that widened the gap between the subcultures of North and South. By midcentury these subcultures were not only distinct but in many areas incompatible: the economic interests of the North were becoming more and more industrial, while those of the South remained agricultural; the values and sentiments of the one had become those of an open class system and individual freedom, while those of the other remained appropriate to a closed and authoritarian class system. The cultural conflict between the two focused upon slavery simply because this was a dramatic, easily understood symbol of the differences between the two subcultures.

The outcome of a civil war determines whether the advocates of change or the defenders of the *status quo* are, temporarily at least, to have political jurisdiction. What the long-run consequences will be, however, is a more complex and less determinate matter. During the Huguenot wars French society lost most of its more enterprising members—the independent and progressive craftsmen, traders, scientists, physicians, etc. Those who escaped to England or Germany often took to these lands advanced craft techniques and the entrepreneurial arts; and, as was earlier observed, there is some reason to think that the Huguenot immigrants were in part responsible for the fact that the industrial revolution came first and developed most rapidly in England. It would, however, be specious indeed to trace to the extermination and expulsion of the Huguenots what subsequently happened in French society—the ill-fated Revolution, the Napoleonic Wars, and the perpetual political dissensions and social apathy that have characterized the French people down to the present time. The immediate consequences of the American Civil War are also clear—the formal liberation of the slaves, the disruption of the entire Southern social system, and the infiltration and rise to economic power of the Northern carpetbaggers; but although the victory of the North in this war was a victory for industrialism, it did not then or for a century bring much in the way of industrialization to the Southern states. Thus while a civil war may express and in a political way resolve marked incongruence within a political entity, it does not lead to a restoration of congruence. Restoration comes, if it does, through more complex, subtle, and piecemeal processes.

The Challenge to Legitimacy

The distinction between civil war and revolution is by no means categorical, and which term is traditionally given to a specific war is often more a matter of historical accident than of meaningful characterization. Moreover, the same war is often designated as civil by some historians and as revolution by others. Thus the series of outbreaks in England against the governments of Charles I, Cromwell, and Charles II are described variously as civil wars and revolutions; and while some English historians prefer to designate the uprising of the American Colonies against the government of George III as a civil war, it is generally known as a revolution, if only because the period during which this conflict took place was one in which the idea of revolutionary overthrow of established government was popular.

A fairly useful conceptual distinction may be drawn, however, between civil war as a militant challenge to the *jurisdiction* of an established government by some area or segment of the population and revolution as a militant challenge to the *legitimacy* of such government by a significant segment of the citizenry. The Huguenot wars were, thus, civil, since there was no question of the legitimacy of the French government but only of its having jurisdiction over religious matters; the violence of 1789, on the other hand, was revolution, since it was directed against monarchy, the long-established system of government, and on behalf of a new form of political organization, parliamentarism. In these same terms, the American Revolution was both revolution and civil war; for it involved secession from the government of Britain and at the same time the establishment of a new form of government, a nonmonarchial one.

Military conquest by outsiders, such as the Nazi conquest of France, has been a common way in which the legitimacy of a political system has been challenged. Rebellion against persons in authority and collective challenging of the jurisdiction of the system of authority seem also to have occurred at various times and in different societies. But revolution, defined as a collective denial by the citizens of the legitimacy of their traditional system, seems to be a form of conflict that has occurred only in recent times. Perhaps the nearest approaches to revolution in premodern history were some of the slave insurrections in pagan Rome, of which that under Eunis in 133 B.C. came nearest to being successful. Yet if the records are correct, these insurrections were directed toward securing greater liberties for slaves, by limiting the jurisdiction of the Roman state, rather than in displacing the political system and replacing it with a different one.

In times past, political systems, like the familial and other forms of organization that government has coercively supported, have invariably been considered expressions of either divine law, as they were in China, India, and in Europe during the Middle Ages, or natural law, as they were in ancient Greece and Rome. Whether it was this kind of ideological support for government that precluded revolution or whether the ideology simply reflected the apathy and conventionality of those who were ruled by established government is not clear. At any event the idea that an established political system can be discarded and replaced at will by the citizenry does not appear in social philosophy until the seventeenth century. Plato, it is true, had proposed that a rationally designed politicosocial system be established, but he had failed to indicate how the transition to such a system would be made. Many rulers had attempted and sometimes succeeded in putting into effect planned reforms in an existing system; but they had not, of course, questioned the legitimacy of the system itself.

The idea that government is a creation of man himself and should, therefore, be abandoned and reformulated if it fails to serve man's interests emerged during the course of the conflicts between English kings and parliaments during the seventeenth century and was expressed most clearly and forcibly by Locke. Those conflicts were essentially conflicts over jurisdiction; but as the jurisdiction of parliament was extended and that of king and aristocracy reduced, a new kind of political system gradually came into being—one in which parliament-made law dominated over tradition and over the authority of the king. It was a hundred years or more before this rather piecemeal English revolution had run its course; and that course had nothing in common with the current Marxian theory of the revolutionary process.

What the English evolutionary revolution accomplished was a shift of political power from the hereditary elite of English society to the nonhereditary middle classes; and it gave legal sanction to the transition, which had begun centuries before, from a system of hereditary positions to an open class system. In England and elsewhere, it was the emergence of the middle class, agents and determinants of social change, that disturbed the internal congruence of the traditional class system that had evolved as feudalism declined. That system had been functionally articulated with an agrarian economy and had been modified in adaptation to the functional needs of medieval guild production and trade only to the extent of providing new positions for craftsmen and traders; like peasants, aristocrats, and churchmen, craftsmen and traders were dedicated to stability, both technological and organizational.

As has been noted, the individual entrepreneurs of one sort and another who began to emerge and to gather around them independent functionaries of various kinds, including liberal philosophers and embryonic scientists, soon found themselves hampered on all sides by customs, conventions, and laws that reflected the interests of the established classes—the peasantry, guildsmen, churchmen, and aristocrats. Thus almost everything that these independents did and represented brought them into conflict with one or another and often with all of the established classes. With some striking exceptions, of which the Huguenot wars are the most dramatic, this conflict was for long individual and largely nonviolent; but as the forces of change intensified and the numbers of the middle class increased, an ideology of revolution developed, and violent attacks upon the existing political systems began to occur.

Although the time, the course, and the direct consequences of the various revolutions that have so far occurred around the world have varied enormously, the conditions that have given rise to them have been everywhere much the same—the existence of a closed class system represented and maintained by the political order and a growing body of men with ambitions, values, sentiments, and education that put them into irresolvable opposition to the class system, and, hence, to the political order. The enterprise of these men, whether as independent producers and distributors of goods, as physicians, as scientists, or as intellectuals, has invariably brought them into conflict with the various representatives of the *status quo* (with the priests, legalists, bureaucrats, etc.) ; and to survive as individuals, they have usually had to maintain an uneasy peace with the forces of stability, accepting a sort of twilight position between two of the traditional classes. Such was for long the position of the *bourgeoisie* in early modern Europe, of the enterprising and individually successful planters and merchants in prerevolutionary America, of the Westernized and educated natives of India under the British, and of the various African colonials under European rule; and such is still the position of physicians, enterprising businessmen, liberal scholars, and would-be scientists in contemporary Spain and, to a lesser degree, in Latin-American countries. It was the existence of a small but dynamic middle class in czarist Russia that led to the Russian Revolution, and it was the emergence of an ambitious but subordinated class of educated men that led to the first and the succeeding revolts against the established political order in nineteenth- and twentieth-century China.

Where and when revolution has finally come, it has been instigated by the members of a newly emerging, nonhereditary class and has been directed, whatever the specific ideology involved, toward the destruction of the hereditary class system and of the political order that represented it.[23]

[23] In *The Anatomy of Revolution* (Prentice-Hall, Inc., Englewood Cliffs, N.J., 1952) Crane Brinton has analyzed four revolutions—the English revolution of 1640 and the American, French, and Russian Revolutions—and finds that all of

Revolution has never involved directly any very considerable proportion of the population. Local and sporadic rebellions, symptomatic of the malfunctioning of a social system, have usually provided revolutionaries with their opportunity to seize power; but revolutionary leaders and the revolution itself have expressed the interests and desires of but a small segment of the population, not in any sense the mass. In no society, not even one in which malfunctioning is acute, have the majority of the members had the sophistication, the foresight, the social courage, and even the sense of desperation that are necessary if men are to destroy what is familiar in the hope of being able to create something more desirable.

The immediate aftermath of every revolution has been social chaos greater than that which gave rise to it. In some instances, for example, after the French Revolution, this intensification of disorders, combined with ineptitude or excesses on the part of the revolutionary leaders or their successors, has produced a counterrevolution with the reestablishment, always in considerably modified form, of the old political order. In even the most successful of revolutions, the destruction of the old class and political systems and the rise of a new elite to power have brought greater rather than less malfunctioning. However inadequate it may have been, the old system did operate; and however venal they may have been, the old leaders were practiced and practical. The new leaders, inexperienced and often inspired by utopian ideas, have usually attempted to build a new society in accordance with some preconceived and untested plan; and their endeavors have inevitably intensified the disorders of the postrevolutionary period. For a decade, perhaps more, after the Russian Revolution production of the necessities of life, especially food, continued to decline and in the end was, in the estimation of some scholars, barely half what it had been during the prerevolutionary period; and so far the recent revolution in Cuba has only intensified the inadequacies that its leaders had so blithely promised to correct.

Revolution has thus never led to the prompt and certain emergence of a more functionally effective social system. Like other forms of war, revolutionary violence is destructive, not constructive. It may, as some revolutions have done, provide an effective if partial lifting of the dead hand of the

---

them grew out of the frustration of the aspirations of an emerging middle class by the closed character of the existing aristocracy. For a detailed account of one such circumstance see Elinor G. Barber, *The Bourgeoisie in 18th Century France*, Princeton University Press, Princeton, N.J., 1955. James C. Davis has recently criticized the traditional idea that it is mass misery that produces revolutionary violence; he holds that historically revolutions have occurred only during periods of *comparative* adversity, following up a long period of increasing social welfare. See his "Toward a Theory of Revolution," *American Sociological Review*, vol. 27, pp. 5–19, February, 1962.

past and serve to disrupt the continuity of social life, and in these and other related ways it may uproot many individual members of the society and free them to some extent from old cultural imperatives. How rapidly and in what directions a new social system has begun to emerge has depended upon the initiative of the uprooted and freed individuals, upon their innovativeness, and upon their willingness to advocate and adopt and, in turn, perhaps discard such innovations as are made available to them.

chapter **15** *Projections*
and Prospects

The revolutions of the eighteenth and nineteenth centuries brought a temporary halt to the centralization and extension of political authority that had been under way in Western societies since the time of the Crusades. These revolutions in considerable measure deprived the hereditary politicomilitary elite of their power and gave it to the economically strong but theretofore politically ineffectual *bourgeoisie*. The resulting change from monarchial to representative government was a change that in social philosophy, and to a significant degree in practice, involved a shift from reliance upon government as an agency of social stabilization to dependence upon the individual members of society as agents of social change. The old political elite, derived from the landed gentry who were the social descendants of the feudal lords, had been dedicated to the twofold thesis that men are by nature incompetent and evil-intentioned and must therefore be coerced by government into subordinating their individual interests to those of the society (a view most fully expressed by Machiavelli) and that the best government is that which preserves intact social practices that have been sanctioned by long custom and tradition. While none of the prerevolutionary governments had in fact been able to prevent social changes from occurring, they had all been dedicated to this end.

The political elite that emerged from the eighteenth- and nineteenth-century revolutions represented and expressed, again in considerable measure, the individualism of those who as a class had for centuries been engaged in working changes in their society—the free and independent merchants, factory operators, financiers, scholars, scientists, lawyers, physicians, engineers and other technicians, and Protestant churchmen. Since all the members of this class were in some degree or other enterprising men, they were, if only by selfish interest, opposed to organized authority of any kind. The Reformation had in the course of centuries brought them comparative freedom from centralized religious authority; but as their freedom in this area enlarged, the growth and centralization of government had tended to impose new constraints upon them. It was therefore functionally appropriate that their view of the nature and the proper relationship of government and the individual was the reverse of the traditional one. They regarded man as a rational and foresightful creature who is prevented from conducting himself in reasonable and socially fruitful ways only by the antirational and socially disadvantageous coercions of government. In their view, government was at best a necessary evil—necessary because the physically strong must be prevented from dominating the physically weak but possibly most socially valuable members of society, but an evil because of its invariable tendency to enlarge and extend its powers at the expense of individual freedom.

The representative forms of government that came to replace monarchy were neither by intent nor in fact equalitarian. They were established to give political effect to the values and sentiments and the ideas and interests of those who had gained social acceptance as men of means and position through their own enterprise (or, as was perhaps more often the case, through the enterprise of their fathers or grandfathers before them) and thus had contributed to the dynamism of their society. While these men believed that government was bad, they believed that change was good and that, such being the case, those and only those who were capable of contributing to change through innovation or the effective advocacy or successful adoption of innovations could be trusted to use the powers of government in moderate and socially fruitful ways—i.e., to protect individual enterprise without jeopardizing it.

For a century or so the ideology of what may for convenience be designated as "individualism" tended to prevail in Western societies; and, as has been seen, every proposed extension of political authority and consequent political infringement upon individual freedom was vigorously, if often in the end unsuccessfully, opposed. The consequences were not, however, quite those that had been anticipated by the early advocates of representative government. Change did occur in all the components of society, change that was unprecedented in both scope and rate; but the advocates of representative government had vastly underestimated the complexity of the processes by which change comes about and overestimated the willingness of men to endure current discomforts, incidental to any change, in the hope of future benefits. Specifically, they did not foresee that many of the social changes which they so heartily favored would produce a functional need for the very thing that they most strongly feared—the centralization and enlargement of political authority; that the growth of government would be accompanied by a progressive extension of political representation until the center of political power shifted from the enterprising elite to the apathetic mass; or that, as a consequence, the governments of Western society would during the twentieth century come to express, not the ideology of individualism, but an antithetical one—the idea that the proper role of government is to assure the physical welfare and peace of mind of every citizen, even if in doing so the conditions favorable to change per se must be destroyed.

Nor did they foresee that, as the pace of social change increased, there would arise men who dreamed only of stability and that one of them, Karl Marx, would become the father of a widely held and socially effective ideology that was based on the assumption that all the desirable changes in technology had already been achieved and that the need for individual enterprise no longer existed. What Marx dreamed of was an end to change, a stabilized society, equalitarian and communal in structure, in which all men would be equal because no man would exert himself either to change his own position vis-à-vis his fellows or to work changes in technology, organization, or ideology. Revolutionary overthrow of what he regarded as capitalistic tyranny would merely be a means to this end; and government, which he decried fully as much as did the individualists, would be but an agent of transition—a necessary evil by which the good and governmentless society would be brought into being, an evil that would somehow wither away when the need for it had passed.

Although Marx is now honored, willingly or from necessity, by perhaps one-third of the people of the world as the father of communism, the savior of the proletariat, and the prophet of the twentieth century, and although *Das Kapital* has officially displaced the Christian Bible in Russia and the Confucian classics in China, Marx himself did not in the least foresee the kinds of changes that would be undertaken in his name. The revolutions of the twentieth century have not led, as he had expected they would, to political efforts to bring into being stable and equalitarian social systems but, rather, to the emergence of highly centralized, totalitarian, and tyrannical governments that are dedicated to the thesis that change is good provided only that it is brought about by government itself. Like the individualists who preceded him, Marx underestimated the complexity of society and of the processes by which social change comes about and overestimated the willingness and ability of men to subordinate their personal interests to the common good.

Social Prediction and Social Change

Perhaps the magic men and priests, the oracles and sorcerers, and the necromancers and prognosticators of the civilizations of antiquity and of the Middle Ages had a reasonably good record of success. The many events of their times and places were characterized by repetitiousness, and change was slight when measured against that of the modern world. At any event, they must on the whole have served their clients well, for they plied their various trades generation after generation. Oracles, prognosticators, and others who purport to be able to predict the future or determine its course have not been lacking in modern societies; and with the rise of science some of them have come to acquire unprecedented skill. Modern physicians, for example, are often able to make highly accurate prognoses as well as diagnoses. Astronomers can now predict the movements of the stars with near-perfect accuracy as far into the future as the mind of man can go. Physicists, chemists, and technicians can predict the future performance of a multitude of mechanical parts, complex electronic devices, and chemical processes with sufficient accuracy that they are able to design, construct, and send off into a predetermined orbit tons of apparatus with which to explore the outer universe.

Predictions in the social sciences, however, are another matter. The sciences that deal with man and his society are still young; and tested and trustworthy knowledge about man and society—psychological, sociological, economic, and political—is still so slight that it is currently impossible to predict social matters with any assurance and so to control them for desired social ends. Methods that might have had some value under conditions of social stability are patently unreliable in an age of constant change; and no methods comparable to those that are used in regard to physical and biological phenomena are yet available. Still, the need, personal and social, for some way of predicting the future, for some way of judging what will follow from a given course of action, is as great as it was in times past and, since ours is a changing and disorganized society, perhaps far greater. Legislators need some way of predicting what will follow from their actions; businessmen need some way of predicting the course of economic events and the consequences of what they do; and individuals everywhere need some way of knowing that what they do today will not be nullified tomorrow.

The need for some means of predicting the social future and affecting its course has led to a reliance by people in every walk of life and by the leaders of all sorts of organized endeavors upon those who, in keeping with the values of our times, profess to be able to read the signs and omens of the times with scientific instruments and to derive their counsel and predictions by tested scientific methods. Many of these social prognosticators are no doubt worldly wise and socially sophisticated and may therefore have an advantage over naïve laymen, whether common citizens or elected officeholders, and thus be able to protect laymen from the worst and most obvious errors of judgment. They may keep an investor from purchasing totally worthless stocks, keep a patently stupid student from trying for a college education, keep an angry wife from divorcing her husband on the spur of the moment, prevent a hysterical parent from dangerously drastic efforts to control a mistrained child, advise a legislative body against passing the most ridiculous kinds of laws, caution an industrialist against plunging into the production of an untried product, discourage a political executive from impulsive acts, and so on.

But none of the social prognosticators is able to foretell the exact consequence of any social act, individual or collective, or precisely to control the social future through choosing from available alternatives the action that is most likely to produce a desired result. Psychiatrists who profess to be able to affect the future conduct of their patients (who predict that a given therapy will aid in restoring the mental balance of a specific individual) seem to have little success. Parole boards that try to discriminate between high-risk and low-risk prisoners and return the latter to private life before their sentences have been served have only a moderately better record. Investment counselers and other financial prognosticators may have the virtue of caution; but their ability to predict the future course of business in general or the future performance of any particular stock is far from impressive. Yet it is on the basis of such uncertain predictions that much individual investment is undertaken, that business leaders make their plans for future operations, and that governments tinker with the economic system; and it is upon even more uncertain predictions of what will follow upon legislative and administrative actions that the various agencies of modern government undertake to shape the future of society—that they enact reform measures, prepare for war, enter treaties and alliances with other governments, etc. A survey of the long-range consequences of major political and military actions that have been taken in the past lends substance to the view that, no matter how rational is the calculation of consequences that enters into political and military decisions, so little is at present known that those decisions might almost as well have been made in a random or fortuitous fashion.

It is not surprising, then, that the early advocates of representative government failed to foresee the course of social change. On the contrary, it is remarkable that they should have understood, if only intuitively, the role that is played by individual initiative and enterprise in social change and the social conditions that are conducive to the emergence and expression of initiative and enterprise. For the same reasons, it is no less understandable that Marx should have misgauged the course of social history and have failed to anticipate the practical uses to which his predictions of the future would be put.

Current Prophecies

During the nineteenth century serious commentators on the future of society —scholars, intellectuals, and even journalists—were commonly of the opinion that the only real danger to the nation came from politicians and that, given reasonable freedom from interference by the tyranny of government, society would continue its steady progress toward perfection. Prophets of doom occasionally raised their voices, usually against the sinfulness and soullessness of modern man; but theirs was the voice of Cassandra, and only ignorant and old-fashioned people paid it heed.

The advent of World War I destroyed the illusion, fostered by nearly a century of comparative peace, that man had at long last learned the futility of war; and with the destruction of this illusion came loss of faith in the inevitability of progress. In the immediate postwar years grave doubts were expressed about the future; and the dismal predictions of such men as Oswald Spengler (in his *The Decline of the West*) and Lathrop Stoddard (in his *The Rising Tide of Color*) were very much in vogue. But as postwar dislocations were overcome and the war itself faded into the past, the tone changed once again; the most-honored of the prognosticators then began to say that we had entered upon a new era of peace and plenty, in which all the old, harsh laws of life no longer operated and in which everyone would prosper without effort. The worldwide economic collapse that began in 1929 brought this dream to an end and a new generation of soothsayers to the fore. Their varied but always grim predictions slowly coalesced into the doctrine of the mature society—the idea that Western societies had reached the zenith of their development, that the age of rapid progress had come to a close, and that what remained to be done was to consolidate the technological and other gains that had been made and through political means assure a reasonably equable distribution of the fruits of a considerably less than perfect society. This doctrine was, of course, but a watered-down version of Marxism; but its Marxian quality was studiously ignored in all Western countries, for it provided a convenient justification for the rapid extension of political controls into previously private spheres of social life and permitted the seeds of welfarism to be planted.

With few exceptions, Winston Churchill being perhaps the most noted and outspoken, British and American prognosticators failed to foresee the outbreak, to say nothing of the course, of World War II. After Munich, Prime Minister Chamberlain airily promised peace in our times; and British and American journalists and scholars were generally contemptuous of the little ex-house-painter Adolph Hitler and his silly Nazi movement. On their side, the German and Italian prognosticators were convinced of the inevitability and desirability of war; but they also predicted that it would be short, victorious, and would leave the whole world cowed and subject to its rightful masters—the Germans, the Italians, or the Japanese.

The prophecies that were made during the course of this war were those that are appropriate to times of war, and few of them bear scrutiny in the light of what actually did come to pass. That they fell so far short of the truth is less important than that the end of the war brought a prompt and decisive falling out among the victors which left two-thirds of the people of the world divided into two great armed camps that have ever since struggled by all means short of total war to extend their influence over the remaining third. The conflict is nominally ideological—communism versus capitalism, totalitarianism versus democracy, Marxians versus Christians. Ostensibly, two great and mutually incompatible systems of social life are fighting for survival, each in jeopardy from the other, each determined to defend itself from impending assault by the other, each claiming to be the one and only way to social salvation.[1] The actual social forces that gave rise to this conflict and that are expressed through it, however, are but vaguely known and little understood; and they seldom enter into the discourse about it. Future generations of historians will no doubt debate the causes of the current condition of world affairs, even as historical specialists are still debating the causes and consequences of the medieval Crusades—assuming, that is, that the course of events does not prevent future generations from existing.

Much current social prognostication concerns the outcome of the present world struggle, and not without reason. It does seem likely that the future of any society, whether that of the primitives of Patagonia or the inhabitants of Great Britain, will be in considerable, and perhaps even major, measure conditioned by what happens to and between the two great world protagonists —the United States on the one hand and Russia on the other. The possibilities as variously described by current social prophets fall roughly into three prospects: total disaster to mankind; the achievement of an uneasy, unprofitable, but peaceful checkmate; and the elimination of the bases for the present conflict through the emergence of a new kind of society, one that will be common to both Russia and the United States and that will eventually come to prevail throughout the world.[2]

THE PROSPECT OF DISASTER

The development during World War II of the technique of releasing atomic energy was the fruition of more than a century of scientific investigation into the nature of matter, but it constituted an unprecedented advance in man's ability to control the forces of nature. Greek fire, gunpowder, nitro-

[1] See Edward M. Burns, *Ideas in Conflict: The Political Theories of the Contemporary World*, W. W. Norton & Company, Inc., New York, 1960.

[2] A number of somewhat more idealistic possibilities are described in Quincy Wright et al., (eds.), *Preventing World War III: Some Proposals*, Simon & Schuster, Inc., New York, 1962. In *The Future of Mankind* (The University of Chicago Press, Chicago, 1961) Karl Jaspers offers the rather unlikely prospect that fear of total destruction will give rise to a new, and presumably worldwide, moral movement that will make peace based on law a political imperative.

glycerin, dynamite, TNT, the sail, the steam engine, the internal-combustion motor, and hydroelectricity were some of the precursors to the atom bomb; each in its turn was proclaimed revolutionary if not disastrous, and each in time did indeed bring marked changes in social life. But the difference between, say, the bow and arrow and the early musket or between the sailing ship and the steamship was slight in comparison to that between the best of the chemical bombs and the thermonuclear bombs that are now available, insofar as their quantitative effects are concerned. Thus it is estimated that just one Polaris warhead (each of our atomic submarines carries sixteen) has destructive energy equivalent to that of all the chemical bombs that were dropped by all the combatants of World War II. The devastation that was caused by the two atom bombs that were dropped on Japan during World War II had no precedent in human experience; yet these two bombs were small by comparison with each one of the thousands of atomic warheads that are now available.

In the years since World War II, first Russia and then Britain and France learned how to make hydrogen bombs; and a new and comparatively cheap method of refining ores and producing bombs will, most probably, soon make it possible for smaller, poorer, and less technically developed nations to join the atom-bomb club. Meanwhile both the United States and Russia have been busy stock-piling hydrogen bombs of various sizes and intended for various tactical purposes. Meanwhile, too, the military rocket has been developed by both countries, and fleets of fast, high-flying jet bombers have been built—both rockets and bombers with intercontinental range. It is a fair inference, although the actualities are known in detail only to the military high commands of Russia and the United States, that before very long Russia and the United States will each have the military capacity to destroy in a few minutes all the major industrial and urban centers of the other.[3] Should the recent course of events continue unchecked, in a few years the various nations of the world would certainly have the joint military capacity to destroy simultaneously all the major concentrations of population in the world—i.e., all the cities of sufficient size to justify the expenditure of a bomb. Such a holocaust would immediately reduce the population of the world by about one-half; and it would leave the remainder without most of the instruments of production except those that are used in agriculture

[3] The data that have so far been released by the United States military services indicate that the United States goal, in addition to the Polaris fleet of the Navy and the intercontinental bomber fleet of the Air Force, is 126 Atlases, 108 Titans, and about 1,500 Minutemen. The explosive potential of these missiles wll be over a *billion* tons of TNT. The estimated number of atomic warheads of all sorts possessed by the United States at the beginning of 1963 was 50,000 (*Time*, January 25, 1963, p. 24). The Russians are presumably striving to stock-pile an equal, if not superior, number of atomic bombs.

and are not dependent upon industrial sources of supply—i.e., not dependent upon coal, oil, electricity, replacement parts, etc.

Even assuming for the moment that there would be no deleterious physiological side effects from this vast release of atomic energy, those people who survived the war would be reduced to preindustrial methods of making a livelihood—to hunting and fishing, premodern modes of agriculture, and the herding of sheep or cattle. The primitive peoples of Africa, the sheep men of Australia, the farmers of Argentina, the peasants of India, Russia, China, etc., would presumably make out fairly well; but the small-town and rural inhabitants of Europe, Britain, and the United States would have difficult going indeed; and before they had learned the old, lost arts of preindustrial agriculture, many, perhaps most, would have died of starvation and physical hardship.

Numerically, and in many respects culturally, the remaining people of the world would be returned to much the same kinds of circumstances and conditions that obtained at the opening of the present era, there to begin again, possibly, the series of technological, ideological, and organizational changes that culminated in the destruction of modern civilization. Our new dark ages would not, presumably, be quite so dark as were the ones that went before. Historical and scientific knowledge, technical knowledge and skills, forms of organizations, etc., would survive in the towns and villages that had escaped destruction; and to revive and reconstitute such knowledges and skills would take far less time than it took to innovate and develop them. Thus it might devolve that within a century or two some people or other would be busily reconquering the world and reestablishing an advanced, industrial social system.

The assumption that the survivors of the atomic holocaust could set about the task of building a new life for themselves and thus ultimately rebuilding the old one or a reasonable facsimile of it is, however, on the basis of our present knowledge untenable; for it is almost certain that there would be deleterious side effects. The by-products of chemical bombs are gaseous compounds of carbon, oxygen, and hydrogen, some of which are normal constituents of the atmosphere, while the remainder are contaminants of the same order as those that are constantly being produced by industry. Some of the by-products of atomic fission, on the other hand, are both destructive of organic life and themselves very long-lived—radioactive substances that pollute the area of destruction and that enter into the atmosphere of the earth, spread widely, and gradually settle on the earth. Organic tolerance for the substances involved in radioactive fallout, of which strontium 90 is the most dangerous, is largely a matter of inference from experimental data; and the long-range effects of heavy bombardment with atom bombs is still a matter of speculation. It is known that some of the radioactive substances can be concentrated in man's food supply, much as DDT from pastures can become concentrated in cow's milk; and there is clear evidence that the experimental bombs that have been exploded since World War II have added significantly to the proportion of radioactive substances in the atmosphere.

Just exactly what, in addition to outright destruction, an atomic holocaust would do to the earth is, however, unknown. Simple projection of what is presently known has led many atomic scientists to conclude that the world would become uninhabitable—i.e., that the survivors of the initial bombing would soon succumb to radiation sickness.[4] Should the result be somewhat short of this, geneticists have predicted on the basis of laboratory findings that the offspring of the survivors would be monstrous sports—that at the very least man as we know him would cease to exist within a generation or two. But simple projection of what is presently known gives highly unreliable predictions. Factors presently unknown could completely change the course of events; moreover, what holds true at one magnitude, say ten bombs, may not at another, say one thousand bombs.[5] Thus it is permissible to hope that presently unknown factors and the unanticipated consequences of the great magnitude of an atomic war would so modulate the predicted effects that man would be able to survive; and it is equally permissible to fear that the catastrophe would be far worse than the worst of current predictions—i.e., that the earth itself would be reduced to cosmic dust. One may with equal reason hypothesize a great variety of consequences between these two extreme possibilities, such as the melting of the polar icecaps and the vaporization of considerable proportions of the sea waters, all of which would be highly adverse to the maintenance of social life. The consensus of scientific opinion, certainly of the opinion of the atomic physicists, is that a worldwide atomic war would undoubtedly bring, in one way or another, the end of mankind; and most scientists seem to feel that the occurrence of such a war is only a matter of time. So prevalent is this dismal view of man's future that some scientists have taken to proposing very unscientific ways by which to save man from total extinction, ways that range from space-rocket migration to some uncontaminated planet of this or some other solar system to man-made worlds traveling endlessly through space.[6]

[4] See John M. Fowler (ed.), *Fallout: A Study of Superbombs, Strontium 90 and Survival*, Basic Books, Inc., Publishers, New York, 1960.

[5] A simple illustration of the unpredictability of phenomena at unknown magnitudes is the fact that the most exhaustive study of the behavior of water at temperature ranges between, say, 40 and 50 degrees centigrade would give no indication at all of what will happen should the temperature rise to 100 (vaporize) or fall to zero (freeze).

[6] The latter way to survival was proposed, apparently quite seriously, by D. M. Cole at the 1961 meeting of the American Astronautical Society. See the news report of his paper in *Time*, January 27, 1961, p. 46. For some other

As a counter to all the dire predictions of the imminent end of man, and hence of human society, it may be observed that the end of the world has been predicted many times in the past, but that so far the end of the world has not come. The bases for the current prediction may be scientific and thus far more impressive to modern people than are the superstitious, supernaturalistic, or metaphysical reasons that were advanced in earlier times; but each dire prediction that was made in the past was in its time and place supported by authority, by the authority of belief or of reason, and yet each in its turn turned out to be false.

MILITARY CHECKMATE AND SOCIAL STAGNATION

The official position of the military and political ideologists in both Russia and the United States has been that the prospect of an atomic attack can be minimized, if not entirely eliminated, by sufficiently enlarging the military establishment and its atomic potential that an attack on it would mean prompt and total counterdestruction. This thesis involves a variety of assumptions, predictions, and beliefs that must be accepted or rejected on the basis of faith alone, since they all transcend actual knowledge and understanding of human affairs. Thus the assumption that one side, contrary to its assertions, is in fact deliberately and calculatingly bent upon using its military force to conquer and enslave the other, which wants only to live in peace, might conceivably be valid for either the United States or Russia, but is in fact accepted, officially at least, by both. And the idea that the aggressive ambitions of one side can be kept in check by fear of massive retaliation by the other assumes a rationality in the conduct of political and military organizations that the history of international relations certainly does not support.[7]

---

proposals, none very hopeful, see Herman Kahn, *On Thermonuclear War*, Princeton University Press, Princeton, N.J., 1960; Edgar A. Mowrer, *An End to Make-Believe*, Duell, Sloan & Pearce, New York, 1961; and Anatole Shub (ed.), *Alternatives to the H-Bomb*, Beacon Press, Boston, 1955.

[7] The United States, and presumably also Russia, is prepared to launch an atomic counterattack upon the first clear evidence of attack. (Apparently no one expects the next great war to be formally declared in advance of actual military assault, for the Japanese sneak attack on Pearl Harbor seems to have convinced even our own military leaders that in modern war, as in love, all is fair.) The hope is that this counterattack can become airborne before the bombs of the enemy have reached their targets; and since the time between evidence of an attack and arrival of the enemy bombs will be very short, elaborate and highly mechanized provisions have been made to analyze evidence of such an attack, reach a decision, and launch the counterattack. But such preparations open the way for catastrophic error, either of human judgment or mechanical failure.

On faith in the validity of the military checkmate theory of preventing all-out atomic war, or perhaps only through crass and calculated appeal to such faith, both the United States and Russia, and with a great deal less enthusiasm the allies of each, have in the years since World War II poured a considerable amount of their social resources into the building and development of atomic weapons, long-range aircraft, intercontinental and other rockets, space rockets, and various space-age devices that are expected to have military value. A large proportion of the scientific, technological, and industrial personnel of each country has been brought into and attached to this endeavor; and the powers, if not the absolute size, of the military establishment of each have grown accordingly. For the United States this has meant becoming for the first time in its history a militaristic nation, since heretofore it has in times of peace maintained hardly more than token forces. For Russia the development has been, on the other hand, but an extension and elaboration of the postfeudal military tradition and military establishment that the Communist government inherited from prerevolutionary times. (For Communist China, largest of the Russian allies, the development of a strong and influential military establishment has been a complete reversal of the old order, in which the warrior was the least respected occupational role and in which war lords and their armies were looked upon as little better than bandits.)

Public acceptance of the thesis of military checkmate came about very rapidly in the years following World War II, at least in the United States; and there has been almost no protest against and even less critical examination of the heavy expenditures that have been made in the name of defense.[8] As a result, those expenditures have continued to rise constantly—from about 4 per cent of the gross national product in 1946 to well over 10 per cent in 1962. Presumably an even higher proportion of the Russian and a very much higher proportion of the Chinese gross national product is directed into military channels.[9] Whatever the circumstances in Russia and China, the expansion of our own military establishment has been occurring during a period

---

One current hazard is that either the United States or Russia might launch an attack on the false assumption that it is in fact a counterattack. A fictional account of this possibility, rather crude in conception, has been provided by E. Burdick and H. Wheeler in *Fail-Safe*, McGraw-Hill Book Company, New York, 1962.

[8] See John Lukacs, *A History of the Cold War*, Doubleday Company, Inc., Garden City, N,Y., 1961.

[9] The Russian government apparently has its own version of double-entry bookkeeping: what is publicly acknowledged on the one hand and what actually happens on the other. For what it is worth, the proclaimed budget of the Russian government for 1963 was 84 billion rubles, of which 14 billion were earmarked for military purposes.

of rising productivity; it has therefore required little if any sacrifice, except on the part of those, mainly older people, who have been living on fixed incomes; and it has, moreover, become linked in the public mind with prosperity itself. As military expenditures have risen, more and more people—scientists, technicians, industrial leaders, and their employees—have become economically and occupationally dependent upon the continuation of these expenditures and thus more or less identified by self-interest with the military establishment. It has, therefore, long since become politically inexpedient for the leaders of our Federal government to attempt to reduce military appropriations or even to check their rise; and it has become almost traitorous to question the idea that the nation is in deadly peril or that the best protection against this presumed peril is an ever-larger military establishment.[10] In the United States and presumably also in Russia and elsewhere national security has become a dominant and dominating political concern.

Whether the threat of counterdestruction, a threat that is maintained by each side and that is constantly increased by enlargement and refinement of its military establishment, will prevent the anticipated outbreak of unrestrained atomic warfare remains to be demonstrated. If it does, and as long as it does, there is the prospect that not only the major nations of the world but other nations as well, including to the best of their limited abilities those that are currently nonindustrial, would become progressively militarized. More and more of the scientific, technological, and managerial personnel of each nation would, presumably, be drawn into the defensive effort; and they and the military leaders upon whom they depend would become, if the process were not somehow checked, the elite of the nation. As this came about, the nonmilitary segments of society would tend to lose political, ideological, and economic power and prestige and to sink into positions of subservience. Since the energies, ambitions, etc., of the new elite would not be expended in warfare, they would be directed toward self-aggrandizement. To some extent this would mean refinement and enlargement of the instruments of war; for the rest, it would mean progressive subordination of the social system to the will of the military elite, expressed increasingly, perhaps, in ceremony and ritual. The end result would be a large-scale and

[10] Various accounts and interpretations of the growth of the military establishment in the United States and of the prospect of the United States becoming a full-fledged garrison state are provided by Arthur A. Ekirch, *The Decline of American Liberalism*, Longmans, Green & Co., Inc., New York, 1955; Samuel P. Huntington (ed.), *Changing Patterns of Military Politics*, The Free Press of Glencoe, New York, 1962; John U. Nef, *War and Human Progress*, Harvard University Press, Cambridge, Mass., 1950; Reinhold Niebuhr, *The Irony of American History*, Charles Scribner's Sons, New York, 1952; Richard A. Preston et al., *Men in Arms*, Frederick A. Praeger, Inc., New York, 1956; and Fred J. Cook, *The Warfare State*, The Macmillan Company, New York, 1962.

vastly complicated parallel to the feudal system that has evolved whenever men have lived under conditions of constant insecurity—as, for example, was the case in Western Europe after the fall of Rome and in premodern Japan and preclassical China.

The salient characteristics of a feudal system, which would presumably develop in every society should the current threat of atomic war drive the various peoples of the world toward preoccupation with military defense, have been analyzed elsewhere. They include the subordination of all social activities to that of defensive preparation against attack; highly centralized and autocratic leadership that represents the military; a sharp division of the social population into military personnel and disfranchised workers; and a high valuation of military arts and human characteristics appropriate to them—physical courage, blind loyalty to the group, submission to authority, and total conformity to the standards and traditions of the system. For contemporary Western peoples this would mean an abandonment of most of the ideals, beliefs, and practices that they have evolved over the past five hundred years. It would also mean an end of the period of rapid social change.

The new feudalism, should it evolve, could not possibly endure for long. If it did not lead directly to self-extermination by the atomic holocaust that it was supposed to prevent, it would certainly wither away as a result of the social stagnation that it induced. Unlike the feudal systems of other times, the new feudalism would be based on an industrial rather than agricultural technology; and, as has been observed, industrial society must constantly change in order to survive, since industrial technology is by nature exploitative and destructive of the materials that are necessary to maintain it—the energy resources, metals, etc.—and at the very minimum must find and develop substitutes for those resources that become exhausted. Moreover, an industrial society is and no doubt would continue to be dependent upon a precarious balance between man and the other organisms that requires contant progress in medicine, public hygiene, etc., if man is to continue his dominance over the other organisms; and failure on man's part to retain his dominance would soon mean a resurgence of epidemic disease, a decline in agricultural production, and a falling off in the numbers and the physical vigor of the social populations.

It may be assumed that as the new feudalism emerged, more and more social effort would go into the production and refinement of military weapons. But the social circumstances that are currently conducive to innovation and to the adoption of innovations would soon give way to organizational rigidity, which precludes the individual enterprise by which innovations, scientific, technological, and otherwise, are achieved and adopted. In a feudal or quasi-feudal society individual freedom is neither possible nor desired; the individual exists for the state, and any deviation from what is sanctioned (and only the established would be sanctioned) is treachery. Hence under the new feudalism, science, which results from the enterprise of free men, would soon disappear; change, ultimately change even in the area of military technology, would come to an end; and marked incongruencies would then arise between the social system and its physical and biological context.

The prospect that the current trends toward military checkmate and toward the development of states dominated by the military will continue unabated until the major peoples of the world are incorporated into quasi-feudal monolithic systems seems very remote indeed. The ideological and other forces that are presently driving the United States and Russia toward a constant expansion of their military establishments are quite likely to be self-limiting; those establishments may very well become ingrown and stagnant before they achieve a position of dominance over the society; a faltering of productivity in the United States or Russia or both, comparable to the world-wide dislocation of economic activities of the early 1930s could distract at-tention from external to internal dangers.[11] Moreover, there is a considerable chance that the concept of military checkmate will prove to be false and the process of feudalization terminated by the war that ends all wars by bringing an end to mankind.

THE CONVERGENCE OF CAPITALISM AND COMMUNISM

Although few of the current social prognosticators take a distinctly hopeful view of the future of man, there are some who forecast a gradual resolution of the present conflict between Russia and its satellites on the one hand and the United States and its allies on the other and, thus, the avoidance of both a world-destroying atomic war and a soul-destroying militarization.[12] Their ray of hope for a long and reasonably comfortable social future springs from the observation, made by Western students of Russian communism, that the Russian social system is not developing according to plan, neither according to the plan that was predicted by Marx nor according to any of the various

[11] Thus a series of crop failures and other economic difficulties seem to have been responsible for the marked—however temporary—reduction in saber rattling by Russian leaders that occurred in 1963.

[12] In this prediction the future international role of Communist China is either ignored or passed over on the grounds that the Chinese cannot possibly become a first-class industrial nation in the foreseeable future. On the other hand, some of our more optimistic seers have concluded from the evidence of some ideological dissension between Russia and China that the latter may be-come a threat to Russia's position within the Communist world and lead to war between Russia and China. This thieves-fall-out hope is perhaps the most fragile of all those that are currently popular.

modified plans for the good and equalitarian society that have been enunciated by successive leaders of Communist Russia. Russian society, they believe, is evolving many of the salient characteristics of modern Western societies, while at the same time changes in the structure of Western societies are bringing them in some respects toward some of the characteristics of Russian society.[13] Thus they believe that the trend of events in both social systems is toward a convergence and that if this trend is not interrupted, there will eventually emerge a new kind of system, neither communistic nor capitalistic, totalitarian nor democratic, but unique—a system of social life that is built upon and functionally more appropriate to industrial technology than is either of those that are currently in existence.

Basic to this moderately hopeful view of the future is the assumption, widely held and previously discussed, that the current conflict between Russia and the United States stems from the fact that the social systems of these two great powers are not only strikingly different but incompatible—that, in the words of the Russians themselves, communism and capitalism cannot coexist. The corollary to this assumption is that if and when the major peoples of the world acquire fairly common basic cultural characteristics, a world society of sorts will have been achieved and the primary causes of war between nations will have been dissolved.

The seed from which the concept of world peace through cultural homogeneity has sprouted is the apparent tendency of Russian society to take on some of the structural characteristics of Western society. Any such tendency is counter to Communist ideology; and when it has been officially recognized, it has been passed off as either a temporary deviation to be promptly corrected or as a temporary concession to expediency. Nevertheless, some of the observed trends have persisted for decades, and there is every reason to believe that present Russian society is very far indeed from the Communist ideal.

The Communist revolution, it will be recalled, was expected to occur in the most industrialized nation of the West, in Britain, and to involve the forcible establishment of a new system of distributing the proceeds of the existing system of production. The revolutionary government, in accordance with this expectation, would simply have taken over the productive

[13] Thus in *The Soviet Citizen: Daily Life in a Totalitarian Society* (Harvard University Press, Cambridge, Mass., 1959) Alex Inkeles and Raymond A. Bauer show that the life and attitudes of Soviet and American citizens are in certain fundamental respects astonishingly similar. Other contributions to the convergence thesis are Amitai Etzioni, *The Hard Way to Peace: A New Strategy*, Collier Books, New York, 1962; William J. Miller, *The Meaning of Communism*, Simon & Schuster, Inc., New York, 1963; and Harrison E. Salisbury, *A New Russian?* Harper & Row, Publishers, Incorporated, New York, 1962.

apparatus of the nation and socialized it in order that goods and services could be equably distributed to all citizens. Thus the change that was contemplated was legal, political, and organizational. Contrary to expectation, the revolution occurred in Russia, which then had very little industry, and that largely destroyed by war, and few of the technicians and skilled workers, few of the industrial managers, few of the scientists, and almost none of the traditions that are essential to an industrial society. Communist Russia started instead with a preponderantly agricultural people and with a body of law and customs, of traditions and ideologies, that were largely postfeudal.

The problem of the leadership of Communist Russia was not, therefore, to provide for an equable distribution of the proceeds of an industrial society. It was, rather, to become industrialized; and since Western Europeans had already devised and developed the techniques of industrial production, both mechanical and organizational, this meant adoption rather than innovation. Thus Russia did not have to go through the long and arduous process by which Western Europeans had evolved their science and technology and their factory production and industrial forms of organization. Russia did not need the high level of individual initiative and the comparative freedom from political and other organizational constraints that are essential if innovations are to be made and developed into useful cultural items. What Russia needed, rather, was vigorous advocacy for the adoption of Western technology and the establishment of conditions favorable to its adoption. There was, therefore, a functional basis for the assumption by the postrevolutionary government of responsibility for the establishment and development of industry, for the education of technicians, for the mechanization of agriculture that was necessary if workers were to be released from the land for industry, etc. The strategy that was adopted for fostering these ends—that of centralized, political planning of changes and coercive enforcement of them—is, of course, quite another matter.

One of the striking distinctions between the revolutions of the eighteenth and nineteenth centuries and those of the twentieth century is that while the leaders of the former were for the most part educated and sophisticated members of the middle class, the leaders of the latter, the Russian, Chinese, and many lesser revolutions, have for the most part been of peasant origins. The difference in the character of leadership reflects, one would suspect, fundamental differences in the nature of the revolutions themselves. The former revolutions, in essence, gave political power to an already well-established middle-class. The latter in each instance displaced an established elite for which there was no qualified replacement and opened the class structure (or power system) to strong-willed, ruthlessly ambitious men who subscribed to no social code and had no social loyalties, to men who were governed only by the desire for power. These men gave lip service to Marxian doctrine, as their successors still do; but expediency was their guide and has been the guide for their successors, one result of which is that Russian society today bears little resemblance to the communal system that was forecast by Marx himself.

Two factors in addition to the nature of their leadership seem to have influenced the strategy that Russia and China have used in their attempts to institute social change. First has been a sense of urgency that could only have stemmed from the fact that Russia and China were obviously backward in comparison to the West; they had, and still have, a great deal of catching up to do, whereas the West during its development had no standard except the social past against which to measure its progress, with the result that any change seemed a remarkable step forward. This same sense of urgency is currently to be found among the political leaders of India, Latin America, and Africa; and where there is a sense of urgency, there is the temptation to try short cuts to objectives—in the case of Communist countries, to try to force the adoption of Western technology and its organizational correlates. In the second place, in Russia at least—and Russia has tended to set an example for China and other non-Western societies—there was a strong tradition of authoritarian political control and no tradition at all of individual freedom and voluntariness. Thus the Communist leaders of Russia inherited the organizational apparatus of political tyranny and a relatively submissive population, the major difference between the old and the new governments being that the leaders of the old were dedicated to the prevention of all social change, while the leaders of the new have been dedicated to maintaining their power, which was possible only through their advocacy of change.

There can be little doubt that the political advocacy of change in Russia (and more recently in China) has been a very important factor in the social development of contemporary Russian society. It is by no means certain, however, that the Russian attempt to force industrialization has been significantly successful; and this uncertainty gives some plausibility to the view of those Western students of Russian society who believe that the course of Russian social development is toward the adoption not only of Western technology but of Western ideology and organization, including political organization. The Russian Communists have now been driving toward industrialization for nearly half a century; the United States, which is fairly adequate for comparative purposes, made fully as much and possibly more progress in this respect, considering the differing states of the industrial arts, in the half century following the Civil War and did so without resort to political coercion—to slave labor, terrorism, secret police, purges, or any of the other coercive devices of a totalitarian state. It is quite possible that the resistance to change that has been generated by coercion, most especially in the peasantry, the gross inefficiencies that are inevitable when men are motivated mainly by fear, and the errors of centralized planning and control have offset whatever advantages the communistic procedure for hastening Russia into the industrial age may have had. Russian progress over the past four decades has, at any event, been considerably less than spectacular and of far less magnitude than Lenin, Stalin, and their successors expected it would be.

Moreover, there is considerable evidence that the social system that is emerging in Russia bears little resemblance to the equalitarian dictatorship by the proletariat which was the professed goal of Russian leadership. The government has not succeeded in eliminating the family as the basic unit of social life, although every effort has been made to break the ties of husband and wife and parent and child. Rather, a nuclear family system, in many respects comparable to our own, has evolved in urban, industrial areas; and among the agriculturalists the old extended family organization has tended to persist. The government has been no more successful in its attempts to eliminate organized religion and religious faith. Although the Church operates in an atmosphere of political persecution and although churchmen are as a class politically oppressed, the people of Russia seem today to be no less religious than are contemporary Americans. The Russian family has changed character during the past half century, and the role of organized religion has definitely declined; thus both family and religion in Russia have followed the same course that they have taken in the societies of the West.[14]

Ownership of the means of production, both industrial and agricultural, is far more highly concentrated in government in Russia than in any Western society; but as even we are beginning to discover, what is important is who controls the means of production and to what end they are put, not who in law owns them. The managers of communal factories and lands in Russia are appointed political bureaucrats, while the managers of our corporations and corporate farms are not under the direct jurisdiction of government; but Russian managers as a class probably differ from our own managerial personnel far less than might be supposed. Both are, or are at least becoming, professionalized; and in both countries they operate as parts of a managerial team rather than as independent entrepreneurs. The fact that the Russian managers are subject to guidance through political directives and are responsible to political agencies is probably no more constraining than are the various private interests—of stockholders, of banks and other fund-providing institutions, of suppliers, of marketing outlets, etc.—that American managers must serve. Moreover, there is a considerable free-enterprise sector in the Russian economy, one which some students of Russian society believe to be growing. Perhaps as much as half of the consumers' goods is either produced or marketed through private rather than governmental agencies; and personal

[14] See Cyril E. Black (ed.), *The Transformation of Russian Society: Aspects of Social Change since 1861*, Harvard University Press, Cambridge, Mass., 1960.

property has very much the same legal status in Russia as it has in contemporary America. Finally, the proportion of the gross national product that is appropriated by government, for military, educational, administrative, welfare, and other uses, has been rapidly rising in Western nations and slowly falling in Russia. Should these trends continue unabated for another two decades, Western societies will be just about as much "socialized" as Russia will be.

What most excites those who foresee a cultural convergence of East and West, however, is the total failure of the Russians to develop a classless, equalitarian society. Early efforts to put into effect the Marxian dictate of from each according to his ability and to each according to his need contributed in considerable measure to the steady decline of economic productivity in the years that followed the revolution. For the first few years this decline was attributed, and was perhaps in fact attributable, to the loss of capital plant and manpower and to the general social chaos that was left by the war and the revolution itself; but the trend continued downward for nearly twenty years. Cultivated land decreased, acreage yields declined, man-hour productivity in industry fell, and there was a pronounced trend in the labor force away from productive jobs into governmental employment. By the end of Lenin's reign, Russia had so regressed economically that the population was in far worse condition than it had been under the czarist regime of the late nineteenth century. Stalin's rise to power signalized a complete abandonment of the communistic goal of an equalitarian society and the adoption of a system of social incentives that in principle differs but little from the incentives of the open class system of Western societies. In the system that has gradually gained form in Russia, class lines are fully as clear as they are in America and just about as open. An individual's income, to which are linked much in the Western manner his social status and prestige, is determined more or less officially by his worth to the society. A man may through his own efforts, and by taking advantage of such politically provided means as formal education, rise in the socioeconomic scale; and through his incompetence he may fall.

There are, of course, no multimillionaires in Russia; but in terms of status, power, and command over consumption goods, the gap between the rich and the poor, between the most honored and the least honored, and between the great and the humble is as great as the gap that exists in American society. Moreover, as is the case in American society and other Western societies, there is movement upward from below and efforts on the part of those who have achieved high status to hold and perpetuate their position for their descendants. The political, economic, technological, scientific, etc., elites of Russia strive as do the elites of America to give their sons every advantage so that they may win in competition with ambitious peasant and working-class lads; and the latter are, even as in the West, encouraged and aided, by such things as free education, to compete with the wellborn.[15]

Some sociologists are so much convinced of a developing convergence of Eastern and Western societies that they predict the eventual emergence of a compromise social system, common to both. It will be, they think, a system of classes and other forms of organization that are peculiarly suited, i.e., functionally appropriate, to industrial technology. The characteristics of this compromise system are vague, even in their minds, but they have designated it, well in advance of its development, as "industrial democracy." Its goal would be similar to that of a modern labor union—the provision of the highest possible wage and the greatest possible security to the workers. It is assumed that to the extent that the system could achieve this goal, all would benefit and none would suffer. What is not perceived is that any such system would result, as did the medieval guild system before it, in technological stagnation and, in the end, total social stagnation.

For the moment, at least, Russian society shows no tendencies toward technological stagnation. Indeed, Russian society appears to be becoming more rather than less dynamic. The period of fruitful borrowing from Western technology and science is probably drawing to a close; and the need is growing for enterprising men who will provide a steady flow of innovations, not alone in rocketry and space exploration, but in all aspects of technology and in organization. It may well be that it is because of this growing need that the Russian government has in some respects relaxed its surveillance of the individual and has at the same time offered new opportunities and rewards for scientific discoveries and technological inventions. Russian society is by no means free as measured by present Western standards, but it has of late years given increasing scope to individual enterprise; and the trend, if there is a trend, is toward the encouragement of individual enterprise.

[15] From analysis of the available data Martin Lipset and Reinhard Bendix (*Social Mobility in Industrial Society*, University of California Press, Berkeley, Calif., 1959) conclude that political ideology has no bearing upon the social mobility within a society. Where the system is expanding, as under industrialization, mobility will be high, in totalitarian Russia or democratic America.

There are a variety of other developments in Russian society that have been singled out as indications that the Russian social system is coming into concordance with that of America: Russian penology, for example, now draws heavily from Western theory and practice; Russian medical care, both technological and organizational, is becoming comparable to American; etc. Some students of Russia have even taken wry satisfaction in the fact that, although Marx and Lenin and many other idols and notables of Russian communism were Jews, anti-Semitism has been developing and is given some political sanction, such as the listing of the Russian Jew on his *carte d'identité* as "Jew" rather than "Russian."

In Western societies, on the other hand, the recent trend of ideological and organizational change has in many respects been counterindividualistic. As has been indicated in earlier chapters, the nineteenth-century ideals of individual enterprise and self-reliance have largely given way during the course of this century to a general acceptance of the idea that security should be the individual's goal and that to achieve it, he should willingly conform to organizational standards, political and otherwise. Moreover, the occasions for and incentives to individual enterprise have been steadily diminishing as a consequence of the progressive bureaucratization of economic activities and the continued enlargement of the scope of political bureaucracy. Whether these and related changes in ideology and organization will in due time bring Western peoples under the uneasy shelter of the total welfare state and so relieve them of the need and opportunity to exert themselves as individuals is not yet evident; but it is clear that Western peoples now passively accept, as their grandparents would not have done, the assumption of responsibility for their welfare by governmental agencies and the consequent reduction in the permissive range and the effectiveness of individual enterprise.

The Fallacy

It is perhaps possible that Communist Russia will continue to acquire more and more of the characteristics of an open society and that Western societies will become increasingly bureaucratized and socialized to the end that at some indefinite time in the future the two trends will meet and Russia and the West will have in common an industrial society organized in a way and to an extent that is neither capitalistic nor communistic, democratic nor totalitarian, individualistic nor collectivistic, but that is, rather, a compromise in all respects between these various ideological extremes. Such a development would not, however, mean an end to the current threat of catastrophic war between Russia and the West.

Those who put their hopes in the concept of convergence assume that the present threat of war stems from the contrast between Russian and Western forms of social organization. What they are assuming rests upon the further assumption that the major cause of conflict between nations is not national differentiation, i.e., not the fact that some people are citizens of one nation and some are citizens of another, each with its own sovereign government, but is a result of differences between the customs, institutions, etc., of the peoples of various nations. There is no doubt that many forms of conflict have arisen out of cultural differences or that war itself has often involved tribes, clans, or nations with markedly different cultural characteristics. But that it is cultural differences that are the *cause* of war and that, ergo, the elimination of such differences will prevent the occurrence of war is a thesis that cannot stand test against the history of wars.

Clans, tribes, and even family units, whose members have differed culturally little if at all from those of antagonistic clans, tribes, or family units have since time immemorial engaged in warfare. The people of feudal Europe, as of feudal Japan, had a fairly common culture and a common form of social organization; but they fought incessantly. During the Crusades, although Christians fought Saracens, they also fought one another, and far more persistently. Recent wars between nations have involved peoples of different nationalities; but the various and ever variable military alignments and oppositions have not been formed on the basis of common or differing cultures. For a century and more the British and the Germans were more or less allied, or, more accurately, intermittently allied, against the French. During the last half century the British and French have twice fought against the Germans with the United States as their ally. The Japanese and the Italians were allies of the British in the first of these wars and their enemies in the second; and the Russians shifted their alliance from one side to the other during the course of the second.

The various peoples of Western Europe and Britain have been in the process of evolving a common, industry-based culture for the past four hundred years; they have a common religious tradition, they share a common scientific heritage, they have a good many common institutional arrangements, they have much the same technology, and they are all highly industrialized. With one another and with the United States they have, in fact, so very much in common that one may speak, and with good reason, of Western society or culture. Nevertheless, the nations of the Western world have gone to war with one another with disastrous frequency. To assume that the leveling out of the present cultural differences between Western nations and the other nations of the world, particularly the Communist nations, will bring an end to war is to hope for the best while all the nations of the world are in fact preparing for the worst.

Even if that assumption could be accepted, the prospects for the future of man would not be markedly improved. As has been pointed out, there is a definite trend, one that has become marked and has been given international sanction and encouragement since World War II, toward industrialization in the non-Western and largely nonindustrial peoples of the world. Russia, which achieved a considerable degree of industrialization between the two great wars, is now numbered among the industrial nations. China and India have begun the process of becoming industrialized, the former under political forced draft. In the Middle East, in Africa, and in parts of South America small starts have been made. At present, however, not more than one-third of the people of the world are in any significant measure industrialized; two-thirds live a peasant, nomadic, or tribal way of life and are directly and totally dependent upon agriculture or herding for their livelihood. Moreover, although the people of the United States constitute less than one-fifth of the industrialized portion of the population of the world, they *consume* considerably more than one-half of the nonorganic energy (the coal, oil, and natural gas) that is produced by the world and an almost equal proportion of the world's output of iron and other industrial materials.

Should the other four-fifths of the industrialized portion of the population of the world become as fully industrialized as the United States, as measured by consumption of industrial resources, the production of energy and of metals, etc., would have to increase nearly threefold; and should the two-thirds of the population who are now nonindustrial become equally industrialized, present production would have to be increased more than sevenfold. Such a drain on the exhaustible resources of the earth would deplete many of them in a generation or two; but as the demand for them increased with the progressive industrialization, their value would certainly skyrocket, and the current international stresses, which are in some measure of economic origin, would undoubtedly become excessive. The presumed cure for war would in this way be only another route to war.

Moreover, the assumption that the danger of an atomic holocaust would be reduced if not entirely eliminated if all the peoples of the world became industrialized and thus in salient respects culturally similar is in quite another way overly sanguine. For among the many assumptions involved is the assumption that industrialization could be accomplished in time to prevent such a war. How much time there will be is unknown, of course; but it is of the magnitude, one might suspect, of decades rather than centuries; and the next few decades are not going to bring the industrialization of such masses of people as those of China and India. Even Russia, which has a comparatively small population, vast territory, and great potential resources and which was to some extent in the Western tradition and had become partially industrialized by the time of the revolution, has needed nearly a half century to achieve its present state of industrialization. China and India lack the basic tradition; they are organizationally and otherwise contraindustrial (their societies are familistic in character); they have made but the feeblest beginnings toward industrialization; and they are burdened with an exceedingly high density of population. Even with everything in their favor—continued peace, continued technological and financial aid from abroad, etc.—they could not reasonably be expected to achieve Russia's present level of industrialization in less than a century. Insofar as the other peoples of the other world are concerned, many of them tribal, a full century of peace and constant assistance would not be sufficient to bring them into the international community of industrial nations.

SOCIAL CHANGE AND THE SOCIAL FUTURE

Speculations such as the foregoing about the future of human society or of any particular social system may be somewhat more sophisticated than were those of the nineteenth-century evolutionists, for they are not formulated in terms of some metaphysical doctrine about the nature of social life. They are, rather, projections into the future of changes that have been occurring and currently are occurring. When the changes so projected are ascertained by reasonably objective study of the social past and present, the speculation has an aura of scientific respectability; and properly qualified, it may serve as a hypothesis for the further scientific study of society. No amount of qualification, quantification, or formalization, however, will convert such a projection of past and current social trends into a reliable prediction of the social future; for as a prediction every such projection currently suffers from two major limitations—it is the product of selective perception, and it does not, and in the present state of knowledge about social life cannot, take into account the possibility that innovations not yet made or not yet adopted may profoundly affect the consequences of present trends.

Selective perception is a commonplace phenomenon: a shoemaker observes shoes, not hats; a physician notes signs of physical well-being, not how the hair is dressed or the body clothed; and social prognosticators tend to note those particular aspects of the social past and present that they regard as pertinent to the social future, not all of those that might be subjected to scrutiny. It is because only a few of the many observable social trends are singled out and projected that one current speculation regarding the social future can vary so much from another and that equally sober and competent students of society can arrive at such mutually exclusive ideas as that total extinction is just around the corner and that a social utopia is well on its way to fulfillment. By selecting demographic trends and projecting them into the future, one may quite logically conclude that before the twentieth century is out there will be so many billions of people on earth that all will be reduced to a subsistence standard of living. By selecting some of the recent trends in agriculture and industrial technology and ignoring all else, one may, on the other hand, with equal reason conclude that, no matter how many billions of people there are on earth at the end of the century, they can all be fed, clothed, housed, and otherwise provided for at a standard equal to or even superior to that now enjoyed by the American people. But should just a few more current trends be added to this latter projection— such as the progressive exhaustion of natural resources—it may again appear that the prospects for man are hunger and impoverishment.

Even if the distorting effects of selective perception were avoided and all current social trends included in a projection, that projection would not, however, provide a reliable prediction of the social future. It would involve the assumption—acceptable to those who believe that change is an immanent process but contrary to the concepts that have been advanced here—that the social future is no more than an extension of the social past and present. It would not take into account the fact that man himself can be an active agent in the making of his society—that he can modify the projected course of present developments by introducing new techniques, ideas, and forms of organization that may aggravate, nullify, or even reverse the future consequences of one or a number of the current trends.

Through most of human history, man's active intervention between his social present and his social future appears to have been infrequent, intermittent, and perhaps to some extent inadvertent. Social change has, in other words, been exceedingly uncertain and erratic, a fact that has, no doubt, been in some measure responsible for the view that man's social destiny is determined by forces beyond his control. The emergence, very recent in the history of mankind, of the physical and biological sciences and the techniques based upon them has given positive proof that man can be an active agent in the shaping of the physical and biological aspects of his life—that he need not let plague run its inevitable course, let the soil grow sterile, or let the harvest fail. The social sciences have not yet so clearly proved their social utility; but there is every reason to believe that scientific knowledge about society and the processes by which it is changed will in time contribute to social changes in a manner comparable to that of the physical and biological sciences and that innovations in the realm of social organization will become less empirical in character and more firmly based upon scientific knowledge, less random and uncertain in their consequences, and more fully in accord with man's desires.

Name Index

Subject Index

Ecology, 230
  social, 30
Education (*see* Public school)
Educators, bureaucratization of, 412, 434
  isolation of, 370
Egocentricity, 135
Elites, social, and history, 49
  industrial, 384
  isolation of, 367
  in plantation system, 360
Energy, 221, 228
Enterprise, of *bourgeoisie*, 314, 349, 380
  constraints on, 359, 462, 474
  of immigrants, 392
  incentives to, 322
  individual, 143, 308
  medieval, 306
  of Middle Western farmer, 360
  opportunities for, 397
  and Protestantism, 313
  in Renaissance, 376, 415
  in Russia, 535
Entrepreneurial system, emergence of, 415
  flexibility of, 417
  and technology, 416
Environment as intervening variable, 213
Equilibrium theory, 73
  criticism of, 35*n.*
Ethic, Chinese, 309
  Indian, 309
  medieval, 309
  Protestant (*see* Protestant ethic)
Eufunctional change, 78
Eugenics movement, 27, 159
Events, social, 45
Evolution, social, 4
  immanent, 139
  modern theories of, 16, 37, 323
Exploitation, 97
  capitalistic, 324

Fad, 59
Familism, decline of, 341
  revival of, 337
  and the individual, 339
  survivals of, 340
Family, as basic unit, 332
  bourgeois, 246, 346
  changes in, 85
  Chinese, 92, 331

Family, extended, 337
  French peasant, 351
  middle-class, 350
  modern, 342*n.*
  nuclear, 337, 341
  petty bourgeois, 350
  in urban context, 397
  working-class, 347
Fashion, 61
Fear of unfamiliar, 176
Festivals, 44, 305
Feudalism, 333
  decline of, 334, 450
  isolation under, 305, 333, 449
  prospects of return to, 530
  war under, 489
Folklore, 299, 314
Food plants, diffusion of, 238
Food preservation, 274
Food tastes, 183
Functional relativity, 71, 81

Gemeinschaft-Gesellschaft, 7
Geographic determinism, 24, 218
Government, 443
  as agency of change, 457, 468
  bureaucratization of, 447, 468
  civil versus military, 446
  as evil, 10, 518
  expansion of, 442, 451, 469
  functions of, 445
  as interdependent variable, 462
  parliamentary, 507, 513
  representative, 518
  and stability, 461
Greenhouse effect, 222
Guilds, medieval, 368, 414
  bureaucratic character of, 404
  political rule by, 451

Heresy, 306, 450
High-energy societies, 221
Historical materialism, 272*n.*
History, 16
  biological interpretations of, 28
  cyclical theories of, 19, 48
  great-man theory of, 47
  little-man theory of, 50

Lighting and urbanization, 277
Linear change, 32
Lutherism, 307

Magic and technology, 272
Maladjustment, personality, 199
Marginality, 154, 200
Marriage, contractual, 337
  evolutionary stages of, 6
Marxism, 11, 272n., 323, 467, 519
Mature society, 467
Medicine, 67, 170, 270
  bureaucratization of, 439
  professionalization of, 432
  socialized, 439
  specialization in, 440
Merchandising, bureaucratization of, 423
  food, 68, 275
  modern forms of, 424
Migration, to city, 389, 396
  war and, 503
Military, bureaucratization of, 411
  conservativeness of, 499
  isolation of, 369
Military checkmate, 527
Military establishment, 483
  conservative influence of, 496
  science and, 500
  and war, 489
  and warfare state, 529
Mobility, social, bureaucratic deterrents
    to, 429
  channelized, 374
  familistic deterrents to, 339
  of individual, 355, 373, 383, 387
  and marginality, 202
  school and, 435
  war and, 505
  spatial, 339
  forced, 389, 505
  incentives to, 388
Models, 73
  equilibrium, 90
  of functional interdependence, 81
  assemblies, 85
  parts and complexes, 84
  social accessories, 83
  social components, 86
  subsystems, 87

Models, of stability, 89
  dynamic incongruence, 99
  stable congruence, 89
  static incongruence, 93
Monopoly, of coercion, 445
  of status, 365
  of writing, 296
Motivation, and closed society, 372
  of innovators, 132
  and welfarism, 474
Motivational research, 156
Movements, 64
  labor, 428n.
  mass, 14, 162
  political, 324
  public school, 158, 435
  religious, 334
Mystique of war, 493
Myths, of breakthrough, 124
  of collective innovation, 125

Nationalization, of European peoples, 491
  of means of production, 463
  of railroads, 464
  of road systems, 466
Natural resources, conservation of, 225
  exhaustion of, 225, 252, 540
  and modern technology, 221
  substitutions for, 227
Neo-evolutionism, 6
Nuclear fission, destructive potential of,
    524
  and fusion, 228n.

Occupational position, ascribed, 365
  monopoly of, 366
Open society, 99n.
  beginnings of, 376
  class system of, 286, 375
Organization, of community, 352
  corporate, 419
  function of, 327
  medieval economic, 414
  professional, 430
  sacred interpretation of, 320
  as social component, 327
  stratification as, 363
  and technology, 272, 408